Great Waterside Vacation Spots
IN THE NORTHEAST
By Betsy Wittemann
And Nancy Webster

Wood Pond Press
West Hartford, Conn.

Readers should bear in mind that prices and hours, especially in restaurants and lodging establishments, change seasonally and with inflation. Prices quoted in this book are for peak season. They are offered as a relative guide, rather than an absolute. Readers should call or write ahead to avoid disappointment.

The authors invite readers' comments and suggestions.

First Printing, April 1987.
Second Printing, April 1988.
Third Printing, October 1989.

Cover Design by Bob Smith the Artsmith

Cover Photo by Nancy Webster: Camden (Me.) Harbor from back porch of Smiling Cow gift shop.

Edited by Richard Woodworth

Copyright © 1987 by Betsy Wittemann and Nancy Webster

Library of Congress Catalog No. 87-050272.

ISBN No. 0-934260-62-1.

Published in the United States of America.
All rights reserved.
First Edition.

Contents

About the Authors

Betsy Wittemann has lived close to water most of her life. Born in Bridgeport, Conn., she attended college in New Rochelle, N. Y. (both on Long Island Sound). She worked as a newspaper reporter in Rochester, N. Y., on Lake Ontario, and taught school in Athens, Greece, where she traveled to several islands of the Aegean. She worked as a journalist in Hartford, Conn. (a Connecticut River town) and lived for two years right on the Atlantic Ocean in San Juan, Puerto Rico, where she was the associate editor of a travel magazine. She and her family live in Glastonbury, Conn., another Connecticut River town. She is the co-author, with Nancy Webster, of the *Daytripping & Dining in New England* books and of *Weekending in New England*. Her travel articles have appeared in several newspapers in the Northeast. She is a Pisces.

Nancy Webster grew up in Montreal, a city on the St. Lawrence River. She spent summers in St. Andrews-by-the-Sea, N.B., and at a girls' camp and a cottage with her family on Lake Memphremagog, Que. During her college years at McGill University, she waitressed at summer resorts on the Gaspe Peninsula, in the Muskoka Lakes region of Ontario and at Jasper Park Lodge on Lac Beauvert in the Alberta Rockies. She worked in London, England, and for a Greek ship owner in Montreal prior to her marriage to an American newspaper editor. She since has lived in Geneva, N.Y., in the Finger Lakes area; in Rochester, N.Y., near Lake Ontario and the Barge Canal, and in West Hartford, Conn., where her family's home is near the lake that gives Wood Pond Press its name. Besides the books she has written with Betsy Wittemann, she is the co-author with her husband, Richard Woodworth, of *Getaways for Gourmets in the Northeast* and of *Inn Spots and Special Places in New England*. She is an Aquarius.

To Our Readers

A room overlooking the harbor, a table with a water view, a stroll along the docks — is there anyone who doesn't like to be near the water?

In our ten years of researching and writing travel books, we have been struck by the universal love for the water. Because we enjoy waterside places as much as you, we decided to find and share the best waterside vacation spots throughout the Northeast.

Naturally, we have included many coastal areas: from the Maritime Provinces of Canada to a wonderful Chesapeake Bay destination in Maryland. But that's just the start. We have also selected several lakes — from Sebago in Maine to Seneca in New York State. We have two chapters focusing on the Connecticut River and one on the Hudson. We look at canals in Bucks County, Pa., and at coves on Cape Cod. Of course there are islands: Nantucket, Martha's Vineyard, Campobello and Cape Breton, to name four — the Champlain and the Thousand Islands, to name more.

In every chapter we have emphasized the restaurants, the inns, the bed and breakfasts which are close to — or have views of — the water. We tell you where you can rent or moor a boat. We advise you about harbor cruises and whale watches, steer you to the best beaches, and find for you the scenic waterfront drives. We cover maritime museums and nautical attractions, fishing excursions and bird-watching places. We even tip you off to rental cottages and who can help you find them. As in our other books, *Weekending in New England* and the *Daytripping & Dining* series, we tell you where to shop, picnic and play.

Every book becomes our favorite, we suppose, but *Water Escapes* has captured our enthusiasm like none before. We have been delighted by all that we have found: from the precious Victorian B&Bs within sound of the surf in Cape May, N.J., to spectacular ocean beaches at the very tip of Long Island. We've idled in a canoe on crystal-clear Long Lake in Maine and savored a picnic high on a bluff above the Hudson River. We've cracked open lobsters on rocks in a Vinalhaven restaurant and dressed for dinner at an elegant inn in Bar Harbor. We've revisited former haunts like the Finger Lakes and St. Andrews-by-the-Sea, and discovered new treasures like Chester in Nova Scotia and the Cabot Trail. And we have enjoyed every minute of it.

Each place included in this book comes with our personal recommendation. Some we like better than others; that becomes apparent in the descriptions. But after more than a year of traveling around the Northeast, we think we have some wonderful secrets to share. If you have comments, we invite you to share them with us. And we wish you good reading and many happy escapes by the water.

Betsy Wittemann and Nancy Webster

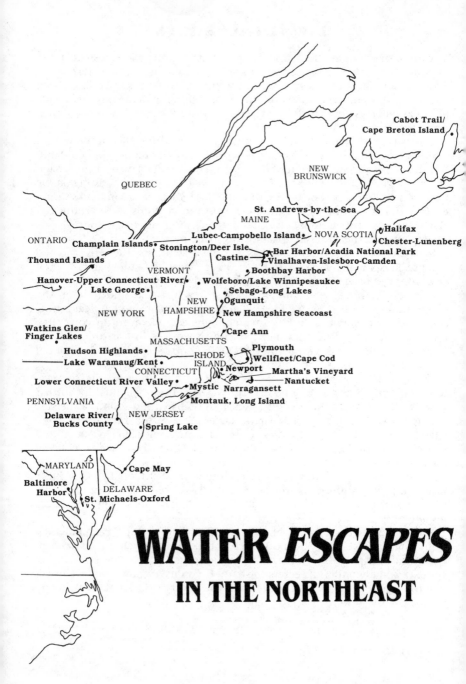

Cabot Trail/
Cape Breton Island

NEW
BRUNSWICK

QUEBEC

St. Andrews-by-the-Sea
MAINE

ONTARIO   Champlain Islands   Lubec-Campobello Island   NOVA SCOTIA   Halifax
                                                                           Chester-Lunenberg
Thousand Islands   Stonington/Deer Isle   Bar Harbor/Acadia National Park
                         Castine   Vinalhaven-Islesboro-Camden
              VERMONT   Boothbay Harbor
Hanover-Upper Connecticut River   Wolfeboro/Lake Winnipesaukee
Lake George   NEW   Sebago-Long Lakes
                     HAMPSHIRE   Ogunquit
NEW YORK   New Hampshire Seacoast

Watkins Glen/   Cape Ann
Finger Lakes
              MASSACHUSETTS
Hudson Highlands   RHODE   Plymouth
Lake Waramaug/Kent   ISLAND   Wellfleet/Cape Cod
              CONNECTICUT   Newport   Martha's Vineyard
Lower Connecticut River Valley   Mystic   Nantucket
                         Narragansett
PENNSYLVANIA   Montauk, Long Island

Delaware River/   NEW JERSEY
Bucks County   Spring Lake

MARYLAND   Cape May

Baltimore
Harbor   DELAWARE
         St. Michaels-Oxford

WATER *ESCAPES*
IN THE NORTHEAST

St. Michaels waterfront from veranda of Hambleton Inn.

St. Michaels-Oxford, Md.

You're sitting on your veranda on a balmy September evening. Gone are the crowds of summer sailors who make St. Michaels the second busiest transient harbor on Chesapeake Bay. Yet to come are the hunters who flock to this area every fall.

Egrets and ospreys can be seen and ducks heard; the Canada geese are all around. Tall Southern pines sway in the breeze. The foliage tends to magnolia, holly and boxwood trees. The homes are pillared and porched. You detect a drawl in the natives' speech.

There's an unmistakable Southern air about St. Michaels and Oxford, its neighbor across the Tred Avon River, as well as remote Tilghman Island between the Choptank River and Chesapeake Bay.

This is Tidewater territory. It's also the Mason-Dixon line, said the woman who checked us in at the Harbourtowne Resort. "People think that with my accent I'm from Virginia, but no, I was born and raised on the Eastern Shore."

Both St. Michaels and Oxford date back to the 1600s and played key roles in the developing nation and its boatbuilding interests before yielding their importance to Washington and Baltimore. For years they languished, relatively undiscovered by tourists and bypassed by the masses headed for Ocean City beaches but beloved by the watermen who make their livelihood from the bay.

The opening of the Bay Bridge out of Annapolis in 1954 forever altered the Eastern Shore's lifestyle. But it wasn't until James Michener penned *Chesapeake* in the area that this choice piece of real estate really took off.

"When I moved here there was one B&B and now there are eight," said ex-Connecticut resident Richard Grunewald, a local businessman and Chamber of Commerce director. There also are new inns, motels, restaurants, shops and, of course, more than enough boatsmen, sportsmen and visitors to fill them. Oxford and Tilghman Island remain less changed, and zoning regulations have just been tightened in the St. Michaels area to keep its waterfront unspoiled.

The focus of western Talbot County — which has an incredible 602 miles of shoreline — is St. Michaels, its landlocked harbor located half way up the Miles River from Eastern Bay toward Easton, the historic county seat. Hidden beneath the clapboards of modernized houses are logs or bricks from the 18th century. When the British bombarded this strategically important town from the Miles River one night in 1813, townspeople blacked out the lights and hung lanterns in the treetops to confuse the invaders. The ploy worked and the British overshot; only the now-famous Cannonball House was hit, and St. Michaels earned a place in history as the town that fooled the British. Today, visitors take historic walking tours through one of America's earliest seaports, enjoy the Chesapeake Bay Maritime Museum and share the harbor with the 20,000 boats that put into St. Michaels annually.

The wildlife that lures hunters and the waters that attract mariners will appeal to you, too. So will the abundance of Eastern Shore oysters and crabs as well as the Tidewater's unhurried lifestyle.

Getting There

St. Michaels is located on the east side of Chesapeake Bay, about 40 miles due east of Washington, D.C. Main approaches are U.S. Route 50 via the Chesapeake Bay Bridge out of Annapolis, Routes 13 and 301 out of Wilmington, Del., and Routes 13 and 50 out of Norfolk, Va. From Route 50 near Easton, take the St. Michaels bypass to Route 33, which leads to St. Michaels and Tilghman. Take Route 333 from Easton to Oxford. To get from St. Michaels to Oxford, use the Bellevue-Oxford ferry.

Where to Stay

Because of its location and its wealth of fish and game, the tourist season is longer in St. Michaels than in more northerly areas (November and December, for instance, are peak periods). Most lodging facilities are open year-round, and most impose surcharges for weekends.

By the Water

St. Michaels Harbour Inn & Marina, 101 N. Harbor Road, St. Michaels 21663. (301) 745-9001. We first thought it a luxury condominium complex, this contemporary structure commanding a superb location at the head of the busy St. Michaels harbor. Not a sign identified it, two months after it had opened in July 1986, and only a chance encounter with a local businessman who mentioned he liked the restaurant at the new hotel led us to investigate. We're glad we did, because this is the kind of full-service inn that St. Michaels needed on the waterfront in the center of town. The L-shaped, three-story structure has 46 guest rooms, many of them two-room suites facing the water. And what suites they are: each has a living room with sofabed, dining table, kitchenette (just a sink and refrigerator — no cooking here) and color television, and a bedroom with two queensize beds, remote-control TV and a large bathroom with double vanities and thick blue towels. French doors lead from each room onto a private terrace or balcony with good-looking chairs and a table overlooking the harbor. After a day of exploring St. Michaels, what luxury it is to have a drink on your balcony before dinner, then after dinner to be able to watch the show of your choice on the bedroom TV while your spouse (this was playoff time) is watching a baseball game in the living room! Smaller quarters on the third floor have rooms with one queen bed; some have kitchenettes. The pleasant **Lighthouse Restaurant** has many tables beside the water and serves three meals a day (see Where to Eat). A small outdoor pool beside the harbor is enhanced by lanterns and yellow mesh chairs, and overnight docking slips are available for 60 boats. An exercise room was in the works. Doubles, $62 to $86; suites, $82 to $134.

Harbourtowne Resort, Route 33, Box 670, St. Michaels 21663. (301) 745-9066. The first new lodging facility in St. Michaels in the 1980s, this was patterned after a similar development at Hilton Head. Hence the resort-like resemblance with an 18-hole, Pete Dye-designed golf course, Olympic-size pool, tennis courts, conference facilities and posh homes all around. Situated a couple of miles west of town and a mile off the road through the luxury 573-acre planned community known as Martingham, this could not be closer to the water — smack up against the rocky Miles River shore on a peninsula with water on three sides. The second-floor rooms of the original 48-unit complex, nicely secluded in several cedar buildings, have brick walls up to vaulted ceilings, spacious dressing areas and private balconies overlooking a tree-lined inlet and lagoon populated by flocks of birds. Some of the 30 new villas in five buildings on the point are right on the shore, the most coveted having water on three sides. The rooms here, with double or kingsize beds, are plush but smaller than was ours in the older section. The large **Harbourwatch** dining room in the main conference center has water views and is perfectly serviceable for three meals a day in a conference-center kind of way. We enjoyed a dinner of rich crab imperial and a tasty shrimp, crab and lobster dish served in a ramekin, but were taken aback when we asked about desserts and the waitress replied, "I think we have brownies back there, and maybe some blueberry pie and carrot cake." Our only real regret was that the air-conditioning in the unit next to ours was so loud that it obliterated the sounds of the birds and water as we relaxed on our balcony and the sliding doors were not screened so we couldn't open them for fresh air at night. Doubles, $65 to $95.

Robert Morris Inn, Morris Street at the Strand, Box 70, Oxford 21654. (301) 226-5111. Built prior to 1710, the home of the important Robert Morris family has been expanded several times since it housed Robert Morris Jr., who was to become a close friend of George Washington and financier of the Revolution. But it remains a study in Colonial architecture and the fame of its dining room and tavern extends far beyond the Eastern Shore. Best of all, for those who seek a Southern experience beside the water, is **Sandaway,** the inn's newly refurbished riverfront mansion with sumptuous rooms, many with porches looking onto the lovely Tred Avon River. Surrounded by treed lawns leading to the river, Sandaway offers several riverfront cottages, a small beach and a view of the Tred Avon Yacht Club. The 19th century house has a small den with TV and seven spacious rooms lavishly furnished with antiques, including kingsize canopy and pencil post beds, large private baths and rocking chairs on screened porches facing the water. The rooms in the 18th century mansard-roofed main inn are more historic but well appointed; one of the nicest, Room 1 with river view and private bath, has a four-poster bed, a sofa and upholstered chair near a working fireplace of English bricks, and hooked rugs over the sloping, wide-board floor. The handmade nails, hand-hewn oak pegs and original Georgia white pine flooring are typical of the Colonial detail throughout the inn. All told, the Robert Morris offers 33 rooms, 16 in the inn and 17 in or around Sandaway, all but five on the inn's third floor with private baths. Non-smoking rooms are available. Innkeepers Ken and Wendy Gibson say they cater to couples — no children or groups. Doubles $40 to $90 in inn, $80 to $120 at Sandaway.

The Inn at Perry Cabin, Route 33, Box 247, St. Michaels 21663. (301) 745-5178. Although known primarily for its dining and party facilities, this historic structure beside Fogg Cove has six upstairs guest rooms for overnighters. You enter via a wide alley of trees from the gate just west of town; an old holly tree — believed to be the Eastern Shore's oldest — shades the brick terrace at the inn's entrance. You'd never suspect that Perry Cabin was built just after the War of 1812 by Samuel Hambleton, first purser of the U.S. Navy, who was aide-de-camp to Commodore Oliver Perry ("we have met the enemy and they are ours") in the Battle of Lake Erie. It was designed to resemble the ship's cabin of Perry, whom he admired and wanted to make feel at home on visits to the Eastern Shore. The original cabin has been expanded several times into a Colonial revival mansion with pillared portico facing the water. It first served as an inn in 1909 and then as the Perry Cabin riding academy, and was the setting in 1928 for the silent movie, "The First Kiss," starring Gary Cooper, Fay Wray and several townspeople. In 1980, it was restored as an inn by Harry and Teresa Meyerhoff. They owned the racehorse Spectacular Bid, winner of the Kentucky Derby, and the **Spectacular Bid Lounge** is filled with racing memorabilia. The original curving staircase leads to the guest rooms, each with private bath and furnished with period pieces; two have sitting rooms and three have water views. Guests share the spacious grounds with gaggles of Canada geese and mallards, and have access to bicycles for trips into St. Michaels. A continental breakfast of sweet rolls and coffee is served. Doubles, $87 to $135.

Hambleton Inn, 202 Cherry St., St. Michaels 21633. (301) 745-3350. A wicker-filled porch facing the harbor runs the length of the second floor of this 1860 B&B, which is very Southern and elegant in feeling. Opened in 1986 by Aileen and Harry Arader, who also have the St. Michaels Inn, it reflects the design flair of Mrs. Arader, who owns the Aileen Arader Boutique. The five guest rooms, each with private bath and harbor view, may have king or queen four-poster beds with pillow covers matching the wallpaper and St. Michaels Pottery accessories; one has a working fireplace and all are ever-so-decorated. Nautical types like the Schooner Room or the Crow's Nest Room at the top, which has a bird's-eye view of the harbor. A continental breakfast of fresh fruit and breakfast cake is served. Doubles, $70 to $85.

Two Swan Inn, Foot of Carpenter Street., Box 727, St. Michaels 21663. (301) 745-2929. This inviting B&B couldn't have a nicer location, its spacious treed lawn sloping to the harbor in full view of all the boating action. Once the home of the Miles River Yacht Club, the 19th century house was renovated by innkeepers Susan and Andy Merrill in 1984. They offer five guest rooms sharing two baths, the three larger ones fronting onto the harbor and one with a fireplace. What Susan calls a sturdy continental breakfast might include baked apples and coffee ring. Swans are the decorating motif and you wouldn't be surprised to find one on the front lawn, which is great for lounging. The inn has boats and bikes for guests' use. Doubles, $49 to $69.

Wades Point Inn, Wades Point Road, Box 130, McDaniel 21647. (301) 745-2500. Very Southern looking, this imposing white brick plantation-style home is surrounded by attractive grounds and backs up to Chesapeake Bay about five miles beyond St. Michaels on the way to Tilghman Island. The original house was built in 1819 by Baltimore shipwright Thomas Kemp. A summer wing was added in 1890 and it has operated as a guest house in the old Bay tradition ever since. "We've been updating it but want it to stay comfy and homey," said effervescent innkeeper Betsy Feiler, who's owned it with husband John since 1984. They offer fourteen guest rooms, two with private baths, and several more with wash basin in the rooms. Most rooms are interestingly if sparely furnished, and the annex is candidly described as a "sophisticated Girl Scout house." The summer wing is what you'd expect to find around Tidewater: rooms with high ceilings (and windows) open off the long corridor, the entrance to each containing a screen door inside the regular door, which guests tend to leave open for cross-ventilation on summer nights. The main parlor is comfortably furnished with two sofas, a piano, a tapestry over the fireplace and more books than a Southern gentleman could possibly have read. Also impressive are the Peruvian hangings in the dining room, and a gorgeous back room filled with white wicker. A continental breakfast of muffins and croissants is included, and guests may use the Roost, the second floor of an outbuilding with rustic furniture and benches like a camp, for BYO drinks. A new rear porch looks onto the river, where Betsy says guests find the biggest crabs off the dock (she'll boil them for you); there's great fishing and you'll marvel at the deer and birds. Doubles, $49 to $69.

The Tilghman Inn and Lodging, Coopertown Road, Box B, Tilghman 21671. (301) 886-2141. A modern motel with condominium units, restaurant, lounge and marina — this is anything but an inn. Yet for those who want creature comforts and a waterfront location where Knapps Narrows joins the Choptank River and Chesapeake Bay, this is the best choice on Tilghman Island. New management has been renovating the 20 rooms, which have two double beds and full baths. Also available are suites with kitchen areas. Caribbean-style rattan furnishings characterize the **Narrows Lounge.** The paneled **Captain's Table** dining room looks onto the marshes and inlet; an open umbrellaed deck overlooks the bay. Three meals a day are served; the fare is considered a bit more current than the area's norm. Doubles, $55 to $75, depending on view and renovation; suites, $85 to $95.

Other Choices

The Parsonage Inn, 210 N. Talbot St., St. Michaels 21663. (301) 745-5519. New in 1986 was this striking-looking inn extensively renovated from a former church parsonage. Check the unusual brick exterior with its many inlay patterns, the Victorian gingerbread trim over the porches and the steeple-type roof above. Four rooms were fashioned from the parsonage and three with separate entrances were added motel-style at the rear. All with private baths including Victorian pedestal wash basins and brass fixtures, they have king or queen beds, plush carpeting and thick towels, Queen Anne-style furniture and Laura Ashley linens and accessories. Three have working fire-places, a couple open onto an upstairs deck and two have television. Oriental rugs and fine Victorian furniture enhance the cozy fireplaced parlor and large formal dining room, where fresh-ground coffee, croissants or pastries and what innkeeper Willard Workman calls the best cantaloupes ever are served for breakfast. A patio has lovely wicker furniture, the landscaping is perfect and the decor reflects the sure touch of the innkeeper's son. Doubles, $68 to $78.

St. Michaels Inn, 208 N. Talbot St., St. Michaels 21663. (301) 745-3303. Two side-by-side buildings dating from the 1870s offer a restaurant with three new guest rooms above and a lodging annex with eight rooms, each with private entrance, private bath, TV and air-conditioning. The inn has been owned since 1983 by Aileen and Harry Arader (she also runs the new Hambleton Inn) and her decorating panache is evident here as well. In the lodging building, a onetime rooming house, a typical front room has kingsize bed with canopied headboard and shuttered windows to block out the street. The new rooms over the restaurant have frilly queensize four-poster beds. A full-menu breakfast is served guests in the restaurant. Doubles, $69.

Kemp House Inn, 412 Talbot St., Box 638, St. Michaels 21663. (301) 745-2243. In 1982, this was the first B&B to open in St. Michaels, and it's said that Gen. Robert E. Lee stayed here long before that. Built in 1805, it has six guest rooms, two on each floor, but no common facilities other than a rocker-lined front porch and a back yard. Period furnishings and candles are in each room, which have four-poster rope beds with trundle beds beneath, patchwork quilts and down pillows. Four rooms have washstands and W/C, others washstand only, and guests share shower rooms on the second floor. Four also have working fireplaces, lit on cool nights. Continental breakfast with hot pastries is taken on trays in the room or outside on the porch or lawn in summer. Doubles, $38.50 to $70.

RENTALS. Grand View Rentals, Box 217, Neavitt 21652, (301) 745-5069, offers fully equipped housekeeping cottages with screened porches and one or two bedrooms on the waterfront. This is a hot spot for real estate and rentals, and many brokers are located in the area. One of the longest established is Benson & Wales, 208 Talbot St., St. Michaels, (301) 745-2936.

Seeing and Doing

Although steeped in maritime tradition, St. Michaels may be too recently rediscovered to have the tourist sights and guides usually associated with such an area. We found no visitor information center and only a couple of brochures with information about the town, although quaint black signs with white lettering point to some attractions at street corners.

On or Near the Water

Chesapeake Bay Maritime Museum, Navy Point, St. Michaels. (301) 745-2916. Founded in 1965 and built on mounds of crushed oyster shells, the expanding museum is the town's major tourist attraction, drawing nearly 100,000 visitors annually. British-born curator Richard Dodds ranks it among the nation's 10 largest, but notes that presently it's bigger in property (18 acres) than in collections. That may change when the future Watermen's Village is developed, detailing life in a typical bay village of a century ago.

For the moment, the museum features the largest floating fleet of historic Chesapeake Bay boats in existence, including a skipjack, log canoe, oyster boat and crab dredger. They're maintained in a traditional working boat shop, where you get to see craftsmen at work and view a small display of primitive boat-building tools.

The focal point is the 1879 Hooper Strait Lighthouse, one of only three cottage-type lighthouses remaining on the bay; its move to St. Michaels was the impetus that inspired the museum. You learn what a lightkeeper's life was like and pass some interesting exhibits of fog signals, lamps and lenses as you climb to the top level for a bird's-eye view of the St. Michaels harbor. The Waterfowling Building contains an extensive collection of decoys, guns and mounted waterfowl, all so important in this area. The 18th century corn crib houses gunning boats now outlawed for use on the bay. The Chesapeake Bay Building traces the area's geological and social history.

Among other sights are the Small Boat Exhibit Shed, a bell tower, a Victorian bandstand where concerts are still staged in the summer, and a small aquarium whose "exhibit population depends on what the museum staff catches as well as what inhabitant has dined upon another," according to the museum guide. It's that kind of a low-key, low-budget place. The museum shop is exceptionally good, containing many books, cookbooks for sailors, decoys, needlepoint coasters and Chesapeake Challenge, an intriguing game.

Museum open daily in summer, 10 to 5, Saturdays to 7; rest of year, 10 to 4; January to mid-March, weekends only. Adults $3, children $1.

Patriot Cruise, Navy Point, St. Michaels, 745-3100. The best way to see and savor this part of the Eastern Shore — most of its meandering shoreline is very private and far from view — is by boat. Baltimore native David Etzel, his wife and two young daughters run the area's only excursion boat, giving a leisurely 90-minute cruise up the Miles River. The two-deck boat with bar carries 103 passengers. Dave advised beforehand that he points out "birds, houses, duck blinds, whatever I see." We saw the Mystic Clipper in the distance, various kinds of bulkheading to prevent shore erosion, several osprey nests on channel markers, the ruins of St. John's Chapel and some mighty impressive plantations and contemporary homes. We learned that the Miles River is not really a river but a brackish tidal estuary of the bay, and that James Michener wrote *Chesapeake* in a rented house along the river; he now has a house outside St. Michaels on Broad Creek. The river was originally called the St. Michaels, Dave said, but the Quakers dropped the "Saint" and local dialect turned Michaels into Miles. Our only regret was that the boat didn't go closer to the sights the guide or taped narration were pointing out on the 11-mile round trip. Cruises daily at 11, 1 and 3 (minimum 15 persons), mid-May to mid-October. Adults $5, children $2.50.

Oxford-Bellevue Ferry, Foot of Morris Street at the Strand, Oxford, 226-4508 or 745-9023. America's oldest ferry (established 1683) crosses the Tred Avon River between Oxford and Bellevue. It's the shortest way to get from St. Michaels to Oxford and, again, the scenery conveys a feeling of the Thames and Great Britain, to which this area was so closely allied. The main ferry holds nine cars; a smaller, older one is pressed into service weekends and in summer. Continuous crossings are provided every 15 to 20 minutes, May to Labor Day, Monday-Friday 7 a.m. to 9 p.m., weekends 9 to 9; Labor Day through April, service stops at sunset. Car and driver, $3.50 one way, $5 round trip.

SAILBOAT CHARTERS. Eastern Shore Yacht Charters, Tilghman Street,

Oxford, 226-5000, rents day and overnight sailboats and power boats, from 13 to 44 feet in size. **Chesapeake Yachting Center Charters,** Town Creek Restaurant and Marina, Oxford, 226-5900, rents the 44-foot Caribbean yacht Foot Loose and the 41-foot Lord Nelson yacht Fitz In by the day or week, and has tugboat charters.

St. Michaels Town Dock Marina, St. Michaels. (301) 745-2400. Outboard runabouts, sailboats, pedal boats and bikes are available for rent or charter on the Town Dock. A 13-foot, 30-horsepower outboard goes for $55 for two hours ($150 deposit required); sailboats start at $18 for two hours; pedal boats are $5 for half an hour, $8 an hour.

Guided fishing and hunting services are offered by countless individuals and outfits in St. Michaels and Tilghman Island.

Other Attractions

St. Michaels Walking Tour. A short self-guided walking tour with map is provided by the St. Mary's Square Museum and the St. Michaels Business Association. It covers the meandering waterfront, including the footbridge from Cherry Street to Navy Point (one wishes there were more footbridges to get from point to point), the Talbot Street business section and St. Mary's Square, an unusual town green laid out away from the main street and apt to be missed unless you seek it out. The map identifies 23 historic houses (none open to the public), churches and sites; you'll likely find equally interesting things along the way.

The St. Mary's Square Museum, On the Green, St. Michaels, 745-9561. One of the town's oldest Colonial houses was moved to this site, restored and furnished. It is joined to an 1860 Teetotum Building, so named because it resembles an old-fashioned top. The museum's display areas of local memorabilia and history are open weekends from 10 to 5, May-October. Admission 50 cents.

Museum of Costume, 400 St. Mary's Square, St. Michaels, 745-5154. Since 1985, Millie Hudson Curtis has been displaying in an 1843 sea captain's home the historic costume collection she started in the 1940s. Outfits of Mrs. Abraham Lincoln and Mrs. Benjamin Harrison, a vest from Clark Gable, a Jean Harlow evening dress and a Mae West shawl are among the prized items dating from 1800 and explained in detail by Mrs. Curtis. Open daily 11 to 5, April-November. Donation $2.

OXFORD. The Strand at Oxford's north side, facing Bellevue, is the only real beach we saw in this area. Few people swim in Chesapeake Bay or its estuaries because of sea nettles which sting everything but the palms and feet, we were told. Once Maryland's principal port, Oxford is a lovely, tree-lined town in which the presence of water on all sides is felt more than in St. Michaels. Never in one small area have we seen so many sailboats, yachts and marinas. Besides marinas and restaurants, there are a few shops, several historic buildings and the small **Oxford Museum,** open Friday-Sunday from 2 to 5.

BIKING. The flat, meandering terrain is good bicycling country. Favorite day trips by bike or car are across the old Tred Avon River ferry to Oxford, which has an ever-so-British yet Southern feeling, or out to a different world on Tilghman Island, where much of the Eastern Shore's famed seafood is caught and the watermen are ubiquitous. Another scenic byway is Route 579 to Bozman and Neavitt. Bicycles are available at **St. Michaels Bike Rentals,** on the town dock, 745-5715, ($3 an hour, $16 all day), or the **Bike Boatique** in the Oxford Mews, Morris Street, Oxford, 820-2222.

SHOPPING. Most of the area's shopping is found along narrow Talbot Street in St. Michaels, and much of it has to do with the area's position as a waterfowl center (the annual mid-November Waterfowl Festival draws 20,000 people to neighboring Easton and is considered the best of its kind in the country). A stuffed bear wearing a St. Michaels T-shirt was mounted outside the **Hunting Horn,** which advertised "olde and newe finds for the sporte in your life."

Hodgepodge Collectibles offers wreaths and baskets of every description, plus other country-cute things displayed on open shelves and hanging from the ceiling. The **St. Michaels Pottery** store speaks for itself, while the **Ship's Store** has nautical necessities and clothing. Among a number of fine shops are **Aileen Arader Boutique, Peas & Carrots** children's apparel, **Woodworks Etc., Lilli's Fair Exchange, Sports and Specialties Shop**, and several including a good kitchen-gourmet shop in the small **Town Hall Mall**.

Where to Eat

This is seafood country, a paradise for lovers of fresh oysters and crabs. Prices are generally modest and frills are few.

Windows on the Water

The Inn at Perry Cabin, Talbot Street, St. Michaels. (301) 745-5178. The most elaborate place in town is this sprawling restaurant and lounge surrounded by treed lawns looking onto Fogg Cove. A ramble of candlelit dining rooms, each individually and richly decorated in antique style, accommodates 110 people upstairs and down; dozens more can be served drinks outside around a large waterfront gazebo featuring live entertainment. Locals consider this a special-occasion restaurant; the continental menu is fancier than most in the area. Appetizers are standard, $3.25 to $5.50 for escargots in mushroom caps to seafood cocktail. A few entrees are a bit more adventurous — veal Biloxi with shrimp, baby rack of lamb au poivre — and priced from $9.95 to $16.95, served with a salad and fettuccine Alfredo. The management especially recommends the crab imperial and seafood Norfolk. Sandwiches, platters and salads are served at lunch in the lounge. Lunch and dinner daily, 11:30 to 10; Sunday brunch from 10.

The Crab Claw, Navy Point, St. Michaels. (301) 745-2900. The first tourist attraction in St. Michaels, this self-styled "tradition" has been operated very successfully since 1965 by Bill and Sylvia Jones, whose daughter Tracy says "we feel responsible for the development of St. Michaels." Certainly they are responsible for feeding hundreds of diners at all hours (except at 9:30 one slow September weeknight when we tried to get in and were told the kitchen had just closed). The knotty pine main room looking onto the harbor has open windows to let in the breeze, a vaulted ceiling crossed by a mishmash of beams, large tables where you sit family style, a bare floor and mallets for cracking crabs. There's more dining in a back room, and in summer you can eat by the water at picnic tables and a raw bar, watching the help steam crabs and shuck oysters. The menu is all seafood, except for hamburgers and fried chicken, and the placemat tells you how to tackle your crab. Fried hard blue crab ($5.95) is the house specialty, but crab also is served in soup, cocktail, salad, backfin crab cake, soft crab sandwich, crab fluff, imperial and even a crab dog ($1.50). There are platters from fried clams and oysters ($9.95) to mixed seafood ($14.95). Beer and liquor are available. The seafood is fresh and priced right, and the atmosphere casual and fun. Open Tuesday-Sunday 11 to 10. Closed mid-November to mid-March. No credit cards.

Lighthouse Restaurant, St. Michaels Harbour Inn and Marina, 101 N. Harbor Road, St. Michaels. (301) 745-9001. A commanding water view in an angled dining room is offered in the town's large new inn. The color scheme is mauve and raspberry with blond wood chairs. The initial menu was fairly standard in the Eastern Shore style. When we dined a couple of months after it opened, service was slow and prone to error. But the price was right: a dinner tab of $35 for two for a bottle of Robert Mondavi chardonnay, scampi Chesapeake sauteed in garlic wine butter but missing the advertised cilantro, and the night's special of two oysters, clams and shrimp stuffed with crab imperial; good rice and crisp long green beans accompanied. Entrees run from $8.95 for broiled flounder to $16.95 for filet mignon. A limited lunch menu was priced in the $5 range, and we enjoyed a stack of apple pecan pancakes for breakfast as we watched the harbor activity. Three meals daily, dinner to 9 or 10.

Longfellow's, 125 Mulberry St., St. Michaels (301) 745-2624. Outside decks with white molded chairs and an interior with large windows take full advantage of the harborfront location at this contemporary restaurant. Inside, the ceiling covered with white and blue beach umbrellas adds to the nautical feeling. Hot crusty rolls and undistinguished salads came with our dinners of six stuffed oysters, incredibly rich and topped with crab and a cheese sauce, and Napoli Nice, a pasta dish topped with succulent soft-shell crabs. Entrees ($8.95 to $14.50) are also accompanied by a vegetable of the chef's creation — in our case, rather oddly, pasta with vegetables. Desserts are primarily homemade vanilla ice cream in many variations; we shared an ample creme de menthe parfait, served with a shot of liqueur on the side. Open daily, 11:30 to 10.

Town Dock Restaurant, 305 Mulberry St., St. Michaels. (301) 745-5577. The locals like this small place, which dates to the 1830s when it was one of the area's first oyster shucking sheds. We found the inside rather dark for lunch, but the picnic tables we had to ourselves outside on the dock were fine. We tried the sampler of three soups ($2.50), crab bisque (so floury as to taste almost like library paste), a spicy seafood jambalaya and a mediocre vichyssoise. The fried oyster sandwich with steak potatoes in garlic butter ($4) and a shrimp and crab salad ($5.50) were only fair, but filling. The dinner menu is vaguely continental (Caesar salad, chicken forestiere, wiener schnitzel and cioppino), priced from $9 to $12.50 for rack of lamb. The dessert list is the town's most interesting, from chocolate decadence with raspberry puree to sherry cream trifle and bananas Foster. Open daily from 7:30 to 10.

Pier Street Restaurant, West Pier Street off South Morris, Oxford. (301) 226-5171. The best restaurant view hereabouts is from the picnic tables on the covered outdoor deck wrapping around this 450-seat restaurant beside the Tred Avon River, facing a broad expanse of Chesapeake Bay beyond. "The sunsets are unbelievable," says owner Anna Siachos. "I've been here six years and still haven't seen enough." We'd choose to sit outside at one of the oilcloth-covered tables and look at all the boats and some impressive houses on the nearby shore; the spacious inner dining room is a bit more formal. The large menu purveys something for everyone, including Florida snapper and shad roe. Entrees range from $7.95 for clam strips or fried chicken to $17.95 for seafood platter. Avoid the wine list, but the beer selection is excellent. Lunch daily, 11:30 to 4:30; dinner from 4:30 and all day Sunday.

Bay Hundred Restaurant Co., Route 33 at Knapps Narrows, Tilghman. (301) 886-2622. A deceptive, small gray building beside the water houses a funky lounge with jukebox and video games and beyond, a rustic dining porch that serves up what many consider the area's best food. It's certainly among the most interesting, prepared from scratch by chef-owner Donelda Monahan, who uses seasonal seafood and local produce. Except for a seafood combo plate, dinner entrees run from $8.50 to $12.50 for Gulf shrimp over pasta, sweet and sour shrimp, chicken tempura, ginger beef, stir-fries, eggplant parmesan and, of course, crab cakes and soft-shell crabs. Oysters Donelda, served over pasta with an oriental flair, won second prize in the Chesapeake Appreciation Days festival. Start with Cajun coconut shrimp and end with grand marnier pudding, the signature dessert for which Bon Appetit magazine requested the recipe. The house salad dressing — a mayonnaise base with curry, thyme, onion and vinegar — is so popular the restaurant sells it by the pint. The wine list, heavy on California vintages, is one of the area's best. The decor is plain with bare tables, cloth mats and candles. Accents are assorted glass jars containing flowers, tools on the walls and other knickknacks given to Donelda and husband Jamie by a supportive community. Homemade soups, salads and pastas are featured at lunch. Lunch and dinner daily.

The Bridge, Route 33 at Knapps Narrows, Tilghman Island. (301) 886-2500. Taking its name from the adjacent drawbridge (said to be the busiest in the world), this attractive restaurant on two levels has some great views, especially from two small alcoves with four or five tables right over the water and a small upstairs crow's nest with glass on all sides. The unusual polished tables made by owner Francis Cole contain inlaid ropes topped with polyurethane. Artifacts and treasures unearthed off the coast of Key West also figure prominently in the decor. Oysters (all you can eat) are $1.95 with any or dinner entree; they also come in fritters, a deep-dish pie, fried or baked stuffed ($7.95 to $12.95). That's the price range for other entrees, from crab imperial to stuffed pork chops or prime rib. An extravagant seafood buffet on Friday nights is $9.95. Homemade desserts like English trifle, Austrian cheesecake, Danish cognac torte and sweet potato pie are on display in a case, as are salads, biscuits and muffins. Lunch and dinner daily.

Harrison's Chesapeake House, Route 33, Tilghman Island. (301) 886-2123. Run for nearly a century by four generations of the Harrison family, this vast restaurant, motel and sport-fishing center is a legend on the Eastern Shore. The 48 overnight accommodations in the inn and motel have seen better days, but the yellow and green hotel-style restaurant divided in three sections is especially well liked by families and bus tours. It seats 220, the hostess said, but "it feels like 4,000 on a Saturday night." Beyond is a covered deck near the water with a bar and carry-out area. Letters posted on the wall of the wicker-filled front porch, where diners wait for a table, testify to owner Buddy Harrison's hospitality. The menu is typically Eastern Shore, with dinner entrees from $7.95 for pan-fried chicken to $12.95 for seafood extravaganza (five seafoods) and the house specialty, fried chicken and crab cakes. Large bowls of applesauce, cole slaw and stewed tomatoes come with the seafood dishes. When we visited, Harrison was planning to build a Harrison Hotel on Baltimore's Inner Harbor at Pier 5 and planned to shuttle visitors back and forth to Baltimore on boats. Breakfast, lunch and dinner daily.

Other Choices

Robert Morris Inn, Morris Street at the Strand, Oxford. (301) 226-5111. No dining reservations are accepted at this landmark inn with a large and popular restaurant. Lunch in the Tavern is an experience straight from the 18th century, the staff in Colonial costumes amid walls of brick, floors of Vermont slate and the Morris coat of arms above the fireplace. Many like to start with a hot buttered rum or the 1710, a mixture of amber rum and fruit juices in a Colonial glass that you get to keep ($6.95). A basket of corn muffins (which crumbled all over the table) preceded our crab soup, a house specialty chock full of vegetables, and a paltry dish of three mushrooms stuffed with crab imperial for $4.25. More filling was a delicious and pure oyster stew ($3.95). You can order anything from a crab cake sandwich platter to prime rib on the extensive lunch menu, $3.75 to $12.95, or mix and match appetizers as we did. The dinner menu, though standard, is even more extensive — from assorted juices (95 cents) to prime rib supreme topped with crabmeat ($19.95), a combination we certainly wouldn't order. As you'd expect, crab is the specialty — from soup to crab cakes, crab Norfolk, crab imperial and a variety of seafood platters. Desserts run from pecan pie to assorted parfaits. The formal, carpeted and chandeliered dining room has well-spaced tables, stenciled chairs and four impressive murals. Lunch, Monday-Saturday noon to 3; dinner 6 to 9, Sunday noon to 8.

The Masthead, Mill Street, Oxford. (301) 226-5303. "We don't own a crab steamer or deep fat fryer," proclaims the sign in front of this hard-to-find restaurant behind the Oxford Boatyard. Instead, the owners hope that simple food, innovative recipes and fresh vegetables might prove a welcome alternative to the ubiquitous fried fish and steamed crabs. There's no view; the main dining room consists of small tables napped in white and blue and set apart in unusual carpeted alcoves. But the Masthead does a large dinner business by reservation, "which is hard to find here," said the host, who called the seven-year-old place a local secret. Chef Sarah MacKenzie's menu is ever-changing, with appetizers like a spicy gazpacho with shrimp and crabmeat, house pate or smoked marlin, and such entrees ($10.95 to $21.95) as filet mignon with a blue cheese-mustard sauce, veal au vin, broiled bluefish, and rack of lamb baked in Guinness stout and served with red currant-horseradish sauce. The dessert tray features house-baked pies, cakes, tarts and cheesecake. Full lunches are served from April 15 to Labor Day; the rest of the year it's a soup and sandwich buffet with salad bar in the lounge. The weekend brunch offers fare like crab Benedict from $3.25 to $6.95. Lunch, Monday-Friday noon to 2:30; dinner, 6 to 9:30 or 10; weekend brunch, 11 to 3.

The Oxford Inn, South Morris Street, Oxford. (301) 226-5220. Since 1984, innkeepers Pat and Jerry Mullins have been offering highly rated fare in two pretty dining rooms fashioned from a century-old country store. Laura Ashley-type printed linens, candles and fresh flowers brighten the main room with its bare floors and original pressed-tin ceiling. The menu mixes appetizers like stuffed potato skins and Texas chili with cream of crab soup laced with sherry and a hint of curry, and entrees ($8.95 to $15.95) like flounder amandine, seafood Norfolk and filet mignon. Desserts include an English sherry trifle topped with fresh cream and walnuts. Upstairs are four air-conditioned guest rooms which have queensize beds and share one bath; doubles are $50, including continental breakfast. Lunch daily, noon to 2; dinner, 6 to 9.

St. Michaels Inn, 208 N. Talbot St., St. Michaels. (301) 745-3303. Three meals a day are served in this restaurant elegantly refurbished by Aileen and Harry Arader. A pleasant lounge leads to three dining rooms, each very different and very decorated. The most formal has pink cloths, rose fanned napkins, candles in tall hurricane lamps and high-back chairs; a small garden room has a canopy on the ceiling, lawn furniture and paper mats, and the largest has brick and wood walls, white fanned napkins and pewter service plates with the inn's logo. The dinner menu varies, becoming more extensive and pricier on weekends. Choices might include deviled crab, seafood Norfolk, scampi on linguini, veal Oscar or roast duckling with a wild cherry sauce, $10.45 to $19.95. Open daily, breakfast 7:45 to 11:30, lunch noon to 3, dinner 5 to 9 or 10.

The Salty Oyster, Route 33, St. Michaels. (301) 745-5151. A schooner in a display case at the entrance to this restaurant run by the adjacent fish market is topped by a sign, "Be kind to cows — eat seafood today." That's what you do at large, heavy wood tables, well spaced and accented with beige napkins, in a setting of hanging plants and lamps. The all-you-can-eat crab feast, including fried chicken and corn on the cob, is naturally popular at $12; so is the special fried oyster platter with two vegetables and bread, $9.25. Chesapeake surf and turf is two crab cakes and fried chicken! The menu goes from $9.95 for crab cakes to $15 for Alaskan king crab. There's a full bar, but no wine list. Open daily, 11:30 to 10 or 11.

Casual St. Michaels Choices: At the **Bread Basket,** 210 Talbot St., newcomer Alice Karakas is up before dawn every day to bake the wonderful breads and muffins that make this a good choice for breakfast (takeout or at a couple of tiny tables). Her sticky buns and cinnamon rolls are the most sought after, but the sourdough and French breads draw raves. Her secret: "I bake just like I was at home and I'm the only one around here to do it from scratch." The **Talbot Street Cafe,** 106 N. Talbot, is casual, with checked brown and white tablecloths inside and picnic tables outside, serving sandwiches from $1.25 to $3.75, homemade crab cakes, malted cones and beer on draft, daily from 11. **Liz's Hoagie Shop,** 116 N. Talbot, has the only Philadelphia cheese steak sandwiches and authentic hoagies on the Eastern Shore. For local color, try the **Cove** at Hudson's Pharmacy, Talbot Street. Beyond the newsstand and sundries are a few tables and a counter where you can hear the gossip and get a cheap meal (we tried the scrapple for breakfast, but almost needed a gas mask as many regulars lit up cigaret after cigaret).

FOR MORE INFORMATION: Talbot County Chamber of Commerce, 7 Federal St., Box 1366, Easton, Md. (301) 822-4606.

Greg Pease/Baltimore Photo

National Aquarium is backdrop for boats in Baltimore Harbor.

Baltimore Harbor, Md.

"Harbor of History," it's called by the operators of excursion boats that ply thousands of visitors daily along the Baltimore waterfront in a variety of craft. They might also call it a harbor of fun. Baltimore's recently transformed harbor has an abundance of both.

For history, consider that the guardian of the harbor, old Fort McHenry, is the place where Baltimore turned back the British in the War of 1812. Had the city not withstood the challenge, the course of American history might have been different. And Francis Scott Key's "Star Spangled Banner," written as he watched the bombardment by dawn's early light, might not have become the National Anthem. The past lives on across the harbor from Fort McHenry in Fell's Point, still a working urban seaport community.

Baltimore's harbor area is making history today. Only a decade ago, it was a wasteland of rotting piers, warehouses and railroad yards, and the city in general was the butt of jokes around the country. Today, the restored Inner Harbor — the horseshoe-shaped recreation area where the Patapsco River moves from downtown out to Chesapeake Bay — is alive with new buildings, boats and people in a transformation that has Baltimore starring on the covers of national magazines.

The focus is hometown developer James W. Rouse's Harborplace, the twin pavilions of shops and restaurants that sparked the renewal of both harborfront and downtown in a joint public-private revitalization effort considered to be the best managed in the nation. On either side of Harborplace, landscaped promenades lead to the Maryland Science Center, the National Aquarium, the vast P.T. Flagg's nightclub and the Pier 6 Concert Pavilion. Pedestrian skywalks link the harbor with nearly a dozen new and renovated hotels, a huge convention center, a Festival Hall where ethnic festivals are staged most summer weekends, and Charles Center. Still to come are the emerging Gallery at Harborplace, the new Fish Market and the Brokerage, lively entertainment and shopping centers.

No wonder Baltimore Harbor now attracts 21 million visitors a year, more than Disney World.

They come to be near the water, of course, and to enjoy a bit of history, in the past and in the making. They also come to have fun — amid the festival atmosphere of Harborplace, the nightclub offerings of the Six Flags' Power Plant, the attractions of the National Aquarium and the Maryland Science Center, the name entertainers at the Concert Pavilion, and any number of watercraft from pedal boats to Tall Ships.

So come along with us and the millions of others attracted to Baltimore's Inner Harbor. Rarely will you find so many things to see and do — most of them fun-oriented — in such a compact and appealing area.

Getting There

Baltimore is a major transportation center served by airlines and trains. Interstate 95 passes under the harbor via the new Fort McHenry Tunnel. Also serving the city are Interstate 83 from the north and Interstate 70 from the west. Well-marked exits lead to downtown, where unusually good (and numerous) signs steer you to the Inner Harbor and other points of interest.

Where to Stay

For a city which had only a few hotels less than a decade ago, Baltimore now has an abundance. Nearly 3,000 hotel rooms have been added since 1984 in the downtown area, most of them near the Inner Harbor. You can get around to most Inner Harbor-downtown attractions by walking the promenades and pedestrian skywalk system, taking a water taxi (see below) or the new Baltimore trolleys, which traverse two routes along Charles Street and the Inner Harbor (fare 25 cents).

Hyatt Regency Baltimore, 300 Light St., Baltimore 21202. (301) 528-1234. Opened in 1981 shortly after Harborplace, which is just across the street, the glittering, glitzy Hyatt with its trademark six-story atrium and outdoor glass elevators was the forerunner of the city's hotel boom. Such is the boom's pace now that — can you believe it? — the Hyatt was already undergoing renovations in 1987, which says more for the competition than for the state of the Hyatt. Nowhere else can you get such a view — if you're lucky enough to get one of the booked-far-in-advance harborview rooms. And no other hotel is so advantageously located for everything near the water. Each of the 500 guest rooms is spacious and furnished in typical Hyatt style. The outdoor swimming pool and three tennis courts atop a roof over the fifth floor are surprisingly popular, given all the attractions around or on the harbor. The lobby is a beehive of activity (especially on the Friday when we arrived to a noisy happy hour with orchestra and a multitude of partakers). Hotel guests get to admire the harbor every time they go up or down the glass elevators; transients have to be satisfied with the view from the 14th-floor rooftop restaurant and lounge, **Berry and Elliot's. The Trellis Garden,** set amid trees and an indoor pond, is considered tops among hotel restaurants in the city, and the lavish Sunday brunch buffet at the more casual **Cascades** restaurant beside the waterfall is one of the city's best (with unlimited champagne, served from 10 to 2, adults $15.95, children $7.95). Cascades also has a $6.50 breakfast buffet featuring "you name it, we build it" omelets. Doubles, $119 to $160.

Harbor Court Hotel, 550 Light St., Baltimore 21202. (301) 234-0550 or

(800) 824-0076. Opulent, personalized, an exclusive retreat — those are descriptions of this elegant, European-style hotel which opened in the fall of 1986. Its understated six-story brick facade fronts onto the Inner Harbor opposite the Maryland Science Center, beneath a towering condominium complex of which it is a part. Each of the 204 guest rooms, including 25 specialty rooms and suites, is a study in luxury with custom-designed furnishings and such amenities as oversize desks, stocked miniature dry bars, bathrooms with large tubs and television sets, separate make-up areas and bathrobes for guests. The seventh-story penthouse suite contains two bedrooms, woodburning fireplace, grand piano, wet bar and whirlpool tub, and rents for a cool $1,500 a night. Meals are served in the **Cafe Brighton** or **Hampton's,** which features upscale American cuisine and seafood. Doubles, $125 to $225.

Admiral Fell Inn, 888 South Broadway, Baltimore 21231. (301) 522-7377 or (800) 292-4667. Located across the street from the working harbor, this is one of the nicest city inns we've seen, albeit located a bit out of the way in up-and-coming Fell's Point. The brick exterior of the three-building complex which was restored in 1985 into an inn gives little indication of its past dating to 1790 as a seafarer's hostelry, the home of a Baltimore mayor, a vinegar bottling plant, a dance hall and a house of ill repute. Inside, all is deluxe, from the fireplaced drawing room in deep hunter green and red where you check in at an antique partners' desk to the comfortable library with its honor bar to the small four-story atrium letting in light to all floors. Each of the original 37 rooms (23 more were being added in 1987) is named for a famous Baltimorean resident (like Edgar Allan Poe) or visitor, with a biography of its namesake on the wall. Owner Jim Widman is from Savannah, Ga., and his background shows in the rooms: rice-carved or pencil-point canopied beds, Federal period antiques or reproductions, and TVs hidden in armoires. Each room is different, and you'll be struck by the various color schemes as well as by the art displays beside the atrium shaft on each floor. The new Admiral Fell Inn restaurant features Swiss cuisine with many dishes prepared tableside, and an English-style pub. There's outdoor dining on an enclosed courtyard. Free van transportation throughout Baltimore is provided for guests. A continental breakfast is served in the bedrooms or the library. Doubles, $90 to $115.

Sheraton Inner Harbor Hotel, 300 South Charles St., Baltimore 21201. (301) 962-8300. Quieter and more sedate than its older neighbor, the Hyatt Regency (which obstructs part of the Sheraton's view of the harbor), this smart hotel opened in 1985 a long block away from the water. Some guests find its restfulness more appealing than the hubbub of the Hyatt. About one-third of the 333 guest rooms in this 15-story structure angled away from the harbor have water views; best are the end rooms which face the harbor straight on. Most have spacious sitting areas; the motif here and in the lobby is muted earth colors, beige walls and rich paneled accents. An indoor health facility contains a sauna, spa and pool, and there's a no-smoking guest floor. **McHenry's** is an all-day American cafe. Doubles, $110 to $140.

Omni International Hotel, 101 W. Fayette St., Baltimore 21201. (301) 752-1100. Busy-busy-busy is the city's largest hotel, actually a two-tower successor to the former Hilton in Charles Center. The busy atmosphere is due, no doubt, to the values offered, including a popular $49 weekend rate

16

for two. Renovated in 1984, the 714 rooms convey the feel of an older hotel, their updating not fully masking the small bathrooms and timeworn corridors. The hotel is about four blocks from Harborplace in the heart of downtown. "We used to have a great view of the harbor but then new buildings blocked it," our guide lamented. One 25th-floor suite has a glimpse of the water, but it's rented by a corporation year-round. Besides an outdoor pool, there's the usual complement of bars and restaurants. Doubles, $99 to $140.

Lord Baltimore Quality Royale Hotel, Baltimore and Hanover Streets, Baltimore 21201. (301) 539-8400 or (800) 228-5152. The old Lord Baltimore was remarkably renovated in 1986 to what management called its original grandeur, after being closed for four years. We can't compare it with the original, but the renovated rooms we saw were quite nice, each with a TV hidden in the armoire, two plush round chairs beside a table, a bathroom with a window and two vanities (one outside the door), and a closet with removable hangers. All told, the hotel has 440 rooms, including suites, and four restaurants. Concierge Level rooms run from the 17th to 28th flooors, with four parlor suites on each floor and a cheery bar on the 17th. Doubles, $85 to $150 (suites).

Other Options. A number of other downtown hotels are located farther from the Inner Harbor, including a Days Inn and a Marriott. The usual motels are scattered around the Baltimore Beltway (I-695) and suburban areas. For bed and breakfast, contact **Amanda's Bed & Breakfast Reservation Service,** (301) 225-0001, run by Betsy Grater, who also has two B&B rooms with private bath in her townhouse at 1428 Park Ave., Baltimore 21217.

Seeing and Doing ⎯⎯⎯⎯⎯⎯⎯⎯ ⟋⟍⟋⟍⟋⟍

Baltimore's Inner Harbor is "a masterpiece of planning and execution," in the words of the American Institute of Architects, which honored it in 1984 as "one of the supreme achievements of large-scale design and development in U.S. history."

Around the Harbor

Harborplace, Pratt & Light streets. The James Rouse-designed marketplace put the Inner Harbor on the map when it opened in 1980. Patterned after Rouse's Faneuil Hall Marketplace in Boston and precursor of his South Street Seaport in New York, this in one way is better than either since it takes full advantage of its waterside location — especially its restaurants, many with outdoor cafes. Here are two glass-enclosed, two-story pavilions linked by a promenade along the harbor. Otherwise, the 135 boutiques and eateries are fairly typical of their genre, with 45 higher-style shops in the Pratt Street Pavilion, and the souvenir shops and most of the 46 specialty eating places, gourmet markets and the mammoth Food Hall in the Light Street Pavilion. You'll likely be struck by all the wares exhorting people to celebrate Baltimore (gone are the days of the city's inferiority complex). Fourteen large restaurants are located in the pavilions. Outside on a plaza between the two are free performances given day and night by a variety of entertainers, from jugglers and mimes to Scottish bagpipers and brass bands. One noontime when we were there, hari krishnas chanted on the grass as a Fuji film blimp floated overhead. Harborplace is at the heart of the harbor and is linked by overhead pedestrian skywalks with hotels and downtown, so it's a busy place most of the time. Shops open daily 10 to 9:30, Sunday noon to 8. Most restaurants open daily until 10, midnight or later; a handful of small eateries open at 8 for breakfast, but most open with the shops.

National Aquarium in Baltimore, Pier 3, 501 E. Pratt St. (301) 576-3810. The crowning jewel of the Inner Harbor is the colorful and architecturally striking National Aquarium in Baltimore, described by Time magazine at its opening as the most advanced and most attractive in the world. Although Congress did not contribute to its funding, it did designate it a national aquarium before the $21 million facility was finished in 1981. In the next five years, it attracted more than six million visitors — 76 percent of them from outside Maryland, and three-fourths of those drawn to Baltimore primarily by the aquarium. Such is its appeal, both to generalists and specialists, that every morning people queue up in long lines for entry every 15 minutes. We visited late on a Friday afternoon, entered immediately and had the place fairly much to ourselves, which is the best way to see it.

The seven-level aquarium is so big that, as one enthusiast noted, you don't walk around it, you walk around in it. Its two large tanks are rings, and you move via escalators and moving sidewalks through the hole in the middle of the rings as fish swim in circles around you. Seals in an outdoor pool and two beluga whales inside the entrance set the stage for things to come. Many people dawdle at the first major attraction, the Open Ocean tank; actually the pool is visible from many points throughout the building, above and underneath, and by the time you're finished the average two-hour tour you may consider its sharks tame stuff. As the recorded glug-glug, squeak and grunt sounds of surf, sea creatures and birds are heard, you wend your way upward through an unusually enlightening mix of descriptions and live displays: the Tidal Marsh, where two fast-moving crabs prance in front of a sign, "No Crabbing or Fishing;" an informative eight-minute slide show called "The Bay at Risk," after which you'll want to join the effort to save the bay; the puffins on the North Atlantic sea cliffs, imported by the director from Iceland; the busy Pacific Reef, populated by colorful fish which you'll try to identify from their pictures above the tank.

The open South American rain forest at the top, enclosed in the 64-foot pyramid of glass that is the structure's most striking architectural feature, provides a tropical-jungle refuge for free-roaming birds, reptiles and amphibians. You're apt to come face to face with a friendly parrot in a ficus tree or be joined by a golden ringed trumpeter hopping onto your platform. On the way back down past the 335,000-gallon coral reef that's among the nation's largest, you'll enjoy a circular parade of fish swimming both ways. One turned and seemed to wink at us, as spotted eagle ray, silver tarpon and shark teams played follow the leader. You may even see a scuba diver floating amid the fish, handing out dinner. Back down on ground level is a good museum shop, specializing in fish and water-related items from necklaces to glassware, stationery to stuffed whales. Nearby is Puffin Place, featuring inexpensive gifts and T-shirts for children. Beyond is the **Aquarium Cafe** (see Where to Eat).

Summer hours, Monday-Thursday 9 to 5, Friday-Sunday 9 to 8; Sept 15 to May 15, 10 to 5 daily except Friday, 10 to 8. Adults $6.75, students $5, children $3.75.

P.T. Flagg's, Pier 4, 601 E. Pratt St. (301) 244-7377. Where fun is the theme, the Six Flags enterprises are likely to follow, and that's exactly what happened in Baltimore. What started as a source of electricity for the city's streetcars in the early 1900s was converted in 1985 into a vast amusement emporium called the Six Flags' Power Plant. On many levels, it was a high-tech extravaganza of arcades, shows, music, eateries, video games, animated characters and non-stop noise. In 1986 a nightclub-disco called P.T. Flagg's was opened to expand its appeal. The Power Plant name and amusement theme gave way in 1987 to P.T. Flagg's, which was being billed as the largest nightspot on the East Coast. Live entertainment, light and laser extravaganzas and special events are featured. Open Tuesday-Saturday 8 p.m. to 2 a.m. in summer, Wednesday-Saturday rest of year. Cover charge.

Maryland Science Center, 601 Light St. (301) 685-5225. The first major attraction at the Inner Harbor, the science center which features live exhibits and hands-on displays has been growing in stature since. Go on a Saturday morning and you'll think all the kids age 10 and under in Baltimore (and their parents) are there, playing games with computers, learning about energy, watching gerbils and the like. There's a good exhibit about Chesapeake Bay, and when we were there we enjoyed the traveling exhibit on dinosaurs, but were sorry the acclaimed **Davis Planetarium** was closed for maintenance so we couldn't see the show on the Red Planet. There are films and demon-strations throughout the day, and the shop here is great fun for kids. To open in the summer of 1987 was a 400-seat **IMAX Theater** costing $5 million. With a 55-by-75-foot screen and a 38-speaker sound system, the center scheduled a variety of spectacular nature and science films. Open daily in summer 10 to 8; rest of year, Monday-Thursday 10 to 5, Friday and Saturday to 10, Sunday noon to 6. Adults $3.50, children $3, family $12.

Top of the World, World Trade Center, Pratt Street. (301) 837-4515. The 28-story, I.M. Pei-designed tower is the tallest pentagonal structure in the world. Its 27th-floor observation deck is a popular place curiously called Top of the World — these Baltimoreans are proud, indeed. From five sides you get a panoramic view of the city and the harbor, and some of the exhibits on Baltimore should prove interesting. Open daily 10 to 5. Adults $1.50, children $1.

U.S. Frigate Constellation, Constellation Dock at Pier 1, Inner Harbor. (301) 539-1797. The first commissioned ship of the U.S. Navy was launched from Baltimore in 1797 and returned to the city in 1955, where it ended up occupying a starring position at a specially designed pier in the Inner Harbor. The oldest warship afloat, it has two months' seniority on Boston's U.S. Frigate Constitution. You can relive the past aboard what envious French sailors back in the 18th century nicknamed the Yankee Racehorse. Go down the old, steep stairs to three decks below, where you'll marvel at the cannons on the gundeck and peer at the barrels in the cargo hold. "Mind your head," warns a sign on the stairway to the crew's quarters, where you stoop to look into tiny bunkrooms with berths, a chair and a bureau. This vessel sure looks, smells and feels old. Open daily in summer, 10 to 8; early fall, 10 to 6; rest of year, 10 to 4. Adults $1.75, children 75 cents.

Baltimore Maritime Museum, Pier 4, Pratt Street. The submarine U.S.S. Torsk and the Lightship Chesapeake, a floating lighthouse, are open for self-guided tours at the end of the pier in what is loosely called the Baltimore Maritime Museum (there being no museum as such that we could find). Instead you board the football-field-length World War II sub, known as the Galloping Ghost of the Japanese Coast, and get an idea of what life beneath the sea was like. At the other side of the pier is the Lightship 116, which served 40 years anchored in coastal waters, mostly off the mouth of Chesapeake Bay, its beacon lantern atop the mainmast a welcome sight to ships' captains negotiating difficult waters. Both operated by the City of Baltimore, they are open daily except Tuesday and Wednesday from 10 to 8 May-October, 10 to 4 rest of year. Adults $2.50, children $1.

Pier Six Concert Pavilion, Pier 6. (301) 727-5580. Summer evening concerts are enjoyed under the stars or beneath the soaring fabric, tent-like structure built in 1981 at water's edge. Performers include the Baltimore Symphony Orchestra, jazz artists like Gap Mangione and Maynard Ferguson, and such name entertainers as Fats Domino, Dionne Warwick, the Kingston Trio and Peter, Paul and Mary. Tickets range from $7 to $15.

Harbor Tours

The Inner Harbor is a continuing and colorful pageant of excursion boats, sailboats, yachts and paddle boats, many available for hire. The choices are legion:

Water Taxis. One of the easiest, most fun ways to get around the Inner Harbor is by water taxi, in this case pontoon boats. They're used both for sightseeing and shuttle service between Harborplace, the Maryland Science Center, the Rusty Scupper, Little Italy, Pier 5 and the National Aquarium. They run roughly every 15 to 20 minutes, daily mid-April to mid-October, and cost 90 cents one-way, $1.50 round trip.

Paddle Boats, opposite Pratt Street Pavilion, Harborplace. Many of those colorful little boats that one sees bobbing around the inner harbor are pedaled by their occupants, and we hear it's hard work. But they're obviously popular, with waiting lines up to 20 minutes for the 80 available boats. Two-passenger boats rent for $4.25 a half hour, $7.50 an hour; four-passenger boats, $7.50 for a half hour.

Trident Electric Boat Rentals, opposite Pratt Street Pavilion. Lazier types will enjoy the electric-powered two-seaters, which rent for $9 per half hour, plus $1.50 for every five minutes overtime. Posted rules are strict; most important is one that says, "Never go left of the aquarium," out into the busy river. The larger vessels have a difficult enough time dodging all the little boats.

The Baltimore Patriot, Constellation Dock, 685-4288. This two-deck (enclosed below, open but covered above) boat gives a 90-minute, 16-mile ride out the Patapsco River past the Port of Baltimore to Fort Carroll and back. Try to sit on the right-hand side since that's the way both the live and taped narration are focused, as we discovered too late. The trip is unusually informative and, on a hot day, refreshingly cooling. Capt. Robert C. Webster was a font of knowledge on local lore and harbor goings-on. He pointed out the Procter & Gamble plant where 28 percent of the Ivory Soap bars are produced, a freighter "offloading" into the Domino sugar plant, the six-sided island Fort Carroll and the Dundalk Marine Terminal, which he credited as the principal reason the port has gone from the tenth to the fifth busiest in the nation. Here the Queen Elizabeth II sometimes docks, 11 giant cranes can lift massive tractor-trailer boxes in two minutes and 50,000 cars are unloaded from ships onto carriers ("last week we watched them offload 4,000 Mercedes-Benzes, all gassed up and with the keys in the ignition," the captain drooled).

You pass Federal Hill, Fort McHenry and Fell's Point, and see the progress of the expanding harbor: the transformation of the old Nantucket Steamship Authority ferry into a waterfront restaurant on Pier 5, the International Yachting Center, the new Anchorage Marina with 1,200 slips priced at $12,000 and up, the site of the Harbor Keys condo development and more. There's lots of activity and we never knew an industrial-city port could be so fascinating. Departures hourly May-September from 11 to 4,; late April and October, 11, 1 and 3. Adults $4.40, children $2.20.

The Baltimore Defender and Guardian, both 85-passenger vessels, are operated by the same company from Memorial Day to Labor Day. They provide shuttle service to Fort McHenry and Fell's Point, where passengers disembark for tours. They run every half hour from the Inner Harbor from 11 to 5:30. Adults $3.30, children $2.20.

The Lady Baltimore, 301 Light St., 727-3113. This 450-passenger showboat offers two-hour lunch and three-hour dinner cruises, as well as special destination and theme excursions (Annapolis or St. Michael's, rock or country music). Very popular are the dinner cruises, where you enjoy a good buffet dinner (roast beef, chicken and seafood), live bands and a musical revue, and everyone usually comes back singing and dancing, according to informants. Lunch cruises, Tuesday-Sunday noon to 2, $14.20; dinner cruises, Tuesday-Thursday 7 to 10, $19.70, Friday-Sunday, $21.90. Moonlight cruises, Friday and Saturday 11 to 1:30, $9.80. Reservations recommended.

Clipper City, 720 Light St., 539-6063. The largest Tall Ship in America licensed to carry passengers gives three-hour sailing excursions at 11 and 2 Tuesday-Sunday, plus 7 and 10 p.m. Friday and Sunday, June to mid-October. There's a Sail-a-way lunch on Wednesday and a champagne brunch on Sunday. Adults $15, children $7.50.

Skipjack Minnie V, Harborplace, 522-4214. The 24-passenger skipjack, part of America's last fleet of oyster boats on Chesapeake Bay, catches oysters in the winter and harbor sightseers in summer. Tour lengths and schedules vary, Tuesday-Sunday in summer, weekends May and September. Adults $5 to $10; children half price.

Schooner Eagle, Pier 4, 962-1171. This three-masted schooner gives 90-minute harbor cruises out to Fort McHenry and back, mid-May to November, daily in summer, weekends in fall. Adults $10, children free.

Princess Myrtle Kate, Pier 4, 659-6797. A 60-foot luxury motor yacht custom-designed for Arthur Godfrey is available for charter as well as for public one-hour tours to Fort McHenry. Adults $10, children free.

Helicopter Tours, Pier 4, 325-1978. Two helicopters give flights on Saturday and Sunday afternoons. The short, five-minute version goes over the harbor to Fort McHenry for $19.50. The longer tour covers much of the city for $40.

Other Attractions

Fort McHenry National Monument and Historic Shrine, foot of East Fort Avenue. (301) 962-4290. "There are 79 million acres of National Park System," says the sign at the Visitor Center entrance. "Welcome to 43 of them." Although small, it's powerful, this star-shaped citadel at the entrance to the harbor where Baltimore held off the British in 1814, and the most cynical cannot help but be moved. Local poet-lawyer Francis Scott Key was inspired to write "The Star Spangled Banner" after watching the historic bombardment from a ship on the river. Visitors are usually inspired to join in song with the U.S. Naval Academy Chorus as the window curtains part to reveal the unfurled flag at the end of an informative 15-minute movie in the Visitor Center. A park ranger then leads a 25-minute tour through the fort, which was restored to its pre-Civil War appearance after serving as the world's largest hospital for returning veterans following World War I. Open daily June-Labor Day, 9 to 8; rest of year 9 to 5. Free.

Little Italy. Out Pratt Street just east of Pier 6 is Little Italy, perhaps the most famous of Baltimore's neighborhoods and the heart of its older restaurant district. The four corners at Fawn and South High streets bulge with four leading Italian restaurants and sidewalk cafes.

Fell's Point. Just beyond Little Italy is the original Baltimore harborfront, now considered unique in America as a surviving Colonial working seaport community. Listed on the National Register of Historic Places, Fell's Point shelters 350 original structures from the 18th century, and nearly half its residents are working seamen. It's rapidly being gentrified with restaurants and shops, but maintains a mixed character. The Art Gallery of Fell's Point is juxtaposed next to the decrepit Port Mission; in the middle of the street is the Broadway Market, one of six municipal offspring of the downtown Lexington Market, the nation's oldest. Savor the past in some of the seamen's bars, the old houses along Ann and Bond streets, the commercial establishments along South Broadway and Thames Street. Still somewhat seedy, Fell's Point will be the Georgetown of Baltimore within a few years, if local restorationists have their way.

Federal Hill. Already a Georgetown of sorts is this nationally designated landmark area just south of the Inner Harbor and the original site of Baltimore's pioneering "dollar-housing" homestead program. For a mere dollar bill, the city sold rundown houses in the 1970s to purchasers who pledged sweat equity. Some of the results can be seen on Federal Hill, where 19th century red-brick row houses have been transformed into places of charm (and are re-selling for more than $100,000). You can walk the quiet residential streets above the Inner Harbor and rest at the hillside Federal Hill Park, which grants a panoramic view of the recreational harbor and the industrial port beyond.

MUSEUMS. A Museum Row embracing two centuries of Baltimore history is emerging within a three-block radius of Jonestown, at the edge of Little Italy a few blocks from the Inner Harbor. It brings together the **Star Spangled Banner Flag House and 1812 Museum,** the **Carroll Mansion** where a signer of the Declaration of Independence lived, the **Peale Museum** (said to be the oldest original museum building in the U.S.), the 234-foot **Shot Tower,** **the 1840 House,** and the unusual **Baltimore Center for Urban Archaeology,** among other historic sites. Farther away are the prized **Baltimore & Ohio Railroad Museum, the Babe Ruth Birthplace, the H.L. Mencken House, the Edgar Allan Poe House** and the outstanding **Baltimore Museum of Art,** which claims the nation's largest Matisse collection.

Festival Hall, 1 W. Pratt St. (301) 659-7000. Weekend ethnic festivals celebrating the diverse heritages of one of America's most diverse cities are conducted in the summer. A Ukrainian Festival with arts and crafts exhibits, songs and dances, music, food and drinks was on when we were there.

Downtown. Pedestrian skywalks lead from the harbor through hotels, office buildings and shopping malls to Charles Center, Baltimore's first revitalization showcase. From there it's a short walk up quaintly posh Charles Street, past the newly restored Brown's Arcade, to Mount Vernon Place. The first Washington Monument is the focus of four tree-shaded squares which provide a verdant front yard for fashionable townhouses, the Walters Art Gallery and the Peabody Conservatory of Music.

Where to Eat

Baltimore was described as the gastronomic metropolis of the universe by Oliver Wendell Holmes. Visitors cherish its crabs and oysters, and have packed into such institutions as Danny's, Haussner's, Olde Obrycki's Crab House and the restaurants of Little Italy for years. The revitalized Inner Harbor has a panoply of eateries popular with tourists; otherwise, locals point to a few standouts in what generally is a sea of sameness in dining choices.

Interesting Dining

Something Fishy, 606 S. Broadway, Fell's Point. (301) 732-2233. New and already planning to expand after its first year, this upscale place with the amusing name provided our best meal in Baltimore. Owned by Martin's Seafood, the state's largest, it is simple but elegant — six tables for four and a small Victorian bar in front and a rear skylit dining room with cathedral ceiling, track lights, bare wood tables and bow chairs. When we were there, the place smelled nicely of seafood and dill. Encouraged by lively proprietor Stevi Martin, 23-year-old chef Nancy Longo changes the short menu every three days; from a repertoire of 600 items, she says, she's never made anything twice. For an appetizer ($6.95), we can vouch for her fried brie and shrimp served with garlic toast croutons and remoulade sauce, and for entrees ($11.95 to $16.50), her homemade (she rolls all her pasta by hand) oyster and shrimp ravioli served with a spinach Alfredo sauce and her grilled salmon with a spicy curry cream sauce. Accompaniments included crunchy French bread with sweet butter, ample salads with side bowls of herbed dressings, steamed carrots, curried saffron rice and potato provencale. The tray of homemade desserts which held Paris Brest, carrot cake, chocolate mousse and a peach tart was nothing out of the ordinary. The wine list was rather strange although fairly priced from $9 to $18. Our Baltimore relatives rave over the pure (no breading) crab cakes ($14.25), for which Bon Appetit magazine requested the recipe. At lunch, you can purchase fish from the adjacent market and for an additional $4, it will be prepared as requested with a vegetable of the day. Open Tuesday-Saturday noon to 1 a.m., Sunday 3 to midnight.

Regi's, 1002 Light St., Federal Hill. (301) 539-7344. Billed as an all-American bistro serving homemade soups, salads, pastas, entrees and sandwiches, this small eight-year-old establishment overseen by Regi Elion is popular with those who like things pure. The bar on one side opens onto the main dining room of tile tables and folding chairs; a little dining room is tucked behind the bar. Supplementing the regular offerings are blackboard specials like pan-fried flounder parmesan, Chesapeake crab cakes, stir-fried chicken, curried chicken breasts and pastas ($8.75 to $9.75). Regi is known for such accompaniments as lemon-dill rice, baked zucchini with bacon and a cauliflower puree as well as her soups, perhaps Lee Bailey's all-vegetable, mulligatawny or mussel bisque. For lunch, try a Philly cheese steak or oyster po'boy sandwich. Her mother helps out at **Regi's Takeout,** a new gourmet deli Regi runs with partner Holly Struven across the street. Concert-goers and sailors can pick up great picnics here; the salmon is home smoked, and an express breakfast of freshly squeezed orange juice, the house coffee and muffin of the day is $2.35. Regi's, Monday-Saturday 11:30 a.m. to 2 a.m., Sunday 11 to 2. Takeout open from 8 or 8:30 a.m. to 10 p.m.

Sisson's, 36 E. Cross St., Federal Hill. (301) 539-2093. Across from the Cross Street municipal market is a lively establishment which owner Hugh Sisson started in 1980 as a beer hall and lately expanded into an upscale Cajun restaurant. You have to pass through a narrow, crowded stand-up bar to get to the rear dining room, where you sit on church pews at tables covered with copper beneath a large map of the world; dozens of labels of beers and ales are connected by strings to their homes on the map. Outside is a pleasant brick beer garden, and upstairs is a small dining room with six linened tables, fresh flowers and votive candles. The blackboard menu features Cajun specialties in the style of Paul Prudhomme — blackened steak or redfish, shrimp etoufee, chicken big Mamoo (in fresh and spicy tomato sauce over green and white pasta) and Cajun sampler, $10.95 to $14.95. The seafood file gumbo and sweet potato pecan pie are highly rated. Dinner nightly, 5 to 11, to 1 on weekends.

Pacifica, 326 N. Charles St., Baltimore. (301) 727-8264. The restored Brown's Arcade houses this trendy open space with balcony, all white linen, glass vases of field flowers, votive candles, and neon and art deco graphics on the walls. New California cuisine is the fare, from gourmet pizzas (voted the best in Baltimore) to mesquite-grilled seafood and pastas. A typical night's specials ($11.95 to $19.95) might be linguini with scallops and red peppers, Florida grouper with julienned vegetables and newburg sauce, yellowfin tuna with crabmeat, braised oysters and basil sauce, grilled red snapper with black bean sauce and sirloin Sacramento with wild mushrooms and julienned onions. Hot cashew pie and a chocolate mousse marquis with creme anglaise are among desserts. Open Monday-Friday 11:30 to 11:30, Saturday 5:30 to midnight.

The Orchid, 419 N. Charles St., Baltimore. (301) 837-0080. In an elegant downtown townhouse, chef-owner Richard Wong combines French cuisine and his oriental heritage for an interesting menu that he calls "the new wave in contemporary cuisine." The extensive menu is written in French but contains Chinese specialties, which makes for interesting reading ("soupe de crabe Maryland" next to wonton soup) and eating. Oriental ingredients and French technique go into "Les Orchid Specialties," among them pan-fried flounder and salmon, brochette of seafood (in a homemade peanut sauce), sauteed veal with bean curd and crisp duck with green peppercorns. There's much more, priced from $9.95 to $15.95, each dish served with potato or rice and two vegetables. The orange bombe is one of the good desserts, and the well-chosen wine list is downright cheap. The setting is elegant: white over peach-orange linens at 12 tables in two small dining rooms with crystal chandeliers, heavy swagged draperies and fresh flowers. Lunch, Monday-Saturday 11:30 to 2:30; dinner, 5:30 to 10:30, weekends to 11, Sunday 4:30 to 9:30.

Fritz's of Fell's Point, 1702 Thames St., Fell's Point. (301) 522-4602. A vaguely Alpine decor of pine paneling and red-clothed tables is the backdrop for some acclaimed German-Austrian cuisine plus Chesapeake Bay seafood. New in 1986, chef Fritz Hofer's restaurant was an instant hit with such offerings as leg of venison with mushrooms and vegetables, roast pheasant in a creamy red wine sauce and his house platter of sauteed veal, pork and beef. Prices are modest, and some of the specialties are served for two. Open daily from 11 to 11. Sunday brunch 11 to 2.

Waterfront Hotel, 1710 Thames St., Fell's Point. (301) 563-9693. The downstairs bar is casual and boisterous, so you almost wouldn't think of going up the side stairs to a room that's surprisingly elegant and formal, with pink fanned napkins on deep blue cloths, blue upholstered chairs, rich paneling, Tiffany glass and Victorian chandeliers. The continental menu runs from $9.25 for flounder francaise to $14.95 for veal Oscar. Tableside preparation is featured upstairs — such things as steak Diane, duck a l'orange, rack of lamb, bananas Foster and cherries jubilee. Lunch, 11 to 3; dinner, 5 to 10 or 11.

Bertha's, 734 S. Broadway, Fell's Point. (301) 327-5795. "Eat Bertha's Mussels," say the ubiquitous bumper stickers, and everyone seems to at this dark and kooky place with brick, tile and wood floors and a million wine bottles overhead. The featured mussels come in a number of ways — perhaps with garlic butter and capers, or with sauces of spinach, tarragon and garlic or anchovy, tomato and garlic, or with Lancaster cream. Prices are $5.75 to $7.75 (for assorted sauces). You also can get three Mediterranean rice dishes including paella, a crab cake platter, shellfish royale and oysters ($8.10 to $16.95), plus soups, salads, omelets and sandwiches. Scottish trifle and pecan-butter tarts are among the desserts. Welsh rarebit and creamed chipped oysters are offered for Sunday brunch, and afternoon tea in the British tradition is served from 3 to 5 for $5.95 (reservations required). Otherwise, it's "turn right and seat yourself," as the sign inside the door advises. Open daily from 11:30 to 11, weekends to midnight.

Alley Oops!, 1043 Marshall St., Federal Hill. (301) 962-8988. Hidden in a brick house at the end of an alley near Sisson's and the Cross Street Market is this airy new restaurant with a wraparound upstairs balcony. Fashioned from an old meat packing house, it purveys casual fare from Mexican appetizers to pita sandwiches to chicken marsala, barbecued ribs and New York strip steak ($8.50 to $11.25). Open Tuesday-Friday 11 to 10, Saturday 5 to 11, Sunday 5 to 9.

Harborside Choices

Aquarium Cafe, National Aquarium, Pier 3. (301) 576-3815. Some of the most interesting food around the Inner Harbor, to our minds, is served at the Aquarium Cafe, and it certainly has a fine location right beside the water. Why we were the only ones dining under the canopy on the outdoor deck on a mild September Saturday we'll never understand, although we did start a trend. It was a special setting for a bowl of crab file gumbo, a Sierra shrimp salad and an excellent duck salad splashed with curacao. For $3.95 to $7.45, you also can get gourmet pizzas (the Hawaiian with cheese, ham and pineapple sounds unusual), pastas, sandwiches, charcuterie selections and for dessert, rhum babas or pecan pie. Wine comes by the glass or liter, beer by the bottle or pitcher. The take-out charcuterie is open daily from 11 to 8; cafe from 11 to 5.

The Rusty Scupper, 402 Key Highway, Federal Hill. (301) 727-3678. The Rusty Scupper chain always seems to have a corner on the waterfront views, and this one is no exception. It's superbly situated right on the water at the foot of Federal Hill, across from all the harbor action. The lengthy menu is typically Rusty Scupper, embracing everything from prime rib and mesquite-grilled salmon to shrimp tempura and pastas ($9.95 to $17.95). Lunch and happy hour on the outdoor decks are popular; it's a busy singles spot at night. Lunch daily 11:30 to 2, dinner 5 to 10, weekends to 11.

Phillips Harborplace, 301 Light St., Baltimore. (301) 685-6600. The largest and most crowded restaurant in the Light Street Pavilion is this offshoot of the Ocean City seafood establishment that started as a beachfront takeout in 1957. Particularly appealing is the sidewalk cafe looking onto the water and the National Aquarium. The enormous menu typical of its genre offers oysters on the half shell or steamed gumbo, shrimp salad and crab cake sandwiches ($3.95). Among entrees ($9.95 to $19.95) are nine versions of crabmeat, three seafood platters and seven lobster dishes. Service is fast (those waterfront seats are coveted); at night you can wait for a table at the piano bar. Open daily, 11 to 11.

Other Harborplace restaurants run the gamut from Food Hall eateries of every description to the rather fancy **Gianni's,** which we thought had the best waterfront deck on the second floor of the Pratt Street Pavilion. It was not as crowded as some of the others the Friday night we dined; our waiter grudgingly obliged when we asked for a candle. The food was passable (canneloni with crabmeat and fettuccine Gianni with scallops, shrimp and lobster butter sauce, $12.50) and the setting exhilarating. Other choices include the **Bamboo House,** with oriental food and a sleek canopied and open-air pavilion; **Taverna Athena,** with an appropriate blue and white Greek look; **Tandoor,** all orange and green with Indian specialties, and back upstairs in the Light Street Pavilion, **City Lights** on one corner and the **American Cafe** on the other.

More Possibilities

Within striking distance of the Inner Harbor are other options. The elegant Peabody Court Hotel's **La Brasserie** is said to present the best Sunday brunch in the city (a claim disputed by the Hyatt Regency), and its **Conservatory** dining room serves acclaimed continental cuisine, a bit pretentiously, we understand. Some Baltimoreans think the Hyatt's **Trellis Garden** is the city's best hotel dining room.

Toucan, new in Brown's Arcade, is a gourmet deli with 10 butcherblock tables amid the plants in a skylit courtyard. **La Provence,** a French-Italian bistro at 9 Hopkins Plaza, has a pleasant sidewalk cafe just off the pedestrian skywalk. **Shogun** at 316 N. Charles St. and **Kawasaki** at 413 N. Charles are recommended Japanese restaurants with sushi bars.

For the ultimate in grazing, don't miss the food stalls at the expanded downtown **Lexington Market.** Purists and those seeking local color find it more to their liking than Harborplace.

The **Owl Bar** at the Belvedere Hotel, a classic pub, is considered *the* place to go for a drink, and Baltimoreans have been going there for years.

FOR MORE INFORMATION: Baltimore Office of Promotion & Tourism, 34 Market Place, Suite 310, Baltimore, Md. 21202. (301) 752-4636. This exceptionally good, helpful office runs a visitor center at Pier 4, Inner Harbor, and publishes a fine seasonal tabloid guide called Baltimore Good Times.

Mules pull barge along Delaware River canal.

Delaware River/Bucks County, Pa.-N.J.

When William Penn came upon Bucks County back in 1682, it so reminded him of Great Britain that he named it after Buckingham, the shire in which he was born.

The resemblance still is clear: A rolling countryside dropping downhill to the wide Delaware River, just as England's does along the Thames River west of London. Crossroads pubs and stone houses that would look at home in the Cotswolds. Narrow, winding roads eliciting rural discoveries at every turn. Even the place names are similar: Solebury, Warminster, Chalfont, Wycombe. Such is the influence of the area's English Quaker settlers.

Although the area straddling the Delaware River became a stagecoach stop on the old York Turnpike linking New York and Philadelphia, it retained its rural heritage and, to this day, remains a surprisingly unspoiled refuge amid sprawling megalopolis.

The tranquil, idyllic setting of river and hills attracted a colony of painters known as the New Hope Artists early in the 20th century. Since then it has lured thousands of visitors, most of them to New Hope, a chic town whose mystique far exceeds its size (about 1,400). Lately, the New Jersey river towns of Lambertville, Frenchtown and Milford are attracting tourists as well.

The arts colony, antiquing and the Bucks County Playhouse are prime attractions. So are several concentrations of small inns and uncommonly good restaurants.

In the midst of it all is the Delaware River, narrow and deserted as it cuts beneath hillsides and cliffs of strange-colored layers of rock at Upper Black Eddy, majestic and lazing at New Hope and Lambertville, mysterious and historic at Washington Crossing. Towpaths and canals flank the river on both sides, and islands occasionally part the river in the middle.

River Road (Pennsylvania Route 32) undulates along the west bank through sharp turns and the odd hamlet a slow 30 miles from Washington Crossing north to Upper Black Eddy. On the east bank, New Jersey's Route 29 speeds motorists the same distance through utterly rural terrain spelled by an occasional town.

The river, the canals and the towpaths lure people for all kinds of rest and recreation — canoeing, rafting, fishing and swimming in the water; bicycling, jogging, strolling and dining alongside. We focus here to the river and immediate environs, acknowledging that other attractions could entice you away.

The river offers so many pleasures, however, that we seldom have time or inclination to yield to the temptations beyond.

Getting There

This area along the Delaware River in Pennsylvania's Bucks County and New Jersey's Hunterdon County is 30 miles north of Philadelphia and 60 miles southwest of New York City. Interstates 95 and 78 plus the Pennsylvania and New Jersey turnpikes are nearby. U.S. Route 202 is the main approach to New Hope and Lambertville.

Where to Stay

Travelers have paused for rest and sustenance at inns and B&Bs along the river since Colonial days. Today, the numerous but small lodging places are booked far in advance, particularly in summer and on weekends, and you won't find any large motels except for a Holiday Inn just west of New Hope. Many inns require two-night stays on weekends (three nights for holiday weekends), and have lower weekday rates when the area isn't so busy. The region could use more inns, New Hope Information Center director Marianne Spersen concedes, and visitors would enjoy a few riverfront motels.

Larger Inns

The Inn at Lambertville Station, 11 Bridge St., Lambertville, N.J. 08530. (609) 397-4400 or (800) 524-1091. In 1985, this area gained a fine, large inn on the riverfront. Following their success with the restored Lambertville Station restaurant, Dan Whitaker and his Philadelphia partners set to building the architecturally impressive, four-story luxury inn on land that had long been an eyesore at the west entrance to Lambertville. More than $3 million went into the inn, and it looks it, from the open four-story-high lobby to the most elegant of suites. You check in at a counter resembling the ticket office of an old train station, perhaps tarry for tea or a drink from the honor bar in the towering lobby (which is higher than it is wide) and get your bags up the elevator to your room. Prized antiques are in the 45 guest rooms, each named for a major city and decorated to match. Ours was the corner New York Suite, high in the trees above a rushing waterfall that lulled us to sleep. The bed is turned down at night and chocolates are left, the bathroom has a whirlpool tub, and around the L-shaped room are heavy mahogany furniture, leather chairs facing the fireplace and TV, handsome draperies, ornate mirrors and fine art. The only thing missing was a good reading lamp. A light continental breakfast with carrot-nut muffins arrived at our door with a newspaper the next morning. Other rooms that we saw were equally impressive, all individually decorated by antiques dealer Phil Cowley, who spared no expense. Though no rooms face the river, occupants on the south side beside the woods hear the sounds of Swan Creek spilling down from the canal; those on the north side view the lights of Lambertville and New Hope glimmering on the river. The large **Riverside Room,** which does face the river with windows on three sides, is used for conferences and Sunday brunch ($15.95 for quite a spread). Doubles, $65 to $85; suites with fireplaces and whirlpool baths, $125.

1740 House, River Road, Lumberville, Pa. 18933. (215) 297-5661. If the Inn at Lambertville Station is the welcome new guy on the block, the 1740 House is the sprightly oldtimer, highly popular and booked far in advance. Its serenity, its quiet location in a quaint hamlet beside the Delaware and its motel-style privacy appeal to repeat visitors who book the same rooms year after year. Opened in 1967 by well-traveled New Yorker Harry Nessler, the 1740 House was built to look old, each room in two wings opening from a front corridor and extending to patios or balconies perched out back at canal's edge. Individually decorated, the 24 spacious rooms have king or twin beds, bathrooms with showers or tubs, comfortable chairs with reading lights, nightly turndown service, and no television or phones to intrude. You help yourself to a buffet-style breakfast in the cheery garden dining room; there's always a hot dish like scrambled eggs or creamed chipped beef. A three-course dinner with choice of three entrees is available to house guests at a single seating at 7 p.m.; you order when you make your dinner reservation and bring your own wine. You'll want time to enjoy the peace and quiet of the river from your balcony or porch, catch some sun around the small pool, read in a couple of small parlors, meander up River Road to the center of Lumberville and walk the canal towpath or cross the footbridge to an island park in New Jersey. Doubles, $62 to $70. No credit cards.

Centre Bridge Inn, River Road, Box 74, Star Route, New Hope, Pa. 18938. (215) 862-2048. Wonderfully situated beside the Delaware across from the pleasant New Jersey village of Stockton, this striking white structure with red shutters built in Colonial Williamsburg style has a large restaurant-tavern and nine sumptuous guest rooms. Fires destroyed inns that had occupied the site since 1705, so this is of early 1960s vintage. After checking in downstairs in the restaurant, you return to the main floor and are let in through a locked door to an enormous formal vestibule, with a fireplaced parlor on the river side. Ahead are a pair of two-room suites, one with a foyer leading into the main room with queensize canopy bed, two plush blue chairs on thick carpeting, TV set, cedar-lined bath and private riverview deck — "our nicest room," according to our guide. Another suite in front has a queen brass bed and sitting room with sofa, loveseat and TV. Upstairs are seven more rooms, many with canopy beds and three with TV. All are air-conditioned, have private baths, and are notable for colorful Schumacher wall coverings. A continental breakfast is served in the suites, the parlor or outside on a deck off the main floor, which has one of the best views of the river anywhere. Doubles, $65 to $85; suites, $85 to $115.

Evermay-on-the-Delaware, River Road, Erwinna, Pa. 18920. (215) 994-9100. A three-story gold and tan Victorian mansion set back on a broad lawn facing the river, Evermay is the bed-and-breakfast and gourmet-dinner venture of Ron Strouse and Fred Cresson, who were known for their cuisine at the

Sign of the Sorrel Horse in Quakertown. Evermay's 16 guest rooms, all with private bath, are furnished in fine Victoriana. We found ours in the Carriage House a bit cold and spare, despite the presence of fresh flowers and a large bowl of fresh fruit. Some inn rooms retain the original fireplaces; walnut beds, oriental rugs, marble-topped dressers, fancy quilts and lacy pillows are among the furnishings. Downstairs in the double front parlor, where afternoon tea is served at 4, a fire often burns in the fireplace and decanters of sherry are at the ready. An excellent continental breakfast is served in the conservatory dining room at the rear; we liked the incredibly flaky croissants and a magnificent compote of fresh fruit. Prix-fixe dinners of five or six courses with a choice of two entrees are served on weekends. We remember fondly an extraordinary fall dinner of lamb noisettes and poached Norwegian salmon, beautifully presented with exotic accompaniments. Doubles, $53 to $90.

Hotel du Village, River Road and Phillips Mill Road, New Hope. Pa. 18938. (215) 862-9911. A Tudor English manor house dispenses renowned French nouvelle cuisine and a converted stable to the rear contains 20 air-conditioned guest rooms and suites with private baths. Old-fashioned beds and quilts are the rule. Guests have access to two tennis courts and a pool on the lovely grounds that were part of a land grant from William Penn. An impressive country estate was built on the property in the late 19th century, and from 1917 to 1976 it was the site of the Solebury School's Lower Campus. Algerian chef-owner Omar Arbani and his wife Barbara converted it into a restaurant and inn in 1978. Across River Road is the canal and next door are the spectacular grounds of Lenteboden, home of bulb specialist Charles Mueller. Doubles, $55 to $70.

Small Inns and B&Bs

Bridgeton House, River Road, Upper Black Eddy, Pa. 18972. (215) 982-5856. This onetime wreck of an apartment house built in 1836 couldn't be more welcoming, having been transformed with sweat and love by Bea and Charles Briggs into a comfortable B&B with a glorious location beside the river. Although smack up against the road, the inn has been opened to the rear for a water orientation. Fresh or dried flowers, a decanter of sherry and potpourri grace the dining room. A rear parlor looks onto the canal. Upstairs are seven guest rooms overlooking the water, each exceptionally fashioned by Charles, a master carpenter and renovator, and interestingly decorated by Bea. Some have four-posters and chaise-lounges; all have country antiques, colorful sheets, fresh flowers and intriguing touches. Third-floor rooms share a new balcony, and everyone gets to enjoy the landscaped terrace by the river. Bea serves an elaborate breakfast of fresh breads or muffins and a hot dish like cheddar cheese omelet or scrambled eggs. Doubles, $65 to $75.

Pineapple Hill, 1324 River Road, New Hope, Pa. 18938. (215) 862-9608. This 18th century Bucks County farmhouse is one of the few places where one can stay south of New Hope. The pineapple motif, symbolizing welcome, appears throughout the house and typifies the personable innkeepers, Randy and Suzie Leslie, who light candles in the windows to add to the warmth. Their seven guest rooms are clustered in separate areas on the second and third floors, affording privacy for families or couples traveling together. Two are two-bedroom suites sharing baths, while three have private baths. Rooms sport country or primitive antiques, stenciling, displays of pewter and perhaps a corner cupboard filled with china or walls covered with quilts. The large fireplaced parlor has a television set and comfortable furniture for lounging. This is also where guests gather for breakfast of fresh fruit salad, croissants and homemade jams. They help themselves to cider, lemonade, beer or wine and munchies from a rear snack and beverage area. Out back are lovely gardens and a wonderful swimming pool built in the stone ruins of a barn, and beyond is the towpath by the canal. Doubles, $45 to $85; no smoking.

The Old Hunterdon House, 12 Bridge St., Frenchtown, N.J. 08825. (201) 996-3632. In 1986, the owners of Evermay-on-the-Delaware turned this exotic Italian villa built in 1865 into a Victorian B&B in up-and-coming Frenchtown. Seven guest rooms, most furnished formally in the Victorian manner, have private baths. The most inviting room on the third floor has a white iron bedstead and a wicker sitting room with a gorgeous Persian rug. Innkeeper Rick Carson serves a continental breakfast of fresh fruit compote, croissants and muffins in the high-ceilinged parlor or outside on the porch, and guests may take weekend dinners at Evermay. Tea, early-evening sherry and cordials put at bedside during nightly turndown service are offered. Guests may relax in the formal study or in the cupola, which grants a bird's-eye view of town and river valley. Doubles, $65 to $95.

Chestnut Hill on the Delaware, 63 Church St., Milford, N.J. 08848. (201) 995-9761. The river lazes past this 1860 Victorian house, considered the grandest in town, and a great place to view it is from the long lineup of rockers on the veranda just a shady front yard away. Linda and Rob Castagna offer three guest rooms and a suite, two with private baths and two with semi-private. The Pineapple Room has a reading area and color TV, and some beds have duvets from Scotland. Guests are served an ample breakfast at the large lace-covered table in the dining room: perhaps a souffle, eggs Roxanne or pancakes with peach sauce. Apothecary wall units in a formal drawing room in the Eastlake tradition contain books and potpourri. Doubles, $55 to $80; no smoking.

CAMPING AND RENTALS. Point Pleasant is the site of the Ralph Stover State Park off Stump Road, which occupies 37 acres of the Tohickon Creek Valley, and the 45-acre Tohickon Valley County Park off Cafferty Road. Both offer campsites, swimming, fishing and miles of unspoiled forests to explore. This is not an area for cottages; what house rentals there are may be arranged individually or by the area's dozen realtors, including Logan Associates, 4 Gazebo Place, Village of Logan Square, New Hope, (215) 862-3385, and John T. Henderson Realtors, 12 S. Franklin St., Lambertville, (609) 397-2800.

Seeing and Doing _____ ✶✶✶

Many are the attractions and varied the appeal of the Delaware River and the narrow canals on both sides. Built in the 1830s, the Delaware Division Canal was used for floating coal and limestone from Easton through New Hope south to Bristol. During its 60-mile course, barges dropped 165 feet through 25 locks and under 106 bridges. New Hope was the only point on the canal where four barges could pass at once, and after 1854, barges shuttled across the Delaware River to Lambertville and the Delaware & Raritan Canal, and on to Princeton and New York. The last shipments were floated down the canal about 1930. These days, there is rarely enough water in the canal for the traditional canoeing except in the immediate New Hope area. Pennsylvania's Delaware Division Canal has become the Theodore Roosevelt State Park and a National Historic Landmark. Most of New Jersey's Raritan canal also is a state park.

On or Near the Water

Walk the Towpath. We thoroughly enjoy walking the canal towpaths along the river, particularly the Pennsylvania portion between Lumberville and Phillips Mill and particularly in spring when the daffodils are abloom. Start in Lumberville at the footbridge to Bull's Island, a New Jersey state park. The Black Bass Hotel's friendly duck may greet you, the gardens and back yards of English-type manor houses are sure to intrigue, and everywhere are wild flowers, singing birds, joggers, picnickers and other strollers. A footbridge leads to the Cuttalossa Inn, where the outdoor terrace appeals for lunch or a drink; you can stop at the Centre Bridge Inn for a drink, or cross the highway bridge to Stockton, N.J., to pick up a picnic lunch at Errico's Market and a bottle of wine at the incredibly well-stocked Phillips wine store. Just downriver is Phillips Mill, an ever-so-British looking cluster of stone houses hugging the River Road, and the colorful grounds of **Lenteboden,** the business and residence of Charles Mueller, the bulb specialist whose gardens full of daffodils, tulips and hyacinths herald the arrival of spring. Like almost everything else along the towpath, they're free and open for the exploring. A word of caution: the towpath walk is lulling and may take the better part of a day; unless you have a car meeting you at the end, you'll have to walk back or hitch a ride, as we did.

Canoeing, Rafting and Tubing. The river is so popular for these pastimes that in 22 years, owner Tom McBrien has turned his **Point Pleasant Canoe Outfitters** enterprise in Point Pleasant, Pa., into the East's largest water recreation facility. Tubing is the biggest operation, with up to 3,500 people a day renting inner tubes for floats of three to six miles (adults $8, children $6). Canoeists are transported up to Tinicum, Upper Black Eddy or Riegelsville for trips downriver of six to eighteen miles ($10 to $15 per person). Rubber rafts and canoes are rented for $15 to $50 per day. McBrien says there's nothing like floating or paddling down the Delaware, watching fish leaping and osprey feeding, and pausing for a swim in the warm, clear waters. When we visited, Richard DeGroot of **River Road Farms** also was hoping to launch a second canoe and tubing center upriver in Erwinna, Pa.

Fishing. Considered one of the best fishing rivers in the East, the Delaware is known to harbor more than 30 species, including trout, bass, muskies and pike. Whenever we visit in the spring, the shad seem to be running and the fishermen are out in force, in boats or in hip boots just offshore in the Lumberville-Bull's Island launch areas. All the activity is a sight to behold from the balcony at the 1740 House.

New Hope Mule Barge Co., New and South Main Streets, New Hope, Pa. (215) 862-2842. Mule-drawn barges bring back the past for hundreds of visitors daily on the old Delaware Canal. The barges have been hauling tourists since 1931 after the canal's commercial usage ended. Spanish-Colombian Leo Ramirez and German Georges Schweickhardt have owned the four-barge operation since 1976. At their outlying farm they care for the nine mules that draw the barges two miles up the river past Colonial homes, artists' workshops, gardens and countryside to the Route 202 bridge and back. A musician-historian relates canal lore and strums folk songs. The one-hour excursions cost $4.95 for adults, $2.75 for children. May 1 to Oct. 15, daily at 11:30, 1, 2, 3, 4:30 and 6; April and to Nov. 15, reduced hours Wednesday, Saturday and Sunday.

Washington Crossing Historic Park, Pa. History was made here in 1776 when George Washington and 2,400 troops crossed the Delaware on Christmas night to attack Trenton. Now it's a large state park in two sections.

The northern Thompson Mill section is two miles south of New Hope. It features **Bowman's Tower,** a 110-foot-high stone observation point that reopened in 1986 with a new elevator (admission, $2). From the top of the site where sentries watched enemy troop movements you get a panoramic view of river and valley. Around the tower is a 100-acre **Wild Flower Preserve,** with 26 acres of trails and habitat areas plus a headquarters building with gift shop and displays. Across River Road are the 1702 **Thompson-Neely House,** requisitioned in 1776 as a battle headquarters and now a museum, a grist mill and picnic areas.

Four miles south is the park's southern section and visitor center. Here a 25-minute film tells the story of how George Washington and his half-frozen troops regrouped at this location from encampments stretching from New Hope to Yardley to cross the river and capture Trenton. The film ends rather abruptly, we thought. Then you can take a walking tour and enter three historic buildings for $1.50. Included are the **Old Ferry Inn,** where Washington is believed to have eaten dinner the night before the Battle of Trenton, the 1816 **Taylor House** and the Thompson-Neely House to the north. One area of this park has a picturesque lagoon populated by incredible numbers of Canada geese and other birds, surrounded by picnicking facilities.

Across the Delaware River bridge is New Jersey's **Washington Crossing State Park,** which has a visitor center, the **Ferry House Inn,** an overlook area, nature trails, an open-air theater for the Summer Festival of Performing Arts, the **George Washington Memorial Arboretum** and the **Nelson House** museum.

Parks are open daily; hours vary.

Around the Towns

Walk New Hope. A compact village, New Hope is made for walking. That's fortunate, because in summer things get unbelievably congested and outlying parking lots charge $4. The small Information Center in the 1839 jail-town hall at South Main and Mechanic streets logged a staggering 6,577 visitors in August 1986. A short New Hope walking tour guides you to the East Ferry Street landing and mill complex, the hub of early village life (now including Martine's restaurant, Farley's New Delaware Bookshop and the Bucks County Playhouse), the historic Logan Inn, the 1784 Parry Mansion (open for tours, Friday-Monday 1 to 5, May-October) and the old houses of West Ferry Street (they're among the town's 243 properties included in 1985 on the National Register of Historic Places). We'd also suggest strolling along the Delaware Canal park and gardens. The narrow streets are lined with art galleries and more shops than we can possibly enumerate. Take our word: if it's for sale, someone in New Hope or environs carries it.

Walk across the Delaware River bridge from New Hope to **Lambertville,** an up-and-coming riverside town of interesting shops and restaurants.

For the ultimate rural small-town experience, walk through tiny **Lumberville** and savor the past, including the historic Black Bass Hotel and Gerald Gordon's Lumberville Store, which dates to 1770 and encompasses the post office, an art gallery, food and sandwiches, books and bicycle rentals.

Wine Bars and Pubs. A favorite pastime of many is stopping at a wine bar, something of a local phenomenon. **The Boat House** wine bar at the Porkyard in Lambertville is nearest the water; the **Swan Hotel** at 43 S. Main St. is a large and extraordinary bar with much atmosphere and limited food service. Another popular spot for English pub food and a pint of bitter is the **Ship's Inn** in Milford.

River Romance Discovery Tours, 18 W. Mechanic St., New Hope, Pa. (215) 862-5217. Guide Stephen Schneer dons period costumes to lead 90-minute walking tours of historic sections of New Hope or Lambertville. He has a champagne tour Saturday and Sunday at noon, and a sunset tour Saturday at 5. Both include refreshments and cost $5, by reservation.

New Hope Steam Railway and Museum, 32 W. Bridge St., New Hope, Pa. (215) 862-2707. The 1891 New Hope train station with its witch-hat peak has been restored as part of a museum that includes a 1906 wooden baggage car with souvenir shop and exhibits. The steam railway takes passengers on a nine-mile round trip up Solebury Mountain to Lahaska and back. Train operates Saturdays and holidays, 1:30 and 3:30; Sundays. 11:30, 1:30 and 3:30, May-October.

Bucks County Playhouse, 70 S. Main St., New Hope, Pa. (215) 862-2041. The old town mill that backs up to the river ceased operating in 1938. It was purchased by local citizens who turned it into a summer stock theater, which debuted in 1939 with Edward Everett Horton in "Springtime for Henry." The 457-seat theater runs an ambitious 30-week schedule from early May to late December, Tuesday-Sunday in summer (with Wednesday and Thursday matinees) and reduced schedules in spring and fall. Tickets, $10 to $14.

ART GALLERIES. The number of galleries has doubled in two years lately in New Hope, long a noted art colony, in the more recent concentration around Lahaska and in newly blossoming Lambertville. The New Hope-Lambertville Gallery Association lists 26 galleries in the area. The River Road Gallery in Erwinna is part of the River Road Farms complex, which includes the distinctive Chachka gift and gourmet shop.

ANTIQUING. The East Coast mecca for antiques is how one advocate describes the area. The largest concentration is in Lahaska, where the Lahaska Antique Courte, for instance, claims 14 distinctive shops and the Bucks County Antiques Dealers Association lists 11 more. Others are in New Hope, Lambertville and small towns on both sides of the river.

Where to Eat

Dining is a big deal along the Delaware, and the choices are legion. Some restaurants do not have liquor licenses, but allow guests to bring their own.

North of New Hope

The Inn at Phillips Mill, North River Road, New Hope, Pa. (215) 862-9919. For charm and consistently good food, this quaint gray stone building

34

right next to a bend in the River Road is tops. Looking as if it had been transported from the British Cotswolds, the 1750 structure has a copper pig above the entrance — a symbol of the stone barn's origin as a gristmill which stood next to the village piggery. Architect Bruce Kaufmann and his innkeeper wife Joyce transformed it into a country French restaurant, plus a cozy inn with five cheerily decorated guest rooms upstairs. The dining setting could not be more romantic: candles augmenting light from the fireplace in low-ceilinged rooms with dark beams, and arrangements of flowers all around. Some nights a young woman in a beret and striped shirt, with a synthesizer around her neck, sings Parisian songs. The house terrine and a mousse of smoked trout and salmon are favored appetizers. We liked the sauteed calves liver in a cider vinegar and the steak au poivre, chosen among 10 entrees from $9.50 to $16.50. A dessert of vanilla mousse with big chips of chocolate and a chocolate fudge sauce made a worthy ending. Dinner nightly, 5:30 to 9:30 or 10. BYOB; no credit cards.

The Frenchtown Inn, 7 Bridge St., Frenchtown, N.J. (201) 996-3300. Opened in 1986 by Robert and Holly Long, this outstanding restaurant and inn-to-be has drawn raves (it had just won a three-star rating from the New York Times the week we were there). And no wonder. Robert Long's food is inventive and superb, the service friendly yet flawless, and the setting comfortable. Arriving for a Friday lunch without reservations, we found the front dining room with its planked ceiling, brick walls and carpeted floors full. So we were seated in the more austere columned dining room in the rear, outfitted with floral wallpaper, crisp white linens and Villeroy & Boch china. Everything on the menu looked great; we can vouch for an unusual and airy black bean soup, the selection of pates and terrines ($4.50 — small but very smooth and good), the corned beef sandwich on brown bread and a sensational salad of duck and smoked pheasant with a warm cider vinaigrette ($6.25), loaded with meat, mixed greens, radicchio and arugula. A layered pear-raspberry tart with whipped cream was a perfect dessert. On the fall dinner menu, the seven entrees ran from $15.75 for breast of chicken with a pheasant mousse finished with fois gras to $24.75 for rack of lamb with a garlic flan. Robert Long was chef at the acclaimed Tarragon Tree in Chatham, N.J., and worked in Paris before finding his culinary niche in Frenchtown. The Longs were planning to add seven to ten guest rooms upstairs. Lunch, Tuesday-Friday noon to 2 (Saturday in the large lounge); dinner, Tuesday-Sunday 6 to 9; Sunday brunch, noon to 3.

Centre Bridge Inn, River Road, New Hope, Pa. (215) 862-2048. The downstairs tavern-dining room with beamed ceilings, stucco walls and huge open fireplaces could not be more attractive, nor the glass-enclosed porch overlooking the river more inviting. Outside by the river is a brick patio with white wrought-iron furniture and a circle of granite tables around a fountain. Here is the ultimate waterside setting, and if some think that the food doesn't necessarily measure up to the surroundings, who cares? The limited French menu is standard: appetizers about $6.50 for house pate, escargot en croute and shrimp-lobster mousseline; entrees ($16.95 to $21.95) like roast duckling bigarade, pheasant Normandy, veal champignon and rack of lamb persille. Cappuccino and international coffees are available, and we recall a happy night sipping after-dinner drinks at the bar as a pianist entertained. Dinner, Monday-Saturday from 5:30, Sunday from 3.

Cuttalossa Inn, River Road, Lumberville, Pa. (215) 297-5082. Another place where the food may not live up to the surroundings is the venerable Cuttalossa, but it's not for lack of trying. New owner Marilyn MacMaster, something of a showperson, travels the world to find new recipes. And the setting is tough to beat: an 1833 stone landmark, with three history-filled dining rooms inside and a large outdoor terrace beside a millstream and waterfall, where we'd gladly have an al fresco lunch anytime. The dinner menu mixes continental and American ($15.95 to $18.95): crab imperial, veal marsala, chicken pollo glace, Peking duck, and steak au poivre; salmon steaks wrapped in parchment paper, braised scallops in champagne sauce on wild rice, and vegetarian plates. You might start with a pumpkin cream soup and finish with homemade strawberry cheesecake. You can stop for a drink in the outdoor bar, illuminated at night by twinkling white lights; with the woods and the stone buildings and the roar of the falls in the background, it's rather magical. Lunch and dinner daily, Sunday brunch 11 to 5. Closed in winter.

Golden Pheasant Inn, River Road, Erwinna, Pa. (215) 294-9595. The glamorous plant-filled solarium once was the setting for a memorable meal, so after the Golden Pheasant had declined, we were glad to hear it was purchased in 1986 by French chef Michel Faure, who was well regarded at the nearby Carversville Inn and Philadelphia's Le Bec Fin. He and his wife Barbara, who oversees the front of the house, have restored the dark inner Victorian dining rooms to the 1850 period, a vast improvement, and were totally renovating six upstairs guest rooms when we visited. We'd still choose the solarium, where you can see the canal and the trees illuminated at night, for one of Michel's dinner creations: perhaps stuffed clams with crabmeat or chicken livers forestiere for appetizers, brook trout amandine, roast duckling with sauce of the day or pepper steak flamed with cognac and creme fraiche ($15.95 to $19.95). Dinner nightly except Monday, from 5:30.

The Blue Ribbon, Bridge Street, Stockton, N.J. (609) 397-4100. This restaurant was opened late in 1986 by Martine Landry, the French owner of Martine's in New Hope. Those who knew it as Le Bistro wouldn't recognize its new layout and exceptionally pretty setting of blue and rose. Martine has decorated with lace from Scotland, tiles from Europe, baskets, stained glass, and a collection of blue ribbons that symbolize the restaurant's name. Even the lampposts outside are painted blue and rose. The menu changes every six to eight weeks. Among entrees ($14.95 to $19.95), we enjoyed the rack of New Zealand lamb and the roast duckling with jalapeno glaze, nicely presented on enormous white plates with red Bliss potatos, lima beans and red peppers and garnished with an edible blossom. The onion-sage bread was excellent, and the vanilla ice cream and raspberry sherbet in chambord sauce most satisfying. Since only two other tables were occupied on a Thursday night, we fervently hoped the Blue Ribbon would fare better than Le Bistro. Dinner nightly except Tuesday, 5 to 10:30. BYOB.

Rare Essentials, 10 Bridge St., Frenchtown, N.J. (201) 996-3633. With its black and white tile floors, hanging green lamps, old stone walls and white formica tables, this tiny gourmet food shop and restaurant in the basement under a gift shop is a welcome addition to the river scene since its 1986 opening. Co-owner Joanna Smyth formerly directed a cooking school in Philadelphia. Her menus are innovative and reasonable; imagine cappellini with smoked salmon and American caviar for $4.50! Other lunch possibilities are shrimp beignets with red pepper salsa and grilled flank steak with Irish whiskey sauce and sweet potato chips. Start with fresh tomato soup with green chilies accompanied by Navajo fry bread. Dinner entrees are $6.75 to $12.95 (for veal scallops with applejack and tart apple slices). Sunday brunch for $8.95 includes appetizer, entree and coffee. In the case are displayed desserts like hazelnut torte, currant mousse, and raspberry and cappuccino cakes. Lunch, Tuesday-Saturday 11:30 to 2:30.; dinner, Thursday-Sunday 5 to 9; Sunday brunch, 10 to 3. BYOB.

The Left Bank, 2 Bridge St., Frenchtown, N.J. (201) 996-4714. Almost next door to Rare Essentials is this little train station converted to a bakery and deli-cafe whose motto is "a home away from home." There are five tables with a river view, and a tiny brick patio by the river. Breakfast brings the world's largest blueberry muffins or french toast made with homemade challah; the Left Bank omelet incorporates peppers, onions, pepperoni and jack cheese topped with salsa. Three or four soups a day are offered; stews, chilis, deep-dish pizzas and all kinds of bagel toppings are hearty fare. The boagie is a hoagie on a bagel. Pick up a loaf of fragrant European peasant bread to take home. Open daily except Tuesday to 9 in summer, to 5:30 or 6 in winter.

Olde Mill Ford Oyster House, 17 Bridge St., Milford, N.J. (201) 995-9411. When a restaurant has an adjacent fish market, you can bet the seafood will be fresh. And that's one reason the Oyster House is highly regarded across the area. Another is the prices, with the most expensive entree (shellfish stew) going for $14.95. The menu is quite simple: dishes like shrimp in beer batter, New England baked scallops and stuffed flounder with shrimp sauce. The many nightly specials might include crab Norfolk, beer-braised rabbit and roast duckling with sweet potatoes and brandied peach orange sauce. A local woman makes the pies, and there's an ice cream crepe with chocolate rum sauce. The three small dining rooms, plain but fresh looking, have oriental rugs and blue and white tablecloths. Fetch your wine from the Milford Liquor Store next door; with a selection of 250 you will surely find what you want. Dinner only, 4 to 9, to 10 Friday and Saturday. Closed Tuesday and month of January. BYOB; no credit cards.

In Town, Near the River

Lambertville Station, 11 Bridge St., Lambertville, N.J. (609) 397-8300. The abandoned 2 1/2-story train station was transformed in 1983 into a stylish Victorian restaurant and lounge that fairly ooze atmosphere. Diners on several levels of the glass-enclosed Platform Room can watch geese glide by on the Delaware Raritan Canal and tiny lights reflecting off the water. With good-sized drinks, our party of four sampled the unusual appetizer of alligator strips ($6.75), which you dip into a mustard and green peppercorn sauce — novel but interesting. Among entrees ($9.95 to $18.95), the jambalaya was spicy, the boneless roast duck was properly crispy and had a mixed fruit sauce, the seafood fettuccine was more than ample and the veal medallions with chanterelles and wild rice were excellent. The honey mustard dressing on the house spinach salad was super. Lime-almond cheesecake and key lime mousse pie were good desserts. The Sunset on the Delaware special, served weekdays from 4 to 6:30, is considered one of the best bargains around: soup or salad, entree and dessert for $8.95. A Victorian lounge is on the mezzanine. Lunch,

Monday-Saturday 11:30 to 3; dinner, Monday-Thursday and Sunday 4 to 10, Friday and Saturday 5 to 11; Sunday brunch, 11 to 3.

The Landing, 22 N. Main St., New Hope, Pa. (215) 862-5711. The only restaurant with a river view in the heart of town is tucked back off the main street in a small house with windows onto the water and a rear lawn that was to be bricked over for a patio in 1987. The limited menu (which arrives in a picture frame) appeals, from shiitake mushrooms stuffed with pork, ginger and water chestnuts to a goat cheese pillow for appetizers, tuna marinated in mushroom sauce and ginger to frog's legs with garlic to rack of lamb with herbed mustard for main courses ($14.95 to $18.95). You might find gingered flank steak, spanakopita, Southwestern chili or a lentil and walnut salad on the lunch menu. Desserts are to groan over: bourbon pecan pie, grand marnier souffle and a frozen mousse with tia maria. California vintages were being added to the wine list. Lunch daily from 11:30, dinner from 5:30.

Mothers, 34 N. Main St., New Hope, Pa. (215) 862-9354. If you can get by the spectacular desserts in the glass case at the entrance and put up with the crowds usually waiting for a table, you'll be rewarded with some of the most interesting food around. The choice is staggering. At dinner, for instance, you could snack on fried almond brie with raspberry sauce, a smoked fish platter or a Cajun-Creole stir-fry. Or you could get a Szechuan linguini or a duck pizza. Or a Cajun duck with potato sausage stuffing, Chinese five-spice strip steak, Creole stuffed blackened trout or salmon filet with champagne-mustard sauce. Or, for dessert, a walnut kirsch cake, banana hazelnut torte or an almond meringue filled with rum butter cream, almonds and chocolate. And that's just for dinner; you can imagine what they do for breakfast and lunch. Prices aren't inexpensive (dinner entrees, $14 to $17.50), but you can mix and match. There's full bar service, the minimum dining charge is $3.50, and the menu warns that "Momma don't allow no cigar or pipe smoking here." The several small dining rooms, all tile and brick with beamed ceilings, are lively and intimate, and there's courtyard dining in back. Breakfast, Monday-Friday 8 to 2, weekends 9 to 2; lunch, 11 to 5; dinner, 5 to 11 or midnight.

Martine's, 7 E. Ferry St., New Hope, Pa. (215) 862-2966. Originally a salt store that was part of the first village center built around a ferry, this mid-18th century structure combines American history and a French bistro atmosphere. The small upstairs dining room is country French with beamed ceilings, small-paned windows, simple wood chairs and delicate stained-glass lamps hanging over handsome tile tables; the downstairs pub has tile booths and a fireplace. The outdoor cafe is popular in season. The classic French menu has some trendy touches: rack of lamb with apricot pommery glaze, grilled veal chop with sundried tomato and pine nut sauce, roast game hen with oyster stuffing ($13.75 to $16). Interesting salads and pastas are featured at lunch, as are omelets and croissants at breakfast. The fancy wine list contains good values. Breakfast, lunch and dinner daily.

South of New Hope

Tosca, 1268 River Road, Washington Crossing, Pa. (215) 321-9000. New in 1986 was this northern Italian restaurant, its beautiful covered outdoor patio overlooking the river across the road. The two attractive small dining rooms are carefully decorated and intimate; you'd never guess that this had been a hot dog stand. The ambitious menu is augmented by interesting specials, red snapper and venison among them when we visited. Entrees embrace everything from roast chicken ($13) to veal scaloppine and steak ($22). The lunch menu is much more limited, listing six entrees from $8 to $10. Lunch, noon to 3; dinner, 5:30 to 11. BYOB.

Odette's, South River Road, New Hope, Pa. (215) 862-2432. For many, this is the ultra Bucks County dining experience: big, lavish, theatrical. The rear outdoor terrace, the glassed-in room facing it and another room above afford gorgeous views of the river. Taped classical or live piano music, beautiful flowers, and formal table settings and service contribute to a perfect atmosphere in which to see and be seen. Three hundred people can be seated in the various dining rooms or in the lounge. The limited menu changes seasonally. You might start with roasted sweet peppers in a casserole, mesquite-grilled lamb sausage or chickory salad before your main course ($12.95 to $19.95), perhaps grilled swordfish with tomato and horseradish puree, mahi mahi, scallops Mexico City (in a spicy saffron cream sauce, baked in a tortilla), fettuccine with smoked turkey or grilled tofu and shiitake mushrooms. Chocolate fudge cake and fruit tortes are among the mainstays on the dessert tray; the wine list is pricey. Salads like Thai beef with spicy peanut dressing and duck with curried vinaigrette make great lunches. Lunch, Monday-Saturday 11:30 to 3; dinner, 5 to 10 or 11; Sunday, brunch 11 to 3, dinner 4 to 9.

Forager House, 1800 River Road, New Hope, Pa. (215) 862-9477. Contemporary decor with track lighting, purple napkins on white linen, well-spaced tables and good-looking prints along the walls distinguish this restaurant. So does the food, which tends to be in the vanguard — Forager House was the first to bring Spanish tapas to Bucks County on Friday nights in 1986, and varying international cuisines were being offered Thursday nights in the winter. The changing menu of chef-owner Dick Barrows typically ranges from Cajun seafood gumbo to grilled loin of pork with peach chutney and loin of lamb with garlic and thyme ($14.75 to $17). Desserts might be a Viennese chocolate torte, fresh fruit sorbet or meringue glace. California's distinguished Trefethen is the house wine, and the wine list is good and fairly priced. Dinner, Tuesday-Saturday from 6, Sunday from 4:30.

Washington Crossing Inn, Washington Crossing, Pa. (215) 493-3634. The area surrounding the inn is full of history, and this stately restaurant and banquet facility has its share. It occupies part of the land where Washington's troops prepared to cross the Delaware, the original hearth room dates to 1760 and the present inn celebrated its 50th anniversary in 1986. Most meals are taken in the Hearth Room, dark and cheery with a large fireplace, or the light and airy Covered Bridge Room, with brick floor and garden-type furniture. The large continental dinner menu runs the gamut from $8.95 for fettuccine Alfredo to $18.95 for lobster tails. Snapper soup, laced with sherry, and roast duckling flambeed tableside are specialties. Lunch features soups, salads, sandwiches and five entrees, priced from $3.25 to $5.95. Lunch, Monday-Saturday 11:30 to 3, dinner 5 to 10; Sunday, brunch 11 to 2, dinner 1 to 8.

FOR MORE INFORMATION: New Hope Information Center, South Main Street at Mechanic Street, Box 141, New Hope, Pa. 18938, (215) 862-5880. Bucks County Tourist Commission, 152 Swamp Road, Doylestown, Pa. 18901, (215) 345-4552. Lambertville Area Chamber of Commerce, 4 S. Union St., Lambertville, N.J. 08530, (609) 397-0055.

Victorian houses face ocean at Cape May.

Cape May, N.J.

Singularly interesting is Cape May — an oasis of exuberant Victoriana not far from the Mason-Dixon line.

Near the end of a peninsula where South Jersey fades away between the Atlantic Ocean and Delaware Bay, America's oldest seaside resort has been reborn into a remarkably diverse charmer that is the closest thing to a Key West up north. Some of the similarities are unmistakable: a salubrious ocean setting with water on three sides, unsurpassed Victorian architecture that designates the entire city a National Historic Landmark, a spate of period bed-and-breakfast inns, outstanding restaurants and, by Northern standards, something of a Southern air.

Time had forgotten Cape May since the late 1800s when it was the playground for presidents and personages from Ulysses S. Grant and William Harrison to Bret Harte and Henry Ford. Fires, new transportation modes and changing lifestyles took their toll; Atlantic City and other more accessible resorts left Cape May languishing as a country town out of the mainstream.

Not until 1970 when a group of citizens banded together to save the landmark Emlen Physick House from demolition did Cape May's fortunes turn. Along came the U.S. Bicentennial with an interest in history and, as local tour guide James Corson tells it, "ours was still standing all around us." Having declined the honor a few years earlier, Cape May in 1976 was designated a National Historic Landmark city, one of only five in the nation, and its future would be forever altered — and preserved.

The Mid-Atlantic Center for the Arts, founded to save the Physick Estate, has left its imprint on the entire community. Two of its longtime officers, Tom Carroll and Marianne Schatz, restored neighboring landmarks into museum-quality guest houses, launching a bed-and-breakfast phenomenon that was a model throughout Cape May and elsewhere.

If B&B is now part and parcel of the Cape May experience, so is Victoriana. Some 670 structures from the late 1800s, the largest concentration anywhere, have been preserved. They range from gingerbread cottages to ornate show-places, from block-long hotels to slivers of guest houses. And everywhere there are front verandas — seemingly all of them in use from late afternoon to sunset or later. So immersed is Cape May in its past that it celebrates an entire Victorian Week in mid-October, not to mention a week-long Tulip Festival, a Dickens Christmas Extravaganza, Victorian dinners, and Victorian house and inn tours. Even the city's welcome center is in an 1853 church.

The Cape May area is one of America's best birding spots, and in season the bird-watchers outnumber beachcombers, fishermen, souvenir shoppers, restaurant-goers and even Victorianophiles.

Such is the annual crush of tourists that one local newspaper wag suggested a spring Festival of Lawns. With tongue firmly in cheek, he wanted to celebrate the last view of grass before it disappeared beneath the influx.

Getting There

Cape May is located at the southern end of the Garden State Parkway, about 90 miles southeast of Philadelphia. From the Delmarva Peninsula, it can be reached via ferry from Lewes, Del.

Where to Stay

The city of 5,000 year-round residents offers more than 3,000 rooms, many of them in efficiency motels and rooming houses. Because bed and breakfast is so much a part of the Cape May experience, we concentrate on some of the more than 30 in town. Most have minimum stays of two or three nights, do not permit smoking and allow access only via the unique combination locks installed in the doors (after all, many of these are museum-quality homes and curious passersby would be an intrusion). Breakfasts tend to be lighter in summer, more formal and filling the rest of the year. The Cape May ritual is for the innkeepers to serve afternoon tea or beverages as well as breakfast, mingling with their guests all the while. As innkeeper John Dunwoody of the Brass Bed said, "We don't just rent rooms; we share our house."

Bed and Breakfast

The Mainstay Inn, 635 Columbia Ave., Cape May 08204. (609) 884-8690. The Mainstay and the Abbey are the two that led the way, and are the most likely to be filled weeks, if not months, in advance. Tom and Sue Carroll began the B&B movement in Cape May at the Windward House, now under new ownership, and purchased the Mainstay in 1975. The 14-foot-high public rooms in the 1872 Italianate villa are furnished in Victoriana right down to the sheet music on the piano. Especially notable is the ceiling of the entrance hall, where a stunning combination of 17 wallpapers makes a beautiful accent. Rooms in the inn and in the pleasant 1870 Cottage next door are named for famous visitors to Cape May like Stonewall Jackson and Henry Ford. Lace curtains, stenciling, brass and iron bedsteads, armoires and rockers decorate the thirteen rooms, nine with private baths and some with copper tubs. The Henry Ford room has its own small porch and the Bret Harte room (with many of his books in a case) opens onto the entire second-floor veranda. Should you not mind a very steep ladder with a wavering rope for a railing, climb up to the tower on the third floor, where, with cushions on two sides and windows on all four, you can get a good view of town. The inn and the cottage, both with wide verandas and rocking chairs, are separated by a brick walk and a handsome trickling fountain; the front gardens are brilliant with flowers. Sue Carroll's recipes for her breakfast and tea goodies are so sought after that she has published a small cookbook called *Breakfast at Nine, Tea at Four*. In summer, breakfast is continental-plus, served buffet-style on the veranda; other seasons it is formal sit-down around the table for twelve in the dining room. California egg puff and macaroni mousse are among the offerings. Tours of the Mainstay ($4) are given Saturday, Sunday, Tuesday and Thursday at 4, after which participants are invited to join inn guests for a formal tea. "Young children generally find us tiresome," the brochure advises sensibly. This is, as Tom Carroll says, "a total Victorian experience." Doubles, $65 to $90; three-night minimum in season. Open April-October.

The Abbey, Columbia Avenue and Gurney Street, Cape May 08204. (609) 884-4506. Relax on the side porch of the Abbey, and you'll likely be a supporting player in someone's video, slide or snapshot. A constant stream of tourists gawk at, and take pictures of, this elegant Gothic villa with its 60-foot tower and incredible gingerbread trim, all painstakingly painted green with deep red and ivory accents. Jay and Marianne Schatz, corporate and academic dropouts, purchased the 1869 Abbey, built as a summer home for a coal baron, in 1979. It's their fourth restoration, and they've done a splendid job. The parlor, library and dining room on the main floor, with ornate 12-foot ceilings and 11-foot windows (decorated with lace curtains and striking lambrequins, designed by Marianne) are filled with priceless items, including the largest freestanding bookcase (which comes apart in 27 pieces) we have ever seen. In the dining room, with its Teutonic sideboard, 14 people can sit around the banquet table; says Marianne, "we have the noisiest breakfasts in town." That's partly because Jay keeps guests regaled both with his stories and his selection of hats from a closet which holds a choice of 150 — perhaps an Australian bush hat or a "Hagar the Horrible" beauty. A continental-plus breakfast is served in summer. In spring and fall, you might have pink grapefruit juice, a dish of fresh peaches and whipped cream, an egg and ham casserole with garlic grits on the side, and buttered English muffins. Marianne also makes a great quiche with a Bisquick crust. The Schatzes preside at 6 o'clock over beer, wine and popcorn on the porch or in the parlor. On the second and third floors, seven bedrooms, all with private baths and interesting period light fixtures, are named for cities. We stayed in the Savannah, a sweet room with white enamel bedstead, oriental carpets, a white wicker sofa with purple cushions and a small refrigerator in the bathroom. Tours of the first floor are given Thursday-Sunday at 5. In 1986 the Schatzes purchased the building next door and planned to make it into a somewhat less formal B&B than the Abbey. Doubles, $60 to $90; three to four-night minimum stay in season. Open April-October.

Windward House, 24 Jackson St., Cape May 08204. (609) 884-3368. The Mainstay's Tom and Sue Carroll got their start here, but today's elan is provided by Owen and Sandy Miller, she a collector of vintage clothing, who runs fashion shows and spreads her wares ingeniously all over the house. Her eggcup collection in the dining room and the beveled and stained glass all around are extraordinary as well. The eight guest rooms, all with private baths, are furnished with antiques. One of the most requested is the third-floor Empire Room with the best water view and access to a large sundeck looking toward the ocean. The place is decorated but not overwhelming; it's cool and cheerful and "guests get a great sense of being at home," says Owen. Breakfast is simple but homemade, the fare tending to health foods, and guests rave about the granola, hot breads and Philadelphia sticky buns. Doubles, $65 to $80. Open year-round.

The Brass Bed, 719 Columbia Ave., Cape May 08204. (609) 884-8075. Guests are welcomed into an attractive enclosed sunporch or a delightful small parlor with an old victrola and a desk topped by an old Corona typewriter, two pairs of spectacles and a small globe. Eight guest rooms with 19th century brass beds, period wall coverings, oriental carpets and lace curtains are offered by John and Donna Dunwoody. Two rooms have private baths and two have half baths. "We did the total restoration ourselves," advised Donna, rolling her eyes skyward. The result is cozy and homey. Egg and cheese strata or banana pancakes might be the fare for breakfast, served at a long table in the dining room. Doubles, $50 to $80. Open year-round.

Captain Mey's Inn, 202 Ocean St., Cape May 08204. (609) 884-7793. Named for the Dutch explorer for whom Cape May is named, this 1890 structure with a spectacular wraparound veranda filled with wicker furniture is run very personally by Carin Feddermann of Holland and Milly LaCanfora. "We tie in Dutch flair with Victoriana," says Carin, showing their remarkable Delft Blue china collection, the chestnut oak Eastlake paneling, beautiful dining room fireplace, a hand-painted medallion above a chandelier in the parlor and, the crowning touch, five kinds of Tiffany stained glass with a wreath in the front door. A soldier pops out of a cuckoo clock at appointed intervals. The eight upstairs guest rooms, two with private bath, are decorated with similar flair: Dutch lace curtains, handmade quilts and European antiques. You'd never guess that the interior once was all painted white, or that the women refinished the entire house (an album of before-and-after photos traces their progress). Sherry or white wine is offered in the afternoon. Breakfast is an event, served by candlelight with a fire in the fireplace on cool mornings (or outside on the veranda or new courtyard). It's a typical Dutch meal with imported cheeses, breakfast meats, yogurt, egg dishes and possibly french toast with grand marnier, Dutch potato pancakes or scalloped apples. Doubles, $65 to $90. Open year-round.

The Queen Victoria, 102 Ocean St., Cape May 08204. (609) 884-8702. At the head of the stairway to the second floor is a basket of amenities and essentials labeled "In Case You Forgot." It's one of the thoughtful touches offered by Joan and Dane Wells in their luxurious inn with twelve rooms, eight with private baths. The new Carriage House Suite in the rear is the largest, but the Queen Victoria Room on the main-floor front corner is no slouch: two brass beds joined together, armoire, settee and two Victorian chairs at a small table in an alcove. Furnishings in the public rooms are not so high Victorian as in other inns. Sherry is served in a front parlor with brick fireplace and heavy furniture; a cozy reading room offers books and magazines, a popcorn popper, setups and glasses. The library contains volumes on architecture, art and history collected by Joan when she was executive director of the Victorian Society in America. Baked eggs, a spinach or corn casserole and homemade breads are served for breakfast at a long table in the dining room. Doubles, $69 to $110. Open year-round.

The Manor House, 612 Hughes St., Cape May 08204. (609) 884-4710. After all the Victoriana, the Manor House comes as a refreshing change of pace. The impressive, gambrel-roofed house with warm oak and chestnut foyer and striking furnishings seems almost contemporary in contrast. "We're not trying to be high Victorian," explains Mary Snyder, innkeeper with her husband Tom. "This is more homey and we want people to feel comfortable." Guests spread out for punch or tea in a living room with a colorful stained-glass-front player piano or a library with two plush loveseats in front of a fireplace. Upstairs are ten guest rooms, six with private bath, furnished in antiques, brass and wood beds, handmade quilts and light Victorian print wallpapers. The Snyders offer a choice of two entrees at two breakfast seatings — perhaps buttermilk pancakes or Mexican souffle, Mary's crumb buns and non-stop monologue by Tom, who rivals the Abbey's Jay Schatz as a standup comic and conducts walking tours of town. Doubles, $55 to $95. Open year-round.

Motels

Cape Motor Inn, Beach Drive and Grant Street, Cape May 08204. (609) 884-4256. Locally considered to be the best of the lot, this family operation run by Ruth and Bob Escher is pleasantly restrained in architecture and luxurious in accommodations. Nearly half the 52 rooms are two-room efficiencies with sitting rooms and balconies; the third-floor suites with vaulted ceilings and oceanfront views are nicest. Rooms contain two beds and modern oak furniture. The Eschers have added an elevator and were planning to expand and renovate the older section of the motel by 1988. There's an attractive pool. Doubles, $70 to $121. Open May-October.

La Mer Motor Inn, Beach Drive and Pittsburgh Avenue, Cape May 08204. (609) 884-2200. This appealing, low-key motel with shingled roof has 62 units on two floors in a rather out-of-the-way location along the ocean on the north side of town. Second-floor rooms face the ocean; those on ground level look at the pool. Rooms have been redecorated and some have kitchens. There are a new children's playground, a miniature golf course, barbecue area, laundry facilities and a family restaurant and lounge called Water's Edge. Doubles, $85 to $110. Open May to late October.

Montreal Inn, Beach Drive at Madison Street, Cape May 08204. (609) 884-7011. Opened in 1966 with 27 units, this oceanfront motel has grown to four floors with 70 units, plus Promenade restaurant and lounge, a package store, large pool, sauna and mini-golf layout. The Montreal connection is unclear, but the values are — especially in the off-season, when we got a fine room for $36. The only minus was the noise of a carousing group of fishermen in a suite next door. Doubles, $59 to $94. Open March-November.

Hotels

The Chalfonte, 301 Howard St., Cape May 08204. (609) 884-8409. Cape May's oldest hotel (1876) and in many ways its most revered is somewhat hard to find — a block away from the ocean at the edge of the historic district — and we bumped into it quite by accident on a walking tour. New owners Judy Bartella and Anne LeDuc are upgrading both the public rooms and guest quarters. Although the rambling three-story hotel has 103 rooms, only 78 are rented. They're conceded to be rustic and threadbare in the endearing manner of an earlier era. Each has a sink, but most of the baths are down the hall; 11 have private baths. The front porch is lined with rocking chairs, and one TV and two phones are available for guests' use. Four generations of the Dickerson family have been cooking Southern food served family style in the long, echoing dining room since 1876. Helen Dickerson, head chef for 40 years and now in her late 70s, is assisted by her daughter, Dot Burton. Helen's cookbook, *I Just Stop Stirrin' When the Tastin's Good*, typifies her style. The Virginia country breakfast ($6.50) includes spoonbread and biscuits. Two-entree Southern dinners with a set menu and all the trimmings are $14.95 and gentlemen are requested to wear jackets. "It's really still like a large boarding house," Judy Bartella concedes, and guests keep returning for the experience. Doubles, $59 to $110 MAP. Open summer through September, weekends in October.

Congress Hall, Beach Drive and Perry Street, Box 150, Cape May 08204. (609) 884-8421. An imposing National Historic Landmark that once served Presidents and Congressmen (Benjamin Harrison made it his Summer White House), this 102-room hotel is gradually being renovated by the grandsons of the longtime owner, the head of the Christian Beacon Press, who also owns the Christian Admiral Hotel at the north end of town. John Phillips Sousa is said to have been so charmed by the building that he composed "The Congress Hall March" in 1882 after performing on the hotel's lawn for seven nights. Billed as the nation's oldest seaside hotel, its first structure was built in 1812 with a 700-foot-long piazza fronting on the sea. The enormous lobby with marble floors is filled with wicker and a sea breeze. Best rooms are the 25 Cottage and 14 oceanfront Presidential rooms. You enter the Cottage rooms off a long, wide hall through a louvered door and an inner door; inside all is white wicker, a thick carpet, a bed, a bathroom with shower, windows onto the ocean, a prominently displayed Bible and not much else. The Presidential suites include a room with a day bed between the main bedroom and bath; oriental rugs, plain white walls and wood floors comprise the decor. Breakfast and dinner buffets are served in the large dining room, and the **Tussie Mussie Shop** off the lobby offers Victorian-style gifts. The spacious lawn has a pool, shuffleboard and croquet area. Doubles, $39 to $80; unrestored rooms, $35 to $45. Open mid-May to mid-October.

The Colonial Hotel and Motor Lodge, Beach Drive at Ocean Street, Box 338, Cape May 08204. (609) 884-3483. Operated continuously since 1893, the Colonial is younger than the Chalfonte "but in better condition," longtime owner Robert Fite says proudly. Considered ultra-modern for its time, it had the first elevator in town and electric bells from rooms to front desk. Today the Colonial offers a choice: 100 rooms in the turreted, five-story hotel or 50 rooms in an adjacent three-story motel. The oceanfront motel rooms have private balconies, air-conditioning, TV and refrigerator. Most hotel rooms, except those on the fifth floor, have private baths and half face the ocean. A typical corner room offers a double and twin bed, a small sitting area in an alcove beside the wash basin, maple furniture and a tiny bathroom with tub. A second-floor deck looks onto the ocean, but most regulars prefer the main-floor porches filled with rockers. Windows on all sides of the long, 300-seat dining room open for cross-ventilation. Nightly entertainment is provided in the **Colonial Lounge,** as in the old days when John Phillips Sousa and his band played nightly during the dinner hour. Out front is a curved pool and a smaller children's pool. Doubles, in hotel, $62 to $89 MAP, $42 to $69 EP; in motel, $77 to $89, EP. Open mid-April to November.

SUMMER RENTALS. Many summer houses are available for rent, particularly in the Cape May Point area. The owners of the Windward House inn, for instance, offer a house sleeping six people one door from the beach for $675 a week. Rentals top out at about $750, alhough some condominiums charge $1,000 a week. Among real-estate brokers handling rentals are Cape May Realty, 311 Pittsburgh Ave., 884-2700; Sol Needles Agency, 512 Washington St. Mall, 884-8428, and Tolz Realtors, 4 Victorian Village Plaza, 884-7001.

Seeing and Doing

Besides enjoying the beach, which is as far as some unknowing souls get, there's enough in Cape May and environs to keep one busy for days. No wonder the minimum-stay requirements don't bother most; many come for a week or more and return season after season. Incidentally, Cape May's season — from Memorial Day to mid-October — is extending every year as new events are staged and more inns and restaurants stay open longer.

Touring Cape May

There are no Gray Line bus tours here — only old-fashioned trolley tours and walking tours sponsored by the Mid-Atlantic Center for the Arts (MAC), which seems to have a hand in just about everything that's good in town.

Guided Trolley Tours, MAC, 884-5404. Leaving regularly from Ocean Street opposite the Washington Street Mall, they take half an hour and cover the East End (the best tour if you only have time for one) and the West End. Our guide, tenth-generation resident Jim Corson, told about the town's bad luck with hurricanes and fires and pointed out his house, "which cost more to paint this year than it did to buy it in 1904." He explained that the Washington Inn was moved three times, showed how Victorian cottagers were trying to outdo each other (including his favorite house, the Abbey, where the original owner was not content to compete only with his neighbors but also with himself on every side), and pointed out the largest mansion in town, the George Allen House, and its prized outhouse, a two-seater with cupola. His comments made our subsequent wanderings much more informed. Moonlight trolley rides (unguided) also are given at 8 o'clock many evenings. East End and West End tours, adults $3.50, children $1. Early spring to late fall.

Walking Tours. Following maps or instinct, you can explore on your own, but the guided walking tours offered by MAC are more entertaining and informative. Geared to those who like to see history close-up, the 90-minute tours are led by knowledgeable resident guides like innkeeper Tom Snyder, who share insights into Victorian traditions and customs. Tours leave from the Washington Street Mall information booth weekends and some weekdays at 11. Adults $4, children $1.

Mansions by Gaslight. Four of Cape May's finest homes are open for self-guided tours Wednesdays from 8 to 10 p.m., mid-June to mid-September. Included are the Physick House, the Mainstay Inn, the Abbey and the Wilbraham Mansion. MAC's shuttle bus runs a continuous transit loop starting from the Emlen Physick House, where tickets were purchased. Adults $10, children $5.

Cottages at Twilight. Five more charming Cape May homes are open for self-guided tours on Monday evenings from mid-June to mid-September. Tickets are purchased at the eclectic Dr. Henry L. Hunt House, 209 Congress Place. Also open are the Joseph Q. Williams House, Franklin Hughes House, Windward House and Gothic Gables. Adults $8. children $4.

Inside Cape May. Four Cape May inns offer combination tours under their own auspices in the mid to late afternoon every Friday and Saturday and some Mondays and Wednesdays in season (adults $8, children $2). On tour are the Duke of Windsor Inn, Alexander's Inn (also a restaurant in which the professional kitchen is a tour high spot), Captain Mey's Inn and the Summer Cottage Inn.

Christmas Tours. Seven year-round B&Bs are decked out in their Yuletide finery, each in a way that tells a part of the Christmas story: an elegant Christmas setting at Alexander's, a children's Christmas at the Brass Bed, a Dutch Christmas at Captain Mey's, the lights of Christmas at the Manor House, the history of Victorian decorations at the Queen Victoria, the music of Christmas at the Summer Cottage and vintage fashions for the holidays at Windward House. Afternoon and evening semi-guided tours are offered certain days in December. Adults $10, children $4.

Emlen Physick House and Estate, 1048 Washington St., 884-5404. The place where Cape May's restoration effort started (and now the headquarters of MAC, the group whose arts offerings funded the restoration) is open certain days for guided tours in summer and weekends in spring and fall. The 16-room house was designed by Philadelphia architect Frank Furness in 1879 for a young physician (an eminent surgeon's grandson, who never practiced and never married) and his mother. Many of the original furnishings have been retrieved and returned to the house. The family parlor has the original fireplace, sofabed and pipe organ. A crazy tureen in the corner of the formal parlor was a housewarming present. The upstairs library has striking Japanese wallpaper, even on the ceiling. Tapestry curtains, porcelain lamp fixtures and chandeliers are all around. We liked best the owner's bachelor bedroom beside a sunken marble bathroom; right next door is Mother's bedroom, her fan collection framed over the fireplace. Don't miss the costume collection across the hall. The tours take about 1 hour and 15 minutes or longer, our informant advised, if you get "a long-winded tour guide." On weekends, the tour of the 8.5-acre estate also includes the Carriage House, now home of the venerable Cape May Colony Art League, and a small barn displaying antique tools. Adults $4, children $1.

On or Near the Water

BIRDING. The city lies on the heavily populated Atlantic Flyway and more than 400 species of birds, plus the entire migration of monarch butterflies along the East Coast, heads south through Cape May Point. Spring and fall are the peak migration seasons, but many species stay year-round. Off Sunset Boulevard south of town is **South Cape May Meadow,** a 180-acre wildlife preserve and migratory bird refuge owned by the Nature Conservancy. A U-shaped trail across the meadow into the dunes, with grazing cattle at the side, is one mecca. A more popular one is **Cape May Point State Park,** where a platform beside a pond provides a pleasant and cooling spot to watch for birds and listen to the surf. A professional hawk counter and hawk banders can be seen at work, and a scoreboard is posted in the hawk-watch area charting the number of species counted the previous day and the year to date. Another bird-watching spot is the **Higbee's Beach Wildlife Management Area,** 600 acres of dune forest along Delaware Bay. The **Cape May Bird Observatory,** run by the New Jersey Audubon Society, conducts bird walks in the fall. Just north of Cape May off Stone Harbor Boulevard is the **Wetlands Institute and Museum,** surrounded by a 6,000-acre salt marsh. Included are an observation tower, a touch museum called Wetlandia, saltwater aquaria, a gallery with changing art and crafts shows, library and marsh trails.

Cape May Point State Park. Located near the lighthouse in the quaint summer colony of Cape May Point, this is a favorite with birders, naturalists and those who like to walk the dunes, beaches and three miles of trails. MAC had plans to restore the 1859 lighthouse, open it to the public and develop a maritime museum on its small grounds. Some visitors say not to miss the small museum containing information about birds and beach erosion (a particular problem around Cape May). Do walk out to the World War II bunker built with guns to guard Delaware Bay from enemy attack. Today it is an open "fortress" with benches and picnic tables above the surf. The beach here is unprotected and swimming is discouraged, although some sunbathers ventured into the water the late-September afternoon we visited. Nearby, St. Peter's-by-the-Sea is a tiny gray Episcopal chapel with fancy trim behind the dunes that line the beachfront.

Sunset Beach. At the end of Sunset Boulevard is a sheltered beach with free parking and a hodgepodge of snack bars and souvenir stands. Just offshore is the shell of the USS Atlantis, one of twelve concrete ships built during World War I and brought to the point in 1926 to serve as a breakwater; it ran aground in a storm and has been trapped ever since. The beach may yield the Cape May diamonds, semi-precious stones of pure quartz which are found only here; they can be polished, cut and set to make attractive jewelry.

SWIMMING. The aforementioned beaches, including Higbee's, are more secluded than Cape May's strand, but the latter is where the action is. Most inns and motels give their guests beach passes; the beach is patrolled in season so no one gets in free. A boardwalk flanks the beach and provides a view of the goings-on.

FISHING AND BOATING. More than 30 species of fish are said to inhabit the waters of the Atlantic, Delaware Bay and the inland waterways which separate the barrier resort islands from the mainland. Entered in Cape May's year-long fishing tournament are everything from winter flounders to mako sharks; the Canyons, said to be one of the world's great white marlin areas, are easily accessible. Boat rentals and charter boats are plentiful, and launching ramps are available along the waterway and Delaware Bay. The center of fishing activity is Fisherman's Wharf, where the commercial fleet unloads beyond the Lobster House restaurant. Six boats offer day and night fishing at the **Miss Chris Fishing Center,** Third Avenue and Wilson Drive, 884-5445 or 886-8164.

Boating is concentrated on the inland waterway near the Cape May Bridge at the north end of town. Sailing from the Miss Chris Fishing Center is the 65-foot oyster schooner **Delta Lady,** 884-1919, which offers three daily three-hour cruises at 10, 2 and 6 for $22. Barefoot cruises in which guests help sail the boat are given Sundays in summer from 10 to 4 for $40 per person including buffet lunch. **Twilight Cruises** off Wilson Drive, 884-0433, has daytime fishing excursions and nightly sightseeing-dinner cruises at 6; customers tour the waterway and dine at the Anchorage Inn for $17. In summer, **Capt. John Wilsey,** 884-8347, takes passengers aboard Summer Sun, a 27-foot catamaran, off Sunset Beach. **Cape Island Sailing Cruise,** 884-8347, offers leisurely afternoon or evening sails, viewing Cape May from the ocean and from the bay.

Other Activities

ARTS AND ENTERTAINMENT. The Mid-Atlantic Stage, 884-2787, presents professional theater on the outdoor Theatre by the Sea stage in an amphitheater surrounded by hedges and towering trees at the Physick Estate six nights a week (excluding Sunday) in July and August. A typical season might include "Deathtrap," "George M!" and "Godspell," presented in rotation two nights a week (adults $6). Victorian vaudeville revues are presented on the outdoor stage on Sunday evenings in late July and August. Vintage films from the 1930s and '40s, starring such favorites as Fred Astaire and Katharine Hepburn, are held Tuesday evenings in summer in the auditorium at Victorian Towers, the city's only high-rise apartment building at Washington and Ocean streets. For 14 summers, **band concerts** have taken place Wednesday and Saturday evenings and some afternoons at the Rotary Bandstand. For those interested in more mundane pursuits, the Arcade at the boardwalk offers the usual diversions.

SPECIAL EVENTS. From **Crafts at Tulip-time** in late April at Congress Hall to the **Christmas Candlelight house tour** the Saturday after Christmas, Victorian Cape May is alive with scheduled activities and events. **Victorian Week,** a 10-day extravanganza encompassing two weekends in mid-October, includes house tours, fashion shows, evening stained-glass tours, an antiques show, a crafts show, a Victorian dance, and lectures on Victorian architecture and decorative arts. **Victorian dinner feasts** for $35 are served in high style to 24 guests five times a year in the Emlen Physick House. A **Victorian Fair** is a mid-June highlight.

SHOPPING. Shopping is big business in Cape May, and the city's famed Washington Street Mall — one of the first to be closed to traffic in 1971 — is filled with pedestrians, particularly on rainy days. The small City Center Mall even has an atrium and an escalator (one-way, up). You'll find all kinds of stores, from swish to tacky. Our favorites:

The Whale's Tale is a nifty ramble of rooms containing everything from wind sockets to coffee mugs to shell magnets to an extraordinary collection of cards. The owners' previous emphasis on gourmet cookware has been eclipsed, since their offspring arrived, by children's games and accessories.

McDowell's Gallery of Gifts is literally that, its walls between marble floors and high ceilings brightened by colorful kites and wind sockets; there's an interesting assortment of jewelry, glass, crafts, wood products and games.

The Victorian Pink House Gift Shop, a local landmark, is open only mornings and evenings; the afternoons are for restocking. It has an incredible array of Victoriana. "We look back on the past with pleasure to things that were pleasurable," owner John Miller said in explaining it all. The lace baskets, nosegays, mini-ballerina slippers, modern reproductions on cards and more are pure nostalgia.

Imported from Portugal has fine handknit off-white fisherman sweaters, handmade rugs, ceramic bowls and tiles. Next door is **Trade Winds,** with jewlery, art and cultural items from exotic places like Panama and Kenya. **Swede Things in America** offers just what it says, mainly small items but some furniture. The **Washington Street Gallery** has Cape May and beachy posters; we almost sprang for a photo poster called "99 Bottles of Beer on the Wall" for a nephew.

Where to Eat

The choice in Cape May is staggering and the prices generally quite reasonable, all the more so at many places which do not have liquor licenses but allow you to bring your own wine. Many are open seasonally, with reduced hours in the spring and fall.

Near the Ocean

The Mad Batter, 19 Jackson St. (609) 884-5970. For more than 10 years, some of the most creative meals in town have been served in the appealing covered sidewalk cafe, the large dining room divided into two parts or on the rear porch amid white garden furniture, statues and greenery. We found the sidewalk cafe warm enough for candlelight dining on an early May night — a special treat, what with the view of the passing scene, the roar of the surf muted by classical music, and food so assertive that we returned the next morning for breakfast. The menu is fun and eclectic, from blackened sirloin Louisianne to calves liver Quebec. Our terrine of five seafoods was dense and smoky, if light on the advertised caviar and creme fraiche, and the whole wheat french bread was crusty and hearty. Dancing devil shrimp stir-fried with pecans, kumquats and black bean sauce and a fettuccine tossed with snails, asparagus and baked garlic were sensational. From a tempting dessert tray, we enjoyed the cheesecake with dates and prunes soaked in port. Breakfast the next day produced a gorgeous fruit plate and excellent whole wheat peach pancakes. Entrees on the changing dinner menu range from $11.50 to $22.50. Breakfast-brunch-lunch, daily 8 or 9 to 2:30; dinner, 5:30 to 9:30 or 11. Open late March-November, closed Monday in spring and fall. BYOB.

Restaurant Maureen, 429 Beach Drive. (609) 884-3774. Consistently good food and flawless service are high points of this sophisticated place run by Maureen and Stephen Horn on the second floor of what was once a bath house and saloon. Particularly inviting is the enclosed porch with smashing view of the ocean, all pristinely white with pink napkins; inside is a long chandeliered dining room. The Horns have attracted quite a following after seven years in Philadelphia and six in Cape May. Crab Versailles, tournedos royale, baked pheasant, veal au poivre and seafood cassolette are among the entrees ($14.75 to $22). Start with shrimp oriental or scallops seviche and cap off your meal with one of the pastry chef's desserts. Downstairs is **Summers,** a more casual place serving brunch, lunch and dinner and catering to bathers right off the beach. The bar is open daily from 11:30 to 2 a.m. Maureen, dinner 5 to 10; Summers, lunch-brunch 11:30 to 3, dinner 5 to 10, entertainment after 9:30. Open April-November.

The Lobster House, Fisherman's Wharf. (609) 884-8296. One of the largest enterprises we've seen, this includes an enormous restaurant, an outdoor raw bar, the schooner American, a take-out counter and the best seafood market around. The inside is packed for lunch and dinner; we preferred to lunch on the 143-foot-long schooner anchored on the inland waterway, although we felt somewhat on display for those at window tables inside. The schooner menu is unfortunately limited and boring; most people go there for drinks, and we found the tuna melt ($5.25) and shrimp salad croissant ($6.75) mundane at best. Better would have been snacks from the **Rigging Loft** raw bar — crab soup for $2.50, clams casino for $4.25 or a clambake dinner with clams, lobster tail, shrimp, mussels and corn, $8.75. Even better would be the **Dockside Take-out,** offering goodies from the seafood market like snapper soup and soft-shell crab sandwich. Inside, the oversize menu offers something for everyone in the old-school tradition, from fried oysters with pepper hash ($11.25) to fisherman's platter ($18.25). The house specialty is baked crab imperial, $8.75 at lunch. $13.95 at dinner. Lunch, daily 11:30 to 3; dinner 5 to 10, Sunday, 2 to 9. Open year-round.

Ocean Deck Restaurant, On the Promenade at Convention Hall Pier. (609) 884-8826. The expansive outdoor deck over the beach is the place to be in the thick of the waterfront activity. A seagull may wander in the open door of the lounge and on into the windowed dining room of leather booths and not much else. The food is traditional and ordinary — something to please everyone, the management says. Best bet may be for breakfast: omelets, waffles or pancakes, under the umbrellas beside the sea. Open daily in season, 8 a.m. to 9 p.m.

Away from the Water

410 Bank Street, 410 Bank St. (609) 884-2127. What could be more magical than dining in an outdoor courtyard, surrounded by plants, tiny white lights and Victorian lamps? That's the joy of this restaurant, which opened in 1984 (and expanded in 1986 with the opening of Frescos for seafood and pasta next door). A gumbo of New Orleans and French dishes, many grilled over mesquite wood but all with Cajun-Creole overtones, is offered at 410 Bank. We loved the special seviche and blackened quail for appetizers, and found both our entrees of blackened redfish and snapper with pecan sauce, served with crisp vegetables and rice pilaf, too much to eat. After all, we had to save room for the key lime pie, which was the real thing. So is everything else, from Cajun crawfish popcorn to possibly the best bread pudding you'll ever taste. If you can't eat outside, settle for one of the narrow screened porches or the small, intimate dining rooms adorned with New Orleans posters inside the restored 1840 house. Appetizers are in the $3.95 to $5.95 range; entrees, $12.95 to $17.95. Dinner nightly except Tuesday, 5:30 to 10. Open May-October. BYOB.

The Bayberry Inn, Congress Place and Perry Street. (609) 884-8406. A former Mad Batter chef, Joe Lotozo, presides over an international menu at the Bayberry, located in a corner of the Congress Hall Hotel but not a part of it. The outdoor patio, with fir trees in pots on the tile floors and lacquered tables with fish patterns, is fun on summer evenings; inside, the large high-ceilinged room has bare floors, wainscoting painted a deep burgundy, and deep green tablecloths to match the paint of the mismatched chairs. Dried flowers and stenciling add accents, and the well-spaced tables have patio candles lit at night. We were told the service could be erratic, but ours was fine. A serving of the Thai chicken wings was more than enough for two, with six big and spicy wings, crisp as could be, to dip into a blue cheese sauce. The white and whole wheat rolls are hot and crusty, and your white wine is served properly in an ice bucket. The Siamese chicken bangiampo, although tasty, suffered from an intense saltiness, but the shrimp and scallops in green sauce, a Portuguese dish garnished with mussels and chorizo sausage, was superb. A popular appetizer is the Szechuan dan dan noodles in a peanut sauce. Appetizers and salads (including one of roast duck, capellini and snow peas) are $3.75 to $5.95 and entrees, $11.75 to $17.50 (for a seafood stew in a sauce of wine, tomato and saffron). A few specials every night might include a sea trout in oriental sauce or grilled swordfish with mustard, wild honey and cream. Changing desserts are listed on a blackboard; chocolate caramel cake, lemon cheesecake with fresh blueberries and bread pudding were a few at our visit. Dinner nightly except Wednesday, 5:30 to 10. Closed January to Easter, open part-time until Memorial Day. BYOB.

Alexander's Inn, 653 Washington Ave. (609) 884-2555. If the combination lock at the front door makes you suspect you're entering a museum, the interior will confirm it. Arguably Cape May's most formal restaurant and certainly its priciest, Alexander's has been expanding since it opened in 1977, adding four elegant guest rooms with private baths upstairs and planning to nearly double the dining capacity in 1987. The owners' success at auctions across the country is evident in the furnishings in the high-ceilinged front parlor, the chandeliered dining room and the porch beyond, each individually decorated. The porch shows off the chef's wicker baskets filled with plants, the dining room her draperies and fringing. Tuxedo-clad waiters, burgundy and gold English china on lace mats over huge cloths, fringed lamps and red roses on each of the five interior tables complete the high Victorian setting. The continental menu seems fancier than when we dined there nearly a decade ago and Alexander's reigned alone as the best in town. Appetizers run from $5.95 for sausage nut-strudel to $11.95 for steak tartare; entrees from $17.95 for breast of chicken stuffed with apple, almond and brandied pineapple to $26.95 for rack of lamb. Entree prices include a garden salad with a Caesar dressing and a fresh fruit sorbet to clear the palate. We remember the brandy Alexander pie, still a fixture on the extensive dessert menu. Dinner nightly except Tuesday from 6; Victorian Sunday brunch, 10 to 1. No smoking.

The Washington Inn, 801 Washington St. (609) 884-5697. Considered the best of the larger restaurants in town, this historic white building is surrounded by banks of impatiens and inside all is elegant. Dining is in several areas, including a pretty wicker-filled front veranda done up in pink and candlelight, a Victorian greenhouse, dark interior rooms and a Victorian cocktail lounge. The extensive menu starts with clams casino and crab Louis (both $4.50) and runs from $10.95 for chicken saute to $17.95 for petite filet mignon and lobster tail. The serviceable wine list is reasonably priced, and diners like to finish with international coffees. Dinner nightly, 5 to 10.

Small and Intimate

Peaches, Perry and Jackson Streets. (609) 884-0202. They don't get much smaller than this delightful cafe sandwiched into a tiny space between the restroom and the entry, and spilling outside onto the sidewalk in front of Stumpo's Pizzeria. It seats only 20 inside and 16 outside, and is immensely popular, so much so that they ran out of many dishes the Saturday we lunched there. Nevertheless, we thoroughly enjoyed sampling an enormous bowl of creamy clam chowder, a house salad with a zingy dressing, chicken salad in a pita pocket and crabmeat in a croissant, finished off with a chilled pear-ginger pie, the luncheon highlight. At night, the cafe is transformed into an art work of white and royal blue. The Mad Batter heritage of the chef is evident in his dinner menu, which includes sauteed shrimp with ginger and rice, grilled duck with peaches and such specials as Thai shrimp with scallops, rock Cornish game hen in ruby port wine and Norwegian salmon with red wine sauce ($9.95 for vegetarian pastas to $22.50 for rack of lamb). Lunch, 11:30 to 2 and dinner from 5:30 in season, weekend brunch; closed Tuesdays. BYOB.

A Ca Mia, 524 Washington St. Mall. (609) 884-1913. Acclaimed northern Italian cuisine is offered by formally trained chef Paolo Nota from Torino, Italy, and proprietor Clint Gangloff, who have created a pleasant Mediterranean-style garden cafe with murals and umbrellas inside and a more formal enclosed porch. The chef likes to combine crabmeat, oysters, shrimp and lobster in various fish dishes; his Cornish game hen is served with a cognac duck liver sauce, his rack of lamb with mint hollandaise. Other entrees ($10.50 to $19.95) include two vegetarian and three pasta dishes, all outstanding. The breads come from La Patisserie in front, but the other baking is done in a 40-foot-wide brick oven downstairs. Desserts include creme caramel, cheesecake and profiterole. Light meals are available in season on the sidewalk patio, and an interesting brunch menu is offered. Dinner nightly except Tuesday, 5:30 to 10; Sunday brunch, 9 to 1. BYOB.

La Toque, 210 Ocean St. (609) 884-1511. A stained-glass rendering of a chef is in the window of this intimate French bistro, crammed with glass-topped, pink-linened tables and a partially open kitchen. Fresh croissants and breads, authentic french toast, soups and salads, creative dinners and desserts are the fare. Omelets with a croissant are $4.95 to $5.75, depending on filling (crabmeat and salmon are two). The seafood linguini or the California sandwich make a good lunch. Dinner entrees from $11.95 to $14.95 include blackened redfish, shrimp francaise and steak au poivre. Danish apple cake, raspberry cheesecake and chocolate raspberry cake are among desserts. Breakfast and lunch served til closing, dinner from 5. BYOB.

Louisa's, 104 Jackson St. (609) 884-5882. A tiny storefront with incredibly colorful flowers banked around its window, Louisa's serves some of the most innovative and affordable meals in town at a handful of tables covered with bright calico cloths and surrounded by molded plastic chairs in wild colors. The changing seasonal menu might offer hot and spicy ginger sesame noodles, local asparagus vinaigrette or new tomatoes with feta for appetizers (about $3.50). For main courses ($8.50 to $10), how about sea trout with rouille sauce, bluefish poached in white wine and dijon mustard, scallops with sherry and ginger, or marinated chicken with balsamic vinegar and rosemary? Among desserts for $2.75 are chocolate mousse pie, bread pudding and figs in port and spices. It's no wonder the place is usually jammed and there may be quite a wait for a table. Louisa's is not the place to go to if you feel like having a private conversation. Dinner nightly from 5. BYOB.

FOR MORE INFORMATION: Cape May Chamber of Commerce, The Depot, 609 Lafayette St., Cape May, N.J. 08204, (609) 884-5508; Welcome Center, 405 Lafayette St., 884-3323. Mid-Atlantic Center for the Arts, P.O. Box 164, Cape May, 884-5404.

Boardwalk parallels ocean beach at Spring Lake.

Spring Lake, N.J.

Quiet. Unhurried. Gracious. And very pretty. That's the way we think of Spring Lake, almost an anomaly on a New Jersey coastline that is more apt to be noisy, crowded and honky-tonk.

This town on the north Jersey Shore, south of Asbury Park and north of Bay Head, must have had some hard-headed members of its Zoning Board over the years. Houses are large, imposing and architecturally interesting. Lawns are in pristine condition. Flowers bloom. And neon signs are non-existent.

Yet the attractions to the tourist are clearly here: a beautiful ocean strand and a wide, well-maintained, two-mile-long boardwalk; a charming lake crossed by two rustic wooden bridges and surrounded by a small green park in the center of town; wide, flat tree-lined streets perfect for bicycling; good restaurants, and a fine selection of accommodations from Victorian B&Bs to breezy summer hotels.

Summer is the season. Oh, some of the places open as early as March (most not until May) and many remain open into October, but June, July and August is prime time. When New York and Philadelphia and Pittsburgh become steamy, Jersey's exceptional coastline beckons. Of course, in some spots, it's hard to find the advantage for cottages are cheek-by-jowl, the bands blare, and the beer flows.

Here in Spring Lake, a calm, cool difference is apparent. Settled by upper-class Irish families, and still called the Irish Riviera, the town is welcoming to those who choose — and can afford — to come. Seasonal rentals are not inexpensive and short-term ones are hard to find. High-priced beach badges ($8 per day on weekends; $7 during the week) deter casual daytrippers and hordes of kids.

You will notice the difference dramatically if you drive north on Ocean Avenue from Spring Lake to Belmar, the next town, in the evening. A large pair of brick pillars is the line of demarcation; after you've passed through you're in a world of fudge and taffy, frozen custard, and a McDonald's on the beach. You'll see crowds of college and young working people (group rentals) strolling around with beers in hand. Rock music is blaring from tiny cottages, cars and the beach.

Spring Lake will have none of that. There is a tranquility to the town. Of course, you can head south to Brielle or Point Pleasant Beach to find party boats for deep-sea fishing; you can head out to see the trotters at Freehold or the thoroughbreds at the Monmouth Park Jockey Club; you can spend some time shopping in pricey stores or even "slum it" at the amusement-ride area in Point Pleasant. You can do all of those things, but you may not need to.

You may just want the beach, the boardwalk and the lake. You may be so relaxed that you don't need any diversions beyond sunny weather and good food, both of which we've found in abundance here. You may want to schedule a weekend for a second honeymoon — the town is perfect for strolling hand in hand — or a week for a summer vacation. You may even want to bring some elderly relatives or friends with you (they'll love it).

Spring Lake has been a dignified summer resort for more than 80 years and it looks as if it's going to stay that way for many more.

Getting There

About 35 miles due south of New York City, Spring Lake is about 75 roundabout miles by car. Take the Garden State Parkway to Exit 98 and Route 34 south to the second traffic circle; there, follow Route 35 south to Spring Lake, watching for Warren Avenue, which will bring you into town. Frequent train service is provided from New York City. For information about rail or bus service, call (201) 762-5100, in New Jersey (800) 772-2222.

Where to Stay

No Jersey Shore town except Cape May offers a wider selection of bed-and-breakfast facilities than Spring Lake. These are fun for singles and couples; families with children are usually wiser to select a larger summer hotel where amenities like pools, tennis courts, shuffleboard and ping-pong help to keep the troops entertained.

The grand old dame, the **Essex and Sussex Hotel** ("E&S" to the locals), was undergoing renovation when we visited in 1986. Some expressed doubt it would ever reopen to its former glory, but its great location right on the ocean makes us hope it will fare well.

On or Near the Water

The Normandy Inn, 21 Tuttle Ave., Spring Lake 07762. (201) 449-7172. This Victorian B&B is clearly the cream of the crop, both for its location, just a half block from the ocean, and the purity of its restoration. Susan and Michael Ingino left an ice cream business in Bayville in 1982 to take over this imposing olive green mansion with 20 bedrooms in the main house, and two more in a carriage house out back. Most have private baths; all have been beautifully decorated and sport such items as brass beds, oak bureaus and pretty floral wallpapers. Deep red carpeting splashed with roses makes for a dramatic entry, and the red velvet furniture in the front parlor adds to the setting. Guests enjoy a full breakfast in a cheerful breakfast room on the main floor (for those not staying here, the privilege costs $5.95 per person). White wicker furniture on the broad front porch beckons; from a few rooms there are distant views of the ocean. Doubles, $58 to $100, open year-round;

weekend reservations in July and August accepted seven days in advance only.

The Sea Crest, 19 Tuttle Ave., Spring Lake 07762. (201) 449-9031. This large white Victorian B&B is right next door to the Normandy Inn, a few steps closer to the beach and boardwalk. A few rooms have water views, and a large airy porch is filled with wicker furniture for lazing away the afternoon. Breakfast is served family style in a breakfast room. All rooms have TVs. Doubles, $60 to $80; weekly, $325 to $375.

Ashling Cottage, 106 Sussex Ave., Spring Lake 07762. (201) 449-3553. Halfway between ocean and lake, this charming Victorian B&B was built by George Hulett in 1877 with lumber from the dismantled Agricultural Exhibit of the Philadelphia Exposition of 1876. Hulett was responsible for many of Spring Lake's late 19th century homes; this he built for his own use. Now Goodi and Jack Stewart lend their special flair to innkeeping at this 10-room charmer. We love the bright pink impatiens that hang from the glassed-in solarium where guests take their breakfast (served buffet style in the nearby parlor). Here are wicker tables and chairs and a white, pink and blue color scheme that is delightful. The Stewarts offer impromptu wine get-togethers and the use of a pleasant side yard where guests may use a gas grill for a simple picnic. Goodi, who loves to cook, was thinking of offering Saturday evening dinner for guests in the summer months since restaurants are so difficult to deal with at the height of the season. Eight of the ten rooms have private baths, one of them sunken; all have furniture with a period feeling, and the peach room is very popular. You can see the lake from Rooms 1 and 4. Doubles, $65 to $95. Closed January and February.

The Shoreham, 115 Monmouth Ave., Spring Lake 07762. (201) 449-7100. An ambitious restoration under new owners is making this venerable summer hotel even more inviting. The hotel overlooks the lake and has a wide front porch shaded by sprightly blue and white striped awnings; this is where guests sit on Sunday mornings reading the newspaper. To the side at street level is a pretty kidney-shaped swimming pool and Pool Bar in an enclosed terrace area. Many of the 108 rooms have kingsize beds and most are decorated quite attractively. We are especially fond of the main lobby with its terra cotta painted wicker furniture and peach accents. The large main dining room with Ionic columns harkens back to the genteel days when Spring Lake was at its height; there is also a piano bar. A few rooms share baths. Doubles with private bath, $126 to $144 MAP. A family suite with two bedrooms and connecting bath, accommodating four, is $64 to $72 per person. Deduct $14 a day for EP. Open May to mid-October.

The Warren Hotel, 901 Ocean Ave., Spring Lake 07762. (201) 449-8800. This large brown and white turreted hotel, with bright yellow and white striped awnings and American flags displayed in front, is less than a block from the ocean. It is also being spruced up. By the summer of 1986 the bedrooms on the upper two floors of the four-story hotel had been renovated along with the public rooms at main level. White wicker furniture with bright green cushions set on a green patterned carpet make the lobby crisp and inviting; the all-white dining room — right to the tablecloths and napkins — is stunning and cool. College students are waitresses, bellhops and elevator operators among others, and are cheerfully accommodating. Outdoors, a pool area with bar, tennis court, shuffleboard court and nine-hole putting green are fun for guests; next door is the popular **Beach House** (see Where to Eat). Bicycle rentals are available for guests, $12 for the day, $3 per hour. Doubles. $126 to $188, MAP in July and August; deduct $15 per person EP. Open May to mid-September.

The Beacon House, 104 Beacon Blvd., Sea Girt 08750. (201) 449-5835. Ern and Ginny Westphal operate two large white, green-shuttered houses — with an attractive pool between — in neighboring Sea Girt, just a short walk from the town's lovely beach and boardwalk. In one of the houses rooms are rented for the season only; the other has week-long and occasionally weekend rentals. Everything is green and white, cool and clean in this place, and it is one of the most attractive offerings in the area (although it is hard to get a room). We peeked into one triple (most rooms have three singles or a double and a single bed) where all of the four-poster beds were covered with white puff quilts with a pink and green stencil design. The Beacon House is just across the street from the Parker House (see Where to Eat). A complimentary continental breakfast is included. Doubles, $68 to $78. Open May through mid-September.

Other Good Bets

Victoria House, 214 Monmouth Ave., Spring Lake 07762. (201) 974-1882. This charming bed-and-breakfast inn has a big front porch where guests often have their breakfast; fresh fruits, home baked breads and beverages are set out on the dining room table. Stained-glass windows in the stairwell remind you that the house dates from 1882; gingerbread accents and carpenter gothic shingles add more clues. Some guest rooms have private baths. Doubles, $65 to $85.

Villa Park Guest House, 417 Ocean Road, Spring Lake 07762. (201) 449-3642. Alice and David Bramhall are welcoming hosts at this small hostelry with five guest rooms, a bit off the beaten path in Spring Lake. The walk to the beach is a few blocks, but the friendly warmth of this house highly recommends it. A fireplaced living room and an oak-filled dining room where breakfast is served add to the comfort. Doubles, $53 to $65.

The Carriage House, 208 Jersey Ave., Spring Lake 07762. (201) 449-1332. Tom and Marie Bradley are the enthusiastic hosts at this guest house, just a few steps from the center of the village, and two or so blocks from the beach. Here are eight airy rooms including one single, four doubles, and three extra-large rooms which can accommodate up to four persons. Complimentary coffee is served daily; on the weekends there are pastries or donuts, which guests take to the inviting front porch. Doubles, $42 to $68. Open year-round.

The Chateau Motel, 5th and Warren Avenues, Spring Lake 07762. (201) 974-2000. This splendidly kept-up Victorian brick house with veranda and pretty hanging plants plus a more modern addition is at the foot of the lake, not too far from village shops. A very inviting green and white lobby, plus individual patios for many of the rooms, make it a good choice. The accommodations range from kitchen suites and two-room suites to simple double rooms. All have refrigerators. Three-night minimums are required in July and August. Doubles, $69 to $97. Open year-round.

RENTALS. There aren't too many houses to rent in Spring Lake and those there are come dear. It is not unheard of to charge $25,000 for a seasonal rental, a real-estate agent told us; more common are monthly rentals at $5,000 to $6,000. New Yorkers camp out on Saturdays in January and February, trying to find the perfect place. Check with the Charles F. Coffey Agency in Spring Lake, (201) 449-2300.

Seeing and Doing

This is not an area filled with historic monuments, art colonies and museums. This is the beach, and most people spend their days on or near it. There are also good shopping, deep-sea fishing, biking, and the like; a car tour around Spring Lake and Sea Girt is highly recommended.

THE OCEAN. The Atlantic is the draw and the beach at Spring Lake, while suffering yearly ravages and erosion, is still quite good. Small dunes anchored by beach grass and flowers are touted, but they're too small to look much like dunes to anyone who's seen the National Seashore on Cape Cod. Nevertheless, the beach is fine here, and two pavilions (one at the south end, one at the north end of the stretch) sell refreshments and beach badges. These badges ($8 per day weekends, $7 daily during the week) are necessary from mid-June through Labor Day; most hotels and guest houses sell them at a discount to overnight guests, or include them in the price of the room. A saltwater pool is located at each of the pavilions on the beach, but we are told that only residents of Spring Lake may use them. The beach at Sea Girt (next town south) is very nice, but quite a bit smaller; badges must also be purchased for about the same price as in Spring Lake. Again, nearby hotels or guest houses usually provide them free or for a small fee. The beach at Point Pleasant is backed by a boardwalk with amusement park rides; that at Bay Head has no boardwalk and huge weathered "cottages" overlook it. Again, badges must be purchased.

THE LAKE. Spring Lake's lake is very pretty, with weeping willows planted in areas along the bank, and two rustic bridges to walk across. Benches overlooking the lake are placed at comfortable intervals and evening strolls are popular. Ducks and swans are fun to watch. The lake is said to be spring-fed.

Sea Girt Lighthouse, corner Ocean and Beach avenues, Sea Girt. This is the only lighthouse on this portion of the Jersey Shore. Perched atop a brick house, the light began to beam in 1896 and continued until 1955. It has been restored but is not open to the public. However, it makes a nice background for photographs.

St. Catharine's Church, West Lake Drive at Third Avenue, Spring Lake. This Roman Catholic church, a smallish replica of St. Peter's in Rome, is very ornate and worth a visit.

Spring Lake Trolley. A jaunty orange and green trolley ferries tourists and others around Spring Lake. The 30-minute route is covered from 11 a.m. to 7 p.m. daily, Memorial Day until Labor Day. A ride is 50 cents and you can hail the trolley and get off any place along the route.

Ocean Grove, an oceanfront religious community which still clings to its Methodist past, is a 20-minute drive north of Spring Lake via Route 71. Drive around and look at all the tiny gingerbread houses and the larger gingerbread boarding houses and hotels. Read the street names: Pilgrim's Pathway, Mt.

Tabor Way, Mt. Carmel Way. Look at the auditorium where religious meetings are held weekly throughout the summer. On Thursday and Saturday evenings performers such as Debbie Boone or an orchestra playing Mozart are scheduled. The auditorium is being restored and is on the National Register of Historic Places. Next to Ocean Grove (when we were in college the kids called it "Ocean Grave") is Asbury Park, a portion of which, we're told, is going to be restored.

DEEP-SEA FISHING. Party boats in search of blues, flukes, sea bass and mackerel go out year-round from Brielle and Point Pleasant. **Bogan's Boat Basin,** at the Manasquan River Bridge just off Route 35, Brielle, 528-8377, has the largest fleet of party boats in the area. Capt. John Bogan, who started his trips more than 50 years ago, overseas the Paramount, Jamaica, Paramount II and Jamaica II. Cost is about $15 for a half-day, about $24 for a full day. Night trips are also offered. The nearby bait and tackle shop is open every day of the year and if Capt. John is in, he'll give you other advice (such as the best restaurants in the area). Party boats also leave from **Ken's Landing** at Point Pleasant Beach, also just off Route 35, 477-6441 or 892-5358. Half-day fluke trips and half-night blues trips are offered. Daytime trips are $15; nighttime blues trips, $21.

BOAT RIDES. One-and-a-half-hour shore cruises of the ocean just offshore are offered weekdays at 2 during the season aboard the Miss Point Pleasant II, leaving from Ken's Landing in Point Pleasant Beach, 447-6441. Adults $6, children $4. The Norma K II leaves at 8 nightly for 90-minute moonlight sails. Adults $6, children $4.

BICYCLING. The flatness of these towns makes them especially appealing to cyclists. Bicycles can be rented from **Point Pleasant Bicycle,** 2701 Bridge Ave., 899-9755. Some hotels and guest houses also rent or lend bicycles to guests. Bikers are allowed on boardwalks from 6 to 10 a.m.

OTHER SPORTS: Windsurfing. If you're really anxious to get out on the water, contact Windsurfing Bay Head at 899-9394 in Bay Head for lessons or equipment.

Golf. Public golf courses include the Bey Lea Municipal Golf Course on Bay Avenue, Toms River, and the Bel-Aire Golf Club, Allaire Road and Highway 34, Wall.

Horse Racing. Monmouth Park, Oceanport Avenue, Oceanport, has been bringing thoroughbred racing to New Jersey for more than 40 years. The season is early June to the end of August with 10 races daily Monday-Saturday.

SHOPPING. Most shops are on 3rd Avenue with a few on Morris Avenue. Because of the town's Irish heritage, it's fun to stop at the **Irish Centre,** 1120 3rd Ave., and check out the handmade Irish woolen sweaters or other crafts. **Silent Poetry** at 304 Morris Ave. offers contemporary handcrafted jewelry, pottery, blown glass and other special items. The **Fireside Book Shop** at 1212 Third Ave. is chock-full of hardcover and paperback books and also has a lending library. Toiletries and cosmetics can be found at the **Crabtree & Evelyn** shop next door. The **Camel's Eye** for women and **Village Tweed Inc.** for men are shops with preppy clothes.

Where to Eat

There is a disconcerting aspect to eating at the Jersey Shore. Most restaurants don't take reservations, resulting in waits of up to two hours on Friday and

Saturday nights. If you don't like to wait, plan to arrive before 7 or after 9:30 when the crowd is usually thinner. Also, check whether the restaurant has a liquor license. Several do not, but you are welcome to tote your own bottle of wine.

By the Sea

The Yankee Clipper, Ocean Avenue, Sea Girt. (201) 449-7200. Ask anyone in the area where you can dine with a view of the ocean, and this will be the response. The view from huge windows in the main **Surf Room** on the upper level is fantastic. Downstairs, the **Sand Bar Pub** has a view of the water from the windows in front, but it's not nearly as dramatic. Nevertheless, the pub is popular, especially with all of the beachers who throw T-shirts on over their bathing suits and cross the road for a drink or a quick lunch. A big barrel of peanuts greets you at the door to the pub and the beer drinkers scoop them up by the handful. The decor is wood (tongue-in-groove paneling around the side), brass and plants around a bar in the center of the room. Our party of three had tasty lunches of clams on the half shell, tacos, and a roast beef on rye; prices range from $3.50 to $8, and you can have breakfast here. A special pub drink is "Surf's Up," vanilla ice cream with melon liqueur and rum. Upstairs in the Surf Room, entrees include veal dishes, steaks and seafood in the $15 to $18 range. One consistent complaint about the Yankee Clipper is that service tends to be slow; ours certainly was. Surf Room, lunch and dinner, Tuesday-Saturday; Sunday, brunch noon to 3, dinner 4 to 9. Pub is open year-round.

The Beach House, 901 Ocean Ave., Spring Lake. (201) 449-9646. Operated by the Warren Hotel and "chefed" by George Schreck, this is the most popular spot in Spring Lake for dining (and drinking). The turreted brown shingled Victorian building (check the crazy chimney architecture on the roof) attracts a crowd for lunch, happy hour and dinner. The bar in front and the two picnic tables outside have the best view of the ocean and boardwalk just across the street. Two pleasant dining rooms with pressed oak furniture and black and white tiled floors are in back. A wraparound, glassed-in porch on the side also offers great views at small tables for two. No reservations are accepted for dinner at the Beach House and the lines can be discouraging. The creative menu usually includes a half dozen appetizers such as country pate with cornichons and French bread croutons for $4.25 and iced jumbo shrimp with horseradish sauce and tarragon mayonnaise for $5.95. Usually two salad choices are offered: possibly sliced tomatoes with red onions in basil and olive oil or watercress and endive with a walnut vinaigrette dressing. Entrees include shrimp baked with spinach and feta cheese for $13.25; loin lamb chops with fresh mint sauce for $16.25 and a breast of chicken stuffed with Black Forest ham and Swiss cheese at $12.75. There is always a hamburger choice on the dinner menu, priced at about $5.50. Lunches are heavy on salads and sandwiches (a jumbo hot dog with caraway sauerkraut is $3.25). Lunch and dinner, May-September.

The Wharfside, Channel Drive, Point Pleasant. (201) 892-9100. Overlooking the busy Manasquan River channel, this restaurant is one of several owned in New Jersey and Florida by Jack Baker. Another is the **Lobster Shanty,** (201) 899-6700, right next door. Popular with tourists, these restaurants provide standard water lovers' fare: a good range of seafood, a water view, bustling conviviality and rational prices. The Wharfside is usually packed, but we managed to be seated within 20 minutes by arriving just before 7 on a Saturday evening. Orange shell-motif lamps hang in both restaurants and rough pine wood booths are also standard. The Lobster Shanty is a bit more open, with a slightly better view. The menus are virtually identical and include such items as baked scallops ($8.95), shrimp and chicken stir-fry ($9.95, and pronounced superb by our teen-aged daughter), seafood florentine (shrimp and fish filet on creamed spinach topped with Monterey Jack cheese sauce, $8.95) and the Wharf combo (a casserole of shrimp, scallops and fish fillet, broiled, for $8.95), which was good but not great. Surf and turf (filet mignon and rock lobster tails) goes for $16.95. Tasty corn fritters and garlic bread come to the table in a basket; the meal also includes cole slaw, a potato choice, and a tossed salad mixed at the table by a "salad bar waitress" and served with the house dressing, Italian. There is a small section for outdoor dining. The Lobster Shanty features an "all you can eat" seafood buffet on Fridays for $16.95. Open daily, noon to 9:30.

Barmore's Shrimp Box, 75 Inlet Drive, Point Pleasant Beach. (201) 899-1637. People around here proclaim this their favorite for seafood with a view. "We Overlook Nothing But the Harbor" is the motto at this restaurant which overlooks the busy Manasquan River. Complete dinners are the rule, with an appetizer of shrimp and mussels, salad bar, potato, dessert and coffee included in the price of the entree ($10 to $17 range). The menu includes many expected seafood items; one of the most popular, we're told, is fluke florentine for $14.95. Dinner nightly, spring to late fall.

Other Good Choices

The following restaurants do not boast a water view or proximity to the waterfront, but the food is fine — in many instances better than what can be found at water's edge.

Scarborough Fair, 1414 Meetinghouse Road (off Route 35), Sea Girt. (201) 223-6658. It started as an 1880s house, was added onto and changed into a gift shop and, a few years ago, bought by Michael Fotinos, of a Greek-American restaurant family with other properties in New Jersey. The restaurant, multi-leveled and brick inside and out, with stained-glass window accents and a huge skylit atrium entrance, is very California in atmosphere. The cuisine is inventive and we had one of our best lunches ever here. The emphasis is on fresh foods with lots of fruits and vegetables. For example, the chicken salad plate ($4.95) was surrounded by bananas, watermelon, oranges, kiwi, plus walnuts atop the generous mound of chicken salad. "The Vegetarian" is sauteed eggplant and zucchini with Swiss and cheddar cheese and tomatoes on French bread, baked in the oven, for $2.95. Our son's Midwesterner, pronounced excellent, was roast beef, provolone cheese and bacon on toasted rye, baked in the oven, and again, served with a large platter of fruit for $4.75. Dinner entrees include sauteed veal with shallots and crabmeat ($15.50), chicken stuffed with ham and banana, dipped in coconut and served in a sweet and sour sauce ($13.95) and tournedos ($17.95) or New York steak ($16.95) served with a variety of sauces. An art gallery is next door. Lunch, Monday-Friday; dinner, Monday-Saturday. BYOB.

The Peachtree, 2517 Route 35, Wall Township. (201) 223-4844. The Peachtree takes reservations and so, of course, we made them. The restaurant's outside appearance — a square box in a small shopping center off the main drag — is countered by the prettiness inside. Patrons step down from the entry area into one dining room, which is on a couple of different levels; another dining room in back is windowed and looks out, unfortunately, onto the parking lot. Tiny white lights strung on ficus trees, pleasant peach and deep green color combinations on the tables, rattan chairs, and white vases filled with pink carnations create an appealing setting. Small mirrors and paintings on the walls add to the feeling of elegance. The Peachtree is well-regarded by sophisticated diners in this part of the state for new American cuisine. On the holiday weekend when we dined here, the place was crowded, which we hope was the reason for the rather uneven service. Menu items were inventive: pheasant in walnut, apple and applejack sauce (tasty but not boneless as described); scallop and shrimp jalapeno (sauteed in white wine sauce with fresh tomatoes, hot pepper and topped with cheddar sauce), and liver sauteed with mushrooms, onion and bacon, and topped with a burgundy wine sauce. Our complaints were that the shrimp bisque had too heavy a cheddar cheese base and the beef filet was charbroiled to the point of blackness. Entrees range from $8.95 to about $16 and are mostly in the $12 to $14 bracket. Warm sourdough rolls were good and the creamy peppercorn house dressing complemented the mixed salad. The carrot cake (a bit high priced at $3.75) for dessert was the best we've tasted. Lunch and dinner are served.

The Breakers Ristorante, 1507 Ocean Ave., Spring Lake. (201) 449-7700. The emphasis is Italian at the popular restaurant in the Breakers hotel, a waterfront hostelry owned by Cosmo Scardino, who also owns Cosmo's restaurant in town. Located to the rear of the main hallway leading from the summery lobby, the restaurant, alas, has no view. A low wall separates diners from the rest of the traffic; lighting is soft, and the noise level acceptable. Prices for entrees range from $11.95 for filet of sole francaise to $17.95 for New York strip steak. Veal dishes are emphasized, including veal rollatini, marsala, parmigiana, saltimbocca, francaise and piccata. A la carte salads can be Caesar (for two) at $5.50 or mixed tomato and onion for $2.50. Zuppa di clams is $5.95 as an appetizer; a cold antipasto for two is $7.50. Dinner nightly except Monday, year-round. BYOB.

If you want to take out fabulous sandwiches, muffins, giant cookies and scrumptious salads (you can eat them there, too), stop at **Bakin' Around** on 3rd Avenue in Spring Lake.

At **Susan Murphy's Old Times Ice Cream** at 601 Warren Ave., father Don dishes up creamy ice cream from an old ice cream machine and has all his daughters and nieces helping him. People stand in line on hot summer evenings to eat Milky Way ice cream and green apple sherbet. Our toasted almond cone reminded us of Good Humors from days gone by. Open daily April-October from 11 to 10.

For breakfast, the mobs go to **Perkins' Pancake and Steak** at the corner of Route 35 and Warren Avenue and we know why. Those buttermilk pancakes are delicious. Service is fast and courteous, and the menu includes eggs, too. Open daily year-round.

After hours, the yuppies and others gather at the huge white and green **Parker House** in Sea Girt for drinks on the porch, in the bar, or downstairs where there's a happy hour with music just about every day. The **Osprey** in Manasquan attracts a happy-hour crowd as well.

FOR MORE INFORMATION: Spring Lake Chamber of Commerce, Box 694, Spring Lake, N.J. 07762. (201) 449-0577.

Montauk Lighthouse is at tip of Long Island.

Montauk/Long Island, N.Y.

For many of us, Long Island conjures up images of asphalt and anguish, crowds and crush. Except for the Hamptons, of course — money, money, money. The geography intrigues us — that long sandbar jutting out into the open ocean — but we wonder what could be left of it? Haven't those voracious New Yorkers devoured it all?

The happy answer is: no. There's lots of open land and open ocean to be enjoyed, especially at the very tip of the island in Montauk. Surrounded by water on three sides, including a saltwater "lake" and a huge pond, and crowned by a lighthouse at its tip, Montauk is the epitome of an oceanside resort.

Resort status came relatively late, not until 1920 when entrepreneur Carl Fisher decided to turn Montauk into a "Miami Beach of the North." High on Signal Hill he built the Tudor-style Montauk Manor, which for many years was a popular luxury hotel, in spite of its distance from the ocean. Somewhat braver — and smarter — developers built motels right along the sandy beaches, now the prime real estate in the town.

Today, Montauk is mostly beach motels, two stories high, set one after the other along a splendid ocean strand where the rollers rush in and bathers ride the waves. It is a very accessible beach, with plenty of parking — either free or for a small charge. In season the beach is crowded, but not crushingly so. After Labor Day, it is exquisite: the air has that special tang and the sun is in a mellow mood.

Montauk Village is a bit of Hyannis with a slice of New York. Good Jewish delicatessens serve up lox and bagels and kippered herring. Visitors walk into the IGA store in bathing suits and plastic thongs. Dressing for dinner means climbing into jeans or a denim skirt. Everyone, it seems, is on vacation.

Montauk Village is on the ocean side; a few miles across, on Long Island Sound, is the harbor that boaters know. (One of Carl Fisher's more successful ideas was to dredge out what is called Lake Montauk and make a huge protected anchorage.) Sport-fishing boats, yachts and sailboats stop here in great numbers, and you can spend a couple of hours just looking at them while roaming the docks. In fact, more sport fishing is done from this port than from any other in the world.

Few visitors get this close to the tip of Long Island without going all the way. Follow Route 27 to the end to Montauk State Park, where you can take a variety of paths down to a rocky beach for views of the great lighthouse at land's end.

There's history here, too. Indians were the earliest settlers, but as far back as the 17th century the gently undulating grasslands were used as grazing land for cows and sheep owned by inhabitants of towns farther west. Montauk claims to be the birthplace of the American cowboy.

The best part about Montauk is the sense one has of being close to the end of the world. Sea grapes and beach plums line the roads, the dune grass bends in the wind, the ocean is everywhere. The pretentiousness of the Hamptons ends at their borders. In its place is a relaxed attitude that is very refreshing.

Getting There

Montauk is about 135 miles east of New York City. Follow the Long Island Expressway to Exit 70, then Route 111 south to Route 27 East. From New England, take the ferry from New London, Conn., to Orient Point, drive to Greenport to pick up the ferries to Shelter Island and Sag Harbor. From Sag Harbor drive to East Hampton and then pick up Route 27 to Montauk.

Where to Stay

You will probably want to be on the ocean — or the lake — and that's quite possible as long as you commit to three or four days minimum during the summer months. Several motels with oceanfront terraces line the beach; you fall out of bed and you're practically on the sand. Many have efficiency kitchens and barbecue grills. Inns and B&Bs haven't been developed in Montauk; the price of real estate may forever preclude their arrival. But what's available serves quite well the needs of visitors: a clean bed, a shower, and access to the magnificent ocean.

The Panoramic View, Old Montauk Highway, Montauk 11954. (516) 668-3000. A half dozen buildings — all white clapboard with green roofs — are set into the steep hillside leading down to 1,000 feet of private ocean beach at this spectacular yet simple complex. Located on the road which hugs the ocean, the Panoramic View is enormously popular both for its location and the impeccable care which it's given. All 120 accommodations have a view of the ocean and a terrace from which to enjoy it. The plantings are particularly pleasing; we were charmed by red and white begonias in the shape of a whale, and masses of red impatiens near the check-in area. You can stay in a one-and-one-half-room unit with bedroom and small kitchenette, a two-and-a-half-room suite with bedroom, living room and kitchenette, or an oceanfront house with wood-burning fireplace, two bedrooms and two baths, accommodating six. Barbecue grills are tucked discreetly into the shrubbery. A free-form heated swimming pool is about halfway down the hill between road and ocean. Rooms are mostly wood paneled and have wall-to-wall carpeting, air-conditioning, cable TV and telephones. If there is a negative it is the steepness of the walk back up the hill after you've spent a day on the beach; avoid it by staying in the closest building, Salt Sea. Rates are quite rational and off-season weekends are bargains (doubles, $120 to $184 for two nights). Doubles, $88 to $155 daily in season (minimum stay, five days). Open early April-October. Reservations are taken after March 1.

Montauk Yacht Club & Inn, Star Island, Montauk 11954. (516) 668-3100 or (800) 351-5656. Built around what was once a working lighthouse over-looking Lake Montauk, this full-service resort is now a part of Horizon Hotels Ltd., the group which also runs the Equinox in Manchester, Vt., and other distinctive hotel properties. While not on the ocean, the inn has a great marina setting on Star Island, which juts out into the lake, connected by a causeway; boaters can pull their craft right up to the dock and spend a few luxurious days ashore. Of a total of 107 accommodations, 84 are in the main complex and another 23 are in "villas" — five houses that were renovated by the hotel in the early 1980s and are located a short walk along the water from the main area. Rooms are in weathered contemporary buildings with large decks, most of which are waterfront. All have kingsize or two double beds and sliding glass doors leading to the patios. The villa area — with its own pool — features larger rooms, lush lawns and a quieter away-from-it-all atmosphere. Four tennis courts, an indoor pool with jacuzzi and sauna, game rooms, a luxurious and tasteful lobby decorated in earth tones, plus a small beach where sunfish may be used free of charge make this a place to play. There's a second outdoor pool at the main complex. Greens fees at Montauk Downs, the local golf course, are included; if you want to sail a 16-foot Hobie cat or take out a windsurfer, you're charged extra. A good restaurant, the **Club Terrace,** and a casual outdoor dining spot, the **Cafe Potpourri,** are open to the public. The only minus at this resort is that to get to the ocean beach, you have about a five-minute drive. Two-night minimums are required in season. Doubles, villa rooms, $205 to $225; main complex, $195 to $210. Open early April-late November.

Gurney's Inn and Spa, Old Montauk Highway, Montauk 11954. (516) 668-2345. Probably the best-known place in town and the oldest, this sprawling hillside complex celebrated its 60th anniversary in 1986. Too glitzy for our tastes, with its Italianate statuary and wrought iron, Gurney's attracts a nouveau-riche, sun-bronzed crowd in search of eternal youth (which it tries to provide through its European spa program and special calorie-conscious meals). Alto-gether 125 rooms are located in a half dozen buildings, plus four fireplaced cottages on the beach. The beach is that next door to the Panoramic View, but at Gurney's the climb is not quite as steep. Its indoor heated saltwater swimming pool is central to a therapeutic spa program and those not staying at Gurney's can pay daily rates. Conditioning beach walks, hypnotherapy, physical therapy, aquatic exercises, aerobics and so on are offered. Gurney's also will sell you seaweed skin-care products, vitamin supplements and even introduce you to T'ai Chi Chuan, a Chinese system of exercise, meditation and health preservation. Now a time-sharing cooperative, the inn includes suites, staterooms, studios, a duplex and the cottages. Except for cottage occupants, all guests take two meals a day in the spacious, oceanview dining room which is part of the large administrative building at the top of the hill.

Interior decorators have color-coordinated each of the buildings (the Forecastle is mauve and blue) which have sunken living rooms, often two TV sets (for the living room and the bedroom) and carpeted terraces overlooking the Atlantic. It may all appear a bit much, right down to the Sevilles and limos in the parking area, but it certainly throbs with activity. The dining room, featuring a European menu with a range of seafood, beef and veal, is quite well rated and open to the public. Doubles, $220 to $290, MAP in summer. Open year-round.

The Ocean Surf, Route 27, Montauk 11954. (516) 668-3332. This 26-unit complex appeals because of size and situation. Small and fairly quiet, it is located right on the ocean as you're entering Montauk from the Hamptons. Like most of the other oceanfront motels in town, the Ocean Surf has gone co-op, so that each unit is individually owned. It is managed like a motel, however. The two-story structure has rooms with two double beds or a queensize bed with pullout couch, a two-burner stove and refrigerator, and a terrace overlooking the surf. A nice-sized pool with brick walkway all around is set right into the sand out back; just a few steps farther is a wonderful beach with chaise lounges for reclining and sunning. Four-night minimums are the rule on summer weekends (three days midweek). Doubles, $120. Open mid-April to mid-October.

Driftwood, Route 27, Montauk 11954. (516) 668-5744. This weathered gray co-op motel with two sprawling buildings, a pool, tennis courts, shuffle-board and ping-pong is also out on the highway before you get into the downtown area. The 57 units come in several configurations: two-and-one-half-room suites, single bedrooms or studio efficiencies and there's even one two-bedroom cottage (it does not have an ocean view). Rooms in Driftwood, which stretches along the oceanfront, have views of the surf; those in Drift-wood East overlook the pool and gardens. Individual owners have varied the decor, but all units have refrigerators and cable TV. A strip of green indoor-outdoor carpeting leads from the front desk out back to an area with chaise lounges on the beach. Three-night minimums on the weekend, prepaid, are required. Rooms are $97; studios, $106, and suites, $115. Open May-September.

The Royal Atlantic, South Edgemere Street, Montauk 11954. (516) 668-5103. Located right in town — and on the ocean — this spot is for the visitor who wants to be within walking distance of restaurants, nightlife and the beach. The large two-story complex with a pool sits right on the beach; across the street, with its own pool, is its sister motel, the **Royal Atlantic North,** (516) 668-5597. Accommodations range from regular to oversize rooms and three-room suites accommodating up to four, with standard motel decor. All units have carpeting, TVs, in-room coffee makers and refrigerators plus terraces overlooking the water; units at the Royal Atlantic North also have kitchenettes. A lounge and restaurant are open to the public, and once again, the beach is terrific, if a bit more crowded because of its in-town location. Doubles, $99 to $122; Royal Atlantic North, $135 to $165; suites, $900 to $975 weekly. Open April-October.

Malibu Motel, . Elmwood Avenue, Montauk 11954. (516) 668-5233. We spent one night at this motel (after moving from an unacceptable B&B which will remain nameless) and found it quite satisfactory. The two-story, U-shaped motel is located across the street from an in-town stretch of beach. Some units have full ocean views; some, like ours, have a distant view; a few look out toward the town. There are two double beds, a small table with chairs, a refrigerator, and a pleasant terrace; it is relatively quiet here and convenient to town. Three-night minimums are standard in season. A midweek special including a room, two breakfasts and two dinners at nearby restaurants was featured at $69.95 per person for two nights in season. Doubles, $90; three-night weekend, $250.

East Deck Resort Motel, Dutch Plains Road, Montauk 11954. (516) 668-2334. This low-key, one-story family motel was one of the first in Montauk. Located east of town on a quiet and gorgeous stretch of beach, it is raised from the sand a few feet and surrounded on all sides by one vast deck where guests lounge and chat. If you want privacy, do not choose this resort, for its convivial, open, communal spirit is its strength. Absolutely basic furnishings — linoleum-covered floors and 1950s dinette tables, for example — make these units perfect for sweeping out the sand and keeping dinner hour as simple as possible. An Olympic-size pool is a major plus and teenagers love the surf at the beach; if you don't take a surfboard along, you may find yourself buying one in town. The 30 accommodations include one and two-room efficiencies, motel units (no cooking allowed) and three-room suites. The prices are relatively low, but we're not talking about luxury here — just a basic spot at the beach with location, location, location. Doubles, $80 to $90.

The Ocean Beach, South Emerson Avenue, Montauk 11954. (516) 668-4000. Touting its 450-foot beach as the longest in the village, this co-op motel has 80 units divided among four buildings. Rebuilt and redecorated in 1984, it offers an indoor pool in a glassed-in atrium building (the roof slides back to allow in the natural rays of the sun on clear days). All accommodations are studio apartments with a double bed, a sofabed, an efficiency kitchen and a terrace overlooking the ocean. Rates, $110 to $130 daily or $715 to $845 weekly. Open mid-March to late November.

RENTALS. They're not cheap, but they are available; all kinds of striking weathered contemporary houses perch along the shore or a bit farther inland. You'll have to sign up in January or February and you'll pay $3,000 a month (the minimum for a small place) to $10,000. John Keeshan Inc., (516) 668-9090, and Edward Pospisil, (516) 668-5200, handle many of them.

CAMPING. Hither Hills State Park, off the Old Montauk Highway, Montauk, is an exceptional situation for campers: a wonderful ocean beach, a bathhouse and a playground for children. But it's hard to get in because it's naturally popular. The 140 sites are assigned by a lottery system in January. Those who want one must write the State Park Commissioner in Babylon, N.Y., the previous December. Cost is $8 a night, $56 a week, with one-week maximums. RVs are welcome, but there are no hook-ups. This offers just a very simple camping week at the beach — but what a beach!

Seeing and Doing

THE BEACH. The beach runs the entire length of the south shore and it's one of the best in the Northeast. Both sand and surf are found in abundance. If you're a serious surfer you'll probably want to go to **Ditch Plains Beach,**

east of Montauk Village (there's a sign off Route 27). If you're a people watcher, go to the beach in town. If you'd like to have the amenities of **Hither Hills State Park** available to you, pay the day rate of $3.50 and enjoy. A $5 parking fee is charged in some beach areas; in others, if you can find parking along the road, you're welcome to it.

BOATING. Uihlein's Boat Rentals on West Lake Drive Extension, Montauk Harbor, 668-2545, has a wide range of craft for rent, ranging from 16-foot skiffs at $15 an hour with a 6-horsepower motor to a 19-foot T-bird with a 200-hp motor at $60 an hour. Boats can be rented for one to four hours at an hourly rate; there are also half-day and full-day rates.

FISHING. The Viking Fishing Fleet, West Lake Drive Extension, Montauk Harbor, 668-5709, offers several deep-sea fishing trips, including four-hour fluke fishing trips on the Viking Starlite (adults $18, children $10). Trips leave at 8 and 1. Special tuna trips are scheduled on Wednesdays, either from 3 a.m. to 2 p.m., or from 3 p.m. to 2 a.m. These cost $75 per person with a 30-passenger limit. Night bluefishing trips leave at 7:15 and return at 2 aboard the Viking Starship. The cost is $30 per person. The Viking fleet also runs a passenger ferry (no cars) between Montauk and Groton, Conn. A sunset cruise aboard the ferry leaves Montauk at 6:30 and returns at 9:45 ($10 per person).

Charter boats are widely available, especially at Tuma's Dock off Flamingo Road, Montauk, 668-2707. Prices are in the range of $250 for a half day; $550 a whole day. Usually six passengers can be accommodated.

The Appledore, 668-5700. This 86-foot, gaff-rigged schooner sails from the Viking Landing. Two-hour sails from noon to 2 or 3 to 5 cost $16 for adults, $8 for children. A twilight sail at 6 is $20 for adults, $10 for children. An overnight cruise to Block Island on selected Mondays in July and August is $110 to $120 per person, including meals.

Okeanos Whale Watch Cruises, 728-4522. The Finback II leaves from the Viking Landing daily at 10. Adults $25, children $15.

Horseback riding. Two stables, right across Route 27 from one another east of Montauk Village, offer horseback riding and take groups along the beach on the Sound side. We thought the horses at **Indian Field Ranch** looked a bit healthier. Ninety-minute rides leave every two hours starting at 9:30; reservations are advised, 668-2744, and remember to wear long pants. The other spot, the **Deep Hollow Riding Academy,** 668-5453, is connected with the Suffolk County Park. Rides leave hourly.

See the Oceanfront by Moped. Fortune Mopeds on Montauk Highway, 668-4040, one-half block east of the circle green in the center of town, charges $11 hourly to $99 for a week. Mopeds are in demand, so make arrangements early.

The Montauk Lighthouse, east end of Route 27. Built in 1796 and perched above the rocks and churning waves of the Atlantic, the magnificent light has a spectacular view over the ocean and Block Island Sound. This is land's end, and you feel as if you're at the end of the world when you stand here. Parking in a nearby lot is $2.50; from there you walk down one of several paths to the beach, and gain several vantage points for viewing the white lighthouse with its cummerbund of red.

Second House Museum, Montauk Highway (Route 27), Montauk. Built in 1797 and virtually as old as the lighthouse, this was one of the original three houses in Montauk (the first burned to the ground; the third is part of the Montauk County Park). They were used by cattlemen and their families while caring for the herds of sheep and cows brought out to Montauk to graze. The weathered Cape is a charmer, and visitors are treated to a tour by a Montauk Historical Society member. Visitors view candle molds, a cranberry scoop, a courting couch and a number of other 18th and 19th century artifacts and furnishings. A rope handrail leads to the second floor, where five bedrooms are furnished in period style. On the first floor, a small room attached to the kitchen is furnished as a school room, for it was in this house that Montauk's children were first schooled. After the sand, the sun and the fun of Montauk, visiting Second House is a nice change of pace. The gorgeous lawn outdoors, and the herb garden in back, are refreshing places to wander. We spread our cloth and picnicked here as well. Open daily in summer, 10 to 4.

Suffolk County Park, Route 27, Montauk, 668-5022. This large county park, stretching from Montauk Highway north to the beach on Block Island Sound, offers a few diversions. The park office is located in a rambling wood building, parts of which are the original **Third House,** constructed in 1806. Here you'll see photographs of Teddy Roosevelt and the Rough Riders who were stationed at Montauk following the Spanish-American War. Also on the site are an **Indian Museum** which is supposed to be open weekdays (but was not when we visited), picnic areas, a large pond for freshwater fishing (small electric motors permitted, but no outboards) and a bicycle hostel. Guided walks are offered summer weekends at 8 and noon along four miles of nature trails. Only county residents may camp in the park.

SHOPPING. Gosman's Dock at the mouth of the harbor is more than just a restaurant (see Where to Eat). It's a village of shops, some of them quite tony, such as **Summer Stock,** which sells high-priced and sophisticated rhinestone-studded denim items and has soft pastel Montauk sweatshirts for about $18. In Montauk Village, stop at **Plaza Sports** on the main drag for your Reeboks, thongs, beach towels, Jams and other casual clothes. Here you can also rent bicycles for $2 an hour ($12 a day), tennis rackets for $5 and surfboards for $10. Check out the teddy bears, dolls and antique doll carriages at the **Carriage House** in the village, and you'll find wet suits, windsurfers and beachy duds at the **Wind and Surf Shop,** also in town.

Where to Eat ⎯⎯⎯⎯⎯⎯⎯⎯⎯⎯⎯ ⟋⟋⟋⟋⟍

Considering the prices of the rentals and the motels, and the sophistication of the clientele, we expected more of Montauk's restaurants. On the other hand, several places take advantage of the water. You may not have the dining experience of your lifetime, but you won't go hungry — and you'll have fun in the process.

The Boathouse, South Emery Street, Montauk. (516) 668-5574. Margaret and Bob Lachmann opened their restaurant, on the shore of Fort Pond in Montauk Village, in 1981 to a rousing welcome from the locals, who have remained fans. Coveted tables are those on the wraparound porch with yellow directors' chairs, and reservations are often snapped up far in advance for weekend nights. The water view (and the sunset) are particular draws, but the food is well regarded. A boneless duck (Long Island, we presume) a l'orange at $12.95 is a favored entree for dinner. The stress, however, is on seafood, and dinners include scallops or broiled stuffed shrimp at $11.95, swordfish at $13.95, and flounder, $9.95. At lunch there's a good range of sandwiches, salads, soups (both Manhattan and New England clam chowders), quiches and specials like fish and chips ($6.95), fried clams ($8.25) and chili ($3.95). Boathouse mud pie at $2.50 is the preferred dessert; chocolate mousse pudding and chocolate mousse cake sound equally absorbing. Then there's the rum cream pie! Out front are paddleboats and rowboats for rent. Open daily noon to 10, except March 18 to May 1.

Port Royal, Navy Road, Montauk. (516) 668-3599. A little hard to find (take Second House Road to Navy Road) on the shore of Fort Pond Bay, this restaurant has a festive air and a fun spirit. Outdoors, as you enter, is a deck with picnic tables, a jaunty blue and white striped awning and tiny white lights. Inside are a tiled floor, beamed ceiling, wood-plank polyurethaned tables with blue director's chairs, and such nautical touches as a ship's wheel and red ship's lanterns along one side, green lanterns along the other. Votive lights flicker on each table. Overhead fans keep the air moving, and the proximity to the water means it rarely gets too steamy. Waitresses in white shirts and khaki shorts recite the specialties. The menu is smallish, with an emphasis on seafood including a charbroiled fish of the day; when we were there it was swordfish ($14.95). Other choices included shrimp parmigiana with pasta ($13.95), pasta pesto ($9.95), chicken marsala ($16.95) and crisp Long Island duckling ($12.95). The salad bar was quite complete, but we didn't like the cold rolls. Montauk chowder is always on the menu; the night we visited it had a cream base, but our waitress said it is sometimes Manhattan style. A baked potato comes with the entree; vegetables are a la carte (rice with broccoli and carrots when we were there). Cheese, carrot and chocolate mousse cakes and large sundaes finish off the meal. Dinner, late spring until October.

The Windjammer, Edgemere Avenue, Montauk. (516) 668-2872. A blue and green decor, with blue napkins and wooden tables with ropes embedded into the edges under a polyurethane coating, don't quite add up to a nautical atmosphere, but the view of Fort Pond is great. Tables are set at a couple of different levels and you can see the water — and a few ducks swimming around — from almost every one. Still, this has more of a city than a beachy feeling and lots of New Yorkers in dressy duds dine here. The menu is varied, with a Greek bent (moussaka and baklava) not surprising when you hear the owners' names: Tricia and Socrates Hiotakis. Fish preparation is especially good here; our flounder was moist and succulent, and a generous portion to boot. You can start with stuffed grape leaves ($3.75) or spanakopita ($3.95); there's also the ubiquitous Manhattan clam chowder ($2.25). A Greek salad is $3.75 — unfortunately, a salad does not come with the dinner, but must be ordered separately. Hearts of palm salad, another choice, is available at $6.75. Among entrees in the $10.95 to $16.75 range are broiled scallops, flounder florentine, bouillabaisse, moussaka and roast Long Island duckling. Vegetables in lieu of salad were creamed spinach or carrots in orange sauce, both excellent. The rolls were flaky and hot, but had to be requested. Open for three meals daily year-round.

Gosman's Dock, Montauk Harbor. (516) 668-5330. The location of this restaurant, at the mouth of the harbor with views of the passing parade of boats, makes it Montauk's most sought after. You will probably have to sit at one of the outdoor tables with a drink before a table is ready, but that's part of the fun. The dining area — open but covered — is casual. The menu emphasizes fish, much of it fried. Fried shrimp in a basket with slaw and french fries is $9.25, fried clams, $8.25, and fried scallops, $9.95. You can have a lobster, broiled or steamed, for $15.50 (a two-pounder is $26) or lobster Newburg served with steamed rice and a salad for $13.25. Among other choices from $8 to $15.50 are swordfish, sea trout, broiled chicken and sirloin steak. The selection of wines is basic. Desserts include homemade pies, carrot cake, cheesecake and fresh fruit. An even more casual atmosphere is available in **Topside,** a rooftop dining spot where you sit under Cinzano umbrellas and eat cioppino ($8.95) or lobster in the rough ($12.95). Salads — chicken with tarragon at $6.95 or avocado stuffed with shrimp at $7.95 — are also featured. Topside is open from noon until dark; larger dining area, noon to 10 daily.

The Inn at Napeague, Montauk Highway, Amagansett. (516) 267-3332. For 17 years Monty and Muriel Grossman (and now son, Mark) have been catering to the tastes of the summer people; before that, Monty was a chef at Quo Vadis in New York City. The "inn" is actually a rather plain little roadside building that warms up once you're inside: a stone fireplace, wooden captain's chairs and tables, and bare wooden floors set the mood. There's a view of the dunes across the road from the window tables, but the water is out of sight. Muriel is the hostess, who wishes people wouldn't come to dinner wearing shorts; if they do, she will try to seat them in the bar, rather than one of the two dining rooms. A Sunset Dinner — for $10.95 complete — is available weekdays from 5 to 6, Saturdays 5 to 5:30 and Sundays 4 to 5:30. Among appetizers are a hot antipasto, mussels marinara or a selection of different soups. For entrees, choose from the Neptune's Locker section of the menu, The Continental or Grill and Roast. Continental dishes — a change of pace from all of the seafood in the area — include Hungarian beef goulash, sauerbraten with red cabbage, and curried chicken. A Dutch-oven chicken baked in wine sauce and served with buttered noodles or Texas-style barbecue chicken is on the Grill and Roast menu. Seafood includes the inn's special bouillabaisse and baked bluefish Sicilian style with linguini. Entrees are priced from $10 to $22. Lunch and a takeout service are also part of the attraction here; why not pick up a Coney Island hot dog ($1.50) on your way to the beach? Lunch, noon to 3; dinner, 5 to 10 or 11, Sunday from 4. Open May-October.

Omasa, Montauk Highway, Montauk. (516) 668-2524. Masaru Yamada, a great sushi chef who has another restaurant in Hartsdale, owns this attractive Japanese restaurant in the center of the village. It's quite well regarded, although one local woman complains "the prices are higher than in Manhattan." The bar, mostly black, not very attractive, and with video machines, is countered by the prettiness of the restaurant proper with pink tablecloths and hydrangeas. Among the entrees are unagi futomaki, a large roll of smoked eel with rice and seaweed, $15.90; shrimp tempura, $13.90, and chicken katsu, breaded and served with a sweet sauce, $11.90. Lunch and dinner. Open May-October.

Club Terrace, Montauk Yacht Club and Inn, Star Island, Montauk. (516) 668-3100. The popular dining room, booked in advance for weekend nights, is also famed for its elaborate Sunday brunch ($17.95), served from

11 to 3. For dinner, entrees run from $17 for broiled weakfish with a scallion-ginger sauce to $21 for sea scallops or split rack of lamb. Mesquite-grilled yellowfin tuna with roasted peppers or mako are local favorites; veal medallions with a rosemary shallot sauce are also mesquite-grilled. Pasta entrees include chicken tenderloin with mushrooms and walnuts on pumpkin fettuccine or prosciutto and wild mushrooms on lemon fettuccine. Open daily from 7 a.m. to 10:30 p.m.; jacket required.

The Lobster Roll Restaurant, Montauk Highway at Napeague Beach, Amagansett. (516) 267-3740. A short distance down the highway from Montauk, this unpretentious restaurant has a sign on top that simply screams "Lunch!" There's outdoor dining at umbrellaed tables on a deck on two sides with a view of, alas, the highway; inside are small tables with brown and white checked tablecloths. This is the place to get clams on the half shell (six for $3.95, a dozen for $7.50), steamed mussels (appetizer order $5.50, dinner size $9.95), or New England clam chowder by the cup, bowl or quart (to go). However, the best-known items on the menu are the "Roll," the "Bowl" or the "Platter" of lobster, mixed seafood, shrimp or tuna salad. Lobster rolls cost $5.95, bowls $8.95 and platters $10.95, and the lobster is chunky and fresh. Side orders include tempura veggies, fried mozzarella fingers and creamy cole slaw. A landlubbers' menu offers grilled cheese, frankfurters, burgers and roast beef or baked ham sandwiches. Heineken is on tap, and there's wine, too. Open daily, noon to 10.

O'Murphy's Pub on the circle in Montauk Village is the place to go for drinks, burgers and Irish breakfasts. **Mr. John's Pancake and Steak House** on the main street of town is a good breakfast spot. And the **Four Oaks General Store** in Montauk Harbor is perfect for homemade muffins, coffee and deli items to go.

FOR MORE INFORMATION: Montauk Chamber of Commerce, Box CC, Montauk, N.Y. 11954. (516) 668-2428.

Rondout Belle takes passengers onto Hudson River.

The Hudson Highlands, N.Y.

The Hudson River, tidal and navigable from New York to Albany, is perhaps the most interesting river in the Northeast. Endlessly fascinating, its traffic ranges from huge oil tankers to tiny sailboats. It was on this river that the steamboat got its start: Robert Fulton sailed the Clermont from New York to Albany in 32 hours in the early 1800s. But it was Henry Hudson who, back in 1609, explored the mighty stream from its mouth as far north as Albany and put it on the map.

Some of the river's splendor comes from the beauty of its banks: in the Hudson Highlands area, of which we write, the river winds between steep western slopes and rolling eastern farmland. Because of its navigability, villages sprang up early and several grew into cities. The Hudson was so important a passageway for the Colonists that its defense became critical in the Revolutionary War; at the winding turn in the river known as West Point, a contingent of the Colonial Army was stationed. Later, in 1802, the U.S. Military Academy was founded on that strategic site, high above the Hudson.

In the 19th century, the magnificent views and high vantage points along the Hudson attracted the rich, who built castle-like homes and mansions to which they retreated in the summer. Today some are opened to the public as museums: among them, the homes of Eleanor and Franklin Roosevelt, the artist Frederick Church, and Frederick Vanderbilt, one of the Commodore's grandsons.

The extraordinary light which plays over the Hudson River Valley attracted artists in the same century that it attracted the wealthy. Those whose landscapes celebrated the wonders of nature — not only with the river as the focus, but in the western United States as well — were said to belong to the Hudson River School.

Interest in the river is high today, after a difficult period in the middle of the century when the Hudson, like many other rivers in America, became polluted, and many of its towns and cities seemed to be decaying and declining. A cleanup of the water, spearheaded by an active environmental group headquartered in Poughkeepsie, is only part of the story. Renovations of historic buildings in towns along the Hudson, the presence of several attractive inns and restaurants, and a great variety of things to see and do — many of them on the river — draw travelers to the Hudson River Valley as never before.

This Hudson is humbling and awe-inspiring. It is moody, one day glistening in the sunlight, and another, brooding darkly under low gray clouds. Its waters may be tranquil one moment, stirred to whitecaps the next.

If there is any frustration in a trip to the Hudson Highlands, it is in not being able to see or reach the river often enough. The moments when you do, therefore, become all the more dramatic, and you will take home with you memories of a place unlike any other we know.

Getting There

The area included in this chapter lies between the Bear Mountain Bridge to the south and the Kingston-Rhinecliff bridge to the north. It encompasses both sides of the river, the western side along Route 9W between Highland Falls/West Point in the south and Kingston in the north; along Routes 9 and 9D in the East, from Garrison-on-Hudson in the south to Rhinebeck and Rhinecliff in the north. The region is reached by the New York Thruway and Interstate 84.

Where to Stay

There are not enough interesting hotels and inns, particularly near the water. You can stay in any one of the places suggested and quite easily access the entire area. No one town is best in terms of location, but for the charm of being close to the river and having decent shopping available, we like Cold Spring.

The Hudson House, 2 Main St., Cold Spring 10516. (914) 265-9355. At the foot of Main Street, right across from the river, the Hudson House offers both smashing views and cozy, country charm. Billing itself as the second oldest inn in continuous operation in New York State, it was taken over by Mary Pat Sawyer in 1981 and renovated with great taste. A red, white and blue decorating scheme is carried out with homespun fabrics and mini-prints. Several of the 15 guest rooms have a river view and those on the second floor also have small porches for sitting and enjoying it. The wallpaper matches the dust ruffles on the beds; there are overhead ceiling fans, simple pine bureaus and bare polished wooden floors. Tin molds (some heart-shaped) adorn the walls, and all rooms have private, modern baths. A dining room across the front of the main floor offers breakfast, lunch and dinner and river views. Options at lunch range from a hamburger for $6.95 to veal medallions for $14.95, and based on the crowd on a Saturday afternoon in late September, we'd say it's popular. At dinner the dishes include a duck and coriander salad at $12.95, a shellfish assembly and rack of lamb, both for $16.95. The **Half Moon Bar** takes up a third of another large room off the main lobby; a couple of sofas in a conversation group form a nice spot for sipping a cocktail with friends. The other part of the room is used for dining. Across the street from the Hudson House is the town park and gazebo; it is pleasant to walk along the waterfront, or to sit on a park bench and watch the river traffic. Doubles, with continental breakfast, $75 to $85. A suite (two bedrooms with bath) rents for $110 to $130. Open year-round except January.

Olde Post Inn, 43 Main St., Cold Spring 10516. (914) 265-2510. This appealing bed-and-breakfast inn is a few steps from the train station and Manhattanites often come by rail for the weekend. Former schoolteachers George Argila and Carole Zeller rescued the 1820 house from near disaster in 1983 and have come up with a unique concept. George, a graduate of the Juilliard School and a drummer, operates a jazz club in the cellar on weekends, bringing in top talent from New York. Pianist Ray Bryant and bass player Marty Rivera are among those who've played; as the drummer in residence, George accompanies his guest artists. They've got a full liquor license for their 50-seat spot and there's a $4 cover charge. From Wednesday through Sunday drinks are served; on Fridays and Saturdays, jazz is heard. Carole is "front of the house" and bread baker. She serves breakfast to guests in an appealing front parlor with several tables, all adorned with dried flower arrangements. To one side is a comfortable area for reading and chatting, with piano and wood stove. The six bedrooms share two hall baths; the two attic rooms with skylights, finished most recently, are in demand. All are simply and agreeably furnished. Doubles, $60 on weekends and holidays, $45 midweek.

The Golden Eagle Inn, Garrison's Landing 10524. (914) 424-3067. This rosy brick bed-and-breakfast inn has a veranda across the second floor with a wonderful view of the river. In fact, the property goes right to the river's edge, and there's additional waterfront property next door. Host George Templeton thinks "people like to be near water because we all came from water." West Point is directly across the Hudson and the Golden Eagle, understandably, is booked far ahead for fall football weekends. George, a watercolorist, and his wife Stephanie, a decorator, have brought considerable flair to their five-room inn. A shop known as the **Sporting Image** on the ground floor shows George's watercolors as well as art items (pillows, lamps, etc.) for people who go duck hunting, trap shooting and the like. It is where continental breakfast is served to inn guests (croissants, breads, fresh fruit, tea and coffee) at sprightly little white tables and chairs. Nearby is a parlor with bookcases, card tables and games like Trivial Pursuit. Two guest rooms have private baths and two share, all on the second floor; a "garden suite" on the first floor features a cheerful sitting area and private bath. Guests often enjoy cocktail hour on the veranda. They may also use a rowboat or, if experienced, a canoe on the river. Doubles, $60 to $75; suite, $90.

The Bird & Bottle Inn, Nelson Corners, Route 9, Garrison 10524. (914) 424-3000. Built in 1761, this inn offers authentic Colonial charm and is a favorite of many. The main-floor dining room and tap room, starkly simple, are known for fine foods (see Where to Eat) and are a popular destination for weekend drivers. At the end of a dirt road just off busy Route 9, the white-trimmed, yellow inn has two guest rooms and a two-room suite on the second floor, plus a cozy cottage on the grounds. Decorated in early American style with antiques, the rooms have working fireplaces and private baths. The emphasis is clearly on food, however, and room rates include breakfasts and dinners. Doubles, $165 MAP; suite or cottage, $190.

The Beekman Arms, Route 9, Rhinebeck 12572. (914) 876-7077. Dating from 1766, the Beekman Arms bills itself as America's oldest inn. Both George Washington and Aaron Burr are said to have slept here, and we think they would have been comfortable. The inn has been added onto several different times and so has a rambling quality, with dining rooms on different levels, and true Colonial flavor. One addition we find a bit incongruous is a greenhouse dining room which stretches across half the front of the building. Bedrooms are smallish in the main inn. Up the street is the **Delamater House,** also owned by the inn, a charming confection of a place in the American Gothic (gingerbread) style. Stay there if you can. Also available behind the Delamater House are a couple of other buildings of more recent vintage. Most of the 18 rooms have private baths. Doubles, $50 to $84.

Hotel Thayer, West Point 10996. (914) 446-4731. Located on the U.S. Military Academy grounds, the Hotel Thayer sits high above the Hudson River and offers splended river views from many rooms. It's quite large and bustling, catering to the thousands of tourists who visit West Point annually, who might just drop in to look around or eat a meal, or who may stay here while visiting a son or daughter or while touring the area. A bit overwhelming are the large bus tour groups, particularly during fall foliage season, which is also football season. Sunday brunch is said to be quite good. Doubles, $50 to $60; two-bedroom suites, $105.

Plumbush, Route 9D, Cold Spring 10516. (914) 265-3904. Known for fine dining for a decade, this elegant Swiss-owned inn opened three guest rooms, all with private baths, in 1986. Two newly completed rooms, the Washington Irving Room and the Marquesa, are located off a wicker-filled (and not very warm) sitting room on the second floor of the inn; the Hendrik Hudson room, also on the second floor, is set apart and has a more settled feeling. Decorating has been done with a Victorian theme; there are oriental rugs and queensize beds. The Marquesa, which is considered a suite, has a sitting area filled with red plush sofas and chairs. Because of the popularity of the restaurant (see below), inn guests may find the atmosphere somewhat busy, although the guest rooms do have a feeling of being away from the world. Continental breakfast is served to guests in their rooms. Doubles, $95; suite, $125.

West Point Motel, 361 Main St., Highland Falls 10928. (914) 446-4180. Basic, clean and fairly new, this two-story, 22-unit motel is located less than a mile from the Thayer entrance to West Point. Each room has two queensize beds. It is understandably popular for football weekends, when room rates rise from $60 to $82 per night.

Seeing and Doing

The Hudson Highlands area can keep you busy for days. Attractions include mansions and historic homes, the Rhinebeck Aerodrome where vintage airplanes (World War I and older) are flown in air shows on weekends from May to October, the Storm King Art Center, a maritime museum and restored waterfront area, hiking trails and nature walks, West Point, antiques and crafts shops, and boat trips on the Hudson. We keep our focus close to the river and think everyone should get out on the water at least once during a visit.

On the River

The Hudson River Maritime Center, Rondout Landing, Kingston. (914) 338-0071. This is as good a place to start as any. Begun as a small storefront exhibit hall in 1980, the center is gradually growing, and is the only waterfront educational center on the Hudson. A small museum is worth a walk-through (it doesn't take long and you won't mind giving the $1 admission fee to a worthy cause). Old photographs showing Hudson River activity, a model of the steamer James W. Baldwin, poster-sized color photos of the steamer Alexander Hamilton, and a videotape on the steamship era are fun. A small gift shop offers river-type souvenirs. Next door is a boat-building shop.

The Rondout Belle, Rondout Landing, Kingston, 338-6280. From the landing, this small excursion boat takes sightseers on Sunday brunch cruises from noon to 2 for $15 each, as well as cruises to the Rondout II lighthouse Saturday at 1 and 3 for $8 per person. Dinner cruises are often scheduled during the summer.

Trolley Rides, Trolley Museum of New York, Kingston, 331-3399. Forty-minute trolley rides along Rondout Creek, which enters the Hudson nearby, are offered on an antique trolley from the Trolley Museum, a stone's throw away. Open daily from noon to 5 July-August, weekends in late spring and early fall. Adults $1, children 50 cents.

Hudson Highlands Cruises and Tours Inc., Highland Falls, 446-7171. The jaunty, canopied M.V. Commander takes passengers out on the Hudson daily between West Haverstraw and Peekskill, with stops at West Point. A favorite cruise leaves the West Point dock at 12:30 daily, sailing past Bannerman's Island, and returning at 5. Adults $5, children $4. The boat is also available for charter by large groups. Cruises, May-October; reservations required.

Hudson River Cruises, North Ohioville Road, New Paltz, 255-6515. All-day cruises from Kingston to West Point and back, with a 90-minute stop at West Point, are offered daily from late June to early September and Sundays only in late spring and early fall. The M.V. Rip Van Winkle leaves the Kingston dock at 9:30, reaches West Point at 1 and returns to Kingston by 6. It's possible for passengers to take a one-hour tour of the Military Academy while at West Point. You can bring your own lunch or purchase food from a deli-bar on board. Adults $15, children $8. Also offered on Friday and Saturday evenings are music cruises from Kingston. Tickets, $12.

Great Hudson Sailing Center, at the Hudson River Maritime Center, Kingston, 338-7313. Myles Gordon is an entrepreneur who has all kinds of schemes to get you out on the Hudson with a tiller in your hand. In addition to a sailing school, he offers two-hour sunset cruises for 15 passengers on Friday, Saturday and Sunday evenings in summer. Wine, cheese and music are included for $18 per person. Day rides on a 43-foot yacht, with a visit to the Rondout II lighthouse, are offered at 2 and 4 for $18. Finally, for the diehard who really wants to see the river, there are three-day cruises, where passengers live on board and learn to sail, or help to sail. These are limited to six people plus a captain, and cost $320 per person, including food. Small sailboats may be rented from the center for $15 an hour and up.

Ring Maritime Inc., c/o Hudson House, Cold Spring, 265-9355. Jackie

Ring is a U.S. Coast Guard captain who runs a small advertising agency but whose real love is sailing. To indulge it, she offers weekend sunset cruises from the Hudson River Sloop Club on the waterfront in Beacon aboard her 32-foot sail-power ketch, the Claddagh. Cheeses, breads, fruit, drinks and other goodies are supplied. The capacity of the sailboat is six plus the captain. Two-hour sails at noon and 6 are $25; reservations required.

Shearwater Cruises Inc., Mountain View Road, Rhinebeck, 876-7350. Marty Ward also has her U.S. Coast Guard captain's license. She teaches sailing on the Hudson, and also offers two-hour pleasure sails where passengers may participate in the sailing of the boat if they wish. Two to eight persons are accommodated aboard the 28-foot yacht and snacks, lunch or dinner may be included. Prices for lunch and dinner sails range from $14 to $20. The yacht leaves from the Norrie Point Yacht Basin, Route 9, four miles south of Rhinebeck. All trips must be reserved in advance.

The Warner House and Constitution Island, West Point. A worthwhile two-hour visit to this 19th century mansion on an island owned by the U.S. Military Academy includes a boat ride, a tour of the Anna B. Warner Memorial Garden, an escorted tour of 15 rooms of the Warner House with guides in Victorian-style costumes and a short walk to the ruins of Revolutionary War fortifications. The house was the home of the Warner family from 1836 to 1915. Two of the children, Susan and Anna Warner, became quite well-known writers of their time. The house is furnished with original Warner family possessions. The boat leaves from South Dock at West Point at 1 and 2 Wednesdays and Thursdays. Reservations must be prepaid; call (914) 446-8676 for reservations from 10 to 11:30 Monday through Friday. Adults $5, children $2.

Constitution Marsh, a nature sanctuary, is located in back of Constitution Island and reached from Route 9 on the river's east side via Indian Brook Road, an unmarked dirt road a quarter mile south of Boscobel. There are several nature trails and a boardwalk through the marsh. The walk from the parking area to the boardwalk is an easy half hour. Owned by the Taconic State Park Commission, it is managed by the National Audubon Society. Open daily 8 to 6 year-round.

Manitoga, Route 9D, Garrison, 424-3812. This sanctuary and contemporary house were created through the vision of the industrial designer and landscape architect Russel Wright. Today the 80-acre site is open to the public primarily as a nature sanctuary with several marked trails. At two spots in particular visitors have fabulous vistas of the Hudson River. Included among the trails is an access route to the Appalachian Trail, a portion of which cuts through the property. House tours are occasionally offered. Open Wednesday-Friday 10 to 4 and weekends, 10 to 6 or dusk. Adults $2, children $1.

Riverfront Access. If you just want to see the river from close up, not sail on it, you have fewer options than you'd probably like. The waterfront park at Cold Spring is particularly attractive and you can see West Point across the river. The imposing stone walls of West Point are also visible from Garrison's Landing. The Beacon waterfront is being revived. In Kingston, you can see the Hudson by going to Kingston Point Beach at the end of Delaware Avenue. It's rather a seedy drive to get there, and the beach isn't extraordinary, but it is sandy, there are lifeguards and changing areas, and there's a boat launch area as well. We saw windsurfers on a cool Sunday morning in

September. The West Point docking area, located below the academy grounds (the road is quite easy to find), is also a good place from which to view the river. Best of all will be the beach at Stony Point located in Hudson Highlands State Park, off Route 9D in Cold Spring. This is expected to have lifeguards and amenities for the 1988 season.

The Houses

Several magnificent houses situated high above the Hudson offer wonderful river views. They also are of great interest in themselves.

Franklin Delano Roosevelt Home and Library, Route 9, Hyde Park. (914) 229-8114. The boyhood home of Franklin Delano Roosevelt is the most intimate of all of the great homes to be seen in the Hudson River Valley. Roosevelt's father bought the house in 1867 and had it redesigned in 1915 to add the south wing. It is an intensely personal place, left just as it was when the President died in 1945, and an incredible peek into what life was like for this extraordinary man.

The small Snuggery on the first floor, where his mother Sarah organized her household, is revealing. The enormous living room, down a couple of steps from the hallway, with massive fireplaces at each end, was where the family played, rested, read and entertained. Upstairs are the bedrooms, including that in which young Franklin was born, all remarkably unassuming and homey. His Presidential office, which was used as a Summer White House, is on the main floor and viewed from outdoors. Visitors may press a button and hear the President's voice.

Nearby is the pleasant shuttered stone building which is the **Roosevelt Library and Museum.** Established in 1939, it contains an exceptional exhibit of the President's "First Fifty Years." Starting with the wicker bassinet he used as a baby, and including touching letters in his childish hand to his mother, as well as those he wrote from the Groton School and Harvard, the entire exhibit is absorbing. Other displays contain portions of FDR's massive collection of sea memorabilia. Still another is devoted to his years as President.

Outside in the rose garden are the graves of Franklin and Eleanor and their little dog, Fala. Not too far distant, and reached by buses from the main site, is **Val-Kill,** the unpretentious and warm property used by the First Lady as a retreat while her husband was alive, and more or less full time from his death until hers in 1962.

Visitors are introduced to Val-kill and to Mrs. Roosevelt through a 20-minute audio-visual presentation in a building known as the playhouse. Also on the property are the Dutch Colonial house used by Eleanor until she died, and the larger white building, the Factory, erected by her and her friends for use by local craftspeople who made early American-style furniture here for some years. The First Lady's home is most memorable for the photographs covering the walls, tables and just about every possible space. They provide a glimpse into a life devoted to people.

Combination ticket for main Roosevelt site and Vanderbilt mansion (see below), $2; Val-Kill, $2.50. Roosevelt home and library are open daily 9 to 5 except Thanksgiving, Christmas and New Year's. Val-Kill is open April-November.

Vanderbilt Mansion, Route 9, Hyde Park. (914) 229-9115. A short distance north of the Roosevelt site, and with an enchanting view of the Hudson

River, this 54-room mansion was the home of Frederick W. Vanderbilt, grandson of Commodore Vanderbilt. It was Frederick's brothers who built the Marble House and the Breakers in Newport, R.I., and the guide told us that this was the most modest of the Vanderbilt mansions built during the gilded age. An Italian renaissance palace created by the architectural firm of McKim, Mead and White, it was used during the spring and fall by Frederick and his wife, Louisa, a social woman who entertained — didn't they all? — lavishly. The circular plan of the first floor, with a dining room which could be turned into a ballroom, and where the Roosevelts' only daughter Anna was once feted, is in marked contrast to the home of FDR. Perhaps it's the marble that makes it seem so formal; this is a pretentious place which just doesn't appear lived in. The surrounding property, however, is especially nice. A road leads down to the riverfront, where there are picnic tables along the river's edge and ample parking. The "guest house" of 16 rooms is now a visitor center. A short slide presentation precedes a visit to the house. Open 9 to 5 daily except Thanksgiving, Christmas and New Year's.

Boscobel, Route 9D, Garrison. (914) 265-3638. One of the best museums of the decorative arts of the Federal period, Boscobel was saved from the wrecker's ball — through the generosity of Lila Acheson Wallace, co-founder of the Reader's Digest, among others — and opened as a house museum in 1961. Located on 45 acres high above the Hudson, Boscobel was the dream of States Morris Dyckman, a descendant of Dutch settlers, who with his wife began construction of the house in 1804. His heirs lived in the house until 1888, after which it deteriorated and was almost torn down by the middle of this century. Thanks to Mrs. Wallace, it avoided that fate and lives today as a handsomely reconstructed monument to the Federal period. It is filled with outstanding examples of New York Federal furniture, including pieces by Duncan Phyfe and other leading furniture makers of the day. The house's exquisite gardens (thousands of tulips and flowering fruit trees bloom in the spring), its fabulous views of the river, and its outbuildings, including a gatehouse where spinning is demonstrated, all work together to make a worthwhile place to visit. Open daily from 9:30 to 4 except Tuesdays, Thanksgiving, Christmas, January and February. Adults $4, children $2.

Mills Mansion, Old Post Road, Staatsburg. (914) 889-4100. This is an example of one of the great estates built by financial and industrial leaders at the turn of the century. Ogden Mills, whose wife Ruth Livingston Mills inherited the property, had the prestigious architectural firm of McKim, Mead and White remodel and enlarge the home which already occupied the gorgeous site above the river. Completed in 1896, the new house was very different from its former self, with two large wings and balustrades, pilasters and floral swags added as exterior ornament. Inside the decoration is in the style of Louis XV and Louis XVI, rich with marble fireplaces, oak paneling and gilded ceilings. The mansion was given by Mills's daughters to New York State. The parklike grounds are marvelous and the views of the Hudson quite stunning; you can walk to the water's edge. Open Memorial Day weekend through Labor Day, Wednesday-Saturday 10 to 5 and Sunday 1 to 5; September and October, Wednesday-Saturday noon to 5 and Sunday 1 to 5. Free.

Washington's Headquarters, 84 Liberty St., Newburgh. (914) 562-1195. You drive through what looks like a war zone in downtown Newburgh to reach the spot where George Washington had his headquarters from April

course of their schooling. The menu changes with every meal, and its offerings are so creative that you'll have trouble choosing — as we did at lunch — because everything is enticing. For appetizers, who could decide between chicken and turkey pate with fresh tomato relish for $3.75 or a Savannah Bay hot scallop salad for $4? Then there are soups, such as chilled melon-berry or pecos bean for $2.25 or a sampling of all three for $2.50 for the indecisive among us. Luncheon entrees might be blackened red snapper with frog's legs and hush puppies ($12), a New England seafood steamer pot with garlic sourdough toast ($12.25) or a pan-fried chicken breast with black bean sauce and jicama salad ($10.75). Desserts also are exciting: chocolate-dipped strawberries on orange custard sauce ($3) or Florida lemon and lime cake ($2.25). A specialty is American Bounty wine cream cake ($2.25). Dinner is by candlelight and entrees in the $13 to $16 range might include sauteed scallops New Orleans and San Francisco-style seafood medley with saffron dumplings. An *American Bounty Sampler Cookbook*, featuring some of the recipes, may be purchased for $3.50 from the maitre-d. American wines and beers are served. Lunch, 11:30 to 12:30; dinner, 6:30 to 8:30. Closed Sundays and Mondays. Reservations required.

The Escoffier Room, Culinary Institute, Route 9, Hyde Park. (914) 471-6608. The original CIA dining room is formal and French in style. Gold and white latticework walls, handsome brass chandeliers and comfortable black leather-like chairs and banquettes put you in the mood for a fancy luncheon or dinner. Three revolving menus consist mostly of classic French items. Lunch is $18 prix-fixe and dinner, $36, and considering that at lunch you'll have almost everything offered at dinner (except for the fruit and cheese course), it's a bargain. At each meal you choose from five or six appetizers, four soups, eight or nine entrees, and several rich desserts. The appetizer choices might include galantine of pheasant, coquilles St. Jacques, oysters Rockefeller, or hors d'oeuvres varies — a selection from the cart of at least 10 items. Soups might be onion (always on the menu and fabulous), gazpacho, vichyssoise and creme Senegalese. Entrees might be trout, lamb chops, grilled salmon bearnaise or English mixed grill at lunchtime. Dinner entrees include tournedos Rossini and rack of lamb Nicoise, and there is always a game dish. A house salad with herb dressing is served after the entree and if you've any room left you may try French pastries, tortes and rich cakes for dessert. Open Tuesday-Saturday, noon to 1 and 6:30 to 8:30. Reservations with deposit required.

Bird & Bottle Inn, Nelson's Corners, Route 9, Garrison. (914) 424-3000. This was the inn selected for location scenes in the movie "Kiss Me Goodbye" with Sally Field, which may or may not mean anything to you. The atmosphere is strictly Colonial, in keeping with the history of the structure built as a tavern in 1761. Wide plank floorboards throughout the main floor and a stark simplicity set the scene in the main dining room, with its white tablecloths, and the more intimate tavern rooms. The prix-fixe dinner at $33.50 lists smoked trout with horseradish cream, quiche Lorraine and mussels in sour cream and dill among the appetizers. Entrees include tournedos Helder (two filets on lightly breaded eggplant served with an artichoke bottom and a mushroom cap with bearnaise sauce); sauteed breast of chicken with sherry, mushrooms, prosciutto and thyme, and roast pheasant with a Madeira wine sauce. Homemade pastries are on the dessert tray. For the three-course prix-fixe ($14.95) Sunday brunch you might start with a chicken liver terrine or a ratatouille Nicoise, have an omelet, seafood crepes or chicken divan as the entree, and end with cheesecake, creme caramel or almond apple tart. A ploughman's lunch of homebaked bread, cheddar cheese, pickled onions and chutney is $4. Lunch, noon to 2:30; dinner 4 to 7. Closed Tuesday, also Monday in winter and part of January.

Plumbush, Route 9D, Cold Spring. (914) 265-3904. Celebrating its 10th anniversary in 1986, Plumbush is highly touted as one of the best restaurants in the area. Its Swiss owners, host Gieri Albin and chef Ans Benderer, concoct an elegant dining experience inside the striking plum-colored house with gold trim. The five Victorian dining rooms range in style from dark wood paneling to elegant rose-splashed wallpaper. In summer there is also dining on a wraparound porch. The oak-paneled bar is dark and intimate. Dinner may be ordered a la carte or prix-fixe for $30. Appetizers ($5.25 to $7.50) include shrimp in beer batter with pungent fruit sauce, a country terrine with cumberland sauce or an aspic of fresh salmon. House specialties among entrees include veal Oscar ($23.50), classic trout au bleu with sauce mousseline ($21.50), stuffed roast squab ($21.50) and a whole roast duckling with brandied plum glacee ($40 for two). Swiss apple fritters at $4.50 are always a dessert choice; daily specials might be a chocolate praline mousse or a frozen orange souffle grand marnier. For lunch, entrees in the $8 to $12 range include poached eggs with crabmeat and hollandaise sauce, shrimp in beer batter with fruit sauce, a smoked trout platter and chef's salad. Lunch, noon to 2:30; dinner, 5:30 to 9:30; Sunday, brunch noon to 2:30, dinner, noon to 8. Closed Tuesday, also for lunch in winter and month of January.

45 Fair Street, 45 Fair St., Cold Spring. (914) 265-3166. Not much to look at from the outside, but highly recommended by the locals, this small restaurant has an interesting menu with the emphasis on Italian. Located at the end of a nondescript side street in Cold Spring, it has a distant view (across the railroad tracks) of the Hudson, and a pleasant interior with hanging plants and cheerful brown and white checked tablecloths on small tables. Dinner entrees include linguini with white clam sauce for $6.50; filet of sole florentine, $9.75, and stuffed scampi for $10.25. Each night the chef prepares veal a different way for $12.95, and chicken cordon bleu at $9.50 and London broil with garlic toast at $7.95 are a couple of other reasonably priced choices. For lunch (and on the Saturday we visited it was busy), there's a simple sandwich and burger selection plus a few specialties like omelets and quiches, a chicken salad or shrimp salad plate, and potatoes cordon bleu. Prices at lunch range from $3.75 for a hamburger to $6.95 for the potatoes. Open daily for lunch and dinner.

Roundout Golden Duck, 11 Broadway, Kingston. (914) 331-3221. This enormously popular Chinese restaurant just a block or so from the water at Rondout Landing in Kingston is considered one of the best in the region. Chef-owner Paul Wong has been cooking in China and this country for more than 20 years, and a menu notation says he does it all without additives like monosodium glutamate. Dinner specials include Szechuan, Cantonese and Mandarin foods — plus a few dishes from Shanghai. Among the offerings are crispy chunked chicken and shrimp imperial for $8.95; pan fried noodles (a house special) for $7.95; Szechuan sauteed scallops and shrimps, $8.95, and chicken with garlic sauce at $6.25. The regular luncheon is $3.50 and a dozen choices include shrimp with Chinese vegetables and roast duck with mixed vegetables as well as the ever-in-demand moo goo gai pan. Lunch, Monday-Friday; dinner nightly, 3 to 9:30. An all-you-can-eat buffet is served Sunday from 11:30 to 2:30.

Ship to Shore, Roundout Landing, Kingston. (914) 331-7034. Ricky and Michelle Polacco, a young couple, have opened this bar with sandwich menu to a very appreciative audience. Located in the Rondout area not far from the maritime museum, this is a pleasant spot for lunch or light supper, its small tables covered with sprightly flowered cloths. Soup of the day was chicken with barley when we looked in; sandwiches served with chips and garnishes are $4.50. Desserts are homemade. All-day menu served from noon to 9.

Schneller's, 61-63 John St., Kingston. (914) 331-9800. The dining room of this venerable German restaurant in downtown Kingston is reached after walking through the undistinguished bar and climbing the stairs (note the unusual mural-style wallpaper). The room looks as if it has not changed in 40 years. A couple of clocks, at least one of them a cuckoo clock, and a large poster with verses to "Schnitzelbank" are on the walls; a few large beer steins are set here and there on tables or buffets. Simple chandeliers, one of which had several bulbs missing, hang from the high pressed-tin ceiling. But, oh, the food! And, oh, the prices! You can eat so well and so reasonably here that it is worth the effort to find it. Entrees include eight schnitzel varieties, sauerbraten and Austrian goulash, all in the $8 to $9 range. Wursts at $5.95 are served with two choices among potato pancakes, sauerkraut, cucumber salad, potato salad, cole slaw or green salad. Our sauerbraten came with red cabbage which tasted as if it had simmered for several days in the pot, and spaetzli, the delectable German homemade noodles — scrumptious, but too much to finish. We didn't have room for apple strudel, but did accept the waitress's offering of a glass of tasty apple schnapps, which comes as a bonus with all meals. Lunch, Monday-Saturday; dinner, Wednesday-Saturday.

FOR MORE INFORMATION: Dutchess County Visitors Bureau, 41 Main St., Poughkeepsie, N.Y. 12601, (914) 485-4690. Ulster County Public Information Office, Box 1800, Kingston, N.Y. 12401, (914) 331-9300.

Mohican plies waters of Lake George.

Lake George, N.Y.

The popularity of the place is unbelievable. On the Fourth of July — admittedly, the peak of the summer season — you can barely move in Lake George Village. College kids, teenagers, families, young couples, all crowd onto Canada Street until it is a challenge to keep a spot on the sidewalk. You don't exactly walk; you're carried along by the momentum. You've never seen so many T-shirts. The traffic is snarled. Horns honk, radios blare, friends call to friends.

The carnival atmosphere that prevails in the village, at the southwestern corner of the 32-mile-long lake, diminishes — but doesn't completely disappear — elsewhere around the area. Many of the people who visit Lake George are from the New York metropolitan area and are used to crowds. They apparently don't mind sharing their vacation with thousands of others as the year-round population of 3,500 swells to 70,000 in summer.

Motels are crowded cheek-by-jowl along the waterfront and are completely booked for big weekends. On the lake, powerboats skim along, pulling waterskiers, unnerving canoeists, flying past sailboats. Excursion boats ply the waters, crowded to the gunwales. Parasailers tied to big white and red striped sails float above the scene. Amusement parks like Great Escape are nearby.

North along the western shoreline, including Diamond Point and Bolton Landing, the crowds thin out a bit, and there are some fine self-contained resorts. Even more remote are the northern and eastern areas, populated principally by families who return to summer cottages season after season.

Discovered in 1646 by the French Jesuit missionary, Father Isaac Jogues, Lake George has been the scene of action — military and otherwise — almost ever since. The name which finally stuck was bestowed in 1755 by General William Johnson, an Englishman engaged in the French and Indian War, when the two countries fought for control of Lake Champlain and Lake George, which together formed such an important waterway from the north. George, of course, was King George III, who was later considered no friend of the Colonists.

The lake, which is long and narrow (one to three miles wide), is surrounded by the dramatic Adirondack mountains, making for great vistas. Its summer

86

temperature is salubrious, 65 to 70 degrees on average, and its waters — in spite of the crowds — are clear. It is dotted with some 300 islands, which make it a boater's paradise (and a camper's also, for the state maintains some of the islands as campsites). Fishermen pull trout, salmon, bass and northern pike from Lake George.

Its early history has left a few monuments: Fort Ticonderoga at the northern end, Fort William Henry in the south, among them. Today's vacationers may visit the forts, but the focus of their trips tends to be on the boating, swimming, fishing and amusements to be found in the area. We, too, concentrate on the diversions in Lake George Village and along the southwestern shore of the lake.

Getting There

Take Interstate 87, the Adirondack Northway, to Exit 22. Route 9 leads into Lake George Village. Route 9N along the western shore of the lake, north of the village, leads to Diamond Point and Bolton Landing.

Where to Stay

You won't have trouble finding a room, although most will be in motels. There are no country inns and almost no bed-and-breakfast establishments. A couple of true destination resorts — and a few others which are oriented that way — are good choices if you want to relax and be waited on. Campers have a wide selection, and there's even a youth hostel.

Canoe Island Lodge, Route 9N, Box 144, Diamond Point 12824. (518) 668-5592. For more than 40 years, Jane and Bill Busch have been providing a special brand of hospitality at their resort on the shores of Lake George. The ambience is peculiarly, and perfectly, Adirondack in character. There is, too, an alpine flair evident in the architecture of the buildings, the dress of the staff on special occasions, the fact that some guests speak only German (the Busches oblige). A Maifest on Memorial Day weekend usually promises maiwein and beer on tap. From the stone fireplaced main lodge, with dining room overlooking the lake, to the several wood and stone cabins and cottages nestled on the hillside leading down to the water, Canoe Island Lodge is cozy and welcoming. The waterfront is very busy and guests can take sailing, windsurfing and waterskiing lessons, go off on a cruise in one of the lodge's boats, or — and this is really special — catch the shuttle to a five-acre island owned by the lodge (one of only 18 on the lake which is privately owned). Meals are memorable, too, especially the weekly Thursday chicken barbecues on the island, and the extravagant Friday night buffet dinners. Not surprisingly, many of those who have discovered Canoe Island Lodge return year after year. In addition to waterfront activities, there are tennis courts, a hiking trail to a lookout high above the lake, shuffleboard, a country tavern for pre- and post-dinner drinks, and planned nightly events including square dancing and video movies. Two meals a day are included in the rates (before July and after September, make that three). Rooms have king, queen or twin beds. Accommodations range from rooms in the main lodge at $54 daily per person to the upper level of the Chalet Erika at lakeside with private sundeck and stone fireplace at $102 per person. MAP. Open May 20 to Oct. 20.

The Sagamore, Bolton Landing 12814. (518) 644-9400. A resort in the grand manner of the late 19th century, the Sagamore was restored to its Victorian elegance in 1983. Now an Omni Classic hotel, it is located on an island a short bridge length from the mainland, but once you cross that bridge, you're in another world. Gleaming white and turreted, the hotel crowns the island's highest point, and looks south down the lake from its majestic position. Several contemporary lodge buildings behind the hotel have rooms with balconies and eastern views of the lake. From the grand piano and marble-topped tete-a-tete tables in its **Veranda Lounge** with panoramic lake view to its green Adirondack chairs out front on a terrace above the water and its green and white umbrellaed tables by the pool, this is a first-class resort. You won't have to leave the hotel property — unless you want to play golf at the Sagamore's nearby championship course — if you don't want to. A large year-round pool (it's indoors but there's a sundeck adjacent), tennis and racquetball courts, sailboats, the Morgan yacht for rides around the lake, a fitness center and other planned activities (like aerobic walks and horseback riding) are part of the package. Guests may dine at any of four different restaurants, including the Sagamore dining room, **Mr. Brown's** (a more casual cafe), the **Club Grill or Trillium** (see Where to Eat), a beautiful room favored by gourmets; a surcharge is added to guest bills when dining here. Dinner also can be enjoyed aboard the Morgan yacht, and breakfast is often available on the outdoor terrace. For night owls, **Van Winkel's** is a sophisticated downstairs nightclub done in pink and black with a big-city feeling. The Sagamore is open year-round and has cross-country skiing in the winter. The hotel caters to substantial convention business in the spring and fall, but summer is oriented to individual guests. Doubles, $188 to $318 daily, MAP. Open year-round.

Melody Manor Resort Motel, Lake Shore Drive (Route 9N), Bolton Landing 12814. (518) 644-9750. Stucco motel buildings with wood trim and balconies carry out the Bavarian feeling at this resort, located directly on the lake. In fact, it's the exceptionally nice 300-foot lakefront — along with the impeccable care given the entire property — that sets this place apart. Marzella Hamm, yet another of the German hoteliers to be found in the Lake George area, runs a tight ship. The two buildings on a knoll above the lake (with a pool beside them) have 40 rooms in all. A steep stone staircase (or more gentle driveway) leads down to the water's edge, where there are rowboats for the use of guests and a manicured lawn area for sitting or sunning. A rushing brook borders one side of the property. **The Manor**, an adjacent restaurant, with red tablecloths and roaring fire on chilly nights, offers dinner nightly. German specialties include sauerbraten and wiener schnitzel; steaks and seafood are also on the menu. Doubles, $60 to $88, EP. Open May-October.

Marine Village Resort Motel, 350 Canada St., Lake George 12845. (518) 668-5478. Right in the heart of the village, this motel also boasts a sandy lakefront beach, a heated pool overlooking the lake, and free rowboats and paddle boats for guests. The Coon family, owners for 15 years, keeps the place immaculate. The 85 units are located in a one-story or a two-story building leading down to the lake from the street. A separate honeymoon cottage for two with a good view of the lake rents for $98 a night. Doubles, $80 to $135. Open year-round.

Lake Crest Motel, 366 Canada St., Lake George 12845. (518) 668-3374. Also in the heart of the village, the Lake Crest has two two-story buildings leading down to the lakefront with units accommodating from two to four persons. A heated pool and color cable TV are additional attractions. There's a coffee shop on the property. Family units for up to six persons are available for $155. Doubles, $96 to $145 for a lakefront unit. Open year-round.

Alpine Village, Lake Shore Drive, Box 672, Lake George 12845. (518) 668-2193. This log cabin resort is north of Lake George Village on the road leading to Diamond Point and Bolton Landing. An older and quieter facility somewhat removed from the frenzy of the village in midsummer, it offers clean but sparse accommodations in a variety of log buildings, ranging from a lodge with a dozen rooms to several small cabins for two or four. There are guest rooms as well in the main building, which has a dining room for breakfast and dinner with a nice distant view of the lake. Rowboats and canoes are free for guests; paddle boats cost extra. There are a small, sandy beach, a tennis court and an outdoor ping-pong table. The large lobby in the main building with fieldstone fireplace is pleasant. But the towels are the see-through sort that seem to have been around for several years, and the metal shower stalls could use updating. Doubles, $55 to $72 EP, $90 to $100 MAP. Open year-round.

East Cove Log Cabins, Route 9L and Beach Road, Lake George 12845. (518) 668-5284. This log cabin community on the southeastern side of the lake is not on the water, but its adjacent restaurant (see Where to Eat) is a particular attraction. Most of the eight cabins with Indian names (like Mohawk and Iroquois) are large enough for four people; Stumpy is just big enough for two. Some have fireplaces. Cabins rent for $250 (Stumpy) to $370 (Seneca) per week in season. Open year-round.

Sue's Bed and Breakfast, 106 Mohican St., Lake George 12845. (518) 668-4480. One of few B&Bs in the area, this meticulously clean place a few blocks back from Canada Street is run by Sue Jensen, who serves breakfast to guests on an outdoor terrace when weather permits. Her favorite: Finnish pancakes and syrup with fresh fruit and coffee. Five guest rooms share two baths. Doubles, $35 to $40.

An **American Youth Hostel** operates in the summers at 176 Montcalm St., Lake George, on the grounds of St. James Episcopal Church.

CAMPING. Hearthstone Point, a state operation for serious campers (no plug-ins are available), has campsites on both sides of Route 9N ($8.50 for those on the lakeside, $7 for those across the road). The 268 sites can be reserved through Ticketron in New York State and are available from May 16 through Labor Day. A lovely long beach on Lake George makes the area particularly attractive.

Mohawk Camping, Route 9N, RR 2, Box 2386, Lake George 12845. (518) 668-2760. This campground north of the village and on the shore of the lake features city water and electricity at each site, hot showers, a campground store, and a swimming area with sandy beach. No campsites are directly on the water. Open Memorial Day through mid-September.

Seeing and Doing

The focus is clearly on the lake, with excursion boat rides, boat rentals, swimming, windsurfing and parasailing all popular. Besides strolling in the village, a much loved activity, there are amusement parks, a terrific mountain drive, and some good small museums. Don't overlook rafting down one of the nearby Adirondack rivers for a little excitement.

On the Lake

The Lake George Steamboat Company, Steel Pier, Lake George Village, 668-5777. Carrying passengers on Lake George since 1817, the company has three excursion boats, the Ticonderoga, the Mohican and the paddlewheel steamboat, the Minne-ha-ha, running from early May to mid-October.

A full-day excursion to the northern end of the lake at Ticonderoga is offered aboard the **Mohican,** which leaves at 10:30 and returns at 3:15. It's possible to take the boat one way and get off at Ticonderoga. Adults $9.75, children, $4.75.

The largest boat, the **Ticonderoga,** has two cruises daily to the island area in the Narrows, about half way up the lake. This is an especially pleasant trip, with comfortable deck chairs on an open-air upper deck, or sheltered mid-deck area. Passengers are told of the various people who built homes on Millionaires' Row on the western shore of the lake, and sites are pointed out along the way. A particularly good view of the Sagamore resort is available from the water. These tours leave at 11 and 2:15. A dinner-jazz cruise from 6:30 to 8:30 offers a buffet at an optional extra charge. Adults $8.25, children $4. On Thursday, Friday and Saturday nights there's a moonlight cruise with a Dixieland jazz band from 9:30 to 11:30. Adults, $9.25.

Finally, the sprightly **Minne-ha-ha,** whose steam calliope plays merrily as it sails along, offers one-hour shoreline cruises six times a day from 10 to 7:30. Adults $5.25, children $2.50. A two-hour moonlight cruise with Dixieland jazz band is also offered on fine nights. Adults $9.25, children $4.50.

Shoreline Cruises, 2 James St., Lake George, 668-4644. Two smaller cruise boats, the Defiance and the Algonquin, offer several variations: a sunset supper cruise, a bay cruise, a narrows cruise, a fishing cruise and a moonlight cruise. The fishing tour departs at 6 a.m. Tuesdays and Thursdays in summer and lasts three and a half hours. Adults, $9; children, $4. The sunset supper cruise, leaving at 5:45 and returning at 8, costs $10.95 for adults, $7.75 for children, and includes a fried chicken and ham dinner. The boats operate from Memorial Day Weekend to Columbus Day weekend, with a reduced schedule from early May and again into late October.

Want to try a pirate ship? The feisty red **Buccaneer,** 668-5351, sails several times daily from the dock at the foot of Amherst Street where the Boardwalk restaurant is located. This is an hour-long sail with a difference: the ship is prone to lie in wait in hidden coves and then come out firing its harmless but booming cannons. It's fun for the not-so-faint-of-heart.

Parasailing is offered from the Shoreline Cruise dock at Canada Street and Beach Road, 668-4644. The courageous pay $35 for a 10-minute "sail" high above the waters of the lake. They are picked up and returned to a large floating platform in the center of the lake. Jet ski rentals are also available at $26 per half hour.

BOAT RENTALS. Lake George's Finest, Beach Road, Lake George, 668-9234. Sixteen-foot runabouts with 35-horsepower motors seating six rent for $40 an hour; with 70-hp motors and seating eight, $46. A 19-foot boat with 165-hp engine seating 10 is $54 an hour.

In Bolton Landing, **Chic's Marina,** 644-2170, has a wide variety of boats for rent. They range from canoes and rowboats at $10 an hour ($24 a day) to speedboats with 200-hp motors at $73 an hour. The marina also rents water ski equipment. The **Water's Edge** on Sagamore Road, 644-2511, has 17-foot Grumman canoes plus rowboats for rent at $6 an hour or $25 a day. Powerboats are also rented from $14 to $43 an hour.

SWIMMING. Lake George Beach State Park, Beach Road, Lake George, is quite a nice strand, with bathhouse, snack bar, picnic grove and plenty of parking ($2.50 per car). Locker rentals and showers are $1 and it costs 50 cents to enter the beach. Located at the southern end of the lake, with lifeguards and roped-off areas for children, this is a lively place for swimming, sunning and people watching.

Other Attractions

A View From the Top. A fabulous view of Lake George, the surrounding Adirondack mountains and — if the day is clearer than ours was — other lakes in the area can be enjoyed from from the the 2,030-foot summit of **Prospect Mountain.** Starting from Route 9 south of the village, the 5.5-mile drive up and down Prospect Mountain Road is not rigorous, and several scenic overlooks are good for stops along the way. At the top are picnic tables (tote your own food, for none is sold); you can view the remains of an old hotel and the world's largest cable railroad. A little open-air trolley bus takes passengers from the parking lot to the actual summit. Cars pay $3 apiece and the trip is well worth it.

RIVER RAFTING. Rivers in the Adirondacks are popular for whitewater canoeing and river rafting, and as long as you're here, you might as well try it. We joined our teen-aged daughter and her friend for a trip down the Sacandaga River with **Adirondack Widwaters Inc.,** (518) 696-2953. Ten passengers in bathing suits or shorts and T-shirts (you're going to get wet, so dress appropriately) plus one guide from AWI get into a raft at a dam on the Sacandaga in Hadley (about a half hour from Lake George). The group then paddles, floats and screams its way down more than three miles of river, stopping midstream for water fights with other rafters or for a swim. The trip takes about an hour and is great fun. You can purchase a photo of yourself in the raft at the end of the trip. Trips are run hourly Monday-Saturday 9 to 4 and cost $8.50 per person. AWI also runs a Hudson River trip.

Great Escape Amusement Park, Route 9, Lake George. (518) 792-6568. More than 100 rides, shows and attractions are touted at this fun park, including the "Steamin' Demon" roller-coaster. Open daily 9:30 to 6, late May into early fall. Adults $12.80, children $10.90.

Water Slide World. Routes 9 and 9L, Lake George. (518) 668-4407. This family-oriented, water fun park has a 16,000-square-foot wave pool, slides, a bumper pool lagoon, a toddlers' lagoon and restaurants on site. Open daily 10 to 6:30, June to Labor Day. Adults $11.95, children $9.95.

Fort William Henry, Beach Road, Lake George. (518) 668-5471. Living history tours conducted by guide-historians include demonstrations of musket firing, a grenadier-bomb toss, a cannon firing and musketball molding. The fort was constructed by the English in 1755 to block an anticipated French advance from Canada into the colonies. The fort's history, including its destruction by the French forces under Montcalm in 1757, was used by James Fennimore Cooper in his famous classic, "The Last of the Mohicans." Open daily 10 to 10 July-August, 10 to 5 May-June and September-October. Adults $5, children $3.

SHOPPING. Most of the stores on Lake George Village's Canada Street (and there are a lot of them) are into T-shirts, postcards, junky souvenirs, film and fudge. You can get fabulous caramel corn at **Karamel Korn**, good ice cream cones, cakes and cookies at **Cookies and Cream**, and **Janet Vito's Boutique** has better than average clothes. **Beach and Beyond** is the place for waterfront necessities. **The Adirondack Connection** on Route 9 south of the village has Adirondack-style furniture and accessories. **Sutton's** (see Where to Eat) has a fine array of crafts, foods and clothes in a country-store atmosphere. **Dexter** and **Dunham** shoe outlets are located on Route 9 south of the village.

Where to Eat

Considering the sheer numbers of visitors, the dining opportunities (except for fast food and pizza) can be disappointing. You will always be able to grab a snack, but it's hard to find *our* kind of restaurant, one with a little flair, a good chef and a water view. Still, we've found some neat spots.

Algonquin Restaurant, Lake Shore Drive, Bolton Landing. (518) 644-9442. You can't get any closer to the water, and the Algonquin takes advantage of its lakeside location. Outside is a patio with tables decked out in cheerful yellow and white striped umbrellas. Indoors the **Pub Room** downstairs has a flagstone-look floor, red tablecloths and an informal menu, while upstairs, the **Topside** room with pink linens and bentwood chairs is more formal. You can pull your boat right up to the docks in front if you'd like, and diners love watching all the lakefront activity. Opened in the mid-19th century as a tearoom for guests of the Algonquin Hotel, the restaurant has been in the Smith family for a couple of generations and is run with professionalism and attention to detail. For lunch we enjoyed a turkey croissant with Swiss cheese and lemon mayonnaise ($4.50), a "Totem Pole" cheeseburger with lettuce, tomato, onion and mayonnaise ($4.75) and a taco salad ($5.95). All were good, served promptly by young waitresses in khaki skirts and white shirts with nautical flags. Also on the menu are omelets and a good selection of salads and sandwiches. Upstairs, silk flower arrangements adorn the tables, soft blue wallpaper the walls, and a beautifully varnished wood canoe hangs from the ceiling. Here diners enjoy choices including oriental shrimp stir-fry at $13.95; scallops marsala for $12.95, or sole Algonquin — sole wrapped around broccoli spears, baked and topped with a lobster sauce — for $13.95. Veal Andrew is another house specialty: lightly breaded veal sauteed with artichoke hearts and covered with a basil, lemon and brandy flavored brown sauce, $12.95. Open daily for lunch and dinner in summer, closed Monday and Tuesday in winter. Reservations are advised, especially for dinner.

Log Jam Restaurant, Route 9, Lake George. (518) 798-1155. This typical Adirondack log building is deceiving from the front, for it extends back with a large addition in the rear. The spirit is very much that of the Adirondacks, with a huge stone fireplace in the lounge, bare plank floors, and such touches as snowshoes hanging on the walls. The idea was to give it the flavor of a logging camp in the mountains, and since its opening in 1976, both its attractiveness and consistently good food have won a large following. One caution: no reservations are taken, and while the restaurant is open by 4:30 in the summer, it is usually filled within an hour, so get there early or be prepared to wait. We did arrive early, but it was Fourth of July weekend so we had to wait in the pleasant lounge. A favorite house drink is a "Strawberry Shortcake" made with amaretto, cream and strawberries, and these were being downed with enthusiasm by drinkers all around. Once seated for dinner you can choose from the Menu Gazette such standards as prime rib, steak teriyaki, shrimp scampi or New York sirloin ($7.95 to $18.95). A small printed menu for the day added some nice specials: blackened redfish, seafood casserole au gratin, veal Marsala and chicken Oscar among them. The salad bar is stocked with cast aluminum plates which keep the offerings icy cold; there are three crusty loaves of bread from which to slice as much as you'd like. You ought to save room for the desserts — this menu comes attached to a twig! — which include a house specialty, pecan pie with chantilly cream (sour cream and heavy cream mixed with vanilla and grand marnier and absolutely heavenly) for $3.25. Or you might try the Adirondack Log, a fudge brownie with ice cream, hot fudge sauce and whipped cream, $2.25. Open nightly in summer, 4:30 to 10:30; rest of year, 5 to 10, closed Monday and Tuesday.

Ridge Terrace, Route 9L, East Lake George. (518) 656-9274. Yet another log building houses this rather large restaurant a 20-minute drive to the east of the lake. The varnished log interior with mounted deer heads carries out the Adirondack mountain theme and the locals all rave about the food prepared by the Rios family. Father Raymond works with sons Michael, the chef, and Richard; sister Virginia also gets into the act. The 1920s building, originally a tavern, is open for dinner only. Diners may choose the enclosed wraparound porch with flagstone underfoot, or the large interior dining rooms with polished wood floors. Tablecloths are white; chairs are wooden with green seats. The overall atmosphere is subtle — an appropriate backdrop for very good food. Veal is definitely the specialty, says Michael, who prepares it in several ways, many of them named for family members. Other preparations include veal cordon bleu, wiener schnitzel, veal Oscar and Black Forest veal, the last sautéed in butter with sliced eggplant and finished with special Ridge Terrace sauce. Other options include steaks, pork chops, chateaubriand, German pot roast, lobster, scallops and other seafood in the $9 to $15 range. There is a salad bar. Dinner nightly from 5, Sunday from 1, May to mid-October.

East Cove, Route 9L and Beach Road, Lake George. (518) 668-5265. Still another quaint Adirondack log cabin houses this popular dining spot a little off the beaten track on the southeast corner of the lake. Pete and Debbie Smith are the longtime owners of the restaurant, which started out in 1970 as a hamburger stand and grew to a full-service dining spot with two additions in 1979 and 1980. Flags of several nations adorn the ceiling, adding a colorful touch to the interior. The menu doesn't forget the restaurant's origins — you can order a hamburger or a Russian royal burger (with sour cream and sautéed mushrooms) as well as a full meal. Daily specials usually include a veal, a beef and a seafood dish. Standard dinners range from sliced tenderloin at $10.95 to schnitzel a la Holstein at $14.95. You might also choose shrimp scampi, center-cut pork chops or prime rib ($15.95 for an oversize cut). The salad bar is available with meals, or by itself for $5.25. Seafood bisque is a featured soup. Dinner nightly, 5 to 11, Sunday from noon; Sunday brunch in summer; dinner on weekends only in the winter.

Tired John's, Lake Shore Drive (Route 9N), Diamond Point. (518) 668-9232. This small restaurant three miles north of Lake George Village is great for families — and anybody who likes barbecue. Don't be put off by the white oilcloth table coverings or the paper plates and cups, for it's what's on and in them that counts. The restaurant's splendid New Orleans-style barbecue sauce with a bit of a tang covers the chicken, the pork ribs and even the BBQ meatballs, all of which can be ordered in a number of ways. Our group of four enjoyed the family-style salad, which was not just the standard lettuce and tomatoes but included hunks of cheese and pieces of Granny Smith apples as well. We tried variations on the rib, chicken and rib, and chicken dinners ($5.95 to $8.95), all of which came with a baked potato, and washed them down with ample amounts of beer. Other possibilities include BBQ country sausage with beans for $5.75, an overstuffed BBQ pork sandwich for $4.50 or a combination of ribs, meatballs and seafood for $9.95. Save room for the outstanding desserts, including the house specialty, apple strudel; there are also frozen Carioca rum pie, chocolate peanut butter pie, French cheesecake or Black Forest cherry torte, $1.50 to $2.50. There is nothing tired about John's food, which is also available for takeout beginning at noon daily. Lunch and dinner are served.

Trillium, the Sagamore, Bolton Landing. (518) 644-9400. This is probably the fanciest dining spot in the area. The chandeliered, columned room has an outdoor dining area overlooking the lake, where guests dine when the weather is warm. Inside all is elegant, with potted palms and soft lighting. Typical menu items ($18 to $25) include roast rack of lamb with mustard seeds and herbs; Atlantic salmon marinated in dill, flamed with aquavit and served with a mustard dill sauce, and mignonettes of beef in port wine and sweet garlic. Warm duckling salad, $8, or asparagus salad with truffles, $6, are typical accompaniments. The lunch menu, served May-October, is priced in the $10 to $15 range. Lunch, noon to 2:30; dinner, 6 to 9:30; closed Sunday.

Sutton's Country Cafe, Route 9, Glens Falls. (518) 798-1188. "Go to Sutton's for breakfast," we were advised by our waiter at the Log Jam, so we did. Arriving on Saturday morning about 9, we had to wait more than a half hour for a table. But those who wait have the pleasure of browsing in the large country store adjacent, with its bakery, green grocer, gift shop and clothing boutique. Tasteful items ranging from regional cookbooks to candles to homespun table linens to delectable baked goods make good purchases. And the heady aroma of breakfast items tantalizes the hungry. The restaurant is simple and contemporary, in contrast to the country store, with green-topped, wood-edged tables and simple wooden chairs, overhead ceiling fans and a cathedral ceiling. Small baskets of African violets are on the tables. Only the loudspeaker announcing the next party to be seated is off-putting at this extraordinarily popular spot. Diners may sit indoors, as we did, or outside on a terrace which can get a bit steamy if the day is warm. Juices are creative; we loved our strawberry-apple juice, all pink and frothy and reminiscent of a daiquiri, and our orange cream, orange juice whipped up with Ben & Jerry's vanilla ice cream — scrumptious! The breakfast menu is extensive, including "flap jacks" in various guises — plain, banana, blueberry, apple and chocolate chip. A Farmer's Stack is four pancakes layered with ham, sausage and bacon for $4.95. Eggs in omelets, with steak, breakfast meats or by themselves are

94

available, of course, and the home-baked goodies are legion — cider donuts, grilled raisin bread, fresh croissants, blueberry muffins. We OD'ed on grilled raisin toast and the muffins along with omelets served with wedges of watermelon on the plate. A sandwich and salad menu is most interesting at lunch time. Breakfast, 7 to 11:30; lunch, 11:30 to 3.

Two restaurants we liked for their proximity to the water:

The Boardwalk, Amherst Street, (518) 668-3242. We had a late supper at the Boardwalk the night of the Fourth of July, and sat on the upstairs deck overlooking the docks and the lake. Furnished with white bentwood chairs and tables with red and white checkered oilcloths, the spot has a beer-garden feeling, and lots of young people imbibe by the pitcherful. A string of red light bulbs is hung overhead and there are marine lights on either side of the door leading to the upstairs lounge. Live music begins around 9:30. You can get hot dogs, hamburgers, barbecued spare ribs, fried scallops and chicken, among the meals priced from $3 to $10. While you munch, you enjoy the flickering lights on the water and, for us, since it was the Fourth, the informal fireworks display on the other side of the lake, as you wait (you do wait; service is slow). The Boardwalk definitely has a great location; food and service are secondary.

The Shoreline, off Beach Road, (518) 668-4644. We enjoyed a fine lunch along with a view of the lake from this contemporary restaurant, which opened in 1986 as an add-on to an old house by the water. An outdoor umbrellaed deck is popular. Cajun specialties are served at night. For lunch we had a Bird of Paradise salad — curried chicken in a pineapple shell with walnuts for $7.95 — which was outstanding, and a pasta salad with seafood, which was equally good. New Orleans Po' Boys — shrimp, soft-shell crab or oyster served in French bread — were $4.95. Tomato stuffed with shrimp at $4.95 was another lovely offering. While we were pleased with our meals, the restaurant was still in its shakedown phase and could not be adequately appraised.

Highly recommended, but a bit farther afield, is the **Friends Lake Inn** on Friends Lake in Chestertown, (518) 494-4251. This 100-year-old, antiques-filled inn overlooking Friends Lake is run by an energetic couple who restored the place in the early 1980s. Main-course offerings include sole with artichoke hearts, steak au poivre, beef Wellington and salmon with dill hollandaise. The red snapper en papillote is especially well regarded and the shrimp gamache, made with artichoke hearts, broccoli and simmered in vermouth and spices, is a favorite. Tempting desserts include bananas Foster, raspberry charlotte and double chocolate patent leather cake! Dinner nightly; Sunday brunch, 11 to 2.

FOR MORE INFORMATION: Lake George Chamber of Commerce, 312 Canada St., Lake George, N.Y. 12845, (518) 668-5755. The Chamber information booth is located south of the village on Route 9 (across from the road to Prospect Mountain).

Tour boat passes beneath Canadian span of Thousand Islands Bridge.

The Thousand Islands, N.Y.-Ont.

The quaint overhead "welcome" signs at the entrance to each village in the Thousand Islands region are distinctive:

Alexandria Bay's sign lights up in neon, a garish reminder of the resort heritage of this touristy village, which, though tacky, is endearingly so. The signs for Clayton and Gananoque are old-fashioned wood, reflecting a more low-key tradition. The small sign at the entrance to the hamlet of Rockport has a homemade look, evidence of a simpler way of life.

The Thousand Islands region is a watery venue of rocky, forested islands straddling two nations and marking the beginning of the storied St. Lawrence River as it leaves Lake Ontario to head northeast toward the Atlantic Ocean.

Many of the Thousand Islands — actually they number nearly 1,800 — are mere rocks with a tree, too small for habitation or more than a single cabin. Others are large enough for many cottages, and Wellesley Island contains a Victorian village, several state parks, a major resort and hundreds of summer homes.

The region's vacation centers are as varied as the islands themselves. The focus on the American side is Alexandria Bay, or Alex Bay as it's called; here is an old-fashioned, once-moneyed resort in the genre, perhaps, of the New Jersey shore. To the west is Clayton, its poor-boy cousin, a mecca for fishermen and campers.

The Canadian side is more low-key and more scenic. Its focus is Gananoque (Gan, as the locals call it), an up-and-coming town of inns and restaurants. To the east, tiny Ivy Lea and Rockport retain the look of a generation ago. In the heart of the area, Wellesley Island in New York and Hill Island in Ontario provide the bridge and highway links between the two nations and two very different shores.

Fishing and boating are the islands' chief attractions for many. Bass, northern pike and muskies keep the anglers happy, and no fewer than 75 sightseeing excursion boats ply the river waters.

You can rent a houseboat or ride a water taxi. Watch ocean-going freighters pass along the St. Lawrence Seaway. View the islands from the Skydeck tower or a touring airplane. Attend vesper services by boat. Take a shuttle boat to shop at the Boatcak on Bluff Island or to dine at a lodge on Carleton Island. Camp in a cabin on Canoe Island or a tent on Mary Island, and island-hop between campsites in Canada's St. Lawrence National Park.

You can visit North America's largest inland Shipyard Museum, see first-rate theater at a playhouse beside the water, take in the wonders of the Wellesley Island nature center, reminisce in the Victorian homes and ambience of Thousand Island Park, and enjoy the local Thousand Island salad dressing and River Rat cheese.

And everyone ogles Boldt Castle, the $2.5 million monument to a man's love and a broken heart on Heart Island, an omnipresent landmark off Alexandria Bay.

Just as the islands and towns vary, so do the people who visit or populate this busy summer vacation area. All types can find their place among the myriad islands and attractions of the mighty St. Lawrence.

Getting There

The Thousand Islands region is located approximately 100 miles north of Syracuse, 200 miles east of Toronto and 100 miles southwest of Ottawa. The closest nearby cities, Watertown, N.Y., and Kingston, Ont., are each about 30 miles away. Interstate 81 and the Trans-Canada Highway 401 are the main access routes to the area. The two soaring spans of the Thousand Islands International Bridge connect the American and Canadian shores (toll, $2).

Prices are quoted in local currency, and American funds stretch quite a bit farther in Canada.

Where to Stay

What you do and how you enjoy the Thousand Islands likely will depend on your choice of accommodations, which range from resort to motel to cabin to campsite. The area is highly seasonal, and generally battens down the hatches for the winter.

Resorts

Pine Tree Point, Alexandria Bay, N.Y. 13607. (315) 482-9911. This 30-year-old resort is on a 40-acre peninsula thick with pines, and has what we consider the most enticing public setting in the islands. Still personally overseen by the founding Thomson family and situated off by itself away from town, the 83-room complex has a main inn with 21 guest rooms, a cocktail lounge and several dining rooms (see Where to Eat), plus motel-style buildings (many with idyllic waterfront balconies), a picturesque outdoor dining terrace beside a quiet cove for boats and a shady pool area. The corner Victorian room and the 22 balconied Cliffs units at water's edge are most prized, but even the more modest rooms without water views have television and share the verdant setting. Doubles, $52 to $110. Open May to mid-October.

Thousand Islands Club, Wellesley Island, N.Y. (315) 482-2551. This venerable Mediterranean-style resort has undergone several incarnations in its 86 years, recently as a Treadway inn and then as the Thousand Islands Resort; it is emerging grandly again as the Thousand Islands Club and Conference Center, thanks to a $3.5 million expansion and refurbishing by new owners, seven investors from Syracuse. They first renovated the aging public rooms, then built 64 contemporary villa units which could be mistaken for condos along the golf course greens, and planned to remodel the 44 hotel rooms (which could use a sprucing up) for the 1987 season. Expanded marina facilities, an 18-hole golf course, tennis and a large heated pool are attractions. The large dining room has been stylishly done over (see Where to Eat), and there's nightly entertainment. Doubles, $68 to $108. Open mid-May to mid-October.

Glen House Resort and Motel, Thousand Islands Parkway, Box 10, Gananoque, Ont. K7G 2T6. (613) 659-2204. The Canadian side's largest resort, this rustic complex sprawls in motel-style on either side of the main turn-of-the-century Glen House along the quiet riverfront, well away from the parkway. Most of the 70 nicely furnished rooms with color TVs have water views. There are a heated pool at river's edge as well as an indoor pool and sauna, and a dining room and cocktail lounge with panoramic views. Doubles, $62 to $80. Open year-round.

Edgewood Resort, Box 218, Alexandria Bay, N.Y. 13607. (315) 482-9922. Occupying its own 75-acre peninsula across the bay from downtown, the Edgewood has 160 rooms in a variety of motel-style buildings clustered around a lively central clubhouse. The waterfront rooms are as sought-after as those at the more sedate Pine Tree Point. The heart-shaped pool, three cocktail lounges and nightly entertainment set a young-at-heart theme, and the weekend specials — a Friday night seafood buffet, the Saturday night all-you-can-eat prime rib buffet ($13.95 per person) and two Sunday brunches ($8.50 in the dining room, $10 with unlimited champagne in the Gazebo) — pack them in. Doubles, $50 to $90. Open early May to mid-October.

Bonnie Castle Resort, Holland Street, Box 219, Alexandria Bay, N.Y. 13607. (315) 482-4511. Under the auspices of Baldwinsville muffler-chain owner Don Cole, the old Holland estate has blossomed into "the showplace of the Thousand Islands" (its words). The emphasis is on big-name entertainment (Al Martino and Les Elgart, when we visited) in the new Showplace of the Stars nightclub. The Chandelier Terrace dining room, right over the water, is glamorous and glitzy, the nightclub is noisy and the bar between the two is crowded. We were reminded of Atlantic City, without the jingle of the slot machines. A new luxury "hotel" (its words) is really a motel with 100 spacious rooms (each with wet bar, some with heart-shaped tubs) set back from the river overlooking parking lots, a pool and roofs of a boatyard and marina. And, spare us, please, there's a tanning bed in the beauty center, and a replica of the Statue of Liberty on the grounds. Doubles, $90 to $135. Open year-round.

Inns

The Athlone Inn, 250 King St. West, Gananoque, Ont. K7G 2G6. (613) 382-2440. A red brick and gingerbread structure built in 1874 houses the region's best dining room (see Where to Eat) and four elegant guest rooms, each sumptuously furnished in Victoriana with poster beds and sitting areas.

At the side are six well-appointed motel rooms. Each room has an eagle over the bed, television, good reading lamps and enough personal touches to show that innkeepers Gerald and Barbara Schothuis care as much for their overnight guests' comfort as they do for their diners' palates. Doubles, $50 to $80. Open year-round.

Ivy Lea Inn, Thousand Islands Parkway, Lansdowne, Ont. K0E 1L0. (613) 659-2329. A rustic cocktail parlor with blazing hearth, a nautical wraparound dining room, a riverside cocktail terrace, great grounds and the care of the Dekker family make this inn-motel-cottage complex appealing. One of the few local places built as an inn, the century-old main lodge has 11 upstairs rooms, rather spartan and some with the original bedsteads, some with private baths and all quaintly un-color coordinated. More comfortable are the 12 units in the motel, off by itself with the river beyond the pool, or the eight cottages set back in the trees along a stretch of the 2,000-foot waterfront, which has a concrete fishing pier and an impressive swimming area with freestanding diving platform. Old-fashioned arrow signs point the way to the mini-store, the game room and other attractions. Doubles, lodge $28 to $45; motel, $42 to $52; cottages, $310 to $525 a week. Open April to mid-October.

Gananoque Inn, 550 Stone St. South, Gananoque, Ont. K7G 2G6. (613) 382-2200. Nicely situated on the river a few blocks south of downtown, this complex has 30 rooms in the 100-year-old main structure plus 20 motel units. Most popular are the 14 new waterfront units, as well as the inn rooms with brass beds and balconies. Private baths, TV and air-conditioning are modern touches in a building that otherwise shows its age. There's a gorgeous outdoor cocktail deck, as well as a large cocktail lounge in the rustically old-school motif. Doubles, $60 to $125. Open year-round.

Bach's Alexandria Bay Inn, 2 Church St., Alexandria Bay, N.Y. 13607. (315) 482-9697. Super-keen fishing enthusiast Virginia Bach had been coming here for years from New Jersey to participate in her favorite sport. In 1986 she took the plunge and bought the old Dixie Inn, now running it with her son Robert — and, of course, has little time to go fishing anymore. This is the area's first real B&B and the somewhat decrepit Victorian house, the village's oldest extant building, is being nicely redone. The enthusiastic Mrs. Bach serves continental breakfast with homemade rolls and breads in the morning and afternoon lemonade or tea in the living room or on the wicker-filled side veranda. Antiques, an 1856 encyclopedia set, a Persian rug and new lavender carpeting are caring touches. Eight of the ten rooms have private baths. Mrs. Bach scorns linens from a linen service (as do we) and provides pretty patterned sheets and properly large, thirsty and colorful towels. Doubles, $50 to $100. Open year-round.

St. Lawrence Grande, 9 Market St., Alexandria Bay, N.Y. 13607. (315) 482-9877. The sign in front of the long front porch was the suavest thing about this old inn under new ownership in 1986. The breakfasts are great, with 16 omelets priced from $1.95 to $3.75; our breakfast for two on the porch added up to a bargain $5.03. The two dining rooms are plain, the bar often noisy and the crowd young, as you might expect from a look at some of the 18 rooms. Seven have private baths and all are somewhat threadbare and reached via a maze of hallways. Doubles, $45.

Thousand Islands Inn, 335 Riverside Drive, Clayton, N.Y. 13624. (315)

686-3030. Built in 1897 across the main street from the river, this three-story place is popular with fishermen and advertises all kinds of fishing packages. The 18 rooms vary; 13 have private baths and television and the rest are "just sleeping rooms," according to the manager. The pleasantly rustic dining room has received Silver Spoon awards. Doubles, $33 to $40. Open mid-May to mid-October.

Riverhead Lodge, Carleton Island, Box 142, Cape Vincent, N.Y. 13618. (315) 639-3311. Fishing and hunting packages are the chief attraction here, but the 1880s lodge at the head of Carleton Island also advertises overnight accommodations and gourmet dining for transients. Up to 10 overnight guests can be housed and dine together around an old mission oak table. Free boat transportation to the island is offered by reservation for outside parties of four to twelve for dinners — six courses with wine for $30 per person. Lodging, $80 per person, MAP. Open May-November.

Motels

Capt. Thomson's Motor Lodge, end of James Street, Alexandria Bay, N.Y. 13607. (315) 482-9961. The Thomson family which also owns Pine Tree Point and the Uncle Sam Boat Lines runs this motel, where the riverfront (Main Channel) rooms are blessed with an unbeatable location right over the water with a view across to Boldt Castle. As you watch all the boating activity or take in the sunset, the waves lap at the rocks and birds land on your private balcony (and at one point the hook — with worm — on the fishing line of the young lad fishing from the balcony next door swung around and imbedded itself in our balcony as well). The 117 rooms are spacious and comfortable; ours had a full bathroom with an extra sink, but also had those dreadful skimpy linen-service towels that you can almost read through. There's a pool out front beside the parking lot. Doubles, $45 to $85. Open May to late October.

Riveredge Resort, 17 Holland St., Alexandria Bay, N.Y. 13607. (315) 482-9917. If advertising billboards everywhere make a difference, the Riveredge would win hands down. It's evolved from a pancake house (great breakfasts) to an open steak pit (acclaimed barbecues) to a motel with treed grounds and a pleasant pool and a hot tub. "Resort" is a misnomer, however, for this is really a motel with 82 riverfront rooms, a few facing the open river but the rest on the harbor. All are air-conditioned and have cable TV. Doubles, $69 to $88. Open mid-April through October.

The Ledges Resort Motel, Box 245, Alexandria Bay, N.Y. 13607. (315) 482-9334. Its location set back from the riverfront near Pine Tree Point rates this 24-unit motel a cut above many of the Bay's others. The swimming pool has a water slide, and guests can fish from the docks. Doubles, $48 to $78. Open May to mid-October.

Torchlite Motel, Box W451, Wellesley Island, N.Y. 13607. (315) 482-3550. Eighteen comfortable motel and efficiency units are available at this secluded waterfront location, on Wellesley Island almost under the American span of the Thousand Islands International Bridge. The view is what sells the place, although a free continental breakfast and a pool help. Doubles, $54 to $64. Open mid-May to mid-September.

West Winds Motel & Cottages, Route 12E, RD2, Box 56, Clayton, N.Y. 13624. (315) 686-3352. Sloping lawns down to the river, an attractive pool and fairly sprightly motel furnishings make this a good bet in the Clayton area. Twelve motel units have one or two beds, and there are eight good-looking efficiency cabins and housekeeping cottages, two near the water. Doubles, $40 to $45; cottages, $45 to $55. Open mid-May through September.

RENTALS. Island cottages and houses can be rented, through private auspices or real-estate brokers. Efficiency cabins by the week or month abound on both the American and Canadian mainlands; rentals are generally $250 to $500 a week. R. Kemp Realty at 39 Church St., Alexandria Bay, N.Y., (315) 382-9241, and at 507 Riverside Drive, Clayton, N.Y., (315) 686-3409, is the islands' largest realtor.

Houseboats can be rented for $375 to $1,400 a week from Remar Rentals, 510 Theresa St., Clayton, N.Y.; Rebob Houseboat Rentals in Rockport, Ont., or Houseboat Holidays Ltd., R.R. 3, Gananoque, Ont.

Camping

STATE PARKS. Some of New York State's finest parks are in this area and offer campsites among their facilities. Wellesley Island State Park, (315) 482-2722, is by far the largest, with 438 campsites and a public golf course. From a marina here you can rent a boat to get to campsites on Canoe or Mary islands. One of the more pleasant sites is Keewaydin State Park, (315) 482-3331, a 179-acre former private estate sloping down to the river west of Alexandria Bay and boasting an Olympic-size pool and a marina among its amenities. (It's also the headquarters of the Thousand Islands regional state park office, where camping reservations are computerized through Ticketron).

Those who prefer not to rough it in tent or camper may rent cabins by the week at DeWolfe Point and Canoe Island. At DeWolfe Point State Park, (315) 482-2012, where one of our families spent many a happy vacation in the 1950s, 14 two-room cabins for four are scattered along the Lake of the Isles shoreline. They're basic and bare, with nothing more than refrigerator, bunk beds and two electric lights. Weekly rentals are $62 and the cabins are fully booked for the summer by a January lottery drawing.

Among the larger private campgrounds are the Ivy Lea KOA in Lansdowne, Ont., (613) 659-2817, and the Rockport Camping and Trailer Park in Rockport, Ont., (613) 659-3402, each with 120 sites. The Jolly Oaks Island Park at Fine View, Wellesley Island, N.Y., (315) 482-2424, has 110 sites with dockage available.

Limited camping is offered in St. Lawrence Islands National Park, Canada's smallest national park, which consists of 19 islands and Mallorytown Landing on the mainland northeast of Rockport.

Seeing and Doing

The water, and the islands, are the lure. The passing traveler might wonder what the attraction is, since you really have to get onto the river to see the islands and sense their mystique.

On the Water

BOAT TOURS are the thing in the Thousand Islands, and 77 tour boats from six cruise lines offer 90-minute to five-hour trips of up to 52 miles as often as every hour in season. Sometimes it seems there are more tour boats than private craft in this area seemingly made for powerboats (sailing vessels are far less in evidence — about as numerous as the enormous lakers and ocean-going freighters plodding to and from the Great Lakes through the St. Lawrence Seaway via the American Narrows off Alexandria Bay).

Tour boats vary in size and length of trip. Some, particularly **Ivy Lea** and **Rockport** lines in Canada and **Paul Boat Lines** in Alexandria Bay, boast of small boats that go where the larger ones can't. The three-decker **Gananoque Boat Line** vessels and the two-deck **Uncle Sam Boat Lines** boats out of Alexandria Bay let people move around for various vantage points. High points are the millionaires' row cottages around Alex Bay, the Canadian palisades area where the greenish waters are 250 feet deep, and some of the smaller, fancily landscaped islands containing a single home and boathouse; youngsters might get bored after awhile, but we enjoyed hearing all the tidbits about who owned the houses and islands. Tour prices are in the $7 to $9 range and include unlimited stopovers at Boldt Castle.

Boldt Castle on the appropriately named Heart Island was to be the testimony of the love for his wife of George C. Boldt, a Prussian immigrant who became the most successful early hotel magnate in America, owning the Waldorf-Astoria in New York and the Bellevue-Stratford in Philadelphia. He had spent $2.5 million on a six-story, 150-room Rhineland-style castle with enormous boathouse and power plant when she died in 1904 — mysteriously. No one ever tells the cause, although our young boat guide suggested cancer. Work was stopped and visitors wander through the huge, empty rooms, imagining what might have been. The castle is reached by boat tours or water taxis from Alex Bay. Open daily, 10 to 6 July-August, 10 to 4:30 from mid-May and in September. Adults $2.25, children $1.50.

You also can see the Thousand Islands by water taxis, day sailing expeditions, U-Drive Boats, airplane tours and the 350-foot Thousand Islands skydeck on Hill Island (adults, $2.95). The best auto route is along the Thousand Islands Parkway on the scenic Canadian side, with beautiful vistas and frequent picnic spots; the American side, alas, is almost devoid of river views from the road.

FISHING is popular, from Alexandria Bay ("bass fishing capital of the world") to Clayton. Our boat tour guide said 85 species, from pan fish to sturgeon, have been caught, and the world's biggest muskie was landed in the Shoals region. Numerous guides lead fishing parties on chartered boats.

Half Moon Bay Vesper Services. Since 1887, non-denominational vesper services have been conducted by visiting ministers in a secluded bay off Bostwick Island near Gananoque. The congregation arrives and remains in small boats, including canoes, for an hour of hymns and meditation at 4:30 on summer Sundays amid a natural water setting gouged in granite by the glaciers. Water taxis leave by reservation, (613) 382-8058, at 4 from the Bay Street Dock in Gananoque.

Waterside Attractions

Thousand Islands Shipyard Museum, 750 Mary St., Clayton. (315) 686-4104. Started in 1964 as the outgrowth of the oldest antique boat show, this non-profit institution has grown into the largest freshwater maritime museum in the country. Boating enthusiasts have a field day exploring the rambling riverfront buildings containing all manner of wooden boats, the local St. Lawrence skiffs, old birchbark canoes, exotic yachts, runabouts, outboard motors and such. The more than 150 small craft show the ingenuity of builders in adapting to the tricky St. Lawrence waters, our informant said, and you'll marvel at the importance boating has had here over the years.

One yacht in the new Cleveland Dodge launch building rests on blocks so visitors can peer under as well as in via ramps. The Stroh beer family's commuter boat was being readied to go back in the water in 1987. The 1902 antique Elco glass cabin cruiser, the **Narra Mattah**, takes visitors for half-hour river rides three times a day in summer. There's a fine shop with books and nautical gifts.

Considered a sleeper with great potential as a destination site, the museum is well worth the $4 admission charge. Open mid-May to mid-October, daily in summer, 10 to 5.

Minna Anthony Common Nature Center, Wellesley Island State Park. Eight miles of trails and walkways crisscross through 600 acres of wooded wetlands, marshes, swamps and rocky knobs for closeup views of varied wildlife — perhaps a thorny porcupine in a tree, or beavers splashing in ponds or white-tailed deer loping into the woods. The center's staff offers special trail hikes and nature walks. Perched on a plateau of the reddish-brown Potsdam sandstone characteristic of the area, the museum includes live collections of fish, reptiles and amphibians, plus mounted waterfowl and a beehive with live bees.

WATER DRAMA. The Thousand Islands Playhouse, fashioned from the old Gananoque Canoe Club building, is right on the river in Gananoque. In 1986 it celebrated its fifth season in an enlarged, 350-seat theater with five plays, one of which was the delightful "Have Some Madeira, M'dear" with the songs of Flanders and Swan. The cast is professional, curtain is at 8:30 and tickets, $9. Also popular in 1986 were the **River Barge Productions,** hour-long touring shows featuring New York and North Country actors in an original musical titled "The Slick of '76," a 10-year look back at the 1976 oil spill in the Thousand Islands.

Thousand Island Park. Founded in 1875 as a church colony, this slice of Victoriana at the west end of Wellesley Island is on the National Historic Register and reminiscent of the campground at Oak Bluffs on Martha's Vineyard. It's well worth a visit for a look at the colorful old cottages and the spacious green, and a stop at the boutiques upstairs in the restored Wellesley Hotel or the ice cream parlor across the street.

For the Youngsters. The Thousand Islands Wild Kingdom on the north side of Gananoque is one of the area's newer attractions. A baby black panther from India, snow monkeys from Japan, and a 380-pound Siberian tiger are among the more unusual animals, birds and reptiles, viewed from a nature walk blending cages and animal pods with the landscape. Open daily 9 to 7; admission, $5. **Water Fun Village,** an elaborate new complex of amusement rides, shops and restaurants at the foot of the Thousand Islands Bridge in Collins Landing, N.Y., was closed suddenly in 1986 because of insurance liability problems, but hoped to reopen.

SHOPPING is not among the area's strengths. There are no boutiques or galleries, unless you consider **La Boutique** and the **Riverbarge Gallery** in Alexandria Bay examples of their genre. Instead, Alex Bay is full of ice cream parlors, candy stores, trinket, T-shirt and curio shops, and an arcade. The Hill Island discount stores leave much to be desired, and Gananoque holds few bargains, though some Americans are intrigued by Canadian stores and you may buy English china and woolens at prices lower than in the States. The Gold Cup Farms store at 528 Riverside Drive in Clayton is worth a visit; we bought the local River Rat cheddar cheese (the extra-sharp is great) and tried a couple of the sensational truffles which come packed in an egg carton. For a different experience, try the Boateak, a shop above owner Cookie and Matt Tomaivoli's boathouse on Bluff Island off Clayton. Reached via a shuttle boat by appointment, it features American arts, crafts and antiques, including Sid Bell wildlife jewelry, stuffed animals and pierced lampshades.

Where to Eat

Dining in the Thousand Islands region tends to the surf-and-turf syndrome with, surprisingly, Maine lobster and prime rib heading the list. Local fish is rarely on restaurant menus; even Thousand Island dressing is seldom mentioned. For the best dining, knowledgeable locals head for Gananoque.

The Best for Food

The Athlone Inn, 250 King St. West, Gananoque, Ont. (613) 382-2440. Tops on gourmands' list for two decades is this charming Victorian inn, personally run by Dutch chef-owner Gerald Schothuis. His two ornate, high-ceilinged dining rooms are handsomely appointed in burgundy and pink with rose and white china, cream-colored lace curtains, a large tapestry and velvet draperies between the two rooms. Chef Gerald calls his dinner menu French-continental, with the emphasis decidedly on the French. Start with his house pate or French onion soup before trying the likes of poached salmon with hollandaise, Dover sole meuniere, scallops and mushrooms in wine sauce, veal cordon bleu or entrecote Paris (entrees, $13.95 to $18.95). Meringue glace, pear Helene and parfait Athlone (Haagen-Dazs vanilla with Baileys Irish cream and whipped cream) are worthy endings. The wine list is mainly French. Although the prices are higher than most in the area, so are the results. Dinner nightly, 5 to 10; closed Monday October-April and month of November.

The Grand McCammon Inn, 279 King St. West, Gananoque, Ont. (613) 382-3368. Almost across the street from the venerable Athlone is a promising newcomer, which opened in the summer of 1986 in a magnificently restored 1872 red-brick house. An elegant parlor, two handsome dining rooms linked by a grand piano and a veranda for outdoor dining overlooking the lovely rear gardens are the setting for appealing fare from a wide-ranging menu. For starters, consider chilled strawberry and rhubarb soup, baked brie or rumaki; for entrees ($8.95 to $19.95), lemon chicken, baked salmon with dill and watercress, pepper steak or beef Wellington. There are pastas for dinner, and the lunch menu is one of the area's few that's "with it," as is the wine list. Co-owners Ray Crosby and Gary Cousins hoped eventually to offer overnight lodging. Lunch and dinner daily except Wednesday.

Golden Apple Inn, 45 King St. West, Gananoque, Ont. (613) 382-3300. A gray stone building with gray and yellow trim dating to 1830 has been home to a local dining tradition since 1928, and we doubt that the menu has changed much over the years. The two older dining rooms in particular are terribly quaint, and the garden terrace with different-colored umbrellas couldn't be nicer. Old-fashioned, home-style cooking and meals are the rule: roast leg of lamb with mint sauce, ham steak with pineapple ring, roast chicken with dressing and gravy, accompanied by vegetables or stewed apples, sticky buns and tea biscuits, followed by pie squares, rice pudding or Grandma's apple nut cake. You get the idea, and traditionalists love it. Complete dinners are $15.95 to $19.95; a la carte lunches (which are more like dinners), $5.95 to $8.95. There's a standard beverage list. Lunch, noon to 2; dinner, 6 to 8:30; closed Tuesdays and mid-October to mid-May. No credit cards.

Wellesley Hotel, Thousand Island Park, Wellesley Island, N.Y. (315) 482-9400. Thank goodness for this charming summery spot in a restored 1903 hotel. Reopened by Rochester school teacher Jim Finger in 1984, it has the American side's most interesting restaurant, some small and unusual boutiques upstairs and four spartan but serviceable guest rooms. Candles glow, classical music plays, formally attired staff serve and there's a wondrous blend of the up-to-date with yesteryear. Chef Myla Seitz offers the regional standards (beef and lobster) on one side of the limited menu; she gets creative with her four nightly specials. Our dinner began with a complimentary dish of vegetables: olives with fennel seeds, pasta salad with pecan shrimp, carrots in raspberry vinaigrette, celery with liver pate and marinated cauliflower, followed by a hot, oversize loaf of bread and a mixed salad with choice of raspberry or orange vinaigrette or champagne dressing. The specials of linguini with seafood and basil and brochette of scampi were accompanied by snow peas and a garlicky zucchini-almond concoction. We wished they hadn't run out of the whipped applejack mousse; it probably would have been better than the kahlua torte. The wine list is reasonable and well-chosen. Lunch, Tuesday-Saturday 11:30 to 2:30; dinner, Monday-Saturday, 5 to 9; Sunday brunch, 11 to 2.

Thousand Islands Club, Wellesley Island, N.Y. (315) 482-2551. Under new owners, the pretty dining room alongside a super terrace beside the water and a pool has been upgraded with new tableware and linens and a more innovative menu. Carpaccio, baked oysters Remick and a pastry shell of escargots, chopped tomatoes and snail butter are among appetizers. For entrees ($12.95 to $19.75), consider crab stuffed shrimp with dill butter, lamb chops with a sauce of cognac and wild mushrooms or "operetta of seafood" (a Mediterranean stew). Dinner nightly, 6 to 10.

All-American Choices

The Clipper Inn, Route 12, Clayton, N.Y. (315) 686-3842. The locals think this modern restaurant beside the highway east of Clayton serves the best food on the American side. The interior is contemporary with stained glass, skylights, hanging plants and cane and chrome chairs at blue-linened tables. The menu offers something for everyone, from potato skins and nachos or shrimp cocktail to veggie Alfredo, veal parmesan, chicken Alaska, frog's legs and sole Oscar to kahlua parfait and key lime pie. Entrees are $8.95 to $21.95. Lunch in season, dinner 5 to 10, mid-May to November.

Cavallario's Steak and Seafood House, 24 Church St., Alexandria Bay, N.Y. (315) 482-9867. The other favorite of the locals is this large establishment with valet parking and ersatz medieval decor inside and out. The extensive menu includes pastas, blackened redfish, peppercorn swordfish and bouillabaisse amid a sea of beef and fish offerings, but Frank Cavallario says "most of the people come here for lobster and prime rib." Entrees are $12.50 to $22.50. Dinner nightly, 4 to 11, Sunday 1 to 10.

Admirals' Inn, James and Market Streets, Alexandria Bay, N.Y. (315) 482-2781. For casual dining, the wraparound sidewalk terrace here is popular. The menu is like most of the others in town (that is to say, uninspired), but you can find almost anything traditional from spaghetti to surf and turf. Lunch and dinner daily.

Down by the Riverside

Pine Tree Point, Alexandria Bay, N.Y. (315) 482-9911. We can think of no better setting for brunch than the outdoor terrace surrounded by pines and water or, for dinner, the small Sunset Room off the larger Voyageurs dining room at Pine Tree Point. Here, amid half a dozen tables, we watched freighters pass and the sun set as we warmed up at a mediocre salad bar and sampled an adequate rack of lamb and a filet mignon, each garnished with grapes and a good, zesty mix of tomatoes and zucchini. We thought the highly touted pastry cart ordinary, but liked the creme de menthe parfait, big enough for two and a bargain at $1.75. Choices ranged from $9.95 for chicken Kiev to $21.50 for beef and reef. Lunch, noon to 2; dinner, 6 to 10.

Bamford's, 504 Riverside Drive, Clayton, N.Y. (315) 686-3519. A sign in the window of its nondescript exterior indicates that you cannot see the dining room beyond the bar. If you enter, you'll find a pleasant enough room at the rear, with windows onto the St. Lawrence and a breezy outdoor deck, its picnic tables covered with oil cloth. For lunch, we found the bloody mary spicy, the chicken salad routine and the Philly steak sandwich special nothing like the grand and goopy creations you find in Philadelphia. But the prices are most reasonable, and as a dinner special they offered breaded Canadian smelt ($6.95), one of the few regional fish entrees we saw. Lunch and dinner daily.

The Gananoque Inn, 550 Stone St. South, Gananoque, Ont. (613) 382-2200. The best riverfront view in Gananoque is afforded from the dining room and a gorgeous outdoor cocktail deck with tables topped by yellow umbrellas. At noon, the food is standard: a good sandwich list, plus lunchy items from omelets ($3.95) to crab Louise ($6.95). We enjoyed a reuben and a chef's salad topped, appropriately, with Thousand Island dressing — it was the only time it was offered. At night, the two large dining rooms are gussied up with tall orange napkins in orange water glasses on white linen; each table had a potted begonia wrapped in tinfoil when we visited. Lunch and dinner daily. Open year-round.

Boathouse Restaurant, Rockport, Ont. (613) 659-2338. Right on the water in the placid hamlet of Rockport is this informal restaurant with outdoor deck, serving breakfast, lunch and dinner in an atmosphere of oilcloth-covered tables and lamps made of ship's steering wheels. Jimmy's fish-fry special includes two pieces of local white fish, french fries, cole slaw and rolls for $5.95. Sauteed salmon steak is $8.95, as is roast beef with gravy and all the trimmings. Afterward, stop downstairs at the ice cream bar for an 80-cent cone of tiger tail (described as black liqueur, orange sherbet and vanilla) or bubblegum ice cream.

FOR MORE INFORMATION: Thousand Islands International Council, Box 400, Alexandria Bay, N.Y. 13607, or Box 69, Lansdowne, Ont. K0E 1L0. In the U.S., phone (800) 8-ISLAND. Alexandria Bay Chamber of Commerce, Box 365, Alexandria Bay, (315) 482-9531. Gananoque Chamber of Commerce, 2 King St. East, Gananoque, Ont. K7G 2L7. (613) 382-3250.

Youngsters cavort in waters of Havana Glen.

Watkins Glen/Finger Lakes, N.Y.

"The Glen Is Back," the advertisements all around New York's Finger Lakes region proclaim.

They're referring to the Watkins Glen International racetrack, which is busy once again following its revival from a bankruptcy that nearly destroyed the illustrious resort status of the village of Watkins Glen when the track closed in 1980.

The ads might just as well be referring to the Watkins Glen area as a whole. The area, blessed with a scenic location at the foot of the most sparkling of the Finger Lakes and poised between booming Ithaca to the east and Corning to the southwest, is a slumbering giant reawakening.

It's long had its natural attractions — Seneca Lake, towering waterfalls, awesome gorges and placid glens. In the last decade, it has developed an unusual concentration of small wineries. And now the home of auto road racing is back on track for race-car enthusiasts.

There's a new dynamic in an area that has seen better days.

It started in 1983 with Timespell, a million-dollar outdoor laser and sound show that draws upwards of 1,000 people a night into the lower depths of the Watkins Glen State Park gorge. It continued a year later with the opening of Seneca Market, a bonanza of shops and eateries in an old machine shop complex on the Seneca Lake waterfront, and with the resumption of auto racing at the renovated Watkins Glen racetrack under the aegis of Corning Glass Works. It mounted in 1985 with the opening on the lakefront of a 75-slip marina and a 330-foot-long fishing pier crowned with a Victorian gazebo.

The pace heightened in 1986 with a new excursion boat serving Seneca Lake, the restoration of a dilapidated hotel in neighboring Montour Falls, planning for a 150-room lakefront hotel, and the sprucing up of a decaying downtown with plantings, cobblestone walkways and Victorian-style street lamps.

The problem of housing visitors adequately is just being addressed. Schuyler County, of which Watkins Glen is the county seat, had 35 lodging establishments, but all were built prior to 1960 and look it. A dozen or more small bed-and-breakfast establishments have popped up in the last five years. But until the $1.5 million Montour House restoration provides 30 European-style hotel rooms in Montour Falls and a private developer builds the Watkins Glen waterfront hotel — or a savvy chain motel operator enters this area where the only non-indigenous establishment is a lonely Burger King — visitors will find the lodging and restaurant pickings rather slim.

That's unfortunate, because, as Sandy Schmanke, co-owner of the Red House Country Inn in nearby Burdett, says: ''The southern Finger Lakes are a paradise untapped.'' And Watkins Glen is at the heart of it all.

Getting There

Watkins Glen is at the southern end of Seneca Lake, longest of the Finger Lakes, about 80 miles southeast of Rochester and 75 miles southwest of Syracuse. From the New York Thruway, take Route 14 south from Geneva. Watkins Glen also can be reached from the south via Route 14 off the Route 17 expressway at Horseheads-Elmira.

Where to Stay

Accommodations are varied but limited, considering the vast numbers of visitors to this area in summer and early fall.

Motels and Lodges

Glen Motor Inn, Route 14, Box 44, Watkins Glen 14891. (607) 535-7262. The area's only modern, full-service motel, this has 40 comfortable units in two buildings separated by a swimming pool and a third building one level higher. Located down a sharp hillside and shielded from the highway above, they overlook a parking area and the lake below in the distance. Thirty units have balconies, and all have color cable television (rare for the area). Run by five generations of an Italian family, the motel started with a two-bedroom flat rented for $3 a couple in 1937, says owner Helen Franzese, who's proud that 12 Franzese grandchildren work in the motel or adjacent restaurant. She's also proud of the racers pictured in the motel-restaurant lobby; "we've been catering to celebrities since the first race in 1948," says she. "I'm the momma to all the racers." Doubles, $60 to $65. Closed in winter.

Rainbow Cove Resort Motel and Restaurant, Route 14, Himrod 14842. (607) 243-7535. Twenty-four rooms in two structures have patios or balconies and access to lovely grounds leading to the lakefront across Plum Point Road. Our room in the original one-story section built about 1950 was smaller than the rooms in the "deluxe" two-story section built about 1970. Having access to the lake and an impressive pool behind the restaurant are distinct pluses; a TV set that gets only one channel is not. The restaurant is known for good prix-fixe dinners served family style at 7 for $8; at breakfast, others are likely to join your table as well. Longtime owner Dot Plubell may tell you the story of how the original house and the Four Chimneys winery homestead up the road were part of a Hollywood retreat envisioned by Mary Pickford and Douglas Fairbanks Jr. Doubles, $37 to $44. Open May-October.

Chalet Leon Motel-Resort, Route 414, Box 388, Watkins Glen 14891. (607) 546-7171. Hector Falls is right beside this eleven-room motel and nine rustic cottages above Seneca Lake. The two-story motel has large rooms with full baths and television; the cottages have showers but no tubs. The roar of the falls lulls to sleep all except those in one northside room to which we were assigned. Steep paths lead to the three cascades of Hector Falls, to picnic tables and all the way down to the lakefront, which has a dock, beach and a canoe. A continental breakfast is served in the main building. Doubles for motel, $35 to $55, cabins $29 to $45.

Seneca Lodge, South Entrance to Watkins Glen State Park, Watkins Glen 14891. (607) 535-2014. In the late 1940s, lawyer Donald Brubaker quit his practice after his wife died and bought the former White City Tourist Camp, added a log restaurant-bar and called it Seneca Lodge. He and his sons have run it since, and his sister Mary Cobean registers guests at the front desk. The complex across from the state park's South Entrance bears a faint resemblance to a national park lodge. Nestled in the woods away from the road are 20 motel units in two strips opening onto shared front decks, plus A-frame housekeeping chalets and upwards of 40 cabins that have seen better days. To the rear are tennis courts and an appealing spring-fed swimming pool; to the front are a crowded lodge-style restaurant and an enormous bar popular with racers. The motel rooms are large and comfortable. Everything appealed until we found the TV set barely received two channels and those marginally, a neighboring family noisily barbecued hamburgers on our common deck, and another young group partied outside our window until 2 in the morning. Doubles in cabins, $24; motel, $38. Open seasonally.

Inns and B&Bs

The Red House Country Inn and Store, Picnic Area Road, Burdett 14818. (607) 546-8566. Joan Martin and Sandy Schmanke left careers in Rochester to open their charming B&B inn in an 1844 farmhouse in the Hector National Forest. Indeed, they and their guests are the only humans in this preserve full of birds and wildlife. Three goats, four dogs, a donkey and chickens are part of the entourage; so is a fine gift shop, one of three the pair operate (others are the Country Store along Route 14 in Hector and a section of the Morning Glory Cafe in Watkins Glen). Five lovingly furnished guest rooms share four baths, two up and two down, each outfitted with perfumes, powders and soaps. Guests sip sherry in the living room, make snacks in a guest kitchen and savor the restful life on a wicker-filled veranda. By advance reservation the innkeepers will serve dinner (for a bargain $14, country vegetable chowder, cheese muffins, salad with poppyseed dressing, roast Long Island duckling with fresh raspberries or beef bourguignon, and butter pecan tart or six-inch-high Viennese cheesecake, plus Hazlitt or Wagner wines and dessert sherry). Hearty breakfasts start with local melon with raspberries, pumpkin or lemon yogurt bread, eggs with slab bacon and the partners' own jellies and jams. Chairs are scattered around the five acres of lawns and gardens; party games are the entertainment at night. Doubles, $32 to $55. Open year-round.

The 1819 Red Brick Inn, Route 230, RD 2, Box 57A, Dundee 14837. (607) 243-8844. The winemaker and general manager of Glenora Wine Cellars, Raymond J. Spencer, bought this striking red Federal farmhouse with 15-inch-thick brick walls specifically to open a B&B in 1984. Guests have the run of two antiques-filled parlors, an upstairs Vintage Room for games and reading, and a family dining room in which breakfasts featuring grape juice, sausages made by Ray's father, and eggs or pancakes are served. They also can view in his cool, clean cellar the new Barrington Champagne Co., which he thinks is the smallest commercial winery in the state and the only one devoted exclusively to the "method champenoise" production of sparkling blanc de blancs. "A purer, more natural wine will not be found anywhere," says he; tours and tastings are by appointment only. Two of the four upstairs bedrooms have private baths. The Burgundy Room has a huge oak bedstead and rocking chairs; the Bordeaux has lovely hand-stenciling and a grapevine wreath. All the rooms are tastefully decorated and accented with grape art and handmade quilts. Doubles, $46. Open year-round.

The Muse, 5681 Middle Road, Horseheads 14845. (607) 739-1070. Way out in the middle of nowhere in the hills above Montour Falls is the 1838 family home of Dick Castor, an Elmira dentist and Montour Falls school board member, his wife Diana and four children. When the last of the children left the nest in August 1986, the Castors decided to share three bedrooms in their large and country-elegant home, a carriage house they moved to the site and 10 acres of grounds with B&B guests. The home is a lived-in masterpiece, from its stenciled walls and period antiques to early rope beds and a welcoming entry room that could be straight out of a house museum. Diana Castor serves fruit drinks in the afternoon, an evening candlelight snack and a full breakfast with french toast or an egg and cheese casserole, plus granola. The three bedrooms share one bath. The rooms are large and meticulously furnished with Sheraton highboys, old coverlets and Williamsburg wallpapers. The Hearth Haus across the road has a living and kitchen area and a loft bedroom; a gazebo and patio are out back. The property includes a pond with a cable-swing, gorgeous gardens, a tennis court and hiking trails. Doubles, $55 to $85; Hearth Haus, $110. Open year-round.

Willow Cove, Glenora-on-Seneca, RD 4, Box 87, Dundee 14837. (607) 243-8482. Who could want a more fortuitous location, directly on the expansive lakefront in a family compound with the Glenora Glen falls as a restful backdrop? George and Jean Van Heusen have run a B&B since 1984 in a house built in 1828 as the Glenora Inn. You'd barely know it, although the four third-floor guest rooms sharing one bath remain as they were when her grandparents bought it in the 1920s. Coffee cake, muffins and cereal are served at a huge, lace-cloth-covered table in the formal dining room or outside on an open porch. Above the lower floor is a large living room with fireplace and a super porch for viewing the lake. The third-floor Canopy Room has windows stretching to the floor and you can hear the waterfall behind the house across the road. Rooms are simply but nicely furnished. Guests may use the spacious lawns and the picnic table with a grill beside the water. Doubles, $32. Open April-October.

Glenora Guests, Glenora Road, RD 4, Box 77, Dundee 14837. (607) 243-7686. Just up the road from the lake, with a good view and access to the water below, is the columned home of Tess and Jack Wilgus, who opened it as a B&B in 1984. "Our home is their home," says peppy Tess, who chats with guests while sharing a bottle of Glenora wine on the pleasant porch looking down to the lake. Two double rooms and a single share one bathroom; they are furnished in homey style. "Jack always says the rooms are small but the breakfasts are big," says Tess with a laugh as she reels off a typical menu: juice, potatoes, bacon and sausage, scrapple, omelet and "sweet sticky buns for dessert," plus homemade tomato relish and seasoned cottage cheese. The upstairs den is comfortable for TV-watching. Doubles, $35.

Camping and Cottages

Campgrounds are numerous. **Warren W. Clute Memorial Park** at the southern end of Seneca Lake has complete facilities. Run by the village parks department (303 Franklin St., Watkins Glen 14891, 535-4438), it offers tent and trailer sites ranging from $6.25 for no hookups to $10.50 for full hookups; weekly and seasonal rates are available. **Watkins Glen State Park**, Route 14, Watkins Glen, 535-4511, has 305 campsites in forests above the gorge. South of town, campsites are available at **Havana Glen Park**, Route 14, Montour Falls, 14885, 535-9372, and the **Watkins Glen-Corning KOA**, Route 414 South, Watkins Glen, 535-7404. North of town are **Paradise Park Campground**, Route 14A, Reading Center 14876, 535-9969, and **Smith Park & Campground**, Peach Orchard Point, Hector 14841, 546-9911, with lakefront campsites at $9 daily and $55 weekly. Nine primitive campsites are available at the **Blueberry Patch Campground**, a wooded area next to five acres of blueberries in the Finger Lakes National Forest, Hector.

Five cottages on the lake are offered by **Pedlar Village**, Route 14, Watkins Glen, 546-9736. **Eagleridge**, Route 414, Lodi 14860, 582-6317, has camping and cottages on 75 wooded acres along Seneca Lake. Realtors specializing in lakefront properties include Shoemaker Real Estate, Franklin and Fourth Streets, Watkins Glen, 535-6613, and Strout Realty, 29 Millard St., Dundee 14837, 243-7419.

Seeing and Doing

The lake and the glens are foremost for many.

The longest and deepest of the Finger Lakes, Seneca Lake is flanked by hillsides that reach their peak at the southern end around Watkins Glen. Their steepness has prevented much of the cottage and commercial mishmash that mars the shoreline of more crowded Finger Lakes (namely Canandaigua and Keuka).

"Seneca Lake is quieter and less developed because of the cliffs," notes Mary Ellen Andrews, executive director of the Schuyler County Chamber of Commerce. "We rather like it that way."

The hillsides also make perfect growing sites for the vineyards and orchards that crisscross their slopes, creating an unforgettable canvas. Creeks that slice through crevices as they rush toward the lake have forged waterfalls and glens, no fewer than 400 in the southern Finger Lakes alone.

The Lake and the Glens

Watkins Glen State Park, Route 14, Watkins Glen. (607) 535-4511. This is the biggest and best-known of all the gorges. Stone walkways and trails traverse the gorge, which drops 700 feet in two miles from the park's upper entrance to the tunnel entrance in downtown Watkins Glen. Sometimes called the eighth wonder of the world, it has sheer cliffs, rock caverns, grottoes and 18 waterfalls and cascades that create the greatest pageant of waters in the East. It's an easy, though sometimes wet and slippery walk with about 800 steps, most at the lower end. For those who want to walk only one way, a shuttle bus ($2) runs between the two entrances every 15 minutes until 6 p.m. A shorter walk goes as far as the South Entrance. At the South Entrance, the state park has campsites and an Olympic-size swimming pool with a reported capacity of 2,000 people, for those who like crowds. The pool costs 50 cents for adults, 25 cents for children. Park open daily from 8 a.m. to 10 p.m., mid-May to mid-October. Parking fee, $2.50.

Timespell, White Water Development Corp., Franklin Street, Watkins Glen. (607) 535-4960 or 535-2466. Watkins Glen State Park comes alive at night in a $1 million sound and light extravaganza in which the audience is guided part way into the darkened gorge. With considerable pomp and circumstance, the show traces the history of the gorge through an inspired (if overly dramatic) documentary. Dinosaurs and lighting effects are splashed onto the darkened cliffs and waterfalls, and Aaron Copland music resounds from a sound system all around. Most visitors find what is advertised as the only outdoor show of its kind worth the tab, especially since the laser images became animated in 1986. Two shows nightly, first at dusk, second 45 minutes later, May-October. Admission, $4.

Other Falls. Four nearby falls and glens have their devotees, though fewer in number. **Chequagua Falls** tumbles 186 feet — just eight feet short of Niagara — into downtown Montour Falls and presents a startling sight at the end of the village's Main Street. Just south of Montour Falls is **Havana Glen,** a village park with 37 waterfalls. Here the visitor emerges after a two-minute walk into an open glen where youngsters wade in a pool and cavort behind a 75-foot-high waterfall. Along Seneca Lake are two other glens and falls, which are less accessible to the public. **Hector Falls** tumbles 165 feet in several cascades above and below Route 414 next to the Chalet Leon motel in Hector. The privately owned **Glenora Glen** meanders through cascades and swimming holes from Route 14 down to one last waterfall in the lakefront hamlet of Glenora.

Captain Bill's Seneca Lake Cruises, foot of Franklin Street, Watkins Glen.

(607) 535-4541. Hour-long boat cruises have been popular for years on the 50-foot mock steamer that lives up to its name, Stroller IV. They were augmented in 1986 by a sprightly blue and white double-decker vessel with a capacity of 150, the Columbia. It offers a two-hour lunch cruise, a three-hour dinner cruise, a late-evening cocktail cruise lasting past midnight on weekends, and even a teen dance cruise. Capt. Bill Simiele still gives 50-minute cruises hourly with a minimum of eight customers on the Stroller IV, hourly from 10 a.m. in summer. Columbia cruises by reservation: Lunch, Tuesday-Friday noon to 2, $15; dinner, Tuesday-Saturday 6 to 9, $24; weekend Dixieland brunch, noon to 2, $15. Stroller IV, adults $4.95; children $2.50. Season, May 15-Oct. 15.

BOATING. Sailing and powerboating are favorite sports in the Finger Lakes. Boaters can use the first 75 slips in the new Watkins Glen marina, which eventually will have 75 more, located next to Captain Bill's. Powerboats and sailboats may be rented from Glen Harbor Marina, Fourth Street at the canal. The Montour Falls Marina, one of the few civic projects of its kind, offers 175 docks and campsites shaded by willows, as well as access to Seneca Lake through the Seneca Lake Inlet canal.

SWIMMING. Swimmers who eschew the pool at Watkins Glen State Park will find the real thing — meaning cool, clear and deep water — in Seneca Lake. Fortunately, it is more accessible than are many of the Finger Lakes. The village operates W.W. Clute Memorial Park, named after the founder of the local salt industry that remains here and there in evidence, at the southern end of the lake. A stony beach (all the Finger Lakes shores are lined with rocks and gravel), a wooded picnic area and campsites across Route 414 are offered. Just up the lake in Hector is a secluded town beach and forested picnic grove at Smith Park, at the foot of Peach Orchard Point.

FISHING. Fishermen prize the lake trout, rainbows and Atlantic salmon among 35 varieties of gamefish that thrive in the deep waters of Seneca Lake. Catherine Creek, which spills through the area, also is known for its rainbows. Capt. Harvey R. O'Harra, 535-2390, conducts full or half-day fishing charter trips ("guaranteed fish") on an aluminum cruiser.

The Wineries

Seneca Lake's deep waters and steep hillsides have produced a winegrowing region that has been called "the American Rhineland." Since New York's Farm Winery Act of 1976 allowed vineyardists to bottle and sell wine, 11 wineries have opened on the southern half of Seneca Lake alone. They vary in size and stature, but all are relatively small and specialize in European and California-style viniferas rather than the fruity blends for which the Finger Lakes have been noted. All are open for wine tastings and sales, and some offer tours (new since the previous time we visited are $1 tasting charges levied by some — refundable with purchases — ostensibly to discourage freeloading tipplers).

Largest is **Wagner Vineyards** in Lodi, where owner-entrepreneur Bill Wagner has parlayed a spectacular vineyard setting overlooking the lake into an architecturally striking octagonal winery and the adjacent **Ginny Lee Cafe,** a tent-covered outdoor deck perfect for lunch or a snack and sipping wines at vineyard prices.

Across the lake, **Glenora Wine Cellars** specializes in prize-winning white viniferas and offers a short talk and tour. The new winery at the **Hermann**

J. Wiemer Vineyard is very small and very serious, and has many national awards to show for it.

Up the lake, the **Four Chimneys Winery** at Himrod produces organic wines, including an Eye of the Bee blend of Concord grape and honey. This unusual commune-style establishment has a new gourmet deli and hosts weekend chamber music concerts and candlelight dinners (see Where to Eat).

Two small wineries on the east side of the lake also are worth a visit. **Rolling Vineyards** in Hector, the closest to Watkins Glen, offers one of the best lake views, although there's no outdoor deck from which to enjoy it. Nearby, **Wickham Vineyards** has a deck but no lake view and offers a new haywagon tour of the vineyard.

Other Attractions

Bird and wildlife watching is offered in **Queen Catharine Marsh,** an 890-acre state-owned wetland, fish and wildlife preserve. It's accessible by boat, foot or car off the east side of Route 14 between Watkins Glen and Montour Falls.

Hiking and camping are popular in the **Finger Lakes National Forest,** which embraces 13,000 acres of wildlife and forestry management land in Hector. It has 25 miles of trails (part of the 650-mile Finger Lakes Trail network) for hikers and horseback riders.

Watkins Glen International, Box 500, Watkins Glen. (607) 974-7162 prior to June 1, (607) 535-2406 after June 1, or (800) 382-808. The widely known Watkins Glen auto races, which started on the village's hilly streets in 1948 and became world-famous with the annual Grand Prix in October, a three-day weekend of Formula One racing and bumper-to-bumper partying and drinking, ended in bankruptcy in 1980. A subsidiary of Corning Glass Works bought the hilltop racetrack four miles southwest of town in 1983 and invested more than $1 million in badly needed renovations. In 1986, four weekends of major road racing were scheduled, and races or entertainment of some kind were planned at the track every weekend in what was billed as the Glen's biggest season ever. The racing crowd, upon which the town so depends, is a mixed blessing. It fills the business coffers while despoiling the area's peace and quiet, imbuing the village with a schizophrenic character. Race schedule and prices vary each year.

Watkins Glen Racing Museum, 110 N. Franklin St., Watkins Glen. (607) 535-4202. Established in 1974, this is a small downtown museum with ten racing cars, classic engines, a model collection and historic photos and memorabilia. It's open daily from 10 to 5 in July and August and all race weekends. Adults $1, children 50 cents.

SHOPPING. The choices are limited, unless you go on wine-buying sprees as we do at the area vineyards. Otherwise, the best location is Watkins Glen's new **Seneca Market,** a keystone of the lakefront development envisioned by the Watkins Glen Tomorrow plan, which reflects the interests of the Rouse Company that designed it. The old three-story Frost Machine Shop building at the foot of Franklin Street and an adjacent courtyard and shed are alive with farm-market stands, fast-food eateries and souvenir shops of the ilk that appeal to youngsters. It does, however, offer some of the most interesting snack food in a town that generally lacks it. A treat for many is a large **Corning Glass Outlet Store** on East Third Street.

114

Where to Eat

This area is woefully lacking in good dining facilities. You can imagine the situation when some townspeople say the best dinners are to be had at a pizza parlor.

Food with a View

Seneca Landing Restaurant, at the Showboat Motel, Himrod. (607) 243-7434. Since acquiring the rundown Showboat Motel complex with 45 units in three buildings in 1984, suburban Syracuse school principal David Hoey and partner Jack Brown have upgraded the facility, especially the waterfront restaurant. You can't get closer to the water than the outdoor deck at Seneca Landing; why we were the only dinner patrons to eat outside one summer night we'll never know. The candlelit tables, the absence of bugs ("we have more trouble with flies inside," David conceded) and the placid water scene at dusk were memorable. The trout amandine and broiled pork chops, accompanied by salads with choice of six dressings, carrots and rice pilaf or french fries, were not especially memorable, but were priced right ($7.95 and $8.45, respectively). You can get anything from homemade chowders and soups to sandwich platters, spaghetti or strip steak on the dinner menu ($4.25 to $11.75). Reservations are accepted nightly except Friday, which is fish fry night, and David recommends highly the Hermann J. Wiemer Vineyard offerings on his wine list. Open daily in season, breakfast 7 or 8 to 11, lunch noon to 4 and dinner 5 to 9 or 10. Closed rest of year.

Ginny Lee Cafe, Wagner Vineyards, Route 414, Lodi. (607) 582-6450. The spacious tent-covered deck with view across vineyards and lake is idyllic as ever, even if the food isn't as creative as when we first visited after it opened in 1983. Gone are the weekend dinners and the scallops seviche and fettuccine primavera we recall so fondly. Never mind. The French bread with herb-flavored butter, the turkey croissant and a chef's salad laden with cheese, ham and turkey strips made a fine lunch. We lingered over a bottle of Wagner seyval for $4.50. And extraordinary as ever were the peach pie and cinnamon-flavored coffee, which you might need to get through the rest of the afternoon. Open Monday-Saturday 11 to 4:30, Sunday 2 to 5 and brunch, 10 to 2.

Glen Motor Inn Restaurant, Route 14, Watkins Glen. (607) 535-9776. The Franzese family has long been proud of their lake view from their spacious motel-style dining room and ebullient hostess-owner Helen Franzese likes to tell you about all the racing celebrities they've entertained over the years. But in 1986 host Patrick Franzese's emphasis was on the fresh seafood turned out by new executive chef Bernard Navarra, a veteran of San Diego waterfront restaurants. His fresh trout, salmon and tuna offerings were highly touted, as were the restaurant's traditional pasta and veal entrees. Entree prices run from $8.95 for chicken roasted a la mama Helen to $14.95 for steak and scampi. Open from 7:30 a.m. to 9 p.m.; closed in winter.

Rainbow Cove Restaurant, Plum Point Road, Himrod. (607) 243-7535. The family-style dinners served nightly at 7 have a loyal following among motel guests and residents, who say the food is well prepared and the best bargain around ($8 per, with children $3.50). The dining room with view across the lawn toward Seneca Lake is a mishmash of fancy Victorian draperies and oilcloth-covered tables. But the food is down-home good and plentiful, served on heaping platters and with seconds offered. The fixed menu changes daily: Tuesday is baked chicken night with mashed potatoes, gravy, rice, carrots, marinated beans, peas, pumpkin bread and fruited Jello. When we stayed, regular visitors from Westchester County were looking forward to the Wednesday night fare of lasagna and baked pork chops, finished off with sherbet. The roast beef and apple pie dinners offered Thursdays and Sundays are most popular hereabouts; the baked ham with scalloped potatoes on Mondays and Fridays is a close second. No liquor is served. Dinner at 7.

Other Choices

The French Quarter, at the Montour House, Main Street, Montour Falls. (607) 535-2494. Former Keuka Lake restaurateur Walter Jones moved his French Quarter restaurant to Montour Falls in 1986 as the first step in a $1.5 million restoration of the 1854 Greek Revival hostelry into a European-style luxury hotel with 30 large guest rooms, a restaurant and a gift shop. Only the downstairs was open when we visited in August 1986 and that was in a state of flux, the dining room having moved from place to place as renovation evolved. A canopied front porch offered dining tables with a view up the street to Chequaga Falls. The main L-shaped dining room was smartly outfitted with white linens, ironstone plates with a country French pattern and large wine globes. The dinner menu is continental with Cajun overtones — blackened redfish and shrimp Creole amid a parade of king crab Grenobloise, veal chasseur, scampi au vin and roast duck grand marnier ($10.95 to $18.50). The ice cream crepes are acclaimed, and bananas Foster is flambeed tableside for two. The extensive wine list is heavy on New York vintages. Lunch daily from 11; dinner from 5. Open year-round.

Seneca Lodge, South Entrance to Watkins Glen State Park, Watkins Glen. (607) 535-2014. No reservations are accepted and you may have to wait in the congenial Bench and Bar Tavern Room and listen to an authentic nickelodeon while waiting for dinner at the Seneca Lodge. Many locals think it has the best food in town; it certainly is the "real Watkins Glen," as one writer put it. The emphasis is supposed to be on natural foods and vegetables "for a way of life harmonious with the natural order of the universe," according to the brochure. We found the salad bar uninspired, the fresh breads good, the lamb kabob and chicken Kiev too much to eat, and the vegetables cooked beyond redemption. But the spacious and rustic lodge-style dining room is pleasant enough, dimly lit and full of local color — tables full of tourist brochures on one side, vintage posters of Formula One racers in a side room — and the prices are from yesteryear. Breakfast, lunch from 11:30 and dinner from 5 to 9 daily in season. Closed rest of year.

Morning Glory Cafe, 300 E. Fourth St., Watkins Glen. (607) 535-4408. A Victorian-style house with vine-shaded front porch is the setting for some of the area's best lunches and brunches. Homemade soups, salads, sandwiches and desserts are the fare; you might try the fruit bowl or veggie pasta, an apple cheese melt or shrimp salad, at prices from $2.50 to $4.95. We stopped for breakfast on the day when the two women owners were catering a breakfast cruise on the tourboat Columbia and their cafe was closed; we hear the croissant filled with mozzarella and mushrooms is delicious, and such desserts as chocolate or cinnamon croissants, Barbara's pie and Cindy's cheesecake irresistable. Open 9 to 3; closed Monday.

Scuteri's Pizzeria and Ristorante Italiano, 400 N. Franklin St., Watkins Glen. (607) 535-4254. Take-out pizzas and submarine sandwiches are popular fare here, but the locals also like such complete dinners as tenderloin strips marsala, stuffed squid in tomato sauce, chicken or veal parmigiana and baked haddock, served with a side of spaghetti or baked potato and salad, for $5.50 to $7.95. You also can get complete Italian dinners at lower prices, and Sicilian cannoli or homemade spumoni for dessert after a hefty portion of garlic pizza. Italian wines and domestic beers are featured. Open daily from 4 p.m.

Wine Country Provisioners, East Third Street, Watkins Glen. Opened in 1985, this specialty food store expanded in 1986 with an addition offering tables for luncheons and snacks. The foods are generally not made on the premises, but the salad plates for $3.50 and $4.50 and the sandwiches with potato or macaroni salad for $3.25 are hefty. The oriental chicken, pasta pesto and seafood salads particularly appealed. Open daily from 8 to 7.

Four Chimneys Winery, Hall Road, Hinrod. (607) 243-7502. It's not a restaurant, but the weekend post-concert dinners offered by reservation and the gourmet deli intrigue. "People were always asking where we could eat," the Korean woman behind the counter explained, "so we decided to serve food ourselves." The crowning achievement is what they call post-concert dinner wine tastings following the Seneca Lake chamber music series concerts on Saturdays in August and Saturdays and Sundays in September in the winery. After the 7 p.m. concerts, diners adjourn to the Four Chimneys homestead for regional nouvelle dinners with five wines at a prix-fixe $30. The opening night included the Four Chimneys paté, scallops and pine nut sauce with fresh pasta and lemon basil, an organic strawberry sorbet to cleanse the palate, boeuf en daube with Basque potatoes and miniature vegetables, a summer salad, cheese, and Norwegian cream cake with fresh organic peaches. The wine feast starts with chardonnay and ends with late harvest Delaware.

FOR MORE INFORMATION: Schuyler County Chamber of Commerce, 1000 N. Franklin St., Box 330, Watkins Glen, N.Y. 14891. (607) 535-4300.

Shoreline setting is tranquil along Lake Waramaug.

Lake Waramaug/Kent, Conn.

It's long been said that there's no tonic like the Housatonic, a reference to the river that cuts beneath forested mountains in Northwest Connecticut toward Long Island Sound. The same might also be said for Lake Waramaug, one of Connecticut's most picturesque lakes, enveloped in hills just east of the Housatonic.

The tonic provided by the Housatonic — indeed the entire triangle-shaped area from Kent to Cornwall to Lake Waramaug — is a rural respite from the pace of nearby metropolitan areas. Here, less than 100 miles from New York City and 50 miles from Hartford, is an utterly tranquil, unspoiled piece of land that beguiles artists, literati and weekenders.

The Housatonic is at its most scenic in the 20-mile stretch between Connecticut's only two covered bridges remaining open to automobile traffic, at West Cornwall and Bull's Bridge. In between are Kent Falls, the state's highest waterfall, other state parks good for hiking and camping, the Appalachian Trail and a section of water known for canoeing and kayaking.

At the center is tiny Kent, where the late artist Eric Sloane designed his Sloane-Stanley Museum and where people like Henry Kissinger now live. Here are the riverside campus of the private Kent School, and a short main street of art galleries, antiques dealers, shops and restaurants interspersed among historic homes.

Lake Waramaug is less than five miles as the crow flies from Kent but nearly 15 miles by car unless you know the back ways. A narrow, winding road hugs the sheltered eight-mile circumference of Connecticut's second largest lake. Here, you can easily imagine yourself in Europe as you sit on the terrace of an alpine inn and gaze at one of the East's least spoiled shorelines. The lake has attracted several establishments and a small winery there are no commercial intrusions to mar Waramaug's charms.

"This area is very rural and the residents want to keep it that way," says Phyllis Dietrich of the new Country Goose B&B. It's also "a very exciting, creative area in which a tremendous number of weekenders are into new things," adds entrepreneurial shopkeeper Joanna Seitz of New Preston, a quaint little hamlet enjoying a mini-boom at the edge of Lake Waramaug.

Long may the rural charms and creative excitement co-exist.

Getting There

Lake Waramaug and Kent are located in the Litchfield Hills section of northwest Connecticut. Kent is on Route 7, the main highway between I-84 at Danbury and the Massachusetts Turnpike at Lee. Lake Waramaug is off Routes 202, 341 and 45, east of Kent between Warren and New Preston.

Where to Stay

More than many such places, this is a four-season destination. Sophisticated dining, shopping and winter sports (downhill and cross-country skiing) attract visitors year-round.

On the Lake

Boulders Inn, Route 45, New Preston 06777. (203) 868-7918. A grand lakeside setting, an excellent dining room (see Where to Eat) and fine accommodations are hallmarks of the Boulders under the personal guidance of innkeepers Jim and Carolyn Woollen, transplanted Indianans. They adapted to New England with flair, expanding and upgrading the old-fashioned country inn into one of privacy and sophistication. With an expanse of windows looking onto Lake Waramaug, the living room couldn't be more comfortable, its wing chairs and small tables grouped for afternoon tea or cocktails and off in one corner shelves of books and a stereo. Beyond is a small den with color TV; downstairs is a game room for ping-pong and skittles. The spacious grounds include a tennis court, a beach house with a hanging wicker swing, and waterfront for swimming, sailing and canoeing. The five upstairs guest rooms, all with private baths, are richly furnished with antiques; two facing the lake have queensize beds, loveseats and cushioned window seats, and a suite in back has a sleigh bed and separate sitting room. All the eight contemporary-style chalets scattered along the hillside in the woods behind the inn have decks, most with good views of the lake. Most sought-after in winter are the four with sofas and chairs grouped around free-standing fireplaces. Full breakfasts are served in the new six-sided Lake Room. Doubles, $138 MAP. Open year-round.

The Inn on Lake Waramaug, North Shore Road, New Preston 06777. (203) 868-0563 or (800) 525-3466. The granddaddy of area resorts (dating as an inn to 1880), this is for those who like lots of activity. For 35 years, it was run very energetically by the Combs family, who sold it late in 1986 to Baron Country Inns of Avon, Conn. A management group that owns six other large inns in New England, it appointed John and Karen Koiter as innkeepers. The inn has long been known for a busy schedule of special events and promotions from lake excursions on the inn's 50-passenger Showboat in summer to horse-drawn sleigh rides in winter. Swimming is offered at the beach or in an indoor pool with a whirlpool. There are five guest rooms in the inn and twenty in newly renovated motel-style guest houses on the lawn below, the choicest being those with canopy beds, fireplace and lake view. The inn's main floor is a ramble of inviting early American parlors, the Honeycomb gift shop and two dining rooms, one all in blue and the other in pink, where three meals a day are served. The extensive dinner menu favors the traditional, with entrees from $11 for roast turkey or chicken cordon bleu to $17 for English mixed grill and steak Diane. Doubles, $130 to $188, MAP; many packages available. Open year-round.

The Hopkins Inn, Hopkins Road, New Preston 06777. (203) 868-7295. Part of a striking hilltop lineup of structures you can see from across the lake, this Federal-style building erected in 1847 as a summer guest house is the most imposing of all. It's home to a highly popular dining operation (see Where to Eat), but also offers nine guest rooms and one apartment. As befits a summer country house, the rooms are light and airy, decorated with Colonial papers and furnished with country antiques. Innkeeper Beth Schober apologizes for their spareness and prices them accordingly, but we found them rather appealing with brass or wood bedsteads and thick carpeting. Seven have private baths, while two on the third floor share. All are warmed only by small heating units, so the inn closes in winter. There's a private beach on the lake for guests. Doubles, $39 to $47. No credit cards. Open April to mid-November.

The Birches Inn, West Shore Road, New Preston 06777. (203) 868-0229. If you want to be right on the water, the three rooms in a lakeside cottage at the Birches may be for you. Across the road from the main inn, they share an extended back porch directly over the lake. One that is good for families has a loft area with four beds. The large guest room in the inn has two double beds, an assortment of chairs, and windows looking onto the lake. Five smaller rooms, all with private baths, are in a guest house behind the inn. Innkeepers Heinz and Christa Hull offer a private beach, boat dock, canoes and bicycles. They also oversee a fair-sized restaurant operation, Christa in the kitchen and Heinz at the cozy bar, which has a fine lake view. Entrees ($9.95 to $18) include four chicken dishes, plus sauerbraten, wiener schnitzel, filet mignon and chateaubriand. Doubles, $98 to $130, MAP (European plan available midweek or weekly). Open year-round.

Kent

Flanders Arms, Route 7, Kent 06757. (203) 927-3040. Listed on the National Register of Historic Places, this sprawling, good-looking house dating to 1742 is located in the historic Flanders section north of Kent. Operated since 1984 as a B&B by well-traveled owners Marc and Marilyn DeVos, it is decorated to the hilt in Laura Ashley fabrics and wallpapers, all neatly color-coordinated down to the sheets and shower curtains. The four guest rooms, two with private baths and two sharing, are in the original 1742 part of the house and reflect it, from the inside window shutters to the sloping bare oak and pine floors and ceilings. Striking bouquets of silk flowers and a selection of good magazines are in each room. Although there is no common room, guests gather at an impressive marble table in the family dining room for a continental breakfast of croissants and fresh orange juice. Doubles, $65 to $75, by reservation only. Open year-round.

The Country Goose, Route 7, Kent 06757. (203) 927-4746. Another historic (1740) house with an unusual double-pillared entrance was opened as a bed and breakfast in the fall of 1986 by Phyllis Dietrich and her IBM-executive husband, a restorer of antique cars. A six-month renovation created a welcoming place with a library full of old National Geographics and tavern puzzles, a formal parlor and a breakfast room with a working beehive oven in the original kitchen. Upstairs off an enormous center hall are four guest rooms (one a small single) sharing two large baths. Antique furnishings and interesting touches like country goose shade pulls, dear little wreaths, watercolors by local artists and a carriage filled with dolls enhance the rooms. The aroma of baking greets afternoon visitors (Phyllis puts out a plate of fresh cookies on a table in the upstairs hall). She also bakes muffins, breads, croissants or mini-bagels for the continental breakfast. Out back on five acres looking up to the towering St. Johns Ledges are sheep, chickens, a myriad of birds at an assortment of feeders, and paths to the Housatonic River. Doubles, $60. Open year-round.

Fife 'n Drum Inn, Main Street, Kent 06757. (203) 927-3509. Part of a thriving restaurant and gift-shop complex are seven motel-style rooms on the second floor above the rustic shops. Each of the air-conditioned rooms is decorated individually; one with canopied four-poster is next to another much more modern room with a chair and loveseat. The corner room, No. 6, has a high ceiling with track lights on exposed beams, white iron frames around both a double bed and a frilly sofa bed, a high white rattan chair, dressing area and modern bathroom with clawfoot tub. All rooms have color TV and complimentary coffee makings and canned juices. Doubles, $75. Open year-round.

CAMPING. The area is a paradise for tent campers, at sites along the Appalachian Trail or in state parks beside the Housatonic River and Lake Waramaug. **Housatonic Meadows State Park** in Cornwall Bridge has 104 campsites in a heavily forested area beside the Housatonic. **Macedonia Brook State Park** in Kent, known for its hiking along the Appalachian Trail, offers 84 campsites. **Kent Falls State Park** has 12 sites in open meadows near the foot of the falls. **Lake Waramaug State Park** has 88 sites in woods and fields near the lake, plus a camp store and full facilities.

RENTALS. The pages of the Litchfield County Times and the Lakeville Journal, two of the best weekly newspapers anywhere, are filled with ads for some of the priciest real estate you ever saw. Seasonal rentals may be listed privately or with three agencies on Main Street in Kent: DeVoe Realty Co., 927-3571; David L. Bain, 927-4646, and Gordon Casey Real Estate, 927-3591; or Klemm Real Estate, Routes 45 and 341, Warren Center 06754, 868-0505.

Seeing and Doing

In terms of the usual tourist attractions, this area has few. It's a do-it-yourself type of place where you canoe the river, cycle around the lake, poke through the galleries and shops, relax and bask in the rusticity of it all.

Sloane-Stanley Museum, Route 7, Kent. (203) 927-3849. When artist Eric Sloane died in 1985, he left an enormous legacy — not the least of which is the Kent museum that bears his name and displays a collection of his beloved early American tools. The barn-like structure was designed specially by the artist-writer to house the collection. The wooden shovels and bowls, the baskets and pitchforks, the axes, yokes and scythes are grouped in a most ambient setting. Visitors love the dog-powered butter churn. Horse-drawn sleighs and other early artifacts are shown in a gallery, as are several of Sloane's paintings. A new wing houses a reproduction of the artist's studio. Also on the site are the remains of the Kent Iron Furnace and a small cabin that Sloane built in two weeks when a TV film was being made of his book, "The Diary of an American Boy." Adults $1.25, children 50 cents. Open Wednesday-Sunday 10 to 4, May-October.

Hopkins Vineyard, Hopkins Road, New Preston. (203) 868-7954. Ex-dairy farmer Bill Hopkins and his wife Judy converted their dairy barn into a winery with a fine gift shop of wine-related items and an upstairs Hayloft Gallery with changing art exhibits. The winery produces a superior seyval blanc, which has won many awards, among seven varieties from their 20 acres of French-American hybrid grapes in a vineyard above Lake Waramaug. The Yankee Cider is available in fall for those who like apple wines. You can get a quick, self-guided view of the winery operation from a vantage point off the tasting room; buy a bottle or two for a picnic outside at tables overlooking the lake. Open daily 11 to 5, May-December; weekends rest of year.

Housatonic Railroad Co., Canaan Union Station, Canaan. (203) 824-0339. Scenic train excursions along the banks of the Housatonic depart from the Canaan station. The trains pass through Falls Village and West Cornwall, with occasional extensions to Cornwall Bridge, on the former Berkshire Division of the New Haven Railroad. The company was planning soon to serve Kent as well. The standard round trip from Canaan to West Cornwall is $6 adults, $4 children. Departures at 10 and 1:30 Saturday and Sunday, late May through mid-November.

For the Active

River Expeditions. Canoeing and kayaking, both whitewater and flatwater, are favorite pastimes on this section of the Housatonic. **Clarke Outdoors**, Route 7, West Cornwall, 672-6365, rents canoes and kayaks ($26 a day) and offers shuttle service ($8) to the launch point at Falls Village. The river trip ends 10 miles downstream at Housatonic Meadows State Park and takes three to four hours; vans pick boaters up there and return them to West Cornwall. Warns proprietor Mark Clarke: "If you're not prepared to swim the river, don't canoe it!" Also providing similar shuttle and rental services is **River-running Expeditions Ltd.** on Main Street, Falls Village, 824-5579.

Kent Falls State Park, Route 7, Kent. North of the village is the 200-foot cascade of Kent Falls Brook. A little covered bridge leads from the parking lot onto an open meadow with picnic tables scattered about. Visitors may take a winding but wide pathway to the head of the falls, a short hike from the parking area. There's fishing, but no swimming.

Other Parks. Housatonic Meadows State Park is fortuitously located along the Housatonic north of Cornwall Bridge. Besides 104 campsites, the park offers boat access, hiking and fine picnicking facilities. **Macedonia Brook**

State Park, with 2,300 acres in the mountains northwest of Kent, provides views of New York's Catskills and Taconic mountains, camping at 84 rustic sites, stream fishing and hiking along the Appalachian Trail, which parallels the river on the west side of Route 7. **Lake Waramaug State Park**, on the northwest shore of the lake, is exceptionally appealing, with picnic tables scattered along the shore under the trees, a fine swimming beach, and camping at 88 sites. Another good swimming spot is the pond at **Mount Tom State Park**, east of Lake Waramaug off Route 202 near Woodville. Besides an uncrowded beach, pleasant picnic tables beside the lake and good boating, the park has a trail to a stone summit tower that affords great views of the hilly countryside.

Country Arts and Shops

KENT. Already fun for browsing, Kent's Main Street is being rapidly upgraded by local merchants, according to Carol Hoffman of the **House of Books**. Featuring books by local authors, her store in the old Masonic Hall has a framing gallery in the rear and is adjacent to **Sport Scene**, outdoor outfitters. Across the street are **Country Clothes** and **Foreign Cargo**, a large emporium of imported clothing, jewelry, home accessories and antiques, plus a new back room of American antiques. The **Heron American Craft Gallery** has strikingly different pottery, gargoyles, weavings and handmade paper. At **Strobel Baking Co.**, Patsy Strobel makes everything from scratch; her breads and pies are said to be the best around. The new **Kent Town Center**, a retail and office complex designed around a three-story atrium, was scheduled for a late 1987 opening.

Kent Station Square is a cluster of shops near the century-old train station. The **Paris-New York-Kent Fine Art Gallery** displays changing exhibits to great advantage in a caboose behind the station. We were intrigued by a trompe l'oeil exhibit by Ann Osenga at prices up to $12,000 for a green door that opened. Beyond is the **Kent Antiques Center** in a restored 150-year-old farmhouse. Across the street are Audrey Traymon's excellent **Fife & Drum Gift Shop** and **Mimi's Boutique.**

South of town is **Bull's Bridge Glass Works,** where Stephen Fellerman exhibits his glass art, from lamps to perfume bottles, and may give a glass-blowing demonstration.

WEST CORNWALL. Always a quaint rural spot beside the covered bridge, West Cornwall's center has had its ups and downs with its few restaurants and shops coming and going. Lately it has been up with the opening of Freshfields in the former Deck restaurant site and the arrival of the Cornwall Bridge Pottery Store (see below). Located in the Toll House next to the covered bridge, **Ian Ingersoll Cabinetmakers** constructs reproduction furniture in the Shaker tradition, specializing in chairs, stools and rockers. **Poor Farm Gifts** has Shaker-style boxes, baskets, wooden trays and other items made by local artisans.

Cornwall Bridge Pottery Store, West Cornwall. This is the showplace for the works of local potter Todd Piker and two assistants, whose pottery operation in Piker's home above the Housatonic at Cornwall Bridge is one of New England's most prolific. Since 1972 he has been making nearly 30 tons of functional stoneware each year in a 40-foot-long woodburning kiln, one of the largest of its kind. Known for pottery glazed inside and out and decorated with fine brushwork, he produces items ranging from tiny teacups to garden pots, serving bowls to lamp bases. His pottery operation off Route 7 is open daily from 10 to 5, although the day we visited we found no one around. The West Cornwall store, which also features Simon Pearce glass and leather purses made by Todd's wife Ivelisse, is open Thursday-Sunday 10:30 to 5:30.

NEW PRESTON. This hamlet at the southeast end of Lake Waramaug is below the lake. A few years ago, there was no reason to pause on your way to the lake; now there is. Preservationist Barbara Corey Tippin converted an old grocery store into **Brittania Books,** a wonderful two-level place in which to browse through British and Irish literature, sheet music, old post cards and prints. British flags fly from the second-story deck over the narrow East Aspetuck River, which flows downhill from the lake to meet the Housatonic at New Milford. On the other side of the stream is a delightful British garden walled in stone. Below Brittania Books is **Timothy Mawson Bookseller,** specializing in gardening, landscape architecture and English country life, plus food and wine books, herbs and potpourri. **Trebizond Rare Books** is above an art gallery next door.

J. Seitz & Co. is just down Main Street in a converted garage, where Joanna Seitz shows an eclectic array of clothing from all over the world (designer dresses from Canada, coats from Australia), twig furniture, French glassware, handloomed rugs, unusual tableware, fancy pillows, hand-painted cupboards made in New Mexico and local crafts. A large window in the rear of the high-ceilinged shop looks onto a big waterfall. Next door, Mrs. Seitz runs **Zoom,** a trendy clothing boutique for children.

Worth a side trip from New Preston on Route 202 toward New Milford is the **Silo** at Hunt Hill Farm, Upland Road. Here, conductor Skitch Henderson and his wife Ruth run an art gallery, a noted cooking school and a shop full of gifts and gourmet delights.

Where to Eat

Boulders Inn, Route 45, New Preston. (203) 868-7918. Crisp white linens and single tall white candles in shiny brass holders set the stage for some of the area's consistently best food. The intimate inner dining room with its walls of boulders is warming on a chilly night; the airy, glass-enclosed six-sided Lake Room beyond, where every diner has a view of Lake Waramaug, is delightful anytime. And the outdoor patio is perfect for summer lunch. The limited dinner menu is supplemented with up to a half dozen specials. Among entrees ($10.50 to $16.25), consider chicken paprikasch, Kashmir lamb, skewered shrimp grilled with garlic and coriander, boned duck breast maconnaise or tournedos Madeira. The three-mushroom salad, sweetbreads with watercress sauce and artichoke hearts with smoked trout mousse are appealing appetizers, and we've enjoyed a wonderful brandied orange nut cake and meringue glace Pavlova. The interesting lunch menu features oriental, Mediterranean, curried chicken and chef's salads, a charcuterie plate, five hot entrees and three sandwiches, one called "a Mexican thing," from $4.50 to $8.25. Dinner, nightly except Monday 6 to 8:30, Memorial Day-Labor Day; Tuesday-Saturday, September-October; Wednesday-Saturday, rest of year. Lunch, daily noon to 2, Memorial Day-Labor Day; Sunday brunch, Labor Day-Memorial Day.

Hopkins Inn, Hopkins Road, New Preston. (203) 868-7295. Waitresses in dirndls, fires in the hearths and an interesting continental menu testify to chef owner Franz Schober's Austrian background. Here is a place we like to take visiting relatives. The warm European country inn atmosphere inside the 1847 Federal structure and the idyllic outdoor terrace under the giant chestnut tree, with the waters of Lake Waramaug shimmering below, both appeal. Who wouldn't appreciate the trout meunière, backhendl with lingonberries, wiener schnitzel, sweetbreads Viennese or calves liver and bacon at long-ago prices of $10 to $14.50? The appetizers are downright cheap (pate, $1.75), but we always make sure to save room for the fantastic desserts, perhaps the meringue glace, pear Helene or strawberries Romanoff. The wine list is extensive and reasonably priced. Lunch, May-October, Sunday 12:30 to 8:30; closed January-March. No credit cards.

The Milk Pail, Route 7, Kent. (203) 927-3136. An ancient sled and old milk pails flank the facade of this small brown house in the center of Kent. The milk pails are repeated inside, where they hang from the walls and contain lights that illuminate the beamed ceiling. A blazing corner hearth and well-spaced knotty pine tables with brown woven mats and fresh flowers make for a comfortable country setting. When we last visited, owners Penny and Ernie Schmutzler were enclosing their side deck into a glass greenhouse affair — good for cool weather, but we'll miss the outdoor dining. The blackboard menu runs from $10.25 for mustard chicken or chicken cordon bleu to $16.50 for filet mignon; you also might order bluefish bearnaise, veal forestiere, crab-stuffed shrimp or veal saute with applejack sauce. Penny's desserts are renowned, especially her fresh fruit pies and rum chocolate mousse. The lunch offerings range from $4.25 for soup and salad to $6.50 for shrimp salad or a special swordfish stir-fry. Lunch, Tuesday-Saturday 11:30 to 2:30, dinner 5 to 9:30; Sunday, brunch noon to 3, dinner 4 to 9.

Fife 'n Drum, Main Street, Kent. (203) 927-3509. A continental menu, a taproom with fireplace and framed Eric Sloane prints, a candlelit dining room set with pewter service plates and owner Dolph Traymon at the piano. That's the formula that draws patrons in great numbers to this well-known establishment, which recently expanded with seven inn rooms and an excellent gift shop. Tableside preparation of Caesar salad, fettuccine Alfredo and flambeed roast duckling and Cornish game hen is featured (and fairly pricey). The menu runs from $11.50 for roast chicken with herbs to $17.95 for steak au poivre. There's a blackboard menu at lunch, and the taproom menu offers everything from nachos and potato skins to cold poached chicken, drunken drumsticks and pasta. Lunch, 11 to 3; dinner 5:30 to 9:30 or 10:30; Sunday, brunch 11 to 3, dinner 3 to 9; closed Tuesday.

Kent Station Cafe, Main Street, Kent. (203) 927-4751. Half of Kent's old train station houses this new-in-1986 cafe, light and airy with pale peach walls, muslin curtains and pretty hand-stenciling — done by a Kent artist — running up and down the sides of windows and along the wainscoting. A rough pine hutch bearing copper pots, pottery and wine bottles serves as a divider at the entrance; a ficus tree and a few pictures and copper pans on the wall comprise the rest of the spare decor. Except for the glass-topped tables and fans whirring overhead, we enjoyed an autumn lunch of tortelli with roasted red pepper and smoked ham with salad and a turkey melt, both $3.95. We hear that chef Barbara Kobler, a local caterer, does nice things like chicken marinara, shrimp casino style, Cajun blackened strip steak and Ozark fried chicken for dinner ($10.95 to $16.95). Homemade desserts might be pumpkin flan, apple crisp or chocolate whipped cream cake. Lunch, Tuesday-Sunday 11:30 to 2:30; dinner, 5:30 to 8:30 or 9:30.

Freshfields, Route 128, West Cornwall. (203) 672-6601. Here is a fresh country bistro with a deck beside a waterfall, where the menu is so innovative that you'd need a large party to try to taste everything that sounds appealing. Consider one October night's menu: sauteed curried shrimp, jalapeno chevre chicken, New York strip steak with blueberry ketchup, roast baby pheasant stuffed with apple and maple walnut sauce, barbecued Norwegian salmon with oriental sauce, and grouper steamed in a stew of fall vegetables — those were less than half the entree choices, with a wide range of prices from $8.95 to $18.95. At other dinners, lunch or brunch you might find grilled catfish with roasted tomatillo butter, venison stew, lamb-stuffed cabbage, omelet with basil and goat cheese, clam and almond soup, arugula salad, grilled Malpeque oysters, cioppino and grilled swordfish with refried black beans and spicy melon. You get the idea that chef Steve Mangan, a former instructor at the New England Culinary Institute in Vermont, has quite a reach and owner Cheryl Matthew and her partners give him a free hand. The kitchen is open to the windowed dining room, divided into sections with blond wood tables and bow chairs. The outdoor deck beside the waterfall is great for lunch, and the upstairs bar with its huge mural of baby blue skies, puffy clouds and Cornwall's hills is fine for a drink or dinner overflow. The wine list, arranged by year, is as interesting as the menu. Since it opened in 1985, Freshfields has been enormously popular. Lunch, Wednesday-Saturday noon to 2:30; dinner 5:30 to 9 or 10; Sunday, brunch 11:30 to 2:30, dinner 5 to 9.

Bull's Bridge Inn, Route 7, Kent. (203) 927-3263. One October Saturday afternoon when everyplace else was either booked or had closed, we were glad to find Bull's Bridge still open for lunch at 2:30. From a large menu in the $5 to $7 range, we had an unusually thick and tasty quiche Lorraine served with a good house salad, and crepes a la reine with a wild rice mixture and julienned green and yellow squash. Burgers, soups and a meatball ravioli were other choices for lunch, served in the paneled and cozy lounge and rear dining room looking onto the parking lot. Dinner in the front dining room appears to be more formal. Lunch and dinner, Tuesday-Saturday 11:30 to 9 or 10; Sunday, brunch noon to 3, dinner 5 to 9.

Fillipo's, Kent Green, Kent. (203) 927-3774. The blackboard specials and a casual, family atmosphere attract locals to this new restaurant in a shopping area. The chef-owners from Rome and Sicily mix styles of cooking, one specializing in veal and chicken and the other concentrating on seafood and tomato sauces. Entrees are $8.95 to $11 for osso bucco, chicken abruzese, fettuccine with bacon and onions in a creamy meat sauce, tortellini in white cream sauce, and zuppa di pesce. Homemade desserts include chocolate mousse, peanut butter pie and traditional Italian desserts; finish with espresso or cappuccino. Fillipo's also offers grinders, calzones, and regular or Sicilian pizzas. Open daily, 11 to 11.

FOR MORE INFORMATION: Litchfield Hills Travel Council, Box 1776, Marbledale, Conn. 06777. (203) 868-2214.

The Lower Connecticut River, Conn.

Boat docks beside Victorian Goodspeed Opera House.

As it travels south, the Connecticut River cuts a wider swath — and dominates the countryside more. From Middletown to Essex, it is a major factor in the life of towns that developed on its shores. Essex is, in fact, a sailing center, its harbor filled with graceful craft that sail the waters of Long Island Sound, into which the river flows. (An Essex resident was a member of the crew of Stars and Stripes, winner of the America's Cup in 1987.)

Connecticut's river towns have an impressive heritage. Many were settled in the 1600s, so their sense of history is strong and much of their real estate is impressively aged. Essex is almost "museum quality," its main street lined with Colonial homes and an 18th century inn that is one of the nation's oldest continuously operating hostelries.

East Haddam is home to the famed Goodspeed Opera House and a couple of vintage bed-and-breakfast inns. Day excursion boats cruise from here down the river and across Long Island Sound to several Long Island ports.

Chester, connected by a tiny car ferry to Hadlyme on the eastern bank of the river, has nifty shops, fine dining and experimental drama at the Goodspeed-at-Chester theater. Across the river, high above the water, is Gillette Castle, the incredible edifice which was home to actor William Gillette.

Middletown, a small city, lately has taken charge of its waterfront, located at a bend in the river allowing for wonderful views from a new restaurant and a town park. The Wesleyan University boathouse is nearby; crews can be seen practicing in spring and fall. Wesleyan's cultural offerings are an additional attraction for visitors. Deep River, Ivoryton and Centerbrook are other river areas awakening to their tourism potential.

127

Bed and breakfasts are springing up, good restaurants abound, and shops and antiques stores attract weekend browsers from early spring to late fall (hardy souls who really like quiet pick winter).

Because Connecticut is our home state, and because we love this section of the river, we're excited about the developments. We hope you will be, too.

Getting There

The area occupies a stretch along the river about 20 to 40 miles southeast of Hartford. Route 9 is a divided highway from I-91 in Cromwell, just north of Middletown, to I-95 in Old Saybrook, just south of Essex. It parallels the river and brings visitors to all the towns along it.

Where to Stay

Stonecroft Inn, 17 Main St., East Haddam 06423. (203) 873-1754. This 1832 Federal-style house, painted soft beige with white trim, was a private residence until 1985 when ex-banker Paul Higgins of Boston took over. Aware of the amenities demanded by the modern tourist, Higgins had the house rewired and replumbed, the most important feature being up-to-date private bathrooms for all five guest rooms. Virtually all the antiques in the house are family pieces. The first-floor guest room has a double bed and a fireplace; our favorite second-floor room with a canopied bed and chaise lounge has a working fireplace and is charmingly decorated. The smallest guest room has been given its own book-lined sitting room. While he claims his only culinary training was a stint as a cook in the Army, Higgins whips up complete breakfasts including — by his own description — "fabulous french toast." Guests eat in a cozy, fireplaced breakfast room adjoining the kitchen. Doubles, $75 to $85.

Bishopsgate Inn, Goodspeed Landing, East Haddam 06423. (203) 873-1677. A bit further east on Route 82 beyond Stonecroft, Bishopsgate is an 1818 Colonial with a soft beige facade, cocoa trim and a red door. Taken over in early 1987 by a Brooklyn couple, Dan and Molly Swartz, Bishopsgate appeared to be in good hands. Its theatrical bent (former innkeeper Julie Bishop was connected with the Goodspeed Opera House) seemed assured since Dan ran a performing arts center prior to becoming an innkeeper. The six guest rooms (two downstairs, four up) are furnished mostly with period pieces — many of them antiques from the Swartzes' Brooklyn brownstone. A suite with bath, sauna, its own entrance and a deck is comfortable. Three of the other five rooms have private baths and four have working fireplaces. Light breakfasts in summer — and dinners for guests who want them — are served in the former 1860 kitchen, which has a little fireplace and baking oven. Says Molly: "Having dinner before the theater can be crazy; I'd like to provide dinner to guests if requested ahead of time." Guests dine at two four-foot trestle tables in the period kitchen; they also relax in a downstairs living room and a second-floor parlor. Doubles, $65 to $70; suite, $95.

Riverwind, 209 Main St. (Route 9A), Deep River 06417. (203) 526-2014. This rosy peach inn, renovated and opened in 1984 by innkeeper Barbara Barlow, a former junior high school teacher who grew up in Smithfield, Va., was to gain a four-room addition by mid-1987. The 1850 main house, which was in dilapidated condition before Barbara began to apply her talents to it,

128

is now the coziest and most original place imaginable. The daughter of a farmer who raises hogs in Smithfield, she has one standard item at her country breakfasts, Smithfield ham. This is accompanied by biscuits, often cut into the shape of pigs, homemade breads and jams, fruit (cold in summer, hot in winter), coffee and tea. They are served at a wonderful old harvest table beneath a candlelit chandelier in a fireplaced room filled with antiques. In the inviting front parlor, a unique lighting fixture, which seems to be a cross between a weathervane and a chandelier, has animal cutouts holding candles; there are a piano with all sorts of sheet music, hooked and woven rugs, quilts, and comfortable sofas and chairs. A wicker-filled, enclosed front porch appeals in summer. All four bedrooms in the original house — one on the first floor and the other three up a steep flight of stairs — are enticingly decorated. The second-floor Smithfield Room, all red, white and blue, has bluebirds stenciled around the wall and a stained-glass window in the adjoining bathroom. Zelda's Room, with carved oak furniture, has a decidedly Gatsby flavor; the Havlov Room, named for Barbara's parents' farm, has a pine bed and a crazy quilt. The new addition, built as an ell off the main house, was to have three more common areas including a dining room and a fireplaced keeping room. The Riverwind Inn formerly included an antiques shop on premises; now a friend from Virginia manages the shop elsewhere in the village. Doubles, $70 to $80.

The Inn at Chester, 318 West Main St., Chester 06412, (203) 526-4961. David Joslow, who has lived in the 1776 John B. Parmelee House out in the country west of town since 1955, turned his property into a sophisticated inn with an acclaimed dining room in 1983. That turned out to be just the start of his innkeeping ventures; he now owns and manages the Gelston House in East Haddam and the Town Farms Inn in Middletown (read on) as well as the Lord Jeffery Inn in Amherst, Mass. All are in the Connecticut River Valley, and Joslow, who grew up in Springfield, Mass., says "I love the river. The attitudes along the river are different from other places; there's a real culture here." The Inn at Chester is contemporary with a traditional look. Colors are soft, furniture is reproduction Colonial (plus a few antiques), and bathrooms are furnished with baskets of shampoo, soap and bath foam. The 47 rooms in two wings have carpeting, air-conditioning, and white George Washington-look spreads on the beds. Two of these and guest rooms in the original farmhouse have fireplaces. A cathedral-ceilinged living room/lounge with a huge stone fireplace, oriental rugs, reproduction sofas and wing chairs, and a piano — where pianists entertain nightly — is located off the dining room (see Where to Eat). A "living hall" on the second floor is where guests are served continental breakfasts on Sundays. Complimentary newspapers are a nice touch. The dining room serves a full breakfast menu. Doubles, $80.

The Copper Beech Inn, Main Street, Ivoryton 06442, (203) 767-0330. Although known primarily for its dining room (see Where to Eat), the Copper Beech Inn has 13 guest rooms. Four are in the sprawling white main house, and nine in a carriage house restored in 1986. Those in the main house have been decorated in country fashion with TLC and good taste by innkeeper Louise Ebeltoft; the old-fashioned baths have been kept intact for a feeling of nostalgia. A suite decorated in rich shades of blue has a canopied kingsize bed, a loveseat and a chaise lounge; there's a large table for two in the front dormer window. Out in the Carriage House, where original supporting beams have been exposed, rooms have an elegant country atmosphere with contemporary touches. Some have cathedral ceilings; each has a large jacuzzi tub and French doors leading to a deck. Several queensize beds are canopied; others are four-posters. A complimentary continental breakfast is served in one of the three dining rooms, which has a view of the great copper beech tree for which the inn is named. In season, the large greenhouse behind the inn, full of colorful garden furniture and plants, serves cocktails and after-dinner drinks. Doubles, $70 to $110 in inn, $90 to $125 in Carriage House.

The Griswold Inn, Main Street, Essex 06426. (203) 767-0991. Built in 1776 as Connecticut's first three-storied structure, the "Gris," as it's fondly called, oozes charm. Its first-floor dining rooms are fascinating; its tap room with steamboat-Gothic bar, potbellied stove and antique popcorn machine is a place to linger. The 22 guest rooms in the main inn, the annex and a house are less charming — just simple, old-fashioned and, in some cases, rather small. One upstairs room facing the street in front has beamed ceilings and sloping floors, a marble-topped table, and a small bath with shower. Suites are a bit classier: the Oliver Cromwell features a living room with two sofas, coffee table and fireplace, four-poster bed in the bedroom, a kitchenette and a small porch from which you can look over rooftops to the busy river. A continental breakfast buffet of juice, coffee and Danish pastry is served in the dark paneled Library (our favorite dining room) where the table next to the fireplace is favored in chilly weather. Other dining rooms feature an extraordinary collection of Currier and Ives steamboat prints on walls and ceilings, and there's a musket-filled Gun Room as well. The food, described in the inn's own brochure as "typically country" with "no pretenses," has not been highly rated lately and its famed Sunday Hunt Breakfast is fairly unexciting. If atmosphere is all you want, you'll enjoy dining and staying here. Doubles, $68; suites, $90 to $110.

The Gelston House, Goodspeed Landing, East Haddam 06423. (203) 873-1411. The 1852 Gelston House, which has been the primary restaurant to serve patrons of the Goodspeed Opera House for years, was acquired in 1984 by David Joslow of the Inn at Chester. Six new, air-conditioned guest rooms on the second and third floor, reached by a curving staircase from the front lobby, have been furnished in period pieces. On the second floor are a double room and a two-room suite done in American Empire furniture; they are carpeted and have up-to-date bathrooms, but we wish they were cozier. Both with queensize beds and white bedspreads, they do have good views of the river. On the third floor are a large two-room suite facing the river, another suite, and two rooms in back. Doubles, $80; suites, $120 and $140.

The Town Farms Inn, Silver Street, Middletown 06457. (203) 347-7438. In 1987, this elegant restaurant (see Where to Eat) was being given a large two-story brick addition with 48 guest rooms decorated in Georgian style and overlooking the Connecticut River. (Said owner Joslow when he bought the restaurant, "I'm really in the lodging business.") The addition has an exercise room and two conference rooms. A path was planned for walks along the river. Doubles, $80.

Seeing and Doing

There is plenty to keep a weekender — or a week-long visitor — busy in the lower Connecticut River Valley. You'll want to get out onto the water

— or at least as close as possible. There are special museums to visit, and be sure to leave time for shopping.

On the River

Camelot Cruises Inc., Marine Park, Haddam, 345-8591 or 345-4507. Cruises to Long Island have long been pleasurable summer trips. The M/V **Island Clipper** and M/V **Yankee Clipper**, both 500-passenger excursion boats, sail down the Connecticut River and across Long Island Sound to Greenport or Sag Harbor, N.Y. Trips to Sag Harbor go daily except Wednesday and Thursday, when the destination is Greenport. Boats leave Haddam at 9, arrive in Long Island at noon, leave Long Island at 3 and return at 6. Adults $15, children $7.

A new ship, the **M/V Camelot**, with a 300-passenger capacity, was to begin luncheon and dinner cruises on the Connecticut River in 1987, leaving from Marine Park. Luncheon cruises were scheduled daily from noon to 2:30; evening dinner cruises daily except Saturday from 5:30 to 7:45 and 8:15 to 10:30 (Saturday cruises one hour later). A full meal with a selection of appetizers, entrees and desserts was planned. Luncheon cruise, $18; dinner, $38.

Harborpark Cruises, Route 9, Middletown, 526-4954. The Deep River Navigation Company offers luncheon, afternoon and cocktail cruises from summer to late October, leaving from Harborpark. The daily schedule includes a one-hour luncheon cruise at noon ($3.50); a two-hour cruise at 2 ($5) and two 90-minute cocktail cruises at 5:15 and 7 ($5). After Labor Day, on Saturdays, a four-hour cruise to Hartford leaves at noon ($8.50); on Sundays, a four-hour cruise goes to East Haddam at noon ($8.50). Both Saturdays and Sundays in the fall include a 90-minute cocktail cruise at 5 ($5). The foliage can be quite spectacular along the river's banks.

Canoe the River. North American Canoe Tours Inc. of Niantic, 526-5492, rents canoes and gives guided weekend tours from Hadlyme. Canoes rent for $16.50 a half day, $21.50 a day and $38 for two days. On the guided tours starting Friday, tour operator David Harraden says canoeists paddle about a half hour to Selden Island where they set up camp for a weekend of canoeing and hiking. Food, canoes and tents are included in the $90 cost per person.

If you have your own canoe and want an outing on the river, **camping** is permitted at Hurd State Park, Gillette Castle State Park and Selden Neck State Park. For reservations, contact the Parks and Recreation Division of the Connecticut Department of Environmental Protection at (203) 566-2304 or 526-2336.

Steam Train and Riverboat, Valley Railroad Company, Essex, 767-0103. You can ride a vintage steam train along the Connecticut River shoreline, and even board a riverboat for part of the trip. The summer schedule allows you to hop a train at 10:30, 11:45, 1:15, 2:45 or 4. All but the last connect at Deep River with an optional one-hour boat cruise. Train rides take 55 minutes; the combined trip a little over two hours. Kids love these rides and, we confess, so do we. Santa is aboard special trips running from Thanksgiving to Christmas. Train rides, adults $6.95; children $2.95; train-boat combination, $9.95 and $4.95. Daily in summer, limited schedule in spring and fall.

The **Chester-Hadlyme ferry** operates between the towns of Chester and Hadlyme. The small ferry takes about four cars plus a few passengers for the five-minute trip and operates "on demand" April-November. Car and driver, 75 cents; each additional, 25 cents.

For another vantage point, **Eagle Aviation** at the Goodspeed Airport in East Haddam, 873-8568, takes three passengers on a small airplane up and down the river. The regular 20-minute flight costs $15 per person or $30 for a group of three.

Near the River

Goodspeed Opera House, Goodspeed Landing, East Haddam 06423. (203) 873-8664 (box office, 873-8668). The landmark white Victorian confection that sits high on the banks of the river in the tiny town of East Haddam was originally built by William H. Goodspeed, who had shipping, banking and other mercantile interests in the community but who also had a great love for opera and theater. Built in 1876, it thrived until 1920. The building was saved from demolition by preservationists and rededicated in June 1963, when it began its second — and very active — life (that alone is reason enough to visit this area). Since then three musicals — revivals and new tryouts — each running for about three months have been produced each season; among the 11 which have gone on to Broadway are "Man of La Mancha," "Shenandoah" and "Annie." People travel from across the state for "an evening at Good-speed," which can include dinner in the area and the show. At intermission, the audience loves to munch old-fashioned popcorn or sip champagne from the Victorian-style bar and stand on the open-air porch overlooking the river. There's usually a breeze, and it's fun to see the lights on the water as well as the structure of the old bridge soaring overhead. Guided tours ($1) are offered Mondays from 1 to 3, July-September. Shows are Wednesday-Friday at 8, Saturday at 5 and 9 and Sunday at 2 and 6. Tickets, $15 to $24. Productions April-December.

Goodspeed-at-Chester, the Norma Terris Theater, North Main Street, Chester. This "second stage" for new musicals is connected with the Goodspeed Opera House. Works of new (and often young) playwrights are produced in an attractive theater in an old factory building. Tickets are available through the Goodspeed box office.

Gillette Castle State Park, Route 148, Hadlyme, 526-2336. Here is one of the most interesting state parks anywhere. William Gillette, a Hartford native and well-known actor early in the century, built the house of his dreams on the last of a series of hills known as the Seven Sisters above the river. Since his parcel of land included the southernmost hill, he called his house "The Seventh Sister." He never called it a castle, but that's what it is, a massive stone building which came from Gillette's own inventive mind. He drew all the architectural plans for the 24-room castle and then designed all of the furniture for it, too. Most of it is heavy, hand-hewn oak. The dining room table moves on metal tracks on the floor. Some bedroom furniture is built into the structure of the castle itself. Stout oak doors are fastened by intricate wooden locks and there are intriguing stone terraces and fireplaces. The actor-architect, who was in his 60s when he built it, had the most fun, it seems, designing himself a railroad. A small train ran around the castle grounds on a three-mile-long track, from "Grand Central Station," a depot which survives as a picnic spot in today's park, through a forested glen, to "125th Street Station" and finally back to Grand Central. Gillette was usually at the throttle, and we're told he was no overly cautious engineer. The train has been moved to the Hershey Lake Compounce amusement park and most of the tracks have been dismantled, but it's fun to hear stories about it on your tour. A guided walk through the building takes about a half hour, after which you can enjoy trails along the river, gorgeous views of the water below, and picnicking at tables scattered throughout the park. The park is free. Castle tours, adults $1, children 50 cents. Open daily 11 to 5, mid-May to Columbus Day; sometimes, weekends from Columbus Day to Christmas.

Connecticut River Museum, Foot of Main Street, Essex, 767-8269. This small museum is located in an old warehouse with a graceful cupola and porch overlooking the river; outside you can walk on docks and view the passing parade of boats. Besides an exhibit of shipbuilding tools, there are half-models and full-rigged models of ships that sailed on the Connecticut, plus a life-size reproduction of David Bushnell's American Turtle, the first submarine. Models, prints, paintings and broadsides with a connection to the Golden Age of Steamboating form a nice collection; the warehouse has hoist barrels and sacks of Valley produce. Open Tuesday-Sunday 10 to 5, April-December. Adults $1.50, children 50 cents.

Pratt House, 20 West Ave., Essex, 767-8987. There is a sweet herb garden behind this center-chimney Colonial, which contains an outstanding collection of American furnishings of the 17th, 18th and 19th centuries, including Connecticut redware and Chinese courting mirrors. Open Thursday, Saturday and Sunday 1 to 5, June-September. Adults $2.50, children free.

The Stone House, South Main Street, Deep River, 526-2609. The 1840 house is a museum of 19th century furnishings and local history. It contains a Charter Oak piano, marine room, locally-made cut glass and Indian artifacts. Open Tuesday, Thursday and Sunday 2 to 4, July and August. Donation.

Davison Art Center, Wesleyan University, off Route 66 (Washington Street), Middletown. The Zilkha Gallery and the Davison Art Center building offer changing exhibitions. Open Tuesday-Friday noon to 4, weekends 2 to 5. Closed academic holidays. Free.

SHOPPING. Essex is the first place to stop if you're a shopper (or perhaps the last, if you want to have any money to spare). Its fine stores offer pricey and preppy men's and women's fashions (**The Talbots, Country Shop of Madison, Silkworm**); great children's clothes (**The Red Balloon** is about our favorite such store in Connecticut); nautical items (the **Boat House** at Dauntless Boat Yard); jewelry (nice Greek necklaces at **Aegean Treasures**), and gifts. **The Queen's Museum** is an extraordinary gift shop at Champlin Square. It is one of those rare places where you want just about everything you see; there are enormous stuffed fabric tulips, California necklaces, placemats with historic scenes, tote bags, dolls, china, glassware and lamps. The **Clipper Ship** bookshop has a good nautical collection, and **Seaflour Foods** sells breads, muffins, cakes, pastry, salads, sausages and coffee by the cup (something we usually stop in for). You can pick up a loaf of crusty French bread here.

Chester is another great shopping town. **Hands All Around** has to be one of the best women's clothing stores in the area, with unusual and beautiful items. The **Chester Book Company** is tranquil and lovely. **The Red Pepper** is a pretty little shop with kitchen items, many of them European. We liked some hand-decorated Portuguese eggcups the last time we stopped.

In East Haddam, both the **Seraph** and **Parsnip Hollow** are gift shops

133

worth poking your head into. The Seraph is in a Victorian mansion and has kitchen items, fashions, Crabtree & Evelyn soaps, and fun travel specialties. Up the hill (take Route 82 past the junction with Route 151) is a red antiques shop run by Gerry Miller with a good selection of used clothing, including furs (mostly Persian lamb when we visited).

If you cannot pass up a Christmas shop, try one of the best and biggest we've seen — the **Holly Loft** on Route 81 south of Chester. The antiques shop, **Never Say Goodbye**, on Route 81 in Killingworth is also highly recommended for costume jewelry and vintage clothes.

Where to Eat

Fine Bouche, Main Street, Centerbrook. (203) 767-1277. Since 1979, Steve Wilkinson, chef-owner of this restaurant in a small house in the center of town, has provided exceptional meals in an area known for good dining. Outside the house both French and American flags are flying; you walk past two small patisserie cases to three dining areas seating a total of 50. Our fireplaced room with off-white walls, white tablecloths and Queen Anne chairs with deep rose seats was tranquil and appealing for a winter dinner. The enclosed wraparound porch with latticework and rattan chairs with chintz-covered seats also is inviting. Dinner may be ordered prix fixe ($34.50) or a la carte (appetizers $5.50 to $9.50, entrees $16.50 to $19.50). The menu offered appetizers such as smoked duck with curly and Belgian endive, and goat cheese in a blueberry vinaigrette with fresh chervil; a terrine of duck fois gras with port-flavored aspic, and a winter salad of celery root, beets, baby carrots and radicchio served with a light pommery mustard vinaigrette. We decided on soup this especially cold evening — a cream of artichoke and hazelnut soup was fabulous; the other choice, soupe de moule provencale (a julienne of vegetables with tomato, mussels, white wine and saffron served with herbed toast rounds) was pronounced equally scrumptious. For entrees, we chose rack of lamb roasted with a breadcrumb, parsley and garlic coating, which arrived a bit too rare (it was whisked off and came back appropriately pink), and sliced veal filet with fresh noodles and a julienne of fennel and cream, which was outstanding. Other choices included bay scallops and scallop-filled ravioli in a light white wine sauce, veal sweetbreads and mushrooms in a cream and sauterne sauce, quail stuffed with a chicken and truffle mousse, and roast New York strip steak, sliced and served with a celery root mousse and zinfandel sauce. Entrees were preceded by simple green salads and came with pureed butternut squash and snow peas. Crusty, warm rolls were served and replenished by our accommodating waiter. His suggestion of a Russian River Valley chardonnay from the extensive wine list was just right. Desserts are also creative; the night we visited a pumpkin cheesecake, carrot cake, and the house specialty, marjolaine, described by our waiter as "a chocolate confection of unsurpassed wonder," were available. Service is nicely paced and the menu changes every two weeks, bringing diners back again and again. Lunch, Tuesday-Friday noon to 2; dinner, Tuesday-Saturday 6 to 9.

Restaurant du Village, 59 Main St. Chester. (203) 526-5058. This restaurant is reminiscent of one in a French village. Its blue facade, with ivy geraniums spilling out of window boxes and the bottom half of the large windows curtained in a sheer white fabric, is on the main street of tiny Chester. Although there had been concern that partners Charles van Over and Priscilla

Martel might have spread themselves too thin since taking over the restaurant Au Musee in Hartford's Wadsworth Atheneum, Restaurant du Village seems to have kept its act together. The small, square dining room has stucco-type walls and two sets of French doors onto the side brick walk; they are kept open for breezes on hot summer nights. The decor is simple: white tablecloths, small vases of field flowers, votive candles, salt and pepper dishes, and blue-sprigged Laura Ashley service plates. The French bread is the best we've had, crusty and chewy, made from a Canadian golden wheat flour that gives it a somewhat nutty taste and a slightly darker color, and served with crocks of sweet butter. The changing dinner menu includes six appetizers ranging from pureed vegetable soup at $4 to snails cooked in mushroom caps with a garlic cream sauce at $7. Other choices are a salad of native smoked wild duck with hazelnut dressing, smoked haddock with a lime vinaigrette and marinated French goat's cheese, baked and served on a bed of greens. Entrees are priced from $19 for braised boneless lamb served with baby vegetables and a poached pear. Others might be an Alsatian choucroute of smoked pork loin and garlic sausages braised in sauerkraut, boneless breast of chicken stuffed with sweetbreads and served with a mushroom sauce, and sauteed scallops with julienned carrots and leeks in a ginger butter sauce. Salads, usually mixed greens with a vinaigrette dressing, are served first. The notable desserts change daily. Chocolate mousse cake, lemon mousse, lemon curd cake, orange chanteler and raspberry tart are among those which regularly appear. A strong French roast coffee is a nice way to complete the meal. Dinner, Tuesday-Sunday 5:30 to 10. Closed Tuesday in winter.

Copper Beech Inn, Main Street, Ivoryton. (203) 767-0330. Louise Ebeltoft runs this inn and restaurant while husband Paul commutes to a financial job in Hartford. The Ebeltofts had a tough act to follow when they took over from Jo and Robert McKenzie, who garnered for their inn a reputation as one of New England's best dining places. Comparisons were odious and for the first few years, the restaurant suffered from them. Now, we're happy to report, the word is out that the Copper Beech is fine once again. The inn's three elegant dining rooms are all quite formal, but each has a different feeling. The blue Copper Beech Room with Empire chairs has blue oriental carpeting; the Ivoryton Room (with rose carpet and flowered wallpaper, and the Comstock Room, popular) with its Chippendale furniture and paneled walls, has a decidedly masculine feel. Chef Paul Gaffney's food, as described by Louise Ebeltoft, is "in the classic tradition, but lighter." A recent dinner menu lists hors d'oeuvres ranging from a country pate at $6.95 to Beluga caviar at a whopping $32 for one ounce. Other choices include crepes filled with sour cream, shallots and caviar, and sauteed shrimp in a cream sauce with diced tomato, brandy and tarragon. A pate of fresh foie gras, poached and served with an aspic and madeira wine, shallots and truffles, was listed at $19.75. Entrees include poached salmon garnished with shrimp for $21.50, broiled swordfish and bouillabaisse. Roast baby pheasant under glass, filled with minced mushrooms, shallots and butter and served with a sauce of game stock, red wine and wild mushrooms, is $20.75. Other choices include sauteed veal sweetbreads, beef Wellington served with a madeira wine sauce and truffles, and noisettes of lamb with fried garlic. Entree prices include a house salad and vegetables; Lyonnaise potatoes are a favorite accompaniment. Dinner, Tuesday-Saturday 5:30 to 9, Sunday 1 to 8.

Fiddlers Seafood Restaurant, 4 Water St., Chester. (203) 526-3210. An attractive, small restaurant getting good marks for its consistent and interesting food, Fiddlers is located in a wood-frame building and offers a cheerful cafe atmosphere. The curtains are blue and white checked, there are cane and bentwood chairs, and pictures of sailing ships add a nautical touch. The lunch menu lists three soups: a cream-style crab, Rhode Island clam chowder, and a soup of the day. There's also mesquite-grilled, poached or pan-sauteed fresh fish in season — usually priced about $6 — plus specials such as baked brie with almonds, mussels in puff pastry, and a Max-Burger served with steak fries. At dinner, along with the soups and fresh fish, add baked stuffed shrimp ($13.50), filet of sole garnished with shrimp ($11.95), and bouillabaisse ($12.95). Scallops with black mushrooms or Pernod, lobster au peche, and oysters imperial are other seafood choices; landlubbers can choose New York sirloin, lamb brochette or two chicken dishes. Chocolate mousse terrine with lingon-berries and a lime mousse are popular desserts. Lunch, Tuesday-Saturday 11:30 to 2; dinner, 5:30 to 9 or 10, 4 to 10 on Sunday.

The Inn at Chester, 318 West Main St., Chester. (203) 526-4961. A most attractive high-ceilinged barn is the main setting for dining here; there are also a couple of smaller rooms and a garden room for warm weather. Walls are of dark, rough wood but light pours in through a greenhouse-window addition. The room has a rustic but elegant feeling, with accent colors of deep blue and fresh flowers on bare wood tables. Dinner starts with a selection of rye rolls and biscuits with sweet butter in tiny cups. Appetizers include a five-mushroom strudel, the house specialty ($6.75), and smoked Scottish salmon for $8.95. A black bean soup is always on the menu. The house salad of mixed greens is tossed in a mustard vinaigrette. For entrees, try rack of lamb served with a merlot brown sauce ($23.50) or, at the other end of the scale, breast of chicken with seasonal mushrooms ($15.50). Other choices are veal scallops with lobster, sea scallops braised in vermouth, and New York sirloin. On the luncheon menu you'll find a roast beef or deli sandwich (in the $6 range), spinach salad, stir-fried chicken or cheese rarebit; most entrees are priced at $7 to $8. Lunch daily, noon to 2; dinner, 6 to 9; Sunday brunch, 11:30 to 2:30.

The Gelston House, Goodspeed Landing, East Haddam. (203) 873-1411. This 1853 structure with good views of the Connecticut River from its main dining room (called the Porch) has been a dining fixture for years. Granted, there's a captive audience in town prior to Goodspeed events right next door, but since David Joslow took it over in 1984, its reputation has improved. The coat rack in the lobby as you enter is a little off-putting, and the floors look as if they've been scuffed once too often, but in general the Gelston House is a pretty place. The Porch, with its three sides of small-paned glass over-looking the river, is large and convivial when full. The colors are pleasing: a cinnamon patterned rug, pale peach tablecloths, deeper peach fanned napkins, bentwood chairs and a single peach rose in a vase on each table. Votive candles flicker at night. Two smaller dining rooms have the same color scheme; one sports a mural showing the river and the Goodspeed. American cuisine is served. At lunch, that translates to appetizers of chilled shrimp served with both cocktail sauce and a horseradish dill sauce for $5.95 and almond brie served with fresh fruit (wouldn't a Vermont cheddar be more American?) for $3.95. Cold selections include a chicken salad platter, a Plymouth turkey sandwich, and a lobster salad plate, which is the most expensive at $7.50. Hot entrees include Yankee beef pot pie ($6.95), Lake Champlain calves liver ($6.95) and Kansas City open-steak sandwich ($8.25). You might also try the omelet of the day, seafood turnovers, or honey baked chicken. Dinner appetizers range from $3.95 for the almond brie to $5.95 for beer batter shrimp. Entrees might be grilled lamb steak or pork loin medallions (both $14.95), Columbia River salmon steamed in parchment ($15.95) and veal medallions topped with smoked ham and mozzarella cheese ($15.95). In the outdoor beer garden beside the river, you can order barbecued chicken or spareribs, a steak sandwich, a fruit and cheese sampler or a Greek salad. Lunch, Monday-Friday 11:30 to 2:30, Saturday noon to 4; dinner, 5:30 to 9 or 10; Sunday, brunch 11 to 2, dinner 3 to 8.

Town Farms Inn, River Road, Middletown. (203) 347-7438. Another David Joslow venture, the Town Farms was in the middle of a major renovation on our last visit. In addition to adding two brick wings with guest rooms, Joslow planned to change the main floor of the 1839 structure to retain our favorite dining room, the Indian Room, and add two others, the Captain Mather Library and the Commodore McDonough room. Gone is the high-ceilinged and chandeliered River Room (which we always found too formal and cold), part of which was to be added to a new lobby. Both the Indian Room, with its deep red walls and Indian artifacts, and the Commodore McDonough room are fireplaced. Although by day you can see the river, our most recent visit for dinner was after dark when the cheery warmth of the Indian room pleased us; alas, the fires in the Delft-tiled fireplaces were fake. A single peach rose on a white tablecloth, ladderback chairs, bare wooden floors and hammered-tin chandeliers combine to create an appealing room. We shared an appetizer of baked brie with fresh fruit ($4.50) from choices including pepper-grilled shrimp or smoked goose breast (both $6.95). Both the catch of the day, scallops in a tomato sauce with tarragon ($17.95), and the poached salmon served with a creamy dill sauce ($16.50) were excellent. Other offerings included Cajun trout and brace of quail. The rolls seemed to have been around too long, but the creamy Italian with cheese house dressing for our mixed green salads was excellent. With our entrees came a mixture of peppers, celery and tomatoes. We shared an exceptionally creamy cheesecake slice for dessert. Lunch, Monday-Saturday noon to 2; dinner, 6 to 9 or 10; Sunday, brunch 11:30 to 2:30, dinner 5 to 9.

Middlesex Opera House Restaurant, College Street, Middletown. (203) 344-3439. In 1984 three young owners, Robert P. Byrne, Philip T. DeRing and Lauren J. Higgins, combined forces to renovate the 1892 Middlesex Theater, nee opera house, into a restaurant. Very pink and not a little pretentious, the Middlesex offers dining on several levels, with the top floor reached by a wide curving staircase into whose well hangs a huge crystal chandelier. Gold-rimmed white china on the pink-clothed tables, potted palms, white stucco-like walls and gold trim here and there make it feel very dressy indeed. Lemon slices float in the water glasses and live piano music is heard in the background. Young waiters and waitresses try hard but seem unable to rise to the occasion; a more serious objection is that the tables are too close together for privacy. The menu has a theatrical tone: Act I is appetizers, Act II, entrees; the salad

137

is Intermission. We chose herring in sour cream at $4.50, a very generous slice, and shrimp in beer batter with an orange horseradish sauce ($5.95) as appetizers; both were fine. Our entrees were the sole Danoise ($13.95) and baked pork chops with a stuffing of apples, almonds and celery ($11.95). The latter proved quite dry and tough. Prime rib, shrimp marinara, veal francais and pasta primavera are other choices. The house wine, a French bordeaux, was quite nice. Dessert choices ($3.50) were linzer torte, Black Forest torte, peach melba and ice cream sundaes. Lunch, Monday-Saturday 11:30 to 2:30; dinner, 5 to 9 or 10; Sunday, brunch 11 to 3; dinner 11 to 8.

The Chart House, West Main Street, Chester. (203) 526-9898. This pretty salmon building with cream trim overlooking the Pattaconk River was once the Rogers & Champion Brushworks factory. Remnants of the water-powered factory remain: old mill works are still seen overhead in one of the large dining rooms on the second floor. Customers enter via a wooden footbridge across the river, from which you can see and hear a waterfall. The main floor is devoted to the bar and lounge; an outdoor dining terrace overlooks the river. One upstairs dining room in an addition to the building sticks right out over the water, affording the best views. Tabletops are nautical charts under polyurethane edged in wood; chairs are Windsor and captain's styles; there are exposed brick walls and in some cases single bare light bulbs with exposed filaments hang above tables. All in all it's a rather rustic and pleasant country atmosphere. As in others in the national chain, the emphasis here is on steaks and seafoods. The limited menu has three appetizers: clam chowder ($2.95), lobster bisque ($3.50) or shrimp cocktail ($6.75). Salads are brought family style to the table. The most popular entree is the prime rib, $14.95 for a regular cut or $17.95 for an oversize cut. Teriyaki steak, filet mignon, shrimp teriyaki, swordfish and Australian lobster tails (two for $23.95) round out the entrees. A boneless breast of chicken at $9.95 is the most economical choice. Mud pie and cheesecake are among desserts. Dinner, Monday-Thursday 5:30 to 9, Friday and Saturday to 11, Sunday 4 to 9.

Harbor Park Restaurant, 81 Harbor Ave., Middletown. (203) 347-9999. The best view of the river from any area restaurant is an attraction at this rather new place smack beside the river. Even on a Saturday afternoon in winter, the porch area with the window tables was busy; we all watched seagulls floating downstream on ice floes and two kayakers paddling like mad. Blue chairs with white turned rod arms, a raised platform in the center of the room with a mast and boom to give the impression of a sailboat, and other nautical touches appeal. Food is mediocre. A small plastic container of cheddar cheese spread and assorted crackers come to the table before the meal. At lunch we could start with a bowl of clam chowder or chicken noodle soup; the noodle was really a chicken vegetable soup and was delicious. The large house salads are sprinkled with mozzarella cheese, but ours tasted as if they'd been preassembled and waiting in the fridge. For lunch you can have a spinach or a chef's salad, pasta of the day, croissant sandwiches, or entrees such as a seafood crepe. In the evening, you might try broiled scallops, fried seafood platter, baked stuffed sole, chicken teriyaki or prime rib in the $10 to $15 range. The large first-floor bar is popular with singles. Lunch, daily 11:30 to 3; dinner, 5 to 9 (to 11 on weekends); Sunday brunch, 11 to 3.

FOR MORE INFORMATION: Connecticut Valley Tourism Commission, 70 College St., Middletown, Conn. 06457, (203) 347-6924.

Mary Anne Stets Photo/Mystic Seaport

Last whaleship is focal point of Mystic Seaport.

Mystic, Conn.

Think of Mystic and the word "seaport" probably comes to mind. It should, for this is the home of famed Mystic Seaport, the nation's premier maritime museum. Think some more and you might add shipbuilding, whaling, fishing, clipper ships and sea captains' homes. You might even think of tourism, now the area's biggest business.

Although Mystic is a mere village and a post-office address straddling the Mystic River — a political nonentity enveloped in the larger towns of Groton and Stonington — it is important beyond its size.

Historically, the Mystic River has been a site for shipbuilding since the 17th century. In the mid-1800s, the village of 1,500 owned 18 whalers and the boatyards produced 22 clippers, some of which set sailing records that have never been equaled. Later, many of the nation's fastest sailing yachts and schooners were built here, and submarines still are made along the banks of the Thames River on the western side of Groton.

Today, Mystic thrives on its legacy of having produced more than 1,000 sailing vessels, more noted captains and more important sailing records than any place of its size in the world.

Its quaint neighbor to the southwest, Noank, reflects its heritage as both a shipbuilder and a lobster fishing port. To the southeast, the tiny borough of Stonington — as historic a seaside village as you'll find along the East Coast — is the home port for about 30 draggers and lobster boats, Connecticut's only surviving commercial fishing fleet.

With a notable maritime tradition chronicled by Mystic Seaport, it's no wonder that little old Mystic has become the state's largest tourist destination. In addition to the Seaport, visitors are drawn to the Mystic Marinelife Aquarium, the submarine Nautilus and the U.S. Naval Submarine Base in Groton, and the U.S. Coast Guard Academy across the Thames River in New London. The result is a heady melange of motels and guest houses, seafood restaurants and fast-food eateries, eclectic boutiques and souvenir shops, and other attractions that bring still more tourists.

In the midst of it all is busy downtown Mystic, the only place we know of where U.S. Route 1 traffic is stopped hourly while the rare bascule bridge over the Mystic River is opened to let sailboats pass. But then, Mystic is also one of the few places we know where motorists stop all along Main Street for pedestrians — tourists, most of them — to cross.

Getting There

About 50 miles east of New Haven, the Mystic area stretches along Long Island Sound in southeastern Connecticut from New London to the Rhode Island border. U.S. Route 1 meanders through the heart of Mystic, while Interstate 95 crosses its northern edge. State Route 27 links the two. Regular train service is provided by Amtrak, whose shoreline route between Noank and Stonington is one of the more scenic around.

Where to Stay

Accommodations in Mystic are numerous and vary widely in size, type and quality. Except where noted, they are open year-round.

Tops for Luxury

The Inn at Mystic, Route 1, Mystic 06355. (203) 536-9604. Even when this was the Mystic Motor Inn, we thought it the nicest accommodation in town, with its superb location atop a hill beside Pequotsepos Cove and its appropriately weathered, shingled look. Now that it has been rechristened the Inn at Mystic, and upgraded to boot, it is even more appealing. Sisters Jody Dyer and Nancy Gray, whose father started this as Mystic's first motor inn of size in 1963, have totally revamped the 12 rooms in the East Wing, all with Federal-style furniture, queensize canopy beds, wing chairs and fireplaces, plus balconies or patios with views of the water. Six rooms here have huge jacuzzis in the bathrooms with mirrors all around; these are booked far in advance for romantic getaways. In the inn's 1904 pillared mansion atop the hill are five large and antiques-decorated guest rooms, some with fireplaces and all with whirlpools or spas. In summer on a wicker rocker on the inn's spacious veranda, gazing out over English gardens, orchards and the water, or in winter sitting deep in a chintz-covered sofa by a fire in the drawing room with its 17th century pin pine paneling, you may feel like a country squire. Behind the inn, the guest rooms in the secluded Gatehouse are also being redone in a country look, with Ralph Lauren sheets and coverlets. The 38 rooms in the original two-story motor inn are handsomely furnished as well. In yet another building on the hilly 12-acre property, the inn's **Flood Tide** restaurant (see Where to Eat) is well regarded. A tennis court, a small pool and rental rowboats are other pluses at this ever-changing complex (as if this weren't enough to keep them busy, the sisters also are adding 50 rooms to their elegant B&B called the Harraseeket Inn in Freeport, Maine). Doubles, $85 to $95 in motor inn, $100 to $135 in inn, Gatehouse and East Wing.

The Mystic Hilton, Coogan Boulevard, Mystic 06355. (203) 572-0731. Opened in 1986 to the tune of $15 million, this is not your typical Hilton in terms of head-on, high-rise architecture. Across from the Mystic Marinelife Aquarium, its low red-brick exterior and peaked roofs emulate the look of 19th century mills and warehouses. Inside, all is luxurious, from the grand piano in the fireplaced lobby with intimate sitting areas next to an open courtyard to the **Mooring** restaurant (see Where to Eat). The 187 standard and kingsize guest rooms are decorated in rose and green, each bearing two large prints of Mystic Seaport scenes commissioned from artist Sally Caldwell Fisher. Five deluxe jacuzzi rooms have queen beds and a sitting area plus big jacuzzi tubs in the extra-large bathrooms; they also have separate vanities and enormous closets. The meandering, angled layout puts some rooms an inordinate distance from the elevators but also contributes to peace and quiet; we walked the equivalent of several blocks to our corner room, but never heard a sound all night. Facilities include a small and shallow indoor-outdoor swimming pool and a fitness center. Doubles, $70 to $125.

Red Brook Inn, 10 Welles Road, Box 237, Old Mystic 06372. (203) 572-0349. Take a 1768 stagecoach-stop tavern in Groton, dismantle it, move it to Old Mystic and reassemble it piece by piece. The result is the large new-old building at the expanded Red Brook Inn, as fascinating an historic inn structure as we've seen. After a year's painstaking restoration, innkeepers Verne Sasek and his wife Ruth Keyes, transplanted Californians, added the Haley Tavern in 1986 up the hill behind the original red 1770 Creary homestead they opened as a B&B in 1983. Interestingly, Nancy Creary, who was born in the homestead, married the son of Elija Haley, "so we brought the tavern back into the same family," Verne says. The tavern structure has six luxurious guest rooms, all with private baths (one with a jacuzzi), and three with working fireplaces. Each is handsomely appointed with period antiques, color-coordinated stenciling and fresh flowers. The Ross Haley Room has a 200-year-old Shaker chest that still opens as easily as ever. The several downstairs common rooms are furnished with Ruth's fine collection of old lamps, hand-blown glass, pewter and such. Although this could almost be a house museum, it's comfortably lived in. The innkeepers offer afternoon tea and after-dinner brandies, and are converting the original taproom into a game room. Full breakfasts of fresh fruits and walnut waffles or apple pancakes are served in the keeping room. Here, in the enormous open hearth, breads and pies are baked for Saturday night candlelight Colonial dinners available to houseguests by reservation in winter. The original Geary homestead has three large guest rooms with working fireplaces; two adjoin and share a bath. Doubles, $70 to $105. No smoking.

The Palmer Inn, 25 Church St., Noank 06340. (203) 572-9000. The imposing 16-room mansion built in 1907 in pillared Southern plantation style for Robert Palmer Jr., when the Palmer Shipyards were among New England's largest, was restored in 1984 as a B&B by Donald and Patricia Cornish. Guests play checkers in the library or gather for afternoon tea in the parlor, where Patti has put out a variety of guides to the house and the area. In the dining room she serves a continental-plus breakfast of homemade granola, breads and muffins. From the impressive main hall with its 13-foot-high ceilings, a mahogany staircase leads past one of many stained-glass windows to the six second-floor and third-floor guest rooms. The huge Master Suite has a large fireplace, a rare rocker, a fancy satin bedspread and a canvas ceiling, while the white and blue Wicker Room has a private sitting area. Step up to the balconies off a couple of front rooms for a good view of Long Island Sound. The Cornishes sponsor winter theme weekends and arrange for lobster bakes on a sailboat, picnic cruises and the like. Doubles, $80 to $115.

Moderate Range

The Shore Inne, 54 East Shore Road, Box 3487, Groton Long Point 06340.

(203) 536-1180. Wonderfully homey is this "inne on the water," facing Long Island Sound in a community of fine old summer homes. Helen Ellison offers seven pleasant bedrooms, three with private baths and four sharing two, in the summer-home style. Her wicker-filled living room, a library with TV and a dining room with a telescope in the picture window are most comfortable. Cereal and homemade muffins are served for breakfast. A large lawn has chairs for enjoying the view, as well as the shade of a beautiful copper beech tree. The Shore Inne grants guests access to two private beaches which Helen calls "the best swimming beaches in Connecticut," a nearby fishing dock and eight tennis courts. Doubles, $40 to $50. Open April-October.

Harbour Inne & Cottage, Edgemont Street, Mystic 06355. (203) 572-9253. In an area in which few public accommodations are near the water, here's one that is — although the harbor is cluttered with moored boats and the property with lobster traps and fishing paraphernalia. Bearded commercial fisherman Charles LeCouras (Charley to the guests who have filled his scrapbook with fan letters) runs this small, quirky place. The main house contains four paneled guest rooms with small private baths, cable TV and air-conditioning (one room even has a stereo system). Facilities for guests include a small living room with a wood stove next to an open kitchen where they have kitchen privileges, and a prominently displayed washer and dryer. An adjacent quonset-type cottage finished in cedar has a bedroom with two double beds, a sofabed in the living room, a kitchen and a deck with redwood furniture. Outside are picnic tables beside the water, canoes and rowboats. Doubles, $35 to $65; cottage, $160.

Days Inn, Route 27, Mystic 06355. (203) 572-0574. As far as Days Inns go, this is a cut above, and so are its prices. Part of the motel row near Exit 90 off I-95, it's located well back from the highway and high atop a hill sets this 118-central corridors on two floors. Rooms in the motel were refurbished in 1986 in beige, brown and orange; they're rather small, but have either two double beds or a kingsize bed with a sofabed and a desk. Besides an outdoor pool, the motel has a restaurant that was being upgraded. Doubles, $72 to $82.

Seaport Motor Inn, Coogan Boulevard, Box 135, Mystic 06355. (203) 536-2621. Its location back from the highway and high atop a hill sets this 118-room motel apart from others along motel row. The rooms are pleasant enough (five are two-bedroom suites good for families), the outdoor pool is large and **Jamm's** restaurant serves lunch and dinner. Doubles, $58 to $75.

Whaler's Inn & Motor Lodge, 20 E. Main St., Mystic 06355. (203) 536-1506. For those who want to be in the thick of the action in downtown Mystic, this is the place. There are 40 rooms in the old main building and two newer motel buildings surrounding a courtyard. Rooms and rates vary widely. The Macbeth family also owns the Binnacle Restaurant, the outdoor Flying Bridge dining patio and the Ship's Hold gift shop, all parts of the complex just east of the Mystic drawbridge. Doubles, $38 to $85.

Taber Motor Inn and Guest House, Route 1, Mystic 06355. (203) 536-4904. Located in a quasi-residential area, this has 34 rooms in a basic motel, a restored 1829 guest house, a remodeled farmhouse and even a private two-bedroom guest house. Doubles, $55 to $70.

Cove Ledge Motel, Route 1, Pawcatuck 06379. (203) 599-4130. Sixteen

142

basic motel and efficiency units are offered at this older motel with a cove view, a 50-foot swimming pool, boat dock and picnic tables. Doubles, $40 to $50; efficiencies, $40 to $70. Open May-October.

The Adams House, 382 Cow Hill Road, Mystic 06355. (203) 572-9551. Ron and Maureen Adams opened a B&B in 1986, offering four rooms with shared baths and a separate country suite that can accommodate four. The rural 18th century house has fireplaces in the living room, dining room and TV room, and a swimming pool. Continental breakfast is served. Doubles, $40 to $55. No smoking.

Baker's River Lodge, 25 School St., West Mystic 06388. (203) 536-7296. Also new and on the river is this boat haven and small guest house with six rooms sharing baths. Continental breakfast is served. Doubles, $55 to $60. Closed in winter.

Farnan House, 10 McGrath Court, Stonington 06378. (203) 535-0634. Ann Farnan runs a five-room B&B (one with a private bath) in the 1906 home built by her late husband's father. She serves muffins or sweet rolls for breakfast beside the big wood stove in the kitchen. The upper rear porch affords a view of the water. Doubles, $40 to $53.

CAMPING. Seaport Campgrounds, Route 184, Box 104, Old Mystic 06372. (203) 536-4461. A swimming pool, pond fishing, rec room, playground and miniature golf are attractions at this 130-site campground with hookups and separate tenting area two miles north of I-95. **Highland Orchards Resort Park**, Route 49, North Stonington 06359. (203) 599-5101. Closer to the highway is this large RV area with pool, fishing pond, playground, basketball court, fireplace lounge and more.

RENTALS. Among the many real-estate brokers in the area, several specialize in summer rentals, including Mary J. Meader Real Estate, 22 E. Main St., Mystic 06355, (203) 536-3417, and Manmon Realty, 18 Crescent St., Groton Long Point 06340, (203) 536-1183.

Seeing and Doing

Fish and Ships

Mystic Seaport Museum, Route 27, Mystic. (203) 572-0711. From a local marine historical museum with one building in the old Greenman family shipyard in 1929, Mystic Seaport has evolved into the nation's largest maritime museum, an impressive testament to the lure, the lore and the life of the sea. The 17-acre site along the Mystic River contains more than 60 historic buildings, 300 boats, a planetarium and significant collections of maritime artifacts. Together they create a mix of a working seaport village, a museum of massive proportions and a must-visit attraction for any sailor worth his salt.

Landlubbers among the 500,000 annual visitors like the re-creation of a 19th century seafaring community. Trades of the era are demonstrated in the cooperage and shipsmith, shipcarver and model shops. You can poke through the Mystic Bank and shipping office (the second oldest bank in Connecticut), see handbills being published in the Mystic Press print shop, and visit the hardware store, schoolhouse, the old drugstore and doctor's office, and the delightful Fishtown Chapel. Guides cook on the open hearth of the Buckingham House kitchen, sing chanteys and demonstrate sail-setting, whaleboat rowing and fish salting.

Everyone likes to climb aboard the Charles W. Morgan (1841), the last of America's wooden whaleships and a remarkable example of the seaport's ship restoration efforts; the full-rigged training ship Joseph Conrad (1882), and the 1921 fishing schooner L.A. Dunton. About 300 small craft, the largest such collection in the country, are on display in the Small Boat Exhibit and North Boat Shed. Others are afloat along the seaport's docks or can be seen from a visitors' gallery as they undergo repairs in the Henry B. duPont Preservation Shipyard.

Sailors, historians, collectors and those with an interest in things nautical cherish the three-story Stillman Building, which houses ship models, scrimshaw, paintings and an informative exhibit called "New England and the Sea," which traces the region's maritime past. The shipping and shipbuilding businesses are explained in the Mallory Building, and other collections are displayed in more buildings than you can possibly comprehend in a day.

Don't miss the wonderful scale model of Mystic as it appeared in the mid-19th century. Take a ride on the steamboat Sabino (see below), and visit the excellent Museum Store, which offers all kinds of nautical items, a new art gallery and one of the best maritime bookstores anywhere.

Among special events are a May lobster fest, a horse and carriage weekend and an antique and classic boat rendezvous in July, an October chowder fest, and daily Yuletide and evening Lantern Light tours in December. The last are particularly charming as guides with lanterns lead tours to selected exhibit areas and ships, where costumed staff portray Christmases past.

Museum open daily except Christmas, May-October 9 to 5 and November-April 9 to 4. Adults $10, children $5.

Mystic Marinelife Aquarium, Coogan Boulevard, Mystic. (203) 536-3323. Two Steller's sea lions cavort in an outdoor pool at the entrance to the stark gray building a gull's glide from I-95. Inside are 38 aquariums of various sizes containing 6,000 specimens, themed according to adaptation methods and aquatic communities (New England, tropical and Pacific coast waters). Each is well labeled and highly instructive, and the inhabitants get bigger as you move on, finally reaching the beluga whales and dolphins.

Guides lead periodic tours of the outdoor Seal Island complex, which occupies 2.5 acres of land right beside the interstate (the five species of seals and sea lions seem oblivious to the roar of passing traffic). A marsh pond between the aquarium and Seal Island features a variety of waterfowl, including some colorful redhead ducks. Beyond is the site of the aquarium's planned $4.3 million **Whale Study Center,** the first in the world.

Alone worth the price of the admission is the hourly demonstration in the 1,400-seat **Marine Theater** upstairs. Aquarium officials call it a training demonstration; the audience calls it quite a show. In one segment, Skipper, a 500-pound sea lion, twirled a ball on his nose, applauded and balanced his entire weight on one flipper; then he bounced a ball as he turned, rolled and slid, finally saying "oh yeah," on command. One of the performing dolphins cleared a hurdle held over the trainer's head, soared through a hoop, tossed a ball and did both a front flip and a one-and-one-half laid-out back flip. As visitors leave the theater, the performers are on view in the tanks downstairs. From that vantage point, little would one suspect how talented they are.

Open daily, 9 to 6 in summer, 9 to 4:45 rest of year; closed Thanksgiving, Christmas and Jan. 1. Adults $6.25, children $3.25.

The USS Nautilus Memorial/Submarine Force Library and Museum, Naval Submarine Base-New London, Route 12, Groton, (203) 449-3174. The storied Nautilus, the world's first nuclear-powered submarine, was built at Groton's General Dynamics Electric Boat Division shipyard in 1954. Returned to its birthplace, it has been opened to visitors after cruising faster, deeper, farther and longer than any craft in history. The submarine museum traces the history of underwater navigation, showing a submarine control room, working periscopes and models depicting submarine style and development. The highlight for most is a short tour of portions of the 319-foot-long Nautilus. The lines may be long, but you get to see the operations deck, torpedo room, dining quarters and berth areas. Open daily except Tuesday 9 to 5, April 15 through September; rest of year, 9 to 3:30 weekdays and 9 to 5 on weekends; closed every Tuesday and the first full week of January, April, July and October, plus Thanksgiving, Christmas and New Year's Day. Free.

USS Croaker, 359 Thames St., Groton. (203) 448-1616. A better look inside a submarine is afforded by this World War II beauty also berthed near its birthplace. A non-profit memorial association opens the 312-foot-long vessel for tours of the torpedo rooms, engine room, control room, officers' quarters, the 65-foot periscope and the berth room in which 32 crewmen bunked in four tight rows stacked four high with barely enough room to turn over. Seeing how 76 men lived underwater is fascinating for those who don't get claustrophobia. Open daily, 9 to 5 mid-April to mid-October, 9 to 3 rest of year. Adults $3, children $1.50.

Boat Tours

S.S. Sabino, South Gate, Mystic Seaport, 572-0711, Ext. 251. The 57-foot, two-deck Sabino is the last coal-fired passenger steamboat operating in the country. Built in 1908 and long used on Maine's Casco Bay, it was acquired in 1974 by Mystic Seaport for passenger excursions. Half-hour river cruises are available to 100 Seaport visitors hourly from 11 to 4; adults $2.25, children $1.50. The Sabino is at its best after hours when it gives 90-minute evening cruises down the Mystic River past Noank and Masons Island to Fishers Island Sound. It's at its very best during the summer musical cruises: Dixieland jazz on Sundays, barbershop quartets on Thursdays and chantey singers on Wednesdays. Regular cruises, daily at 5, mid-May to mid-October, also at 7 in July and August. Adults $5.50, children $3.50. Musical cruises, $6 to $8.50.

Out O' Mystic Schooner Cruises, 7 Holmes St., Box 487, Mystic, 536-4218. (800) 243-0416. The Mystic windjammer fleet is known for the **Mystic Clipper** and the **Mystic Whaler,** which offer seagoing vacations on board. The newer, 125-foot-long Mystic Clipper carries 125 day passengers and can house 56 overnight in private and coed quarters. Trips of one, three or five days may go to Newport, Block Island, Sag Harbor or Greenport. Rates run from $45 for one-day sneak-away cruises and $59 for overnights to $385 to $525 for five-day cruises. Those with less time enjoy three-hour quarterdeck dinner cruises on the Whaler and Clipper Fridays, Saturdays and Sundays at 5. Full dinners with wine cost $39. The Mystic Clipper sails Chesapeake Bay out of Annapolis, Md., in spring and fall. Operating season in Mystic, early May to late October.

Voyager Cruises, Steamboat Wharf, Mystic, 536-0416 or (800) 243-0882. Designed and built by owner-captain Frank Fulchiero, the replica of a 19th century packet schooner gives everything from half-day sails to three-day cruises, depending on reservations. The Voyager has 10 private cabins (with running water and rare hot-water showers) and a professional chef known for his clam chowder and lobster bakes. Two-day cruises, $179 to $249; three-day cruises, $249 to $329. Operates June-October.

Noank Rose, 52 Riverview Ave., Noank, 536-8372. Capts. Ben and Frank Rathbun give short sails as well as three-day sails on their charter sloop for three to six people. They personalize their cruises so you can sail where you wish, and offer sunbathing or swimming ("suits or au natural as desired," according to their brochure). Day sails from 8:30 to 4:30 are $55 each, including lunch; three-hour evening sails from 5:30 to 8:30 are $20; three-day cruises, $185.

River Queen, 193 Thames St., Groton. 445-8111. "See Submarines by Boat," is the pitch for the open but covered River Queen. It plies the Thames River as it passes the USS Nautilus nuclear sub, the USS Croaker, the U.S. Coast Guard Academy and the U.S. Naval Submarine Base, and you may see new Trident subs under construction at the Electric Boat Division of General Dynamics. It's billed as a friendly one-hour harbor tour, but all the subs and Navy ships look rather unfriendly. Tours at 11:15, 12:30, 1:45 and 3 on weekends in spring and fall, also 10 a.m. and daily in summer. Adults $4.75, children $2.75. The River Queen has two-hour Dixieland jazz cruises Saturday evenings at 7 and sunset dinner cruises Wednesdays and Fridays.

Other Cruises. The 42-foot Ketch Majestic, 27 W. Main St., Mystic, 536-1943, provides day, evening or overnight sails. The Sea Duck, Noank, 274-2511, offers full or half-day charters for sightseeing, cruising and fishing.

Land Tours

Auto Tape Tours of the Mystic area are available on cassette. Tapes may be obtained for $10.95 at the Mystic information center in Olde Mystick Village and at tourist attractions and stores.

Sightseeing Tours are given by **Out O'Mystic Tours,** Mystic information center, 572-0070. Local guides provide the narration on nine-passenger minibuses for land and sea tours, including Mystic, Noank and the Nautilus sub. Tours start daily at 10; prices $5.95 and up.

Mystic Walking Tour. A guide to the historic homes along Gravel, Clift and High Streets on the west bank of the Mystic River is available from the Chamber of Commerce's depot office. Many of the large white homes with dark shutters are visible from the other side of the river or from Mystic Seaport. For an up-close look, a leisurely walking tour takes about one hour and points out what the guide calls "the little differences of each house."

STONINGTON. There's no tour as such, but a stroll along Water and Main streets and cross streets is a must. The Stonington Historical Society has marked with signs many 18th and 19th century structures, including the home where the mother of artist James Whistler and later poet Stephen Vincent Benet lived and the birthplace of Capt. Nathaniel Brown Palmer, discoverer of Antarctica. The borough is full of large homes crowding their lots right up to the sidewalks; the architecture is an intriguing mix of gambrel roofs, old Cape Cod and pillared Greek Revival. At the end of Water Street is the **Old Lighthouse Museum,** the first government lighthouse in Connecticut. It houses the Stonington Historical Society's collection of whaling and fishing gear, articles from the Orient trade and an exquisite dollhouse. Today, Stonington is home to a number of celebrities who cherish its quiet charm, which you can best appreciate by walking its streets.

Other Attractions

SWIMMING. Most of the shorefront in this area is privately owned, and beaches are few. For surf swimming, head across the Rhode Island state line to Watch Hill and Misquamicut, which face the open ocean. A protected beach called **Esker Point** at Groton Long Point has picnic tables in the trees; there's no surf, but it's uncrowded and open to the public.

WINERIES. Southeastern Connecticut's mild climate and its proximity to water have spawned several small boutique wineries. **Clarke Vineyard**, Taugwonk Road, Stonington, offers wine tastings and sales Tuesday-Sunday 10 to 5. Also along Taugwonk Road (Exit 91 north off I-95), **Stonecrop Vineyard** offers a casual winery tour and wine tastings weekends, Tuesdays and Thursdays from 10 to 5. **Crosswoods Vineyards**, Chester Main Road, produces excellent chardonnays among its California-style viniferas and may take visitors by appointment (535-2205).

ART. The **Mystic Art Association Gallery** off Water Street beside the river features changing exhibitions and special events in the summer. The **Mystic Seaport Museum Store** has a new art gallery and a variety of nautical arts and crafts. **Framers of the Lost Art** in Factory Square is one of several galleries. Mystic hosts the annual **Mystic Outdoor Art Festival**, scheduled the second weekend in August and considered one of the largest in the East.

SHOPPING. Mystic is one tourist area without a shopping plaza or mall as such, and yet it has an uncommon concentration of good stores.

Olde Mystick Village, Route 27 at I-95, has 46 shops in a nicely landscaped, built-to-look-old complex. Here is a catch-all of boutiques, gift shops and such to appeal to tourists, and catch them all they do. It's a sightseeing attraction in itself, the carillon music from its Anglican chapel lending a happy air and the ducks in a pond beside the water wheel keeping youngsters amused.

Across Coogan Boulevard are the new **Clockworks Factory Outlets,** where Manhattan, Van Heusen, Swank, Quoddy and Bali-L'Eggs-Hanes are among those represented. Nearby on Route 27 is **Seaport Fabric & Gifts,** full of designer fabrics for draperies and upholstery (seconds and overruns), most from $5.95 to $14.95 a yard. Many of our Hartford friends do their fabric shopping here.

Water Street in West Mystic has small shops in the restored **Factory Square** buildings, as well as the **Emporium,** three floors of zany items. Its shopping bag proclaims "Shop Until You Drop," and you just might as you open some of the more offbeat (and offcolor) cards. Further out Water Street at 375 Noank Road is **The Market,** a nifty gourmet deli and market in which classical music plays as you pick out gift baskets with Abbott's Lobster in the Rough products, a placemat saying "Bone Appetit" for a pampered pet, or luscious desserts, available by the slice.

In Stonington, more antiques shops pop up every time we visit. **Grand & Water** is one of the best. We're partial to the **Hungry Palette,** whose screened fabrics are turned into beautiful skirts that match the wall hangings displayed in the window; we coveted some of the corduroy ones for winter. **Quimper Faience** has firsts and seconds of the popular handpainted French china, while **Sugar and Spice** doles out everything from vinegars and coffee beans to English bangers and Portuguese bread.

In downtown Mystic, **Whyevernot** has unique things, from jewelry to fabrics, and we picked up a few gifts at **Peppergrass & Tulip**, which stocks a choice selection of McBeeton's preserves, wood carvings, lacy pillows and baskets; owner Mary Ellen Grills will make up gift baskets for any occasion. **Wind and Wood** has interesting crafts, some in a cat motif, and the **Company of Craftsmen** offers American crafts. **Everything But the Stamp** purveys a large selection of paper goods, and we chuckled over Humphrey Beargart and Lauren Bearcall, dressed-up bears in the window of **Good-Hearted Bears. Mystical Toys** lives up to its name. **McMonogram** has nice bags, purses and totes. **The Bermuda Shop, William Bendett, Pentangle Fashion Boutique** and **Waves Fashions** offer elegant to trendy clothing. **Nantucket Mills** stocks wool and cotton sweaters at discounted prices. The **Irish Currach** has everything Irish from tea to overcoats.

Where to Eat
Fancy Dining

The Harborview, Water Street at Cannon Square, Stonington. (203) 535-2720. Southeastern Connecticut's first restaurant of distinction is still going strong in its second decade. It's French, has a good view of the water and a convivial spirit, especially in its popular tavern. The large dark-paneled main dining room with blue linens, pink napkins and fresh flowers is the setting for fine food offered by owners Jerry and Ainslie Turner, who look to Brittany for their inspiration. Dinners run from $11.95 for breast of chicken with tarragon cream to $16.95 for a classic bouillabaisse. The veal sweetbreads in a vol-au-vent pastry are superb, as are the curried shrimp, the lobster baked with pernod creme and mushrooms, and the veal with chestnuts, green peppercorns and bordelaise sauce. Many dinner items are available at lunch (entrees $5.95 to $8.95), and the rustic bar offers daily specials and lower-priced entrees. We like the lavish Sunday brunch buffet ($11.95), which has interesting hot dishes (wonderful omelets full of fresh crabmeat, seafood en croute) and enough food to keep us happy for a couple of days. Lunch daily, 11:30 to 3; dinner 5 to 3; Sunday brunch, 11 to 3; closed Tuesday in winter.

J.P. Daniels, Route 181, Old Mystic. (203) 572-9564. Flawless service and consistently good continental cuisine are the hallmarks of this off-the-beaten-path restaurant, a favorite with locals who like the candlelit elegance of a converted dairy barn. Some find its high ceilings a bit cavernous; others pay more attention to the white-linened tables and what's on the plate, and everyone appreciates the light fare offered in the lounge nightly except Saturday. Dinner entrees in the $14.95 to $16.95 range include coquilles St. Jacques, broiled scallops and bouillabaisse. We hear the curried shrimp, veal Oscar and several filet mignon presentations are good, and the wines are moderately priced. Dinner nightly, 5 to 9:30 or 10; Sunday, 4 to 9:30.

Flood Tide, Route 1, Mystic. (203) 536-8140. A new porte cochere, entrance and lobby lead into this popular restaurant at the Inn at Mystic. Past the airy lounge with its leather chairs is the spacious two-level dining room with handsome patterned wallpaper, brass chandeliers, sturdy captain's chairs and large windows to view Pequotsepos Cove. Tables are appointed with white linens, a single rose in a small vase, etched-glass lamps and hammered silverware. Executive chef Peter Schroll's interest in fine wines is evident in the wine list. We were impressed with his $8.95 luncheon buffet, which had everything from seviche, caviar, seafood salad, eggs Benedict, seafood crepes and beef bourguignon to bread pudding and kiwi tarts. Dinner is where the chef shines, with appetizers ($3.95 to $6.95) like smoked fisherman's platter, a crepe filled with lobster madeira or herbed mushroom soup Diana. Shrimp primavera or tempura, mixed grill, veal Zurich vol au vent and duckling with peach glaze are some of the entrees, priced from $10.95 for a vegetarian fiesta to $21.95 for baked stuffed lobster. From a large dessert menu you may choose things like Jamaican coffee jelly with tia maria, peppermint profiteroles or strawberry parfait amour. Lunch, Monday-Saturday, 11:30 to 3; dinner, 5:30 to 9:30; Sunday brunch, 11 to 3.

Seamen's Inne, Route 27, Mystic. (203) 536-9649. Adjacent to Mystic Seaport is this large and popular establishment, now under the ownership of Jon Kodama, who also has the Steak Loft in Mystic and Dave & Eddie's in Newport. The menu changes quarterly, the wine list offers more than 400 varieties, a new **Riverfront Terrace** operates in summer and there are two restaurants, **Felicity's** and the more casual **Atlantic Ocean Grille.** The latter is a particularly fetching place for lunch or supper. It's properly time-worn with a pressed-tin ceiling, bare wood floors and tables, rich red velvet-cushioned bentwood chairs and a greenhouse window filled with plants. We thoroughly enjoyed a lunch of clam chowder (thick and delicious for $2.50 a bowl) and two appetizers, poached mussels with salsa ($3.95) and nachos Atlantic ($6.50), the latter such an enormous portion of tasty shrimp, scallops, cheese and crisp tortilla chips that we couldn't even try the lemon-ginger or orange mousses for dessert ($2.50). An excellent complimentary seafood dip with melba rounds precedes each meal (ask the hostess for the recipe for your next party). Main courses here are in the $7.95 to $10.95 range. Felicity's is larger with ladderback chairs, carpeting and white tablecloths. Among dinner entrees ($11.95 to $17.95) are lobster pasta, seafood stew, rack of lamb and an interesting sounding dish of sea scallops stir-fried with lobster, snow peas, scallions, ginger, garlic and water chestnuts. Start with grilled shrimp with leeks ($4.95) and finish with chocolate marquise cake or hearts of cream (creme fraiche, cream cheese and raspberry sauce, $2.50). The wine list is exceptionally varied and exceptionally reasonable, with a number of offerings in the $10 range. Open daily from 11:30 to 9 or 10, year-round.

The Mooring, Mystic Hilton Hotel, Coogan Boulevard, Mystic. (203) 572-0731. A comfortable three-level dining room with arm chairs and banquettes in deep blue looks onto an outdoor courtyard. On the main wall is a striking sculptural relief of overlapping oars. The menu is limited and nouvelle. Some natives complain that the portions leave them hungry, but we were satisfied after our dinners of roast rack of lamb — four nice pink little chops accompanied by new potatoes, pieces of grilled yellow squash, zucchini and eggplant, and half a broiled tomato — and medallions of venison with a sauce of port wine, sage and chanterelles, plus green beans and carrots. Good crunchy French bread and salads of mixed greens and radicchio (with pieces so large they had to be cut with a knife) preceded. For dessert, the almond lace cookie filled with chocolate mousse and liqueur was enough for two. Dinner entrees are priced from $13.75 for five-spice roast chicken to $19.50 for braised lobster with sweetened red cabbage, champagne and truffles. The all-American wine list contains bargains like a Fetzer zinfandel for $10.50. For other meals, the continental breakfast at $4.50 seems overpriced; at lunch, a grilled duck and spinach salad with spiced pecans for $5.75 or a seafood pasta for $6.75 does not. Lunch, Monday-Saturday 11:30 to 2:30; dinner, 6 to 10 or 10:30; Sunday brunch, noon to 3.

The Fisherman, 937 Groton Long Point Road, Noank. (203) 536-1717. A good view of the water and an elegant nautical decor are offered by Christine Walker, who took over the old Yankee Fisherman and upgraded both the facility and the menu. About 150 diners can be seated in two dining rooms, the side room with the best view handsomely outfitted in blue, the larger rear dining room in gray and maroon. Once you sit in the unusual cushioned chairs that swivel and rock, you may never get up. Dinners run from $12.95 for chicken francaise or whitefish supreme to $19.95 for beef Wellington duxelles, tournedos, lobster thermidor, a fried fisherman's platter and surf and turf. The sole layered with crabmeat and mushroom pate, surrounded by puff pastry and topped with bearnaise sauce, sounds interesting. The house salad is tossed with a strawberry-amaretto dressing. The lounge offers light fare, and entertainment on weekends. Lunch daily, 11:30 to 3; dinner 5 to 10.

Captain Daniel Packer Inne, 32 Water St., Mystic. (203) 536-3555. Once a stagecoach stop on the New York to Boston route, this restored 1756 inn receives mixed reviews, but you can't fault the historic atmosphere recreated by young owner Richard Kiley. Downstairs is a crowded tavern where a light pub menu is served amid the original walls of brick and stone. The main floor has a couple of handsome dining rooms with working fireplaces, and a new second-floor room handles the overflow or private parties. The dinner menu, with entrees from $9.75 to $17.95, contains some surprises: pork chops Calabrese or Greek-style lamb chops (both seasoned with oregano and garlic), pepper steak glazed with Jack Daniels, veal Sicilian and shrimp dijon, served French style at the table over rice pilaf. Homemade cheesecake is a favored dessert, and there's a new Sunday buffet brunch for $9.95. Lunch Monday-Saturday, 11:30 to 3; dinner, 5 to 10; Sunday brunch, 11 to 2:30.

More Casual Places

Noah's, 113 Water St., Stonington. (203) 535-3925. Small and homey, the two dining rooms here are usually packed with regulars who appreciate good food at refreshing prices. Regional or ethnic specialties are posted nightly to complement dinners on the order of broiled flounder, cod Portuguese, pork chop, pasta and breast of chicken, with everything priced under $10. Lest we mislead: the fare is interesting, from the house chicken liver pate with sherry and pistachios ($2.65) to the Greek country or farmer's chop suey salads at lunch. Save room for the homemade desserts. Noah's is fully licensed, offering most wines around $10. Breakfasts are a bargain as well, the thick wedges of french toast made from challah bread going for $2.50. Breakfast, 7 to 11; lunch, 11:15 to 2:30; dinner 6 to 9 or 9:30. Closed Monday and month of February.

Skipper's Dock, 66 Water St., Stonington. (203) 535-2000. You'll be hard-pressed to find a better waterside location than the outdoor deck at this casual restaurant operated by — and right behind — the Harborview. That the food is so appealing and reasonably priced is a bonus. On a sunny November day we sat beside the water (the plastic sides on the canopy-covered deck were down to cut any chill) and enjoyed a lunch of Portuguese seafood stew and a tasty linguini with shrimps and clams, studded with black olives, red pimentos, artichokes and capers (both $5.95). The bloody mary was enormous, the bread so good we asked for seconds and the main portions so ample we didn't want dessert. The lunch menu is a smaller version of the dinner, when entrees are in the $10.95 to $12.95 range. The name and much of the nautical-historical motif came from the original Skipper's Dock in Noank; a rainbow of colorful buoys hangs from the exterior. Lunch daily 11:30 to 4, dinner from 4. Open April-November.

Abbott's Lobster in the Rough, 117 Pearl St., Noank. (203) 536-7719. It's altogether fitting that this old lobstering town would be the home for 40 years of a lobster pound like those you dream of (and occasionally find) in Maine. Right beside the Mystic River as it opens into Fishers Island Sound and casual as can be with picnic tables of assorted colors resting on mashed-up clam shells, this is the place for lobster — as well as steamers, mussels, clam chowder, crab rolls and the like. You line up to place your order inside, then take a seat and sip a drink or wine (BYOB) as you await the freshest seafood around. It's not inexpensive (a complete seafood dinner, last we knew, was $16.75), but we always find the experience worth it, and Abbott's mail-order sales of specialties like clam chowder testify to its success. Open daily, noon to 9, May-September. No credit cards.

Cove Fish Market Takeout, Old Stonington Road, Mystic. (203) 536-0061. There's no atmosphere or view — a lineup of picnic tables beside Route 1 — but the prices are right at this takeout stand that's an adjunct to a fish market. You can get a crab pattie burger for $2.55, fish and chips for $3.75, fried clams for $6.50 or splurge for a single lobster ($6.75) or twin lobsters ($12.25). Open daily, May-September. BYOB.

Sailor Ed's, Old Stonington Road, Mystic. (203) 572-9524. Billed as Mystic's oldest seafood restaurant (1924), this large place is near the Cove Fish Market and popular with families. They like the touristy-nautical decor and the fresh-off-the-boat seafood, most of it priced under $10. When we stopped, a shore dinner with chowder, steamers, boiled lobster, corn on the cob and Indian pudding was going for $10.95, and the weekend prime rib specials were $10.95 and $12.95. An old-fashioned Sunday brunch is $10.95. Open daily from 11:30 to 9 or 10; Sunday brunch, 11 to 3.

Seahorse Restaurant, 65 Marsh Road, Noank. (203) 536-1670. You'll likely mix with yachtsmen and fishermen at this out-of-the-way establishment which looks like a gin mill but serves up good steaks and seafood. The lively bar is filled with locals, but at tables or booths in the two-level dining room you can order anything from sandwiches to cold seafood plates to sirloin steaks or shrimp florentine (both $10.95). The setting is basic and so is the food, but the entire menu is available all day. When did you last see a steak or cold roast beef sandwich for $1.95, or a plate of fried clams for $4.25? Open daily, 11 to 10.

Anthony J's, 6 Holmes St., Mystic. (203) 536-0448. The old Mischievous Carrot has turned into a small, pleasant Italian restaurant, with about 15 tables on either side of a lively bar, where you can order from a small bar menu that includes Philly steak. The food is rated well locally, especially the veal and shrimp dishes in the $9.95 to $12.95 range. Most of the Italian standards are on the rather extensive menu, including pastas served with salad and bread for $5.95 to $7.95. Lunch, 11:30 to 2:30; dinner, 5:30 to 9:30 or 10. Sunday, 4 to 9:30.

Other Mystic Choices

Mystic's Main Street has more than its share of restaurants catering to tourists. Take a look at the crowds inside the **BeeBee Dairy** restaurant — which, incidentally, is known for its ice cream — and you'll see what we mean. The **Flying Bridge** at the Whaler's Inn is a busy spot for outdoor casual dining. Otherwise, you might as well be in any restaurant in any tourist town. **Giaco's Ships Lantern Restaurant** at least has some interesting daily specials (on one winter night, grilled yellowfin tuna, broiled red snapper and veal sauteed with grand marnier, $10.95 to $12.95). That's more than can be said for either the **Landing at Steamboat Wharf** or the **Mystic River Tavern**, both relatively new establishments blessed with riverside locations but marred since their beginnings by inconsistency, ownership changes and erratic menus, although we heard changes for the better were in store.

Two standbys are **Margaritaville**, the Mexican restaurant and watering hole run by the Chuck's Steak House chain, serving inside and out daily from 5 at 12 Water St. in Factory Square, and the ever-popular **Steak Loft,** a classic of its genre, open daily from noon at Route 27 and Coogan Boulevard, beside Olde Mystick Village.

Two Sisters Deli, 4 Pearl St., 536-1244. Kate Halsey and Cindy Halsey Shaw make up for what their nearby competitors lack in creativity with their popular New York-style deli and restaurant seating 35. So successful is their formula that they have branched out to Captain's Walk in New London as well. After placing your order at a counter, they call you by your first name to pick up an oversize sandwich, a salad or, in our case, a hodgepodge lunch of shrimp and crab newburg with side salads of winter vegetables and lentil with orzo ($8.95 for two). You might find pizza rustica, hamburger stew or spinach ricotta quiche, but whatever you find will be good and pleasantly priced (chicken divan with a stuffed potato, $3.25). Desserts and bagels are scrumptious. For breakfast, try a bagel with scrambled egg, 99 cents. Open daily from 7 a.m.

Kitchen Little, Route 27, Mystic. (203) 536-2122. Last but not least is this tiny gem, where people line up to get in for breakfast on hottest summer or coldest winter days. We waited our turn in the January chill for a memorable breakfast of scrambled eggs with crabmeat and cream cheese ($3.65), served with raisin toast, and a spicy scrambled egg dish with jalapeno cheese on grilled corned beef hash ($3.25), accompanied by toasted dill rye. Everything was absolutely yummy — and we could barely eat lunch. The coffee flowed into the red mugs, the folks occupying the nine tables and five seats at the counter were jovial, and two window tables even look onto the Mystic River. You can eat outside at a few picnic tables in season. Florence Brochu's open kitchen measures 19 feet square, but what creations she puts out, all in the $1.95 to $3.95 range. Breakfast daily, 6:30 to noon; Sunday, 7:30 to 1.

FOR MORE INFORMATION: Mystic Chamber of Commerce, Railroad Depot, Route 1 at Broadway, Box 143, Mystic, Conn. 06355. (203) 536-8559. The large Mystic and Shoreline Visitor Information Center, Old Mystick Village, 536-1641, has materials for Mystic as well as for much of Southern New England.

Youngster digs in sand at Narragansett Beach.

Narragansett, R.I.

Although most people don't realize it, the Narragansett of nearly a century ago was a society resort rivaling Newport.

The New York Times commented in 1877 that Narragansett was "an American watering place in the truest sense of the term." A writer for Harper's Weekly wrote in the late 1800s: "The habitues of the place are, in general, people of the same social standing as those of Newport and have in the main less money."

Aristocratic vacationers from New York, Philadelphia and points south frequented no fewer than 10 major hotels, built summer "cottages" only slightly smaller than Newport's mansions and reveled in the recreational and social goings-on at the Stanford White-designed Narragansett Casino. They enjoyed what they considered a simplicity and lack of pretension, as opposed to the more affluent Newport across Narragansett Bay.

A fire in 1900 destroyed the large Rockingham Hotel and the adjacent casino. More fires, financial difficulties and changing vacation patterns wiped out the other hotels in the first part of this century. The hurricanes of 1938 and 1954 left standing only a few reminders of the resort's colorful past.

The landmark granite Towers spanning Ocean Road at the entrance to the old Casino and the high-rent district remain as a symbol of the Narragansett that was. So do a number of spacious, often hidden mansions of modern-day Newport proportions.

Today, with less of an identity and "less money" than Newport, as the Harper's writer put it, Narragansett is often overlooked by out-of-staters. It's a mecca for Rhode Islanders who cherish its beaches, its boating and its fishing, and its active, do-it-yourself style.

"People who get lost on their way to Newport are beginning to discover us," said the woman in the Chamber of Commerce information office in the Towers. "This is getting to be the up-and-coming place."

For beaches and sportfishing, Narragansett and its South County neighbors

153

have few peers — at least on the mainland — and they imbue the area with an unusual character. There are few swank hotels, restaurants, shops and other accouterments of the Newport type here — just lots of sandy strands and fine fishing grounds and the kinds of tourism that accompany them.

Amid nature's splendors are remnants from the area's 350-year history. The Narragansett Indian Statue, the Old Narragansett Church, the Gilbert Stuart Birthplace and Snuff Mill, the 1750 Casey Farm, the quaint living-museum village of Wickford and the working-fishing village of Galilee are reminders of another era.

Getting There

At the west entrance to Narragansett Bay opposite Newport, Narragansett is located on Scenic Route 1A off U.S. Route 1. It is 15 miles east of Interstate 95 and 30 miles south of Providence.

Where to Stay

This is a highly seasonal area, and lodging establishments react accordingly. Summer weekend rates are highest; midweek and off-season may be lower.

By the Water

The Village Inn, 1 Beach St., Narragansett 02882. (401) 783-6767 or (800) 843-7437. Built in 1984 as part of an urban-renewal facelift that has changed the look of Narragansett, this three-story motor inn is just across the road from the town beach, the village green and the historic Towers — and right in the thick of the action. Many of the 57 rooms have ocean views; all are comfortable and contemporary with soft sand colors, color TV, side chairs and small private balconies. We particularly liked Room 320, nicely angled (even the bathroom is angled) and claiming a great view of beach and water. Originally known as Durfee's at the Pier, the inn was acquired in 1986 by the Patel family, who changed the name, leased out the dining room and turned the coffee shop into a pub. The heated indoor pool and jaunty outdoor dining and drinking deck remain. Doubles, $110 to $130. Open year-round.

Stone Lea, 40 Newton Ave., Narragansett 02882. (401) 783-9546. Former New Bedford restaurateur Brian Crete and his wife bill this as "the ultimate bed and breakfast," and in Narragansett terms, they're right. Designed in 1883 by the architectural firm of McKim, Mead and White, this brown shingled mansion is right beside the sea, down a side road off Ocean Road a mile south of town. The large entrance hall with its parquet floor is most impressive, as is the beautiful staircase in the shape of a harp. Nine large guest rooms on the second and third floors have private baths — one, with an old pedestal sink, is about the largest we've seen. One of three oceanfront rooms has two double beds and an enormous window seat for savoring the view. All rooms have at least a partial ocean view, and the sea breeze is cooling on warmest days. Shortly after opening in 1986, Brian still was putting finishing touches on the furnishings — "my truck pulls over by itself and stops at any antiques sale," he quipped. He serves a full breakfast of the guest's choice on quilted mats at four tables in the dining room. Upon request, he also offers dinners. Guests enjoy a spacious front parlor, a wicker-filled porch and a terrace and lawns outside. Doubles, $95 to $125. Open mid-April to late October, weekends rest of year. Closed Dec. 20 to Feb. 13.

Pier House Inn, 113 Ocean Road, Narragansett 02882. (401) 783-4704. The former Neptune Motel and bar were turned into the Pier House Inn in 1986 by Anna Toro and her husband, Jay, a professional musician. His interests explain the light jazz series they launched that first summer in their refurbished **Tiffany Lounge** and restaurant. The likes of Dave Brubeck, Dizzy Gillespie and Herbie Mann were on the docket every other week or so in what they compared to "an intimate private party," that they planned to repeat throughout the year. Decorated with an air of elegance are three dining rooms and lounge seating a total of 190; the breezy new terrace has an outdoor barbecue grill and serves lunch and drinks. Upstairs in the inn are eight large guest rooms, all with private baths and three with oceanfront porches. Anna Toro had plans to upgrade the mismatched furniture here, as well as to redecorate the 18 motel units behind the inn. Doubles, $85 to $95 in inn, $75 in motel.

Atlantic Motor Inn, 85 Ocean Road, Narragansett 02882. (401) 783-5534. Fourteen of 34 units face the water at this motel and all have access to the second-story porch over the entry and to the lawns down to the ocean. Most rooms go off an interior hotel-style corridor; furnishings are serviceable if a bit plain (no closets; a hanger rail beside the bed). Doubles, $54 to $59. Open mid-April to late October.

Away from the Water

The Phoenix, 29 Gibson Ave., Narragansett 02882. (401) 783-1918 02882. One of the first of Narragansett's many small B&Bs, this is also one of the largest and nicest. Five guest rooms share baths in an 1888 Stanford White-designed summer cottage facing a vast lawn and a near-replica at the other end. Nestled behind tall hedges among similar homes in a quiet residential compound initiated by New York restaurateur Louis Sherry (who ran the Newport Casino dining room), the Phoenix has a big wraparound veranda where afternoon sherry is served. Its fireplaced living room is a comfortable combination of upholstered leather and wicker furniture, and high-back velvet chairs flank the tables in a paneled dining room. An upstairs vestibule doubles as a small library. Two guest rooms go off either end of the upstairs hallway, with shared bath between corridor and rooms. Dutch wooden shoes scattered here and there are accents. Innkeepers Joyce and Dave Peterson serve a full breakfast that might include eggs Benedict or lobster quiche. Doubles, $30 to $50. Open year-round.

Larchwood Inn, 176 Main St., Wakefield 02879. (401) 783-5454. Situated away from Narragansett in the midst of expansive lawns in bustling Wakefield, the Larchwood Inn is the area's only real inn (operating since 1926), and is known locally for its dining. Surrounded by a collection of ginkgo, copper beech, mountain ash, Japanese cherry and mulberry trees, among others, the three-story 1831 manor house has twelve guest rooms, seven with private baths, each individually decorated with period pieces. Across the street is the inn's recently acquired **Holly House**, an 1830s residence with seven renovated guest rooms, three with private baths, The Scottish heritage of earlier owners is reflected in the **Tam O'Shanter** cocktail lounge; excerpts from the poems of Robert Burns are found there and in the Crest Room, and his annual January birthday celebration is a bigger draw than New Year's Eve, according to innkeepers Frank and Diann Browning. Three meals a day are served in four dining rooms seating a total of 225. Doubles, $40 to $67. Open year-round.

Dutch Inn, Port of Galilee, Narragansett 02882. (401) 0789-9341. With its windmill at the entrance and its tropical indoor pool, this 100-room motel is a bit of an anomaly in in the midst of the simple fishing village of Galilee. The rooms are among the area's better accommodations. Most are in a two-story building outside but a few are grouped inside around the pool; all have dressing-room vanities, and some have bathroom phones. Off the plant-filled pool area are a sauna and exercise room and a large Tahiti-style cocktail area. A nice touch: the pool is reserved for adults three hours a day. The **Wheel-house** restaurant offers a large, mostly seafood menu, with entrees from $6.95 to $12.95. Doubles, $79 to $103. Open year-round.

The Sparrow's Nest, 470 Annaquatucket Road, Wickford 02852. (401) 295-1142. Slightly removed from Narragansett is this 1800s farmhouse, once a working farm with nearly three acres of gardens. Oceanographers Mary Worobec and Peter Doering have three rooms for overnight guests. They give guests suggestions for interesting marshes, tidal pools and such to explore. A continental breakfast is served in the dining room or underneath the apple tree. Doubles, $40 to $45. Open year-round.

Other Alternatives.

Many of the other lodging options are bed and breakfast, generally living up to the true sense of the word — residents opening a couple of rooms for overnight guests. "All the interesting people here run B&Bs," said our informant at the Chamber of Commerce.

Among them are historical society president Sallie Latimer, who owns the **Louis Sherry Cottage** at 59 Gibson Ave., a National Register-listed landmark, 783-8626, and **Wagon Wheel** at 16 Mathewson St., 783-7178, home of artist Marjorie Vogel, whose etchings of local scenes are displayed around town.

West Highland Cottage at Box 24, Saunderstown 02874, 294-3808, is the headquarters of **At Home in New England,** a regional B&B reservation service.

The Chamber of Commerce lists nearly a dozen cottage colonies, with rentals by the week or longer. Rooms and efficiencies also are listed.

Camping. Long Cove Marina Family Campsites offers 150 sites at Long Point Marina off Point Judith Road (Route 108). Fishermen's Memorial State Park has 147 trailer and 35 tent sites near the beaches off Point Judith Road.

Seeing and Doing

THE BEACHES. These are the big attraction, and the natives say they're the best in New England. There's one for every taste: quiet beaches, noisy beaches, people beaches and secluded beaches. The **Narragansett Bathing Pavilion,** the town beach right in the center of town, is the most crowded and often has good surfing (regional surfing competitions are staged annually). **Scarborough State Beach** and the **Roger Wheeler State Beach** at Sand Hill Cove are less crowded, sandy beaches. Many saltwater coves provide receptive areas for scuba divers.

WATER SPORTS. Narragansett Surf & Sports, Pier Village, 789-2323, rents sailboards, surfboards and diving equipment. So does the Watershed at 409 Main St., Wakefield, 789-1954. The Narragansett Pier Dive Shop, 145 Boon St., 783-2225, rents diving and snorkling equipment.

FISHING. Some of the world's most fertile fishing grounds are found off the Rhode Island coast, particularly the famed Block Island and Cox's Ledge areas. Galilee and Point Judith are known as the tuna capital of the world; the annual late-August tuna festival is a major attraction. The area is the third largest exporter of lobster in the world, and it has one of the oldest fishing co-ops in New England and is a major fishing port in New England. Other catches include bluefish, cod, flounder, shark, swordfish and marlin. A number of large open party boats sail daily at 6 a.m. and charge by the person, no reservations needed; prices range from $15 to $30. Charter boats are reserved for the day and the price is the same whether for one or six persons; bait and tackle are provided in the charter fee. Cost ranges from $200 to $700. The Chamber of Commerce lists 10 charter boats; sailing from Galilee or Jerusalem.

BOATING. You can rent a boat from a number of marinas to sail the waters made famous by the America's Cup races. And be sure to take the ferry for at least a day trip to Block Island.

M/V Southland, State Pier, Galilee. (401) 783-2954. Eleven-mile nautical sightseeing cruises on the two-decker Southland are offered in season out of Galilee. The 145-passenger boat goes through the Galilee Breachway into the protected Harbor of Refuge, on to the Point Judith Lighthouse and back past Jerusalem and Snug Harbor into the Great Salt Pond. One-and-three-quarter-hour cruises are scheduled at 11, 1, 3 and 5. Adults $4.

Interstate Navigation Co., Galilee State Pier, Point Judith. (401) 783-4613. (Mailing Address: Box 482, New London, Conn. 06320). Eight cruises a day to Block Island are offered from 8 a.m. to 7 p.m. in peak season. The island is one of the most beautiful in the Atlantic and makes a good day trip. Its long shoreline contains good beaches and one of the best harbors in the Northeast; the town of Old Harbor is fun to explore, and the bicycling is great. Sailing time is a little over one hour. Round trips, adults $8; children $4.

Cultural Attractions

Theatre-by-the-Sea, Route 1, Matunuck. (401) 789-1094. Founded in 1933, this is one of the oldest barn theaters in the country and is listed on the National Register of Historic Places. Stars from Eve Arden to Mae West have graced its stage; the 1986 summer hits included "A Chorus Line" and "The Unsinkable Molly Brown." The theater offers dinner and an after-show musical cabaret. Children's musicals are given Fridays at 11 and 1; all seats $2.75. The season runs from late June to early September, evenings except Monday and Wednesday matinees.

Summer concerts are offered periodically at the gazebo on the village green near the Towers at Narragansett Pier, Fridays at 7; at the Peace Dale village green Wednesdays at noon and Sundays at 6, and at Fishermen's State Park Saturdays at 7.

Historic Attractions

The area is steeped in history, although it doesn't flaunt it.

Canonchet Farm, Strathmore Street, Narragansett, across from the Narragansett Bathing Pavilion off Beach Street, is the new home of the South County Museum. The 174-acre park is a 19th century working mini-farm with wildflower garden and a cemetery with graves dating to 1700. Devoted to preserving the rural life in old Rhode Island, the museum has an extensive collection of tools, farm implements, utensils, vehicles and mechanical devices depicting life a century ago. An old print shop shows how newspapers were produced at the turn of the century. Adults $2, children $1, family maximum $5. Open Memorial Day through Labor Day, Wednesday-Sunday 11 to 5.

The **Narragansett Indian Statue**, a 23-foot-tall carved landmark in Sprague Park at Kingstown Road and Strathmore Street, is a visual stunner for passing motorists. Carved from a single Douglas fir by Peter Toth, it is one of a series of 41 throughout the country honoring the American Indian and reflects Narragansett's Indian heritage.

Casey Farm, Route 1A, Saunderstown, 294-8182. An unspoiled farm that was the site of Revolutionary War activity, this still-functioning farm has an assortment of animals and a fine collection of barns. The 200-year-old Casey homestead contains original pieces of furniture, family paintings, prints, china and documents from the 18th through 20th centuries. Operated by the Society for the Preservation of New England Antiquities, it is open in the summer Tuesdays, Thursdays and Sundays from 1 to 5. Adults $1.50; children 75 cents.

Gilbert Stuart Birthplace and Snuff Mill, Gilbert Stuart Road, Saunderstown, 294-3001. Born here in 1755, Gilbert Stuart was the foremost portraitist of George Washington. His deep red clapboard, Dutch Colonial-style house is turned away from the road to face a mirror-like millpond which is approached via a footbridge. The house contains few of his art works and is maintained more as a Colonial house museum than an art gallery. You also can tour the first snuff mill in America (1751), which is on the lower level of the house. Afterward, rent a rowboat and row up the Mettatuxet River to a 78-acre pond. Open March-November, daily except Friday, 11 to 5. Adults $1.25, children 50 cents.

WICKFORD. The entire village of Wickford is worth touring. Old churches, quaint shops, beautiful gardens and historic homes combine to present an image of life unchanged over the years. Named in 1662 and laid out in 1707, this is an historic town through and through, made all the more charming by the glimpses of Wickford Cove here and there. The Old Narragansett Church (1707) on Church Lane is the oldest Episcopal Church standing north of Virginia. A sign out front says tour guides are on duty from 11 to 5 in July and August; a small graveyard is adjacent.

SHOPPING. To our minds, Wickford has the most interesting shops in the area. We particularly like the **Wickford Gourmet Foods**, the **Green Ink** women's store, **Potpourri, Hands All Around, the Toy Cellar, Canvasworks, Cubby Hole** and the **British Connection.**

The **Pier Marketplace**, Ocean Road, is the shopping mecca for beachgoers in Narragansett. There are stores with trendy names like **Signatures Ltd., Body Talk, Fantaseas** and **Doubledecker Gifts Ltd.**, but sometimes the names are trendier than the stock. **Mariner Square** off Point Judith Road, Narragansett, has stores of the shopping center variety, and a large new mall was about to open nearby.

Where to Eat

Basil's, 22 Kingstown Road, Narragansett. (401) 789-3743. Consistently good and crowded is this small establishment in quarters formerly occupied by La Petite France. Basil Kourakas, who had been a chef in Vail, Colo., took it over in 1984 (to be closer to Europe, he said). Here he does all the cooking himself, offering a French-continental menu with no fewer than seven veal dishes, including his specialty with a cream and mushroom sauce. Other entrees ($10.95 to $16.95) include tarragon chicken, sole meuniere, duck à l'orange, pepper steak and steak Diane. Start with steamed mussels Brunoise, seviche or herring Lucas and finish with a French chocolate mousse, coupe Basil, a parfait or baked Alaska. The wine list is good, the dining room intimate and lovely with striking wallpaper and ornate-framed paintings. Dinner nightly.

Mercedes Ocean House, Mariner Square, 120 Point Judith Road, Narragansett. (401) 789-3380. The 15 nightly seafood specials chalked on the blackboard are reasons enough for visiting this good-looking restaurant in a shopping center. Chef-owner Chip Munro gets creative with things like Cajun saute, sole Carlsburg, blackened tuna and lobster Mercedes, the last a specialty in which lobster meat is sauteed with garlic and relishes and served over angel hair pasta. The regular menu includes bouillabaisse (the most expensive item at $14.95); broiled sole is $8.25, and three dishes are provided for "fish frowners." The wine list is excellent and reasonably priced. Dark paneled and cathedral ceilinged, the dining room and bar are outfitted with dark wood tables, Tiffany lamps, comfortable chairs and booths, and etched-glass drawings of Mercedes Benzes, as well as a single Ford. Lunch, Monday-Saturday from 11:30; dinner 4:30 to 10.

Center Cafe, 12 Tower Hill Road, Wakefield, (401) 789-3070. White cloths, maroon paper mats and fresh flowers give a sparkle to the small café off to one side of a seafood store and raw bar. Here again the most interesting items are the blackboard specials listing American and regional cuisine, things like Cajun tuna or salmon, mako shark au poivre citron, scallops Creole and egg fettuccine with mussels, priced from $9.50 to $13.95. More standard fare is available on the regular and takeout menu. Desserts here are exceptional: Italian rum cake, chocolate truffle cake, chocolate chambord cake and Bailey's Irish Cream mousse cake. You can BYOB from a package store nearby. Open Monday-Saturday, 11 to 4 and 5 to 9.

Antipasto's, Mariner Square, 140 Point Judith Road, Narragansett. (401) 789-5300. Would you believe there are six shrimp and scallop dishes among the blackboard specials at this small shopping-center cafe, which has a "super salad bar" in the rear corner, complete with turkey, ham and cheese. The regular menu offers a good selection of chicken, veal, beef and seafood dishes in interesting sauces, $7.95 to $11.95, plus the locally popular Buffalo wings. Dessert specials include cannoli and raspberry cheesecake. The 12 tables are covered with blue cloths and white napkins, and wines are available from a tiny bar. Lunch, Monday-Saturday from 11:30; dinner nightly.

Casa Rossi, 90 Point Judith Road, Narragansett. (401) 789-6385. Chef-owner Peter Rossi converted a house into a pleasant restaurant with orange walls, brown linen, and beige and brown sheer curtains. The emphasis here is on the food, based on family recipes passed down through the generations: homemade pastas, Italian breads and seven veal specialties. The menu lists about 20 interesting pastas, $3.95 to $12.95, served as entrees with bread and tossed salad. For $7.50 to $13.95, you also can get chicken marsala, baked stuffed shrimp, Sicilian flounder, steak zingarella and bracciole. Four Italian combination plates are available for $9.95. Open daily, 4 to 9 or 10, Sunday 1 to 9.

On the Water

Coast Guard House Restaurant, 40 Ocean Road, Narragansett. (401) 789-0700. We always enjoy lunch here on the upstairs deck beside the ocean, watching all the swimmers in the distance on the Narragansett beach and all the windsurfers riding the waves. In fact, one of us had our first lobster dinner here as a child and gave it short shrift to go outside onto the rocks to watch the pounding surf. The setting in the National Register-listed landmark beside the Towers is more interesting than the fare. At lunch on the deck, we enjoyed a seafood kabob and a sausage, pepper and onion sandwich, and admired the snail salad and the raw bar. The large dinner menu ($8.95 to $15.95) starts with escargots bourguignon and oysters Rockefeller, includes pastas and continental items like chicken cordon bleu and veal marsala, steaks and a dozen seafood dishes, and finishes with parfaits and international coffees. A fireplace warms the large cocktail lounge filled with velvet sofas and Victorian chairs. Lunch and dinner daily from 11:30; Sunday brunch, 11 to 2. Deck open until about 10.

Long John's Marina Park Restaurant, Salt Pond Road, Wakefield. (401) 789-4050. The lower outdoor deck and raw bar overlooking Great Salt Pond is the place for a snack or drink on a nice day. The quiet cove full of moored yachts is a tranquil sight. Limited fare ranges from shrimp (85 cents each) to hot dog, hamburg and lobster roll ($6.50). Upstairs, the long enclosed porch overlooking the water is a good spot for dinner, which ranges from $8.75 for poached scrod to $13.95 for boiled lobster and steamed mussels. Bouillabaisse and fried seafood dinners are other offerings. Lunch daily 11:30 to 3; dinner nightly 5 to 10.

The New Lighthouse Inn, Ocean Road, Point Judith. (401) 783-5422. An ocean view on three sides commends this restaurant under new management in 1986, beside the lighthouse at Point Judith. Large windows, crisp white and green linens and hanging plants are the setting for traditional fare: veal marsala, chicken cordon bleu, lobster pie, shrimp brochette Cajun style and baked scallops Nantucket ($8.95 to $13.95). There's plenty of fried seafood as well, and the large cocktail lounge has one of the area's best ocean views. Lunch and dinner daily, dancing on weekends.

Windsor's, Ocean Road, Point Judith. (401) 783-1522. The largest cocktail lounge in Southern Rhode Island, with dancing seven nights a week, shows where the emphasis is in this big and contemporary restaurant that opened in 1985. Dark pine tables dressed in white linen and burgundy paper mats, gray and burgundy banquettes, a vaulted ceiling and a central atrium-type staircase comprise a crisp decor. Second-floor tables have a water view, and an outdoor deck is used in summer. The menu ($8.95 to $12.95) features fresh seafood (the combination of shrimp, clams, scallops, crabmeat and scrod is served over linguini), pastas, veal, and surf and turf. Open daily from 11:30 to 10, year-round.

Enzo's at the Village Inn, 1 Beach St., Narragansett. (401) 783-6767. Vincenzo Donato, a Boston area chef for many years, took over the restaurant when ownership changed at Durfee's on the Pier. The airy, circular dining room is done up in beige and burgundy, with nicely spaced tables getting views of the ocean across the green. There's a small outdoor deck for lunch or drinks, and the continental-seafood menu offers something for everyone. Lunch and dinner daily.

Pier House Inn, 113 Ocean Road, Narragansett. (401) 783-4704. The new umbrella-studded dining terrace in front of the renovated Pier House Inn catches the eye; people who remember the old Neptune wouldn't recognize the inside dining rooms in their Victorian finery. The menu in Tiffany's restaurant and lounge is like so many in the area: heavy on veal, seafood and pasta, $9.95 to $14.95. The baked seafood platter is a favorite. Lunch and dinner daily.

George's of Galilee, Sand Hill Cove Road, Galilee. (401) 783-2306. An institution run by the Durfee family since 1948, this rustic establishment is closest to the water and fishing-boat action in Galilee. The upstairs deck is good for lunch or drinks; when we were there in off-season, you ordered at the take-out counter and took your food to a table upstairs, while the bartender slipped you a beer from inside the **Topside** cocktail lounge. The clam cakes are large and puffy, the clam chowder thin, and the scallop and clam rolls just fine. The two inside dining rooms offer things like baked stuffed shrimp, broiled sirloin and fish and chips. Open daily in summer 6 a.m. to 10 or 11 p.m.

The Fo'c's'le, Sand Hill Cove Road, Galilee. (401) 789-6905. A large gray deck with picnic tables and an inside dining room that looks something like a living room distinguish this place in Galilee. Outside you can get fish burgers for $2.35 and a lobster roll for $6.95. Inside, the all-day menu offers sandwiches and dinners from $4.95 for fish and chips to $13.95 for a shore dinner with lobster. Open daily.

Other Choices

Wickford Gourmet Foods, 21 W. Main St., Wickford. (401) 295-8190.

Wickford folks think the best place to eat in town is at this specialty food shop with a deli, one of the nicest we've seen. You can get sandwiches for $2.50 to $3.50, a ploughman's platter for $2.95 or a pasta salad for $3.25. Take it outside to the tables out back or to a secluded spot along the harbor and enjoy. Open daily from 9:30 to 6:30, Sunday to 5 and Friday to 7.

Amelia's, Pier Marketplace, Narragansett. (401) 789-3000. A tiny cafe with lace curtains and a large take-out section purveys interesting picnic baskets, fresh breads and pastries, and good light fare. For lunch, try the tri-pasta salad ($3.95) or a curried turkey plate ($4.95). Open daily for three meals.

Nana's, Pier Marketplace, Narragansett. (401) 783-9630. What's a beach without ice cream and sweets? Since 1985, this has been *the* place for them in Narragansett. Nana is the mother of owner Grace Falk, who with husband Bill dispenses quite a variety of pastries, cookies and ice cream creations. Try the Jamestown Bridge, a whipped concoction of vanilla ice cream, orange sherbet and orange juice, or the Towers, twin cookies joined by ice cream and rolled in jimmies (both $1.95). We restrained ourselves and cooled off with a watermelon sherbet cone and a berry glace made from tofu — 100 calories, not including the homemade cone.

FOR MORE INFORMATION: Narragansett Chamber of Commerce, The Towers, Box 742, Narragansett, R.I. 02882. (401) 783-7121.

Preservation Society of Newport County Photo

The Breakers is largest mansion along Cliff Walk.

Newport, R.I.

As America's yachting capital, an historic seaport and the birthplace of the U.S. Navy, Newport is a nautical city like no other.

After its founding in 1639 at the tip of Aquidneck Island as a religious refuge (the first Quakers and Jews in the New World settled here), Newport was one of the nation's leading ports in the 17th and 18th centuries. The first Navy boats sailed from its harbor into Narragansett Bay and the Atlantic. In the 1800s, the Vanderbilts, the Astors, the Morgans and others of America's 400 created a seaside summer resort unmatched in opulence. In the 1900s, the Navy increased its Newport presence to the point where it has become the area's largest employer, with 10,000 military and civilian personnel at 32 commands and installations.

The revered Newport-to-Bermuda races, the Tall Ships and the America's Cup extravaganzas merely solidified Newport's place on the international maritime map.

The nautical presence is all-pervasive. You sense it among all the wharves — both old and quaint, and rebuilt and trendy — along Thames Street. It's glittering and glamorous along the Cliff Walk behind the Bellevue Avenue mansions, where the 400 summered. It's rugged and up-to-date along the 10-mile Ocean Drive around the peninsula where today's 400 live. There are sailboats everywhere and regattas all season. The beaches are fine for swimming

162

and surfing. The new Museum of Yachting has opened; the Newport Yachting Center and Sail Newport promote things nautical.

The phone book's Yellow Pages devote nearly four pages to boating, from building to rentals. Restaurants and stores take up the theme in their names: The Mooring, the Pier, the Ark and Rhumb Line, the Armchair Sailor Bookstore, Cast Offs, JT's Ship Chandlery and the America's Cup Gallery.

Myriad pleasures are to be found by anyone interested in the water, history, sports, good living, shopping, fine dining and the like. The summer playground of the Astors and Vanderbilts has become a year-round vacation escape for the multitudes, as well as a place for investors to park their dollars in all the condominiums and time-sharing resorts popping up as nowhere else in New England.

Much as we like Newport, there are times — especially on summer weekends — when it overwhelms. That's when we'd don the T-shirt we found in one of the Newport shops: "Frankly, Scallop, I don't give a clam."

Getting There

Newport occupies the southwest tip of Aquidneck Island, the point where Narragansett Bay meets Rhode Island Sound. Some 40 roundabout miles south of Providence, it's reached via Routes 114 or 138 from the north and east; via I-95 or Route 1 and Route 138 across the Jamestown-Newport Bridge (toll $2) from the west.

Where to Stay

Newport has an incredible range and number of accommodations, the Chamber of Commerce listing 24 hotels and motels plus more than 50 inns and guest houses. Rates vary by season (highest in summer, which in some cases runs from mid-May to mid-October), and weekend rates may be higher than weekdays. Most facilities are open year-round.

Hotels-Motels

Sheraton Islander Inn & Conference Center, Goat Island, Newport 02840. (401) 849-2600. This is Newport's all-around resort hotel, from its banquet room, conference center and underground garage to its indoor and outdoor pools and tennis courts. That it happens to be on a narrow island between the Jamestown-Newport Bridge and Newport Harbor and surrounded by water on three sides (the other end of the island has marinas and new condominiums) is an advantage. A disadvantage is that you have to use your car or walk a distance to visit the rest of Newport. Most of the 253 rooms on six floors have views of the water. Ours didn't, unless you consider the indoor pool a water view. The huge pool area is light and airy with high arched-glass roof and a busy cocktail area where imbibers can watch the swimmers. The outdoor saltwater pool beside the tennis courts is fine. The seventh-floor **Rodger's Roost** is a great place for drinks and harbor-watching. The **Cafe Regatta** coffee shop is open all day for meals and snacks, and the **Windward** dining room, which has a greenhouse terrace beside the water, is well regarded locally. Dinner entrees run from $13.75 for broiled scrod to $17 for steak au poivre or rack of lamb with herb sauce; the medallions of veal, pork and venison served with woodland mushrooms is a house specialty. Doubles, $150 to $190.

Inn on Long Wharf, 142 Long Wharf, Newport 02840. (401) 847-7800. Blessed with a superb waterfront location, all 40 suites in this time-sharing resort built in 1985 face directly onto the harbor. In fact, if you open the sliding glass doors, only a railing separates you from a fall into the drink. All rooms on four floors open off a corridor into the bedroom; beyond are a bathroom opposite a small kitchenette equipped with refrigerator and microwave, and beyond that a comfortable living room decorated in earth tones with a grape-colored sofabed, chair, TV and that sliding door opening onto the water. The view couldn't be better, unless it's the one from the second-floor **Spinnakers Lounge** off the lobby, where breakfast, lunch, snacks and drinks are available; here, at tables beside the windows, you're perched right over the water. Although the suites lack outdoor balconies, there's a sundeck on the roof. Doubles, $170 to $180.

Inn on the Harbor, 359 Thames St., Newport 02840. (401) 849-6789. Only five years old in 1987, this older sister to the Inn on Long Wharf was being totally renovated — apparently, time-sharing and transient guests take their toll. The new furnishings are like those at the Inn on Long Wharf, and so are the layouts of the 58 suites on five floors above a parking deck. All Newport is on view from the sixth-floor sundeck. Each room has sliding glass doors that open onto a railing with moored boats and harbor beyond, although you don't feel as close to the water as at the other inn. Besides a health club on the third floor, there's a waterside restaurant called **Astor's,** where the menu was in transition from Italian to more seafood and more casual. Doubles, $170 to $180.

Newport Bay Club and Hotel, America's Cup Avenue and Thames Street, Newport 02840. (401) 849-8600. This is another of the time-sharing resorts whose pitches are varied (discounted visits for some, perhaps a free meal if you tour the facility). Although it doesn't face the harbor head-on like its aforementioned peers, it has 36 larger and more luxurious units, ranging from one-bedroom suites to two-bedroom townhouses. The fourth-floor townhouses have balconies upstairs and down, with side views of the harbor. Fashioned from an old General Electric mill and listed on the National Register of Historic Places, the building retains high wood ceilings and paneling. Each condominium-style suite has a complete kitchen including dishwasher, large living room with a sectional pullout sofabed plus a dining area, a marble bathroom with jacuzzi and a queensize bedroom. There's nightly turndown service, and continental breakfast is served. The Perry Mill Market shops are on the ground floor. One-bedroom suites, $125 to $185; two-bedroom suites and townhouses, $195 to $295.

Holiday Inn Crowne Plaza, 25 America's Cup Ave., Newport 02840. (401) 849-1000. Newport's biggest hotel yet was under construction for a summer 1987 opening on Long Wharf, with the harbor across the street and the new Gateway Center behind. The Crowne Plaza is the top of the Holiday Inn line. The $38 million luxury hotel with ground-floor specialty shops facing the wharf has a seven-story atrium, a health club, an indoor pool and 308 rooms, including a deluxe concierge level on the top floor. Three restaurants were planned: the casual **Atrium Cafe,** the **Misty Harbor Restaurant** and lounge overlooking Narragansett Bay, and **F. Scott's Restaurant** for fine dining. The **Mischief Lounge** with a sound and lighting system was being billed as Newport's liveliest nightclub. Doubles, $160 to $190.

Treadway Newport Resort & Marina, 49 America's Cup Ave., Newport 02840. (401) 847-9000. The first of Newport's big waterfront hotels, this is the oldest (and may convey a bit of a tired feeling, in comparison with its competitors), but there's no denying the location, on the harbor and central for walking almost everywhere. Half the 134 rooms in the handsome weathered gray wood structure face the harbor and cost more; the rest face what the hotel euphemistically calls city, wharf and park but most would call parking lot and street. Some of the harborside rooms have balconies and cabanas. There's a rather austere indoor pool. The bar and restaurant were being totally renovated in 1987. A continental breakfast is served in the lobby. Doubles, $130 to $190.

Easton's Inn on the Beach, 30 Wave Ave., Newport 02840. (401) 846-0310. Billed as Newport's only hotel on the beach, this is across the street from busy Easton's Beach; its restaurant, beach bar and sidewalk cafe cater in summer to the beach crowd. Converted from an apartment house, the rambling brick and wood structure has 41 guest rooms of varying size, shape and condition. A couple of corner rooms facing the ocean (and the noisy street) are attractive with two double beds and TV; a couple of small suites are good for families. Only about half the rooms have water views, and only half have been renovated, a few with stenciling, to convey more of an inn feeling; some of the original rooms share baths and appear threadbare. In 1987, the inn was adding an elevator, moving the lobby to the front of the building and planning to raise the roof to add 11 more rooms on the fourth floor. Downstairs, the large **Greenhouse** restaurant is cheery with white linens and hanging plants. The choice of salads at lunch is one of Newport's best (Mexican, Greek and fruit, among them), and dinners run from $8.95 for broiled scrod to $16.95 for bouillabaisse. Doubles, $58 to $106.

Sea View Motel, Route 138A, Box 392, Newport 02840. (401) 847-0110. A good view of Easton's Pond and the ocean from a hilltop away from the road commends this older motel of 1950s vintage. In fact, it's the only one of Newport's many standard motels that's close to the ocean; others farther out Routes 138 or 114 in Middletown could be in Anytown, but the prices are lower than in Newport proper. This has 40 rooms on two floors, all with balconies or motel-style patios to enjoy the view. Rooms have paneled walls, two double beds, a couple of wood and leather motel chairs and color TV. A coffee shop serves breakfast only. Doubles, $55.

Inns–Guest Houses

Harborside Inn, Christie's Landing, Newport 02840. (401) 846-6600. If you want to be on the water, you can't get much closer than this, right in the heart of the wharf area off downtown Thames Street. Ten suites and four rooms overlook the water or the landing; be sure to specify. Best are the waterside suites which have balconies, queensize beds, sitting areas with two modern upholstered chairs and an ottoman, and another queensize bed in an upstairs loft reached by climbing almost straight up a ladder. The Harbor Room has windows on three sides with deck chairs for lounging and tables for continental breakfast. Doubles, $115 to $135; suites, $165.

Thames Street Inn, 400 Thames St., Newport 02840. (401) 847-4459. The newest venture of Don Glassie of the Yankee Peddler Inn (the Harborside almost across the street is another), this opened in 1986 in the former St. Mary's Church convent, which was moved to the site to be saved from demolition. Its shingled square facade is so unassuming that people hesitate to venture in; those who do find a luxurious restoration which the nuns would not recognize. They also wouldn't recognize the state-of-the-art elevator or the rooftop sundeck. Eighteen air-conditioned rooms of different shapes on three floors are simply but nicely furnished with one or two queensize beds (each is covered with four pillows, and the colorful patterns on the top pillows match the sheets), antique bureaus, TVs, telephones and private baths. We particularly liked a third-floor room with skylights, a view of the harbor, wicker chairs and a private deck. Continental breakfast is served in a front room with high-back chairs and a monastic look. Complimentary tea is served on weekends; drink mixers with cheese and crackers are put out nightly in summer. Doubles, $105 to $125.

Sanford-Covell House, 72 Washington St., Newport 02840. (401) 847-0206. It would be a treat to stay in this lavish Victorian mansion with a wide piazza on three sides from which to take in the view of the water. An old-fashioned glider hangs on chains from the ceiling of the rear porch; beyond is a small lawn with a new swimming pool and a jacuzzi, and beyond that a dock stretching into the harbor. That's enough for us, but the inside is an architectural dream — shortly after it was completed in 1870 by Boston architect William Ralph Emerson (cousin of Ralph Waldo Emerson), a Boston newspaper called it "the most elegantly finished house ever built in Newport." The four-story tower entry hall rises 35 feet to the ceiling above the fourth floor; small balconies project at several levels, and the stenciling is incredible. The original woods remain, as do many of the furnishings, including a dining set once owned by the founder of the U.S. Naval Academy at Annapolis. Some of the walls have seen better days but a lot of restoration is going on. Don't miss the redone ceiling in the dining room with its silver stars. One guest room and a two-bedroom walk-out basement apartment have private baths; three rooms share an enormous bath. A second-floor apartment has a huge sitting room and alcove looking onto the water. A continental breakfast is served in the dining room. Both guest rooms and public rooms are richly furnished by California owners Anne and Richard Cuvalier, descendants of an early owner. Doubles, $95 to $110; apartment, $200.

The Inn at Castle Hill, Ocean Drive, Newport 02840. (401) 849-3800. An out-of-the-way location atop a hill overlooking Narragansett Bay gives a sense of seclusion to this local institution which calls itself "a country inn by the sea." Innkeepers Paul and Betty McEnroe have decorated their fine Victorian inn with flair and sophistication, including well-aged oriental rugs, paintings by Newport artist Helena Sturdevant, and splashy coordinated prints on the wallpaper, draperies and everything else in the guest rooms. Seven of the ten rooms have private baths; most are huge and have sitting areas with views of the bay. A continental breakfast is served in a lovely breakfast room. Guests (and the public) enjoy a stunning corner bar, whose tall windows take in a grand view of the bay, and the three-sided dining porch which juts out toward the water (there are two other dining rooms as well). The continental menu with a touch of nouvelle is priced from $18 to $24 for such entrees as filet of sole stuffed with scallop mousse or sliced duck with raspberry sauce. Jackets are required for dinner. Lunch also is served in summer, and a Sunday jazz brunch on the lawn is popular. In summer, six motel-like units are available in the adjacent Harbor House. Eighteen beach cottages, right on the water, are available by the week and rented a year in advance. Doubles, $80 to $170; beach cottages, $550 to $600 weekly.

The Inntowne, 6 Mary St., Newport 02840. (401) 846-9200. Paul and Betty McEnroe's in-town version of their Inn at Castle Hill is centrally located at Thames and Mary streets. It, too, has a rooftop sundeck like those of so many downtown Newport inns, but there are no elevators nor phones nor TVs in the 26 rooms. All are ever-so-decorated in colorful matching fabrics, canopy beds, upholstered wing chairs and wicker furniture. Side rooms facing busy Thames Street and those on the third and fourth floors each a glimpse of the harbor. The inn's nearby Restoration House at 20 Mary St. has a basement apartment and six upstairs rooms and suites. A continental breakfast of croissants and muffins is served amid antiques and oriental rugs in the inn's small dining room; tea and cookies are served in the afternoon. Doubles, $90 to $125; suites and apartments, $100 to $150.

Cliffside Inn, 2 Seaview Ave., Newport 02840. (401) 847-1811. Ebullient Kay Russell from San Diego bought this cottage, built in 1880 by the Governor of Maryland, and after extensive renovation since 1981 has turned it into a fine 10-room inn. Her Victorian parlor, done in cheerful tones of green and peachy-orange, is where guests eat continental breakfast at two big round tables or congregate in front of the fireplace. A wide front veranda with wicker furniture affords glimpses of the ocean. All rooms have private baths, although some are miniscule and ingeniously tucked into old closets (with a sink in the bedroom). All are furnished with interesting pieces and most have some of Kay's collection of fans on the walls. Miss Beatrice's Room is the largest; she was a well-known artist who summered in the house and the flowers she painted on the door panels have been left for guests to admire. The bathroom for this room was once a bedroom so it is huge — and the toilet looks like a throne behind lacy eyelet curtains. The Wicker Room on the third floor has pieces from a platform rocker to a lampshade shaped like a bonnet. Also on this floor is a tiny sitting room with a TV (so the men can watch the ballgame while the wives go shopping, says Kay) and a library-landing with books and games. Iced tea is put out on the veranda on summer afternoons. Doubles, $65 to $85. Closed November-April.

Other Choices

Mill Street Inn, 75 Mill St., Newport 02840. (401) 849-9500. Although two blocks from the harbor, the upstairs decks of the townhouse suites afford a view of the water from this 19th century brick mill restored in 1985. Listed on the National Register of Historic Places, it has 23 suites furnished in high-tech style in white and gray — most with an original brick wall. The rather austere sitting rooms are accented by interesting museum posters of seashore scenes. Afternoon tea and morning coffee and muffins are served in a basement breakfast room. Suites, $135 to $165.

Cliff View Cottage, 4 Cliff Ter., Newport 02840. (401) 846-0885. The water can be seen from a side veranda and two upstairs rooms in this 100-year-old house in a residential section above the Cliff Walk. John and Pauline Shea offer four rooms, two with private baths, furnished simply but pleasantly with sprightly accents. A continental breakfast of English muffins and pastries is served. Doubles, $55 to $65.

Halidon Hill Guest House, Halidon Avenue, Newport 02840. (401) 847-8318. Another house in a residential section — this one a large pillared affair in the Ocean Drive area — has two double rooms and a two-bedroom apartment for guests. Helen Burke serves a continental breakfast, and lets guests use the family's rear deck for cookouts beside the swimming pool. Doubles, $75; apartment, $95.

Cliff Walk Manor, 82 Memorial Blvd., Newport 02840. (401) 847-1300. We've always thought this white and garish-red mansion at the entrance to the Cliff Walk, overlooking Easton's Beach, had seen better days; now we hear that better days are ahead. Although it was closed for the season when we visited, local people say the 19 rooms have been nicely refurbished and the former emphasis on bar and restaurant is giving way to more of an inn feeling. Doubles, $89 to $175. Closed in winter.

Tack House at Dolphin Gates, Coggeshall Avenue, Newport 02840. (401) 849-2473. The tack room for the stable that once belonged to Marble House has been converted into a guest cottage in the heart of the mansion district opposite Champs Soleil Estate, not far from famed Bailey's Beach, which guests can use. Owner Noreen O'Neil likens hers to a summer cottage at a lake, with a living room with a queensize sofabed, a bedroom with a double bed and a galley kitchen and dining area. Cottage, $70 to $100.

RENTALS. Rooms, condos, time-sharing units, waterfront houses and others are listed by Public Relations of Newport, 169 Broadway, 849-4325. Private Properties, 174 Bellevue Ave., 847-1331, also deals in rentals. Among seven reservations services are Access to Accommodations, 9 Broadway, 846-9443, and Newport Reservation Service, Box 518, 847-8878.

Seeing and Doing

On or Near the Water

America's Cup Avenue and Thames Street are a sea of humanity in summer, as boat people and tourists jam the streets and the wharves that jut into the harbor at every opportunity. The harbor and Narragansett Bay are filled with powerboats and sailboats. Regattas are scheduled every summer weekend and sometimes during the week. The Newport Yachting Center off America's Cup Avenue is the scene of occasional boat shows and special events.

HARBOR CRUISES. Viking Tours. Goat Island Marina, 847-6921, offers one-hour sightseeing tours on its 49-passenger **Viking Princess** or its 140-passenger **Viking Queen.** Summer cruises leave daily at 10, 11:30, 1, 2:30, 4, 5:15 and 7; fewer cruises off-season from May to Oct. 23. Adults $4, children $2. The **M/V Amazing Grace,** Oldport Marine, America's Cup Avenue, 849-2111, gives one-hour narrated cruises of Newport from a marina adjacent to the Mooring restaurant daily in summer at 10:30, noon, 1:30, 3, 4:30, 6 and 7:30 (limited schedule in spring and fall). Adults $4, children $2. **Newport International Sailing School and Cruises,** Dockside, Sheraton Islander, Goat Island, 683-2738, offers two-hour sailing cruises daily at 10, noon, 2, 4 and 6 for $15 per person; half-day and full-day sails also can be arranged at $25 and $50 respectively. The 42-foot sailing yacht **Copacetic,**

Bowens Wharf, 846-0565, gives day sails for up to six people, $275 for a half day and $425 for a full day.

The Museum of Yachting, Fort Adams, Newport. (401) 847-1018. A special place for yachtsmen is this emerging museum which opened in 1985 in a 19th century granite building on a point at the end of Fort Adams. The goal is to have a center of yachting, says retired marine historian Edward B. Smith, uncle of executive director Tom Benson; "in fact, as you look over the harbor in the summer, this is the center of yachting." Yachting costumes, memorabilia, photos, paintings and models trace the history of sailing inside what was once an Army mule barn. The fascinating photo exhibit called "The Mansions and the Yachts" focuses on the sailing roles of the Vanderbilts, Astors and Morgans ("while the women were here for the social life, this is what the men did," Ed Smith explained). The Hall of Ships displays old wooden boats beneath a model of the boat that won the first America's Cup perched near the ceiling. Upstairs is a Hall of Fame for Singlehanded Sailing and a library detailing ocean voyages. In the harbor is the museum's latest acquisition: the prized Shamrock V, captained by Sir Thomas Lipton as the 1930 America's Cup entry; called the last of the famed J-boats, it's considered the largest floating ship of its kind in the world. The museum sponsors the annual Classic Yacht Regatta on Labor Day weekend for older boats. The museum is small, but it's designed to appeal to laymen as well as sailors. Even if you're not into sailing, you'll get a feel for part of Newport's heritage and the hilly waterside site is spectacular. Open Tuesday-Sunday 10 to 5, mid-May through October. Adults, $2.

Fort Adams State Park, Fort Adams Road off Harrison Avenue, 847-2400. One of the nation's largest seacoast forts and guardian of the head of Narragansett Bay from 1799 to 1945 is open for picnicking, fishing, swimming and guided tours. Named for President John Quincy Adams, the fort was designed to accommodate 2,400 soldiers and 463 mounted cannons, and the fortifications can still be seen. The hilly point juts into the bay and provides as good a vantage point today for yacht-watching and the Newport skyline as it did for soldiers defending their country. Tours are given Wednesday-Sunday from 11:30 to 4:30 in summer for a nominal charge; period garrison drills are staged Fridays at 6 and Sundays at 2:30 and 4 in summer. Open daily during daylight hours; parking, $1.

Naval War College Museum, Coasters Harbor Island, Gate 1, Naval Education and Training Center, 841-4052. The U.S. Navy is such a presence in Newport that, of course, the first museum of its kind would be located here in Founders Hall (1820, first site of the Naval War College), a national historic landmark. Exhibits on the history of naval warfare and of the Navy in the Newport area are featured. Open weekdays 10 to 4:30, weekends noon to 4, June-September. Free.

Brenton Point State Park, Ocean Avenue. Benches are placed strategically all along a bluff for contemplating the ocean in this scenic park. Stairs lead down to the rocks, an area popular with fishermen, sunbathers and divers. The grounds along the shore contain picnicking areas, restrooms and parking lots.

Ocean Drive. The 10-mile Ocean Drive is the East Coast's version of California's 17-Mile Drive in Carmel. It meanders past rocky points with crashing surf, spectacular scenery that provides an awesome setting for equally spectacular mansions and contemporary homes, and a couple of beach clubs including the fabled Bailey's Beach where the 400 sun, swim and socialize.

The Cliff Walk. For an intimate look at the ocean and the backs of the mansions, the 3.5-mile Cliff Walk is a must. Although you can get onto the walk at several points, we prefer to start at the foot of Narragansett Avenue, where you walk down to the ocean on the Forty Steps. The first couple of miles are well-maintained and quite easy; the last part near Bailey's Beach requires good shoes and a stout heart since the path disappears and the going is rocky (we paid for our perseverance with torn stockings). You also must pass through a couple of dark, wet tunnels, and you may be greeted outside the fenced-in Doris Duke estate by a surly guard and the fiercest watchdogs ever. The faint-hearted might better take the first half of the walk and retrace their steps.

BEACHES. Although the Ocean Drive beaches are private, you can sunbathe in Brenton Point State Park. For swimming, head for **Easton's Beach** (also known as First Beach), a wide and sandy three-quarter-mile strand from the Cliff Walk to the Middletown line. There's an amusement rotunda, and bathhouses may be rented. Parking costs $3 weekdays, $5 weekends. Beyond Easton's Beach in Middletown are **Second Beach** (where surfing is permitted) and **Third Beach;** both have lifeguards and similar parking fees. **King Park** along Wellington Avenue in Newport is on a sheltered harbor with pleasant lawns, a pier, a good supervised beach for children, a raft with slides and a free bathhouse. **Fort Adams State Park** has a small roped-off area for swimming; parking $1. At all beaches, lifeguards work weekends starting Memorial Day, and daily from mid-June to Labor Day.

Other Attractions

Guided Tours. Viking Tours, 184 Thames St., 847-6921, offers four different tours daily April-October, ranging from a 90-minute scenic tour past 150 points of interest (adults $7.50, children $4.50) to a deluxe four-hour mansion tour and a land and sea tour (adults $13, children $6.50). **United Tours,** 1 America's Cup Ave., 849-8005, offers a trolley tour past the mansions (adults $6, children free), plus a land-and-sea tour using the yacht Amazing Grace ($12). At least two auto-tape tours are available at prices from $7 to $9.50. Local tour guide Arthur Mattos, 846-7880, offers **taxi tours** of Newport for one to five people.

Walking Tours. The Newport Historical Society, 82 Touro St., 846-0813, guides walkers through Colonial Newport, with visits to its **Wanton-Lyman-Hazard House** (1675), the oldest surviving house in Newport, and the **1699 Friends Meeting House,** Newport's oldest religious structure. Tours leave Friday and Saturday at 10. Adults $3, children free.

Mansion Tours. The Preservation Society of Newport County, 118 Mill St., 847-1000, offers guided tours of its seven mansions and a topiary garden. The most popular is the 72-room **Breakers,** the summer home of Cornelius Vanderbilt and the most opulent of Newport's "cottages." It resembles a northern Italian palace and its vast lawn stretches down to the Cliff Walk. From its upper loggias, you can see the Elizabeth Islands far out to sea on a clear day, and you get to tour the kitchens and butler's pantry — an area larger than most houses.

Other choices are romantic **Rosecliff** of "The Great Gatsby" fame, whose living room doubled as a ballroom; William K. Vanderbilt's **Marble House,** where the hostess gave a 10-course dinner party for 100 of her friends' dogs, and the museum-like **Elms,** with the finest of Newport's grounds. Also open are the 1852 **Chateau-Sur-Mer,** the 1748 **Hunter House,** and **Green Animals** in Portsmouth, considered the best topiary garden in the country. If you've seen the grander mansions, you may like best the 1839 **Kingscote,** a charming Victorian which looks lived in and livable.

Mansion schedules vary: limited schedules in April, daily 10 to 5 May-November; open til 7 some evenings in summer. Marble House, the Elms and Chateau-Sur-Mer open weekends from 10 to 4 in winter. Admission: Breakers or Marble House, adults $4.50, children $2; other sites, $4 and $2. Combination tickets run from any two ($7 and $3) to all eight ($25 and $9).

Several other mansions are open under private ownership. **Astor's Beechwood,** 580 Bellevue Ave., is perhaps the most extravagant. It's an 1851 Italian-style seaside villa that was home to the woman who coined the term "400" for the number her New York ballroom would hold. Mrs. Astor had 281 diamonds in her stomacher and looked like a walking chandelier, according to our guide. Open daily 10 to 5 June-October; adults $5, children $3.50. **Belcourt Castle,** now the home of the Tinney family, is shown by costumed guides and visitors may stay for tea. Open daily 9 or 10 to 4 or 5 mid-February through December; adults $4.50, children $3.50.

Hammersmith Farm, Ocean Drive, 846-0420. The 28-room Auchincloss mansion is where Jacqueline Bouvier Kennedy spent her summers and President Kennedy used one of the second-floor rooms as his Summer Oval Office. The home has more of a seaside country feeling than most Newport mansions and one of the nicer settings — across the island from Bellevue Avenue, overlooking a meadow to Narragansett Bay. We like the beautiful tiled fireplaces in almost every room, the lavish flower arrangements and the huge deck room, where a crowd of grownups and children could find their own niches. The grounds are worth a stroll, and there's a small gift shop in the old children's playhouse. Open daily 10 to 5, April-October; 10 to 7, June-August; weekends in November and March. Adults $4.50, children $1.50.

International Tennis Hall of Fame, 194 Bellevue Ave., 849-3990. The stately Newport Casino, a masterpiece designed by Stanford White, was the home of the U.S. lawn tennis championships before they were moved to Forest Hills. Now it's the site of the world's largest tennis museum, housing displays and memorabilia covering more than a century of tennis history. Visitors can watch occasional tennis tournaments, see court tennis as played by Europeans in the 13th century, and play on one of the dozen well-maintained grass courts for a fee. Open daily 10 to 5, May-October; 11 to 4, rest of year. Adults $4, children $2.

Historic Sites. Newport has more than 400 structures dating from the Colonial era on Historic Hill and the Point. Among them: the 1763 **Touro Synagogue,** the oldest house of Jewish worship in the country; the Christopher Wren-inspired **Trinity Church** (1726), which has the second oldest organ in the country; the 1739 **Old Colony House,** locally believed to be the real Independence Hall (Rhode Island was the first colony to separate from Britain and the Declaration of Independence was read from its balcony); the 1748 **Redwood Library,** oldest in the country; the old stone mill that some believe was built by Norsemen in Touro Park; the 1772 **Brick Market**, and the 1741 **Newport Artillery Company Armory and Museum**, headquarters of the oldest militia organization in America.

SHOPPING. With all its other attractions, one might not expect to find so many shopping opportunities, but Newport does not disappoint. The main shopping area is along Thames Street, Brick Market Place, and Bowen's and Bannister's wharves. Lately, the hot spots are along lower Thames Street, where shops are burgeoning out to the new Wellington Square and beyond, and Spring Street, home of some exotic galleries and boutiques. Bellevue Avenue near Memorial Boulevard is where the 400 used to shop and still do. We enjoy browsing in the shops along the wharves — **Marblehead Handprints, Spring Pottery, Sarah Elizabeth** (where cute country things are displayed amidst a wonderful spicy aroma), **Operculum** (a trove of shells, with seahorses and mermaids in the window) and **Fabric Works**. Lower Thames is now worth a stroll, too, with the terribly sporty **Newport Polo, the America's Cup Gallery** (which even has boxer shorts emblazoned for the Cup), **New Zealand Sport**, the **Armchair Sailor** marine bookstore and **Stone Bridge Dishes**. Along Spring Street, we were taken by **Lily's of the Alley** (fragrance factory), the **Liberty Tree** for contemporary folk art, and the **Native American Trading Co.**

Where to Eat

Newport's concentration of yachtsmen, big-spenders, high society and tourists has spawned an enormous range and number of restaurants, with new ones popping up every year. Again we concentrate on those near the water.

Fine Dining

The Black Pearl, Bannister's Wharf. (401) 846-5264. **The Commodore Room**, whose small-paned windows overlook the water, dispenses regional-nouvelle cuisine (entrees from $13 for paillard of chicken with beurre blanc to $22 for medallions of venison with grand veneur sauce). More casual is the cozy and noisy **Tavern**, where people line up for the great clam chowder ($2 a cup, and seemingly better every time we order it), crab Benedict, a tarragon chicken salad and the famous pearl burger in pita bread with mint salad ($4.75). Most popular in summer is the outdoor patio, where you sit under colorful umbrellas and watch the world go by. You can get most of the tavern fare outside, with heartier entrees (Cape scallops, filet of sole Marguery, calves liver and tenderloin bearnaise, $11 to $15) available inside at both lunch and dinner. Desserts are few but scrumptious. Although the service may be so fast as to make you feel rushed (the world's smallest kitchen serves up to 1,500 meals a day in summer), we've never been disappointed by the fare. Tavern and outdoor cafe open daily from 11; dinner in Commodore Room from 6. Closed a few weeks in February.

Le Bistro, Bowen's Wharf. (401) 849-7779. Regional American cuisine and an airy, elegant decor in the second-floor and third-floor dining rooms with windows toward the water make this fancier than the usual French bistro. We've enjoyed a fine salad Nicoise ($6.25) and a classic bouillabaisse ($9.95) from a luncheon menu on which everything looks good. At night, the changing fare is among Newport's most interesting, priced from $11.95 for breast of chicken bordelaise to $19.50 for tenderloin saute au poivre. Fresh pasta jambalaya, duck with fresh figs, grilled smoked pork loin beaujolaise and veal sauteed with fresh herbs and cream appeared on our latest visit. Start perhaps with shrimp and scallops in cabbage with caviar ($7.95) and finish with Creole bread pudding or Ivory Coast chocolate rum cake. Lunch daily, 11:30 to 2; dinner, 6 to 11; bar menu served from 11:30 to 11 on third floor.

Clarke Cooke House, Bannister's Wharf. (401) 849-2900. Proprietor David Ray now owns Boston's Locke-Ober, so don't be surprised to find lobster Savannah on the ambitious menu here or to learn from the clipping posted out front that this 1790-vintage Colonial restaurant has style, as defined by the newspaper ''W.'' Downstairs is the **Candy Store Cafe,** a bistro-like bar which offers an informal menu ($6.50 for codfish cakes to $14.95 for New York sirloin, plus pastas, sandwiches and light dishes). Those who want to see or be seen go upstairs, to the formal dining room or, we'd suggest, to the breezy but elegant, canopied upper deck with a great view of the waterfront. The service can be haughty, but the fare appeals. Entrees ($15.25 to $22) include sauteed breast of pheasant, poached salmon with sorrel sauce in raspberry glaze, sweetbreads with morels and lobster, and rack of lamb persillade. Carpaccio of lamb and warm salad of lobster and foie gras are among appetizers; desserts include Locke-Ober's Indian pudding and a raspberry charlotte. The wine list is as pricey as the rest of the offerings. Dinner nightly, 6 to 10; cafe, 11:30 to 10 in season.

The White Horse Tavern, corner of Marlborough and Farewell Streets. (401) 849-3600. This is the oldest operating tavern in the United States (1673), beautifully restored by the Newport Preservation Society and now run as a fancy restaurant by Texas owners with sailing interests. Although our Colonial ancestors would be appalled by the prices, the warm and historic atmosphere captivates, particularly on chilly days or in winter. We've enjoyed lunch and dinner splurges here, but be forewarned, dinner entrees start at $17 for breast of chicken with pine nuts, cepes and ham, and rise rapidly into the $20s for lemon veal, Dover sole, beef Wellington and grilled sea scallops. The mixed green salad is $5, and the cheapest appetizers (escargots or shellfish medley) are $7. At lunch, the shrimp tempura is $11 and tasty; the chicken salad in an avocado is $7 and bland. Lunch, daily noon to 3; dinner, 6 to 10 (jackets and reservations required); Sunday brunch, noon to 3.

The Southern Cross, 514 Thames St. (401) 849-8888. A sleek new upstairs dining room has spread out the crowds in the popular restaurant opened by Australian Peter DeCaux in time for the 1983 America's Cup races. The setting is more sophisticated than in the downstairs cafe-style room. The food is billed as new American with a touch of Down Under. Dinner entrees ($10 to $19) range from sea scallops sauteed with lime and butter or seafood fettuccine to baby New Zealand lamb chops and bouillabaisse. Deep-fried brie and gravlax are among appetizers; desserts could be a classic Pavlova or chilled passionfruit souffle. Fine Australian wines, ports and beers are included on the drink list. Dinner, nightly 6 to 10 or 11; Sunday brunch, noon to 3.

Seafood by the Water

The Mooring, Sayer's Wharf. (401) 846-2260. Ensconced in a building which once served the New York Yacht Club, this has one of the best waterfront locations in town. The brick patio with blue umbrellas and an upper deck covered by a green and blue canopy take full advantage. If the weather's bad, sit inside by the windows or in a cozy area with a huge fireplace opposite the famed oak bar; beware, though, the curved-back chairs that rub you in all the wrong places are uncomfortable. A very spicy bloody mary served in a pilsener glass may help; the all-day menu, while extensive, may not excite you. For a winter's lunch, we finally settled on a cup of the restaurant's award-winning clam chowder (which we'd rank behind those of the Black Pearl and the Main Brace) served with half a good lobster salad sandwich ($8.50), and a bowl of "The Salad" ($5.50), an enormous concoction of lettuce, mushrooms, sprouts, cheese, carrots, olives, cherry tomatoes and a whole hard-boiled egg, served with a dijon vinaigrette. The dark green tables are bare (without even a mat), the decor is nautical with old photographs and prints, and the Mooring is obviously popular; we just wish the plain old steak and seafood menu with something for everyone had something more interesting for us. Lunch and dinner daily, 11:30 to 10 or 11.

Dave & Eddie's, Brick Market Place. (401) 849-5241. This contemporary seafood grill and raw bar owned by a Mystic (Conn.) restaurateur purveys the freshest of seafood. It's fairly large, with a lounge, two dining rooms on several levels and an outdoor sidewalk cafe. For dinner, votive candles flickered on white tablecloths as we sampled a shrimp dish chosen for its preferred ginger (which we couldn't find a trace of) and a special of baked sole stuffed with crabmeat and artichokes that sounded more interesting than it tasted. Steamed new potatoes or rice and a fine winter medley of sauteed zucchini, snow peas, carrots and summer squash accompanied. The fresh fish specials (their origin is listed on the blackboard) run from $9.95 to $12.95 range are best; regular dinner entrees run from $11.95 for chicken supreme to $18.95 for surf and turf. The seafood selection is extensive, from fried calamari to lobster thermidor, and the wine list has some unusual offerings at appealing prices. Lunch daily from 11:30 to 4; dinner from 4 to 10:30 or 11:30; closed Tuesday in winter.

The Main Brace, 100 Long Wharf. (401) 849-4397. A rather ordinary downstairs tavern is upstaged by a raw bar (which we wished we'd seen before we ordered our tavern lunch) and a high-ceilinged and beamed upstairs dining room with an outdoor deck overlooking the harbor. Our winter lunch of a fine clam chowder, a chicken salad ($5.95) with more cashews and greens than chicken and a huge "chili in a boule" ($4.25), served lukewarm inside a bowl of bread with melted cheese, was okay. But we'd return for dinner or a lunch of mussels, steamers or oyster stew on the outdoor deck. At night, the dining room offers appealing choices ($8.95 to $17.95) like pasta shu shu, shrimp and scallops Portuguese over linguini, blackened bluefish, cioppino and salmon steak with a dill-pernod sauce. Lobsters up to two or three pounds are a house specialty, and there's a good American wine list. Lunch daily from 11:30, dinner from 6.

Christie's of Newport, Christie's Landing, Thames Street. (401) 847-5400. This is Newport's oldest waterfront restaurant, evolving out of a fish market in 1941. The hostess said 450 people can be seated comfortably in the main red and white dining room, a tiered upstairs dining room, on the large outdoor deck or at picnic tables beside two shacks containing a raw bar and a cocktail bar on the pier. Pictures of famous visitors grace the walls, and the chaplain's

174

corner where Navy chaplains sat beneath a stained-glass window still draws an 80-year-old monsignor three times a week. Dinner fare is standard steak and seafood, priced from $9.95 for two chicken dishes to $21.95 for bouillabaisse or a baked lobster stuffed with scallops. Broiled swordfish, baked stuffed shrimp with petit filet mignon, and a clambake ($19.95) are house specialties. Prices are relatively high (most lunch items are $5 to $8), but the tourist trade doesn't seem to mind. Lunch daily, 11:30 to 3:30; dinner 5 to 10 or 11.

The Pier, West Howard Wharf, Thames Street. (401) 849-3645. Another favorite with tourists is this low-slung establishment dating to 1964 and proud of its Silver Spoon awards adorning the entry. The beamed main dining room is dark at night with tables topped by red paper mats and red patio candles; windows at the end look onto the water, and there's a patio bar. There's no denying the values: a broiled seafood platter is $11.75, bouillabaisse is $13.95, roast duckling is $9.95 and filet mignon, $13.50. Even the chateaubriand for two is only $25.85. Each item on the dinner menu is accompanied by a wine recommendation. Lunch fare ranges from $4.50 for eggs Benedict to $7.95 for seafood pie. Although it's not our kind of place, we have friends who swear by it. Lunch, 11:30 to 3; dinner, 4:30 to 10 or 10:30, Sunday noon to 10.

New and Casual

Amsterdam's Rotisserie, 466 Thames St. (401) 847-0550. A branch of the two Amsterdam's Rotisseries in New York City, this trendy place opened in early 1987 in a small storefront space. The tablecloths are woven red and white and the chairs are black lacquer, the walls are pressed tin and that's about it for decor, except for an amazing light fixture of a ship's figurehead holding two globes. Start with duck liver mousse with lingonberries and sliced orange or smoked brook trout with freshwater caviar sauce, both $3.95. Entrees ($6.25 to $11.95) include a roasted half chicken with fresh green herb sauce, roasted Norwegian salmon or roasted shell steak with a caper mustard sauce. These are served with a three-greens salad and fried potatoes. Desserts like lemon pie and tarts come from the Wave Cafe down the street. Initially it was BYOB, but the owners were hoping for a beer and wine license. Dinner, 5 to 11 daily in summer; Wednesday-Sunday off-season.

Puerini's, 24 Memorial Blvd. W. (401) 847-5506. We kept hearing about this from other restaurateurs, who think it is the best place in town for Italian food. Chef-owner Dan Puerini's cafe-like restaurant has about 17 tables in two small tiled-floor dining rooms with lacy white cafe curtains. Antipasti, all under $3, include marinated mushrooms, pepperoni and cheese calzone, spinach pie, pesto bread and sweet roasted peppers in oil and garlic. Pasta dishes are a gentle $4.95 to $6.95; chicken and shrimp dishes go up to $9.95. Linguini with pesto (voted best in the state), spinach fettuccine with pesto, breast of chicken and artichoke hearts, and sole rolled and stuffed with pesto and crabmeat are some yummy entrees. Desserts again come from the Wave Cafe; one is a seven-layer pie. There's no liquor license but you may bring your own wine; espresso and cappuccino are available. Open daily from 4 to 9, 10 or 11. Closed one month in winter. No credit cards.

Cafe on the Green, Thames and Church Streets. (401) 846-8528. We hope this restaurant lasts longer than the several that have come and gone (mostly gone) in this space in the last few years. The large square room with a few length tables on a small balcony is airy in summer, when many of the floor-length windows — outlined in tiny white lights — are open to the breeze. There are lots of tequila drinks, and two big screens on the side wall are used to show games and movies. Several blackboard specials supplement the all-day Mexican-American menu. The fare runs the gamut from stuffed quahogs to ultimate nachos to avocado burger to fried clam roll. Prices are moderate, with dinners like Mexican beef pie, taco tossup and fiesta plate in the $4.95 to $6.95 range. Open in summer for breakfast, lunch and dinner; winter hours more limited. Sunday breakfast all day.

Cappuccino's, 92 William St. (401) 846-7145. Six tiny round marble tables are where you can partake of some of the fare of this neat little breakfast and lunch cafe, but it's a takeout place as well. We brought home slices of the day's broccoli quiche, one of the best we've tasted. Breakfast casserole squares, sandwiches like smoked chicken and havarti, croque monsieur, pasta salads and wonderful cookies and pastries are set up on the counter; herbal teas, fruit nectars, hot mulled cider and Italian soft drinks go with. Open Tuesday-Saturday 8 to 6:30, Sunday 8 to 3.

Wave Cafe, 580 Thames St. (401) 846-6060. This small cafe and bakery is also the home of Ocean Coffee Roasters, with a large selection of beans, from $5.49 to $21.99 a pound (for Jamaican Blue Mountain), and all the coffee accoutrements. The cafe is basically a takeout place but there are a few tables on the black and white linoleum floor. Handmade bagels, a vegetable cheddar board, spinach ricotta pie, hummus, three-cheese calzone, pizzas, pesto bread and, of course, those good desserts supplied to other restaurants are offered. Chili with bread and butter is $2.95. Open for breakfast and lunch.

FOR MORE INFORMATION: Newport County Chamber of Commerce, 10 America's Cup Ave, Box 237, Newport, R.I. 02840. (401) 847-1600. The Visitor Center will be part of the new Gateway Center, under construction in 1987 on Long Wharf. Two helpful free guides are *Newport This Week* and the *Pineapple Post.*

Sea captains' homes are on view from observation deck at Edgartown harbor.

Martha's Vineyard, Mass.

We've come to the Vineyard in the sun and in the rain, in fog and in storms, in summer and autumn and in the late spring (never, yet, in winter).

Each time, it has presented a different face; if weather is fickle in all of New England, it must be most fickle on the islands off Cape Cod. Most recently we arrived on the ferry to Oak Bluffs in pea-soup fog a few hours before a hurricane was scheduled to hit. Later in the day the rain and the wind pounded the island, and at night we joined others at South Beach to watch the storm's fury.

Our first trip to the island was during one of our college summers, when we'd lined up a job as a waitress at an Edgartown hotel. Between serving three meals a day, there was time for swimming and sunning at Lighthouse Beach across the road. At night there were bonfires and beach parties with other college kids. There were afternoons spent at the Gay Head cliffs, and evenings spent rowing around Edgartown Harbor. In September, back at college, it all seemed magical and a little unreal.

It is those feelings of magic and unreality that have consistently drawn visitors to the Vineyard. Its variety alone, from the beautiful old whaling homes and brick sidewalks in Edgartown to the wildly colored gingerbread cottages and honky-tonk of Oak Bluffs, suits many moods. There is busy, bustling Vineyard Haven (so busy on a rainy day that you might as well forget it) and charming, picture-perfect Menemsha, the only true fishing village on the island. There are the gorgeous clay cliffs at Gay Head, a town in which many residents are of Indian descent, and surprisingly agricultural Tisbury and Chilmark. There are fabulous beaches, fine restaurants, scores of guest houses and inns, paved bikeways, wonderful shops and good harbors. And everywhere, there is the sea.

Because of all it has to offer, Martha's Vineyard has been discovered. The rich and the famous — Jackie Onassis, Mike Wallace, Art Buchwald and Patricia Neal, for example — own summer homes. Condominiums crowd close to

177

South Beach, where once there were just dunes and beach grass. Summer rentals are sky high, and accommodations and dining are not cheap. The cars and the clothes attest to the affluence of the visitors.

If you want a summer vacation away from it all, you'll be hard-put to find it on the Vineyard in season; wait until the fall, which is luscious. But if you don't mind crowds and having to make ferry reservations months in advance, if you're willing to share your sidewalk when you shop and your beach when you swim, then you will love the Vineyard in summer. Move beyond the annoyance of the masses and focus on what brought you here in the first place. You will enjoy the sunning and the surfing, the gorgeous views and the wonderful walks. You'll dine elegantly and enjoy sophisticated shopping. You'll sleep deeply and awaken to the scent of the sea. The island will exert its hold on you.

Getting There

The ferry from Woods Hole is the most popular way to reach the island, although it has an airport with scheduled flights from major East Coast cities. There are also ferries from New Bedford, Falmouth and Hyannis (passengers only).

The Woods Hole, Martha's Vineyard and Nantucket Steamship Authority, Box 284, Woods Hole 02543. (617) 540-2022. Approximate costs for cars are $26.50 each way; for passengers, $3.75 each way. Car reservations must be made far in advance, especially for late June through early September. The trip from Woods Hole to Vineyard Haven takes approximately 45 minutes and departures are frequent. Four boats a day operate between Woods Hole and Oak Bluffs.

From Hyannis, the **Hy-Line,** (617) 775-7185, operates a passenger boat to Oak Bluffs three times a day in summer. One way, adults $9, children $4.50. From Falmouth, the **Island Queen** (617) 548-4800, makes several sailings daily to Oak Bluffs. Round trip $7.50.

Where to Stay

Bigger than most people realize (twenty miles long and nine miles wide), the island is full of delightful B&Bs and inns. Your lodging choice will depend on location and style. Many visitors like to stay in Edgartown because of the old whaling homes, colorful harbor and good shopping; if you don't have a car, you may opt for Edgartown, too, because there's so much to do on foot. Be advised, however, that the beach is a bit of a hike; you'll have to take the shuttle bus, which runs frequently, or perhaps a bike or moped.

Oak Bluffs, the first real resort town of the island, was given that status because of the religious enthusiasts who developed a Methodist Camp Meeting. The ornate, colorful gingerbread cottages near the present-day Tabernacle are a must for the sightseer. Oak Bluffs has several B&Bs, plus a couple of larger summer hotels. There are a nice beach within walking distance, a movie theater, a merry-go-round and funky shops.

Vineyard Haven is more commercial, but tony shops and restaurants have found their way onto its main street. Most ferries land here, making it a convenient location. You'll have to ask about the small beaches nearby, or take a longish drive to the island's south side ocean beaches, which are favored by most visitors.

Menemsha is charming and small. There's a beach in town and if you're staying in a local inn, you'll probably be given a beach pass to the wonderful Lucy Vincent Beach.

Vineyard Haven

Thorncroft Inn, Main Street, Box 1022, Vineyard Haven 02568. (617) 693-3333. Lynn and Karl Buder, formerly of Simsbury, Conn., said goodbye to the corporate life a few years ago and opened this fine B&B inn just a mile up Main Street, toward West Chop. Previously the Haven Guest House, the name was changed in 1986 to reflect the inn's origin as part of the Thorncroft Estate owned by a Chicago grain merchant in the early part of the century. This house, which was used to accommodate relatives and dignitaries visiting Thorncroft, was built in 1918 and is described as a classic craftsman bungalow. Thorncroft is one of the Vineyard's few inns that includes a full breakfast in the rate, and Karl is proud of his. Among specialties are almond french toast, quiche Lorraine and a spinach, sausage and cheese pie. Homemade granola is always available. Breakfasts are served in a formal, fireplaced dining room where soft blue mats and napkins grace the table. The front parlor is filled with wicker, and the inn has a Victorian feeling with pieces of pressed oak and appropriate floral wallpapers. All ten guest rooms in the main inn, and three others in a separate building, have private baths, some with clawfoot tubs. All are decorated with antiques, Lynn's taste being reflected in the decor. All guest rooms and public rooms in the inn are designated non-smoking; two first-floor guest rooms with their own entrances are rented to smokers. Guests can walk to Long Point Beach; upon their return, an outdoor shower is available. Doubles, $90 to $120. Open year-round.

Captain Dexter House, 100 Main St., Box 2457, Vineyard Haven 02568. (617) 693-6564. Here is elegance indeed. This gorgeous house, built in 1843 by a sea captain, was opened as a gracious inn by Beyer and Lara Parker in 1983. The imposing white house with green shutters and porch, and with a yard filled with bright impatiens and other flowers and plantings, is just a block from the shops. Eight bedrooms, filled with antiques and all with private baths, are exceptionally attractive; many are done in shades of deep green and rose. Brass candlesticks with white candles are placed on each stair of the curved staircase to the second floor. One room has a working fireplace and canopy bed; the two-room Captain Dexter Suite at the head of the stairs features wall-to-wall carpeting and Colonial Williamsburg prints. Continental breakfast with coffee cake, strawberry bread or croissants, fresh orange juice and herbal tea or coffee is served in a beautiful formal dining room with Queen Anne chairs. Doubles, $80 to $110. Open year-round.

Hanover House, 10 Edgartown Road, Box 2107, Vineyard Haven 02568. (617) 693-1066. Mark Hanover — with help from his accommodating mother — runs this pleasant inn, located a bit out of town. Since opening in 1979, Mark has renovated twice, and now has fifteen rooms, including five housekeeping units. A wicker-filled front sunporch, decorated in shades of blue and peach, is where a continental breakfast is served to guests. Several rooms in the main house, plus a few units in another building separated by a terrace, are decorated mostly in earth tones. All accommodations feature private baths and color TVs; guests also can use picnic tables and barbecue grills outside. Doubles, $68 to $87; efficiencies, $88 to $95 for two, $95 to $105 for four. Open year-round.

North Tisbury

The Bayberry, Old Courthouse Road, North Tisbury (Mailing address: RD 1, Box 546, Vineyard Haven 02568). (617) 693-1984. Rosalie Powell, an island native and descendant of Thomas Mayhew, the first settler, runs this exceptional B&B located in a charming Cape Cod house that looks antique, but is not. A former home economist, Rosalie opened the Bayberry in the early 1980s. When we visited one summer morning, she was ironing linens in front of the huge fireplace in her keeping room-kitchen, which is where guests are served a full breakfast. Rosalie had just made a favorite, "Dream Boats," puffy pancakes filled with fresh fruit and yogurt. Other breakfasts might be blueberry waffles, omelets or souffles. Tea is served daily at 5 — outdoors with a view of an open field in nice weather, or inside in the comfortable living room crowned by a grand piano. "Sometimes I serve on a silver tray; I love to use nice things," enthuses Rosalie. She also sees that all rooms have fresh flowers. One of the five guest rooms has a private bath and two have semi-private. Two rooms on the main floor — one with four-poster twin beds and the other with a canopied double — share a bath. Upstairs, a blue and pink room with private bath, a kingsize bed and heart-shaped, lace-edged pillows is perfect for honeymooners. The setting is bucolic — there's a horse in the pasture next door. Doubles, $70 to $90. Open year-round.

The Island Epicure, State Road, North Tisbury 02568. (617) 693-1650. Louise Tate King, who ran one of the island's best restaurants back in the 1960s and early 1970s and who still does some catering, hangs out her shingle in the summer and rents two rooms in her 200-year-old house with its large fireplaced living room and huge, work-in kitchen (perfect for the chef that she is). This is a very personal operation and Mrs. King not only bakes the pastries for the continental breakfast, but also turns down beds and leaves chocolates on the pillows. Charming and knowledgeable about island life, she offers a twin-bedded guest room on the first floor, plus a room with a double bed on the second floor. Guests share a bathroom. There's an outdoor shower, a pleasant deck, and a yard with an herb garden. Doubles, $65.

Menemsha

Menemsha Inn and Cottages, Box 38, Menemsha 02552. (617) 645-2521. Thirteen cottages and a seven-room inn on eleven acres are set back from the road, approached by a dirt driveway, above the fishing village of Menemsha. Richard and Nancy Steves run a homey operation at a place that has been welcoming visitors for about 50 years (Alfred Eisenstadt, the Time-Life photographer, has been coming for 48 of them). People rent cottages for a week at a time; inn rooms may be available for shorter periods. The complex spreads over the hillside in a treed meadow, down toward a beach. All but two cottages have water views; only two inn rooms do. While there is a rustic, camplike quality to the setting, the cottages are bright and attractive with floral bedspreads, crisp curtains and scatter rugs. All have screened porches, grills, picnic tables and kitchenettes. There are nine studios, two one-bedroom and two two-bedroom cottages. The inn's rooms share two baths. A nicely old-fashioned dining room is where guests are served continental breakfast. It's also open to the public for dinner (reservations required; BYOB). Bare wooden floors, white painted wood chairs, an open beamed ceiling and fresh flowers on the tables create an attractive country setting. Son Woody

Steves is the chef. Prices range from $13.95 for chicken francaise to $18.95 for broiled swordfish. Smoked bluefish is a popular appetizer. Doubles, $60 to $65 in inn. Cottages, $575 to $675 weekly. Open mid-April to mid-November.

Oak Bluffs

The Oak House, Seaview Avenue, Box 299, Oak Bluffs 02557. (617) 693-4187. This marvelous, sprawling 19th century summer home is located directly across from the water and most of the 10 rooms have water views. They also have the most elaborate oak woodwork we've seen. Our family of four was cozily ensconced on the third floor in a huge room, the Surf Suite (double bed at one end, two twin beds at the other, separated by a bureau and screen), with walls and ceilings covered in beautiful oak paneling with great detail. A tiny private balcony afforded a view of the shoreline. The ten rooms share four baths, which have been updated; some have tin ceilings and clawfoot tubs. Public rooms on the main floor have elaborate oak paneling and Victorian-style furnishings. There are a huge front parlor and a formal dining room (where guests breakfast, unless they want to carry their coffee to the front porch). Our only disappointment was that the breakfast juice came in little cartons and the coffee cake was pre-packaged as well. But innkeepers Marcia and Stuart Haley are friendly and helpful, and the location is superb. Doubles, $68; family of four, $100. Open May-September.

The Beach House, Seaview Avenue, Box 417, Oak Bluffs 02557. (617) 693-3955. Perfectly named, this inn has a beachy feeling and a nice beach is just across the street. Of the same vintage, but with not quite the elaborate woodwork of the Oak House, it features a cozy alcove with pink patterned window-seat cushion, and a large open front porch with a telescope for viewing distant ships. All seven rooms have marble sinks; they share hall bathrooms. Some rooms are paneled and others are painted white. They are simply furnished and it looks easy to sweep out the sand. Innkeepers Pamela and Calvin Zaiko offer complimentary morning coffee and pastries. Doubles, $50 to $60. Open mid-May to Columbus Day.

The Wesley Hotel, Lake Avenue, Oak Bluffs 02557. (617) 693-6611. A landmark for years, the Wesley has been refurbished and renovated by Peter Martell, who also owns the Pequot Hotel in Oak Bluffs and was part-owner of the Colonial in Edgartown. Completely redone in 1985, the hotel has 58 rooms in the main building which overlooks the Oak Bluffs harbor, and a wide front porch with rockers. A separate building out back has 20 more simply furnished rooms, which share baths. Rooms in the main building have wall-to-wall carpeting, one or two double beds, and fresh quilts and curtains. The main lobby is done in the Victorian style with red velvet sofa and chairs in a conversation grouping amid marble-topped tables, oriental rugs on bare floors, and elaborate light fixtures suspended from colorful ceiling medallions. A raised-platform breakfast area overlooks the lobby. This is a busy hotel with lots of coming and going through the lobby; the activity of the harbor is also a draw. Doubles, $45 to $95. Open mid-May through September.

Edgartown

The Charlotte Inn, South Summer Street, Edgartown 02539. (617) 627-4751. The most elegant place to stay on Martha's Vineyard, the main inn, white clapboard with black shutters, was a sea captain's home and dates from the mid-1800s. From the moment you walk up to the front door, you know you're in for something special. The two front rooms inside are an art gallery; fine art also hangs in hallways and some of the rooms. Rooms here are decorated with French and English antiques and fine reproductions, and have four-poster beds, candlewick bedspreads and fresh flowers. Most rooms have an attractive sofa-sitting area. Rooms are slightly less formal in the other buildings, the Carriage House (with cathedral ceilings and French doors), the Garden and Summer houses. All rooms in the Garden House have brass beds, and a first-floor bedroom with its own porch looks out on a colorful garden. Suites with fireplaces are coveted in fall and winter. Innkeepers Gery and Paula Conover run their 24-room inn with great attention to detail. A fine classic restaurant, **L'Etoile**, is located in the inn (see Where to Eat). Doubles, $98 to $195, including a continental breakfast; suites with fireplaces, $175 to $250. Open year-round.

The Victorian Inn, South Water Street, Box 947, Edgartown 05363. (617) 627-4784. Victorian cream tea — served in the afternoon by reservation in a flower-filled brick courtyard — was new at this wonderful old inn in 1986. The $10 charge produced such delights as cucumber sandwiches, fresh strawberries with clotted cream, home-style preserves, scones and a selection of teas. Jack and Marilyn Kayner, who winter in Vermont, run this beautiful inn in the center of town. Its rococo style is unusual in Edgartown, which was settled in an earlier era and boasts mostly more traditionally Colonial styles. A small front parlor opens into two dining rooms where a full breakfast is served. Two favorite items are the homemade granola and the banana and apricot crepes. The 14 rooms, all with private baths and furnished with antiques, have twin, double, queen and kingsize beds, and some are canopied four-posters. Room 10, which has a kingsize bed and a porch overlooking the harbor, is understandably popular. Doubles, $80 to $165. Open April-October.

Point Way Inn, Main Street at Pease's Point Way, Box 128, Edgartown 02539. (617) 627-8633. Through the white swinging gate on the corner, and past the shrubbed and flowered yard, you walk up to this lovely old sea captain's house-turned-inn. Although there's no view of the water, things are very nautical inside — no doubt related to the interest of innkeepers Linda and Ben Smith in the sailing life (they'd just sailed into Edgartown harbor after a 4,000-mile, year-and-a-half cruise, when they found the house in 1979 and decided to make it over). Point Way has 12 rooms in various configurations: all have their own baths, some have original fireplaces, and some have canopied four-poster beds. A two-room fireplaced suite has an outdoor deck. Continental breakfast is served in a cheery yellow room with ladderback chairs and there's a living room-library with a large fireplace where guests can relax or have a drink. The Smiths used to host sailing trips in the Caribbean in the winter, but they now devote full attention to the inn. Doubles, $85 to $165. Open year-round.

The Harbor View Hotel, Starbuck's Neck, Edgartown 02539. (617) 627-4333. Two large gray-shingled structures with an unimpeded view of the Edgartown Light and the entrance to the harbor are the signature buildings of this resort complex. With seven large "cottages" and a lanai with motel-type rooms surrounding the pool, the hotel provides a total of 117 rooms.

Built in 1891 and updated in 1984, the Harbor View has a commanding position on Starbuck's Neck, a prime piece of Edgartown property. The location — and the amenities of a full-service resort — bring guests back. Rattan furniture in the lobby gives it a light summery mood and 30 rooms in the main building are furnished rather contemporarily and attractively in neutral hues. Ask for a room in front for a view of the lighthouse and the water traffic. A path leads to a private beach by the lighthouse, just a short walk from the hotel. **Starbuck's**, a big, gracious dining room decorated in green and white with bentwood chairs, is well recommended. Open for lunch and dinner, it reflects the European training of its Swiss chef; popular entrees include veal saltimbocca, rack of lamb with chevre, and medallions of veal with crabmeat and wild mushrooms, in the $15.95 to $18.95 range. A good selection of fish is on the menu, and desserts are hard to resist. The view from the dining room of the lighthouse and the water is stunning. The Harbor View is owned by Allan Jones, a former state senator from Massachusetts, his son Stephen and an attorney friend, Bob Welch. Together they oversee Regency Inns, a group of New England hotels headquartered in Cape Cod. But lest you think this means absentee management, Senator Jones is frequently on the premises, keeping his eye on everything. Among the extras are two tennis courts, and windsurfing lessons and rentals at the dock. Doubles, $145 to $185; suites, $260 to $284; lanai rooms, $160; cottage suites, $200 to $385. Open May to late fall.

The Colonial Inn, North Water Street, Edgartown 02539. (617) 627-4711. Considering the location, the Colonial is a bargain. Situated on prestigious North Water Street — a street lined with stately white whaling homes — and just a few steps from shops, restaurants and the waterfront, this large summer hotel with broad porch and window boxes filled with petunias and geraniums is a classic. We stayed here for Fourth of July weekend one year and had a bird's-eye view of the charming Edgartown parade. Opened as a hotel in 1911, the Colonial has been operating in the same mode since. Some rooms have private baths, some semi-private, and a few share hall baths. All are simply furnished and basic. Doubles, $60 to $85. Open mid-May through September.

The Daggett House, 59 North Water St., Edgartown 02539. (617) 627-4600. Because the Daggett House was built as an inn in 1750, it exudes a charm that eludes many other hostelries. Also, because it has been run for nearly 40 years by Fred and Lucille Chirgwin, it has a settled, comfortable feeling. The main building is square and shingled with seven guest rooms, all of which have low ceilings, wainscoting, mini-print wallpaper and appropriate furnishings. A period parlor on the entry level is for the use of guests; downstairs is a mammoth brick fireplace in the Chimney Room, which opens into the back yard leading directly to Edgartown Harbor. Antique artifacts adorn this room, where a continental breakfast is served guests. Also part of the complex are the 14-room Capt. Warren House, which has some efficiency units (good for families), and a three-bedroom garden cottage. The long, narrow back yard of the Daggett House leads to a postage-stamp beach. Lounge chairs are available for guests, and from here you get the best possible view of the On-Time ferry, which runs across the street at the channel to Chappaquiddick Island. In fact, the traffic lines up along the street at the side of the Daggett House. Doubles, $50 to $135. Main inn open year-round.

The Edgartown Inn, 56 North Water St., Edgartown 02539. (617) 627-4794. A nice variety of accommodations is available here, from the 11 antiques-decorated rooms with private baths in the main inn to the more simply decorated rooms with shared baths in the Captain's Quarters and Barn beyond a terrace out back. Built in 1798 as a residence by Capt. Thomas Worth, the house became an inn in the early 1800s. Among its distinguished guests have been Daniel Webster, Nathaniel Hawthorne and John F. Kennedy. An optional breakfast is served guests in a cozy rear room or on the terrace. A porch out front is a good place to sit and watch the North Water Street traffic. Doubles, $65 to $110 in inn, $45 in Barn, $38 in Captain's Quarters. Open April-October.

Mattakesett of Edgartown, South Beach, write to Mattakesett, 252 Main St., Hyannis 02601, (617) 778-1101. Here's a place to rent a condominium or home right at what's considered the best public beach on the island. Altogether 91 units with tennis courts and pool form what is like a private tennis club for the renters. The condos and homes, which have attractive gray-shingled exteriors with white trim, come with linens, blankets, towels, kitchen utensils and housecleaning service (both prior to and after the week of rental). The beach is just a few steps away. All homes have three bedrooms, each with private bath. The condos have three bedrooms sharing two baths. Rents range from $1,500 to $3,500 weekly in season.

Reservations services help visitors to find accommodations: Dukes County Reservations Service, Box 1495, Edgartown 02539, (617) 693-6505, or Martha's Vineyard Reservations, Box 1769, Vineyard Haven 02568, (617) 693-4111.

HOUSE RENTALS are on the high side — $700 to $1,500 weekly. Barbara Nevin, (617) 693-2174, and Macomber Real Estate, (617) 627-8030, are two active agencies.

Camping

Webb's Camping Area, RD 2, Box 100, Vineyard Haven 02568. (617) 693-0233. Located off Barnes Road, in roughly the center of the island, Webb's has 131 wooded sites, 25 trailer hook-ups and a separate area for cyclists and backpackers. Each site has a picnic table and natural stone fireplace, and bikes can be rented. A few sites have views of Lagoon Pond, where there's a small public saltwater beach as well. Sites with water views, $17 nightly and $119 weekly; other sites, $15 and $105. Open May 15 to Sept. 20.

Martha's Vineyard Family Campground, Box 1557, Edgartown Road, Vineyard Haven 02568. (617) 693-3772 or 784-3615. This campground is located off the Edgartown-Vineyard Haven road, closer to Vineyard Haven. Campsites are $15 per day and trailer sites are $18. Tent trailers may be rented on site.

Seeing and Doing

Martha's Vineyard has much to offer. Each of the major towns has its own identity and spirit and deserves to be explored. The beaches are wonderful. Sailboats and sailboards, rowboats and motor boats can be rented. A ferry goes to Chappaquiddick, which has a very good beach at the far end. Shopping is interesting. Historical homes and sites can be visited. There are movies and artistic performances. Art galleries are especially good. Enjoy!

Getting Around

A car is useful, but hundreds of visitors come just with bicycles; 25 miles of bike paths are well-maintained. Bike rentals, widely available, average $7 a day for a 3-speed; $10 for a 10-speed.

Mopeds have hit the island and big. Just up the street from the ferry in Oak Bluffs are two rental places. King's Taxi and Rentals charges $35 for a full day, double, and $25 for a single. Oak Bluffs Bike & Moped Rentals charges $35 double, $20 single. Others are available in Vineyard Haven.

Buses operate on a regular schedule connecting Vineyard Haven, Oak Bluffs and Edgartown, mid-May to mid-October. They run at least twice an hour from mid-June to Labor Day, hourly the rest of the season. Buses stop on Union Street in Vineyard Haven (straight ahead from the steamship wharf), at the traffic circle in Oak Bluffs and at the police station in Edgartown. Shuttle buses between Edgartown and South Beach operate frequently during the summer. In July and August, a shuttle leaves Church Street in Edgartown for Gay Head with stops at the airport, West Tisbury and Chilmark; cost is $3 one-way, $6 round trip. Taxis meet all incoming ferries at Vineyard Haven and Oak Bluffs and pick up passengers anywhere on the island.

Sightseeing buses leave the ferry terminal areas in Vineyard Haven and Oak Bluffs almost hourly during the summer months and cover the island. Tours take about two hours; adults $5.50, children $3.

Photo tours are offered for avid shutterbugs by the Martha's Vineyard School of Photography, (617) 693-2170. Daily four-hour tours are led by a staff photographer who takes each group to a different spot on the island and discusses film speed, control of light, use of filters and tripods, and so on. Each person drops his film off at the school for overnight processing and receives an analysis of his work the next day. Cost, $35.

The Beaches

Most people love the Vineyard for its beaches. Waters off the shore are relatively shallow, and the Gulf Stream and protection from Cape Cod assure rather warm waters for seasonal swimming. Several beaches are open to the public. Others are reserved for town and summer residents and a sticker is required. Among the best:

Oak Bluffs Town Beach is a calm, shallow and supervised beach on the Vineyard Sound side of the island and is open to all; it stretches from the ferry terminal to the first jetty heading toward Edgartown. **Joseph Sylvia State Beach** is two miles of a clear, mild beach between Oak Bluffs and Edgartown. **Lighthouse Beach,** the small harbor beach at Starbuck's Neck in Edgartown, is reached via a paved path from North Water Street.

Katama Beach (more familiarly known as **South Beach**), three miles of public barrier beach on the south shore at Edgartown, has fine ocean surf on one side, plus a protected salt pond. **Menemsha Public Beach** is a gentle beach with clear, bright water typical of the North Shore.

Several other beaches, including Lambert's Cove Beach, Lucy Vincent Beach, Squibnocket, Lobsterville and Gay Head Town Beach, are open only to town residents.

The Cape Pogue Wildlife Refuge and Wasque Reservation (East Beach) at the tip of Chappaquiddick is considered one of the best. It's open subject to regulations of the Trustees of Reservations.

Boating

Several large yacht charters are available. **Gale Force Charters,** Edgartown Harbor, 627-3091, offers captained yacht sails aboard a 45-foot cruising ketch during the day and at sunset. Charges are $200 for the first two hours and $50 for each additional hour.

The 38-foot friendship sloop, Irene, and the 50-foot ketch, Laissez Faire, put out from Vineyard Haven for half-day sails on Vineyard Sound, day sails to Tarpaulin Cove, and overnight trips to Cuttyhunk or Nantucket. Contact John Clarke at the Lothrop Merry House in Vineyard Haven, 693-1646.

Learn to sail or rent a sailboat yourself at the Harborside Inn in Edgartown Harbor, 627-4321. Sailing lessons and sightseeing are offered at $30 per hour or $150 for a six-lesson, six-hour series, which includes a one-hour solo and sailing certificate at the end. The 17-foot O'Day day-sailors can be rented for $25 an hour, $50 a morning or afternoon, or $75 for a full day. Powerboats (15-foot Boston Whalers with 25-hp outboards) are $25 per hour, $50 a morning or afternoon, or $90 a day.

Sailboards are the way to go on Lagoon Pond or on Vineyard Sound. They can be rented from the Selfni Sailing Center on Beach Road, between Vineyard Haven and Oak Bluffs, 693-4252. Sailboards or sunfish cost $12 an hour, $50 a day or $150 a week.

Fishing charters are widely available, among them: Clyde's Beach Charters, Edgartown, 627-8181; Captain Gerolamo, Oak Bluffs, 693-0617; Larry's Tackle Shop, Edgartown, 627-5088.

Walking Tours

In **Edgartown,** be sure to see the Vincent House, built in 1675 and now operated as a museum; the Old Whaling Church on Main Street; the Dukes County Historical Society, a Colonial home decorated with period furniture, and the giant pagoda tree on South Water Street (brought as a seedling from China and planted in the mid-1800s). Climb to the observation deck at the Town Wharf for a good view of the harbor. See the Old Sculpin Gallery, housed in an old boat shop. St. Andrews Church on North Summer Street has stained-glass windows designed by Lewis Tiffany and its pulpit is the bow of a boat. Ogle all the beautiful whaling homes; we especially like to stroll up North Water Street to Starbuck's Neck from the center of town.

In **Oak Bluffs,** the many gingerbread cottages painted in vivid colors are a delight to see; just wander the streets as you will. Don't miss the Tabernacle at Trinity Park. Originally designed for wood, the open-air auditorium was built of wrought iron and replaced a one-ton tent. On Illumination Night in August hundreds of lanterns glow from the eaves of the cottages nearby. Check out Ocean Park with its gazebo and the Civil War statue on Seaview Avenue. The Oak Bluffs harbor is busy and colorful. Take a ride on the Flying Horses, one of the oldest carousels in the country. And don't miss Circuit Avenue with its shops and its fudge stands.

Other Attractions

ART GALLERIES. Many on the island are of high quality. **John Stobart,** the marine painter, maintains a gallery in Edgartown. The **Old Sculpin Gallery** in Edgartown represents several different island artists. The **Harness and Reed Gallery and Workshop** in Edgartown displays leather, baskets, jewelry, glass and imports. The **Tiasquam Gallery** on Middle Road in Chilmark shows

19th and early 20th century American paintings. The **Edgartown Art Gallery** on South Summer Street exhibits works of distinguished American artists.

ANTIQUING. A brochure, "Antique Shops on Martha's Vineyard," lists no fewer than 17, most of them in Edgartown.

FLYING. Soaring and biplane adventures are offered by Soaring Adventures at the Edgartown Airfield, 627-3833. The cost is $39.95 per person, with a two-person minimum.

SHOPPING. The stores are almost irresistible. Boutiques and pricey clothing shops are mostly in Edgartown, though they're making appearances in Vineyard Haven as well. Funky clothes and T-shirt shops are located in Oak Bluffs. The **Bunch of Grapes Bookstore** in Vineyard Haven is where everyone goes, and on a rainy day you'll be hard put to shoehorn your way in or out. Sweaters are to be found at **Northern Isles** in the Tisbury Inn in Vineyard Haven. Basics — raingear, Jams, jeans, shoes and such — are available at **Brickman's** in Vineyard Haven and Edgartown.

The Vineyard has a vineyard, **Chicama Vineyards** in West Tisbury, where you can tour and buy wine, as well as specially flavored vinegars. **Lorraine Parish**, a designer of interesting women's clothing, has her own shop "up island" in Chilmark (next door to the restaurant, Feasts).

In Edgartown, the **Country Store of Concord** is popular, and we think **Petunia's** has great clothes. **A Gift of Love** on North Water Street, a shop for hostess items, games and gifts, has impeccably tasteful items. **Rags** in Edgartown is another place to check out for clothes, and **The Fligors'** with its many rooms and levels is almost a department store. You can spend a half day browsing on Main and Water streets, but don't forget your wallet.

In Oak Bluffs, we love Circuit Avenue. Walk past Murdick's at the lower end and go all the way to the top of the street to **Hilliard's Kitch-in-vue** store where they roll out caramel, "paint" it with chocolate, and sprinkle nuts on top to make butter crunch; fudge is great here, too. Part of a three-store candy chain, this has the original family firmly in charge. Other shops on Circuit Avenue include a terrific Army surplus store, a vintage clothing store, a children's store, and T-shirt emporiums. If you have teenagers, drop them off here for a few hours.

Where to Eat

More and more trendy, pricey restaurants are dotting the island and are very popular; reserve a table well in advance. There are also casual spots, and one of New England's great pizza places, too. Liquor is served in restaurants in Oak Bluffs and Edgartown only; other towns are BYOB.

Fancy Dining

L'Etoile, in the Charlotte Inn, South Summer Street, Edgartown. (617) 627-5187. There are many reasons to dine at L'Etoile, newly opened in the island's most elegant inn. Occupying the spot formerly known as Chez Pierre, L'Etoile is the creation of its friendly and serious young chef, 26-year-old Michael Brisson. White bentwood chairs with cane seats are placed at white-clothed tables in the conservatory dining room; on the greenery-filled terrace a fountain trickles and thriving plants add color. Michael especially likes the place settings of gold-rimmed white Villeroy & Boch china, Reed & Barton silverplate and fluted crystal wine glasses. Forty diners can be seated inside, with another 45 on an outdoor terrace. The $40 prix-fixe dinner menu changes seasonally and offers about five entrees, plus a nightly special. The chef takes great pride in what he does with lamb, pheasant and quail. For a summer dinner the offerings included roasted baby pheasant with a pecan bourbon sauce and wild rice; rack of lamb with port, shallot and black pepper sauce served with warmed goat cheese, and grilled swordfish with champagne and shrimp sauce and a tricolor pepper stir-fry. Other imaginative choices were a saute of lobster and mussels in puff pastry with a lobster and saffron cream sauce, and a grilled sirloin steak with soy-cured ginger and potato-turnip gratin. One might start with chilled avocado soup, sauteed soft-shell crab with tomato and basil butter sauce or a marinated artichoke and mushroom salad. An unusual appetizer was quail glazed with sherry wine vinegar on corn and chive brioche. Save room for dessert, perhaps a wild blueberry sorbet with champagne sabayon, hazelnut cream peach tart with cognac chantilly or raspberry Bavarian on chocolate genoise with framboise sauce. Arriving at L'Etoile is part of the fun, for it is tucked behind the inn's art galleries, allowing you to browse before or after your meal. Dinner nightly in summer. Open year-round.

Warriner's, Post Office Square, Edgartown. (617) 627-4488. Bookcases filled with books, dark paneled walls, Queen Anne chairs with green seats, white tablecloths and tiny bouquets of fresh flowers on the tables create the aura of an Englishmen's clubroom. Tables are set with striking Dudson china from England; small brass lamps with pleated shades add a homey touch. Sam Warriner, who once ran the Dunes restaurant at the Katama Shores Inn, rocketed to the apex of the island restaurant scene after opening this in December 1984. The location is a small white house, and dining is in several intimate rooms with a total seating capacity of 60. Appetizers range from marinated hearts of palm at $4 to escargots en croute for $5.50. Duck and leek soup is one of the special soups. Entrees range from sole amandine at $12 to tenderloin of veal with pignoli and spinach, $19. Also offered are black bass Grenobloise, stuffed shrimp, medallions of lamb provencale, and duck steak with a plum and ginger sauce. Entrees include a mixed salad, vegetable and potato; Warriner's also boasts an exceptional wine list. For dessert, try chocolate mousse with raspberry sauce, apricot ice cream with a cinnamon ginger sauce, papaya with lime rum sabayon or chocolate truffles. Dinner nightly 6 to 9, two seatings in summer (at 6 to 6:45 and 8 to 8:45). Reservations required. Open year-round.

Beach Plum Inn, North Road, Menemsha. (617) 645-9454. One hears lots of things about the Beach Plum Inn, ranging from "don't miss it" to "it's overrated." After a summer dinner, we share both feelings. An unpretentious clapboard house, the inn is reached via a long, rather private driveway. You park your car and walk around the house to the entry; suddenly you are in a two-level dining room, one end of which affords distant views of the water. You've been told the entree offerings when you reserved so that you can order ahead (the prix-fixe dinner is $35). You bring a bottle of wine (no liquor is served at this end of the island). Since the restaurant is quite in vogue, we felt we were among people who want to be seen at the right places. The tables are beautiful, covered with white tablecloths atop which are mismatched Italian pottery plates and plum napkins. Among soup choices were cold cucumber with dill, tomato-orange or a sweet and sour soup, served hot. We loved the cucumber with dill but thought the tomato-orange a little muddied. Salads, beautifully presented, were lettuce and crudites, with a choice of a divine creamy dill, dijon-roquefort or Italian dressing. Our entrees of tournedos with bearnaise sauce and a baked scallop dish were fine. Other diners were enjoying huge steamed lobsters, and the crisp scallop duckling with a honey-curry sauce is said to be wonderful. For dessert, pecan pie and creme brulee were excellent, and the blueberry cream pie sounded good. The downside to the meal was that it was rushed service. For such an evening, one should be allowed to linger, yet our young waitress whisked away plates as soon as the last morsel was eaten and served the next course almost immediately. Dinner nightly, 6 to 9:30. Open May-October. Reservations required. No credit cards.

Martha's, 71 Main St., Edgartown. (617) 627-8316. This is an unusually pretty restaurant with both a first-floor and a second-floor dining room and a tiny porch upstairs overlooking Edgartown's busy, narrow Main Street. Bare wooden floors, glass-topped tables over flowered print tablecloths and peach walls with a green border make it very au courant. New Yorkers Bart Fleishman and Gerald Ottinger began this successful venture in 1981. They serve the crowds of Edgartown virtually all day long (an extensive luncheon-appetizer menu is available from 3 to 6). Lunch, which is in the $4 to $8 range for most items, concentrates on sandwiches, omelets, quiches and a few special entrees such as egg-dipped filet of sole with grilled potatoes or chunky chicken salad and grapes served in a melon wedge, both $7.25. In the evening you might try a salad like seafood Monterey ($14.95) featuring seafood, avocado, cherry tomatoes and fresh rotelle pasta in a lemon dijon vinaigrette. Or you can order bouillabaisse a la Martha at $24.95; a sushi platter for $14.95; steak au poivre, $20.95, or baked chicken citron with a citrus herb marinade, $13.95. A large selection of pasta dishes is in the $14 range. There's no view of the water except for that which flows down the mirror in the second-floor bar, but this spot is attractive indeed. Breakfast-lunch, 10:30 to 3; dinner, 6 to 10; Sunday brunch, 10:30 to 3:30. Open April-November.

Feasts, Chilmark at the Four Corners. (617) 645-3554. This trendy, two-level dining spot has a gourmet market and a thriving catering business as well. The high barn-like atmosphere of the interior is sophisticated with pale pink oilcloth squares over white tablecloths, cane-back chairs and fresh flowers. Seats upstairs afford a view of the entire scene. Mesquite-grilled and Cajun foods are among the exceptionally wide range of offerings: just looking at the menu can make you dizzy. House specialties include North Carolina barbecued ribs ($16.95), loin lamb chops ($19.95), seafood kabob with swordfish, tuna, sea scallops, onions, red peppers and mushrooms ($17.95) and mesquite-grilled teriyaki chicken ($13.95). There are salads (classic spinach and Feasts Caesar among them); soups (gazpacho, quahog chowder, seafood stew); seafood entrees including yellowtail tuna steak and soft-shell crabs from Maryland; meat entrees such as breast of duck or teriyaki steak; pastas with all sorts of sauces, and desserts such as the Feasts obscene brownie. If you can waddle to the door after dining, you're to be cheered. Open for lunch and dinner in season. BYOB.

Le Grenier, Main Street, Vineyard Haven. (617) 693-4906. The classic French restaurant above La Patisserie Francaise is run by French chef Jean Dupon of Lyon and his partner, Robin Salisbury. The small porch overlooking the street is the place to dine if you can. Dress is a step up from casual, but no jacket or tie is required. Among the hors d'oeuvres are a pate de campagne ($4.50), a terrine of vegetables in a tomato sauce ($4.75) and slices of salmon marinated in wine and chives ($6.50). Entrees range from $14.95 for classic frog's legs in garlic butter to $22.95 for lobster thermidor. Also available are filet mignon Wellington, salmon sauteed with cream of leeks, veal scallops with asparagus, crabmeat and bearnaise sauce, and steak au poivre flamed with cognac. Desserts, some of which are special pastries from the bakery downstairs, include peaches in raspberry sauce on meringue, creme caramel and chocolate mousse cake. Dinner nightly from 6. Open mid-March to mid-October. BYOB.

More Casual Choices

The Home Port, North Road, Menemsha. (617) 645-2679. Overlooking the water in the quaint fishing village of Menemsha, the incredibly popular Home Port offers the best seafood platters on the island and prepares its food simply and honestly. Owner Will Holtham has not deviated from his original concept since he opened 10 years ago. In the last two weeks of August it is not unusual, we're told, for the restaurant to turn away 200 would-be diners a day. The place is simple: bare wooden floors, captain's chairs, seating for 135. There is a small waiting area with raw bar outside where you can have drinks if you've brought your own. The blue and white menu is not elaborate but it covers the basics: lobsters are available in eight variations including a jumbo (three pounds) for $40 and a Home Port shore dinner (one-pound lobster, corn, stuffed quahog, steamed clams or mussels, $20). A fish platter of fried shrimp, fish, scallops and oysters plus a boiled lobster and a stuffed quahog goes for $21. Other specialties ($14 to $20) are baked stuffed shrimp, broiled bluefish and broiled Menemsha swordfish. Baked or french-fried potatoes come with the entree, as does an appetizer (quahog chowder, steamed mussels, fruit cup, cranberry juice) and a tossed salad or cole slaw. Desserts include home-made pies and ice cream. Dinner, 4:30 to 10. Open May to mid-October. Reservations required.

The Square Rigger, at the Triangle, Edgartown. (617) 627-9968. Building on his success with the Home Port, Will Holtham opened this restaurant in an old house in Edgartown in 1986. It has a quite different atmosphere — and the food is prepared differently — but we found it very cozy and pleasant. The larger of two dining rooms has tables arranged around an open brick hearth where the cooking is done; the tiny, four-table room at the rear is Colonial with mini-print wallpaper and candles on the tables. Our meal began with a chewy, dense and crusty loaf of bread brought to the table with a crock of butter. Complete dinners, priced from $16 to $26, include an appetizer (clam chowder, marinated scallops, or a small shrimp cocktail), a tossed salad, an entree and a dessert. Among entrees were bouillabaisse, a lobster salad plate with lobster meat, shrimp, crabmeat and whitefish (plus crisp garden veggies), baked stuffed shrimp, broiled Vineyard scallops, which were superior, and thick lamb chops, cooked to a pink perfection. We could not resist the dense, rich cheesecake nor the chocolate mint pie. Dinner, 5:30 to 10:30. Open year-round.

The Black Dog Tavern, Beach Street Extension, Vineyard Haven. (617) 693-9223. We stopped at this harborside place for lunch on a rainy, blustery day and found the rustic, cozy environment perfect to prepare for a hurricane.

190

No reservations are taken and you may have to wait, as we did, for a table. The dining porch running along the side overlooks the water and the ferry slip (in bad weather, heavy plastic sheeting is rolled down). Inside are bare wood floors and varnished square pine tables with captain's chairs; the kitchen is in view and servers scurry back and forth. Specials are posted on a blackboard. When we visited there were sauteed zucchini with pesto and rice, nachos with salsa and beans and chef's salad ($4.50 to $5.95), plus burgers and sandwiches of the usual sort. For dinner, seafood is featured in interesting variations ($12 to $17), such as baked West Tisbury oysters parmesan, filet of flounder francaise with sage, charbroiled swordfish steak with anchovy butter, and fresh halibut with shrimp and sweet red pepper sauce. Desserts are good, too; try fudge-bottom pie, Black Forest cherry cake, peach cobbler or Spanish vanilla cake. Breakfast 6 to 11, lunch 11:30 to 3, dinner 5 to 10; Sunday brunch, 7 to 2. Open year-round.

Louis' Tisbury Cafe and Take-Out, 102 State Road, Vineyard Haven. (617) 693-3255. This is a low-key hit; the dining room is in the back with red and white checked tablecloths on as many tables as can be crowded in. Out front is a take-out counter offering homemade pasta dishes, pizza, barbecued chicken and ribs, gazpacho, subs, clam chowder and so on. Dinner specials ($5.95 to $10.95) include barbecued half chicken, barbecued chargrilled shrimp, and pastas (the one with seafood is popular with the locals). Dinner nightly, lunch in season. No credit cards. Open year-round. BYOB.

The Brass Bass, Circuit Avenue, Oak Bluffs. (617) 693-3300. Besides being fun, this has arguably the best seafood in Oak Bluffs. The bar features 40 types of beer and the chance to join the "Around the World Beer Club" — members must have tried all 40, after which they get a T-shirt and a chance to have their photo posted on the wall. The bar also has a complete collection of Simba beer cans with pictures of wild animals from Africa displayed for all to see. We enjoyed Bavarian Weissbier, served with a wedge of lime, and some good skiing conversation with the bartender, who's skied all over the world. The large, open dining room next to the bar is Victorian in feeling with overhead fans, fluted pillars painted pale green, white balloon curtains, high-backed wooden booths and wooden tables. The restaurant serves light fare from 3 to 5, after which the dinner menu is in force. Selections ($10.95 to $17.95) include Cajun blackened bluefish, shrimp scampi over linguini, sole stuffed with broccoli and steamed lobster. Besides a chicken entree and barbecued ribs, you can get a burger if you insist ($6.95). All are served with french fries and cole slaw. Among above-average desserts, key lime pie is a favorite. Dinner nightly, 5 to 11.

The Ocean View, Chapman Avenue, Oak Bluffs. (617) 693-2207. This is a favorite family restaurant located near the harbor but, as far as we could see, without any view. The simple gray building with burgundy awnings and trim is basic inside, too: paneled walls, wooden tables with captain's chairs, a predictable salad bar, and efficient waitresses (unfortunately their numbers are flashed on an overhead board by the kitchen door when orders are ready). Patronized mostly by the locals, the Ocean View features plain cooking and seafood. Entrees include shrimp and scallops Ocean View (in a somewhat gelatinous white sauce) at $11.95 and swordfish, veal marsala and boiled lobster, all $12.95. An enormous piece of herring in sour cream was a nice appetizer. Portions are ample, if not inspired, and service is fast. Open for lunch and dinner year-round.

Papa John's on Circuit Avenue in Oak Bluffs has the best pizza on the island, we think, and it's a cut above many places on the mainland. Patrons sit at long tables, drink from pitchers of beer, and order pizzas with almost anything on them (including pineapple). This is a favorite spot of teenagers and college students.

Good ice cream can be found at any of the several **Mad Martha's** establishments around the island. "Oreo cookie nookie" for $3.25 is Oreo cookie ice cream with hot fudge and marshmallow sauce, topped with whipped cream and a Hershey kiss. The Vineyard Surprise is orange pineapple ice cream laced with tequila. And for the big eater, there's "Pig's Delight," one dozen scoops of ice cream with toppings, "hosed down with whipped cream." Order by saying "oink." The cost is $14.95.

The Scottish Bakehouse on State Road, going up-island about 1.5 miles from Vineyard Haven, is a wondrous little spot. Breads, scones, shortbread, steak and kidney pies, scotch meat pies, sausage rolls, and cakes and pastries all taste as if they've just been taken out of the oven in Edinburgh, my lads! Makes for a good picnic lunch.

Among the Flowers Cafe on Mayhew Lane in Edgartown has homemade waffle cones and ice cream and good light lunches. You can sit indoors or outside on a pleasant little terrace.

Happy Hour and Later

The Wharf Pub in Edgartown, on lower Main Street, is the place to rub knees and elbows with just about anybody who can push his way in. This place has piano music nightly.

David's Island House on Circuit Avenue in Oak Bluffs should not be missed. Small bare wooden tables, Tiffany-style lamps and bentwood chairs provide the atmosphere at the bar and restaurant owned by David Crohan, the well-known blind piano player. David tickles the ivories nightly and everyone comes to listen and sip.

Hot Tin Roof, Carly Simon's night spot at the airport, brings in a variety of entertainment. Call 693-1137 to find out what's on.

FOR MORE INFORMATION: Chamber of Commerce, Beach Road, Box 1698, Vineyard Haven, Mass. 02568. (617) 693-0085.

Pavilion awaits swimmers at Cliffside Beach Club.

Nantucket, Mass.

Everything about Nantucket epitomizes an island at sea. No point on the 14-mile-long island is more than a mile or two from the ocean. From historic Nantucket Town to beachy Surfside across island, from quaint Siasconset on the east to remote Madaket on the west, you can feel the breeze and smell the salt air (and almost touch it in times of pea-soup fog). Nearly everywhere you see the dunes, moors and heathlands honed by time, and hear the sounds of the sea.

Here is an island of history and romance nearly 30 miles off Cape Cod, with no land visible on the horizon. Historically it's been known as the "Little Gray Lady of the Sea," but we think of Nantucket in the preppy pink and green of its more contemporary veneer, as well as in the azure blue of its waters and the gold of its sandy beaches.

Nantucket was settled in the early 1600s, harbored fortunes as a whaling port in the 19th century, and carries its history and affluence well today. That's partly due to its relative isolation and an inherent sense of preservation, and partly due to the resources of Walter Beinecke Jr. of the S&H Green Stamps family.

Variously considered Nantucket's visionary or villain, he started in the early 1960s to turn the town around to face the waterfront that had been abandoned over the years. When he sold his holdings to First Winthrop Corp. of Boston in late 1986, he had built or restored three lodging establishments, the Nantucket Boat Basin, 40 cottages on the wharf and 36 retail buildings in the downtown area. He was a principal force behind the Nantucket Historical Trust and the Nantucket Conservation Foundation, which set the twin themes for the preservation of Nantucket.

Seldom has one man so greatly influenced the look, feel, fate and fortune of a place as Bud Beinecke has for Nantucket, in the words of Yesterday's Island newspaper. Recognizing the small size of the island and its finite quantities, he managed its growth by limiting access. Nantucket became an upscale, year-round community, not a seasonal carnival midway.

Daytrippers do come to Nantucket — for a price. But they return on the late-afternoon ferry to their tour buses in Hyannis, leaving the island for those who are willing and able to pay up to $150 for dinner and an equal amount for overnight lodging.

For the good life that Nantucket offers, the price may be worth it. Whether you're into beaching or boating, luxury lodging or fine dining, the arts, history, nature or wildlife, Nantucket is one island that has it all.

Getting There

Nantucket is reached by ferries or airlines.

The Woods Hole, Martha's Vineyard & Nantucket Steamboat Authority, Box 284, Woods Hole 02543. (617) 540-2022. Called simply the Authority (in more ways than one), it has four trips a day in summer between Hyannis and Nantucket (2 1/2 hours) and one trip from Woods Hole and Nantucket (3 1/2 hours). Costs for each one-way trip are $66.50 for cars and $8.50 for passengers (auto reservations are imperative, far in advance, for peak season).

Hy-Line, Ocean Street Dock, Hyannis 02601. (617) 775-7185. Faster crossings (two hours, without vehicles) for passengers are provided by the smaller Hy-Line ferries, which have six sailings daily in summer, three in June and September, and one in May and October. Seats are guaranteed for the return on same-day round-trip cruises. One-way, adults $9, children $4.50.

Nantucket's airport, we're told, has become the second busiest in Massachusetts, serving commercial jets from New York and Boston and an inordinate number of smaller airlines and private planes.

Where to Stay

Near the Water, In Town

Cliffside Beach Club, Jefferson Avenue, Box 449, Nantucket 02554. (617) 228-0618. Nantucket's niftiest waterfront accommodations, we think, are in the 14 new "hotel" rooms at the old Cliffside Beach Club, dating to 1924. Here on a glorious 400-foot strand, members waited years to reserve one of the prime sections of the west beach, and the same umbrellas and chairs are still in the same spots, according to general manager Robert F. Currie. Some of the old-fashioned changing rooms have been transformed into airy contemporary guest quarters with cathedral ceilings and modern baths. All the beds, tables, vanities, doors and even the pegs for the beach towels were built by Nantucket craftsmen; angled wainscoting serves as the headboards for the built-in queensize beds. The woodwork from the old bathhouses is handsomely accented by dark green colors and prints by local artists. Some rooms have decks facing the beach, and all have cable TV. Continental breakfast is served in the spectacular lobby, full of smart wicker furniture and planters, and topped by quilts on the ceiling. Lunch and dinner are available at **The Galley** (see Where to Eat), the beach club's appealing waterfront restaurant across the sand. Twelve kitchenette apartments in four cottages were being renovated for 1987, and three new two-story suites and an indoor swimming pool were in the works. Doubles, $185 to $275; apartments, $135 to $395 (also available by the week). No credit cards. Open Memorial Day to Oct. 15.

The White Elephant, Easton Street, Box 359, Nantucket 02554. (617) 228-2500. A few detractors say the White Elephant lives up to its name, based on the small size of its 22 main-hotel bedrooms and the lofty level of its prices. But even they concede the charm of the 15 rose-covered cottages scattered about the property, and must be impressed with the 26 magnificently refurbished rooms in the Breakers annex. A superb harborfront location offers lush lawns, fancy walkways lined with hedges and plantings that focus on a white elephant statue in the middle, two nine-hole putting greens and a pleasant pool beyond the outdoor terrace and restaurant. Who wouldn't adore the cozy weathered-shingled Spindrift cottages done up in wicker, their living rooms with bay windows overlooking the water? Who wouldn't want to indulge in the sumptuousness of the nē plus ultra Breakers, outfitted in Ethan Allen furniture and modern baths with twin sinks? Here, complimentary wine and cheese are served in the lounge, as is continental breakfast, and your refrigerator is stocked with champagne and mixers. You even receive Breakers canvas tote bags to remember them by. Third-floor rooms have patios and decks, but some rooms here and many of the cottages do not have water views — be sure to specify. Doubles, main building, $160-$195; cottages, $105 to $425; Breakers, $235 to $375. Open Memorial Day to Oct. 12.

Cliff Lodge, 9 Cliff Road, Box 2452, Nantucket 02554. (617) 228-9480. A harbor view from three of the nine crisp guest rooms (one an apartment), five common rooms on three floors, two patios and a rooftop deck are attributes of this new guest house, which opened in 1986. Built in 1771 on a hillside overlooking the harbor, the onetime whaling master's mansion is notable now for paint-speckled floors and Laura Ashley wallpapers. All rooms have private baths, TVs hidden in cabinets, and many have kingsize beds and fireplaces. But all the sitting rooms, reading porches and well-furnished patios set Cliff Lodge apart. "People don't want to be cooped up in their bedrooms all the time," avows manager Mary Coughlin, "so we provide lots of common rooms and mixing areas." A complimentary breakfast of granola, fresh fruit and homemade breads is served. Cliff Lodge is owned by Nantucket Roosts, which also rents five kitchenette cottages known as Still Dock Apartments on old North Wharf, $140 to $180 a night, $1,100 to $1,300 a week. Doubles in lodge, $75 to $105. Open year-round.

Westmoor Inn, Cliff Road, Nantucket 02554. (617) 228-0877. A distant ocean view from a hilltop is afforded by this striking yellow 1917 Vanderbilt mansion, which was reopened by the Romano family in 1985 as a glamorous, antiques-filled B&B. Up a grand staircase are six rooms and three suites, handsomely appointed with a mix of antique and more modern furnishings — a canopied four-poster and a peach-colored chaise lounge in one, a double and a single bed and working fireplace in another. A deluxe suite has a sitting area, a jacuzzi and sliding doors leading to the side lawn. The formal living room is wrapped in draperies that drag the floor in European style; here, near a grand piano, wine and hors d'oeuvres are served every evening. A library, furnished in antique white wicker, has books, cable TV and VCR. An atrium breakfast porch is the scene of gourmet country breakfasts: perhaps cantaloupe and Welsh rarebit, or fresh berries and eggs Benedict with asparagus hollandaise. Outside, guests enjoy two acres of grounds, including a back garden full of birdbaths; there's garden furniture for taking in the view. Doubles, $90 to $135; suites, $165 to $200. Open early May-October, plus Thanksgiving and Christmas Stroll.

Nantucket Landfall, 4 Harbor View Way, Nantucket 02554. (617) 228-

0500. Nantucket's only B&B located across from the water was opened in late 1985 by Gail and David More in an old house with a great front porch furnished in white and navy wicker and a wide side yard full of white garden furniture. All five guest rooms have private baths, a couple of them ingeniously tucked into cubicles because "this is a small house and we had to use every inch," Gail relates. She made up for lack of space with interesting decor and colorful comforters. Two second-floor rooms have sitting areas overlooking the harbor, and a downstairs room has its own private patio. The living room has a fireplace and library. The Mores mingle with guests at one big table over a hearty continental breakfast of juice, melon, hard-boiled eggs and muffins. Doubles, $70 to $110. Open year-round.

Brass Lantern Inn, 11 N. Water St., Nantucket 02554. (617) 228-4064. The large, new contemporary rooms are best at this in-town B&B, which is closest-to-the ferry docks — a consideration for baggage-toting visitors without cars. The ten older guest rooms in the front of the 1846 Greek Revival house vary in size, and all but two share baths. We like the eight luxury rooms built by innkeeper Ben W. Garneau's son, a contractor — especially the extra-large room with cathedral ceiling, queensize bed, and sitting area with two white wicker chairs, a skirted table and a sofabed. Guests have access to a living room with TV and books. A light continental breakfast (very light — one of us had to have another at the Morning Glory Cafe to last the morning) is delivered to the rooms; we asked to have ours at a picnic table on the small side lawn. Doubles, $85 to $135. Open mid-April through October.

Wharf Cottages, New Whale Street, Box 1139, Nantucket 02554. (617) 228-4620. Twenty-five harborfront cottages on Swain's and South wharfs were refurbished by Sherburne Associates, the Walter Beinecke-inspired company which also owned the White Elephant and the Harbor House. Celebrities often rent them by the month or season, but single nights may be available (by chance and without reservations). Some transformed from old fishermen's shacks, the cottages vary from studios to three bedrooms, and are right on the water amidst all the yachts. Each has a kitchen, telephone and hookup for cable TV, and some have pleasant touches like skylights in the kitchen, living rooms with decks over the water, or brick patios. As the brochure says, "you're part of the scene, right on the harbor," with boats and boatpeople traipsing by, for better or worse. Cottages, $135 to $325 daily; 10 percent less by month, 20 percent less by season. Some cottages open through December.

Tuckernuck Inn, 60 Union St., Nantucket 02554. (617) 228-4886 or (800) 228-4886. The old Center for World Affairs has been gutted and turned into a motel-like inn with 17 guest rooms, a main-floor breakfast room that innkeeper Ken Parker hoped would become a restaurant, a third-floor library-common room and a rooftop deck with a wide-angle harbor view beyond the adjacent lumber yard. Rooms that smell of newness have comfortable furnishings, cable TV and private baths; most have queensize beds. Ken and his wife Barbara, who also own the **Parker Guest House** at 4 E. Chestnut St., planned to attract the conference business. Doubles, $85. Open year-round.

On the Water, Out of Town

The Summer House, Ocean Avenue, Box 313, Siasconset 02564. (617)

257-9976. Eight romantic, rose-covered cottages of the old school were delightfully upgraded by new owners in 1986 and present an idyllic oceanfront scene straight out of Bermuda on the south side of 'Sconset, as the islanders call it. The complex includes a heated pool beside the beach across the road, and an acclaimed restaurant (see Where to Eat) in the veranda-fronted main house that was formerly the Moby Dick. Continental breakfast is served to overnight guests. Under a canopy of trees and ivy, the quite-private cottages have been sweetly redecorated with English antiques, colorful wallpapers, eyelet-embroidered pillows, lace curtains and such. Interesting roof lines, painted floors and chests, stained glass, leaded windows, and little nooks and crannies add to the charm. Co-owner Vicki Osier says her favorite cottage is the one with a small lanai with table and chairs, a queensize bed, a step-up bathroom, a sloping floor and a decor of ribbons and flowers. Cottages have one or two bedrooms, two have kitchens, one has a sitting room and another a fireplace. Cottages, $125 to $175. Open May 24-Oct. 15.

The Wade Cottages, Sankaty Avenue, Siasconset 02564. (617) 257-6308. Eight guest rooms, five apartments and three cottages are offered in this venerable, family-run summer compound atop the 'Sconset bluff, with a private beach below. Old-fashioned chairs on the spacious lawn, typical of the 'Sconset tradition, afford magnificent ocean views. Room guests are served continental breakfast in the Card Room of the beautiful main house, much of it still occupied by the Wade family. Accommodations range from guest rooms with private or shared baths, apartments (one with the tiniest kitchen ever) and housekeeping cottages with three to five bedrooms. Doubles, $80 to $105; apartments and cottages weekly, $800 to $2,300. Open May-October.

Star of the Sea Youth Hostel, Surfside, Nantucket 02554. (617) 228-0433. The 1873 Surfside Life Saving Station, one of the few remaining in the United States, is listed on the National Register of Historic Places. Now it offers 72 beds in single-sex dorms for up to three consecutive nights. Accommodations are open to American Youth Hostel members or to travelers who purchase a temporary guest membership card. The hostel rents sheet sacks and provides blankets, mattress and pillow and usually a stash of free food left by fellow travelers. Open April-October.

Away from the Water

Jared Coffin House, 29 Broad St., Nantucket 02554. (617) 228-2405. One of New England's grand inns and the one against which others in Nantucket traditionally have been measured, the Jared Coffin House has 58 rooms in a complex of six historic homes at the edge of downtown. All have private baths and most have television; most deluxe are the queensize canopy rooms in the Swain, Coffin and Grey houses. The public rooms are a sight to behold, furnished in priceless Chippendale and Sheraton antiques. The downstairs **Tap Room** and outdoor patio have good food at reasonable prices. Doubles, $90 to $135. Open year-round.

76 Main Street, 76 Main St., Nantucket 02554. (617) 228-2533. Innkeeper Shirley Peters has upgraded the old White Eagle Inn into an elegant B&B in the midst of historic Main Street. Off the grand entry hall are a formal Victorian parlor and a kitchen with dining area where continental breakfast is served. Upstairs are 12 handsome guest rooms with private baths. Outside is a sheltered courtyard and a motel-like annex with six more rooms designed for families ($85 to $95). Doubles in inn, $95 to $125.

Harbor House, South Beach Street, Box 1048, Nantucket 02554. (617) 228-1500. Local purists are not partial to this luxury motor lodge and time-sharing resort put up by the Beinecke interests, but visitors who appreciate their creature comforts are. Amid some fancy landscaping are a total of 54 guest rooms with phones and cable TV in the motor lodge, Garden Cottage or Springfield House. Most coveted are the newer 57 rooms in six townhouses, built to resemble early Nantucket homes (but the sea captains would scorn today's amenities). The Harbor House has a heated pool, putting green, conference facilities and restaurant. Doubles, $115 to $175; motor lodge open all year.

Dozens of other guest houses and cottages are available on the island. The only real motel is the **Beachside** (not on the water) on North Beach Street, (617) 228-2241, 88 units from $105 to $175, unless you include the Harbor House or the large new **Nantucket Inn at Nobadeer,** a Koala enterprise with indoor and outdoor pools, a fitness center and a rooftop restaurant beside the airport at 27 Macy's Lane, (617) 225-6900, doubles $155 to $185.

Two central sources for details are Nantucket Accommodations, 6 Ash Lane, 228-9559, and Nantucket Vacation Planning Service, Airport Tower Building, 228-9010.

RENTALS. The pages of the Inquirer and Mirror, Nantucket's weekly newspaper, are filled with real-estate advertisements for properties generally priced from $200,000 to more than $1 million. Rentals are fewer, and range from $700 to $3,000 a week; the prevailing rate is $1,000 to $1,500 a week. We saw classified ads asking $4,000 a month and $13,000 a season. Among the score or more of Nantucket realtors with rental listings are Nantucket Vacation Rentals, 6 Ash Lane, 228-3131; Coffin Real Estate, 51 Main St., 228-1138; Congdon & Coleman, 57 Main St., 228-0344, and the Maury People, 35 Main St., 228-1881.

Seeing and Doing

What you do in Nantucket depends somewhat on where and how long you're staying. Daytrippers and weekenders probably will want to stay close to Nantucket town. Those staying longer and those with cars can explore the island. Here is a sampling of its attractions.

Touring

Getting Around. If you have a car, it's easy to see the island, though the heart of town is congested and parking is limited. Bring your car by ferry — be sure to reserve well ahead — or rent a car from Island Rentals (228-4316), Barrett's (228-0174) or Young's (228-1151). On our latest two-night trip, we rented a car for 24 hours (noon to noon) for $40 from Barrett's, which gave the best deal, and were able to cover all the island that we hadn't already walked or biked. There are taxis and private bus services, and more bicycles and mopeds than you can honk your horn at.

Sightseeing Tours. Barrett's Gray Line, 20 Federal St., (617) 228-0174, offers six bus tours daily ranging from one to four hours, from Nantucket town to a full island tour. All but the full island tour have morning and afternoon departures, and have been operated for more than 60 years by descendants of Nantuckets whaling captains. Prices start at $6 for adults, $3.50 for children. Barrett's also runs a beach bus to Surfside seven times a day, roughly hourly, $2.75 for a round trip. **Island Tours**, Straight Wharf, 228-0334, has six 75-minute tours of Nantucket town and the east side of the island out to 'Sconset, adults $8, children $4, May-October. **Nantucket & Sconset Bus Line**, 20 Federal St., 228-3118, runs five trips daily to 'Sconset for $3 round trip: four 90-minute sightseeing tours of town and 'Sconset (adults $7, children $4), and trips every 30 minutes (75 cents) to Jetties Beach.

BICYCLING. Bikes or mopeds are the best way to see the outskirts of Nantucket town (the cobblestone streets of downtown present a problem there), as well as a good way to get out to Surfside. The ride is flat, on a path bordering the roadway. Our favorite trip is out the bike path bordering the road to Siasconset, an easy eight-mile straightaway past the airport with the wind generally from behind. The beguiling east-end village perched on a rose-dotted bluff is a world away from busy Nantucket town. The sand dunes, the azure-blue ocean, the golf courses and the birds a-twitter between vine-covered cottages present "a magical setting like that of Bermuda," as Summer House manager Vicky Osier reminded us. Instead of retracing your path, return via the winding, sometimes up-and-down loop road past Sankaty Light, Quidnet and Polpis. Here you'll see cranberry bogs and ponds, striking homes and rolling moors, and you'll get a sense of the real island.

Bike and Moped Rentals. Young's Bicycle Shop, Steamboat Wharf, 228-1151, is in one of the first buildings one passes upon leaving the ferry. Rent wheels, grab your bag and you're on your way. Three- and ten-speed bikes go for $2 to $3 an hour (two-hour minimum), $8 to $10 a day. Single and double mopeds are rented by the hour ($8 and $12), four hours ($18 and $28), and day ($24 and $36). **Nantucket Mopeds** off South Water Street rents three-speed bikes at $5 for four hours, $7 a day and $9 for 24 hours, and mopeds for $8 an hour, $18 for half a day and $24 daily. Also handy for bikes is **Cook's Cycle Shop**, 6 S. Beach St., 228-0800.

Walking Tour by Roger A. Young. 26 Easy St. (617) 228-1062. A number of self-guided tours of Nantucket town are available — or just meander in any direction, and you won't be disappointed. Best for local color is the tour sponsored by the Nantucket Historical Association and led by Roger Young (of the Young Bicycle Shop family). By appointment, the energetic semi-retiree gives two-hour tours after which participants receive little blue cards saying the bearer "has successfully completed the leisurely walking tour through some of the lanes and byways of Nantucket town." You arrange to meet under the tree at the Peter Foulger Museum. He won't be in Nantucket pinks ("those are for the summer folk," his wife advised), but you'll recognize him by his MAA (Madaket Admiralty Association) cap and the walking cane he uses as a pointer. A former town selectman and a civic leader, he knows everyone in town and everyone knows him, which makes the tour that much more interesting as he waves to the bank president and jokes with a young shopkeeper. "I go where the buses don't," he said as he led our group of seven down a two-foot-wide walkway beside the newly restored 1809 South Church (Unitarian-Universalist), where he arranged for a special viewing of the interior, in which the 1843 trompe l'oeil painting is quite a sight. He relates the inside scoop on all the history and personalities of Nantucket, from the mother of Ben Franklin to the Macy who founded the department-store chain. Tours daily at 9:30 or 1:30 (the first caller sets the time); adults $6.

On or Near the Water

Nantucket Harbor Cruises, Straight Wharf. If you've already arrived by ferry, this may seem redundant, but at least you find out what you're looking at. Cruises depart at 10, noon, 2, 4 and 6 for $12.50 each.

Fair Tide Charters, Slip 18, Straight Wharf, 228-4844. Capt. Lee Groth and crew sail out of Fort Lauderdale in winter but say they like Nantucket better — the island provides a shelter for Nantucket Sound that the coast lacks, giving "a strange combination of flat ocean but a lot of wind." Sailors know that, but landlubbers enjoy a a short cruise on their 43-foot oceangoing yacht. "After you've been to so many restaurants and clubs, you get restauranted out and this becomes a nice afternoon off," said crewman George Smith. The main two-hour sail departs daily for Great Point or Madaket at 10, 1, 3:30 and 6:30 (sunset), $25 a person. A three-hour Sunday brunch cruise anchors in the harbor after a sail for fruit, muffins, quiche and coffee ($35). Day, overnight and weekly charters are also available.

Harbor Sails & Rentals, Slip 15, Straight Wharf, 228-5585. Capt. James Genthner offers a variety of cruises on his 31-foot Friendship sloop Endeavor. One or one-and-a-half-hour sails cost $12.50 to $17.50 per person. A three-hour beachcomber cruise to Coatue, where you're rowed ashore for swimming or shell-collecting, costs $210 for one to six people.

Fishing charters. Flicka & Albacore, Straight Wharf, 228-9224, takes one to six people for $70 an hour, supplying everything but the food. "We're fishing 10 minutes after we leave the dock," Capt. Gibby Nickerson said. Bob Walin, 228-3329, conducts two trips daily via Wagoneer to Nantucket's best surf-fishing spots. If you call to check as we did, you may get a recording "gone fishing." That's the Nantucket way.

Jeep Expeditions. Whitney Mitchell, 15 Masaquet Ave., 228-2331, takes people to Great Point in the morning for surf fishing, beachcombing or swimming. Beach Excursions, 228-3728, will pick people up at their door in a jeep for surf-fishing or beach excursions and picnics at Great Point. The point is a remote and desolate stretch, Nantucket has an inordinate number of jeeps, and everyone wants to go out there, we were told. On the way, you'll see clamming and oyster ponds, eagle and tern nesting grounds, and bayberry forests as you ride the dunes to the ruins of America's oldest working lighthouse, now being restored.

Windsurfing. The lack of choppy seas that sailors enjoy also is attractive to windsurfers on Nantucket's north shore, particularly around Jetties Beach. Indian Summer Sports at Jetties Beach, 228-9401, rents windsurfers, surfboards and sunfish, and offers instruction. Madaket Harbor, Dionis and Pocomo Point are also popular with windsurfers. We're told that several have windsurfed all the way to Martha's Vineyard, some 30 miles away. For surfing, the south shore around Surfside is challenging — big waves but strong rip currents going the other way.

BEACHES. Despite the allure of great restaurants, inns, shops, history and such, the beaches are what entice most to Nantucket. And there's quite a choice. The north shore beaches facing Nantucket Sound tend to be calmer and more tranquil than those facing the open ocean on the south shore. Waters are warmer (up to 75 degrees in summer), the ocean bottom slopes more gently and the beaches are wider. Just north of town is **Jetties Beach,**

the best all-around for calm waters and named for the jetties that jut out into the ocean from its sandy shore. Bathhouses, lifeguards and a snack bar are available. **Children's Beach,** closer to the center off Harbor View Way, lives up to its name and has a playground. More secluded and harder to reach on the north shore is **Dionis,** a harbor beach favored by snorkelers. On the south shore, our favorite all-around is **Surfside,** four miles south of town. It has lifeguards, a food concession, bike racks, changing areas and an impressive surf — the beach is most expansive, of course, at low tide. Less crowded and more private is **Siasconset Beach,** a pleasant strand along the east shore. The beaches at **Great Point, Coskata and Coatue** are popular with those who can get to them, either by boat or jeep. At the island's west end is **Madaket,** a great place for sunset-watching and isolated beaching; here the water deepens rapidly.

Wildlife Refuges. A total of 21 miles of ocean, harbor and sound shoreline are protected by the Coatue, Coskata-Coatue and Great Point-Nantucket National wildlife refuges. Mainly barrier beaches, marshes and dunes, they harbor a variety of birds, shellfish and even jack rabbits. Visitors are welcome, but are warned that swimming may be dangerous. Coatue is part of the Nantucket Conservation Foundation, which has protected more than 6,100 acres of the island.

Church Tower Tour, First Congregational Church and Old North Vestry, 62 Centre St. Church officials say that you get a bird's-eye view of town and can see the entire island from the church tower atop Beacon Hill in the center of town. Open weekdays 10 to 4, June-September.

Historic Sites and Museums

Historic Nantucket, Box 1016, Nantucket. (617) 228-1894. Dating to 1659 when Thomas Macy arrived as the first settler, Nantucket town has more than 400 pre-1840 structures, the greatest concentration in the country. Walk up Main Street for a look at the Three Bricks, Georgian mansions built by whaling merchant Joseph Starbuck. Thirteen buildings of special significance are open to the public and maintained by the Nantucket Historical Association. Tickets may be obtained individually or by combination. On the outskirts, don't miss the Oldest House (1686) on Sunset Hill, the Old Mill (1746) and the Old Gaol (1805). Five period houses of different eras and three museums (see below) are opened by the association as well. Combination visitor pass good for entire season: Adults $6.50, children $2.50.

Nantucket Whaling Museum, Broad Street. The single largest attraction in town is the Whaling Museum, as befits a community that was a major whaling port. The story of Nantucket whaling is detailed in the inviting red-brick building just off Steamboat Wharf. The museum opened in 1930 as an outgrowth of the private collection of summer resident Edward F. Sanderson and has expanded since. The extensive exhibit includes a 43-foot finback whale that washed onto the north shore in 1967, an 18-foot whale jaw, what's said to be the only candle press in existence, the original lens from the Sankaty lighthouse, a room full of scrimshaw, whalecraft shops, whaling implements and whalers' finds, along with portraits and memorabilia of those who made Nantucket the third largest port in the United States at the time. You leave the rambling structure via an outstanding museum shop. Open daily

10 to 5, Memorial Day to mid-October; weekends in fall and spring. Adults $2.50, children $1, or combination visitor pass.

Peter Foulger Museum, Broad Street. Next door to the Whaling Museum is this folk museum named for the grandfather of Benjamin Franklin. It traces Nantucket's history from farming community to summer resort. Paintings, articles from the China trade, 'Sconset as a fishing village, the old railroad, Nantucket silver and furniture, lightship baskets, textiles, Indian artifacts and more are shown. Open daily, 10 to 5, Memorial Day to mid-October; Monday-Friday, spring and fall. Adults $1.50, children 50 cents, or visitor pass.

Fair Street Museum, Fair Street. Located next to the 1838 Quaker Meeting House, this 1904 structure was built to house the Nantucket Historical Association collections, which since have been dispersed throughout its properties. It is now the town's art museum, hosting special exhibits of local cultural heritage and decorative arts. Open daily 10 to 5. Adults $1, children 50 cents, or visitor pass.

Maria Mitchell Association, 1 Vestal St., 228-2896. The birthplace of America's first woman astronomer, who discovered the Mitchell comet, remains as it was in 1918. Next door is a memorial observatory open Wednesday evenings. The scientific and historic center also has a natural science museum at 7 Milk St., featuring local wildflowers and birds, and an aquarium at 28 Washington St. Hours vary. Combination tickets: adults $3, children 75 cents.

Music and Arts

Nantucket Musical Arts Society, Box 897, Nantucket. Since 1959, the society has sponsored weekly summer concerts and recitals on Tuesdays at 8:30 in First Congregational Church, 62 Center St. Series and individual tickets are available by mail, at the door or at Tiller Antiques on Easy Street. Informal "Meet the Artists" gatherings, co-sponsored by the Nantucket Artists Association, are held the night before the concert at 8:30 at the Kenneth Taylor Gallery. **The Theater Workshop of Nantucket,** 62 Centre St., 228-4305, presents four varied productions in the summer in Bennett Hall; tickets are $7.50.

'Sconset Casino, New Street, Siasconset, 257-6585. The casino's theatrical tradition which began in 1900 has been revived by the Terrapin Theatre Co. of New York, which spent the summers of 1985 and 1986 in residence here. Shakespeare comedies, George Bernard Shaw farces and an American folk musical, "The Robber Bridegroom," were presented in two-week segments about every other night in 1986. Tickets, $4 and $6.

SHOPPING. Nantucket is a paradise for shoppers, and every year new stores open (in 1986, residents were bemoaning the arrival of Benetton, the first mainland chain store other the Country Store of Concord and Crabtree & Evelyn, both of which pass muster (as does the vital A&P supermarket on the wharf). Fine small shops, boutiques and galleries are scattered along the wharves, Main Street and side streets. Among standouts are **Erica Wilson Needle Works, Kenneth Taylor Gallery,** the **Bowler Co. of Boston** for men's sportswear, the **Forager House Collection** of folk art and accessories, and **Nantucket Looms,** with beautiful, whimsical woven items. **The Lion's Paw,** one of the nicest shops we've seen, is too elegant for words. **The Hub** newsstand and sundry store is a local institution. Other local institutions are Nantucket faded pink pants worn by men, while women tote Nantucket's famed lightship baskets on their tanned arms. The baskets come in assorted shapes and sizes, and are carried in many shops. At Michael Kane's **Carvers Guild** shop, we looked at a small $800 number without the ivory and decided to pass. Instead, we picked up a couple of nice-looking sweaters at a good discount at **Nantucket Mills**, a small store at 1 N. Beach St.

Where to Eat

For an island with a year-round population of 7,000 (augmented by up to 40,000 high-livers and free-spenders in the summer), Nantucket has an uncommon concentration of uncommonly good restaurants. Even the summer-long vacationer would be hard-pressed to visit them all — and might go broke in the process. But every visitor, whether ensconced in an in-town inn or a Surfside cottage, makes a point of dining out at least once. Most of the top restaurants require or advise reservations. We concentrate on those near the water, or those with a particularly summery air.

On or Near the Water

Chanticleer Inn, New Street, Siasconset. (617) 257-6231. Renowned across the world for world-class dining, this elegant French restaurant on two floors of a large 'Sconset cottage has been considered tops since Jean-Charles Berruet acquired it in 1969. A-la-carte lunch (entrees $13 to $16) in the outdoor garden, at tables beneath trellised canopies of roses and beside impeccably trimmed hedges, is a 'Sconset tradition, as is an after-dinner drink accompanied by piano music in the beamed and nautical Chantey Bar. Amidst heavy silver and pretty floral china, dinner is served in the lovely fireplaced dining room opening onto a greenhouse or upstairs in a pristine peach and white room. Although you can order a la carte, prix-fixe dinners are $45 "and worth every cent," townspeople informed us. Regulars put themselves in the hands of a knowledgeable staff to steer them to the right choices on an ambitious and complex menu. Feast, perhaps, on a mousse of Nantucket scallops and salmon topped with a cream of tomato and watercress sauce, a stuffed Nantucket pheasant or grilled breast of Nantucket duck with a juniper berry and spicy current sauce, salad and cheese, and a lime meringue pie in the Creole style. The possibilities are limited only by chef Jean Charles's imagination and the sensibilities of his kitchen staff of eleven. The $25,000 wine cellar contains 800 selections, priced from $14 to $400. Lunch, noon to 2 in summer; dinner, 6:30 to 10; closed Wednesdays. Open late May to mid-October. Reservations required.

Straight Wharf Restaurant, Straight Wharf, Nantucket. (617) 228-4499. Marian Morash of television and cookbook fame is the force behind this seasonal restaurant on the waterfront, specializing in fresh seafood and produce. We wish that the June night we dined had been warm enough to eat outside on the canopied, rib-lighted deck beside the water, that the service had been more prompt and that the acclaimed vegetables were more exciting and seasonal than broccoli and carrots. But the complimentary bluefish pate, the grilled salmon and the lobster crepes were first-rate, the peach Bavarian laden with raspberry sauce excellent, and the elaborately written bill was served with two chocolate shells. The shiny parquet floors and the soaring, shingled interior walls topped with billowing canvas create a summery feeling. With candles in hurricane lamps and classical music in the background, dining here is a real treat. Entrees start at $20. Dinner nightly except Monday, 6:45 to 9:30. Open mid-June to late September.

The Second Story, 1 South Beach St., Nantucket. (617) 228-3471. The pink and green decor (including a pink-spattered, green-painted floor), enormous hurricane lamps and a harborview-window alcove awash with pillows are all very striking and glamorous. At night, candles are the only illumination. The dinner fare, changing nightly, is a mix of Mexican-Spanish, French, Italian and Cajun. We enjoyed the good hot monkey bread, and a thick slab of country pate that was piping hot and bathed in a creamy green peppercorn sauce. Among entrees starting at $18, the Thai shrimp with black bean and coriander sauce was super spicy, and the scallops au gratin so ample that we needed neither salad (extra, as in many Nantucket restaurants) nor appetizer. Our amaretto souffle had barely a hint of amaretto and tasted more like a mousse; pears in puff pastry with caramel sauce might have been a better choice. Dinner nightly, 7 to 9:15; Sunday brunch, noon to 2 in summer. Open April-December. Reservations required.

The Galley on Cliffside Beach, Jefferson Avenue, Nantucket. (617) 228-9641. Nantucket has no better waterfront setting for a restaurant than this canopied, flower-lined deck on the beach beside the ocean. Rimmed with red geraniums and hanging plants, the jaunty navy blue deck chairs and striped cloths make an enticing setting against a background of azure water and fine sand. Mediterranean cuisine is featured, especially pastas and seafood ($14 to $21), although you can get veal marsala, scampi with garlic butter, sole angevine and sweetbreads with truffles. In the Casablanca-style interior, Ralph Strain plays the piano and sings nightly. At midday, take a beach break for a lunch of cold pasta salad, carpaccio, eggs Benedict or assorted smoked fish ($7.50 to $10), finishing with an airy lemon mousse. Lunch daily, noon to 2:30; dinner, 6:30 to 10. Open mid-June through mid-September.

The Regatta at the White Elephant, Easton Street, Nantucket. (617) 228-2500. A harborfront terrace beside the pool — with a feeling rather like that of a yacht club — makes this another good bet for lunch, though we thought our seafood and chicken salads were too small and we had to ask for seconds on rolls. The dinner menu gets fancier in an elegant peach and white dining room on several levels, some with water views. All is serene and lovely amid exotic silk flowers, brass-rail and column dividers, draped niches, chandeliers and tiny lamps. The dinner menu changes nightly. A typical menu runs from $14.50 for breast of chicken with lime to $24.50 for steamed lobster with drawn herb butter. Other choices might be shrimp boursin, sauteed quail with cassis and rosemary, or noisettes of lamb with artichoke bottoms and truffles. For dessert, take a fresh pastry ($3.50) with coffee and a cognac on Nantucket blue sofas surrounded by etched-glass elephants in the lounge. Lunch daily, noon to 2:30; dinner, 6 to 10. Open May 23 to mid-October.

The Summer House, Ocean Avenue, Siasconset. (617) 257-9956. The former Moby Dick restaurant has gone all summery with beachy furniture and an idyllic, Caribbean-style decor of white, pink and dark green. Hanging baskets of flowers, flickering candles and a display of desserts and cognacs add to the romance. At $19, filet mignon with a pink peppercorn sauce is the cheapest entree on the dinner menu, which includes fricassee of seafood with two sauces, Nantucket pheasant and red Spanish shrimp. Begin with baked oysters with salmon caviar in a vodka cream sauce or a salad of greens, wild mushrooms and quail eggs ($7 and $8 respectively) and you might not need dessert. They start at $4 for ice cream and go up to (gasp!) $9.50 for fruit and cheese. A white satin torte or chocolate apricot gateau each cost $5.50. You can lunch at the raw bar beside the pool and ocean below, although after shelling out $4.50 for a strawberry daiquiri and $2.50 for a beer we thought better of spending another $3.50 for a hot dog and decided to go elsewhere. Light lunch daily in summer, dinner nightly.

The Westender, Madaket Road, Madaket. (617) 228-5197. If you find yourself near the west end of the island, at the beach or simply OD'ed on high prices, consider this lively five-year-old establishment run by scallop fisherman Peter Dooley and his wife Annie. Casual lunches and takeout picnics are the daytime fare for beachgoers, who also can eat at picnic tables in the garden. The menu gets fancier at night, with items like Cajun seafood gumbo, chicken piccata, poached salmon and fettuccine with seafood ($13.95 to $17.95), served in a plain dining room with 10 shiny pine tables or in a canopied outdoor patio bar. Lunch, 11:30 to 3; dinner, 6 to 10; light fare 3 to 10; closed Tuesday except for takeout and light fare. Open May-October.

Other Choices

More options, from elegant to casual:

Le Languedoc, 24 Broad St., Nantucket. (617) 228-2552. Three serene candlelit dining rooms upstairs and a more casual downstairs room are the setting for what some consider the town's finest meals. The limited menu is supplemented by nightly seafood specials. Of the entrees ($18.50 to $22), we liked the noisettes of lamb with artichokes in a rosemary sauce and the sauteed sweetbreads with lobster in puff pastry, finished off with a chocolate hazelnut torte spiked with grand marnier. Lunch in season, noon to 2; dinner nightly, 6:30 to 10.

21 Federal, 21 Federal St., Nantucket. (617) 228-2121. New in 1985 and an instant hit with gourmands, this restaurant in a grandly restored building with four sleek gray dining rooms on the main floor and a couple more upstairs specializes in what acclaimed chef Bob Kinkead calls new and traditional American cuisine. It's all very innovative, trendy and crowded, but you can graze on a couple of appetizers if you're not up to sauteed sole with broccoli cream and red pepper mousse, grilled rack of lamb with wild leeks or grilled veal chop with grilled radicchio ($14 to $25). It's one of the few restaurants open all year. Lunch daily, 11:30 to 2:30; dinner, 6 to 10; Sunday brunch, 11:30 to 3.

The Boarding House, 12 Federal St., Nantucket. (617) 228-9622. Caterer Sarah Chase (of Que Sera Sarah) and Robert Kuratek, formerly of the India House, have taken over the Boarding House, giving it a striking pink and white renovation downstairs, adding a shady outdoor patio and a cathedral-ceilinged Victorian bar with slate floor and small marble tables, and upgrading the menu into Nantucket's forefront. You might start with herb-crusted lamb carpaccio or warm leek and scallop mousse, feast on brace of roast quail with smoked sweetbreads or confit of duck with strawberry rhubarb sauce, and end with white chocolate marquise or chocolate trilogy. Entrees are priced from $16 to $25. Lunch is served in the bar or patio in season. Lunch, Monday-Friday noon to 2:30; dinner Monday-Saturday 6:30 to 10.

The Club Car, 1 Main St., Nantucket. (617) 228-1101. Inventive chef Michael Shannon is a local institution in his luxurious establishment joined to a red train car used as a lounge and piano bar near the wharf. The inside is as pretty as the colorful flowers in the outdoor window boxes suggest. Appetizers are in the $8 range and entrees in the mid-$20s for such things as grilled Norwegian salmon topped with red pepper lobster butter, swordfish with bearnaise sauce and pecan butter, and breast of muscovy duck with green peppercorns and grand marnier. Dinner nightly in season and weekends off-season, 6 to 10; bar open from noon to 1 a.m.

The Captain's Table at the Ship's Inn, 13 Fair St., Nantucket. (617) 228-0040. Chef-owner John Krebs caters to sailors in this nicely nautical restaurant in the lower floor of the inn. A large fireplace separates the cozy dining room with its small-paned windows from the Dory Bar, where the bar is actually made from an old dory and tavern games like darts and backgammon are played. The fare is straightforward, consistent and fairly priced, from $12 for fish of the day to $17 for strip steak Madeira. Desserts in the $3 range are about half the going Nantucket price, and entrees come with French bread, baked potato, broiled tomato and house salad. Dinner nightly except Tuesday, 6 to 9:30. Open mid-April to mid-November.

North Wharf Fish House, 12 Cambridge St., Nantucket. (617) 228-5213. We had one of our more enjoyable dinners of late in this tiny, crowded place which does not take reservations and where two of us lucked into our own table for four after refusing to be jammed together in a lineup of deuces. An enormous salad served family style, the fresh seafood (sea scallops fra diavolo and a hot and spicy pasta special), the complimentary basket of after-dinner fruit and an interesting wine list made this a relative bargain. Entrees are priced from $11.50 to $16.95, and regulars say you can't go wrong with any of chef Jacques Wilson's offerings. Lunch daily, 11:30 to 2:30; dinner, 6 to 10:30. Open summer only.

Oak Street Cafe, 6 Oak St., Nantucket. (617) 228-0066. Howard Crocker of the now-closed Thistle and British-born Poppy Dean run this small new cafe behind 21 Federal's takeout gourmet store, with one umbrellaed outdoor table where we had a memorable lunch of chilled chive soup, onion tart, salmon quiche and a couple of sensational dessert tarts. The dinner menu ($12.50 to $15.50) offers things like grilled lamb chops, English grill and salmon in parchment with a cucumber watercress sauce. Lunch daily in season, 11:30 to 2:30; dinner, 6:30 to 9.

The Tavern Restaurant, Harbor Square at Straight Wharf, Nantucket. (617) 228-1266. An outdoor patio, an upper deck and several dining rooms are usually bustling and the food has been upgraded since we lunched on nachos deluxe a couple of years ago. No more nachos, says the new management from the Brotherhood of Thieves restaurant. The casual all-day menu is augmented at night by such items as bay scallops, lemon chicken and mako shark ($9.50 to $14.95). You feel as if you're near the water, even if you can't see it. Open daily 11:30 to 9:30, mid-May to mid-October.

The Morning Glory Cafe, Old South Wharf, Nantucket. (617) 228-2212. The quaintness of the wharf patio is exceeded only by the uniqueness of the small inner dining room with striking murals painted on the walls by an artist neighbor of new owner Liz Gracia. The patio is where everyone who is anyone in town seems to congregate at breakfast to exchange gossip of the goings-on in town or the night before. Breakfasts of Morning Glory muffins (which include everything but the kitchen sink) and omelets are memorable, and at night you can BYOB to enjoy with such eclectic fare as Chinese egg rolls, monkfish, Szechuan shrimp or lamb chops parmesan, priced from $7.25 to $10.50. Breakfast, 7:30 to 11:30; lunch, noon to 3; café supper, 6 to 10. Seasonal.

Sconset Café, Post Office Square, Siasconset. (617) 257-4008. Pam Mc-Kinstry, founder of the Morning Glory Cafe, has moved to the Sconset Café, packing her followers in at eight tables for lunches of fajitas salad in a tortilla shell, boboli (a pizza-like creation with pesto and artichoke hearts), and interesting soups and sandwiches. At dinner you might order fresh tuna with tomato-mint vinaigrette, confit of duck with cranberry marmalade or a warm lobster salad ($8.50 to $14). For dessert, try a grand marnier brioche pudding or passion fruit mousse cake. The summery decor is minimal, but the food isn't. A little cookbook of Sconset Café recipes, including those good Morning Glory muffins, is available all over town — we have added the muffins to our repertoire. Three meals daily from 8 a.m. to 9:30 p.m., May-September. BYOB.

Claudette's on the Porch, Post Office Square, Siasconset. (617) 257-6622. If you don't want to sit down to lunch, visit the seasonal little place beside the café to pick up a box lunch for the beach or to eat on a shady outdoor deck facing the square. You can get seafood salad, sandwiches or a piece of celebrated lemon cake (75 cents).

Water Club, end of Straight Wharf, Nantucket. (617) 228-1841. An outdoor patio and two casual waterfront dining rooms are attractions here, if you can put up with the noisy music (dancing after 10). The broad menu appeals, from pastas and salads to blackened salmon and shrimp Creole. Lunch 11 to 3; dinner 5 to 9:30.

Something Natural, 50 Cliff Road, Nantucket. (617) 228-0504. If you are out for a walk or a bike ride, stop here to pick up a great sandwich (a choice of 13, from $2.95 for cream cheese and olive to $4.50 for seafood salad), or a salad. Sandwich garnishes, 25 cents each, range from sliced egg to chutney, and the breads, available by the loaf as well, are sensational. The muffins are good, too, and there's carrot cake, Scotch Irish cake and fresh lemonade. Open May-October, 9 to 6.

Popco, near Nantucket Mopeds, South Water Street. What's a hot dog stand doing in Nantucket? Serving an all-beef hot dog for 95 cents and Nantucket's "one and only $1 salad," that's what. The salad is chock full of greens, cukes, mushrooms, cherry tomatoes and sprouts. You can get a fresh fruit parfait for $2 or yogurt and granola for $2.50 if you really want to splurge.

Two outstanding gourmet specialty shops and delis are **Que Sera Sarah,** now located at the Boarding House restaurant, 12 Federal St., and **21 Federal Specialties,** located behind the 21 Federal restaurant at 2 E. Chestnut St.

FOR MORE INFORMATION: Nantucket Island Chamber of Commerce, Pacific Club Building at foot of Main Street, Nantucket, Mass. 02554. (617) 228-1700. We have not found the Information Bureau at 25 Federal St. particularly helpful on any of our visits.

Cahoon's Hollow is one of four ocean beaches in Wellfleet.

Wellfleet/Cape Cod, Mass.

You're driving up Route 6, the Mid-Cape Highway, toward Provincetown. The traffic is horrendous and the landscape isn't great either: motels, pancake houses, fast-food restaurants, flea markets. You've come to Cape Cod to cool off, relax, put your feet up, find a little space — and you think you've made a mistake.

Then you turn left, following the signs to Wellfleet Center. Immediately, the traffic eases. The road becomes charming, meandering past handsome old clapboard houses and dipping down to the Town Pier. There are authentic Wellfleet fishing boats, plus sailboats and yachts bobbing on the waters of Wellfleet Harbor. You can get a cool drink and sit on the dock. You watch a few sailboarders out on Cape Cod Bay. The breeze is cool and fresh.

This is just the beginning. In the center of town, the shops are small and select. A variety of restaurants — from seafood by the pier to gourmet cuisine in a house-cum-art-gallery — are available. Several good art galleries offer watercolors, oils, Salt Marsh pottery and Wellfleet brownware.

The ocean side of town is no less attractive. Five gorgeous beaches, including one that is part of the Cape Cod National Seashore, beckon. Better still, you can find a parking place and a spot on the sand. This is the Cape as you'd hoped it would be.

Wellfleet has managed to retain the character of the Cape and to reject its blatant commercialism. Located next door to Eastham, and the main visitors' center for the Cape Cod National Seashore, the town has much to offer in the way of sun and sand and surf. And the fishing is fine.

Accommodations such as rental cottages, campsites, a couple of inns and a few motels on the highway suffice. There is no Ramada or Sheraton, no McDonald's or Burger King. You will not be in bumper-to-bumper traffic every time you drive on one of the town roads. The contrast becomes particularly apparent when you pull out onto Route 6 to get to another location. Even early on a Saturday morning — when we needed to take a

208

sick child to a medical care center further up the Cape — the traffic was impossible. By the time we returned to our inn in Wellfleet, we were doubly appreciative of the difference.

Of course, you'll want to drive to Provincetown for a day, or an evening. You will spend time at the National Seashore. You may even visit a shopping mall in Hyannis on a rainy day. But if you want to experience the best the Cape has to offer, you will find much of it here. The pace is more relaxed, the dress more casual, the welcome warmer. We wish you a good holiday in Wellfleet!

Getting There

Wellfleet is located on the lower Cape between Eastham and Truro. If Provincetown is the "fist", this is the "forearm." From the Bourne or Sagamore bridges take Route 6, the mid-Cape Highway, until you see signs for Wellfleet Center. Bus service is available from Boston to Wellfleet.

Where to Stay

The Inn at Duck Creeke, East Main Street, Wellfleet 02667. (617) 349-9333. Three energetic young innkeepers, Bob Morrill, Anne Fortier and Judy Pihl, have put together a most interesting complex: a main inn in which was once a sea captain's house built in the 1800s, several smaller buildings, a duck pond, salt marshes, a fine restaurant called **Sweet Seasons** (see Where to Eat), and a cozy tavern. Popular and appealing, it's wonderfully located — near Route 6 but far enough apart to be quiet and relaxed. Altogether 25 rooms are decorated individually with spool beds, Boston rockers, cane-bottom chairs and painted furniture. Many have mini-print wallpaper and some, like our large family room on the third floor (the old attic), have exposed beams, dormer windows and wall-to-wall carpeting. The front parlor is outfitted with wing chairs and period furniture. A small breakfast room to one side with several tables is where you'll get continental breakfast with coffee cake and muffins set out buffet style, along with coffee and tea. Five of the rooms are in a building out back and two more in a smaller building to the side of the main inn. Most rooms have private baths with showers; a few share. Doubles, $47 to $70; family room for four, $75. Open Memorial Day to Columbus Day.

The Holden Inn, Commercial Street, Wellfleet 02667. (617) 349-3450. Operated since 1969 by the Fricker family, this complex has three buildings: the main white clapboard, black-shuttered inn, a cottage next door, and the Lodge out back with some wonderful views of Cape Cod Bay, especially from a screened porch. Rockers are set along the front porch of the main inn on Commercial Street and guests also relax in a wicker-filled public room. All rooms in the inn and cottage have private baths; those in the lodge share. The Holden Inn can accommodate 50. Room 3 in the main building, on the front, has a double bed with brass headboard and pink printed spread, and wide floorboards indicating the age of the house. No meals are served. Doubles, $35 to $40. Open late June to Labor Day.

The Moorings, Commercial Street, Wellfleet. (617) 349-3379. Innkeeper Sally Scribner comes to the Cape each summer from Syracuse to operate this attractive small complex with two cottages and two smaller cabins out back, plus one three-room suite with private bath in the white house with black shutters. Duck Creeke runs behind the property; it is now mostly marshland, but the harbor and the Town Pier are just a short walk down the street. The main house dates from 1850 and has a welcoming feel to it; coffee and tea are offered to guests mornings in the dining room. The three-room suite with private entrance features a twin-bedded bedroom, a sitting room, and a bathroom with an old-fashioned tub. It rents for $50 a night or $325 per week; the fully furnished three-bedroom cottage with kitchen is $400 per week; the two-bedroom cottage is $375. Two cabins each have a double-bedded bedroom and a private W/C, but share a shower. They are $35 nightly or $215 by the week.

The Wellfleet Motel and Lodge, Route 6, Box 606, South Wellfleet 02663. (617) 349-3535. Located across busy Route 6 from the active Audubon Society grounds, this motel and lodge have been operated for 15 years by Bob and Helen Wilson. The 25-unit motel is the older building; it has pine-paneled rooms (15 of them family size) with refrigerators, color TVs, coffee-makers and air-conditioning. The two-story, 40-unit lodge, built in 1984, is more contemporary and has several two-room suites in two buildings. Attractions here are both an indoor and an outdoor pool, a hot tub, coffee shop, bar, picnic tables and a barbecue grill. Make note that you're only a quarter mile from the Wellfleet Drive-In Movie Theater which is also the site of an active flea market on Wednesdays, Saturdays and Sundays. The grounds include about 12 acres, many of them wooded. Doubles in lodge, $70 to $88; two-room suites accommodating up to three persons, $87 to $125. Doubles in motel, $61 to $76; family-size rooms, $66 to $81. Open year-round.

The Mainstay Motor Inn, Route 6, Wellfleet 02663. (617) 349-2350. Located on busy Route 6, but set back from the road a bit, this two-story, L-shaped motel has 20 pleasant units. Simply furnished, they feature two double beds, television, and air-conditioning. The second-floor units have balconies. Continental breakfast is served in season in a small breakfast area. A plus for beachgoers is an outdoor shower. A shrub-lined, large outdoor pool is also nice. Doubles, $60. Open May-November.

Billingsgate Motel, Mayo Beach Road, Wellfleet 02667. (617) 349-3924. This eight-unit motel is directly across the street from one of the Bay beaches and particularly popular because of the location. The large rooms have TVs and refrigerators. Suites accommodating up to five people with sitting room, two bedrooms and full bath are $100 a night. Doubles, $70. Open late May through September.

Brownie's Cabins, Route 6, South Wellfleet 02663. (617) 349-6881. One of the original, old-fashioned cottage colonies (of many in the area), Brownie's consists of 11 cabins clustered in a pine grove just off Route 6. Operated by the Marshall family of West Springfield, Mass., the cabins come in three configurations: two bedrooms, one-bedroom efficiencies, and one-bedroom overnights, without kitchen facilities. The two-bedroom cabins have one double bed and two twins and fully equipped kitchens; they rent for $275 weekly. One-bedroom efficiencies are $225 weekly, and overnight cabins are $210 weekly. Open Memorial Day to Columbus Day.

CAMPING. The Cape Cod National Seashore does not operate a campground. Private campgrounds in the area include **Maurice's Campground** on Route 6 in South Wellfleet, (617) 349-2029, and **Paine's Campground,**

Old County Road, South Wellfleet, (617) 349-3007.

RENTALS. Many houses are available for rent, ranging in price from $500 to $2,000 weekly (the latter would be large, new and right on the beach) and two-week rentals are the rule, though sometimes you can get a place for a week. Two real-estate outfits that deal with rentals are Cape Cod Realty, Route 6, South Wellfleet, (617) 349-2245, and Wellfleet Real Estate, Briar Lane, Wellfleet, (617) 349-3911.

Seeing and Doing

The beaches are the main draw in Wellfleet. Roads are good for bicycling, and the bay is fine for windsurfing, sailing and small boating. Fishing is great. Rainy-day possibilities include the splendid art galleries, interesting shops and historical society buildings. Just relaxing on the Town Pier deserves some time, too.

Cape Cod National Seashore. Start at the Salt Pond Visitors Center, Route 6, Eastham, where you can view dioramas and get a feeling for these 27,000 acres, including some of the best beaches on the East Coast. An extraordinary resource, the national seashore offers more than fine beaches. In Wellfleet, **Marconi Beach** is part of the National Seashore; it has lifeguards and changing facilities. A full range of guided nature walks, talks and evening programs is also run by park rangers; a schedule may be obtained at the visitors' center. Three of the self-guided trails are designated for horseback riding; horses can be rented at nearby stables. Bikers especially like riding through the seashore; pick up the folder, "Bicycle Trails of Cape Cod National Seashore," so you'll know where you're headed. Surf-fishing does not require a license and you can try your luck at any of the beaches as long as you're not in the lifeguard-protected areas. Open fires are allowed only with a permit, available at visitor centers. Centers are open daily from late spring through fall.

Among the walks recommended in the Wellfleet area is that around **Great Island.** This six-mile round trip will take three to four hours — much of it is in deep sand and is challenging. Pick up the National Park Service's mimeographed map at the trailhead in the parking lot before you set out (maps are kept in a box beside the large metal display map). You should carry your own water. The trail is one of the most primitive in the National Seashore area. Because no vehicles are permitted on Great Island, the only sounds are those of the birds and the surf — lovely.

Wellfleet Bay Wildlife Sanctuary, off Route 6, South Wellfleet. (617) 349-2615. Operated by the Massachusetts Audubon Society, this is a treat. There are five miles of trails through a salt marsh, moor field and pine woods. A full schedule of activities including family and sunset hikes, shorebird walks, early bird walks, night hikes, bird-banding demonstrations and birding programs for beginners is offered.

Swimming and Boating

In addition to Marconi Beach, which is overseen by park rangers from the National Seashore, four other ocean beaches are within the Town of Wellfleet. **White Crest** and **Cahoon's Hollow** are open to the public for a $6 daily parking fee. If you're staying in town for at least a week, you can buy a $15 beach sticker that allows you to park at all town beaches. On Cape Cod Bay, two popular beaches are **Sunset View,** which is next to town, and **Duck**

Harbor. But we prefer the ocean beaches and particularly like Cahoon's Hollow, which is reached after hiking down a dune.

Swimming is easier in the bay than the ocean. In fact, the ocean's high waves and rip tides at this part of the Cape can be awesome and frightening. Small children should not swim here. A lovely place to swim is the fresh-water pond, **Great Pond**, located off Cahoon Hollow Road. A rough-hewn set of wooden stairs leads down to the water, which is clear and blue like the Caribbean. **Gull Pond** is another nice fresh-water pond; a large parking area is next to it, off Gull Pond Road from Route 6.

If you've brought your own boat, you can launch it at the Town Pier at the end of Commercial Street for a $7 fee. Ample parking is available. Very small boats also can be launched at the Indian Neck parking lot at the foot of the breakwater, but any boat with a trailer is best handled at the pier.

A limited number of moorings are kept open each year for transient boats. Those wishing to moor in the harbor can rent moorings from three different companies; a boat livery is provided by two of them. Check with the Harbormaster.

You can rent paddleboats, sunfish, sailboards, canoes and Hobie catamarans from **Jack's Rentals** on Gull Pond, 349-9808. They range from $10 an hour for paddleboat and canoe to $28 an hour for a Hobie 16. All-day rates are $45 for a sunfish, $40 for a sailboard, $30 for paddleboat or canoe; $75 to $85 for a Hobie. Windsurfing and sailing lessons cost $15 per hour. You can pick up a sunfish for a week for $145 from Jack's Route 6 shop in Wellfleet.

Bay Sails Marine at the Town Pier in Wellfleet rents power and sailboats. Sunfish rent at $45 a day, $20 for two hours; a 14-foot catboat is $30 for two hours, $65 per day. Powerboats, including a 13-foot dory and a 17-foot seaway, are also available.

The Wind Gypsy, 255-9640, sails daily from Wellfleet Harbor, leaving at 10 and returning at 3. Charters are limited to six people and include lunch, soft drinks and usually a stop at Great Island for exploring. Adults $30, children $15.

Sport fishing, The Naviator, 349-6003, runs trips to fish for porgies, flounder and blackfish from the Wellfleet Town Pier. Morning trips leave at 9 and return at 1; afternoon trips are from 2 to 6. Adults $14, children $11. Sunset sightseeing trips are offered Tuesday and Friday nights in July and August at $4 per person.

Several **charter fishing boats** also are available. The Quahaug, 349-9000 or 255-0818, is typical. Owned by Steve and Ted Young, it takes six people at $55 each or $190 for the entire boat on trips of five to eight hours.

Whale-watching trips leave from Provincetown on regular schedules. The Dolphin Fleet, 255-3857, operates some 15 different trips daily on several boats. All leave from the Provincetown Pier and most are four hours in length, beginning at 8. Adults $15, children $13. Plans were being made to run two all-day whale-watch trips on weekends.

Other Activities

The **Wellfleet Historical Society** operates a museum on Main Street and the Samuel Rider House on Gull Pond Road. The society's collection of old photographs, maps, documents, marine artifacts, period clothing and household and agricultural items are on exhibit at both places. Several unusual gift items are sold at both as well. Combination fee, $1. Open Tuesday-Saturday from 2 to 5 in summer.

BICYCLING. The Wellfleet Chamber of Commerce issues a map of the town with many bicycle routes indicated. Although fairly hilly, it's quite pleasant to ride from the Town Pier all the way across town to the Atlantic, and then to traverse several trails through the Cape Cod National Seashore. Wellfleet Cycles on East Commercial Street, 349-9322, and Black Duck Sport Shop, 349-9801, rent bikes.

ART GALLERIES. Wellfleet has more than a dozen art galleries, most offering a fine range of work. We particularly like **Left Bank Gallery** on Commercial Street, a spacious place with paintings out front and an exceptionally good pottery room in back. **Salt Marsh Pottery** on East Main Street displays wheel-thrown earthenware and stoneware at attractive prices. The **Brehmer Graphics Gallery** located in a 19th century sea captain's Victorian home on Commercial Street shows the exceptional work of Bethia Brehmer, a printmaker who has had more than 50 one-woman shows around the country. **Wellfleet Pottery** on Commercial Street displays a vitrified, chip-resistant lead-free country china, charmingly decorated with wild grasses and flowers and known as Wellfleet Brownware. We covet a four-cup teapot with floral decoration for $70. Fine artists in glass and ceramics throughout the country display their works at **Cielo**, the marvelous art gallery with restaurant (see Where to Eat), on East Main Street. **Cove Gallery** can be fun to poke around; it's a mixed bag.

SHOPPING. You shouldn't overlook the **Bookstore & Restaurant** on Kendrick Avenue not far from Wellfleet Harbor. We're more interested in the food for thought here; the oceans of used books out back behind the restaurant are extraordinary. We saw comic books for as much as $150 and other collectors' items. The **Higgins House shops** located in a white clapboard house with blue shutters in the center of town include sportswear shops as well as a candy store. **Bank Square** is another house that's been turned into a group of nifty shops, including **Briarmead**, a store for country crafts; the **Corner Cape**, with handcrafted gold and silver jewelry, and **Leather Looks.** **The Glass Eye** on Route 6 in North Eastham offers stained glass, handmade paper featuring Cape plants, and other local crafts.

Up for a movie? The Wellfleet Drive-in on Route 6 at the Wellfleet-Eastham line has a different movie every night in summer. The box office opens at 7 and the movie begins at 8. This is also the site of active flea markets on Wednesdays, Saturdays and Sundays.

Where to Eat

The dining emphasis is on seafood, of course. But you can get it in every way from clambakes-to-go and fried clams on paper plates to rather formal dining in elegant restaurants.

Cielo, East Main Street, Wellfleet, (617) 349-2108. The name means "heaven" and the resident owners, Hayes Black and Richard Polak, are providing that for appreciative diners. Located in a small house across the road from the Inn at Duck Creeke, Cielo operates daily as a full functioning art gallery. At night a five-course, fixed-menu dinner is served to guests who have reserved in advance. The single seating accommodates about 20 diners on the porch overlooking a tidal marsh and a single larger party may be served "in the gallery." The decor is pink and gray, and fresh flowers, grown by Hayes, are lovingly arranged and placed with candles on every table. "This is our home," said Richard as he showed us around the kitchen one Saturday afternoon, "and we treat people as if they're our houseguests." The operation is strictly BYOB and when confirming your reservation about a week before you dine, ask whether the main course would dictate a red or white wine; cocktails are not accommodated. The meal being prepared the day we visited included a homemade chicken sausage with marinated wild mushrooms, something like a dense pate, as the appetizer; a pasta sauced with oysters, bacon and basil instead of a soup course; soft-shell crabs sauteed and topped with crabmeat remoulade as the entree; a mixed green salad garnished with honeydew, cantaloupe and blue cheese and dressed with a mustard vinaigrette, served following the entree, and for dessert an orange and chocolate roulade served with chocolate grand marnier sauce. Other popular entrees include a stuffed loin of pork with plum sauce, coulibiac of salmon, or Polak's own creation: a roulade of chicken filled with prosciutto, cheese and broccoli, sliced and served with a curried chicken sauce. The prix-fixe meal is something of a bargain these days at $32.50. Dinner, Wednesday–Saturday at 8, Memorial Day to Columbus Day.

Sweet Seasons, the Inn at Duck Creeke, East Main Street, Wellfleet. (617) 349-6535. When you make a reservation for a room at the inn, you can, as we did, also ask that a table be reserved at its very attractive restaurant. Entered off the main driveway through a screened porch and then a broad entry lobby wallpapered in a pink Colonial print, the dining room is starkly simple with bare wooden tables and floors, a few plants, dark brown placemats and napkins and pale gray walls on which paintings are shown to good advantage. Lace curtains and mauve draperies add a touch of sophistication. Fresh table flowers are set in white milk glass vases. On weekend nights there is a musician; the evening we dined, a guitarist strummed pleasantly in the background. Often a harpist is featured. A small loaf of bread on a board was brought to the table and promptly replenished after two teenagers had decimated it. Appetizers included a lobster bisque ($3.75), duck pate ($3.50) and Swedish smoked mackerel, peppered and wine-marinated, served with a creamy caper sauce ($5). A house salad costs $2, but was a nice selection of greens tossed with colorful vegetables and served with a vinaigrette dressing. Entrees range from $11 for boneless breast of chicken stuffed with spinach, parmesan cheese and chopped vegetables and served with a red pesto sauce to $17 for tenderloin of beef or a seafood stew with lobster in its shell and other fish and shellfish served in an herb and vegetable broth. Scallops genovese were served with mushrooms and a creamy pesto sauce over linguini and poached salmon with a creamy dill sauce was excellent. A melange of squashes was the vegetable of the day, served properly crisp. A good selection of wines with a wide range of prices is available. For dessert, champagne sorbet with raspberries was the choice of the dieting teenage daughter, while the hard-to-fill-up son chose a chocolate mousse pie with ladyfinger crust, pronouncing it excellent. Dinner nightly, 6 to 10 nightly in season; Saturday and Sunday brunch. Open mid-May to mid-October.

The Wellfleet Oyster House, East Main Street, Wellfleet. (617) 349-2134. This mainstay on the Cape was opened 14 years ago by Tony Costello, who spent the 29 previous years managing a restaurant on Fulton Street in New

214

York City. He runs a restaurant that is equally popular with locals and visitors, often a difficult feat to pull off. The white-trimmed, blue house, with large white letters announcing the name, dates from the 18th century. It is simply furnished inside with tables covered in gold cloths and red napkins. An upstairs dining room is used for overflow or private parties. Wellfleet oysters top the menu, of course, and oyster stew is made on request. Clam chowder is always on the menu. A salad, potato or rice and garlic toast accompany all entrees. According to the owner (who wants everyone to call him Tony), the most popular entree is the Spanish paella at $14.95. Also popular is Poor Richard's Platter, which includes saffron rice, two oysters, scallops, shrimps and crabmeat for $12.95. Steaks and prime rib are also available. The Jamaica mystery cake for dessert ($3.25), the owner's specialty, contains bananas, walnuts and kahlua. Other desserts include a midnight chocolate cake ($3.25) and a fruit fondue with chocolate brandy sauce for dipping, $7.95 for two. "You should try the cappuccino!" says Tony. It is made with Spanish brandy and kahlua and topped with homemade whipped cream. We can't wait. Dinner nightly, 6 to 10 in season; fewer nights rest of year.

Aesop's Tables, Main Street, Wellfleet Center. (617) 349-6450. This restaurant, housed in an 1805 house in the center of town, with tiny white lights outlining the roof, advertises "nouvelle New England cuisine." Owner Brian Dunne has created an elegant looking spot with several dining rooms decorated individually and a porch with pink director's chairs and mauve tables. The fantastic paper constructions of his wife, Kim Victoria Kettler, are displayed on the walls. The menu is slightly pricier than most in the area, with appetizers ranging from $3.25 for soup du jour to $8.25 for a spinach ricotta tortellini served with a walnut gormandise cream sauce. A warm scallop salad at $6.75 or a seafood pate at $7.25 are other choices. Entrees include paupiettes of sole, rolled and filled with a spinach-mushroom mixture and served with a chardonnay cream sauce for $14.75, almond lemon scampi for $16.25 and grilled loin lamb chops, $19.75. Desserts are a specialty and include the popular Death by Chocolate, a chocolate mousse cake with brownie crust served with whipped cream and Belgian chocolate shavings for $4.75, or strawberries with a white chocolate sauce for $3.75. Summer brunch features tofu provencal ($6.75), steak and eggs ($8.25) and salmon Benedict ($8.75). Light fare and desserts are served in the upstairs bar. Dinner nightly in summer; brunch Friday-Sunday 9 to 1. Open mid-May to Columbus Day.

Captain Higgins Seafood Restaurant, Town Pier, Wellfleet. (617) 349-6027. So you want to sit outside on a deck with a view of the harbor? This is the place to do it. For 20 summers Betty and John Balch and their family have run this popular spot, which seats 160 at plain wood barroom-style chairs and tables indoors and another 40 at umbrellaed tables on the deck. We had reserved an outdoor table, but when evening arrived with a chill wind, we were happy to be accommodated at a window table indoors. The menu emphasis is on New England seafood favorites, including deep-fried seafood platters ranging from $9.75 for flounder fillet to $11.95 for the fisherman's platter with scallops, shrimp, clams and a fresh fish in season. Fish may be ordered broiled as well. A shore dinner with New England chowder, steamed clams, a boiled lobster, and fried flounder was $14 the night we were there. Other entrees include baked stuffed shrimp, hot steamed shrimp served in the shell, New Orleans style ($10.95), crabmeat in casserole, au gratin or salad and, for the meat eater, broiled sirloin or southern fried chicken. Baskets of warm rolls come to the table, as do decanters of two salad dressings, Caesar with cheese or creamy cucumber for the mixed salads. Entrees also include baked or french fried potatoes or rice. The house wine is Sebastiani and strawberry margaritas are popular. For lunch, a hot open seafood sandwich with au gratin sauce on an English muffin is $6.95. Lobster, crabmeat and shrimp salads range from $7.95 to $9.50. Open daily for lunch and dinner, mid-June to early September.

Serena's, Route 6, South Wellfleet. (617) 349-9370. Two ambitious young couples and their kids joined forces 10 years ago to create this favorite restaurant right off the busy highway. Paul Johnson and Ed Simpson, who were college roommates, and their wives leased a spot for five years in Yarmouth before being able to build their own place. The decor is simple: wood tables and chairs and booths. Paul invents the cuisine, Ed manages the bar, Linda Johnson manages the front of the house, and Jane is back in the kitchen, presiding over salads and soups. The menu changes with Paul's whims, and included many Cajun specialties when we visited, but there is always an emphasis on seafood. Dinner entrees include seafood fra diavolo, the house favorite with mussels, littlenecks, oysters, scrod, scallops and shrimp in a light wine and marinara sauce for $13.50; broiled haddock in a wine-butter sauce ($10.25), shrimp scampi ($12.50) and grilled shrimp with veal cutlet, served with a mustard butter ($12.95). Veal parmigiana amd veal milanese are among the "Butcher's Block" entrees; pasta selections include ziti or spaghettini with red or white clam sauce, or with sausages or meatballs, in the $6.95 to $8.50 range. You can even get pizza here, ranging from $5.25 for cheese to $8.50 for a special which includes just about everything. Portuguese bread from Provincetown is a popular accompaniment to most meals. Be prepared for long waiting lines in season. Dinner, nightly 4:30 to 10:30 and Sunday from noon in summer; the schedule is pared back slightly in late spring and until mid-November.

Moby Dick's, Route 6, Wellfleet. (617) 349-9795. Three peaked gray buildings set back from the highway with a crushed clam-shell parking lot and lots of nautical memorabilia are the place to get real New England "chowdah," lobster in the rough, and all those other goodies that you must have on a trip to the Cape. Affable Todd Barry, a graduate student in hotel management at the University of Massachusetts, has been running the place for the past four years. The atmosphere is just right: blue and white and red and white checked tablecloths on picnic tables in three dining rooms plus an outdoor deck. Rough wood walls are decorated with nautical charts, lobster buoys and so on. You order at the counter and leave your name; the food is delivered to your table by pleasant young waiters and waitresses. The simplicity of the plastic implements, paper cups and plates, and simple baskets (for some sandwiches) emphasize the fresh goodness of the food. The chowder is creamy and full of clams and costs $1.35 for a cup, $1.85 a bowl. A fried clam plate is $6.95; broiled scallops or shrimp, $7.95; and lobster priced at market rates, but a good value. Hamburgers and chicken are also on the menu and you can get an ice cream cone for dessert. There's a salad bar at night. Open daily 11 to 10 in season. BYOB.

The Tavern Room, Inn at Duck Creeke, East Main Street, Wellfleet. (617) 349-7369. This casual spot, with a variety of live entertainment on weekends, is popular for casual dining and an evening of listening to music. A cozy fireplace and open beamed ceilings add to the ambience. The menu includes appetizers such as stuffed sea clams, chili, steamed mussels and Cajun chicken wings. Entrees in the $10 to $14 range might be Great Island gumbo, seafood pie, broiled scallops or shrimp flamed with tequila. A daily pasta dish is on the menu. Open for lunch and dinner daily in season.

The Lighthouse, Main Street, Wellfleet Center. (617) 349-3681. Everyone stops here at some time, it seems. The little center-of-town restaurant with the lighthouse above the door serves three meals a day in summer. Pictures of lighthouses line the walls and bare wooden tables contain ketchup and mustard bottles; a few more tables are set on a side porch. Soft rock music plays in the background and you can get for lunch anything from a peanut butter and jelly sandwich for $1.35 to an oyster roll for $4.95 and a tuna salad plate for $6.25. Dinner items include fried oysters and plates of fish and chips. Portland lager is served from the bar. Breakfast, lunch and dinner daily in season.

Bayside Lobster Hutt, Commercial Street, Wellfleet. (617) 349-6333. In an old white-shingled oyster shack on the road to Wellfleet Harbor, people dine on lobsters amidst tanks marked "see 'em swim." The clambake, which includes a one-pound lobster, steamed clams and corn on the cob is $13.95; a bowl of chowder goes for $2.50 and you can get steamed clams for $5.95. The fisherman's platter is $10.95. Obviously it's a favorite with families. Open daily, lunch noon to 5 and dinner 4 to 10:30, late June to Labor Day; dinner only in off-season. Open mid-May through September. BYOB.

The Clambake Company, Route 6, Wellfleet. (617) 349-3650. How about a clambake to go? You can get them here, ranging from $18 for one person to $160 for ten, and they'll ship them anywhere in the country ($49 for one; $250 for 10). If you want them to arrive at your friends' on Saturday, it costs more; don't ask us why. Each clambake includes a live Cape Cod lobster, local clams and mussels, codfish, corn on the cob, new potatoes, onions and sweet sausage. They come packed with seaweed in appropriately sized tins; all you have to do is remove the lid, add the beer or white wine and water, replace the lid, bring it to a steam, and cook for 30 minutes. Sounds good to us. The place is impeccably clean and well organized so we'd trust them to deliver. For mail orders, you have to give 48 hours notice. Open year-round.

The Harbor Freeze at the Town Pier is good for soft ice cream, or a delicious ice cream and orange juice mixture, hot dogs, hamburgers and clam rolls. Unfortunately service, for us, was as slow as molasses in winter. **Just Desserts** at Depot Square, open from 4 to 10:30 daily, with a porch overlooking a tidal marsh, serves ice cream in various guises. **The Beachcomber** at Cahoon Hollow Beach is reminiscent of California; surfboards tied to tops of cars, wet-suited guys wandering around, rock music blaring, and hamburgers and beer being enjoyed. There's a small deck out front for daytime, sunny dining or after-the-beach drinking; indoors rock bands set up at night and the kids all come.

FOR MORE INFORMATION: Wellfleet Chamber of Commerce, Box 571, Wellfleet, Mass. 02667. (617) 349-2510.

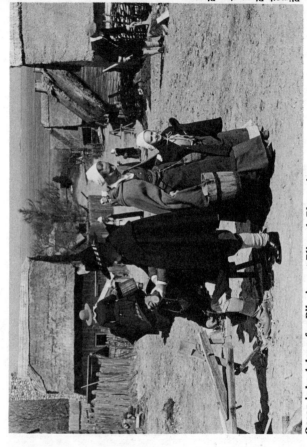

Plimoth Plantation Photo

Ocean is backdrop for Pilgrims at Plimoth Plantation.

Plymouth, Mass.

It was the first permanent settlement in North America. We think back to the Pilgrims of 1620, those hardy souls who braved an Atlantic voyage in the autumn, began to build a village in the midst of a harsh winter, and lost more than half their number before the following summer. We know of their persistence and their piety, their friendliness with the Indians and their first Thanksgiving. We revere the memory; hundreds of thousands of us a year visit the sites at Plymouth to pay our respects.

It is the Plymouth of 1627 that is recreated in Plimoth Plantation, surely the highlight of any visit to this town. The village with its thatched-roof cottages and appropriately dressed interpreters takes one back in history in a most authentic way; a visit to Mayflower II tied up at the State Pier completes the experience.

The rest of the town, sadly enough, does not live up to one's expectations. It has succumbed to commercial interests and not very attractively, at that. Oh, there are some fine historic houses to visit, and Plymouth Rock is on view in its columned protective enclosure. But, considering the layers of history — three and a half centuries of it — where are the quaint historic inns and stagecoach B&Bs? What about restaurants that overlook the harbor? Wouldn't you think antiques shops would abound? And why isn't the town more interesting to walk around?

The answers probably stem from the fact that Plymouth lies along the main route between Boston and Cape Cod and that the rock attracted early entrepreneurs, so it didn't have the opportunity to develop quietly and quaintly. Located on Route 3A, the town has more than its share of fast-food restaurants, tacky souvenir and T-shirt shops, and plastic motels which could be located on an interstate anywhere. There is even a wax museum.

This does not mean you should avoid Plymouth. It is almost a point of national honor to visit at least once. Several historic homes are important and it is possible to find some good meals. Beaches are fine, too, and are often less crowded than those to be found farther south on Cape Cod.

In Plymouth, you have to pick and choose. Here's a guide to help you do just that.

Getting There

About 40 miles southeast of Boston, Plymouth is located at the intersections of Routes 44 and 3A. Take the Route 44 exits from Route 3 and I-495.

Where to Stay

We wish there were historic B&Bs and country inns. Instead, the best accommodations are in motels.

Pilgrim Sands Motel, 150 Warren Ave. (Route 3A), Plymouth 02360 (617) 747-0900. The Pilgrim Sands, a 65-unit motel three miles south of the center of town, is on its own nice beach. It is not far from Plimoth Plantation, away from the commercial hustle and bustle of the town, and the view is wonderful from lounge chairs on a large concrete deck directly behind it and overlooking the bay. Descend a few steps from this deck area to the beach below; in late June we found the water to be quite comfortable, but shallow — you have to walk out quite a distance to swim. The motel has an outdoor pool (unfortunately it's situated in the parking area along Route 3A, which doesn't make it too private), an indoor pool and a whirlpool spa. Complimentary newspapers are available in a comfortable indoor lobby area, and there's a small coffee shop for breakfast. Rooms are standard and come with a kingsize bed, two queens or two doubles, depending on location. All have good-size baths and color TV. There are two levels, and those on the ocean side naturally cost more. Doubles, $72 to $90. Open year-round.

Sheraton Plymouth at Village Landing, 180 Water St., Plymouth 02360. (617) 747-4900. Set amid the colorful shops of Village Landing, not far from the town waterfront (but not overlooking the water), the Sheraton Plymouth is a new and welcome addition to the accommodations in town. Green and apricot are the predominant hues in the sophisticated lobby; these are carried through in **Apricots,** the tony restaurant with its banquette seating and bentwood-look chairs. Creative entrees include such specialties as veal medallions sauteed in cognac with shrimp and pea pods ($17.50) and breast of chicken sauteed in white wine with an apricot-mustard sauce ($11.50); in this area of cranberry bogs, cranberry champagne soup is a natural. Several of the hotel's 165 rooms, with balconies, overlook an indoor pool atrium hung with brightly colored flags; there's also a whirlpool. The Pub with a raw bar is dark wood and English in feeling, and has leather sofas and a fireplace. A nightclub called the Mermaid offers live entertainment nightly, and an exercise room is open daily. Doubles, $90 to $100.

Cold Spring Motel, 188 Court St., Plymouth 02360. (617) 746-2222. This 21-unit motel is located slightly north of the town center on Route 3A, yet its right-angle setting gives it a feeling of privacy. The landscaping is pleasant, there's a picnic area, and its location near a public beach is a plus. Most rooms are simply decorated; some have wood paneling and all have color television and a wall-to-wall carpeting. Several room configurations are available: double bed, kingsize bed, two doubles, two queens. A separate two-bedroom cottage sleeps four and rents for $59 in season. Doubles, $43 to $55. Open March-November.

The Blue Anchor Motel, 7 Lincoln St., Plymouth 02360. (617) 746-9551. A small, four-unit motel is tucked behind the owners' house; it is just a five-minute walk to Plymouth Rock and Mayflower II and the central waterfront area. Privacy and quiet are assured. All units have air-conditioning, TVs and in-room coffee. Doubles, $40 to $55.

Colonial House Inn, 207 Sandwich St., Plymouth 02360. (617) 747-4274. Oscar and Olga Isaacs have been the innkeepers for 42 years at this inviting Federal-style white clapboard house with black shutters. Its manicured lawns lead to a small pool in back. The seven rooms, simply decorated, have private baths. Doubles, $60 to $70.

Seaview Manor, 259 Court St., Plymouth 02360. (617) 746-7459. This turn-of-the-century house (1902), dark clapboard with white shutters and trim, is one of few B&Bs in the area. Five rooms on the second and third floors have air-conditioning and color TVs; several have ocean views. Four rooms share two baths, and one has a private lavatory. A continental breakfast is served downstairs in the dining room. Doubles, $40 to $50.

The Governor Carver, Summer St., Plymouth 02360. (617) 746-7100. **The Governor Bradford,** Water Street, Plymouth 02360. (617) 746-6200. The Governor Motor Inns share literature and have reciprocity of booking. The Bradford is on the waterfront and the Carver has a more in-town location, but both are somewhat nondescript modern hotels with central locations and outdoor swimming pools. The 82-room Governor Carver has a full restaurant, the Hungry Pilgrim, while the 94-room Governor Bradford has in-room coffee. Doubles at the Governor Carver, $65 to $75; Governor Bradford, $65 to $78.

Be Our Guest, Bed & Breakfast Reservation Service, Box 1333, Plymouth 02360. (617) 746-1208. This reservation service places guests in homes in Plymouth and surrounding towns. The obligation of the host or hostess — in addition to providing clean, comfortable accommodations — is to supply at least a continental breakfast. Doubles, $32 to $50.

Camping is available a few miles from town in the huge **Myles Standish State Forest,** (617) 866-2526. Here are 500 campsites doled out on a first-come, first-served basis. Call ahead to see if there are openings, but you must claim your site in person. You can request waterfront, although there's no guarantee. Several fresh-water ponds are within the forest's confines. There are no electrical or water hook-ups and for the most part this is fairly primitive camping. Dirt bikers love the area and are seen zipping all around. A campsite can be rented for two weeks' maximum at $6 per night for two adults and children in one family. Open mid-April to mid-October.

Seeing and Doing

Historic Sites

Plimoth Plantation, Route 3A South, Plymouth. (617) 746-1622. A must to visit (and 500,000 people do so annually), the recreation of the Pilgrim village of 1627 is authentic right down to the animals and the accents of the Pilgrims who dress as they would have at the time and who say they don't "know" anything beyond the time they represent. The two dirt lanes meander between the several thatched-roof cottages; from the top of the hill as you enter, it's possible to see the ocean beyond. The diamond-shaped enclosure was for safety, and there is a sturdiness to the village that helps visitors realize why the Pilgrims managed to survive and prosper.

Visitors are allowed to walk around at will, inspect herb and vegetable gardens and, best of all, question the Pilgrims who inhabit various houses or who are at work doing a variety of tasks. Asked why she wore heavy wool garments on a hot June day, one woman responded that the wool prevented the "grease of your body from coming out," which could be fatal.

Even in the heat of the summer, meals were being prepared over open fires in various houses. We enjoyed viewing the raised beds of the vegetable gardens (all vegetables are those which would have been known and grown in the early 17th century), the goats, chickens and cows, and a primitive lumber mill — boards were being sawed from a log directly over a large, deep pit which caught the sawdust. One woman happily posed with her daughter, and a young couple chatted about their marriage. There is an air of openness and trust that is refreshing: mugs and plates are set out on tables, and various supplies and clothing are left in the houses as visitors wander in and out.

The visit is preceded by an orientation program, a three-screen slide show in a modern educational building, after which you walk past an open field to the village itself. Afterward you can stop at the Wampanoag summer campsite nearby, where "Indians" (who do not speak at all) and English interpreters are engaged in typical activities. While we applaud the concept of the Indian campsite, we were put off by the corpulent Indians, one of whom seemed to have a large surgical scar across his middle; perhaps it's difficult to get males to dress in loincloths and bake fish in blueberry leaves over primitive campfires!

Village open daily 9 to 5, April-November. Adults $6.25, children $3.75. Combination ticket which includes the Mayflower II, adults $8.25, children $5.25.

Mayflower II, State Pier, Plymouth. More costumed interpreters are aboard the replica of the small ship (it seems tiny by today's standards) which crossed the ocean in three months in 1620. In 1957 the replica sailed across the Atlantic from England, where it was built. The visit begins with a dockside exhibit that details the backgrounds and motivations of the small band of colonists who braved the ocean's perils and the uncertainty of a new world for the sake of worshipping as they wished.

The ship is about 106 feet long with a beam of 25 feet — the specifications of a medium-size merchant vessel of the early 17th century. Moored alongside is a 33-foot shallop or workboat like the one brought on the original Mayflower and used by colonists for exploring, fishing and coastal trading. Several "Pilgrims" — who stay in character extraordinarily well — are on the ship and answer questions about the voyage and life aboard the ship during the first winter while the original settlement was being built. Children especially are enchanted by the ship, but all visitors are in awe of the tiny spaces which accommodated the brave band. Open daily, 9 to 5, April-November. Adults $2.50, children $1.50.

Plymouth Rock, Water Street on the waterfront. The famous rock can be disappointing. It is, for one thing, protected by a columned granite enclosure, and visitors stand above and look down upon it. It's hard to imagine that the Pilgrims stepped ashore onto this rock, on which the numbers "1620" are carved. But real or not, the rock is an important piece of the Pilgrim story. On view year-round. Free.

Historic Houses

Mayflower Society Museum, 4 Winslow St., Plymouth. (617) 746-2590 or (617) 746-3188. Be sure to visit this house, which is headquarters of the General Society of Mayflower Descendants. Built in 1754 by Edward Winslow, the great-grandson of Governor Winslow of Massachusetts and a Pilgrim descendant, the house features a remarkable flying staircase with a hand-turned bannister. Bought by the society in 1941, it contains pieces donated by members. Ralph Waldo Emerson married Lydia Jackson in the parlor here in 1835. The house was extensively changed in 1898 when the property was sold to Charles Willoughby of Chicago, who hired the well-known architect, Joseph Chandler; there are Victorian features as well as Colonial. The Jacobean bed in the second bedroom upstairs, dating from 1625, is the oldest bed in Plymouth. Also to be noted are the formal dining room with corner cupboards and Waterford crystal, the molded plaster ceiling in the Tudor rose pattern in the solarium, and the commemorative Staffordshire plates in the display room. We particularly liked the sycamore bedroom with its lighter woodwork; an arch in the ceiling separates the seating area from the sleeping area. Open daily 10 to 5, July to mid-September; Thursday-Sunday 10 to 5, Memorial Day weekend to June 30 and mid-September to mid-October. Adults $2, children free.

Antiquarian House, 126 Water St., Plymouth. (617) 746-9697. This yellow house with black shutters and an expansive front lawn leading down toward (but no longer to) the water is most interesting. Built in 1809 by a merchant ship owner, the house was enlarged in 1830, so the front has two floors and the rear has three. The house features octagonal rooms. A variety of interesting furniture pieces and tableware include an Empire sofa in the formal parlor, a feather bed with canopy, a collection of English china, a Queen Anne lowboy and a children's nursery with early toys and a splendid doll house. Visitors especially enjoy the fully equipped kitchen with beehive oven and open hearth. Quilts, samplers and Hepplewhite furniture pieces add to the 19th century scene. Open daily 10 to 5 and Sunday noon to 5, late June to early September; weekends only, September to mid-October. Adults $2, children 25 cents.

The Richard Sparrow House, 42 Summer St., Plymouth. (617) 747-1240. The oldest house in Plymouth, dating from 1640, the Sparrow House overlooks the historic Town Brook Park. It has a particularly fine early fireplace. The house has been dedicated to crafts and offers demonstrations and classes in hand-built and wheel-thrown pottery. Visitors can observe the loading and firing of a hillside kiln. Open daily except Wednesday 10 to 5, May 24 to Oct. 14. Donation.

The Howland House, 33 Sandwich St., Plymouth. (617) 746-9590. This, the only house in Plymouth where Pilgrims are known to have lived, was occupied by Jabez Howland, one of the ten children of John and Elizabeth Howland, who arrived on the Mayflower. It is believed his parents would have visited, since Jabez and his family built the house prior to his parents' death. The house dates from 1667 but was enlarged in 1750, providing the interesting contrast of two architectural periods. Open daily 10 to 5 and Sunday noon to 5, May 24 to Oct. 14. Adults $1.25, children 50 cents.

Other historic houses include the **Harlow Old Fort House**, built in 1677 with beams believed to be from the old Pilgrim fort, and the **Spooner House** of 1749, home of the Spooner family that included the founder of the Plymouth Cordage Co., once the world's largest rope maker.

The Pilgrim Hall Museum, 75 Court St. (Route 3A), Plymouth, (617) 746-1620. While not an historic house, the museum deserves mention as the repository of the nation's largest collection of Pilgrim possessions. Displays of furniture, household goods, books, paintings and weapons used by the Pilgrims offer visitors an intimate perspective of the Pilgrims' efforts to build their new community. A chair owned by William Brewster, a cradle for the Fuller children and Peter Brown's tankard are among the possessions. There is also the only portrait from the life of a Mayflower passenger, Brownscombe's "First Thanksgiving" painting, John Alden's and Governor Bradford's Bibles are also to be seen. Open 9:30 to 4:30 daily year-round, except Christmas and New Year's Day. Adults $2.50, children 50 cents.

On the Water

Princess Cruise Lines, State Pier, Plymouth, 747-2400 or (800) 242-1304. The 359-passenger **Cape Cod Princess** takes passengers on an all-day cruise across Cape Cod Bay to Provincetown. Passengers can have two agendas: whale-watching on the way to and from Provincetown, and sightseeing and dining in Provincetown during the 4 1/2-hour layover. Boats leave Plymouth at 9 daily and return at 6:30. Adults $13.50, children $7.50. The Princess also offers a sunset Cape Cod Bay music cruise Saturday at 8 and a Cape Cod Canal music cruise Friday at 7:30 (both $8.50). On Tuesday evenings you can catch a lobster clambake-chicken barbecue sunset cruise at 7. It costs $17.95 for lobster or $11.95 for chicken.

Captain John Boats, Town Wharf, 746-2643. Whale-watching cruises are narrated twice daily from June 21 through Sept. 1 by a naturalist on board. Morning trips are from 8:30 to 1; afternoon trips from 1:30 to 6. Adults $15, children $11. Half-day fishing trips for cod, haddock, mackerel, pollack, whiting, flounder and dog fish, depending on season, are offered Monday-Friday at 9 and 2 from the end of June to Sept. 1. Adults $12, children $9. All-day fishing trips on weekends, holidays and Wednesdays are available for $18.50 adults, $14.50 children. A three-hour evening cruise from 8 to 11 on Thursdays features music of the '50s and '60s, $6.50; two-hour cruises on Friday and Saturday from 7 to 9 or 9:30 to 11:30 are $5.

Forty-minute **harbor cruises** are offered at 6:30 evenings, weather permitting, from the Mayflower II dock, 747-2400.

Tripp's Boat Livery at Manomet Point, 224-2009, south of Plymouth and past beautiful White Horse Beach, has 14-foot dories for rent. These classically shaped white boats with green trim come with oars for $20 a day; or with six-horsepower motors for $35. Getting them into the water is a sight to behold. The boats are raised and lowered down an inclined railway atop a wheeled cradle by a powered capstan. The dories are popular with fishermen in search of flounder and mackerel.

Plymouth Marina, one of the largest full-service marinas in the area, can accommodate cruising yachts up to 300 feet.

BEACHES. Plymouth has three saltwater beaches open to the public. **Ply-**

mouth Beach, the largest, is three miles south of town on Route 3A. **Nelson Street Beach** is at the north end of Water Street, and the beach at **Stephen's Field** is on the outskirts of the business district. The best beach, for our money, is **White Horse Beach** in Manomet, a short drive south of Plymouth, a portion of which is open to the public.

Other Attractions

Cranberry World, 225 Water St., Plymouth. (617) 747-1000 or 747-2350. Everything you wanted to know about cranberries — in a beautifully arranged and displayed exhibit — plus a chance to sample juices and to pick up recipes is available at the visitor center sponsored by Ocean Spray Cranberries, Inc. Did you know that "good" berries bounce when being separated (making it easy to discard the bad ones)? Or that cranberry bogs are dry (they're built on peat swamps and all the water is drained from them)? You'll see old cranberry scoops, photographs of bog workers over the years, and other artifacts connected with this important industry in the Plymouth-Cape Cod area. Open daily from 9:30 to 5. Free.

Commonwealth Winery, 22 Lothrop St., Plymouth. (617) 746-4940. Near the Plymouth waterfront, this winery which purchases all its grapes from out-of-town vineyards produces four categories of wines: European varietals, French-American varietals; proprietary blends and fruit wines (including cranberry apple wine). Among several awards touted by the winery is a silver medal for its Dana Vineyard chardonnay in 1984 in the Eastern Wine Competition. The visit includes a tour of the wine cellars, of the winemaking operation, and a tasting in the wine and gift shop. Open weekdays 10 to 8, Saturday 10 to 5 and Sunday noon to 5 in summer; Monday-Saturday 10 to 5 and Sunday noon to 5 in spring and fall; weekends only in winter. Free.

SHOPPING. Lots of touristy shops in Plymouth sell T-shirts and ceramic lobsters. The gift shop at **Plimoth Plantation** has a fairly good selection of books, jams and jellies, and items such as linen tea towels, candles and other gifts. **The Jenney Grist Mill Village** in the center of town boasts a picnic area and several small shops in addition to a working grist mill, where you can buy cornmeal, wheat and rye flours. There's also the **White Goose Christmas Shop.**

Cordage Park Marketplace north of Plymouth, a shopping center in a converted rope factory, has an uneven mix of stores. **M&M Sporting Goods** is really large; **Dillon, Myers & Myers** has a nice selection of antique country furniture and imported clothes. Somewhat cutesy shops are to be found at **Village Landing,** near the Sheraton Plymouth.

In town we liked **British Image** on Main Street with its good selection of British items, including foods such as black current jelly, road maps and bumper stickers declaring "Limeys Are Luvly." The **Onassis Collection** on North Street, a Greek import shop, has pretty sweaters and jewelry.

Where to Eat

Station One, 51 Main St., Plymouth. (617) 746-6001. Located in what was once a working firehouse, Station One is an attractive restaurant with dining on several levels, plus an outdoor cafe area right along Main Street in downtown Plymouth. The brick walls of the old firehouse, overhead fans and hanging plants plus chandeliers with fluted globes make for a pleasant environment. Tables are clothed in white with dark green napkins. Servers wear sprightly outfits — black pants, red suspenders, white shirts and black bow ties — and are quite solicitous. The veal scallops sautéed with shrimp, mushrooms and lemon and flambéed in marsala wine for $11.95 was recommended and very good. One of us had broiled scallops prepared simply with seasoned bread crumbs and lemon butter ($11.25); alas, it was a bit dry. Other choices, ranging from $10.50 for baked scrod to $13.95 for lazy man's lobster, included shrimp with angel hair pasta, duckling baked in a cherry-orange glaze and scallops sautéed with snow peas, mandarin oranges and fresh ginger, and served over angel hair pasta. All pastas are made fresh daily at a sister restaurant, Fiore's, in Hyannis. Salads were enormous and vegetables creative, including as one choice baby carrots, walnuts and raisins. Lunch items are lamb kabobs ($6.25), warm ziti salad ($5.95), fettuccine with prosciutto and peas ($6.95) and a fried clam plate ($7.95). Lunch, Monday-Saturday 11:30 to 3:45; dinner, 4:45 to 10; Sunday brunch, 10:30 to 3.

Marina Landing, Plymouth Marina, 14 Union St., Plymouth, (617) 746-5570. The Deck outside overlooking the marina and Cape Cod Bay has the best view of any waterside dining spot in town. We had lunch here, happily ensconced at our white table with white chairs, on a sunny Saturday in late June. It's a popular spot, serving casual — and just right — foods for outdoor dining. A striped awning allows you to sit in the shade; we sat at one of the umbrella tables to get snatches of sun. The all-day menu includes the "Swanky Frankie," a quarter-pound hot dog stuffed with sharp cheddar, wrapped in bacon and grilled ($4.25). Deli sandwiches come on thick Portuguese bread and you can mix and match the fillings ($4.45). A square lobster roll is $8.45; a marinated breast of chicken sandwich (the marinade is honey and soy sauce) served on that scrumptious Portuguese bread is $4.75. You also can order cherrystone clams at 99 cents each; Ipswich steamers (steamed in beer and herbs) for $5.95 or quahogs at $1.25 each. Many diners were digging into the steamers and accompanying them with ears of corn and beer. Meals are served in a slightly more formal atmosphere indoors and upstairs at Marina Landing, an attractive room paneled in dark teak wood and with a brass bar. Here you can pick and choose from a menu which includes appetizers, salads, soups, sandwiches, dinners and desserts. French onion soup and clam chowder are always available, plus a soup of the day; you can order spinach, antipasto or pasta primavera salads for $4.25 to $5.65. Dinner entrees are priced from $9.95 for chicken marinated in honey, soy sauce, lemon and mustard, to $15.95 for fried lobster meat. Other items include broiled swordfish, a fried seafood platter, fried clams and prime rib. Lunch daily 11:30 to 4; dinner from 4.

Sante, 320 Court St., Plymouth. (617) 747-4226. In a quaint gray and white Victorian house on the north side of town is an unexpected treasure of a French restaurant. David Turin, a graduate of Cornell's Hotel School, is chef; his wife Andrea takes care of the front of the house. David has cooked in Boston (Café Budapest) and New York City — this is the first place he's owned. Sante, which means "health" in French, is quiet and elegant, with two small dining rooms, one upstairs and one down, carpeted in deep blue, with blue velvet chairs and country wallpaper. The linens are white, the china is white with a raised leaf motif and sprigs of freesia are on each table. Entrees in the $15 to $20 range might include lamb tenderloin with spinach and tomatoes, medallions of veal with mustard seed and tarragon, and peppered breast of duck. A few seafood specials are offered every night. Vegetables are intriguing — perhaps baby white turnips, or a bunch of carrots tied with a ribbon of leeks. The house specialty dessert is a chocolate cheesecake, but you might also find a lemon or lime charlotte, a four-layer cookie torte or a tuile filled with white chocolate mousse and strawberry puree. The wine list is mostly French and includes some pricey red Bordeaux vintages up to $250. Lunch, Tuesday-Saturday 11:30 to 2; dinner, 6 to 9 or 10.

McGrath's, Water Street, Plymouth. (617) 746-9751. This shingled one-story building with dark red trim is popular but, we think, overrated — at least in location. It is near, but not on the water — a large paved parking lot intervenes. In fact, you only get a partial view of water from the lounge. It is one of those places which has managed to win the hearts of the locals, however, and large parties converge on the spot on weekend evenings with names called out over a loudspeaker as tables are readied. The decor is simple: pine paneling, captain's chairs and wood-topped tables, red and black carpeting. Seafood, steaks and chowders are served and the price range is $8 to $14. The dinner menu is served all day from 11:30 to 9:30, sometimes later in mid-summer.

Scruples, 170 Water St., Plymouth. (617) 747-3200. This exceptionally attractive restaurant in the Village Landing group of shops is set up high enough so that some of the waterfront can be seen beyond parking lots and waterside restaurants. But you're not here for the view. Maroon flowered curtains and tablecloths dominate the color scheme; a greenhouse room with hanging plants is a pretty addition. Unfortunately the restaurant has had three management changes since it opened in the early 1980s; the most recent came in 1986, and when we visited, things were still shaking down. A "Snacks and Appetizers" section of both lunch and dinner menus included Cajun coconut shrimp at $4.95, fried mozzarella sticks served with a tangy marinara sauce at $4.25 and deep-fried veggies for $3.95. At lunch you might try one of the croissant sandwiches, a gourmet burger (mushroom, chili, club, bacon cheese, etc.), a hot sandwich such as Texas cheesesteak (roast beef with sauteed onions, barbecue sauce and melted jack cheese on a French roll) for $6.95, or broiled scallops for $6.95. Dinner entrees include seafood brochette (roast beef with sauteed onions, barbecue bearnaise ($15.95), prime rib combination (scallops or shrimp with a petite cut of beef) for $15.95 and a fisherman's platter for $13.95. Among desserts are carrot cake, cranberry orange cheesecake and chambord chocolate fudge cake, $2.50 to $3. Lunch daily, 11:30 to 4; dinner, 5 to 10 or 11; Sunday buffet brunch, 10:30 to 2:30.

Bert's, 140 Warren Ave., Route 3A, Plymouth. (617) 746-3422. Bert's overlooks Plymouth Beach, south of town and next door to the Pilgrim Sands Motel. It is highly popular with a wide range of clientele from young single barflies to sedate families who come for Sunday dinner. On the Sunday we were there, Bert's was sponsoring its annual Bathtub Race, so the outside was teeming with college-age kids who were drinking beer and floating around in all sorts of homemade craft. The two dining rooms have both booths and tables, and you can ask for one with a water view. Dark wood tables, baskets of plants and stained-glass accents in the walls make for a conservative setting. The dinner menu (served all day Sunday) includes a selection of sandwiches as well. New England seafood stew containing mussels, clams, oysters, shrimp and cod is $13.45; chicken Margie, a boneless breast of chicken in butter and wine sauce, $9.45, and a lobster roll, $8.45. The emphasis is on seafood: broiled scrod with a crabmeat garnish, seafood casserole with lobster, scallops and shrimp topped with cheese and even a seaman's steak, center-cut sirloin stuffed with crabmeat, scallops and shrimp ($14.95). Dinners come with salad — Caesar or tossed — and potato; they may be preceded by stuffed quahogs, $1.25 each, or mussels in dijon sauce for $4.95. End up with a mocha fudge brownie, pecan pie or cheesecake. Lunches are similar to dinners with two or three specials daily, such as broiled scrod with a newburg sauce for $4.95. Lunch daily, 11:30 to 3; dinner, 5 to 10 or 11.

Mamma Mia's, 122 Water St., Plymouth. (617) 747-4670. The Viscariellos serve up good Italian food at this waterfront restaurant with a view of Plymouth Harbor across the street. Because it's set up high, there is a nice feeling of being out of the madding crowd. Simple decor, formica-topped tables and bentwood chairs are appropriate; large pizza ovens in the back set the scene for some of the best food to be found here. At dinner, large pizzas range from $4.75 for cheese to $10 for specials and you can get virtually anything. Regular dinners ($5.95 to $10) include veal parmigiani, eggplant manicotti, linguini with white clam sauce, stuffed cabbage with pasta, and brasciolettini with pasta — beef rolled and broiled with a blend of spices. Appetizers include meat tortellini, stuffed mushrooms and antipasto for $3.95 individually or $5.75 for the table. Lunch dishes are similar but smaller portions; baked ziti, for example, is $3.95 instead of $5.95 at night. Traditional Italian desserts — spumoni, cannoli and cheesecake — are offered for $1.50. Lunch daily, 11:30 to 3; dinner, 5 to 10.

Souza's On the Wharf, 746-5354, and the **Lobster Hut,** 746-2270, both located near the Town Wharf (the Lobster Hut is closer), offer casual picnic-table dining on lobster, seafood and french fries at rational prices. At Souza's, the tables are set up in the front yard; long lines form to order at the counter, and a boiled lobster can be purchased for $7.50. Fish and chips are $3. You take a number, order and wait for your number to be blared out over the loudspeaker. At the Lobster Hut, beer and wine cost $1; fish and chips, $4.25, and everything else is in that price range. We prefer this because of the whole wharf full of picnic tables; it gets you as close to the water as possible for a roll-up-your-sleeves feast. Open noon to 9.

Farfar's Ice Cream on Court Street, near the intersection with Route 44, is a place to get Danish ice cream cones — the ice cream, made from an old Danish recipe, is creamy and softer than others. It's tucked upstairs into a small space but it's very popular; flavors include orange pineapple, rum raisin, and ambrosia — banana, coconut and pineapple together. Open daily from 11 to 10.

FOR MORE INFORMATION: Plymouth Area Chamber of Commerce, 85 Samoset St., Plymouth, Mass. 02360, (617) 746-3377. The Plymouth Visitor Information Center is on Park Avenue at the intersection with Route 44 A.

227

Swimming is fine at Rockport's Front Beach.

Cape Ann, Mass.

Nowhere does the marriage of sea and land seem more felicitous than on Cape Ann. This chunk of land, which juts into the Atlantic north of Boston, offers a rich melange of seascapes and land views, of working and leisure classes, of dockside activity and sandy strands. We have loved it since we first set foot here years ago and are drawn back again and again. So are thousands of others.

Who can blame them? Cape Ann is split between two markedly different but complementary towns, Rockport and Gloucester. Rockport is a charming, picket-fenced village by the sea, with a colorful harbor, several small beaches, boutiques and restaurants. It is so picturesque that it has drawn artists since the turn of the century and art galleries abound. Motif No. 1, the red fish warehouse in the harbor, is said to be the most painted and photographed waterfront locale in New England.

Gloucester is characterized by the huge bronze statue of the fisherman in foul-weather gear at the wheel along State Route 127. Fishing boats crowd this working harbor and "men that go down to the sea in ships" still sail in great numbers to the rich fishing grounds of Georges Bank. Stores along the city's main street cater to locals, rather than tourists. Rocky Neck, an artists' community in East Gloucester, has colorful galleries and fun restaurants, many with dining overlooking the harbor. Eastern Point embraces the priciest real estate on the Cape Ann and one of its mansions, Beauport, is open to the public as a museum.

Visitors have been coming to Cape Ann for years and so guest houses, inns and B&Bs abound, especially in Rockport. Several attractive motels overlook the ocean in the Bass Rocks section of Gloucester. Dining is dominated by seafood restaurants.

There is much to see and do. Art-gallery browsing and strolling among the boutiques on Rockport's Bearskin Neck takes the better part of a day. Gloucester's Good Harbor Beach is one of our favorites for sunning and swimming anywhere. Whale-watch trips are numerous and there are historic homes to visit. Just driving around the Cape and poking through the charming villages of Annisquam and Lanesville and the section of Rockport known as Pigeon

228

Cove are rewarding. You can walk out to Halibut Point and picnic on a flat rock at sunset. Winslow Homer found inspiration on Cape Ann (he lived for a while in Gloucester), as did T.S. Eliot. Surely you will, too.

Getting There

Cape Ann is located 35 miles northeast of Boston. By car, Route 128 and Route 133 lead to the Cape from Route 1 and Interstate 95. Trains run from Boston to Rockport, one of the few shore towns that still has train service. For schedule and fare information call (617) 227-5070 in Boston or (800) 392-6099.

Where to Stay

By the Sea

Rocky Shores Inn and Cottages, Eden Road, Rockport 01966. (617) 546-2823. Because we first fell in love with Rockport when we stayed here, this seaside inn has a special place in our hearts. Now owned and operated by a warm and friendly German couple, Renate and Gunter Kostka, the inn is almost an anachronism in today's rushed world. A gracious but old-fashioned lobby welcomes guests; soft classical music plays somewhere in the distance, and the breezy salt air blows the light curtains at the windows. Eight of the inn's 10 rooms have private baths and all have TV; there also are 12 housekeeping cottages, eight behind the inn with two bedrooms and four in front with three bedrooms. From a large porch across the front of the inn, guests can look down sweeping green lawns toward the Atlantic and the twin lighthouses on Thatchers Island. While you can walk along the ocean across the road, you really need to drive to the beaches (the closest are Cape Hedge and Pebble Beach). Gunter, the breakfast cook, whips up a delicious repast (apple pancakes and crepes are specialties) for guests to eat in an old-fashioned dining room. The outstanding dark woodwork in the main house, the impeccable housekeeping and the great location appeal. Doubles, $57 to $73 in inn; cottages weekly, $470 for two bedrooms and $570 for three. Open mid-April through October.

Blue Shutters Inn, 1 Nautilus Road, Gloucester 01930. (617) 281-2706. Pat and Paul Earl opened this B&B soon after being transferred to Gloucester with their four children. The children are grown now, but Pat and Paul continue to dispense warm hospitality at this large white, blue-shuttered inn directly across from Good Harbor Beach, the best on the Cape. Everything is blue and white, inside and out: an inviting living room has wall-to-wall blue carpeting, blue patterned slipcovers adorn the sofa and loveseat, and blue pillows are thrown onto chairs and sofas. The breakfast room has a large family-style table clothed in blue; here guests get their own continental breakfast from a buffet spread at one side. All rooms have views of the ocean, which can be quite dramatic. Ours on the third floor had twin maple beds, which white George Washington-style spreads, blue shag carpeting, two white wicker chairs from which we could watch the sea, and crisp white curtains at the windows. A deluxe apartment with living room, kitchen, bedroom and bath rents for $425 weekly for four. Pat is a most helpful innkeeper, dispensing advice and information with not a little good humor. The beach is a short walk from the inn across a picturesque footbridge, and a morning walk along the water's edge is a favorite pursuit of guests. Doubles, $45 for shared bath to $70 for private; two-room suite $85. Open May-October.

Eden Pines Inn, Eden Road, Rockport 01966. (617) 546-2505. Here is a former summer home set so close to the ocean that you're literally perched above the rocks and crashing waves when you sit on the brick deck out back. A knotty-pine living room with fieldstone fireplace is cozy; from it you walk into the breezy, California-style side porch and breakfast room, where a buffet-style continental breakfast of homemade pastries is put out for guests. Out back is a porch above the brick terrace, a great place for tea or cocktails. All six large upstairs guest rooms have private baths; most have two double beds and private balconies over the water, and innkeeper Inge Sullivan's fondness for marble and California fabrics shows. The inn also rents an apartment accommodating five on Bearskin Neck for $525 weekly. Doubles, $76 to $82. Open May-November.

Seacrest Manor, 131 Marmion Way, Rockport 01966. (617) 546-2211. Although this weathered-gray mansion is not at the water's edge, sea views are possible from the second-floor deck above the living room. (The deck is divided into thirds; two rooms each have their own section and other guests share the last section). The lawns and flowers are gorgeous, and guests love to sit and read in the garden. Innkeepers Dwight B. MacCormack Jr. and Leighton T. Saville make you feel as if you're treating yourself very well when you visit — and why not? The intimate breakfast room, warm with red tablecloths and a red brick-look floor, is the site for a full morning meal that Town & Country magazine called one of the 50 best breakfasts in America. It begins with fresh fruit cup, includes oatmeal, bacon and eggs, and ends with a specialty such as blueberry pancakes or corn fritters. A large living room is where afternoon tea is served; there's also a library on the main floor. Six of the eight guest rooms have private baths. All are decorated comfortably and have color TVs. Doubles, $60 to $80. Open mid-February to Christmas Eve.

Yankee Clipper Inn, Route 127, Rockport 01966. (617) 546-3407. This has remained a favorite place of visitors to Rockport for good reasons: location, location, location. The 28-room inn is composed of three spacious buildings, two perched close to the rocky shore and the Bulfinch House across the road. The Wemyss family have been in charge for more than 40 years and do things right. Both the inn and the Quarterdeck (the most modern building) have water views, plus lots of space for lounging in lawn chairs. A saltwater pool is tucked artistically into the landscape. In 1986 the Yankee Clipper began to open its dining room to the public by reservation. Located on a wraparound porch, it is the least attractive of the inn's rooms (the bright orange carpeting underfoot and the royal blue tablecloths are a bit much), but the views are nice. Steamed lobster is available daily; other entrees included maple-glazed corned beef and chicken Kiev. Guests in the inn and Quarterdeck enjoy meals with their rooms, which are lovely and large, often with four-poster beds and decorator touches. You can get bed and breakfast in the Bulfinch House. Doubles, $110 to $175 MAP; $70 to $80, EP. Open year-round.

The Atlantis Motor Inn, 125 Atlantic Road, Gloucester 01930. (617) 283-5808. Highly regarded, this motel is in the Bass Rocks section of Gloucester. Picture windows in the 41 motel rooms look out at the rocky shorefront where waves crash and churn; the coffee shop, furnished in rattan, has fabulous views as well. Rooms are furnished in Danish modern for the most part. There's a pool, and guests can walk across the street and sun on the rocks at water's edge. Doubles, $78 to $80. Open April-October.

Bass Rocks Motor Inn, 119 Atlantic Road, Gloucester 01930. (617) 283-7600. This large brick motor inn with columned facade promises an ocean view from every room. Located next to the Atlantis, the motel has 48 well-furnished and comfortable units plus a heated swimming pool. Views of the rockbound coast are stunning and the decks in front of each room offer a place to watch the sunrise. Doubles, $95 to $105. Open April-November.

The Williams Guest House, 136 Bass Ave., Gloucester 01930. (617) 283-4931. This friendly B&B proves to be a bargain, for it is virtually on Good Harbor Beach (just take the footbridge) and prices are unusually reasonable. The carpeted parlor is warm and inviting; the nearby dining room is where a light breakfast is served. There are four rooms with private and shared baths and three apartment units (one of these is its own little cottage out back). The Williamses make you feel right at home. Doubles, $38 to $45.

On the Beach

Chicataubut Inn, Long Beach, Rockport 01966. (617) 546-3342. So you want to be right on the beach, roll out of bed and hit the sand? This is the only lodging place on Cape Ann where you can do that. The sprawling white beach house is set in the midst of a cottage colony at Long Beach (one of the best, and sandiest, beaches on Cape Ann). Run by the same family for 15 years, the inn has basic but adequate accommodations and great views. All 10 rooms have private baths; there are five efficiency apartments as well. Most rooms have three single beds, and are very simply furnished — the kind you can sweep the sand out of. A fireplace warms the lobby on chilly mornings and evenings. Out front is a terrace with lounge chairs. A small refrigerator is in each room and complimentary coffee is served to guests. Doubles, $63 to $67; efficiencies, $435 to $470 weekly. Open mid-May to mid-October.

Other Choices

Sally Webster Inn, 34 Mount Pleasant St., Rockport 01966. (617) 546-9251. Opened in 1985 by George and Janet Webster (no relationship to Sally), this in-town inn looks like a winner. Affable Janet — a Gloucester school teacher — loves to tell guests the fascinating history of the old white house with red shutters. Sally was the daughter of William Choate, who built the house in 1832. Her picture in the front parlor, known as "Sally's Share" because that was the part of the house she inherited, shows a woman of stern demeanor. There is nothing stern about Sally's inn, however. Rooms are gradually being renovated and made charming by Janet. A small deck off a couple of rear rooms looks onto the spacious (for Rockport) back yard. The dining room with mahogany table and period chairs is gracious; a buffet breakfast is set out for guests. All five bedrooms have private baths. The inn is two-tenths of a mile from the center of Rockport, which tends to be teeming with humanity and short on parking spaces on weekends. The closest beach is Old Garden Beach, a five-minute walk. What this inn lacks in water views, it makes up for in charm. Doubles, $55. Open March-November.

Old Farm Inn, 291 Granite St., Rockport 01966. (617) 546-3237. Until

1986 one of the most popular eating places on Cape Ann, the Old Farm Inn is now being run sans dining room to the everlasting regret of anyone who ever ate there. One of the dining rooms, in fact, has been turned into a parlor with wing chairs and sofas. Of the seven guest rooms, three are upstairs in the main 1799 house and four with private baths and television are in the adjoining Barn Annex. Two upstairs rooms have fireplaces, and are offered as a suite with a sitting room sharing a bath. Its quiet, peaceful location in the Pigeon Cove section near Halibut Point State Park and Folly Cove make the inn especially attractive, as do its spacious grounds. The Balzarini family is still in charge. Breakfast is served in a bright, windowed breakfast room overlooking the lawns and trees. Doubles, $60 to $70; suite, $110.

The Linden Tree Inn, 26 King St., Rockport 01966. (617) 546-2494. Only the cupola atop this huge old Victorian-style home has a view of the ocean, and you have to hike up two steep flights of stairs to get there, but there are other assets. Penny and Larry Olson and children run this large inn, which has 18 guest rooms, most furnished with period pieces; one has twin beds with pineapple posts. All rooms in the main inn have private baths; two in the annex share. An ample continental breakfast is served in the dining room, where the stencil design near the ceiling is a reproduction of that originally found in the house. Guests rave about the lemon nut bread and sour-cream chocolate chip cake that Penny serves on Sundays. The inn is located a couple of blocks from Front Beach and the shops of Rockport. Doubles, $54 to $58 in inn; $44 in annex. Open year-round.

CAMPING. Cape Ann Camp Site, 80 Atlantic St., Gloucester 01930. (617) 283-8683. This private campground overlooks the Annisquam River and is one mile from Wingaersheek Beach. There are 300 mostly shaded tent and trailer sites.

RENTALS. It is difficult to find a short-term rental in Rockport or Gloucester. If you want only one or two weeks on Cape Ann, check with the inns and hotels that have cottages as well (such as Rocky Shores). Monthly and seasonal rentals can be arranged with the help of a real-estate agent. Two who seem to have quite a few listings are Rose Real Estate, 324 Main St., Gloucester, (617) 283-2600, and Virginia Naves Real Estate, 98 East Main St., Gloucester, (617) 283-3823. Rentals are about $2,500 a month.

Seeing and Doing

On or Near the Water

WHALE-WATCHING. Gloucester touts itself as the whale-watching capital of the world and has good statistics to back the claim. Half a dozen boat companies take visitors out in the Atlantic toward the whale-feeding grounds, Jeffrey's Ledge and Stellwagen Bank, where more than 500 whales are said to go annually. The area, some 10 to 12 miles offshore, hosts finback, humpback, right and minke whales. In 1985 more than 200 humpback whales were sighted. Whale-watching is big business; about 125,000 people took the trips. Midsummer trips are often filled, and reservations are advised, especially for weekends. Most trips take about four hours; usually adults pay $15 and children $10. Among the choices:

Cape Ann Whale Watch, 283-5110, leaves from Rose's Wharf in Gloucester daily at 8 and 1:30, May-October

Seven Seas Whale Watch, 283-1776, departs from the Seven Seas Wharf in Gloucester at 8, 9:30, 1 and 2. Sunset whale-watch cruises, with entertainment on board, leave weekend evenings at 6.

Whale Safaris, 281-4163, leave from a dock on the Annisquam River, Gloucester, at Exit 12 off Route 128. Trips are at 9, 1:30 and 5:30.

Gloucester Whale Watch, 283-6089 or (800) 942-5464, sets out from the Cape Ann Marina off Route 133 in Gloucester at 8:30 and 2.

FISHING AND BOATING. The Yankee Fleet, Cape Ann Marina, 75 Essex Ave. (Route 133), Gloucester, 283-0313, offers several deep-sea fishing excursions. They include all-day trips for haddock, pollock, cod and halibut at $24.50 per person, and half-day trips for $13. Evening bluefishing trips from 7 to 1 are offered nightly except Sundays for $25. Distant trips include haddock specials, marathons and two or three-day Georges Bank trips with a Nantucket layover. Priced from $42 to $150, they are offered on varying days.

The **Lady Dianne** leaves from the T Wharf in Rockport Harbor for five-hour deep-sea fishing trips daily at 7:15 from late June through Labor Day. The $14 cost includes bait and tackle.

Sail around Cape Ann on the topsail schooner, the **Norfolk Rover**, 281-3222. Two hour sails from the Ocean Research Docks in Gloucester Harbor leave daily at 9:30, noon and 2:30. Adults $15, children $8. Wine and cheese sunset trips for adults are $20.

Rent a boat from **Captain Hook** on Pirates Lane in East Gloucester, 281-4114. His 16-foot powerboats can be used for fishing or for your own scenic tour of Gloucester Harbor for $12 an hour, $35 for four hours and $60 a day. Add $7 for rod and reel rentals.

A small excursion boat, the **Dixie Belle**, 283-5110, sails around Gloucester Harbor on one-hour tours from Rose's Wharf from noon to 5 daily on the hour. Adults $3.50, children $2.50.

THE BEACHES. We like best the **Good Harbor Beach** on Thatcher Road, Gloucester (close to the Rockport line). This half-mile barrier beach is protected by sand dunes and has a bathhouse and a snack bar. Parking is $5 weekdays, $6 on weekends.

Rockport's beaches are sometimes hard to find, especially **Cape Hedge, Pebble** and **Old Garden** beaches, which are small but pleasant. These do not have changing rooms or snack bars. Find them at **Front or Back Beaches** on Beach Street in downtown Rockport.

Wingaersheek Beach on Atlantic Street in Gloucester is a bit removed from the itineraries of most visitors to Cape Ann. This open, windswept strand is favored by people from surrounding towns. Parking fees are the same as at Good Harbor Beach.

On Shore

Take a Walk. Walking is one of the supreme pleasures on Cape Ann. The center of Rockport, with its old and architecturally interesting houses, its Cape

Leave your car behind when exploring in Rockport. Take the new trolley that was put into service in 1986. Its two routes involve a continuous circuit of the downtown area or a wider trek known as the "scenic sightseeing tour" to the beaches and inns farther out (as far as Cape Hedge Beach to the south and Folly Cove to the north).

233

Cod cottages with picket fences, its art galleries and boutiques, the picturesque harbor and **Bearskin Neck** (the narrow piece of land that juts into the ocean and is crammed with shops and eateries) invite strolling. In fact, the center of Rockport is so crowded you have to leave the car and go by foot. East Gloucester's **Rocky Neck**, another art colony with appealing waterfront restaurants, invites more walking. Hike out to **Halibut Point Reservation** in Rockport for a picnic on the flat rocks or possibly the best sunset ever. Sunsets are also said to be spectacular at **Folly Cove, Lane's Cove and Plum Cove,** to which you drive, then sit.

Drive around all of Cape Ann on Route 127 and 127A, staying as close to the water as you can to find many scenic spots. Sneak down into the little village of **Annisquam** where, once again, you may want to park and walk. The narrow streets and houses are charming.

THE ARTISTS. Gloucester and Rockport have attracted artists since shortly after the Civil War. They come to sit by the shore, to watch the sea and to paint the ineffable beauty of Cape Ann at all times of day and year. Among their numbers have been Childe Hassam, Winslow Homer and Fitz Hugh Lane. Artists are drawn particularly to Rocky Neck in East Gloucester and Bearskin Neck in Rockport, where their galleries are located.

The **Rockport Art Association** at 12 Main St., 546-6604, is open free year-round. It sponsors Tuesday and Thursday evening art demonstrations in summer, changing exhibitions of paintings, graphics and sculpture, and an annual fair.

The **North Shore Art Association** on Reed's Wharf at 197 Main St. in East Gloucester, 283-1857, is active in the summer with exhibits and art demonstrations.

Watercolors seem to be the predominant medium on Cape Ann and Motif No. 1 is the favorite subject. The paintings are for the most part realistic. It is fun to poke around in the galleries, chat with the artists and maybe take a painting home. It's a sure bet that somewhere you'll find an artist and his easel poised at land's edge.

SHOPPING. Stores in the center of Rockport and on Bearskin Neck are crammed with sophisticated fashions, giftware and objets d'art, as well as postcards, ceramic lobster ashtrays and beach towels. The emphasis is upscale, and we often get bogged down by the selections of classic clothing at places like **Lion and Harp** and the **Motif. The Christmas Dove** has intrigued holiday-minded shoppers for years and the **Toad Hall Bookstore** is a great place to browse. **Sarah Elizabeth's** hand-blocked greeting cards at the Whistlestop Mall off Railroad Avenue are wonderful. For homemade fudge and the best saltwater taffy, there's no place like **Tuck's** (two shops in Rockport).

Historic Attractions

Hammond Castle, Hesperus Avenue, Magnolia. (617) 283-2080. This replica of a medieval castle was built between 1926 and 1929 by John Hays Hammond Jr. to house his classic and medieval art collection. It has an exceptional 8,600-pipe organ in the Great Hall, which is the setting for concerts by famed organists from around the world. The hall has two beautiful stained-glass windows, one designed by Jacques Simone and the other a reproduction of a window from Chartres Cathedral. The dining room is styled after a monastery refectory. The courtyard is intended to depict an ancient French church opening into a town square. The pool in the center and the lush plants give it almost a tropical air. Changing exhibits are mounted in several galleries in the castle. A rooftop cafe offers light foods with a view of the rocky Atlantic coastline; just offshore is the "Reef of Norman's Woe" made famous by the Longfellow poem. A gift shop features hand-crafted items. Open daily 10 to 4, May-October; Thursday-Saturday 10 to 4 and Sunday 1 to 4, rest of year. Adults $3.50, children $1.50.

Beauport, 71 Eastern Point Blvd., Gloucester, (617) 283-0800. The Society for the Preservation of New England Antiquities oversees this remarkable mansion, located on the exclusive Eastern Point Boulevard among the most exclusive homes on Cape Ann. Beauport was the home of Henry Davis Sleeper, a collector of antiques and a leading interior designer of the 1920s and 1930s. The house, begun in 1907, was enlarged continually by Sleeper (in collaboration with Gloucester architect Halfdan Hanson) until his death in 1934. The result is a maze of 40 rooms filled with vast collections of American and European decorative arts. The house was bought by Charles and Helena McCann and given by them as a museum — virtually untouched — in 1942. The museum is closed, maddeningly, on summer weekends. Open weekdays 10 to 4, mid-May to mid-September; 10 to 4 weekdays and 1 to 4 weekends, rest of year. Adults $4, children $2.

Sargent-Murray-Gilman-Hough House, 49 Middle St., Gloucester, 281-2432. This 18th century house serves as an example of shipping and other merchant residences that once lined the street. Exhibits of portraits, antique furniture and furnishings and Georgian architecture are of interest. Open Tuesday, Thursday and Saturday 1 to 5. Adults $1.50, children $1.

Captain Elias Davis House, 27 Pleasant St., Gloucester, 283-0455. Six period rooms reflect domestic life during the early 1800s in this three-story, twelve-room house in the Federal style. The house was commissioned to be built in 1796 by Col. Jacob Smith, a master builder whose designs were mainly copied from pattern books. The annual Davis birthday party is held on on a late Saturday in June. Open Tuesday-Saturday 10 to 5. Adults $2, students $1.

Where to Eat

Rockport is dry; Gloucester isn't. Most Rockport eateries allow you to bring wine (which you must purchase in Gloucester if you haven't brought it from home) and may charge a corkage fee.

On the Water

Gloucester on the Waterfront, 17 Rogers St., Gloucester, (617) 281-4416. Jeff Crawford, Neal Packard and Andrew Frazier are chef-owners of this restaurant, which opened in 1986 beside Gloucester Harbor and quickly gained a good reputation. The building is new and the restaurant all blue and white and light wood, with a dining room that's all glass on the water side. The fish is fresh (which lamentably is not true of every restaurant on Cape Ann); we were invited into the kitchen unannounced and shown the most beautiful halibut in its just-caught glory. One dining room faces the waterfront and the other has waterscapes by Gloucester artist John Nesta on the walls. There is no bar, but a full liquor license. Specialties at dinner include baked sole mornay ($10), charbroiled lamb chops with apple chutney or mint jelly ($13), a baked scallop casserole ($11) and a roast breast of chicken with an herb bread and walnut stuffing ($10). Entrees are served with a fresh vegetable and rice or baked potato; a spinach salad with fresh croutons is $2 and a Greek salad is $3.50. At lunch the day we visited, a charbroiled fresh tuna sandwich was $4. A grilled beef Ortega sandwich is a specialty at $5. Half a breast of boneless chicken charbroiled and served with guacamole and Swiss cheese is also $5. Strawberry shortcake, chocolate cheese pie and Indian pudding with hard sauce (all $3.50) are some of the irresistible desserts. The Waterfront Grill serves late-night goodies like hamburgers, steak, smoked fish and native shrimp scampi. Open daily from 11:30 to 11:30.

The Galley, Bearskin Neck, Rockport. (617) 546-3721. Mike Parillo's restaurant, overlooking Lumber Wharf and the harbor, is a small, incredibly popular spot which doesn't advertise much and doesn't have to. The locals send you here because over the years Parillo's standards have remained high. Chowders — "clish" for clams and fish, Atlantic for everything from the sea, and plain old clam — are favorites. The Atlantic chowder, pink and savory, contains hunks of lobster, crab, clams, haddock and scallops, priced from $1.95 for a cup to $3.60 for a bowl and worth every penny. Salad can be ordered with a variety of "additions" such as artichoke or palm hearts, hard-boiled eggs or avocado at 95 cents each. The toasted crabmeat roll at $7.95 is chock full of crabmeat. Another tasty lunch is sauteed mushrooms in garlic butter served on toast ($6.95). For dinner try baked scallops or baked stuffed turbot fillets (both $11.95) or "Galley lobster" priced according to market. The decor is as simple and honest as the food. Fresh flowers in parfait glasses decorate the varnished knotty-pine tables flanked by captain's chairs on a parquet wood floor. Overhead fans circulate the air; a large stone fireplace on one wall promises off-season warmth. Lunch daily 11 to 5, dinner 5 to 8:30; closed Tuesday and January-March. No credit cards.

The Gull, 75 Essex Ave. (Route 133), Gloucester. (617) 283-6565. This is another restaurant favored by locals. Open at 4 a.m. to feed the fishermen who head down the Annisquam River and into Gloucester Harbor from the Cape Ann Marina where it is located, the Gull is another place where the fish is sure to be fresh. Bare wood tables and captain's chairs look out over the water and the marina, where boats are crammed cheek by jowl jockeying back and forth to dock. It's an active scene, just the place to enjoy seafood, fish or clam chowder, all of them rich with cream and butter, but not so thick that you wonder if a little Elmer's has been mixed in. This is good New England seashore cooking and a tank near the entrance has some of the largest lobsters we've seen. You can order two one-and-one-quarter pounders for $18.95, fresh broiled halibut for $9.95 or baked sole with clam stuffing, salad, potato and vegetable for $6.95. A steamship dinner with a one-pound lobster, steamers, corn and clam chowder is $14.95; you'll pay another $4 if the lobster weighs a half pound more. Homemade grapenut pudding is one of the down-home desserts. Open for breakfast, lunch and dinner. Closed November-March.

The Studio, Rocky Neck, East Gloucester. (617) 283-4123. We have always liked the Studio for everything from the artist palette tables and director's chairs in the cocktail lounge to the high-backed booths along the wall to the beautiful view over Gloucester harbor. We also like the piano entertainment at night. A "Salty Dog," a house specialty, is a one-pound boiled lobster with

Table for Two, But Alas, No View

The White Rainbow, 65 Main St., Gloucester. (617) 281-0017. Owned by the people who operate the famed Peg Leg Restaurant in Rockport, this relatively new restaurant is winning high praise. Tucked downstairs from a bookstore and entered more easily from the street behind it, it has two intimate dining rooms (one with white cloths, the other with blue) with oriental rugs on the floors, and gorgeous flower arrangements. There's a small garden for outdoor dining. From appetizers to entrees to salad (served after the entree in the European tradition) this restaurant breaks away from the

My Place, 72 Bearskin Neck, Rockport. (617) 546-9667. This romantic spot perched on the rocks at the end of Bearskin Neck is fine for lunch or dinner or just an afternoon break when you can sit on the deck, sip something refreshing, and look out on Sandy Bay. The pink and aqua color scheme is a distinct change of pace from the nautical motifs around here, and the single rose on each table inside the small dining room is a nice touch. The two flower-lined, umbrella-tabled decks beside the ocean are positively idyllic. Dinner entrees (priced from $8 to $14) include baked scrod, sole and halibut, prime rib, and a poultry dish of the day. Special "feasts" are priced daily and we like the sound of the Down East Feast with steamed lobster, corn on the cob, potato, garden salad, seasonal fruit and breads, all served with "sunset on the rocks," according to the menu. In addition to straightforward seafood presentations, chef Charles Kreis does a gourmet stuffed lobster and other specials. In the evening it's possible to have soup and salad with homemade bread for $5.95; children's entrees are half price, something we like to see. Christull and Robert Sheath, who opened this pleasant restaurant in 1982, have found a formula that works. Lunch daily 11 to 3, dinner 5 to 9:30. Open mid-May through October.

The Outrigger, Rocky Neck, East Gloucester. (617) 281-4998. Paul Schaeffer took over this great spot at the end of Rocky Neck, looking out on Smith Cove and Gloucester Harbor in 1986. The raw bar is especially well-regarded by locals; the pleasant dining room has a good water view. The bar, on the other hand, is dark and somewhat dingy, albeit favored by dart throwers and others. But you can't beat the location and the food is highly rated. The emphasis is on seafood, pasta and steak. Open from 11:30 to 10.

The Rudder, 73 Rocky Neck Ave., East Gloucester. (617) 283-7967. Located in a building that was once a fish cannery, right on the water, the Rudder continues its popularity even though the food's reputation seems to go up and down. A mixed crowd of locals and tourists, young and old, crowds into this convivial place. The rear porch has a view of the water. Other tables are set up in cozy style and diners feast on seafood and fresh vegetables, especially corn on the cob. Service is slow, says the menu, and it certainly can be. Prices are in the $12 to $14 range for dinners of baked fillet of sole hollandaise (a house specialty), fried clams and crab casserole. Lunch, noon to 3; dinner, 6 to 10. Open mid-May to late October.

trimmings, $6.95 at lunch and $9.95 at dinner. At dinner fried clams cost $10.95, fried Maine shrimp, $10.95, and fried or broiled scallops, $12.95. Appetizers range from $1.50 for a cup of clam chowder to $5.50 for clams casino. At noon, try a baked seafood casserole or a crabmeat casserole, both $7.95. Open daily for lunch and dinner.

pack. One appetizer that appeals to us is lobster stew made with brandy, spices and heavy cream ($10.95 for two). Entrees include shrimp capellini (shrimp dipped in egg and sauteed with mushrooms, capers, tomatoes, artichoke hearts and baby corn, served with angel hair pasta for $15.95). You can get tournedos au poivre for $19.95, semi-boneless roast duckling in the chef's sauce of the day ($14.95) and lobster and pasta verde, lobster meat and wild mushrooms in a brandy cream sauce on spinach fettuccine. The adjoining Cafe Wine Bar has a wide selection of wines by the glass. Dinner, Tuesday-Saturday 5:30 to 9:30; Sunday brunch, 11 to 3. Open year-round.

The Raven, 197 East Main St., East Gloucester. (617) 281-3951. This romantic restaurant is decidedly unnautical in feel, with its plant-filled floor-to-ceiling bay window, pink silk flowers on tables and hanging from baskets (we thought the fuchsias were real), black lacquered chairs, pink napkins in the glasses, white tablecloths, and a wallpaper with a black background strewn with tiny pink flowers. Little white lights twinkle on jade plants in the bay window. It is small, intimate, and feels a bit crowded if you're at one of the tables in the center of the room where people have to keep pressing past. The mixed menu offers seafood, veal, beef and poultry dishes. We had one of the more popular items, the Raven Stir-fry, with scallops and shrimp sauteed with pea pods, mushrooms, onions, green peppers and light soy sauce for $11.95, and a lobster special with pea pods and huge chunks of lobster ($13.95). Desserts include the popular Bailey's cheesecake, a mousse of the day (ours was lemon, creamy and delicious) and a fresh strawberry tart, which was disappointing. Service was less than perfectly solicitous, but this restaurant patronized more by tourists than natives has great potential. Dinner, 5:30 to 9:30. Open year-round.

Halibut Point, 289 Main St., Gloucester. (617) 281-1900. Unimposing on the exterior (an old and narrow building built by Howard Blackburn as a tavern in 1900), this restaurant has brick walls, wooden floors and the scrumptious smell of charcoal grilling when you enter. Charcoal-broiled swordfish couldn't be fresher and the charcoal burgers, charcoal chicken breast sandwiches and charcoal-grilled hot dogs are fine. Creamy white clam chowder or Italian fish chowder (a spicy tomato base with vegetables) are specialties. You can get cherrystones or oysters on the half shell ($4.50 a half dozen) or a bowl of shrimp ($3.95) from the Oyster Bar. Prices range from $1.95 for chowder to $9.95 for a full dinner. Sirloin steak is always on the menu, but ask about the seafood specials. And save room for the Low Tide Pie, a chocolate cookie crumb shell filled with coffee ice cream and topped with fudge, $2.50. Open daily, 11:30 to midnight or 1.

Picnicking. Try **Halibut Point Reservation** off Route 127 north of Rockport. You will have to carry your picnic supplies in from the road. You can tote picnics to most beaches. We have enjoyed ours at the end of Bearskin Neck on the rocks (off-season, we must admit). If you want to buy a sandwich to go, the **Greenery Creamery** at Dock Square in Rockport, 546-9593, is where you can get a sproutwich (muenster and cheddar, alfalfa sprouts, lettuce and sunflower seeds, $2.95), or a Middle Eastern (hummus, sprouts, muenster, lettuce and tomatoes, $2.95).

FOR MORE INFORMATION: Rockport Board of Trade, Box 67, Rockport Mass. 01966, (617) 546-6575. Cape Ann Chamber of Commerce, 128 Main St., Gloucester 01930, (617) 283-1601.

Pier at North Hero House faces Green Mountains across Lake Champlain.

The Champlain Islands, Vt.

Its promoters call this area Vermont's West Coast, an appellation that we find appropriate. Viewed from the interstate highway above St. Albans, deep green islands, large and small, fill the expanse of blue water beneath a backdrop of towering peaks as far as the eye can see. Every time we pass this breathtaking vista it reminds us of a similar panorama of the San Juan Islands, viewed from the interstate above Washington's Puget Sound.

They call Lake Champlain the inland sea, which is not all that far-fetched. After the Great Lakes, it's America's sixth largest freshwater lake. But for the presence of mountains all around and the lack of tidal ups and downs, you could close your eyes and imagine yourself near Maine's Casco Bay or Nova Scotia's Mahone Bay.

Given the "West Coast" and "inland sea" attributes, it's amazing how undiscovered — and unspoiled — the Champlain Islands are. Although barely 15 minutes north of Burlington, Vermont's largest city, and an hour's drive south of Montreal, the islands convey a strong sense of isolation. This 30-mile stretch of rural retreat in the middle of the Northeast's largest lake is a never-never land near the international border, too distant for most Americans and another country for Canadians. Thus it has been spared the onslaught that tarnishes similar waterways within development distance of three million people. Grand Isle County, Vermont's smallest, claims a year-round population of 5,000, a few tourist accommodations built years ago, summer cottages and campgrounds, rolling farmlands and apple orchards, abundant shoreline, and not much else.

U.S. Route 2 is the main road through the islands, from South Hero through Grand Isle, North Hero and Alburg. The islands, incidentally, were part of a charter granted in 1779 to Ethan Allen, Ira Allen and others of the Green Mountain Boys. The grant was given the name Two Heroes, referring to the

Allens, and some people still refer to the area as "The Heroes."

These little-known islands are replete with history and a sense of place, as attested by the 470-page history of the Town of Isle La Motte, one of the more remote islands. "There is a certain indefinable spell about it," writes author Allen L. Stratton. "It is a quietness, a sense of peace."

The islands are long and narrow, never more than five miles wide and sometimes, as at the portage point the Indians named Carrying Place, only the width of a road separating lake from bay. They're connected by causeways, bridges and a shared sense of place. On all sides are cool, crystal-clear waters beneath a stage set of mountains — the Adirondacks to the west in New York and the Green Mountains to the east in Vermont. Amid nature's majesty you're likely to feel awed, humble and grateful.

Getting There

The Champlain Islands are in the northern section of Lake Champlain, stretching from about 15 miles north of Burlington to the Quebec border. From Vermont, they are reached via Route 2 from Interstate 89 near Colchester or Route 78 from Swanton. From New York, take the Champlain exit off Interstate 87 east to Rouses Point and Route 2, or the Grand Isle ferry from Plattsburgh.

Where to Stay
Inns and Motels

North Hero House, Route 2, North Hero 05474. (802) 372-8237. The premier place to stay in the Heroes is the waterfront complex around this three-story, mustard-colored frame house, built in 1891 right across the road from the lake. Red rocking chairs are lined up in a row on the hospitable porch. There are six rooms in the main inn, but the coveted ones are in three buildings beside the water, Cove House, Southwind and Homestead. In Cove House, the wallboard was stripped on one wall of each of the six rooms so the original brick and peg beam construction could be seen. Here you can relax on your screened porch right over the water. Downstairs, the old Cobbler's Room is a prized suite, with a fireplaced living room and beamed ceilings. The foundation is Grand Isle granite and the fieldstone walls are three to four feet thick. Of the 23 rooms, only three in the back of the main house do not have water views; all have private baths. Boats moor at the old steamship dock in front, next to one of the few sand-bottom beaches around. Big inner tubes and snorkel gear are available, as are a tennis court, sauna and bicycles. There are also two outboards, four sunfish and a canoe. A restaurant (see Where to Eat), game room/lounge and the **Linnipin Shop,** with locally made goods, maple products, those neat Vermont cow T-shirts and the like, are in the main inn. Longtime owners Roger and Caroline Sorg sold the inn in 1986 to John Apgar, who plans to run it in the same wholesome and friendly way. This is the kind of place where guests get to know each other and return year after year for the same rooms. Doubles, $37 to $67; suite, $87. Open mid-May to mid-October.

Shore Acres Inn & Restaurant, Route 2, R.R. 1, Box 3, North Hero 05474. (802) 372-8722, winter 372-5853. Shore Acres is appropriately named, situated well back from the highway on the edge of a ledge beside Great East Bay, with lovely lawns amid 50 acres of rolling grounds and a half mile of private lakeshore. White with blue trim and blue awnings, it has 19 lakeview rooms in two motel-type wings on either side of the restaurant, plus four new rooms in a guest house annex that operates as a B&B in the off-season. Each room has private bath, color TV, maple furniture and pine paneling. Benches and lawn chairs are scattered about the lawns for viewing the lake and Mount Mansfield beyond. Below are a pebbly beach and a raft. Breakfast and dinner are served in the restaurant (see Where to Eat). Doubles, $42.50 to $65.50. Open May-November.

Sandbar Motor Inn, Route 2, South Hero 05486. (802) 372-6911. Located at the west end of the Sandbar causeway, this is the first accommodation you'll find in the Champlain Islands when you're arriving from the south. In fact, the site has been used for lodging since the 1890s, when the Sandbar bridge toll collector took in guests in his toll house and ultimately added an inn. Now the motel has 37 units, facing Great East Bay across the highway and backing up to the edge of what the locals call the broad lake at the rear. The motel rooms are quite small but adequate, with color TVs and modern baths. Six have kitchens and there are two cottages. Energetic new owners Jim and Lee Metzger and Cliff and Poe Sheard have done some redecorating and have added little touches like vine wreaths and fresh curtains. Now if they'd just get rid of the paper bathmats! They rent bicycles and boats, and plan to expand their marina. There's good swimming from a private dock and beach, or you can drive across the causeway to Sandbar State Park. Breakfast and dinner are served at the Sandbar restaurant (see Where to Eat). Doubles, $40 to $45.

Ruthcliffe Lodge, Isle La Motte 05463. (802) 928-3200. A long way from anywhere but the lake, this lodge with restaurant and motel is good for those who want to be away from it all. It's a family operation, Mark Infante having taken over from his parents who started the lodge in 1951. Three meals a day are served in the lodge, which has a cathedral ceiling opening to a second-floor loft with five guest rooms. Furnished in lodge style, each has a double bed and a half-bath, and shares one full bath. Seven good-sized rooms in the adjacent motel look out onto the lake; they have two double beds and TV on request. Weekly rentals and American Plan meals are available. Doubles, lodge $34, motel $39. Open May 15-Sept. 15.

Holiday Harbor Motel, Route 2, North Hero 05474. (802) 372-4077. Twelve motel units are lined up near the road and an office containing a bait and tackle store and small gift shop. By the shore, six housekeeping cottages, rustic and plain, face the lake. All units have color TVs, barbecues and picnic tables. A small beach, playground area and boat rentals are available. Doubles, $30 to $45; housekeeping cottages, $225 to $250 weekly.

Hislop's Landing, Route 2, RD 1, Box 339, Grand Isle 05458. (802) 372-8229 or 372-8309. Down a long hill from the road are 10 cottages with decks overlooking the lake. The five on the shore are older; five behind them were built in 1979. All have two bedrooms, a day bed in the living room, shower bath, modern kitchen and front decks with picnic tables; two by the shore have fireplaces. There's a sandy beach, and the protected bay called the Gut is fine for sailing and water skiing. Cottages, $200 to $225 weekly.

Aqua Vista Cottages, Route 2, North Hero. Perched atop a little hill looking across the road to the water are nine overnight cabins and one

241

housekeeping cottage. Guests can swim off the dock across the road. The cabins, equipped like motel units, have front porches trimmed with fringed awnings, twin or double beds, carpeting, TV and small refrigerator. The two-bedroom housekeeping cottage is $80 a night or $350 a week. Doubles, $40.

Auberge Alburg, South Main Street, RD 1, Box 3, Alburg 05440. (802) 796-3169. This eclectic place is a B&B, a continental-style café and, planned for 1987, a summer theater. Run by Gabrielle Tyrnauer, an anthropology professor, and Charles Stastny, a political science professor, at Concordia University in Montreal, it exudes their tastes — from a downstairs room full of books to the Russian dinners and entertainment occasionally provided by a Russian woman who is a regular visitor. Upstairs, two large bedrooms each have a double bed and two twins, paneled walls and scatter rugs. In the rear barn, a hideway retreat on the third floor has floor-to-ceiling windows, colorful rugs and private bath. Gabrielle officially serves a continental breakfast of croissants, muffins and bagels, usually brought down from Montreal, but unofficially she's been known to cook eggs or pancakes. A rear deck offers a glimpse of the lake, and it's a short walk to a little beach. At **Café Etcetera,** on the wraparound screened porch, you may order espresso, cappuccino, croissants and continental pastries, plus occasional light meals. Among pastries are cheesecake with apricot and strawberry glaze, sachertorte with fresh whipped cream, kiwi cake, Black Forest pie and strudels, priced from $1.25 to $2.50. Gabrielle said a friend was planning to run a summer theater in her barn in 1987. Doubles, $35.

RENTALS. Individual cottages and houses are advertised in the Islander, the free weekly newspaper. Listings may be available from Billie Tudhope, Realtor, North Hero 05474, (802) 372-6916; Hill Real Estate, Box 102, Grand Isle 05458, (802) 372-5777, or Island Properties, Route 2, South Hero 05486, (802) 372-8880.

Camping

Camping is big in this area. In fact, there are far more campsites than there are guest rooms. Among the best:

Knight Island Campsites, Box 203, North Hero. (802) 372-5436. "We provide the island — you provide the rest," say Lawrence and Mary Tudhope, who live in a farmhouse on Knight Island off North Hero. They share the 200-acre island with campers at seven unserviced sites carefully spaced along the shoreline. People bring their own tents and food; the Tudhopes rent boats and will shuttle campers to the island from North Hero by appointment. The island has five ponds, cliffs and beaches. There are no facilities; you drink from and bathe in the lake. Adults $5, children $2.50; family maximum $15.

Grand Isle State Park, Box 648, Grand Isle 05458. (802) 372-4399. Thirty-five lean-tos are included among the 157 campsites offered in this 226-acre park. Many sites are grouped around a big central lawn. More appealing are the 11 lean-tos on a shoreline ledge, most with views of the lake. The sites have no hookups, but shower and toilet facilities are available. A small playground is beside the beach, and there's a recreation hall. Prime tent sites, $9; lean-tos, $11.50.

North Hero State Park, North Hero 05474. (802) 372-8727. This 399-acre park has 108 campsites and 16 lean-tos amid the trees along three well-spaced loop roads — none on the water, although within walking distance of the swimming and boat launch area. Shower and toilet facilities are available, as are boat rentals. A small gravel beach is popular with wind surfers, and there's a nature trail. Tent sites, $7.50; lean-tos, $10.50.

Private Campgrounds. Cedar Ridge KOA, South Hero 05486. (802) 372-5070. Sixty-five sites, all with water and electricity, are offered here, as are restrooms, rec hall, swimming pool, playing fields and boat rentals. An even better location on a peninsula at the entrance to Mallet's Bay, with a panoramic view of the broad lake, is an asset of **Camp Skyland,** South Hero 05486. (802) 372-4200. Thirty-two campsites are located on six acres along the lakeshore. Also available are eight single-room cabins and four housekeeping cottages, $125 to $150 a week.

Seeing and Doing

Water recreation reigns in this area, naturally. Although there are an 18-hole golf course at **Alburg Country Club,** two smaller courses and a few tennis courts, there's not much else. People are always on the lookout for Champ, the Lake Champlain sea monster whose sightings are front-page news in the Islander newspaper ("Champ must be touring the whole island, for just a few days ago 35 people reported seeing the creature off the YMCA Camp in South Hero," the Islander reported after two sightings off Grand Isle one summer). Visitors who get cabin fever can go off to Burlington or Montreal for the day.

On or Near the Water

BOATING. From canoes to luxury yachts, sailboards to schooners, boats ply the sheltered coves and bays around the Champlain Islands. Great East Bay, that part of the lake between the islands and Vermont mainland, is generally more protected than the "broad lake" to the south and west.

Unfortunately, there are no excursion boats touring the Champlain Islands. The closest boat is the **Spirit of Ethan Allen,** 862-8300, which gives 90-minute scenic lake cruises at 10, noon, 2 and 4 daily from Perkins Pier in downtown Burlington (adults $5.75, children $3.50). Dinner, Sunday brunch, jazz, sunset and moonlight dance cruises also are scheduled. Tour promoters tell visitors to look for Champ. In 1984, 70 passengers aboard the Spirit of Ethan Allen made the largest mass sighting ever of the legendary creature.

Lake Champlain Transportation Co., King Street Dock, Burlington 05401. (802) 864-9804. Another way to see the lake is aboard the Lake Champlain ferries, which connect Vermont and New York on three crossings: Charlotte to Essex, Burlington to Port Kent and Grand Isle to Cumberland Head near Plattsburgh. The Grand Isle crossing leaves from the heart of the Champlain Islands, is the shortest and runs the most frequently, every 20 minutes from 6:40 a.m. to 10:20 p.m. in summer. It's also the only ferry to run year-round. The 12-minute crossing costs $6.25 for car and driver, $1.50 for adults, 50 cents for children, $10 maximum per car.

A number of marinas offer boat rentals. One of the largest is **Tudhope Marine Co.** in North Hero, 372-5545, where you can get a 6-horsepower motorboat for $25 a day, $125 a week; a 20-horsepower boat for $65 and $325, or a 25-horsepower pontoon boat for $100 and $500. Windsurfers rent for $20 a half day, sunfish for $25 and a 17-foot day sailor for $45. **Tudhope Sailing Center,** at the bridge in Grand Isle, 372-5302, has marina facilities and offers sailing instruction and charter services. The islands have eight public boat launching areas from Keeler's Bay in South Hero to Kelly Bay at the Rouses Point Bridge in Alburg.

FISHING. Cool, clear and up to 400 feet deep, Lake Champlain is said to have as large an assortment of freshwater fish as any lake in the world. The annual **Lake Champlain International Fishing Derby** in mid-June helps raise funds for the lake restoration program, started in 1974 to restore fisheries for landlocked Atlantic salmon and rainbow trout. More than 3 million salmon and trout have been stocked in the lake and they're growing fast, according to LCI derby sponsors. In one recent derby, 1,099 fish were registered, among them 350 lake trout, 228 walleyed pike, 180 smallmouth bass, 128 northern pike and 46 Atlantic salmon.

SWIMMING. Lake Champlain's water is so pure that people drink it and so refreshing that some swimmers find it chilly. We don't. Our only complaint is the dearth of sand beaches, as opposed to gravel or rock beaches. Often swimming is done from docks or rafts to avoid the stony bottom. Some of the best swimming is available in state parks. **Sand Bar State Park** at the causeway in Colchester is deservedly popular with daytrippers from Burlington; it has a long beach, shady areas with picnic tables, a snack bar and boat rentals. **Knight Point State Park** at North Hero offers a small, manmade sandy beach, picnic area and shelter, and boat rentals ($1.75 an hour). **North Hero State Park** has a small gravel beach and a few picnic tables for day use ($1 adult, 50 cents children). You also can swim off a beach at St. Anne's Shrine.

BIRDING. Nearly 300 species of birds have been recorded in the area, which lies on one of the major north-south flyways for migratory birds. Herons, eagles, falcons, ravens, osprey, hawks, snowy egrets, cormorants, ducks, geese and songbirds are among the finds. Birdwatchers say the **South Hero Swamp** and **Mud Creek** in Alburg are particularly good sites. The **Sand Bar Wildlife Refuge**, an 800-acre state wildlife management area across from Sand Bar State Park, is known for its duck population.

Other Attractions

Hyde Log Cabin, Route 2, Grand Isle. If Grand Isle has a tourist attraction, this is it, one of the oldest log cabins in the United States. Built in 1783 with an enormous fireplace at one end and an overhead loft, it housed the family of Jedediah Hyde Jr. and his 10 children. Members of the Hyde family lived there for nearly 150 years. In 1945 the Vermont Historical Society acquired the cabin and moved it two miles to its present location along Route 2. Inside you see original furnishings, agricultural and household implements, bedspreads, clothes and such. A guide from the Grand Isle Historical Society informed us that more than two-thirds of the artifacts came from the Hyde family or their descendants and the rest from other pioneer families on the island. We felt we were part of an earlier era, listening to birds twittering out back through the open door and watching cows grazing on the adjacent property. Open Wednesday-Sunday, 9 to 5, July 4 through Labor Day, weekends til Columbus Day.

St. Anne's Shrine, Isle La Motte. (802) 928-3362. Thousands of pilgrims find solace at the Edmundite Fathers' shrine on the site of Fort St. Anne, Vermont's oldest settlement, where the first Mass in the state was celebrated in 1666. In keeping with the island tradition, the shrine is rather primitive: a covered, open-air chapel where Eucharistic celebrations are offered daily, an Italian marble statue of St. Anne housed in an A-frame, a grotto and the Way of the Cross, its stations nestled among tall pines beside the lake. A granite statue of Samuel de Champlain, sculpted in the Vermont Pavilion at Expo 67 in Montreal, now occupies the site where he landed in 1609. There are a no-frills cafeteria and picnic tables, and visitors may swim from the beach or simply relax on a lovely, peaceful piece of land. Shrine is open free, May 15 to Oct. 15.

Isle La Motte Historical Society, Isle La Motte. Originally the South District schoolhouse (circa 1797), this small building now holds local artifacts, looms, spinning wheels and other items collected since 1925 by the historical society. The island is noted geologically for having examples of every known geological period and a few specimens are here, according to assistant curator Edith Andrews, who lives in a house occupied by five generations of her family at the four corners. There are examples of the island's famed black marble which graces the U.S. Capitol and Radio City Music Hall, a piece of coral from a nearby farm field and two pages of Champlain's diary written upon his landing here. Open Saturdays from 2 to 4, July and August, or by appointment. Free.

SHOPPING. Stores are basic and the shops few and far between. We always stop at the **Apple Farm Market** in South Hero, where Judy Allen dispenses cider, apples, gifts (many with an apple theme) and ice cream. You can choose from dozens of kinds of apples (Empires are the best for eating), watch cider being made, and pick up a fresh apple pie to take home. Adjacent is a pizza and submarine sandwich shop where pizzas run from $3.99 for small to $7.59 for large and 10 kinds of grinders are $2.25 to $3. A six-foot-tall green frog is in front of **Green Frog Gifts & Clothing**, Route 314, South Hero. Inside is a little bit of everything from moccasins to Vermont food products, T-shirts to books, plus a large selection of frogs. Amid the array is an old refrigerator covered with "I Love Vermont" magnets. In 1982, Frank and Lynda Clark converted an old hen house into the fine **Hooting Owl Gift Shop**, Route 314, Grand Isle. Here's an intriguing shop chock full of Vermont handcrafts, kitchenware, jewelry, dolls, Christmas decorations and, of course, owls. Through the rear window is a nice view of the lake.

Where to Eat

North Hero House, Route 2, North Hero. (802) 372-8237. A greenhouse dining room decked out in gold and red linens, Villeroy & Boch china and hanging fuschias is not what you'd expect at an historic inn in the Champlain Islands. Nevertheless, it's what you get at the North Hero House unless you're too late, as we were for lunch one afternoon (lunch is served only from noon to 1). We were seated instead in one of two circular screened outdoor gazebos off the lounge and were grateful to be served, there not being many places for lunch in this area. With a glimpse of the lake, we enjoyed a roast beef sandwich on sourdough bread ($4.95) and pie of the day (a shrimp, tomato and brie quiche, $4.45), served with pasta salad and cole slaw. The dinner menu changes nightly with a choice of three entrees priced from $11.50 to $14.95. A typical offering might be London broil on toast points, veal medallions with asparagus sauce and duckling glazed with a sweet and tart plum sauce, accompanied by roasted red potatoes, local Swiss chard and maple glazed summer squash. Appetizers might be chilled peach soup, feta cheese and spinach turnovers or tomato, zucchini, goat cheese and pesto baked in puff pastry. Desserts range from strawberry almond dacquoise to plum puree with blackberry brandy. Fresh whole grain bread and garden salads accompany. Friday night brings a lobster buffet dinner served picnic-style on the steamship dock for $16.95. Sunday night there's a popular buffet for $12.95. Breakfast, 8 to 10; lunch, noon to 1; dinner, 6 to 8.

Steen's, Junction of Routes 7 and 2A, Colchester. (802) 878-3377. Just off the island but worth the trip is this transplant from Stowe, Steen Nilsen from Denmark having moved to and rechristened the former Pierre restaurant in 1985. The main dining room could not be more charming with white linens, blue napkins, Hitchcock chairs, a few booths, candles in pewter sticks and pink lights glowing inside pierced tin lamps. A talk with Steen one morning convinced us that here is a man whose soul is in his food. A dinner the next night confirmed it. Four of us started with good-sized drinks and crusty, soft bread, super salads with Caesar or Swiss herb dressings, a delicate cream of watercress bisque and graved lax (cured salmon) with a maple syrup, dill and mustard sauce. Also exceptional were the lobster Johnny Walker, veal steak with bearnaise, veal scaloppine and a wonderful lamb steak, marinated with coriander sauce, accompanied by green beans amandine and a red potato cake. Entrees are priced from $9.95 for a chicken dish to $14.75 for lobster or filet mignon. The strawberry charlotte was moist and luscious, the pound cake with lemon sauce superb, and next time we might try bananas Foster or blueberries flambee for two. The wine list has a number of good values from $13 to $85. Steen planned to serve lunch in a greenhouse addition in 1987. Dinner nightly except Monday, 5:30 to 9:30. Open year-round.

Gerard's, Route 127, Malletts Bay, Colchester. (802) 879-1000. Gerard is Gerard Rubaud, former president of Rossignol Skis, and his restaurant serves some pretty trendy, fancy food. Made by his French chefs at their Haute Cuisine kitchen in Fairfax, Vt., it is flash-frozen, packaged and reheated here. He took over the renovated Tradewinds restaurant with a perfect location beside Mallett's Bay in 1986. Lunch is served downstairs in a blue and white waterfront cafe and dinner upstairs (or down) in a sleekly elegant room with gray walls and ceilings, pink linens over white and Villeroy & Boch Florida china. Torches light the deck at night, and the sunset over the bay can be sensational. The food is ever-so-with-it. Start, perhaps, with duck pate, salmon rillette or snails and spinach ravioli. For main courses ($12.50 to $17.50), how about lobster mousse, poached Norwegian salmon in a red pepper sauce, seafood fettuccine, braised sweetbreads, veal mignon in a truffle sauce, chicken stuffed with foie gras or leg of lamb fricassee? Desserts from the cart ($3.90) range from charlotte marquise with coffee sauce to pear charlotte. A six-course tasting menu is available if the entire table orders it, $32 per person. Lunch on blue deck chairs at glass tables beside the water could include chicken and rice salad with dill sauce or fettuccine with seafood and lobster sauce, $5.50 to $6.95. A 10 percent service charge is added to the bill. Lunch and dinner daily.

Shore Acres Inn & Restaurant, Route 2, North Hero. (802) 372-8722. The pine-paneled dining room dressed in blue and white linens and fresh flowers has a stone fireplace and looks out onto the lake. The limited menu is priced from $7.95 for chicken of the day to $13.95 for New York sirloin, with most items under $10. Charbroiled swordfish, deep-fried shrimp or scallops, rainbow trout, leg of lamb and charbroiled pork chop are among the offerings, all served with homebaked bread, salad and seasonal vegetables. Appetizers are not all that interesting (Vermont cheese and crackers, clam chowder); desserts include chocolate and other homemade pies, maple syrup sundae and lemon pudding. The wine list contains some unbelievable bargains under $10. Dinner, 5:30 to 8:30.

Ruthcliffe Lodge, Isle La Motte. (802) 928-3200. Meals are served in a rustic, pine-paneled dining room with a cathedral ceiling or on an adjacent outdoor deck with pipe furniture overlooking the lake. Manager Mark Infante handles the cooking chores. Full-course dinners, from juice and soup to dessert, are priced from $9.95 for chicken or stuffed sole to $12.95 for shrimp scampi, broiled swordfish or filet mignon. Homemade desserts include amaretto cheesecake and rice and apple pudding. A fancy wine list, with labels displayed, is very reasonably priced. Lunch is basic: homemade soup and sandwiches. For breakfast, all you can eat is $3.75. Breakfast, lunch and dinner daily in season.

Sandbar Restaurant, Route 2, South Hero. (802) 372-6911. The locals like this homey place with a fire in the fireplace and windows onto the water across the road, and at night it becomes quite attractive by candlelight. The food is good and straightforward, from $7.95 for roast turkey to $13.95 for surf and turf. The "Green Mountain Surprise," a homemade spicy preserve, is served as an appetizer over Vermont cream cheese with crackers, and sold by the jar for $4.95. Dinners come with salad, homemade soup — the split green pea is very hearty and good — and a bread bar with four choices, among them herb and whole wheat. Our New York strip steak and filet mignon dinners were so filling we had no room for dessert. Excellent breakfasts run from $2.50 for yogurt and granola in a parfait glass topped with fruit to $4.25 for eggs Benedict. Breakfast, 8 to 11; dinner, 5 to 9.

St. Anne's Shrine Cafeteria, Isle La Motte. A very plain cafeteria serves very plain food for pilgrims visiting the shrine, passing tourists or swimmers using the beach. You can get bacon and eggs, juice and coffee for $3; a sandwich for about $2, and four complete dinners of shrimp, haddock, chicken or hamburg steak for $6 to $7. Open weekdays from 9 to 4 or 5, weekends from 8 to 5 or 6.

Church Breakfasts. St. Rose of Lima Church at Keeler Bay alternates with **St. Joseph Church** of Grand Isle in offering Sunday morning breakfasts from 7 to noon. At St. Rose, you pay your $2.50 at the door of the church basement, go through a very generous buffet line and sit communally at long tables. We got more than filled up on french toast, scrambled eggs, hashed potatoes, ham, sausage, all kinds of muffins and bowls of fresh fruit. Orange juice and coffee are brought to the table. Even the glutton among us didn't have to go back for seconds. One of the women in charge said 250 to 350 people are served every other Sunday, the biggest rush is right after any of the Masses, and proceeds will go to installing an elevator in the church. St. Rose and other churches occasionally serve family suppers as well.

FOR MORE INFORMATION: Lake Champlain Islands Chamber of Commerce, Box 264, South Hero, Vt. 05486, (802) 372-5566.

Sportsmen take to water in Connecticut River.

Connecticut River/Hanover, N.H.

Ever since our son first went to summer camp in this area, we have been enamored of the 20-mile stretch of the Connecticut River that reaches from Lebanon in the south to Orford in the north. The area includes Hanover, N.H., home of Dartmouth College, and Lakes Morey and Fairlee in Vermont as well as a couple of ponds and waterfalls.

Water may not be its prime attraction, but there is plenty of it, and the river is particularly appealing. It's possible to canoe from inn to inn in one section, to try windsurfing in another. Members of Hanover's Ledyard Canoe Club regularly spend weekends and vacations on the water, kayaking, canoeing, rowing and sailboarding.

While Hanover (and Dartmouth) bring a cultural sophistication to the area — and a fine art museum and performing arts center as well — this is an area for outdoorsmen who dress comfortably and spend their time hiking, biking or engaging in water sports. Canoes tied to the tops of cars are common sights; so are backpacks and hiking boots. The Appalachian Trail runs through Hanover, and the presence of six sports outfitters among the shops in town tells the story.

Accommodations range from fine country inns to simple cottage colonies and include a few bed and breakfast inns as well. For families, there are bargains — good places for camping, and inexpensive cabin arrangements where the kids will have as much fun as their parents. Dining options are varied, from outstanding restaurants to low-key sandwich spots, and, except for West Lebanon, there are no golden arches.

The region is very scenic. The river cuts its swath between the mountains of Vermont and New Hampshire and there are breathtaking views from several spots. Come along with us and explore this upper Connecticut River area, which has so much to offer the vacationer.

Getting There

Hanover is located at Exit 13 off Interstate 91, just north of the I-89 interchange in White River Junction. Exit 15, two exits to the north, leads to Fairlee, Vt.

Where to Stay

By the River

Stone House Inn, Route 5, North Thetford, Vt. 05054. (802) 333-9124. For nearly 10 years, Art and Dianne Sharkey have been running this homey B&B, one of our favorites. The large stone house, set at a bend on Route 5 in the sleepy hamlet of North Thetford, is right beside the Connecticut River, and views are wonderful from a grassy back yard and from several rooms. The Sharkeys started the "Canoeing Inn to Inn" program (see below) and theirs is the middle stop of three inns on the trip. School teachers who taught in various countries around the world, they and their two teenagers have put down roots in Vermont. Art teaches at nearby Thetford Academy and Dianne is a font of information about the area. Seven rooms on the second floor share three baths, one with stall shower. The rear, paneled porch bedroom with windows all around has the best view of the river. A front twin-bedded room with pink and navy flowered wallpaper and soft rose bedspreads is another of our favorites. The main parlor has a welcoming fireplace and there's a gorgeous screened porch for sitting. The porch has two white hanging swings, a few rockers, and pots filled with impatiens. Dianne cooks breads, muffins, scones and other delicious pastries for the ample continental breakfast, which also may include cereal; the basket of breads is always heaping. Breakfast is served in a sunny glassed-in porch out back, next to the kitchen. Doubles, $40. Open year-round.

The Chieftain Motel, Route 10, Hanover, N.H. 03755. (603) 643-2550. This gray wood motel with white trim and yellow doors occupies a choice piece of real estate: a terrace high above the Connecticut River two miles north of town. Most of the 22 pine-paneled rooms have river views; if yours doesn't you can sit out back in a grassy area with chairs and tables and watch the river from there. Trails lead down to the water's edge (although it's a steep hike) and there's a pool for those who want to swim. Each room has two double beds and color TV. There's a simple breakfast room where a continental breakfast (primarily donuts and muffins plus coffee and fruit) may be purchased. Doubles, $40 to $58. Open year-round.

The Sunset Motel, Route 10, Hanover Road, West Lebanon, N.H. 03784. (603) 298-8721. This gray-stained board and batten motel also sits high above the Connecticut; in this case it's a few miles south of Hanover. Most rooms have river views; again, the view is great from behind the motel and there are a few chairs for enjoying it. The 18 rooms feature queensize beds and cable television, and coffee is served mornings in the lobby. Doubles, $55-70. Open year-round.

Lakeside

The Rutledge Inn and Cottages, Lake Morey, Fairlee, Vt. 05045. (802) 333-9722. The Stone family has been operating this rustic inn and cottage complex on the shores of beautiful Lake Fairlee for nearly 20 years. The green-shuttered white inn with screened porch stretching the length of the building, a cozy dining room with red placemats and napkins and flowers on the tables, and a warm fireplaced lobby with sofas you can sink into all spell New England hospitality and quintessential summertime Vermont. The cottages, some of them at water's edge and others climbing up the hillside past the inn, are basic. Some have working fireplaces and a few have screened porches; from many there are splendid views of the lake. The inn is oriented to lakefront activity; canoes, rowboats, water skiing and swimming are available. Large old white Adirondack chairs, set on the grass beside the water, are a good place to read and sun. You can book your room with or without meals. The dining room is famed for its desserts: more than thirty are on the menu, compared with just four or five entrees. The Rutledge attracts many of the same visitors year after year, most for a week or two, and it is often difficult to find a shorter-term accommodation. Doubles in cottages, MAP $88 to $96 nightly, $570 to $610 weekly; doubles with shared bath in inn, $76 daily, $490 weekly. Doubles, EP $45 to $50.

Loch Lyme Lodge and Cottages, Route 10, Lyme, N.H. 03768. (603) 795-2141. Paul and Judy Barker continue welcoming guests to the small inn and cottage community that was run by Judy's parents, the Fultons, from the 1940s until the late 1970s. It's north of Hanover beside Post Pond, where rowboats and canoes await use by guests. Accommodations and rate plans are exceptionally varied: in four rooms in the main lodge built in 1794, in cottages with fireplaces located by the water or stretching up a winding road and hillside to the rear, and in housekeeping cottages. Loch Lyme Lodge is one of the mainstays of the Vermont Bicycle Touring schedule, hosting cyclists on three-day sojourns in the area. In addition to boating and swimming there are two clay tennis courts, badminton and croquet, and a children's play area. A popular Sunday evening lakeside buffet is $7.50. Other meals are served in three attractive rooms in the main lodge in the summer; a la carte meals are $4.50 for breakfast, $5 for box lunch and $11.50 for dinner. In winter, Loch Lyme operates, as Judy says, "as a true B&B country inn" with four rooms in the lodge. Doubles, EP $48 in cabin, $36 in room; MAP $80 in cabin, $68 in room; housekeeping cabins, $205 to $250 weekly. Lodge open year-round.

Inns

White Goose Inn, Route 10, Orford, N.H. 03777. (603) 353-4812. Karin and Manfred Wolf emigrated from Germany, managed inns in Carmel and Monterey, Calif., and eventually found their own place after what they say was a "wild goose chase" in 1984. The White Goose Inn, set in the riverside town of Orford, is stunningly decorated by Karin, an artist. As we approached the imposing brick house with its wide porch (painted green to match the shutters), classical music was playing on the stereo, and a film crew for a country magazine had just left. The inn is picture-perfect, the result of the Wolfs' painstaking renovation from an apartment house. The 19th century brick front and 18th century clapboard back blend beautifully. Karin's stenciling can be seen throughout, and each antiques-filled room has its own charm. Four guest rooms have private baths; three share. Our favorite, the peach room, has a fireplace. Breakfast is described in the brochure as continental, but by Manfred as much more. French toast and Dutch baby pancakes are among his specialties, served in a gracious breakfast room with bare wood tables and chairs. Guests relax in the two front parlors. Outside is a gorgeous yard with comfortable chairs and a small spring-fed pond for swimming. A fishing rod is available for anglers who want to try their luck; several trout have been snagged, then returned to their happy home. Doubles, $55 to $75; no children under 8. Open year-round.

Lyme Inn, Route 10, Lyme, N.H. 03768. (603) 795-2222. The white wicker-filled front porch promises tranquil moments at this beautiful country hostelry run by Fred and Judy Siemons. Canopied beds, chaise lounges, clawfoot bathtubs, braided rugs and antique furniture remind visitors of days when the living was simpler. Ten of the 15 rooms have private baths. Three rooms on the top floor are often booked by families or friends who enjoy the privacy of their own floor and don't mind sharing a bath. Famed chef Hans Wichert (see Where to Eat) provides inventive cuisine in two dining rooms furnished tastefully with bare wooden tables, Hitchcock or ladderback chairs, and woven placemats. The tavern, with a fireplace, is especially popular in winter with skiers from Dartmouth College's own ski area nearby. Doubles, $60 to $85, including breakfast. Open year-round.

The Hanover Inn, Main Street, Hanover, N.H. 03755. (603) 643-4300. An institution along with Dartmouth College, this 102-room Colonial inn is usually host to a few old grads, and even posts a list of those who are in town. Facing the College Green, with a stone terrace where the early claimants sit in rockers and watch the activity, the inn has rooms decorated with period furniture, handmade lampshades and eiderdown comforters. The main dining room is formal; a terrace for dining out front is appealing on nice days and the most popular place in town for the buffet Sunday brunch, and the newly decorated **Ivy Grill** offers a city sophistication with a mixed menu. The front parlor, done in brick red and dark green, features window seats, wing chairs and Chippendale sofas. Doubles, $88 to $104; suites to $150. Open year-round.

Lake Morey Inn & Country Club, Fairlee, Vt. 05045. (802) 333-4311. A little too glitzy for our taste, the Lake Morey Inn nonetheless draws faithful visitors back again and again. Located at the foot of the lake, it offers an 18-hole golf course, a pool and tennis courts. Rooms are available in several wings of the main inn and also in lakeside cottages. Doubles, $120 to $250, MAP.

Camping

The Pastures Campground, Route 10, Orford, N.H. 03777. (603) 353-4579. Dot and Tom Parkington run an immaculate private campground on the banks of the Connecticut River and you can launch a boat at the Orford public boat launch ramp adjoining the site. The sites are mostly sunny, arranged on both sides of the road forming a wide rectangle. In the center is a barn-like building with restrooms and hot showers. Most sites have water and electricity; picnic tables are available and there are large open play areas as well. Nightly $10, weekly $60.

Storrs Pond Recreation Area, Off Route 10, Hanover, N.H. 03755. (603) 643-2408 or 643-2134. Thirty campsites, many of them secluded and wooded, are available in this outstanding recreation area owned and operated by the Hanover Improvement Society. Other features are a 15-acre pond, Olympic-size swimming pool, tennis courts, hiking trails and snack bar. The area is located in Hanover, not far from the golf course, but it feels as if you're way out in the woods. Nightly, $10 for sites with electricity; $6 for tent site, both including driver. Each additional person pays $1. Backpackers, $3.

Seeing and Doing

On the River

Canoeing Inn to Inn, c/o Stone House Inn, Route 5, North Thetford, Vt. 05054. (802) 333-9124. Started a few years ago by the Sharkeys of the Stone House Inn, this program offers canoeists a leisurely two-day, thirty-mile paddle down the Connecticut River from Haverhill to Hanover, with a mid-trip stop at the Stone House Inn in North Thetford. Participants may leave on a Monday or a Tuesday, starting at the Ledyard Canoe Club in Hanover, where the group is met and given information about the trip, then shuttled north to the Haverhill Inn for the first night's dinner and lodging. The trip begins the next morning with the stretch from Haverhill to North Thetford. After dinner and a night's rest at the Stone House Inn, the final leg of the journey takes canoeists to Hanover, where they are driven to Moose Mountain Lodge for dinner and overnight. Groups have included a wide range of ages and Dianne Sharkey particularly remembers the woman who celebrated her 75th birthday and combined it with a family reunion on the water. They even had T-shirts made up for the venture! All-inclusive cost, $200 per person; add $45 to rent a canoe. Trips offered late June to late August.

Canoe Vermont, 496-2409, an extensive program of canoe trips, offers one on the river from Hanover to Windsor, Vt. The three-day trip costs $290 per person.

The **Connecticut River Watershed Council** also offers canoe trips in the region. These are either one-day outings or overnights, and are good values. Plus, you'll learn about the river and how to use a canoe. Day trips cost around $15 (including canoe rental) or $10 when using your own canoe; overnights are $50 with canoe, $40 with your own. Children under 15 pay about half. For information: Canoe Trips, CRWC, 125 Combs Road, Easthampton, Mass. 01027, (603) 643-5672.

The Ledyard Canoe Club, Hanover, 646-2753 or 646-2787. Located on the banks of the Connecticut River and affiliated with the famed Dartmouth College Outing Club, this club rents canoes, kayaks and windsurfers. It's the oldest and best known collegiate canoe club in the country. Founded in 1920 by Dartmouth undergraduates, it continues to be managed by students. The white clapboard clubhouse is open daily from 9 to 7 in the summer and it's here where you rent your boat. Canoes rent for $3 an hour, $15 a day; windsurfers for $5 an hour. A three-day clinic in kayaking and a two-day clinic in windsurfing each cost $30.

The Wilder Dam south of Hanover off Route 10, operated by the New England Power Company, welcomes visitors. Here they receive a tour that involves crossing the dam on a special walkway, seeing the control house, and viewing a new fish ladder. The fish ladders here and at two other sites along the river have been built to encourage the return of salmon to the river. Picnicking and hiking are permitted in the area. Free.

SWIMMING: Even though the Connecticut River is swimmable, there's no public swimming access in this area. Good swimming is available at **Lake**

Fairlee (Treasure Island), **Lake Morey** (public beach) and at the **Storrs Pond Recreation Area** in Hanover.

BICYCLING. This section of the Connecticut River is a cyclist's delight, for both Route 5, following the west bank in Vermont, and Route 10, which parallels the eastern shore in New Hampshire, are scenic. Vermont Bicycle Touring of Bristol, (802) 453-4811, organizes weekend to five-day trips, some in the Hanover-Fairlee area.

Touring

Dartmouth College is a must. Founded in 1769 by the Rev. Eleazor Wheelock, Dartmouth dominates the town of Hanover and provides its character. The large Dartmouth College Green opposite the Hanover Inn is a center of activity. Tours of the campus are offered four times daily, Monday-Friday, leaving at 9, 11:15 and 3 from McNutt Hall, which faces the Green, and at 2 from the Information Booth on the Green. On Saturdays one tour leaves from McNutt Hall at 10.

Hood Museum of Art, connected to the Hopkins Center for the Arts on the south side of the Green, is a fine college museum. As you enter, you see seven ten-foot-high Assyrian reliefs from a palace built between 883 and 859 B.C. Representative pieces from many periods are displayed, including some splendid contemporary art on the second floor. Open Tuesday-Sunday 11 to 5, Thursdays to 8. Donation.

Orford, N.H., is one of the area's most picturesque villages. One of the original "fort towns" strategically placed by the British to control French and Indian uprisings on the Connecticut, Orford was settled in the summer of 1765. The town is known for its architecture, especially the seven so-called Ridge houses dramatically set on a high ridge east of Route 10 in the center of town. These elegant residences were built between 1775 and 1859. The southernmost house (circa 1815) was probably designed by the Boston architect, Asher Benjamin, an associate of Charles Bulfinch. Orford also has a pleasant green with picnic tables.

Take a scenic drive around picturesque **Lake Morey.** The road hugs the lake and the views are lovely.

SHOPPING. Hanover is a fun place to shop. The **Dartmouth Bookstore** on Main Street carries an extensive selection of foreign magazines and literary periodicals, plus cards, tapes, textbooks and an array of all types of books. Dartmouth College sweatshirts and other official college gear can be purchased at the **Dartmouth Co-op.** Other shops with interesting wares include **Bare Essentials,** a women's clothing store where very sophisticated styles are to be found, and **James Campion,** where more traditional women's and men's clothing are sold. **Rosey Jeke's** on Lebanon Street has funky stuff for women.

The **Hanover League of New Hampshire Craftsmen** at 13 Lebanon St. specializes in local and regional crafts and sponsors workshops. The **AVA Art Gallery** at 5 Allen St. is a collective art gallery showing the work of 50 New Hampshire and Vermont artists. Classes, lectures, films and monthly exhibitions are scheduled.

Several antiques dealers and shops are along Routes 5 and 10. The **Powerhouse,** a new shopping center in West Lebanon, N.H., is a mill-like expanse of brick built along a rushing river. The shops are tasteful but a bit pricey. **Great Eastern Sports, Mink Country Outfitters, Rapt in Chocolate**, and several women's clothing stores are fun to explore.

Where to Eat

D'Artagnan, 13 Dartmouth College Highway (Route 10), Lyme, N.H. (603) 795-2137. A handsome dining room located in the basement of the Ambrose Publick House in a small complex of restored offices and buildings 10 miles north of Hanover is the place for some incredibly creative meals. Peter Gaylor, a French-trained chef, and his wife, Rebecca Cunningham, have established a reputation locally for serving outstanding food. Both trained with noted chef Yannick Cam of Le Pavillon in Washington, D.C., before heading north to found their own country French restaurant in 1981. The restaurant seats 60 at simple tables, some of which overlook the rushing stream outdoors. An especially pleasant setting for cocktails is the outdoor terrace, where you can see and hear the water. The prix-fixe dinner ($25) includes appetizer, main course, house salad, dessert and beverage. Among appetizers offered at one Saturday evening dinner were chilled curry of shrimp and scallops with carrot, celery, onion and apple, and cold cantaloupe soup with mint and port. Entrees featured poached halibut with mushrooms and tarragon sauce and sauteed medallions of beef tenderloin in a red wine cream sauce. Rebecca's famed desserts include such temptations as white chocolate mousse with almond-hazelnut praline and fresh figs with red wine vanilla bean sauce. Her desserts have become so well-known that she was about to open a shop in the Powerhouse in West Lebanon to be called The Cool Moose, featuring her ice creams, sorbets and baked goods. Dinner, Wednesday-Sunday, and Sunday lunch. Reservations required.

Cafe la Fraise, 8 West Wheelock St., Hanover, N.H. (603) 643-8588. This 1823 house just off Hanover's Main Street as you drive into town from I-91 offers a variety of options: lunch, dinner, light foods in Le Bar, and a food shop where you can pick up fresh croissants and pastries. The country French decor involves polished dark wood or Windsor chairs and brass and glass lamps against a dark green wallpaper. The dinner menu includes duck in grand marnier orange sauce ($14.75), scallops of veal sauteed with apples and served with a calvados cream sauce ($14.95) and tournedos cooked in mustard, vermouth, shallots and cream, the most expensive at $16. Hors d'oeuvres such as pate, a light fish mousse and a mild baked goat cheese marinated in olive oil and herbs are priced from $4.25 to $5.95. Le Bar offers wine tasting, specially selected cordials and brandies, and a menu of hot and cold dishes from 11:30 a.m. to midnight. The gourmet shop, in addition to baked goods, is a place to buy cheeses, salads and other luncheon items to go. Lunch and dinner, Tuesday-Saturday; gourmet shop, 10 to 5.

Lyme Inn, Route 10, Lyme, N.H. (603) 795-2222. Chef Hans Wichert features some German specialties on the menu at this country inn's dining room. Recent dinner choices included wiener schnitzel, hasenpfeffer and a hunter-style veal as well as beer-batter shrimp and loin lamb chops basted in red wine and garlic. Prices for entrees range from $12 to $16. Also on the menu are "light supper" items such as seafood crepes with vegetable and beverage for $7.95, an idea we find appealing. Appetizers include marinated herring at $2.95 and escargots at $4.95. French onion soup is always on the menu. The Lyme Inn is a most attractive place to go on a summer evening;

after dinner you may be tempted to sit in the wicker-filled front room for a while. Dinner, nightly except Tuesday.

Bentley's, 11 South Main St., Hanover, N.H. (603) 643-4075. A masculine feeling, that of an English club or an old library, is quite appropriate for the Dartmouth grads and faculty members who find their way here. The dark wood paneling and mood are relieved by the flowered banquettes in the back room and the ficus tree adorned with tiny white lights growing toward a skylight, but the bar and the small room up front on the street seem clubby. Old books on a shelf in the bar add to the library feel and there are historic photos of Hanover on the dark green walls. Opened in 1983 by David Creech and Bill Deckelbaum, who have run a sister restaurant since the mid-1970s in Woodstock, Vt., Bentley's attracts a large following. One reason is the menu variety, with light, eclectic fare as well as full meals available at both lunch and dinner. At lunchtime we chose the gourmet chili, thick and spicy and served in a crock with a topping of mild melted cheese ($3.35 alone, $4.95 with a tossed salad and warm bread), while others in our party settled on Bentley's big burger, served with lettuce, tomato and hand-cut Idaho steak fries for $3.95. One of the best summer salads is spinach with scallions, bacon, eggs and poppyseed dressing topped with grated cheese (small, $2.95; large, $4.95). A chicken waldorf salad with sage and seedless grapes is $5.95. A baked wheel of brie topped with almonds and served with crackers and fruit for two is $6.50. Dinner entrees include Cajun barbecued shrimp ($13.95), Caribbean curried shrimp and chicken ($14.95) and Jamaican pecan chicken ($14.95). Out front is a gourmet shop where good soups, salads, chili, pastries and sandwiches are available for takeout. At the very front of the restaurant, with a window onto the street, Ben and Jerry's ice cream is dispensed in waffle or regular cones. On Thursdays, Fridays and Saturdays, folksy entertainers such as guitar strummers and singers hold forth in the bar in the evening. Lunch and dinner daily except Thanksgiving and Christmas.

Five Olde Nugget Alley, 5 Olde Nugget Alley, Hanover, N.H. (603) 643-5081. "The best kept secret in Hanover" is the way chef and co-owner Patty Dodds describes this basement restaurant off South Main Street. Only a solid wooden door and a red canopy proclaim its presence, but Dartmouth students and faculty as well as locals crowd the lounge and 90-seat restaurant for "big drinks and hearty portions." The menu changes every now and again, most recently taking a Cajun turn after Patty and John (husband and co-owner) traveled to New Orleans to sample the real thing. A collection of unusual beer cans is displayed behind the bar. Antique artifacts — old ice skates, a riding hat, a horse collar — are hung from the walls or displayed on a shelf in the two cozy dining rooms. The all-day menu includes appetizers such as cheese nachos and "skinny dips" (potato skins with sour cream), both $2.95; spinach salad with hot bacon dressing, burgers (served with soup, salad or fries), deli sandwiches, and chili quesadillas (giant soft tortillas stuffed with chili, cheese, lettuce, tomatoes and onions, and topped with sour cream, salsa and refried beans for $4.95). Dinner items (available all day) range from $5.95 for vegetable stir-fry to $10.95 for New York sirloin and include chicken and broccoli mornay and baked stuffed shrimp. Sunday brunch is served from 11 to 4 except during the summer. Lunch and dinner daily.

Jesse's, Route 120, Hanover, N.H. (603) 643-4111. Steak, seafood and a salad bar bring so many patrons to this log-cabin-style restaurant that you have to wait for a table as early as 6:30 on a Saturday evening in summer. The young owners celebrated their 10th anniversary in business in 1986 with no obvious slackening of enthusiasm from the local crowd. Hanging plants, Tiffany lamps, stained glass, bare wooden tables with mismatched chairs and subdued lighting lend atmosphere to a spot that seems popular with all ages. Beef, seafood and chicken and ribs are on the dinner menu regularly, but specials such as broiled salmon with dill hollandaise sauce at $10.95 may be the best choices. Three of us chose the salmon, an ample slab and quite delicious. The fourth enjoyed the steak kabob for $8.50. The salad bar, set up in a huge wooden sled, includes good warm breads like pumpernickel-raisin and country wheat. Wild and long-grained rice or a baked potato come with the entrees. Lunch includes sandwiches like turkey, roast beef and a BLT, a teriyaki steak kabob ($4.75) and quiche of the day. Lunch Monday-Friday, dinner nightly.

Molly's Balloon, 43 Main St., Hanover, N.H. (603) 643-2570. Owned by the same people who run Jesse's, this creative and bright place in the center of Hanover offers a light, interesting all-day menu. A greenhouse out front has a bar in the center and booths with upholstered green backs and slatted wooden seats, all set on a tile floor. Decorated with plants and framed prints and posters, Molly's Balloon is fun and upbeat. Helium-filled balloons are handed out to the kids in the group, which seems to bring hordes of them in on rainy Saturdays. "Mollypops," are frosty drinks like the "Yuppie Puppy," 95-octane vodka and tonic, or the peach-almond shake (peaches, amaretto, vanilla ice cream and cream). Snacky dishes like fritto misto, vegetables fried in tempura batter and served with horseradish mayonnaise ($4.95) or potato skins stuffed with Monterey Jack cheese and bacon crumbs and served with sour cream and chives ($4.25) are nice for lunch. French onion soup or a soup of the day can be ordered with a chef's or Neptune salad. Mexican entrees include Tortilla Fats (a giant tortilla filled with taco meat, beans, cheese, green chilis and onions and covered with salsa and melted cheese, then served with guacamole, black olives, and lettuce and tomato) for $5.75. Sandwiches, burgers and dinners (served after 5) such as seafood fettuccine ($9.95) or Molly's marinated sirloin ($10.50) are also on the brightly colored, many-paged menu. Apple crisp is a specialty; other desserts include cheesecake and bananas sauteed in kahlua with nuts and raisins, served over ice cream. The Sunday brunch is quite good; we enjoyed the smoked turkey croissant with Monterey Jack and cranberry sauce for $4.50 and the Mexican three-egg omelet for $5.75. Open daily from 11 to 11.

Peter Christian's Tavern, 39 South Main St., Hanover, N.H. (603) 643-2345. The tiny, tree-shaded deck with flower-filled window boxes and white bentwood chairs and small tables is especially pleasant on a summer's afternoon. Our gazpacho was chunky and spicy; sandwiches were served on wooden boards or pottery plates and included Peter's Mother's Favorite, ham, turkey, Vermont cheddar and tomatoes at $4.25 or $2.25 for a half, and Peter's Father's Favorite, roast beef, cream cheese, horseradish, sliced onions and tomatoes, at the same prices. Salads, yogurt with fresh fruit and honey, and beef stew are also on the menu. Some evenings there are special foods — such as Mexican Night on Sundays. The early-American tavern is all dark wood and booths, tucked a couple of steps down from Main Street. More than 20 beers are available by the glass or pitcher. Open daily from 11:30.

Mascoma River Water Works, The Powerhouse, Route 12A, West Lebanon, N.H. (603) 298-8813. This restaurant in the Powerhouse area is located in a new building made to seem old. A brick exterior, post-and-beam-style structural joists, and belt-driven fans are reminders of days past; the open airy feeling, white walls, and soft gray carpeting are thoroughly up-to-date. Dining is on two levels connected by a large open staircase; window tables overlook the rocky river. Opened in 1986, the Water Works offers a variety of dishes — from Italian to Creole to French in spirit — aimed at pleasing everyone. Our shrimp scampi at $9.25 and stir-fried cashew chicken at $8.50 were quite good, although service was so fast we felt rushed. The most expensive entrees are $11.95 (for tournedoes and New York strip steaks); many are in the $9 to $10 range. All come with salads, rolls, vegetable and rice or a baked potato. For lunch, several interesting salads include poached chicken sliced and combined with avocado, scallions and walnuts and served with a curried mayonnaise for $3.50. Sandwiches are creative as well. Burgers, chili and fish and chips are other options. A good variety of beers, wines and special international coffees are featured. Lunch and dinner, Monday-Saturday; Sunday brunch from 11 to 3:30, dinner from 4.

Lou's, Main Street, Hanover, N.H. (603) 643-3321. Lou's is one of those storefront restaurants, with booths on one side and a counter on the other, that stay full all day because they are reliable. Actually, Lou's is more than reliable, and the baked goods produced by the bakery associated with the restaurant are really good (try the cheesecake). The all-day menu offers sandwiches, salads, burgers, homemade soup, old favorites like lasagna and a hot turkey sandwich, and "breakfast all day." The ubiquitous cole slaw, better than most, has some red cabbage in it; beers and wines please the college kids. Open daily from 5:30 a.m. to midnight, Sunday from 8:30 a.m.

Other recommended restaurants include the **Third Rail** in Fairlee, Vt., casual but reliable, and the **Ivy Grill** in the Hanover Inn, where you can get pizza, burgers, or such delights as baby Coho salmon grilled with shiitake mushrooms and lemon ($12).

FOR MORE INFORMATION: Hanover Chamber of Commerce, Box 930, Hanover, N.H. 03755, (603) 643-3115. The Information Booth is a kiosk on the Dartmouth College Green, where you may meet Mr. Wood, a Dartmouth grad of yore, who is a great booster.

Lake Winnipesaukee is seen through trees from sitting room of Pick Point Lodge.

Wolfeboro/Lake Winnipesaukee, N.H.

Wolfeboro has laid claim to being America's oldest summer resort ever since its last English Colonial governor, John Wentworth, built a palatial mansion on the shore of the lake which bears his name. "Everybody in the country was talking about that house," advised our guide in the Wolfeboro Historical Society museum complex. "He summered here with his hunting and fishing cronies. He was one of those summer people!"

Nestled between Lake Wentworth and Wolfeboro Bay, the east end of Lake Winnipesaukee, Wolfeboro's year-round population of 2,000 triples in the summer, thanks to summer people like Kirk Douglas and David Meredith plus as many tourists as can be accommodated in limited facilities.

Though Wolfeboro is blessed with a magnificent location beneath mountains along New England's second largest lake, it maintains a sedate, small-town atmosphere. Brewster Academy opens its beach to the public in summer. Museums attract just enough visitors to make their opening worthwhile. A peddler dispenses hot dogs beneath an umbrella next to Cate Park at the town dock. The mailboat delivers mail and passengers out to the islands. There are benches for relaxation on the dock and along Main Street. Shopkeepers know their customers by name, and everyone on the street seems to know everyone else.

Happily, there's no schlock. Wolfeboro has resisted the honky-tonk that is the norm along other parts of the lake at Alton Bay and Weir's Beach, for instance, or beyond in the Conways and White Mountains. Zoning is strict and shoreline property in such demand that the pressure of residential real estate has blocked commercial development, according to Dick T. Newcomb, manager of Pick Point Lodge. "What's hurting Wolfeboro is its lack of rooms," he says.

That's just fine with most of the natives, the summer regulars and those transients lucky enough to find accommodations. They enjoy the myriad pleasures of one of the loveliest sections of Lake Winnipesaukee, good restaurants and shops, a fine golf course, a low-key social life, and the homey atmosphere of one of New England's more pleasant villages.

Says Alan Pierce, owner of a bookstore and gift shop aptly named Camelot: "People come back to Wolfeboro every year and are so glad to see that it hasn't changed."

Getting There

Wolfeboro is about 45 miles northeast of Concord at the east end of Lake Winnipesaukee. From Interstate 93, take Route 28 directly to Wolfeboro, or take Routes 3 and 11 to Route 28.

Where to Stay
By the Lakeshore

Pick Point Lodge & Cottages, Route 109, Box 220A, Mirror Lake 03853. (603) 569-1338. The signs get smaller and smaller and the roads narrower and narrower as you drive more than a mile off the highway north of Wolfeboro through a pine forest to the lakeshore. When we told manager Dick Newcomb that we thought we'd never get there, he responded, "that's why we're down here." And once down here, you don't want or have to leave. The family-run resort has ten large, well-furnished housekeeping cottages that are more secluded than many summer homes and an impressive main lodge built in 1924 as a private estate with two inn-style guest rooms, a grand sitting room with a fire blazing in the stone hearth and a full-length porch with a spectacular view through the pines of Lake Winnipesaukee. The club-like atmosphere and the 75 acres of grounds with half a mile of shore frontage appeal to many. "The sun stays with us all day on the beach," Dick says, showing a sandy beach running between two sides of Pick Point. Beyond are lounge chairs on a 200-foot jetty that he calls a sundeck; it has views down three directions of the lake. Rented weekly in summer, the ten lodge-style cottages vary in size from one to four bedrooms; all are pine-paneled, have new early American-style furniture, full kitchens, carpeted bedrooms, color television, porches, outdoor gas grills and daily maid service. The two rooms upstairs in the main lodge have queen or king beds and a color TV, and guests here are served complimentary breakfast in the dining room. There are outdoor and indoor tennis courts, a game room, free boats, a canoe and sunfish, and a wildlife sanctuary with 60 birdhouses, feeding stations and three miles of trails. The Newcombs host a complimentary Sunday flapjack breakfast and a Monday cocktail party followed by a steak or chicken cookout; otherwise guests are on their own. Asked what to bring, the owners say, "yourself, your food and a good disposition, and we'll give you a good time." Cottages, $900 to $1,400 weekly; inn rooms in lodge, $90 for two, $140 for four. Cottages rented by day spring and fall. No credit cards. Open mid-May to mid-October.

The Lake Motel, Route 28, Box 887-B, Wolfeboro 03894. (603) 569-1100. Among the area's few motels, this is the best bet, thanks to its location on tiny Crescent Lake, and it is booked accordingly. Opened in 1956, it has two entries to each of the 30 rooms, one from an interior corridor and the other from the outside. The rear half face the water. All have two double beds, two upholstered chairs and limited cable TV. Five more housekeeping apartments are located away from the water. Situated well off the highway on 16 acres, the motel has a beach and 600 feet of lake frontage, a tennis court, lawn games and boats for rent. **Bailey's Restaurant**, open from 8 a.m. to 11 p.m. daily at the entrance to the grounds, serves the most for the money in town, according to motel owners Allan and Julie Bailey, who run their operation more like an inn than most motelkeepers. Doubles, $56 to $65; open mid-May to mid-October.

Piping Rock Cottages & Motel, North Main Street, Wolfeboro 03894. (603) 569-1915. An eight-unit, two-story motel with balconies and decks overlooks a lawn down to Lake Winnipesaukee. Rooms in the motel, advertised as the newest and finest on the eastern shore, are carpeted, have two double beds and TV, and some have kitchens. Thirteen white and aqua cottages with two to four bedrooms and decks facing the pine trees, some with water views, are scattered about the nine-acre property. By the shore are a sandy beach with raft and boathouse. New owners purchased the property in 1986 and their plans were uncertain. Doubles, motel $85 to $125; cottages, $900 to $1,250 weekly. Motel open year-round.

Clearwater Lodges, Route 109, Star Route 1, Wolfeboro 03894. (603) 569-2370. Now in its 40th season, this rustic resort with 14 housekeeping cottages is on the lakeshore about four miles north of town. The one and two-bedroom cottages have kitchens, fireplaces, shower baths and tiny porches. The cottages are lined up along a road down a hill to the waterfront, where there are rental boats and a recreation hall with television and games. Longtime owners Herb and Anne Vinnicombe also rent a contemporary three-bedroom house with panoramic deck overlooking the lake for $950 a week. Lodges, weekly $410 (one-bedroom) to $530 (two-bedroom); daily rates available off-season; open mid-May to mid-October.

Museum Lodges, Route 109, Star Route 1, Wolfeboro 03894. (603) 569-1551. Ten little brown housekeeping cottages with fireplaces, picnic tables and grills are scattered down a steep slope to the lake, half a mile north of the Libby Museum (we're not sure what connection, if any, the lodges have with the museum, since the brochure refers to the museum as "Libbey"). Cottages have one or two bedrooms, some with twin or kingsize beds, fireplaces and full kitchens. Again the waterfront has a sandy beach, 60-foot sunbathing pier with diving board, boat rentals and a rec hall with games and TV. Lodges, weekly $365 (one-bedroom), $525 (two-bedroom); daily rates off-season; open late May to mid-October.

Lakeshore Terrace, Route 28 & 109, Box 18C, Wolfeboro 03894. (603) 569-1701. Three beaches and a boat basin along a point on Lake Wentworth are assets at this cottage colony. So are the rose garden and the well-kept garden and lawn facing one curved beach. Four of the eight cottages have housekeeping facilities. Nicest is the new Sandbox cottage with living room, kitchen-dining room, twin bedroom and deck. Doubles, $35 to $45; housekeeping units, $48 to $70 (usually rented by the week). Open mid-May to mid-October.

Wolfeboro Inn, 44 N. Main St., Box 215, Wolfeboro 03894, (603) 569-3016. This venerable inn, built in 1812, was under new ownership in 1986, and big plans were afoot for a rear addition with perhaps 40 more. General manager Sandy Taber, a Wolfeboro native who was food and beverage manager for eight years at the renowned Topnotch at Stowe, said the additions would be patterned after the Vermont resort. Already a new front entrance, a rear dining deck, a front parlor and all-around upgrading give indications of things to come. Upstairs on the second and third floors are 13 guest rooms, all with private baths (although some are in the hall). Rooms vary in size and shape, as is the case in older inns, but the wallpaper and furnishings are sprightly and up to date. Room rates include a full breakfast in the inn's good-looking restaurant, serving three meals daily (see Where to Eat). Doubles, $58 to $68. Open year-round.

The Lakeview Inn, North Main Street, Box 713, Wolfeboro 03894. (603) 569-1335. This establishment's name is a misnomer, for trees now block any lake view and it's more a motor lodge than an inn. Three of the 17 guest rooms are upstairs in the restored 200-year-old main house, known for a good restaurant and a striking fan doorway with bull's-eye glass. The rest are in a two-story air-conditioned motel annex with patios or balconies overlooking apple trees and a mountain. All have private baths, color TV, thick carpeting and towels, and four have kitchenettes. A continental breakfast is served to guests in the lounge. Doubles, $60 to $65; efficiencies, $67.50; three-day minimum. Open year-round.

The Tuc'Me Inn, 68 N. Main St., Wolfeboro 03894. (603) 569-5702. An early 1800s village house was acquired in 1985 by Pennsylvanians Tom and Ellen Quinn, who operate it as a B&B. A spacious living room has big sofas, TV and lots of books. Ellen serves full breakfasts of eggs, blueberry pancakes or "the chef's whim" in a pleasant dining room or outside on a porch that's usable late into the fall. Two of the six guest rooms in the rambling house have private baths. Two rooms have access to an upstairs screened porch, and two others share a sitting room with brown sectional and rocker and an old radio. Patterned sheets, colorful towels, frilly dust ruffles, gingham curtains and handmade quilts adorn the rooms. Ellen sells the quilts; 18 of them were snapped up in the first year. Doubles, $56 to $70. Open year-round.

Isaac Springfield House, Route 28 South, RFD 1, Wolfeboro 03894. (603) 569-3529. Located two miles south of town, this 1871 Victorian B&B has four bedrooms sharing two baths. The two front rooms have queensize brass beds and are furnished simply in early American decor. Two rear rooms are smaller and quieter, away from the road. Innkeepers Rose LeBlanc and Andrew Terragni offer a small parlor with books, piano and TV, and a large porch. They serve full breakfasts of eggs or pancakes at tables for two in the dining room. Doubles, $50. Open year-round.

Wentworth Winds, Route 28 & 109, Box 1810, Wolfeboro 03894. (603) 569-1700. Billed as a motel and recreational vehicle resort, the former Allen "A" resort is under new ownership. It has seen better days, or perhaps better days are yet to come. But it was the only place with a vacancy when we visited in August. Some of the 55 rooms have been renovated; ours in the rear faced a ramshackle lineup of green cabins and a dirt road that led to the beach, four tennis courts and who-knows-where. But they're trying: the restaurant in front has bargain meals (and dancing), four-season RV sites were under construction, and the 800-foot beach along Lake Wentworth is pleasant, if a bit spooky when deserted. Doubles, $55. Open year-round.

RENTALS. Private houses and cottages are available through individuals or local real-estate agents, including the Turners Inc., South Main Street, Wolfeboro, (603) 569-1442, and Yankee Pedlar Realtors, 8 Main St., Wolfeboro, (603) 569-1000.

Robie's Campgrounds, Route 109, Wolfeboro, (603) 569-9848 or 569-4354, offers campsites for tents and trailers on Lake Wentworth.

Seeing and Doing

Lake Winnipesaukee, obviously, is the main attraction here. Glacier-formed and spring fed, it is flanked by three mountain ranges and dotted by 274 inhabitable islands. The 26-mile-long lake, New Hampshire's largest and one of the busiest in New England, is more than 60 miles around. Wolfeboro Bay and environs are among the prettiest and quietest sections. Supposedly, more than 15,000 powerboats are registered on the lake, and you see far more of them than sailboats. As we dined by the water one night, we enjoyed the sounds and lights of motorboats after dark — a traditional lake effect we had forgotten after years of vacationing at the ocean.

On the Water

The best way to see this lake and its generally sheltered shoreline away from the road is by boat.

M/S Mount Washington, Weirs Beach, 366-5531. The hulk of this three-level excursion boat is far larger than you'd expect as it cruises ever so carefully up to the Wolfeboro town dock. On board, you're told that the ship was built in 1888 and traversed Lake Champlain from Burlington to Plattsburgh until 1940, when it was moved to Winnipesaukee to replace the original 1872 sidewheeler Mount Washington. In 1982, the ship was cut in half and lengthened to 283 feet, for a capacity of 1,250. The three-hour cruise covers 50 miles and visits Weirs Beach, Wolfeboro and either Center Harbor or Alton Bay, boarding and disembarking passengers at each stop. The narrated cruise takes you through "The Broads," twelve miles long and five miles wide, beneath the Ossipee, Sandwich and Squam mountain ranges on the north, the Belknap Mountain range on the south and the White Mountains in the distance to the northeast. Powerboats come up close to ride the wake; the ship seldom gets close to shore, though you do get a good view of the rocks known as Witches Island and the exclusive Governor's Island community that once housed the German Embassy prior to World War I. The sound of the ship's horn reverberates off the mountains as it prepares to dock at busy Weirs Beach, where most of the passengers board. Just before returning to Wolfeboro after a stop at Alton Bay, it crosses the longest section of the lake; you can see 20 miles up to Center Harbor, and across the bay to the lawns and buildings of Brewster Academy, which identify Wolfeboro from afar. If you time it right, you may get a seat in the Flagship Lounge, where two can lunch on a roast beef sandwich, turkey club and a beer each for $16, including tip. Cruise leaves Wolfeboro daily at 11, also 2:15 in summer; adults $10, children $5.

Blue Ghost, Town Dock, Wolfeboro. Six or eight passengers can join Betsy McKenzie on the U.S. mailboat as she delivers mail for residents to docks on 30 islands on eastern Lake Winnipesaukee. The 60-mile, three-hour cruise gets you up close to the shoreline. The boat leaves at 10:30 and 1:30 daily except Sunday and postal holidays. Adults $10, children $5. Reservations are required through Lakes Region Sports, 569-1114. The powerboat is also available for charter, sunset and foliage tours from early May to late October.

Queen of Winnipesaukee, Weirs Beach, 524-1911. Fifty passengers can ride this new 46-foot sloop under billowing sails. Captain Larry Tanner gives 90-minute sails two to five times daily in summer. Adults $8, children $6. Dinner, island lunch and moonlight cruises also are scheduled.

North Country Charters, Main Street, Wolfeboro, 569-2120. Scuba diving, snorkeling, sightseeing, happy hour — you name it, this 30-foot custom-built dive boat will get you there. Charter rates for up to 16 people range from $95 for a happy-hour cruise from 6 to 8 to $260 for a day cruise from 9 to 5. Sunday evening fireworks cruises to Weirs Beach from 6 to 11 are $165. Dive charters are a specialty. North Country also has lessons and rentals for windsurfing.

CANOEING. Along the lake's 183-mile shoreline are countless coves perfect for fishing, snorkeling and canoeing. The Carroll County Independent newspaper advises canoeists: "Hug the islands and shore for a delightful paddle on the largest lake in the state. Keep out of the Broads, where the wind and big boats will swamp a canoe, and don't chase the loons."

SWIMMING. Most lodging establishments have their own beaches. The public is welcome at **Brewster Beach**, a fine little strand off Clark Road, operated by the town and made availale by Brewster Academy. **Wentworth Beach** is a small sandy beach and park on Lake Wentworth off Route 109 between Wolfeboro and Sanbornville. Swimming and picnicking also are offered at **Wentworth State Park**, six miles east of Wolfeboro.

Other Attractions

RECREATION. Cate Park, a pleasant small waterfront park beside the town dock, is the site of concerts, dances and art shows throughout the summer; a highlight is the annual Artists in the Park arts and crafts fair in mid-August. **Back Bay Recreation Area** has a playground and four tennis courts which are lighted until 10 p.m. Golfers are welcome at the 18-hole **Kingswood Golf Club**, next to the Windrifter Resort off South Main Street.

Libby Museum, Route 109 North, Wolfeboro. (603) 569-1035. Across the road from the shore of Winnipesaukee stands the town-operated Libby Museum, started in 1912 by retired dentist Henry Forrest Libby to house his natural history collections. His original collection includes an alligator, a human skeleton, mummy hands, old surgeon's equipment and paintings from General Wolfe's campaigns, for whom Wolfeboro was named. Visitors have added to the museum, which now has three main exhibits: nearly 600 animals, birds, fish and reptiles in its natural history collection, and 350 Indian artifacts, among them two dugout canoes found in Rust Pond. More than 800 pieces in the Newcomb collection form the basis of Northern New England country living artifacts, which include farm machinery, household items, pottery and Shaker implements. The museum shows free National Geographic nature films Wednesdays at 7 in summer. The museum's annual August cocktail fundraiser is said to be the social event of Wolfeboro's summer. Museum open Tuesday-Sunday 10 to 4 in summer; adults $1, children 50 cents.

Wolfeboro Americana Museums, South Main Street at Clark Road, Wolfeboro. Operated by the Wolfeboro Historical Society, this complex of three museums is worth a visit. The **Clark House** (1778), a Revolutionary farmhouse, was home to three generations of the family, which donated the house to the society in 1929. Everything in it is more or less original, according to our guide. That includes the first piano in Wolfeboro, an applewood four-poster bed, a dining room table from the Wentworth mansion, outstanding pewter, clocks and kitchenware. The **Pleasant Valley Schoolhouse** (circa 1805) contains old school paraphernalia plus a replica of the Wentworth mansion (it burned to the ground in 1820, and there's considerable debate over what it was like). A copy of the New York Herald reporting Lincoln's death is at the door. A replica of the 1862 **Monitor Engine Co. firehouse** was erected in 1981 to house an 1872 Amoskeag steam pumper donated by David Bowers of Wolfeboro, plus five pieces of apparatus, leather fire helmets and horse-drawn sleighs. Museums open 10 to 4:30 daily except Sunday, July through Labor Day, or by appointment. Donations accepted.

Hampshire Pewter Co., 9 Mill St., Wolfeboro, 569-4944. Free half-hour factory tours are conducted on the hour Monday-Friday from 10 to 3 in season at this pewter factory and showroom. Started in 1973 as a crafts shop, Hampshire Pewter has grown into a nationally known manufacturer of quality cast (rather than spun) pewter. Owners Andy and Jane Mulligan are proud that their firm has decorated New Hampshire's Christmas tree at the White House and say Vice President George Bush not only displays but uses his set of six wine goblets, a gift from Wolfeboro. You'll no doubt be impressed, as we were, by the variety of 125 items of handmade pewterware, from Christmas tree ornaments to lamp bases, bells and even a loon. Showroom open Monday-Saturday 9 to 5.

League of New Hampshire Craftsmen, Route 28, South Wolfeboro. The Schoolhouse Shop operated by the statewide league has two huge rooms with everything from handscreened notes to smocked dresses for little girls, stained glass, pottery and jewelry.

SHOPPING. Wolfeboro is a shopping area of quite good taste along its Main Street, the Wolfeboro Marketplace, the new Back Bay Shops and emerging Mill Street.

The **Marketplace** has two levels of shops in an attractive brick-walked complex that's nicely landscaped. **Christmas Presence, Cloud 9 Bed & Bath, the Wolfeboro Book Shop** and the **Irish Tweed Shop** are a few. At the **Cafe-Deli** here are several umbrellaed tables on a patio surrounded by tubs of flowers, where you may have breakfast or lunch. The Wolfeboro muffin, with bacon and havarti cheese, is $2.25; a chef's salad, $3.65. Sandwiches are in the $2 to $3 range, and the chocolate eclair cake is $2.50.

The **Camelot Book and Gift Shop** across the street sports a huge books and colorful nutcracker in front that really livens up the scene — the books, cheeses and gifts are worth a look. At **Cornish Hill Pottery** on Mill Street, stop in to see fine stoneware pottery, from lamps to tableware. Be sure to check out the delicious breads, croissants and pastries at **Bread & Roses Bakery**, just across the street from Hampshire Pewter.

Where to Eat

One local skeptic said the only really good restaurant around is the William Tell Inn on the south shore at West Alton. And a museum staffer said she and her associates go to the cafeteria at Huggins Hospital for the best and cheapest food in town. Wolfeboro has a growing number of serviceable restaurants, however.

Waterside Dining

The Oyster Club, Main Street, Wolfeboro. (603) 569-5534. Aw shucks — they were changing the name of Aw Shucks to the Oyster Club when we visited, as Rex Seley, owner of the acclaimed Woodshed restaurant in Moultonboro, planned to expand his new Oyster Club raw bar and grill concept around New England. Anyway, this is a casual place to eat by the water, outside on a deck beside all the boat action or inside in a raftered bar with a long kayak and stuffed animals overhead. The front dining room has paneled and glass dividers in Victorian style, with mooseheads, old skis and canoe paddles on the walls so you know this is New Hampshire rather than the Vineyard. For a waterside dinner we sampled six oysters ($4.50), served with enough hot sauce for 85 oysters and, alas, no crackers. Good salads with creamy dill dressings and a loaf of bread preceded our entrees of blackened swordfish and beer batter shrimp, accompanied by curly french fries. Entree prices run from $9.95 to $14.95. The Craftsbury Creek chardonnay ($12.95) was a good choice from the all-American wine list, one of New Hampshire's more interesting. Instead of the mocha mud pie and cheesecake, we indulged in a couple of liqueurs as we watched the lights of boats darting to and fro after dark. Lunch daily, 11:30 to 3; dinner, 5 to 10. Open year-round.

Back Bay Boat House, Bayside Village, Mill Street, Wolfeboro. (603) 569-2124. At the rear of a gray shingled contemporary structure, a breezy porch right over the waters of Front Bay has round glass and wood tables flanked by ice-cream parlor chairs. Adjacent is an elegant chandeliered dining room with brass wall sconces, ceiling fans and rattan-type chairs. It's unfortunate that to reach these appealing dining areas, you have to pass through a busy bar, and many apparently won't or don't. A fairly extensive menu offers something for every taste, from chicken fingers and potato skins to chicken breast and prime rib ($9.95 to $15.95), plus nine more entrees "for the more adventuresome" — among them, chicken moutarde, tournedos Rossini, veal hunter's style and charbroiled swordfish teriyaki. The lunch menu consists entirely of burgers and sandwiches, except for appetizers and, strangely, international coffees. The limited wine list, all imported, states not the vintner but the country of origin (valpolicella, Italy; beaujolais, France). Lunch daily, 11:30 to 2; dinner, 5 to 9 or 10; Sunday brunch. Open year-round.

Bailey's Dockside, Town Dock, Wolfeboro. (603) 569-3612. This established restaurant by the Mount Washington landing is not our kind of place, but it's very popular. The pine-paneled dining room with booths and paper mats was packed in late-afternoon with people enjoying sandwiches, salads, any number of ice cream concoctions and a few entrees like fried clams, fried scallops, fried shrimp (or combination thereof), fried haddock, fried chicken and baked ham steak ($4.95 to $9.95), most served with cole slaw, tomato on crisp lettuce, rolls and butter. A take-out counter dispenses ice cream cones, 11 flavors for 80 cents to $1. Open daily, 9 to 9, mid-May to October.

Away from the Water

Lakeview Inn, 120 N. Main St., Wolfeboro. (603) 569-1335. The Lakeview is locally regarded as the town's best restaurant. It's country elegant with wallpaper of flower baskets, swagged curtains, crystal candlesticks and fresh flowers from the inn's garden. A friendly staff serves an appealing menu. Among starters are the chef's favorite Portuguese soup from her mother's treasured recipe, house pate, escargots en croute and artichokes gratinee ($2.95 to $5.95). Three to six nightly specials augment a rather wide-reaching list of entrees, priced from $10.95 for a single lamb chop to $15.95 for scampi alla carbonara, tournedos with snow crab legs and asparagus spears or filet mignon and shrimp. One diner reported she had the best swordfish ever here. Other options include Cajun blackened filet of sole, lobster thermidor, haddock topped with langostinos en papillote and filet boursin Wellington. Salad, homemade breads and vegetables come with. Desserts might be peach cobbler, chocolate mint torte, ice cream puff or hot Indian pudding. Light fare is served in the adjacent lounge, and there's entertainment nightly except Tuesday. Dinner, 5:30 to 10.

Wolfeboro Inn, 44 N. Main St., Wolfeboro. (603) 569-3016. The main side entrance takes you right into the large dining room. Ahead, wagon-wheel walls divide the room from a long wooden bar and lounge where a zesty cheese spread and crackers await imbibers. The contemporary-style dining room is on three levels, the upper level airy with cathedral ceiling and looking onto a new rear deck used for breakfast and lunch, with a glimpse of the lake beyond. Nicely spaced tables are dressed with fine china, linen and vases of freesia. Culinary Institute-trained chef Perrin Long worked in Nantucket, New Orleans and San Francisco before arriving here in 1986. His regular menu is augmented by interesting specials, perhaps a pate of veal, duck livers and chanterelles found by a guest in the woods; a black bean soup with fresh cilantro; blackened swordfish, or beef Wellington with a Madeira sauce. Entrees range from $9.95 for fettuccine carbonara to $14.95 for filet mignon with fresh sage and roquefort cheese. Filet of sole stuffed with a duxelles of tarragon, spinach, mushrooms and boursin cheese, panneed veal, sauteed sweetbreads and blackened duckling are other choices. Desserts by Inez, the baker here for 26 years, include a choice of 60 in the $15 to $18 price range alone. Lunch daily except Sunday; dinner nightly, 5:30 to 9 or 10.

The Cider Press, 10 Middleton Road, Wolfeboro. (603) 569-2028. There's a cider press at the door, and apple trees are out back. Hence the name for this rustic restaurant which started as an inn and has expanded several times under the aegis of Robert and Denise Earle, a young local couple who met while working at the Wolfeboro Inn and have acquired a substantial local following. They now seat 165 diners by candlelight in three country-pretty barnwood rooms and a lounge where there are two chairs in front of a three-sided open hearth which, Denise says with a laugh, "people fight over" in winter. 'Baby back ribs and golden fried shrimp are the specialty,' says Bob Earle, who oversees the cooking; listed on the menu as "the odd couple," they combine for $10.25. The dozen straightforward entrees run from $6.95 for chicken parmesan to $14.95 for steak and shrimp. Halibut Oscar and steak au poivre might be blackboard specials. Most of the desserts are baked on premises, and the tortes and ice cream crepes are the downfall of many. A few house wines are offered; the spiked hot apple cider is more popular. Dinner, 5:30 to 9, Sunday to 8; closed Monday. Open year-round.

East of Suez, Route 28 South, Wolfeboro, (603) 569-1648. Although Charles Powell and his family, some from the Philippines, have operated this restaurant for the past 18 summers, it seems to be almost a secret except for devotees of Asian food. Housed in a building that once was part of a camp, it looks the part — an almost rickety house with a big side porch, set in a field south of Wolfeboro. Decor is spare oriental, with paper globe lamps. The kitchen is huge, and out of it comes a parade of interesting food: $16 will buy you a full dinner of appetizer, soup, salad, entree and dessert, but you may also order a la carte. To start, poached scallops with crab in miso sauce and the Philippine egg rolls known as lumpia are standouts, but you could also choose a tempura of shrimp and vegetables, pork and chicken steamed with soy, oyster and brown bean sauce, or a highly seasoned tikka chicken. At our visit, the day's soup was clam chowder, almost like a New England version, but curiously spicy. The salad bar, except for one oriental dressing, is ordinary and we wonder why they bother. About ten entrees are listed and all sound so good that it's hard to choose. The tempura included a wide variety of vegetables and many large shrimp; the batter was perfect. And the Szechuan shrimp and cashews, stir-fried with snow peas, was great. Korean steak, pancit (a noodle, shrimp and pork dish) and steamed chicken with oyster sauce are other choices. Everything is served with shiny crackers that come sizzling from a pan. For dessert, the "sans rival," a cashew and meringue torte, is a worthy ending. Portions are enormous. Don't eat lunch the day you come, and do bring your own wine. Dinner, 6 to 9:30, June through foliage; closed Monday. No credit cards. BYOB.

The Bittersweet, Route 28 and Allen Road, Wolfeboro. (603) 569-3636. The major choice here, say new co-owners Bill and Joyce Sweeney, is whether to eat upstairs or down. Upstairs, the rambling yellow farmhouse east of town has an airy barnlike dining room with white linen and mismatched chandeliers, pinkish painted wood chairs and farm artifacts on the walls, and a fairly innovative menu. The new downstairs, formerly the lounge, is family-rustic and priced for value-seekers. Kids love the salad bar in an old Coke machine; some of the makings are in pails and a ringer washing machine, and the rolls are stashed in wash buckets. Chef and co-owner Garry Warren does interesting things like French onion soup laced with vermouth or almond shrimp flamed with amaretto for appetizers ($2.75 to $6.50). Norwegian salmon with a seafood mousse in puff pastry or lamb and cider pie for entrees ($10.95 to $16.50). The nightly specials are unusual for the area: grouper en papillote, haddock topped with julienned vegetables, halibut with dill butter and bouillabaisse. The downstairs menu offers snacky appetizers, salads, sandwiches and entrees ($4.95 to $7.95) like seafood crepes, liver and onions, veal parmigiana, chimichanga and steak. The nightly buffet dinner here is $9.95. Desserts are homemade, and the wine list, though small, is serviceable with house offerings by the liter. Lunch daily, noon to 2; dinner, 5:30 to 9:30; Sunday brunch buffet, 11 to 2. Open May to mid-October.

Casual Choices

The Strawberry Patch, 30 N. Main St., Wolfeboro. (603) 569-1212. "Have a berry nice day," says the menu at this breakfast and lunch place where you might be strawberried into oblivion. The decor is all strawberries, from stenciling on chairs to toddler's bibs. So is most of the menu, from strawberry omelet (no thanks) to strawberry pancakes (sensational) and strawberry waffles, piled with strawberries and whipped cream, all in the $3 to $4 range. At breakfast, our orange juice came in a glass covered with strawberries and served with a sliced strawberry. Lunch brings homemade soups, sandwiches, salads and quiche. Upstairs is a gift shop where, you guessed it, everything is in a strawberry motif. Breakfast, 7:30 to 11; lunch 11 to 2:30; Sunday, breakfast only, 7:30 to 12:30.

The Cracked Egg, Clarke Plaza, Route 28, Wolfeboro. (603) 569-4758. An ad for 25-cent coffee attracted us to this out-of-the-way spot in a shopping center east of town. It turns out it was 25 cents per cup, which, for those who like plenty of refills, is not much of a bargain. But everything else is: two eggs, home fries and toast for $1.40, the french toast for $1.60 and the "onezy," of one egg, one bacon, one sausage and one pancake for $1.65. Three melt-in-your-mouth raspberry pancakes with piping hot syrup were a treat for $2.60, as was a cheese and tomato omelet for $2.35. Sandwiches for lunch include barbecued beef, $1.95. The room consists of a long rectangular pine counter ending in the kitchen, three tables for four and one high chair. Breakfast and lunch, Monday-Saturday 5:30 a.m. to 1:30 p.m., Sunday 6:30 to 12:30.

Que Tacos! North Main Street, (603) 569-5377. This is not what you might expect to find in downtown Wolfeboro — a tiny hole-in-the-wall decorated with murals of Mexico and a serape or two. A couple of tables are out in front but most people take out. Nachos, labeled naked, naughty or obscene, are $3.25 to $4.95; tacos are $1.60 each. Burritos, chili and taco salad round out the menu and the que combo, a plate of two tacos, two burritos and naked nachos is $9.95. The relish bar includes mild and hot salsa. Open from 11:30 to 10 or so in summer.

FOR MORE INFORMATION: Wolfeboro Chamber of Commerce, Box 547, Wolfeboro, N.H. 03894. (603) 569-2200.

The New Hampshire Seacoast

Seagulls are fed from excursion boat along New Hampshire Seacoast.

When our forebears were parceling out seacoast, New Hampshire was shortchanged. Since then, she has been striving mightily to make up for it — cramming more visitors into the 18-mile coastline area than it seemingly can accommodate.

Tucked between rockbound Maine and the North Shore of Massachusetts, this is no shy, back-roads tourist area. The New Hampshire Seacost — Hampton Beach in particular — fairly shouts its wares to the world. Motels and summer cottages are crammed cheek by jowl into the downtown area of Hampton Beach, next door to frozen custard, hot dog and fried dough stands (spelled "doe" here). The sandy beach across the street (metered parking means you can stay only for a couple of hours without coughing up more quarters) has had as many as 100,000 visitors on a sunny weekend day in summer, they say. They're probably right.

Bikinis abound. You see them not only on the beach, but on the streets of town, and are one more reason bumper-to-bumper traffic (as early as 10:30 on a hot Saturday morning) comes to a standstill. Tops are down on convertibles, cans of soda and beer are in hand, and car radios blare out hard rock.

They are all ages, but teenagers seem to predominate. There is much to attract them: nightly headliners at the Casino like the Bangles, the Monkees

269

and Eddie Rabbitt; a diet of pizza, Pepsi and popcorn; the chance to meet each other. They hang out, chewing gum, playing arcade games, lying on the beach, shouting from cars.

So what are you, oh sensitive reader, to do here? Go north, for one thing. Get out of Hampton Beach. Drive north on Route 1A, enjoying the vistas of ocean, the thinning crowds. Think about whether you should feel grateful for the State of New Hampshire's "protecting" the coastal area, giving you one state beach after another. When you finally reach Odiorne Point State Park, take the short walk to its rocky shore, perch yourself atop a boulder at sea's edge, and feel the cool breeze on your cheeks. Have a picnic at one of the thoughtfully placed picnic tables. Walk a nature trail, perhaps with a naturalist to show you the way.

Or take a cruise to the Isles of Shoals from Rye Harbor. Listen to the captain narrate the history of these rocky outcroppings, just a little more than five nautical miles offshore. Or go out on a whale watch in the evening, snagging a sunset at the same time.

Eat seafood. Ride bikes. Rent rowboats. Go deep-sea fishing.

Get a tan. Everyone else has one; you may as well. Visit a lovely seaside rose garden. Attend an interdenominational church service in a tiny chapel by the sea.

Take a drive. The back roads, Routes 101C and 101D in particular, offer a surprising contrast to the commercialism of 1A. Here there are horse farms and stone fences, Colonial houses with manicured lawns and quiet, country New Hampshire, far from the madding crowd. Go into sophisticated Portsmouth, tucked just inland on the Piscataqua River, for a good meal or to shop.

Finally, you may discover what brought all of these people in the first place: an exceptionally accessible waterfront. Turn your back to the mobs and gaze out to sea. Taste the salt in the air, feel the breeze on your face. There are redeeming values to be found here.

Getting There

The Seacoast Area is located off Interstate 95 between Salisbury, Mass., and Kittery, Me. Exit 2 brings you into Hampton Beach; from there follow Route 1A north into North Hampton and Rye.

Where to Stay

The New Hampshire Seacoast region lacks fine country inns and charming bed-and-breakfast facilities. For the latter, stay in Portsmouth or the single B&B in the area. Most accommodations come in the form of motels; some of these are downright tacky, but good ones can be found. Two-night minimum stays are the norm.

Rock Ledge Manor, 1413 Ocean Blvd., Route 1A, Rye 03870. (603) 431-1413. Overlooking the ocean from a commanding knoll, the big white house with its sweeping porch offers a view of the sea from each of four attractive guest rooms. Jan and Norman Marineau have operated this B&B for five years and take pride in their complete breakfasts, which may include a fruit compote, home fries, sausages, even a crepe flambe. Croquet on the lawn is a popular diversion for guests. Norm has been restoring the property so you may have to put up with a pile of sand or a sawhorse in the yard, but the location and the warmth of the welcome will likely make up for this. Two rooms have private baths; the other two have half-baths and share a shower. Doubles, $50 and $55. Open year-round.

Rye Harbor Motel, Route 1A, Rye. (603) 964-9054. This smallish, two-story motel looks out on a tidal marsh and is conveniently situated near picturesque Rye Harbor. The 15 air-conditioned rooms are simply furnished but include color TVs and in-room coffee. Second-floor rooms have balconies. Next door to the motel is the **Pilot House** (see Where to Eat), run by the same management. Doubles, $75. Open April-October.

Sea Side Village Motel, Route 1A, North Hampton 03862. (603) 964-8204. This white-trimmed, gray-clapboard complex advertises itself as "the only motel in New Hampshire with direct access to the beach without crossing a street." Its own private beach is just one attraction. The flowers, the lounge furniture on the porch that connects the two main buildings, and the picnic tables out back are others. Although it has been around many years (one guest, we're told, has been returning for 40), most rooms have been redecorated recently. Oceanfront motel unit, $65 nightly ($320 weekly); oceanfront housekeeping unit, $350 weekly; cottage for six, $650 weekly; apartment for four or five, $475 weekly. Open spring to fall.

Town and Beach Motel, 663 Lafayette Road, Route 1, Hampton 03842. (603) 926-2742. Neither in the center of town nor at the beach, but rather on the highway, this motel still is attractive, once you get past the asphalt parking area. Family-owned and operated since 1971, it has 33 air-conditioned units with color TV; there are efficiency units as well. The lobby, with its light pine and traditional furnishings, is inviting, as is a small coffee shop open in the morning. A heated outdoor swimming pool is an asset and it's only a five-minute drive to the beach. Doubles, $56. Open year-round.

Hampton Village Resort, 660 Lafayette Road, Route 1, Hampton. (603) 926-6775. New in 1986, this resort motel has no view (it is on commercial Route 1) but has a pool, sauna and jacuzzis. All rooms have refrigerators, cable TVs and phones, and there's a game and exercise room. Complimentary coffee and donuts are served in the morning. Doubles, $62; suites with jacuzzis, $120. Open year-round.

Hampton Beach Regal Inn, 162 Ashworth Ave., Route 1A, Hampton Beach 03842. (603) 926-7758. Now we wouldn't want to stay in Hampton Beach, but if we did, this is a place we'd select. Sue and Gary Methot own and operate this 32-unit motel, as well as the Hampton Village Resort, and they run a tight ship. There's a restaurant next door for breakfast or for drinks at happy hour. Doubles, $81 to $98. Open year-round.

Hampton Harbor Motel, 210 Ashworth Ave., Hampton Beach. (603) 926-4432. Ring buoys hang from the balconies at this weathered gray, two-story motel at the end of the main drag in congested Hampton Beach. All 23 rooms have refrigerators and color TVs; some are efficiencies. The location is close to the Hampton River for deep-sea fishing boats and convenient to the beach as well. Doubles, $64 to $69, $74 with kitchenette. Open late spring-September.

RENTALS. It's easy to rent a cottage in Hampton Beach, a little harder to find one north of there, but there are still many available. The range is wide, from $450 a week and up. In Hampton Beach, both Monument Real Estate,

43 Brown Ave., 926-5312, and Preston Real Estate, 63 Ocean Blvd., 924-2604, handle many.

Seeing and Doing

The New Hampshire Seacoast prides itself on its activity level. Among the offerings:

On or Beside the Water

BEACHES. New Hampshire owns most of the sand, and offers it in the form of state beaches to residents and visitors. There are six ocean beaches, reaching from **Hampton Beach** in the south to **Wallis Sands**, a smallish state beach in the town of Rye. All charge admission, usually $1 per person, or have metered parking. Of the six, **North Hampton State Beach**, with 1,200 feet of beach and parking for 108 cars, is considered one of the best. There are also **Jenness State Beach**, the Rye Picnic Area with a view of Rye Harbor (but no beach per se) and, in Hampton Beach, both **Hampton North Beach** and **Hampton Beach State Park**, which together stretch nearly three miles along the ocean's edge. Most have restrooms and changing facilities.

Odiorne Point State Park, located at the northernmost point of the Seacoast area on Route 1A — before you drive around to the island of New Castle — is great for walking and exploring, although its rocky shore is not conducive to swimming. Picnic tables are located near the water's edge, offering a fine view of the ocean and the boating activity offshore. The 137-acre site features a system of pathways popular with joggers and nature-lovers through the northern two-thirds of the park. On a steamy July day we went to Odiorne and noticed the dramatic difference in temperatures. When you arrive, check in at the Nature Center to get park maps and information on naturalists' walks. Cars are charged $1 per passenger.

DEEP-SEA FISHING. The Atlantic Fishing Fleet, Rye Harbor. (603) 964-5220. The Atlantic Queen and the Atlantic Sun leave from Rye Harbor for half-day and full-day deep-sea fishing trips. Full-day trips go out for cod, pollock, haddock, cusk and ocean catfish. Half-dayers are fishing for mackerel, bluefish and bottomfish like flounder. All-day trips leave daily at 7; adults $25, children $15. Half-day fishing is offered from 8 to noon or 1 to 5; adults $12, children $8. Day and night bluefishing trips are also available.

Al Gauron Fishing Parties, 1 Ocean Blvd., Hampton Beach, offers several trips on its three boats, the Northern Star, Whitestar and Starfish, leaving from the State Pier. All-day fishing trips ($23 for adults, $15 for children), half-day trips ($12 and $8) and night bluefish trips ($15 and $12) are offered.

Smith & Gilmore, 3-A Ocean Blvd., Hampton Beach, 926-3503, provides deep-sea fishing from the State Pier, with standard full-day, half-day and night bluefishing. A special event is the Wednesday Fishing Marathon, which offers 12 hours of fishing (5 a.m. to 5 p.m.) at $35 per person, one or two Wednesdays per month, May-September.

WHALE-WATCHING. All three deep-sea fishing companies have evening whale watches, usually from 5 to 9. Al Gauron's boat goes out Thursday and Friday at 5:30, Saturday and Sunday at 5; Smith & Gilmore offers whale-watching trips Tuesdays, Thursdays, Fridays and Saturdays at 5; the Atlantic Fishing Fleet takes whale-watchers out on Wednesdays, Fridays and Saturdays at 5.

New England Whale Watch Inc., Hilton's Fishing Parties Dock, 54 Merrimack St., Newburyport, Mass., (617) 465-7165. This outfit located just south of Hampton Beach offers daily whale-watching trips throughout the summer and weekend trips in the fall. Five-hour trips leave at 8; adults $18, children $15. A second trip is offered Friday-Sunday 2 to 7.

Rent a rowboat from Smith & Gilmore to fish or explore Hampton Harbor. Boats take four people and cost $3 per hour.

New Hampshire Seacoast Cruises, Rye Harbor, 964-5545 or 382-6743. A variety of sightseeing trips leave from its dock at Rye Harbor. The daily **Isles of Shoals** trips at 11 and 2 take passengers through the fascinating nine-island group about five miles off the coast. You'll learn some of the history of these barren islands, where marine research projects and a religious retreat center are now located, as is the White Island Lighthouse. Bags of bread are passed out for feeding the seagulls on the way home. Adults $7, children $4.

A 90-minute evening cruise is offered Thursday-Saturday at 5 during the summer. When we took it, the captain's choice was the Isles of Shoals; other times he cruises to Portsmouth Harbor or down to Hampton Beach. Adults $7, children $4.

One-hour lobster trips are offered Monday, Wednesday and Friday at 9. These are short cruises to offshore ledges where one or two lobster traps are hauled aboard the boat and procedures and equipment discussed. Adults $4, children $3. A two-hour cruise is offered Wednesday at 11 to Portsmouth Harbor, north of Rye. The fascinating harbor with its tugboats and activity is fun to see from the water. Adults $7, children $4.

Other Attractions

Fuller Gardens, Willow Avenue, North Hampton (200 yards north of the junction of Routes 101D and 1A), 964-5414. This seaside gem is a two-acre garden on the estate of the late Gov. Alvan T. Fuller. Designed in the Colonial-Revival style in the 1920s by Arthur Shurtleff, with additions in the 1930s by the Olmstead Brothers, the gardens have extensive plantings of roses accentuated by statuary and fountains. In fact, as the All-American Rose Display Garden for New Hampshire, Fuller Gardens offer visitors views of the very latest rose selections. The perennial borders provide color throughout the seasons and from the gardens one can glimpse the ocean. Open daily 10 to 6, mid-May through October. Adults $1.50, children 75 cents.

Union Chapel, a tiny interdenominational house of worship — and favored site for weddings — has a popular 11 a.m. service on summer Sundays. It is located on Willow Avenue across from Fuller Gardens.

The Hampton Playhouse, 357 Winnacunnet Road (Route 101E), Hampton, (603) 926-3073. This is one of the old faithfuls on the strawhat circuit. For nearly 40 years the Hampton Playhouse has been brightening the summer theater life of residents and visitors alike. A recent season saw productions of "A Chorus Line," "Evita" and "Brighton Beach Memoirs," among others. Shows run for two weeks. Monday-Saturday at 8:40, Sunday matinee at 2:30. Tickets, $12 to $15.

Seabrook Greyhound Park, Route 107, Seabrook, 474-3065. Races are run Monday-Saturday evenings at 7:45 and Tuesday, Thursday and Saturday afternoons at 12:30. General admission is $1; admission to the Kennel Club (with restaurant and cocktail lounge), $1.50.

Other Sports. Exeter Country Club, Jady Hill, Exeter, 778-8080, has a public nine-hole golf course. The Exeter Recreation Park on Hampton Road (Route 101C), Exeter, 778-0591, has 10 outdoor tennis courts as well as an outdoor pool and fitness trail.

SCENIC DRIVES. Route 1A should be traveled the entire length, preferably from south to north, to take advantage of increasingly lovely ocean views. Routes 101C and 101D are country roads which take you past Colonial homes, horse pastures and New England stone walls. A drive to **Portsmouth** is definitely in order. Follow Route 1 north to New Castle and then into this exciting small city. Good restaurants, shopping and sightseeing (especially the many historic homes and **Strawbery Banke,** a recreation of an historic section of the city) are to be found in abundance.

SHOPPING. All the T-shirts you can imagine (saying things you can't believe) are available in Hampton Beach. For real clothes, try the factory outlets on Route 1. The best one seems to be the **North Hampton Factory Outlet** with a Dress Barn, Hit or Miss, Bass shoe outlet, Van Heusen store and Kids' Port, where there are good values on children's clothes. The **Rye Fox Boutique** in the center of Rye has upscale clothes. Liquor is a bargain in New Hampshire; the State Liquor Store is at the junction of Routes 1 and 101D.

Our favorite store in this area is **The Aloha Shop** on Route 1A in Rye. For 25 years this shop has been selling an outstanding variety of Hawaiian garb. Antiques shops abound on Route 1. The **North Hampton Antiques Center** in North Hampton is a group of antiques dealers under one roof. **H.G. Webber Antiques** also looks especially nice.

Where to Eat

Carriage House, Route 1A, Rye. (603) 964-8251. Distant ocean views (the restaurant is located across the highway from the coast) add to the many pleasures at what is for many their favorite Seacoast restaurant. Paul Mackey is the young, energetic owner who oversees a first-class operation. The decor is simple and homey. Wooden tables and booths are varnished and shiny, the tables set with deep green homespun placemats; varnished wooden wainscoting on the lower half of the walls, bare wood floors and overhead paddle fans add an old-fashioned touch. Lamps are Victorian in style, with soft, frosted petal-shaped shades at each window booth; candles flicker on inside tables, and soft classical music is heard in the background. Dinners begin with a plate of raw vegetables and a tasty, mild curry dip. The menu is pleasantly varied, but not too large. Among the choices are veal Normandy ($13.95), steak au poivre ($14.25), calves liver ($11.45) and Nantucket pie (with lots of seafood), $14.35. There's also a curry dish of the day. Our orders of veal piccata with mushrooms and broiled swordfish were nicely presented and extremely good, especially the thick and moist swordfish. Dinner includes a nicely arranged mixed salad (hearts of lettuce, onions, carrot sticks, celery, and tomato slices), with a bowl of homemade croutons, almonds and real bacon bits for sprinkling on top. A second choice is an excellent tomato and onion salad: at least two whole tomatoes are cut into chunks and served with onions in an oil-based dressing tasting of oregano, basil and garlic, all sprinkled generously with parmesan cheese. Crusty warm rolls, a crock of butter, and attentiveness to the refilling of water glasses pleased us. With the entrees were served rice or a baked potato and a summer squash. Desserts are wonderful: hot fudge ice cream croissant ($3.25); a hot Tuaca sundae Normandie ($3.45), which is apples sauteed with cinnamon, brown sugar and nutmeg, flamed with Tuaca, a butterscotch liqueur, and topped with ice cream, and an exceptional carrot cake which we split for $2.50. Key lime pie and cheesecakes were also offered. Dinner nightly and Sunday brunch. Open year-round.

Saunders at Rye Harbor, Harbor Road, Rye. (603) 964-6466. The outdoor deck with tables beneath yellow and white striped umbrellas and a view of the activity in Rye Harbor is the place to have lunch or dinner on a nice day. Luncheon includes a lobster club sandwich ($8.25), a half pineapple stuffed with shrimp ($6.95), seafood and asparagus salad ($7.95) and a quiche and salad special ($5.95). You also can get lobster stew ($7.95), boiled lobster ($10.95) or a hearty bowl of fish chowder served with rolls and salad ($4.95). Dinner includes a 1 1/4-pound lobster for $14.95, lobster Newburg ($17.95) and lobster saute ($16.95). Specialties also include haddock pizziola (baked with mushrooms and tomatoes and topped with melted cheddar cheese) at $13.95, and a pasta dish of the day for $12.95. Lunch daily, noon to 3:30; dinner 5 to 10.

The Pilot House, Route 1A, Rye Harbor. (603) 964-8080. Several levels of dining mean a view of the tidal marshes and ocean beyond for most tables at this popular restaurant. A steam-powered dory in the front window sets the nautical mood and seafood is predominant on the menu. The atmosphere is jaunty and casual, with bare wood tables and red napkins, and a jazz pianist offers background music Wednesday through Saturday evenings. Shrimp Zenovia with a mustard wine sauce and shrimp scampi Jamaican with rum, butter and garlic sauce (both $14.95), baked scallops and a scallop kabob (both $13.95) are among entrees. You also may order seafood-stuffed chicken, filet mignon or steak. Dinner nightly, 5 to 10; Sunday brunch.

Widow Fletcher's Tavern, 401 Lafayette Road (Route 1), Hampton. (603) 926-8800. Dark wide-plank pine floors, wooden tables and booths, and British posters on the walls give this well-regarded restaurant the feeling of an English pub. Appetizers set the mood: Baker Street Elite is a baked potato topped with red onion, Canadian bacon, sour cream and cheddar cheese ($3.25) and Piccadilly Squares are English sausages and pepperoni layered in Greek pastry with cheese and a tomato basil sauce ($3.75). An English-cut prime rib at $9.95 leads the list of entrees, but there is also a large selection of seafood dishes including baked scallops ($8.95); scallops, haddock and sole cooked in lemon, butter and white wine ($8.50) and baked scrod ($7.25). Lighter specialties are the Devonshire grill (grilled ham, cheddar and apple on grilled wheat bread) for $3.75 and the Oxford Club (sliced chicken, bacon, tomato and lettuce with avocado dressing or mayonnaise), $3.95. A special English dish is shepherd's pie ($4.95). Also offered are bangers and mash: English sausages on a bed of mashed potatoes with gravy and applesauce ($3.95). Open daily from 11 to 11; Sunday brunch (with every item at $4.95), 11 to 3. Open year-round except Mondays in winter.

Galley Hatch, 325 Lafayette Road, Hampton. (603) 926-6152. Kay and Michael Tinios (and now son John) opened this highway spot in 1970 and have expanded five times until they can accommodate 250 diners and another 150 in two cocktail lounges. It's obviously popular, particularly because all of the elaborate desserts are baked on the premises; a bakery counter at the front sells items to take home. Decor is simple: pine booths and tables with blue woven placemats and hanging plants. The large menu offers incredible variety. Items range from crab cioppino ($13.50) to baked halibut ($10.50) and baked stuffed shrimp ($12.95). Several Syrian choices include a Syrian salad at $4.25, and a "Seriously Syrian" specialty of sauteed fresh vegetables, feta and melted cheddar on Syrian bread for $5.25. The menu is served daily from 11 year-round except Thanksgiving and Christmas.

The Pirate's Cove, 1200 Ocean Blvd. (Route 1A), Rye. (603) 436-8733. Next to Wallis Sands Beach, this nautical spot describes itself as "the only fine seafood restaurant on the beach" and the views of the ocean are among the area's best. Nets, fish and all sorts of nautical memorabilia are draped around; nautical blue tablecloths and captain's chairs add to the decor. Every item on the menu has a cutesy name like "Captain Cook" (twin boiled lobsters, $17.95); "Buccaneer" (baked stuffed haddock, $6.45) and the "Treasure Chest" (a lobster with fried clams, $12.95). The location makes this well regarded by the beach crowd. Open daily from 11:30.

Joseph's Rye on the Rocks, 1505 Ocean Blvd. (Route 1A), Rye. (603) 436-4400. Highly recommended, this restaurant was closed for several weeks during the summer of 1986 due to a fire, and we were unable to review it.

For breakfast, try **Drake's** on Route 1A in Rye where, on Sundays, you can pick up a Boston Globe and read it while you indulge. The High Tide Special is an English muffin with egg, cheese and ham for $2.25. Good homemade muffins are 60 cents each, and omelets and egg sandwiches also are available. Breakfast from 6 to noon weekends, to 11 weekdays; lunch also served.

FOR MORE INFORMATION: Seacoast Council on Tourism, Box 4669M, Portsmouth, N.H. 03801. (603) 436-7678.

276

Ogunquit Beach is a haven for swimmers and sunbathers.

Ogunquit, Me.

The Indians who were its first summer visitors called it Ogunquit, meaning "beautiful place by the sea."

Today's visitor, who is merely passing through or trying to find a room at peak periods, calls it crowded. Thousands of tourists pack its streets and motels, its beaches and Perkins Cove, to the point where the Chamber of Commerce runs a trolley service to shuttle people back and forth.

Which is fine, for you can't really get to know — much less enjoy — Ogunquit's myriad water pleasures by car. You're better off abandoning ship, as it were, and setting off by trolley or foot.

Ogunquit is a walking town, a paradise for people on parade. They walk hand-in-hand on the Marginal Way, tote shopping bags along the Shore Road, and wear bikinis and not much else along Beach Street.

The broad white-sand beach, three miles long and flanked by dunes, is one of New England's finest. Perkins Cove, studded with fishing and pleasure boats coming and going, has fostered artists and intrigued tourists for decades. The Marginal Way, a paved footpath atop the cliffs, links Perkins Cove with the beach area.

Ogunquit offers boat cruises, art galleries, fine shops, one of the original summer playhouses, and an inordinate number of restaurants and places to stay. In summer, many lodging establishments require four-night or week-long stays, which is fine for the regulars who make this their vacation base. The passing overnighter may not find it to his liking, but the off-season is less crowded and, in many ways, just as or even more appealing.

Even in season, however, you can get away — away from the wall-to-wall development and crowds, and into relative seclusion along the Marginal Way, at a hidden beach or on the rockbound cliffs, or at one of the special places to stay beside the water. More than most Maine resorts, Ogunquit is a water place, and it makes the most of it.

Getting There

Ogunquit is located about 20 miles north of the New Hampshire border, 35 miles south of Portland. Take the York or Wells exits from the Maine Turnpike and follow Route 1 to Ogunquit.

Where to Stay

The number of choices is staggering and the variety of lodging places in Ogunquit increases annually. Some would say that Ogunquit is overbuilt. Sheila Stone, manager of the Beachmere, reports that "every time I see another one going up, I don't believe it — and yet we're filled constantly." Four-night and seven-night minimum reservations are the rule in summer, although shorter stays are granted on the spot, based upon availability. Route 1 has numerous motels and the Shore Road some established inns. We think the more interesting are less well known and often hidden along the waterfront.

Waterside Plus

The Sparhawk Resort, Shore Road, Box 936, Ogunquit 03907. (207) 646-5562. This is Ogunquit's top of the line and conveys it, from its large swimming pool and tennis court to its new Ireland House suites and the deluxe penthouse apartment being fashioned from the old Barbara Dean restaurant. "Happily filled," said the sign outside the office when we visited — a nice touch, as is the complimentary continental breakfast served in the old Sparhawk Hall, site of the first Sparhawk hotel built more than 80 years ago. The hotel has gradually been replaced by the main Sparhawk motel units (perched right on the seawall overlooking the ocean), the fancier Ireland House suites and the new inn-style suites and apartments in the Barbara Dean, of which 53 Sparhawk units has a private deck, two Queen Anne-style chairs facing the window, two beds and a small refrigerator in the dressing area. The 20 suites in the two-story Ireland House are angled, so each has an ocean view from its private, nicely furnished patio or balcony; the upstairs front corner is most desirable (and you can take a discreet look at its outside from the Marginal Way, which cuts across the property). Each has two queen beds and a separate sitting area with sofa and two chairs. Doubles, $90 to $100; suites, $100 to $110. Open mid-April to late October.

The Beachmere, Beachmere Lane, Box 2340, Ogunquit 03907. (207) 646-2021. The village's grandest location, without doubt, is occupied by the Beachmere, an inn since the 1920s with 25 efficiency units and apartments, plus a 16-room motel built in 1970. They rest on the outermost bluff along the Marginal Way, facing Ogunquit Beach and with the open ocean on the east. It's easy to see why most guests are repeat; the lawns and private decks provide magnificent views away from the hubbub. The 16 inn rooms are purposely kept old-fashioned ("our guests think the exposed sprinkler system pipes are quaint," manager Sheila Stone says). But each is up-to-date with an outdoor deck, color TV, modern bath and kitchenette. We liked Room 6 with a deck, an enclosed porch-sitting room, a turreted alcove with a dining table, two twin beds and a corner kitchenette with combination sink and stove. Rooms vary in size and price, and 16 motel units have ocean views. Summer rates are weekly, $399 to $1,120. Open mid-April to early December.

The Aspinquid, Beach Steet, Ogunquit 03907. (207) 646-7072. Within easy walking distance but off by itself from the hustle and bustle is this lodge-style resort, all quite contemporary and with a condo look not often seen hereabouts (the complex was fashioned gradually from the old Aspinquid Hotel). Sixty-one spacious rooms are offered by owner Lily Andrews and her two sons in three buildings separated by a heated pool and a lighted tennis court; all have private balconies with water views. The carpeted rooms have television, phones and good-looking rattan-wood furnishings. Doubles, $74 to $82 in motel, $87 to $150 in efficiencies and apartments. Open year-round.

Cliff House, Shore Road, Box 2274, Ogunquit 03907. (207) 646-5124. For the ultimate in seclusion, you can't beat the historic Cliff House. One of the grand old resorts, this is spectacularly located amid 75 forested acres of oceanfront headland atop Bald Head Cliff. Greatly altered from its original 1872 status as the area's first hotel, the main inn houses a spacious dining room serving three meals daily, a modern lounge with a nifty outdoor patio above the ocean, a Victorian library and a lobby. Each of the 105 motel-style rooms has an oceanfront balcony, two double beds, color TV and phones. Although most guests opt for MAP, you can get simply a room. Doubles, $86 to $95, EP. Open April-November.

Terrace By the Sea, 11 Wharf Lane, Ogunquit 03907. (207) 646-3232. Deluxe motel units with loft sitting areas, a four-unit efficiency motel overlooking the ocean and 15 inn rooms with private baths are attractions at this relatively secluded and well-landscaped establishment, all spiffed up in recent years by new owners Donna and Gordon Lewis and Daryl and John Bullard, who also are involved in Sea Chambers Motor Lodge and the Grey Gull restaurant. From the lineup of lawn chairs or from the picture window in the green and rose living room of the main Colonial-style inn you can see the ocean. Most rooms are air-conditioned and have color TV and phones; a complimentary continental breakfast is served, and there's a small angular pool. Doubles, $62 to $110. Open late April to late October. No credit cards.

The Inn at Fieldstone, Hoyts Lane Extension, Box 364, Ogunquit 03907. (207) 646-4998. Built at the turn of the century as one of Ogunquit's first summer residences, this magnificent structure stands on expansive lawns at water's edge. The Mediterranean-style entry looks through a window in a stone wall onto an inviting deck beside the tidal river. To the side is a fabulous living room with leaded windows, TV, wicker groupings and an intricate jigsaw puzzle nearing completion. Beyond is a glorious windowed sunporch, full of a wide range of the day's newspapers as well as deck chairs at tables for continental breakfast of homemade muffins or breads. The 11 guest rooms have window seats, all with a water view, and private baths, angled ceilings and leaded windows; some are efficiencies with cooking facilities. Co-owner Newell Perkins is one of the locally ubiquitous Perkins family. Doubles, $60 to $90. Open May-October.

Sea Chambers Motor Lodge, 37 Shore Road, Ogunquit 03907. (207) 646-9311. It beats us why this L-shaped 43-room motel isn't angled toward the ocean like Sparhawk or the Beachmere; most of its rooms (and those of many motels we're not including) face sideways toward the parking lot and a smallish pool. Second-floor rooms have the best views, and six deluxe rooms and a few ocean-end units face the water. Rooms are comfortable with two beds, two chairs, a large dressing area with sink and an architecturally ingenious, partly open wall above the beds that creates cross-ventilation from all the windows. Doubles including continental breakfast, $84 to $104. Open April-October. No credit cards.

Also on the Water

Riverside Motel, Shore Road, Box 2244, Ogunquit 03907. (207) 646-2741. For years as we wandered through Perkins Cove, we always envied those who were sitting on their balconies at the motel on the far shore. The Riverside is booked far ahead, as you might imagine, and has a three-night minimum, but we lucked into a one-nighter and reveled in the location, a foot-drawbridge walk across the cove to the action (actually, it's quiet at night — the real action is in the beach area). Each of the 37 units has a private balcony with cove view; rooms are standard motel, but the large white towels are extra thick and the shady grounds spacious and attractive. The renovated 1874 House on the property has four guest rooms with private baths and television (doubles, $50). A free continental breakfast of donuts, juice and coffee is set out in the Colonial lobby; you can eat at a table for two inside or at a small round picnic table on a rear deck outside. A few stuffed animals here and there grace the lobby's plush sectionals and sofas. Doubles, $68 to $80. Open May-October.

Ogunquit River Plantation, Route 1, Box 1876, Ogunquit 03907. (207) 646-9611. Best of the increasing numbers of motels lining Route 1 is this new motor inn with 80 units on four floors, each overlooking the Ogunquit River, a tidal lagoon and part of the Rachel Carson Wildlife Preserve. The better rooms are those with private decks or patios and mesh outdoor furniture on the first, second and fourth levels (the third or front ground level compensates for lack of a deck with parking at the door). The spacious rooms are gracefully decorated in shades of rose, sand and blue with Louis XV furnishings; a vanity with toiletries and a refrigerator are in the dressing area outside the bath and, praise be, real hangers are in the closets. Coffee and donuts are served in a small breakfast room, and a small oval pool is flanked by a jacuzzi. Operated by the beachfront Norseman Motor Inn with "a lifestyle akin to what you'd expect from the name," this may be Ogunquit's best value. Doubles, $80. Open April to late October.

Marginal Way House and Motel, Wharf Lane, Ogunquit 03907. (207) 646-8801. Try for one of the six motel units perched above the water at this superbly located place where the lawns slope toward ocean's edge. Twenty-nine rooms are offered in the motel, in the venerable main hotel or in efficiency apartments in three other buildings. Rooms are individually decorated in New England style in the main inn and each has private bath, television and a refrigerator. Doubles, $88 in motel, $53 to $82 in hotel, $686 to $805 weekly for efficiencies. Open late April to mid-October.

The Beachcrest Inn & Restaurant, 16 Beach St., Box 673, Ogunquit 03907. (207) 646-2156. The Andrews family of the Aspinquid took over the Beachcrest Inn just up the street in 1986, upgraded its dining and had plans for improved accommodations. The turreted inn has nine rooms, seven with private baths, and two efficiencies. Lily Andrews showed us "a typical New England room" with twin beds spaced far apart, and wicker furniture, curtains and spreads all in white; the most coveted room is in the third-floor tower. A third-floor common room with TV leads to a deck with a great view. Doubles, $60 to $65; efficiencies, $75. Open year-round.

Norseman Motor Inn, Beach Street, Box 896, Ogunquit 03907. (207) 646-7024. For those who want to be near the beach, you can't get closer than the beachfront units of this 94-room establishment in four buildings also facing dunes, river and street. A typical room has knotty pine walls, shower, phone, color TV, two ordinary chairs and good reading lamps. A long balcony overlooks the beach; the third floor is best for sunning. Doubles, $65 to $98. Open April-October.

The Dunes, Dunes Road off Route 1, Box 917, Ogunquit 03907. (207) 646-2612. One of Ogunquit's more secluded and quiet places is this 12-acre refuge with 17 motel and 19 kitchenette units. The motel description is a bit of a misnomer, since only six units are in a small two-story motel; the rest are nice-looking white cottages with one or two bedrooms, kitchen, bath, TV, screened porch and all but one with a fireplace. Youngsters like the sandy beach, rowboats, pool, shuffleboard court and croquet layout. Popular with families, the cottages are rented for a minimum of two weeks in summer. Doubles, motel, $48 to $75; cottages, $62 to $85. Open mid-May to mid-October.

RENTALS. A number of houses, cottages and apartments are available. Beachmere Apartments, Beachmere Lane, Box 2340, (207) 646-2021, rents 40 efficiencies along the Marginal Way overlooking the main beach. Realtors who help with rentals include the Jean E. Knapp Agency, Route 1 at School Street, (207) 646-4546; Perkins Real Estate, 7 Beach St., (207) 646-5535, and Shore Realty, 67 Shore Road, (207) 646-9345.

Seeing and Doing

THE BEACHES. From a point where the Ogunquit River meets the sea, **Ogunquit Beach** stretches three miles north to the neighboring town of Moody. The beach is broad and the surf strong. The Ogunquit River separates it from the mainland, and provides a back beach for more sheltered swimming. The point where the tidal river enters the ocean is good for families; on the ocean side you have surf swimming and, on the river side, calmer water for children. The beach is free, but parking is $6. Less crowded is the **Footbridge Beach** section of Ogunquit Beach, reached by a footbridge from Ocean Street (you can wade across the river at low tide) or from Ocean Avenue in Moody. Other beaches are **Littlefields, River Side** and **Onito** along the Marginal Way.

BOAT CRUISES. Finestkind, Barnacle Billy's Dock, Perkins Cove, 646-5227. With three boats, Finestkind runs the most tours, daily from July 1 through Labor Day and a limited schedule in spring and fall. Most in demand are the 50-minute lobstering trips to see lobster traps hauled amid a running commentary on lobstering. They leave hourly from 9 to 3; adults $5, children $3. A scenic 90-minute cruise heads south seven miles along the coast to Nubble Lighthouse in York every two hours from 10 to 6:30; adults

$7.50, children $5.50. Finestkind also has five cocktail cruises from 4 to 8:30, a starlight cruise at 9:30 and a breakfast-lobstering cruise at 9.

Also at Perkins Cove, the **Judy Marie II**, 646-3776, runs seal-watching trips to Boone Island from 4 to 7; tickets $10. **Syd's Sailing**, 646-3524, offers private charters from Perkins Cove on the new sloop Jon B; free sailing lessons are included.

DEEP-SEA FISHING. The Town Dock at Perkins Cove is the launching site for at least three deep-sea fishing boats available for individuals and charters. One is the **Judy Marie II** (see above). Capt. Tim Tower runs a 40-foot boat, the **Bunny Clark**, 646-5575, a full day for $30 each and a half day for $20. Capt. Michael Boutet limits his groups to 12 on the **Ruth Bee II**, 646-4074. Capt. Ken Young gives half-day trips for $20 on the **Ugly Anne**, 646-7202. The fishing is mostly bottom fishing for cod, haddock, pollack, hake, cusk, wolffish and occasionally bluefish and tuna.

The Marginal Way. We never tire of walking the Marginal Way, a mile-long paved footpath along the rockbound cliffs beside the sea. It starts inauspiciously enough as a narrow path heading toward the ocean beside the Sparhawk Resort. Then you climb to a point, which affords a glorious view of Ogunquit Beach, and turn to go gently up and down along the ocean to Perkins Cove. Memorial benches provide resting spots along the way; the rocks and what locally are called "the little beaches" offer seclusion or fun for young and old alike. Arches of trees frame views of the sea; the surf pounds into a crevice at one point, and you can admire the wildflowers and private homes all around. This is the easiest way to savor the majestic Ogunquit waterfront. A leisurely walk takes 45 minutes; you can retrace your steps for a different perspective, or return past the shops and galleries along Shore Road (keep an eye out for the old cemetery full of Perkins gravestones). Or take the trolley (25 cents), four of which run every 10 minutes between the beach and Perkins Cove with stops in downtown and side trips to major motels and inns.

Ogunquit Playhouse, Route 1, Ogunquit. (207(646-5511. Billed as America's foremost summer theater, this started in a Shore Road garage as a workshop for aspiring actors and actresses. Now the graceful white barn structure on the southern edge of town is the stage for top Broadway shows and strawhat talent. Its 54th season in 1986 featured "Jesus Christ Superstar," "A Chorus Line" and "The King and I" among seven plays and musicals running from June 23 through Labor Day. Performances are Monday-Saturday at 8:40; matinees Wednesday and Thursday at 2:45. All tickets are $13 for plays, $14 for musicals.

ART GALLERIES. Ogunquit and especially Perkins Cove have been a mecca for artists since the late 19th century, and the galleries along Shore Road are known for quality fine art. The **Museum of Art of Ogunquit**, Shore Road, shows contemporary American paintings and sculpture daily in summer; free. Artists from across the country exhibit at the **Ogunquit Art Center**, Hoyt's Lane. The Art Galleries of Ogunquit brochure has a map and details on 12 galleries. The **Shore Road Gallery**, the **John Bartok Studio**, the **Ted Jaslow Gallery** and the **Barn Gallery** are among the more notable.

SHOPPING. It seems as if everyone is shopping in Ogunquit, especially along Shore Road. The shops get more esoteric as you turn into Perkins

Cove. One of the best is the **Country Shop**, with kitchenware, colorful glassware and jewelry; we liked a nifty tray bearing a seagull. The **Whistling Oyster Gift Shops** (at the restaurant and downtown) have an interesting selection of fine gifts. Farther along in the cove is **Kid 2 Stuff**, where a teddy bear blowing bubbles out front attracts passersby; **Creative Hands**, and the **Cove Bookstore**.

Where to Eat

Many knowledgeable Ogunquit diners consider the two best restaurants currently to be just across the town line in York and Moody. Although restaurants abound in town and along Route 1, we concentrate on those near the water.

Fine Dining

Cape Neddick Inn, Route 1 at 1A, Cape Neddick. (207) 363-2899. Almost everyone's favorite for innovative cuisine is this combination restaurant and art gallery south of town in York. Though not on the water, the setting is artistic and the food creative. The dining room on two levels has Windsor chairs at well spaced tables covered with beige cloths, mismatched china, rose napkins and cobalt blue glasses. Potted palms, fancy screens, flowers in vases, paintings and sculptures give the feeling of dining in a gallery. The limited menu changes every six weeks and is the kind in which every item appeals, from the Indian beef curry or sliced chicken sauteed with pecan pesto for $14 to lobster aioli or chateaubriand with broiled brie and almonds in roasted garlic sauce for $20. Start with goose liver and veal pate or scallops anisette; be sure to save room, as the menu urges, for one of Glenn Gobeille's delicious desserts. The wine list is appealing and fairly priced. Dinner nightly in summer, 6 to 9; closed Mondays and Tuesdays off-season; Sunday brunch.

The Grey Gull at Moody Point, 321 Webhannet Drive, Wells. (207) 646-5701. New owners including Donna and Gordon Lewis of the Terrace in Ogunquit and chef Roberta Pomeroy from Ogunquit's Clay Hill Farm have upgraded this old favorite by the ocean in Moody. Inside the front entrance of the weathered shingled building is a sitting room with a piano and a comfortable, small cocktail lounge. The rest of the totally renovated main floor also is elegant with cane and chrome chairs, oriental rugs and paintings in a couple of dining rooms. The sought-after tables have water views across the road. Robbie Pomeroy's menu emphasizes fresh seafood (pecan-broiled haddock, Maine shrimp pie), but you can get pepper-coated roast tenderloin with a brandy mushroom sauce, chicken piccata or a veal chop with grilled veal sausage ($10 to $16). Black and white mousse is popular among desserts, and the wine list offers good values. Upstairs, five rustic guest rooms share two baths (doubles, $52). Breakfast, 8 to 11; dinner, 5:30 to 9. Open mid-May to mid-October.

Hurricane, Oarwood Lane, Perkins Cove. (207) 646-6348. New in 1986 was this trendy "seafood bar and broiler," owned by the people who run the Horsefeathers restaurant chain (Portland and North Conway). Two small summery rooms are beside the ocean; most appealing is the enclosed but breezy porch. The mood is Caribbean by day, formal and candlelit by night. Jazz was played quietly in the background at dinner as we munched on complimentary marinated peppers, served in a jar on every table. The halibut with pecan sauce was missing the advertised coriander, but the seafood primavera was superb. The changing menu ranges from three-peppercorn chicken ($11.25) to pate-smeared filet mignon ($15.50); Cajun touches, herbs and spices abound. Most of the wines are $10 to $15, and the fresh fruit trifle is a great dessert. We regretted that a place so serious about food did not accept reservations, and that one could wait hours for a window table. Lunch, 11:30 to 3; dinner, 5:30 to 10:30; in-between and late-night menu.

The Whistling Oyster, Perkins Cove. (207) 646-9521. A more glamorous setting taking full advantage of its water view could scarcely be imagined. Rebuilt in contemporary splendor following a 1976 fire, this is one of Maine's oldest (1907) and best-known restaurants, and its well-heeled patrons are dressed to the nines. The airy, cathedral-ceilinged structure has dining on two levels so that everyone can see the cove goings-on as well as everyone else. The fare is expensive and both lunch and dinner menus are grouped under "first plate" for appetizers, "second plate" for soup or salad, and "principal plate" for entrees. Oysters on the half shell and the chef's pate are a whopping $6.95 and $6.50, respectively, and soup of the day is $4.25. Desserts, all $4.75, could be a black bing cherry sundae or vanilla fudge ice cream cake. Dinner entrees start at $12.50 for pasta with fresh vegetables and rise to $19.95 for roast duckling with calvados butter sauce or filet of beef with candied shallots. At lunch, the omelet of the day is $7.95 and soup and a sandwich, $8.95; fresh fish of the day is $14.95. Hey, big spender! The extensive wine list is on the pricey side. Most find the food and atmosphere worth it, although we certainly were taken aback by a $61 bill for two for Sunday brunch a few years ago. Lunch, noon to 1:30; dinner, 6 to 9:30 or 10; dress code. Closed Monday and Tuesday in winter.

Laura W. Tanner House, Shore and Pine Hill Roads, Perkins Cove. (207) 646-5400. The 1874 Tanner House has been grandly restored and furnished with Hitchcock chairs, white-over-beige linens and a small screened porch. Although it seats up to 120, all is serene as guests dine on fresh seafood like grey sole, Laura Tanner's crabmeat, shrimp and lobster pie in a brandy sauce and California cioppino or tournedos forestiere and prime rib, $9.95 to $14.95. On Sunday, the brunch buffet and the evening seafood and prime rib buffet for $10.95 are jammed. A ship's model is behind the piano bar. Dinner, 5:30 to 9:30. Open mid-May to mid-October.

Cove Garden, Shore Road, Ogunquit. (207) 646-4497. The green roof atop this eccentric-looking pagoda on a hill reflects its beginnings as a teahouse. It also boasts the best view of Perkins Cove and the sea from its windows and deck across lovely rock gardens. A tree grows in the middle of the restaurant; it's lighted at night, and has shelves with wines on display. The lattice ceiling and interesting art add to the setting for the chef-owner's northern Italian cuisine. The limited menu (three appetizers, four pastas and five entrees) is reasonably priced — $6.95 for mussels marinara to $12.95 for veal piccata. Dinner nightly, 6 to 10.

The Beachcrest Restaurant, Beach Street, Ogunquit. (207) 646-2156. Chef Bob Campbell took over the dining room with the arrival of the An-drews family in 1986. The new owners added a small porch for outdoor dining to the restaurant, which is nicely done up in blue linens with local art on the walls. The continental menu is supplemented by nightly specials, perhaps scallops saute, lobster fra diavolo, lobster meat tossed with linguini, veal with artichokes and cognac or tournedos with cognac and mushrooms ($9.95 to $15.95). Lobster gratinee is a chef's specialty, and the fresh fruit puff pastry and chocolate fudge fantasy are favored desserts. Breakfast daily, 6:30 to 11; dinner, 5:30 to 10. Open year-round.

Away from the Water

Jonathan's, 2 Bourne Lane, Ogunquit. (207) 646-4777. Everyone loves Jonathan's with its crazy red sign and a houseful of rooms, all different and intriguingly decorated in blue and white. One room has pictures of flowers; the outdoor breakfast area has blue and white umbrellas. Jonathan West's decade-old establishment is whimsical and chef Steven Komacki's wide-ranging menu appeals, from jaeger schnitzel ($9.50) to veal and lobster bearnaise ($16.50). Grilled tuna might be his nightly special and a raspberry colada the bartender's special. Jazz is presented nightly, and the place is favored for after-theater snacks and desserts (it's right around the corner from the Ogunquit Playhouse). Huevos rancheros is a popular breakfast offering; another is — would you believe? — champagne and boiled lobster with muffins, $19.50 for two. Breakfast and dinner daily. Open year-round.

Clay Hill Farm, Agamenticus Road, Ogunquit. (207) 646-2272. "You've found it," declares the sign near what surely must be the end of a winding rural road. Built in 1780, the rambling white house with black awnings is elegant and formal, right out to the deck with umbrellas and a gazebo. Although the chef and some staff departed in 1986 for the Grey Gull, the restaurant retained its menu and popularity. Crab-stuffed mushrooms and smoked trout pate are favorite starters, and the dozen entrees run from $12.95 for chicken mornay to $16.95 for seafood imperial. Entrees in this traditional establishment include baked potato with sour cream and chives, vegetable and rolls. Dinner nightly, 5:30 to 10. Open mid-February through December.

Black Swan Tavern, Route 1 North, Ogunquit. (207) 646-4811. Although the decor is pretty, the food is what really appeals in this long, beamed-ceilinged room with lavender walls and old etched-glass fixtures beyond the piano lounge. Shrimp Diane Cajun style, veal Boheme, roast duckling and mixed grill are among the offerings ($9.95 to $16.95). Chef Jim McAllister's lobster bisque is renowned, as are his changing sauces, and key lime pie is one of his favorite desserts. Dinner nightly, piano from 8:30 to 12:30.

The Common Victualler, Route 1 North, Ogunquit. (207) 646-8209. The food is also foremost at this rustic place with a dark paneled dining room, green paper mats over gold linen and vases of fresh flowers in the bottom of a house surrounded by lovely gardens. The menu is interesting and, for Ogunquit, cheap. Dinners run from $7.95 for pasta primavera to $11.95 for shrimp scampi or steak Diane. Skewered swordfish with a coriander-lime marinade on rice and breast of chicken stuffed with chicken mousse with artichoke-onion sauce are among the tempting choices. Breakfast, 8 to 11; dinner, 5:30 to 10; lounge from 4.

Gypsy Sweethearts Restaurant, 18 Shore Road, Ogunquit. (207) 646-7021. Breakfasts are the main attraction in this old house with an upstairs lounge in the heart of town. Try the scrambled eggs with cream cheese and fine herbs ($2.10) or the Mexican eggs with salsa and cheddar cheese ($3.65). Or get anything from cinnamon toast to eggs florentine. Seafood is featured at dinner, priced from $10.50 for sole meuniere with pine nuts to $13.95 for filet mignon with bearnaise sauce. Breakfast daily, 7:30 to noon; dinner, 5:30 to 10.

Casual and by the Water

Jackie's Too, Perkins Cove. (207) 646-5177. An outgrowth of her original breakfast restaurant on Shore Road, this is the inspiration of Jackie Bevins, who converted an old fish market into a contemporary restaurant with smashing oceanside decks. The surf laps at the shore as you sit on either the canopied or open-air decks; the dark green and white color scheme is striking. The all-day menu includes sandwiches, salads and seafood, plus steak au poivre, smothered chicken and scampi over linguini (dinner entrees, $8.50 to $12.95). As we savored the ocean setting, we enjoyed a hearty lunch of a lobster roll with potato salad and a chicken taco salad, preceded by a Coors Lite and a peach daiquiri topped with a piece of melon and a dollop of whipped cream. Open daily from 11:30.

Blue Water Inn, Beach Street, Ogunquit. (207) 646-5559. A glorious, L-shaped open porch with canopy looking onto the Ogunquit River is colorful in pinks and greens; an old boat for cocktails is moored beside. With a setting like this, who cares if the food is microwaved? There's something for everyone from salads to baked ham, lasagna, fresh seafood and lobster served five ways. Dinners range from $8.95 to $13.95. The bar and lounge in blues, peaches and yellows with stuffed parrots on perches is quite charming, but we'd settle for the porch anytime. Upstairs are seven serviceable guest rooms, three with private bath, for bed and breakfast (doubles, $52 to $67). Lunch and dinner daily.

Barnacle Billy's, Perkins Cove. (207) 646-5575. This is an institution, what with its quaint setting along Perkins Cove and a casual approach whereby you place your order as you enter, take a number, find a table (outside by the water if you can, although many seem to prefer the inside) and then dig in. Lobster is the main attraction; the lobster roll for $6.35 and a crab roll for $4.75, washed down with a couple of beers, made a pleasant lunch. You can feast on steamed clams, barbecued chicken, hamburgers or homemade blueberry pie, on premises or for takeout. Open from 11 to 10 daily, May-October.

Lobster Shack, Perkins Cove. (207) 646-2941. Lobsters, clams and chowder have been dispensed from this rustic place near the end of the cove for nearly 40 years. You feel as if you're beside the ocean at oilcloth-covered picnic tables, even if you can't really see the water. Lobster was going for $6.95 when we visited, a lobster roll was $6.25 and a hot dog, $1.25. Beer and wines are available. Open daily.

FOR MORE INFORMATION: Ogunquit Chamber of Commerce, Box 2289, Ogunquit, Me. 03907, (207) 646-2939. Information Bureau is on Route 1 just south of the center of town, (207) 646-5533.

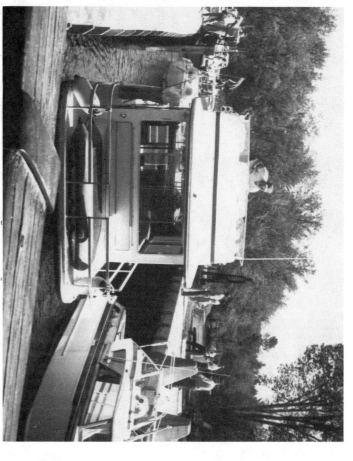

Boats wait to pass through hand-operated Songo Lock into Sebago Lake.

Sebago/Long Lakes Region, Me.

Maine's waterfront is more than the Atlantic. Its inland lakes beckon as well, offering low-key, outdoor vacations — often at bargain prices. While the coastal visitors are apt to be an inn and hotel crowd, a gift-buying, sightseeing and antiquing crowd, visitors to the Maine lakes are often hardy hunters and fishermen, boaters, campers who want to get away from it all, and families who are looking for a vacation on a shoestring.

The Sebago/Long Lakes region is glad to oblige. The second largest of Maine's lakes (after Moosehead), Sebago is a crystal-clear, spring-fed lake that serves as the water supply for the city of Portland. Nearby are Long Lake, beautiful Highland Lake, and several other lakes and ponds known for fishing, swimming and boating.

The mountains of western Maine, which serve as foothills to next-door New Hampshire's giants, rise just northwest of the lakes region, presenting, on a clear day, an especially pleasing backdrop for the shimmering waters. Maine's famed pine trees add another dimension; they cluster near the lake-shores and along the roads. When you hike, it is often on a soft carpet of pine needles.

Sebago and Long Lake are busy; powerboats, parasailers, seaplanes, paddle boats, canoes, sailboats and swimmers all take to the water during the busy summer season. The Songo River, which ties Long Lake to Sebago, allows passage of boats through a hand-operated lock. Highland and Keoka are quieter but no less attractive; Moose Pond and several others deserve attention. Because the lakes offer such marvelous opportunities for recreation, private owners have snapped up much of the good shorefront property. The main routes (302 and 114 in particular) afford but brief glimpses of Sebago and public beaches are hard to find. Sebago Lake State Park is the happy exception: its supervised beach is long and lovely, and there are waterfront campsites as well.

Getting to know the area takes a little doing. There is no one central metropolis, but rather several small villages, ranging from commercial and not-very-pretty North Windham to charming, tiny Waterford. Naples is as central as any, and its causeway on the south shore of Long Lake hums with waterfront activity.

The Sebago-Long Lakes region is one in which the best restaurants, inns and resorts are rather distant from each other. Expect to spend time driving, for you will be rewarded when you do. An outstanding glass and ceramic museum awaits discovery on a hillside well off the main road in Sebago; the last operating lock of the Cumberland-Oxford County Canal is off the beaten path along the Songo River in Naples, and the splendid Shaker Museum at Sabbathday Lake is a half hour away, near Poland Spring. There are antiques and craft shops for those who want to browse.

The mood is mellow, so most visitors are happy to spend their time fishing, sunning, or paddling slowly across a lake in the waning hours of daylight. The season is short, beginning late in June and ending quite abruptly on Labor Day. But for the two summer months, these lakes of Maine are cool, welcome oases for those who want to take it easy.

Getting There

The Sebago/Long Lakes region starts about 15 miles northwest of Portland. From the Maine Turnpike (I-95) in Portland, head for Route 302 west, which goes through North Windham, Raymond, Casco and finally Naples. Naples is as centrally located between Sebago and Long Lake as you can be. On the causeway which stretches between the southern end of Long Lake and the Bay of Naples (from which the Songo River leads down to Sebago) are shops, restaurants, the dock for the Songo River Queen paddle-wheeler, places to rent boats, and the embarkation point for seaplane rides. From here you can travel to Bridgton or Waterford, pick up Route 114 to head down the western side of Sebago, or go into Naples.

Where to Stay

Among a variety of accommodations spread among the several lakes and villages, here are our choices.

Migis Lodge, off Route 302, Box 40, South Casco 04077. (207) 655-4524. Its spectacular 100-acre lakefront location, attentiveness to guests' comfort, and extra touches (such as an island cookout on its own offshore island weekly) make this 70-year-old lodge which has had only four owners our favorite spot on Sebago Lake. Tim and Joan Porta took over full innkeeping responsibilities from Tim's parents 15 years ago. Twenty-five fireplaced cottages clustered around the main lodge have great views of Sebago Lake. There's 1,600 feet of shorefront with a variety of waterfront activities: waterskiing lessons twice daily, sailboats, canoes and rowboats free for guest use, plus motorboats for a slight additional charge. There are three clay tennis courts, a shuffleboard court, three hiking trails and other low-key activities like ping-pong and bingo games. Cabin boys deliver wood and lay a fire in each cottage every afternoon, and guests can have their own cocktail hours — or join others on the flagstone porch of the main lodge. Cottages vary in size from one to three bedrooms; a few larger ones have two bathrooms. They are separated one from the next by low fences of stocked firewood. Spruce, Sunset and Stone's Throw are the closest to the water. Five of the seven guest rooms in the main lodge have private baths. This is one of the few remaining full American Plan resorts in New England, and meals in the lodge's rustic dining room overlooking the water become events in themselves (jackets are requested at dinner and children under 4 are provided their own supervised dinner hour). Menus change nightly but always offer a choice of five entrees (two of them lighter meals). A typical evening's choices are poached salmon with egg sauce, roast leg of lamb, sauteed veal and eggplant parmigiana, cold sliced roast beef with vegetables, and apple and cinnamon omelet. Three cookouts a week (Saturday lunch, Wednesday dinner, Sunday breakfast) as well as optional box lunches vary the meal routine. Cost per person ranges from $55 to $68 daily, AP; weekly minimums in summer, although last-minute cancellations may allow for a few days' stay. No credit cards. Open mid-June to mid-October.

Tarry-a-While Resort, Highland Lake, Bridgton 04009. (207) 647-2522. The Swiss influence of Hans and Barbara Jenni, innkeepers for more than 20 years, makes this special, and Highland Lake, to our taste, is the area's prettiest. Four chalets (most with four rooms and private baths), the Schloss, a large stone house a bit farther away, and the main Gasthaus with its old-world bedrooms, many of which share baths, offer accommodations for 65 to 70 guests at a time. The resort is located above the lake with good views; a road leads down to the secluded waterfront area. Here are picnic tables, a beach, lounge chairs and boats (rowboats and canoes are free; fees are charged for sailboats, windsurfers and waterskiing). A tennis court is next to the main lodge, where guests gather on the porch to enjoy the views and fresh air (it somehow seems particularly invigorating here). A Swiss chef operates the well-known dining room, the **Switzer Stubli**, where guests take breakfast and dinner as part of their MAP rate. The dining room is open to the public as well and is highly regarded in the area. Entrees range from $8.95 for the bratwurst with onions and brown sauce to $12.50 for sirloin steak served with a special herb butter. Also on the menu are fondue bourguignon (for two or more, $14.50 each), cheese fondue, chicken cordon bleu, goulash with spatzli and fresh rabbit in red wine sauce. Rates, $65 daily per person for private baths, $50 for shared baths, MAP. Open mid-June to Labor Day.

The Noble House, Highland Road, Box 86, Bridgton 04009. (207) 647-3733. Located off Route 302, this bed and breakfast is the most attractive of its type in the area. The fabulously furnished, gracious old house provides lake views from most rooms, plus a separate waterfront lot across the street with a dock and boats (and a hammock) for guests' use. You can cook your own supper on a barbecue grill and eat at a lakeside picnic table. Dick Starets had summered on Highland Lake as a young man and finally persuaded his family (wife Jane and three teenagers) to relocate year-round. They offer eight guest rooms (five in the house and three new rooms in an attached barn). The new rooms have wall-to-wall-carpeting, porches, water views and quilted floral bedspreads with matching draperies — Jane's decorative touch. Private baths come with the barn rooms, while those in the main house share. A two-room suite with bath on the top floor is good for families ($95 a night for four). Jane says an ''incredible'' full breakfast is served in a Victorian dining room or a larger fireplaced family room. She cooks, but the rest of the family pitches in also. When we visited the fare included juice, a fresh fruit salad, cheese strata and croissants. Another favorite is ''Noble House eggs'' — a fancy scrambled egg dish. Doubles, $55 to $65. Open year-round.

Sebago Lake Lodge, White's Bridge Road, North Windham 04062. (207) 892-2698. Right on the water with its own dock and a view of boat traffic from many rooms, this lodge scores points for location alone. Debra and Chip Lougee rescued two big old houses (the main lodge is more than 100 years old) from apartment-house status in 1985 and are working hard at making this a pleasant lakeside spot — certainly the best we've seen on the eastern shore of Sebago. Enthusiastic Chip has grand plans for ongoing restoration, but already the white buildings with blue shutters and colorful flowerboxes are inviting. By 1987 all 12 units were expected to have private baths, and Chip was even looking into the possibility of leasing a portion of the main floor out to a restaurant. ''It was one several years ago,'' he explained, ''and it would have great views of the lake.'' When we were there, a small area was set up in the stone-fireplaced main lobby for continental breakfast. A fairly steep hill leads down to the dock and there are picnic tables and barbecues for use by guests. Rowboats are free; motorboats may be rented by reservation. Doubles, $55 to $65. Open year-round.

Kedarburn Inn, Route 35, Box A-1, Waterford 04088. (207) 583-6182. This large white inn with green shutters and colorful flower gardens is not on the water (if you don't count Kedar Brook which runs through the property), but guests can use a private beach on nearby Keoka Lake. There's also a small public beach in the center of Waterford. Taken over in 1984 by Bill Ritchie, a horse trainer, and Edmund Rocheleau, a hair dresser, the inn is filled with marvelous furniture, much of it antique. Four of the seven guest rooms have private baths. A third-floor suite has a double-bedded bedroom, living room and private bath, and a bedroom with kingsize bed and private bath, recently refurbished, is favored by honeymooners. Rooms are comfortable and homey and have color-coordinated towels to boot. The guest living room has a color TV as well as comfortable chairs and sofas and shelves of books. Guests get a full breakfast in an especially pleasant breakfast room; specialties include blueberry pancakes, cheese omelets and homemade muffins. A separate dining room is highly rated and open to the public (see Where to Eat). Kedar Brook is within earshot of the outdoor patio. Doubles, $50 to $60. Open year-round.

Sloan's Round Table Lodge and Cottages, Route 114, North Sebago 04059. (207) 787-2780. Location makes this lodge and cottage community special. Just across the road from its own sandy beach, it's one of few places near Sebago Lake so accessible to the water. Several cottages have full lake views; for those that don't, a fireplaced main lodge has a screened porch where you can watch the lake activity. The beach is equipped with Adirondack chairs, and rowboats and outboard motors may be rented by the day or week. All cottages have nice rooms paneled in knotty pine, full kitchens and electric heat. In the lodge, three attached units with kitchens and one to four bedrooms have picture windows overlooking the lake. These plus 10 cottages clustered nearby rent by the week only in summer and on weekends in off-season. Weekly rentals, $250 to $320 for four in a cottage, $180 for two in a cottage, $320 for four in the lodge units. Doubles, $35 to $40 nightly in spring and fall. Open mid-May to mid-October.

Wind in Pines, Route 302, Box 65, Raymond 04071. (207) 655-4642. These 11 cottages with a clay tennis court and a 400-foot sandy beach are reserved year after year by the same families and we understand why. The location is superb and the owners, the Burnhams, are warm and friendly. In addition to shuffleboard, there's a waterfront area with canoes, rowboats and a float. The cottages flank a quiet, private road leading down to the water. They range in size from Hillcrest, which accommodates two, to Maineholm, which can take eight. Some are two-story and many have fireplaces. Weekly rentals, $250 for two to $475 for eight. Open June-September.

Goodwin's Lodge and Cottages, Route 114, North Sebago 04059. (207) 787-2101. Just up the road from the Round Table Lodge, this pleasant place operates as a bed-and-breakfast cottage colony. Some cottages have wood-burning stoves set up in the fireplaces for evening warmth. Their rustic interiors include one or two bedrooms, a living room and a bath; a few have kitchen facilities. Breakfast is served in the lodge's large dining room, which is open to the public for Sunday brunch. Guests use Nason's Beach down the road (free if you walk to it, and it's close enough to walk) or a separate beach area owned by the lodge about a quarter mile away. One-bedroom cottages, $48 nightly; two-bedroom cottages, $79. Open summer season only.

CAMPING. Many visitors like to camp in the lakes area. The **Bay of Naples Campground** off Route 114 in Naples. (207) 693-6429, is particularly favored and well-run. Its beach on the Bay of Naples (between Long and Sebago lakes) and waterfront campsites are assets. Rates are $12 daily or $75 weekly for tent sites with no hookups, $14 or $88 for sites with electricity and water, and $15 or $95 for full hookups.

K's Family Circle Campground on Trickey Pond has three sandy beaches on this pretty body of water, located off Route 114 in Naples. (207) 693-6881. There are 100 wooded and open sites with water and electric hookups. A laundromat and hot showers are available.

It's first come, first served at the camping area of **Sebago Lake State Park,** off Route 114 in Naples. Sites are $8 nightly for out-of-staters ($6 for Maine residents) and some are on the waterfront. Roll call is taken at 1 p.m., so that's the time to find out what's available. The area stays open until Oct. 15.

Seeing and Doing

The lakes offer a variety of activities to appeal to young and old.

On the Water

The Songo River Queen II, Route 302 at the Causeway, Naples, 693-6861. A replica of a Mississippi River stern paddle-wheeler, this boat gives the most popular sightseeing rides in the area. Two-and-a-half-hour narrated cruises are offered twice daily from Long Lake south through the Bay of Naples (also known as Brandy Pond), down the Songo River and through the Songo lock to Sebago Lake. Passage through the manually operated lock is a highlight of the trip; sightseers stand on the banks to watch the maneuvering of the boat. Trips leave daily at 10 and 4, July–Labor Day, and weekends at 10 in June and September. Adults $7, children $4.

The boat also offers one-hour cruises on scenic Long Lake, daily at 1, 2:30 and 7 in summer. Adults $4, children $3.

Point Sebago Princess, Route 302, Casco, 655-7891 or 655-3821. Two-hour cruises of Sebago Lake are offered daily in summer on an awning-topped, flat excursion vessel. Departure times are 1, 4 and 7, the last being billed as a sunset cruise. Adults $5, children $3.

A **U.S. Mail boat** takes passengers on its rounds daily except Sunday and postal holidays, leaving from the Naples Causeway, Route 302. The three-hour trip on Sebago Lake departs at 2; adults $6, children $3. A two-hour trip on Long Lake leaves at 10:30; adults $4, children $2.

Long Lake Marina at the Naples Causeway, 693-3159, rents paddle boats for $10 an hour and 24-foot party boats (which can accommodate up to 10) for $150 a day. **Mardon Marine** on Brandy Pond in Naples (off Route 302), 693-6264, charges $135 a day for pontoon party boats for groups and also rents canoes and rowboats for $25 per day.

Seaplane rides are offered by the Naples Flying Service at the west end of the Naples Causeway, 693-6591. Cost for the 25-mile, 12-minute ride is $15 per person, with a two-person minimum.

Parasailing. Leave from the Naples Causeway, 693-6861, for a 10-minute ride high above Long Lake. Cost, $25.

Sailboards for windsurfing may be rented from Sunny Breeze Sailboards on Naples Causeway, 693-3867. The hitch here is that the boards may not be used on Long Lake in the causeway area because of all the other traffic; you must transport them (or the store will transport them for you if you are renting for a full day) to a beach of your choice. Cost is $8 per hour; $20 a half day and $30 a day.

The **Sportshaus** on Main Street (Route 302) in the center of Bridgton, 647-5100, rents canoes and water skis. Canoes, rowboats and motor boats also may be rented from **Sebago Lake Camps** at Nason's Beach, Route 114, North Sebago.

BEACHES. These can be tough to find unless you are staying at a place with its own. The **Songo Beach** area in Sebago Lake State Park is a glorious long, sandy strand with lifeguards, backed by a shady picnic grove. There are rest rooms with changing areas and a good snack bar. Cost is $1 per person and on a hot summer Sunday the park sometimes closes by mid-morning because of its deserved popularity. There are also boat launch areas. **Nason's Beach** on Route 114 in North Sebago is a small sandy beach (parking, $4). The water seems exceptionally clear here.

The Lock, Sebago Lake State Park. The lock on the Songo River, which connects Brandy Pond (or the Bay of Naples) to Sebago Lake, is still hand-operated and fun to see. Take the road into the state park from Route 302 and follow the signs to the Songo Lock Camping Area. You'll see the lock just before the bridge that crosses the Songo River. Park and walk across a small footbridge to a grassy island next to the lock where you can watch the action, and even help to close or open the lock if you want. On the Saturday morning when we watched, a crowd of small pleasure boats was waiting to go downstream. The state attendant saw that as many boats as possible packed themselves into the lock, collected $3 round trip for each boat, and began to raise the water level slowly by opening one of the gates. After several minutes, when the level was equal to that of the downstream side of the lock, the gates were reversed, and the boats left. A similar scene was enacted in the opposite direction and was repeated all day.

Frye Island, located south of Route 302 in Sebago Lake, is mostly private. Its 260 homeowners aren't crazy about having sightseers wandering about, but there's a public golf course. Small ferries make the trip every half hour; cars pay $5 each way. Take the road to Point Sebago.

Other Attractions

The Jones Gallery of Glass and Ceramics, off Route 107, Sebago, (207) 787-3370. This is something of a sleeper if you're not knowledgeable about glass and ceramics. For those who are, it is a hallowed place. A rambling, dark green country house holds an exceptional collection of pottery and glassware from across the world. Founder and curator Dorothy-Lee Jones began to collect glass as a child; her collection forms the core of the museum. Exhibits change periodically, although there are many permanent displays as well. When we visited, a most informative special exhibit on Sandwich glass was being presented. Tutorial in nature, it sought to teach viewers the difference between true Sandwich glass and the many copies. The museum has an entire case of glass paperweights, including some from 20th century China and one from the Innsbruck Olympics in 1976. A large case is filled with Chinese export porcelain, including extravagantly decorated 18th century teapots; you'll also see a fine Tiffany glass collection. Even an old green Coke bottle finds its way into the displays.

The gallery shop here is special — all pieces are antiques and collectibles, priced from a few dollars to several hundred. You also can pick up books on glassware, or sit in a comfortable corner and peruse magazines and books on the topic. Outside is a lovely terrace with tables and chairs where you can sit and contemplate the scenic hillside setting. On several days, gallery tours ($5) are given at 2, followed by coffee and tea. Open Monday-Saturday 9:30 to 5, Sunday 1 to 5, May to mid-November. Adults $2.50, children 50 cents.

Antiquing is big in the area. Some 20 shops are listed in the Bridgton environs, most of them off Route 302. The Mansion House in Bridgton seems particularly nice. While most might not have the tony sophistication of the seacoast areas, they are fine for browsing — and buying. Emphasis on Maine along Main Street in Bridgton offers a good collection of handcrafts made by New England craftspeople.

Where to Eat

The Epicurean Inn, Route 302, Naples, (207) 693-3839. New to the lake scene in 1986 and immediately popular (after a Portland newspaper critic gave it four stars, it was virtually impossible to get a reservation on short notice), this green-shuttered, white inn fills a vital niche. Owners Patti and Scott Sparks and Paul Charpentier, who were allied in restaurant ventures in Newburyport, Mass., stress exceptional service and unusual touches with classic French cuisine. Paul is the chef; Scott whips up breads and desserts (his specialty is the chocolate bread and chocolate butter served each table at the start of a meal), and Patti manages the 30-seat restaurant. She also oversees the three upstairs guest suites with private bathrooms, all decorated attractively in the Victorian mode. Rooms are named for famous chefs, and overnight guests are treated to a gargantuan breakfast (doubles are in the $70 range). Back downstairs, Brandy Pond is seen in the distance from the dining porch, a cozy back room with lacy gathered curtains, wood paneling and hanging geraniums. The middle dining room is like yours might be at home, seating only six and quite formal (this is where we ate with our family of four and we loved it). The front room is intimate, with four tables. A single white candle on each table, white linens, flowered china and classical music in the background make an elegant setting. Says Scott, "We really like to entertain people," and that is just what they do. He and Patti attended to our table, reciting specials first, including the Maine shrimp and saffron soup, which was delicate and delicious. With the chocolate bread and butter came dense, moist French bread with a crock of unsalted butter. A light orange sorbet in champagne cleared the palate before the main courses. We had a veal saute with sauce of grapefruit, wine and butter; shrimp margarita, in a sauce of tequila, lime and butter; veal with mushrooms, artichoke hearts, prosciutto and garlic, and tournedos with Stilton. Served after the entrees, the salads were generous portions of greens, red and green peppers, tomato curls and carrots, with Stilton vinaigrette, maple curry or raspberry walnut dressings. Next arrived a tray of assorted cheeses (cheddar, Stilton and Havarti) and fruits (oranges, strawberries and cantaloupe). We declined pastries, but had wonderful, fresh-brewed decaffeinated coffee served at the table in an innovative Danish pot. The check arrived with fresh strawberries dipped in chocolate. Entrees are priced from $13.95 to $19.95; soups are $3.50 and desserts, $3. Dinner nightly, 5 to 9 in season; hours vary off-season.

The Lake House, Routes 35 and 37, Waterford. (207) 583-4182. The restaurant at this old New England inn — the house was built as a tavern in 1797 — has gained a fine reputation since being taken over in 1984 by a young couple, Suzanne and Michael Uhl-Myers. Suzanne, whose previous career was in selling fine wines, is the chef. Michael manages the front of the house and does renovation work (he planned to redo a large guest room upstairs during the winter of 1986-87 — the three simply furnished double rooms go for $55 to $75, including full breakfast). The smaller of two lovely dining rooms has a burgundy print wallpaper above light green woodwork; the paneled back room has a pink and burgundy color scheme. When things are busy, the screened porch that stretches across the front of the inn is pressed into service. Alas, there's no view of a lake. Michael says the inn's name derives from a time when guests came to Waterford for the supposedly curative powers of nearby waters, including Lake Keoka, which is at the end of Main Street. However, the picture-perfect plates created by Suzanne should please the eye sufficiently. A nice range of entrees on the changing dinner menu includes two favorites: veal Waterford (topped with ham, gruyere cheese, pimento and mushrooms) and shrimp New Orleans (sauteed in garlic and served in a cream sauce of basil and fresh tomatoes). Suzanne's soft duck and goose liver pate seasoned with grand marnier ($3.95) is among the creative appetizers. Entrees are priced from $8.95 for tortellini primavera to $15.95 for filet mignon served in a brandied cream sauce with fresh scallions. You should save room for dessert: goodies like parfait pie (chocolate meringue topped with French vanilla ice cream and a rich chocolate sauce, $2.95) or bananas Foster for two, $9.95. Dinner, Tuesday-Sunday 5 to 10; Sunday brunch.

The Lobster Pound, Route 302, Naples. (207) 693-6580. This unassuming wood-paneled restaurant reminds diners that these lakes aren't far from Maine's seacoast. During July and August of 1986, the Lobster Pound sold 32,445 pounds of lobster. Much of it was in the form of the "Lobster Pound Special" — a boiled lobster served with clam chowder, steamed or fried clams, french fries, cole slaw, beverage and ice cream for $15.95. The restaurant also offers fresh lobster at $11.75, fried clams for $8.25, and fried chicken or a plate of clam cakes for $5.25. Clam rolls, pizzas, hamburgers and hot dogs are available. Diners sit at large, varnished picnic tables in this highly regarded spot run for 15 years by the Edwards family, who steam the lobsters in kettles out back. It's an honest value, so it's little wonder that people often are lined up outside waiting to get in. Open daily, noon to 10, July and August only. No credit cards.

The Barnhouse Tavern, Junction of Routes 302 and 35, North Windham. (207) 892-2221. Located in the center of commercial North Windham, this restaurant attracts diners from all around Sebago Lake. Owner Fran Pelletier opened it in 1982, and in 1986 was expanding to accommodate the crowds. Barnwood walls, hanging plants, a loft area and a greenhouse add up to a casual, comfortable atmosphere. Dinner items include teriyaki sirloin ($10.95), baked stuffed scallops ($12.50) and the specialty of the house, prime rib ($14.95). Several items "From the Fry Kettle," such as a clam dinner at $10.95, all include a choice of potato or onion rings, and tossed salad or cole slaw. For lunch, an open-faced crabmeat and Swiss cheese sandwich with tomato, baked in the oven, is $4.95. Lunch and dinner Monday-Saturday, dinner all day Sunday.

Kedarburn Inn, Route 35, Waterford. (207) 583-6182. Bill Ritchie is the chef, while partner Edmund Rocheleau tends to the baking and sometimes the chowders and soups. Soft candlelight illuminates the antiques-filled room, where the innkeepers' collection of copper, brass and baskets is displayed. A sunny breakfast room (for the public as well as inn guests) is also used for Sunday brunch. The most ordered item (and most expensive at $13) is shrimp William, a plate of four jumbo shrimp stuffed with seafood, onions and seasoned cracker crumbs, then wrapped with puff pastry and topped with a cheese sauce. Other entrees include sole florentine, seafood newburg, chicken cordon bleu and a lobster dinner for the gentle price of $8.95. Clam chowder is on the menu daily, and lobster bisque often appears. Appetizers include quiche at $3.25 and a shrimp cocktail for $4.95. Dinner, 5 to 9, nightly in summer, Thursday-Sunday rest of year; Sunday brunch, 10 to 2; breakfast daily 8 to 11 in summer.

Gorham Station, 29 Elm St., Gorham. (207) 839-3354. The former Gorham railroad station was turned into this fun spot a few years ago, and while it is not near the water, visitors to the lake district trek southeast (toward Portland) for dinner quite frequently. The station was extensively renovated; the gray and blue interior colors were originally on the exterior, says owner Tom Colerick, and old railroad posters and photographs add to the flavor.

Specialties include lots of beef, especially prime rib on Friday and Saturday nights for $14.95. Broiled loin lamb chops cost $11.25; a teriyaki steak skewer is $9.50, and a New York sirloin is $11.95. Seafood is also available, sometimes in combination with steak, as in the scallops-steak combo for $13.75. Salad is brought to the table in a huge bowl, family style. It's available as a meal for $5.75 at dinner, $3.25 at lunch. Other lunch choices include hearty sandwiches, and a couple of steak and seafood specials. Open daily except major holidays for lunch and dinner; no lunch on Saturday.

Rick's Cafe, Route 302, Naples. (207) 693-3759. Under the sign with the name of this restaurant is the phrase, "Sunsets and Cocktails," and Rick does pretty well serving up both. New in 1986, this small restaurant with outdoor patio was bustling in the evening with a drinking, music-loving, casual dining crowd. You can't beat the location: on the Naples causeway, directly across the road from all the action on Long Lake (including the docking spot for the Songo River Queen II). We remember fondly our late lunch on a crystal-clear and sunny Saturday. We were able to snag one of the coveted outdoor tables where we could watch the parasailing, seaplane flights, paddle boats and such on the lake. The emphasis is on burgers, Mexican specialties and ribs. A plate of nachos ($3.25) held our appetites at bay until we could dig into sandwiches: a delicious barbecued chicken breast sandwich, a Reuben, a roast beef and a "basic burger," all in the $3.50 to $4.95 range. The blue and white striped umbrellas, white tables and blue and white chairs lend a nautical freshness to the scene. Inside, it's hanging plants, wood and brass, with people crowded around the bar most of the time. Dinners are printed on a blackboard and emphasize the Mexican and barbecue items. Open daily, June to early October.

For breakfast you might want to try the **Log Cabin Cafe,** Route 302 in Raymond, where good values are to be found. **The Tea Room** in the center of Bridgton (open from 9 to 5) is also a find. Located at the rear of the building at 22 Main St., which also has craft items for sale, it offers sandwiches, muffins, sweets, continental breakfast and the like, as well as lemonade, iced tea and coffee.

FOR MORE INFORMATION: Windham Chamber of Commerce, Box 1015, North Windham, Me. 04062. (207) 892-8265. Also, Bridgton Chamber of Commerce, Portland Road, Box 236G, Bridgton 04009. (207) 647-3472.

Lobster traps are a picturesque sight in Boothbay Harbor area.

Boothbay Harbor, Me.

The Boothbay region calls itself "the boating capital of New England" and its harbor will tell you why. On the special weekend known as Windjammer Days (early to mid-July each year), dozens of passenger-carrying schooners add their majesty to the hundreds of smaller boats that crowd around. Even on non-holiday weekends, boating is king. The water is such a compelling presence in Boothbay Harbor that you won't rest until you get out onto it; happily, there's a long list of excursion boats from which to choose.

Settled in the 17th century by English fishermen, the Boothbay area was the one the Pilgrims turned to for help their first winter; they sent a vessel to obtain supplies. Indian hostility eventually caused those first European fishermen to leave, but by 1729 many returned and the area began to flourish. Fishing has been the major industry throughout the years, although ship-

297

building, shipping, ice-cutting, lumbering and farming were important. The way the fingers of the land stretch out into the ocean reveals the story of a sea-dominated society. Fortunately for the visitor, it was one that turned to the tourist trade quite naturally.

The waterfront area of the town of Boothbay Harbor is amazingly small and congested; you really have to park your car and walk. What's terrific about it is the access that the inns and restaurants have to the waterfront; here it is easy to find a spot where you can dine and watch harbor activity. To cross from one side of town to the other, you take a wonderful, long footbridge, which adds to your appreciation of the waterfront.

While Boothbay Harbor will offer many hours of relaxation — dining, walking, watching the harbor activity, and browsing in an amazing array of shops — you'll want to drive all the way down Southport Island to Newagen, southwest of Boothbay proper, and then all the way to Ocean Point, southeast of the harbor, to obtain spectacular ocean views, set off by the pine tree-lined, rock-bound coast. There is a relationship between land and sea which fascinates the viewer; we could spend hours perched on a rock at Ocean Point, watching the waves crash against the shore and the pine trees bend in the wind. And don't forget East Boothbay, a low-key area with another harbor and a good dockside dining spot.

While Boothbay Harbor is one of the most popular of Maine's coastal areas, and while August can be downright crowded, we've never felt unwelcome or hassled. And we're gratified that Boothbay's innkeepers, restaurateurs and shopkeepers know what the visitors want. Clam chowder and lobsters, blueberry muffins and pancakes are always on the menu; local crafts and designs are found in the shops, and the motels and inns take great advantage of water views.

If a vacation on the coast of Maine is what you're after, you may have everything you want in Boothbay Harbor.

Getting There

The Boothbay Harbor area is located about a third of the way up the Maine coast, about 60 miles east of Portland. It is reached via the Maine Turnpike (I-95) and Route 1. From Route 1 near Wiscasset, Route 27 dips down into Boothbay.

Where to Stay

There are terrific possibilities here from full-scale, oceanside resorts to bed-and-breakfast inns and waterside motels. Rarely do we find it so hard to choose!

On The Water

Treasure Island, East Boothbay 04554. (207) 633-3333. What is this Adirondack-style lodge doing on a Maine tidal island with practically a 360-degree water view? John and Phyllis Washington, who live most of the year in New Jersey, found this extraordinary log house 20 years ago and knew it was just what they wanted. During July and August they run a B&B which is downright superior — as long as you're the kind of guest who can appreciate a pipe-smoking moose named Myron above a huge stone fireplace, and the innkeepers' very personalized style. The lodge has a two-story, 50-foot living room with the fireplace, the moose head, and some comfortable sofas and chairs. A steamer chair from the Queen Mary occupies a booked alcove with a view of the ocean

— but there are views of the ocean from virtually everywhere. A stairway to one side takes guests up to the balcony which overlooks the living area and from which three of the four guest rooms are entered; the fourth is tucked around on the first floor. A fifth pair of guests can rent an efficiency in a small building, where John also keeps some boating gear. Bouquets of wildflowers are in all of the simply furnished, twin-bedded rooms, all of which have private baths. There's a great porch across the front for watching the endless parade of water activity; a binnacle is positioned, as if on a ship's bridge, on the lawn out front. Along one side of the island, the Damariscotta River meets the Gulf of Maine; on the other side, little Ocean Harbor has the lobstering activity and a picturesque, casual seaside restaurant. Guests can use a dinghy as well as a float for swimming and sunbathing. Phyllis serves a continental breakfast that often features her own popovers and Norwegian spiced blueberry jam in a cozy breakfast nook. You leave the world behind when you cross the tiny bridge that takes you to Treasure Island, six miles from Boothbay Harbor. Doubles, $50; efficiency with full kitchen and water views from all four sides, $60. Open late June to Labor Day.

Spruce Point Inn and Lodges, Boothbay Harbor 04538. (207) 633-4152. Since 1958 the Spruce Point Inn has been offering its pampered guests the ultimate in an oceanside vacation. Everything is here: a saltwater and a heated freshwater swimming pool, tennis courts, boating, water taxi service across the harbor and into town, wooded paths for walking, and a fine dining room. Now run by Charlotte and John Druce, the daughter and son-in-law of the founders, the Spruce Point Inn has 60 rooms, including 13 suites with woodburning fireplaces. Twelve rooms are located in the main inn, the rest in four lodges and in cottages of two to four bedrooms spread across a pine-tree covered point of land surrounded by water. Photographs of famous visitors line the walls of the inn's large oceanfront living room and there's a huge stuffed bear in the library, courtesy, we're told, of the game-hunting chef. Highly rated meals (breakfast and dinner) are served to inn guests in a large, airy, pine-paneled dining room in summer; dinner for the public by reservation is $17.50, prix fixe. Two or three times a week meals (like lobster bakes or special breakfasts) are served at Sunset Point, an exceptional oceanside dining terrace across the road from the main inn. The saltwater swimming pool is built into another terrace right above the crashing surf. There's a small pagoda for sitting and watching the water activity. Honeymooners would love this place, especially a tiny cottage tucked into the hillside near the water and called Retreat. Walking trails through the pine-scented woods offer guests a chance for a "constitutional." Spruce Point still has a degree of formality that's vanishing these days; jackets are required for dinner. Activities also include movies, bingo and dancing in the evening, as well as exercise programs in the pool and piano entertainment in the cocktail lounge. Doubles, $160 to $210, MAP; $80 to $100, B&B (mid-June to end of June and early to mid-September). Closed rest of year.

Ocean Point Inn and Motel, Ocean Point, East Boothbay 04544. (207) 633-4200. When we first stayed here in 1970, we happened to share a large duplex cottage with some women we think were vacationing school teachers. Our daughter was just one, and her early awakenings not appreciated by the guests on the other side of her bedroom wall; we were delighted to be able to take her for early morning walks along the oceanfront. Since then, the Ocean

Point has grown, adding a 20-unit motel and a 10-room lodge, enlarging the main inn and updating the cottages scattered around on the property. And what a piece of property! Located on yet another point with water all around, Ocean Point attracts repeat vacationers who can't get over the views, attentive service and a good dining room (see Where to Eat). All 58 rooms have private baths, electric heat and color TV. Some are decorated in a traditional Colonial style; others are modern. Many have ocean views (for example, those in the lodge, in Seawinds and Westwinds, and in the inn); be sure to ask when reserving. A pool is located on the property, and there are rocks out front for sitting and sunning. Because the inn property is at the entrance to Linekin Bay, there's a parade of boats back and forth. The Ocean Point Wharf right out front is a stopping point for the Linekin II Ferry, which combines a scenic trip around the bay with a water route into Boothbay Harbor. Those who drive are seven miles, and 15 to 20 minutes, from the center of town. Doubles, $53 to $79, EP. Open May to mid-October.

Lawnmeer Inn and Motel, Southport 04576. (207) 633-2544. Just past the drawbridge on Southport Island, this old-fashioned inn and motel directly on the water is best known for its dining room (see Where to Eat), but its 12 inn rooms, all with private baths, have recently been renovated. There are several more modern rooms in the small two-story motel and there's a cottage for two with a sundeck at the water's edge. All accommodations have two double beds and TVs; all motel units have water views. Considering the location on Townsend Gut, we think this is a good deal. Plus, you've got the good restaurant, a cocktail lounge, and public rooms available in the inn. Doubles, $35 in inn, $46 in two-room inn suite with water view and in cottage, $44 in motel. Open May through late September.

Seafarer Bed & Breakfast, 38 Union St., Boothbay Harbor 04538. (207) 633-4441. Located across the street from the head of the harbor, this B&B is run by Esther and Bob Hunter, who previously had a campground, Holiday Island, in the area for 19 years. Four rooms, two with private baths, are located in this big old house, which is more than 100 years old. Three are on the second floor; one is on the third floor. We like the second-floor front room with gorgeous view. Boxes of cereal, juice, muffins and coffee are available for breakfast, which is taken on the front porch or in the dining room. Doubles, $35 to $45. Open May-October.

Smuggler's Cove Motor Inn, Route 96, East Boothbay 04544. (207) 633-2800. This motel complex right on the water — so close in fact that the unit known as Lantern is built on pilings -- is set on a gentle hillside leading down to the water's edge. Besides a pool with stone terrace situated in the center of the complex, there's a small beach. Rowboats and sailboats are available. The adjoining 1820 Restaurant offers three meals a day, and on nice days lunch is served poolside. Rooms with two double beds are available in four two-story motel units, while the Loft has smaller rooms. Doubles, $45 to $100. Open late spring until early fall.

The Newagen Inn, Southport Island, Cape Newagen 04552. (207) 633-5242. There is a sense of being away from everything when you are here. You don't feel a part of the Boothbay Harbor scene, although you can drive into town in about 20 minutes, and there is an isolated-retreat quality to the location past a spruce forest at the end of Southport Island. The inn has been in business since

1923, so its location is special for those who want quiet. The two-story white inn is simply decorated with rattan furniture and hooked rugs on the bare floors of the lobby; there is a dining room as well. All 25 rooms in the main inn have private baths; most offer ocean views. In addition, there are three cottages; Seacliff with eight rooms, Logholme with three rooms and Spruce with two small bedrooms, a bath, fireplaced living room and screened porch. A large saltwater swimming pool, shuffleboard, croquet and horseshoes, rowboats and charter sailing, plus a 1.5-mile nature trail are among the attractions. Doubles, $55 to $85, EP. Open mid-June through September.

The Harborage, 73 Townsend Ave., Boothbay Harbor 04538. (207) 633-4640. A double-decker side porch extends the length of this large old white house, which is right on the harbor (except that at low tide, it's just mud out there) and a good value. Metal garden chairs and window boxes are set out on the porches. Good parking is available and you can walk into town. The rooms are basic; most have paneled walls and chenille bedspreads, but they make up in location and housekeeping for what they lack in charm. A two-room efficiency with complete kitchen and housekeeping is $75. Doubles with private baths, $52; "economy" rooms with shared bath, $30. Open year-round.

Fisherman's Wharf Inn and **Brown Brothers Motel** are large waterfront facilities that are a bit commercial for our tastes, but they have good locations. Brown Brothers is situated on the other side of the drawbridge; a water taxi can bring you into town. Both have large restaurants.

Other Choices

Topside, McKown Hill, Boothbay Harbor 04538. (207) 633-5404. One of our favorites in the area, this almost could be listed as "on the water," it isn't, but its hilltop, in-town location offers fantastic water views all around. A handsome gray, 19th century sea captain's house with white trim and a large, lawn-level porch, plus two two-story motel buildings (Windward and Quarter Deck) and a separate cottage amid lush lawns and flower beds form the complex. When we visited, a watercolor class at one end of the lawn was painting the magnificent view. All rooms have private baths, heat, wall-to-wall carpeting and refrigerators. Those in the main inn have antique furnishings; Number 8 on the third floor is done in gold and blue and has an extraordinary view of the harbor. Coffee is served on a sunny sunporch in the morning. The Quarter Deck has rooms with two full-sized beds, and a long balcony/deck with blue and white deck chairs for sitting and watching harbor activity. Windward also has two double beds in the rooms, and the views are great. A small cottage accommodating four has two bedrooms, a complete kitchen and full bath. Mr. and Mrs. Newell Wilson have run this outstanding spot for 30 years. Doubles, $85 and $90 in inn, $90 in Windward and the Quarter Deck; cottage, $150. Open mid-May to late October.

Kenniston Hill Inn, Route 27, Boothbay 04537. (207) 633-2159. Situated on the main route between Boothbay and Boothbay Harbor, but set back from the road in a grove of trees, this white clapboard inn with black shutters and a huge American flag hanging from the front is most intriguing. Ellen and Paul Morissette came from Brattleboro, Vt., where he was chef at the Country Kitchen restaurant, to open this elegant B&B in 1983. Paul serves a full country breakfast in the fireplaced dining room; among his specialties is peaches and cream french toast. Guests gather anytime after 8 for coffee in the fireplaced living room;

breakfast is served at 9, family style. Each of the eight bedrooms is distinctively furnished; antiques, oriental carpets and braided rugs make them most attractive. Of the six rooms with private baths, we especially like the Victorian room with its queensize, four-poster bed and working fireplace. The Country Room with twin beds, fireplace, bath and private entrance also appeals. Doubles, $45 to $70. Open April-December.

Coburn House Inn, Route 27, Boothbay 04537. (207) 633-2120. Carl and Muriel Scott — he's a teacher and she works with the elderly-- opened this B&B for the summer months in 1980 and it's going strong. No wonder, for the Scotts are warm hosts who keep adding to the attractions at their inn; in 1986 an above-ground pool was put in. Five of the seven guest rooms have private baths. A large second-floor suite with private deck, skylighted room and new bathroom is more modern than the others. Two rooms are in an attached, motel-like addition directly off the parking area. The rest are in the main inn, many decorated in Laura Ashley prints and wicker. Guests eat a full breakfast at small tables in a large front breakfast area that was once part of a restaurant. Pumpkin muffins, french toast and ham souffle are among the treats that the Scotts whip up. Doubles, $35 to $48; suite, $58. Open June-September.

The Pines Motel, Sunset Road, Boothbay Harbor 04538. (207) 633-4555. Two two-story motel buildings situated on a hillside on the east side of the harbor seem miles removed from the coast of Maine, when in reality they're just a few minutes from town. That is the attraction for those who want to be near activities, but like quiet and relaxation at the end of the day. A heated pool and tennis court are extras. Rooms have two double beds, refrigerators and sliding doors leading to the decks. Only from the second floor of the higher building are distant water views possible. Doubles, $57. Open late April to late October.

Captain Sawyer's Place, 87 Commercial St., Boothbay Harbor 04538. (207) 633-2474. This big yellow sea captain's house in the center of the harbor is for those who really like to be in the thick of things. Known as the Yellow House, the inn has a comfortable common room where coffee and tea are available in the morning. Guest rooms, located on the first and second floors, all have private baths; most rooms have kingsize beds and carpeting. Decoration is adequate, if not inspired; the red carpeting through the halls seems too bright. The front rooms have nice views of the waterfront across the street. The **Admirals' Quarters** up the street is run by the in-laws of Tom Dekker, the innkeeper here. Doubles, $45 to $55. Open April-October.

Green Shutters Inn and Cottages, Boothbay Harbor 04538. (207) 633-2646. This rustic — and a little hard to find -- complex on Bay Street is an old-fashioned summer holiday spot where your grandmother would probably have felt at home. Several cottages, two lodges and the inn are spread on both sides of the street; most are weathered clapboard with dark green trim. Rooms are basic, most with pine paneling or simple wallpaper, a bureau, a chair, and a lamp between the twin beds. We love the look of the dining room: pressed oak chairs painted white at square tables covered in red and white checked cloths, white tieback curtains, and wall lamps with anchor bases. It's like a page out of the 1930s, and is popular with families who want good value. The home-baked breads and cakes are good, and there's a buffet dinner on Sunday. The main inn and two lodges have porches with distant views of the bay. Cottages accommodate two to fourteen and some have living rooms with working fireplaces. Rates, MAP, adults, $27 daily and $159 to $185 weekly; teenagers, $20 and $100; children under 12 pay less. Open late June to Labor Day.

Bed & Breakfast Down East Ltd., (207) 565-3517, is a reservation service with several homes available in the Boothbay area.

CAMPING. **Shore Hills Campground**, Route 27, Box 448, Boothbay 04537. (207) 633-4782. Eighty-five secluded sites carved out of the woods — several on a tidal river where there's a float for swimming — have town water, fireplaces and picnic tables. Electricity is available at most, although several are reserved for tent camping only. Sites with water and electricity are $13 nightly for a family of four; tent sites, $11.

Little Ponderosa Campground, Route 27, Boothbay 04537. (207) 633-2700. Miniature golf is an attraction at this campground, located in a treed area also on the main road which leads from Route 1 into the Boothbay region. Sites with hookups, including sewer hookups, are $13 daily; those without are $11. Open from mid-May to mid-October.

RENTALS. These are both available and affordable. Start by ordering the official Chamber of Commerce booklet that describes several cabins and cottages available for rent. A number of real-estate agencies also list rentals, among them Colburn Realty Co. on McKown Street, (207) 633-2222, and Ethelyn P. Giles in the Bank Building in Boothbay Harbor, (207) 633-4350. The going rate is $300 to $1,000 weekly. August is the busiest month.

Seeing and Doing

This is a busy area and there's lots to do. Many excursion boats go out from the town pier. There is shopping at all sorts of gift stores and boutiques. A railway village with a train ride, an aquarium, deep-sea fishing, art studios and antique shops, plus a chance to see the rocky coast and its dramatic lighthouses are among the attractions. Read on.

Boat Rides

Argo Cruises, Pier 6, Fishermen's Wharf, 633-4925. Five different cruises are offered. A two-and-one-half-hour trip circumnavigating Southport Island and exploring Newagen Harbor sails Thursday, Saturday and Sunday at 10; $7. A 41-mile trip up the Kennebec River to Bath passes seven lighthouses and sails beside the Bath Iron Works, builders of famous Navy destroyers; daily except Sunday at 1:15, $10. A trip to historic Pemaquid Lighthouse and around Seal Rocks leaves Monday, Wednesday and Friday at 10 and Sunday at 1:15; $7. A two-hour cruise to Damariscove and other outer islands guarantees views of seals and waterfowl; Tuesday at 10, $7. A two-and-one-half-hour sunset cruise featuring a chicken dinner leaves daily except Sunday at 6; adults $11, children $6.50. Boat ride without meal, $5.

The Linekin II, 633-4925 or 633-3321, offers a cruise and lobster feast daily at 5; adults $21, children $10. This boat also offers a two-hour cruise around Linekin Bay; usually seals are sighted. Cruises daily at 9, 11, 1:30 and 3:30; no trip Sunday at 9. Adults $5.50, children $2.75.

The Balmy Days, Pier 8, Chimney Pier, 633-2284, visits primitive Monhegan Island. This all-day trip from 9:15 to 4:30 has a four-hour layover on the remote island. Adults $20, children $16.

The Maranbo II, Pier 8, 633-2284, gives one-hour cruises of the harbor islands seven times daily starting at 7. Adults $4.50, children $2.50.

Cap'n Fish's Boat Trips, Pier 1, Boothbay Harbor, 633-3244. A variety of cruises aboard the Pink Lady or the Goodtimes include everything from "Puffin and Coastal Wildlife" to "Cap's Special" for lighthouses, seals and busy harbors. Tours are priced from $5 to $10; children half price. A sunset sail aboard either boat from 7 to 8:15 costs $5.

The Native Son, 633-5440, a water taxi in Boothbay Harbor, will pick up or discharge passengers at a waterfront dock or from a moored boat anywhere in the harbor. It leaves Brown's Wharf every hour on the hour from 9 to 7 and loads and discharges on the half hour at Fisherman's Wharf for the return trip. One way $2, round trip $3.

SAILBOAT RIDES. Ladyslip, Pier 6, Fisherman's Wharf, 633-4925. Sail aboard the friendship sloop Ladyslip on a one-and-three-quarter-hour trip around the harbor and to Mouse and Squirrel islands for seal viewing. Departures daily at 10, noon, 2, 4 and sunset. Adults, $10.

The Appledore III, Pier, 6, 633-4925, a 56-foot windjammer, departs at 9, noon, 3 and 6 for two-and-one-half-hour trips to Seal Rocks. Adults, $15, children $7.50.

The Chesapeake, Brewer's East Marina, Pier 1, 633-6811. This 40-foot yacht sails around the islands and lighthouses of Boothbay Harbor. Two-hour sails leave at 10 and 5 and cost $16; a three-hour sail at 1 is $25.

RENTALS. Brewer's East Marina, Pier 1, 633-6811, has sailboats of 17 to 22 feet for $38 to $45 for half a day, $65 to $75 a full day. Or try a 19-foot powerboat with 85-horsepower outboard for $115 a day or a 17-foot runabout with 50-hp outboard for $95 a day, through **John Ames Associates** at Chimney Pier, Commercial Street, Boothbay Harbor, 633-4188.

FISHING. The Sheepscot Bay area is a fisherman's paradise for tuna, bluefish, sharks, mackerel, cod and pollock. Charter fishing is popular. Walk the docks at Brown Brothers wharf and you'll see many sport-fishing boats lined up, waiting to be chartered. The general range is $180 for a half day and $300 for a full day. Most boats can take six people. The phone at the dock, where you can get information about many boats, is 633-5440.

Half-day fishing trips from **Cap'n Fish's** booth at Pier 1, 633-3244, leave at 8 and noon; full-day trips go from 8 to 3:30.

How about lobster fishing? You can observe it first hand on the 35-foot **Miss Boothbay**, a traditional Maine lobster boat. Ninety-minute trips leave at 8:30, 10:30, 12:30, 2:30 and 4 daily from Pier 6 at Fisherman's Wharf, 633-4925 or 633-5090. Adults $9, children $5.

Other Attractions

SWIMMING. The beaches are few and private. In fact, the waters here are so cold most of the time that it's not a deprivation to pass up the swimming. However, there are a few places where, on a very hot day, you might want a quick dip. Visitors may swim in **Townsend Gut**. Follow Route 27 toward Southport, beyond the Townsend Gut bridge to a circle; turn right and follow Beach Road to the beach where there's calm, shallow water. You might also try **Grimes Cove**, a little beach with rocks for climbing at the tip of Ocean Point.

Railway Village, Route 27, Boothbay, 633-4727. Here's something for the children. The village consists of 30 display buildings, picnic areas, a gift shop, and a steam train giving 14-minute rides throughout the complex. It is the only steam-powered narrow-gauge train left in Maine. The one-and-a-half-mile excursion recreates the type of ride that would have been popular in such areas as served by the Wiscasset, Waterville and Farmington Railroad. The train operates daily at half-hour intervals, and visitors are then welcome to stroll through the turn-of-the-century village, complete with carriage display, fire equipment, an automobile display, blacksmith shop and doll museum. Adults $3.50, children $2. Open daily 10 to 5 mid-June to mid-September, weekends until Columbus Day.

Marine Resources Aquarium, McKown Point, West Boothbay Harbor, 633-5572. The aquarium run by the Maine Department of Marine Resources, although small, is lots of fun. An enormous lobster, a tank of sharks, two blue lobsters (statistically, they're only one in a million), two seals named Saturna and Trumpet who love to frolic in an outdoor pool, and a chance to watch the residents being fed entertain the entire family. There are picnic benches on the shore. Open daily Memorial Day to Labor Day. Free.

Boothbay Region Historical Society, 70 Oak St., Boothbay Harbor, 633-3666. The museum, housed in the Elizabeth Reed House, is good to visit for a little perspective on the area. Exhibits include a collection of 2,000 photographs, a file of local newspapers, an historical library, and artifacts and memorabilia — many of them relating to the fishing in the region. Open Monday, Wednesday, Friday and Saturday 10 to 4. Donation.

The Boothbay Region Art Gallery, in the Old Brick House, Oak St., Boothbay Harbor, 633-2703. This community-supported public gallery presents the contemporary work of outstanding artists of the region and of Monhegan Island. Most works on display can be purchased, and there are three juried shows each summer. Open daily, 11 to 5; Sunday, noon to 5. Adults, 25 cents.

SHOPPING. The Basket Barn on Route 27 in Boothbay has countless baskets (New England hardwood splint baskets, fish baskets, potato baskets) plus wicker furniture, grass rugs and bamboo shades. The **Huckleberry Bookstore** in Boothbay Harbor has a fine selection of Maine authors. **Hand in Hand** on Oak Street offers wonderful pottery and crafts; Edgecomb Pottery (made in the area) is sold there. **Paper Craze** stocks cocktail napkins and paper items.

The Smiling Cow, a gift shop with a branch in Camden, is a landmark. All sorts of nice gifts can be found here and there's a back door leading to the wharf. **Gimbel & Company,** a country store, sells nautical brass items, good Christmas tree ornaments, and all sorts of thimbles for thimble collectors. Stop in **Pine Tree Variety** for nice napkins and paperware, beach balls, towels, yourname-it. **Mountain Tops** on the wharf sells every conceivable variety of T-shirt. The **Mung Bean** on upper Townsend Avenue has fine Maine and New England crafts; in the same area are **The House of Logan** and the **Village Shop** with classic women's and men's clothes.

Where to Eat

We think the Boothbay area is well furnished with good dining spots, many of them perfect for the location. The emphasis is on fresh seafood, especially lobster. Prices are quite reasonable, too.

Water Views

Ocean Point Inn, off Route 96, Shore Road, Ocean Point (207) 633-4200.

The Ocean Point provides the diner with a delightful seven-mile drive from the harbor along Linekin Bay culminating in a good dinner with an ocean view. The dining rooms stretch along the waterfront side of the inn, with large windows and two different levels in the main room, allowing for water views from most tables. The room is divided into various sections by decor; we sat at tables with black floral print tablecloths and pink napkins; another section is done in earth tones. There are ladderback chairs in one area, white bentwood chairs in another. Somehow it is all quite comfortable and if not super sophisticated, at least it works. We lucked out with a window table, even though we didn't have reservations, and our hearty appetites were immediately soothed by an herbed cheese spread which arrived with crackers. Specialties of the day change (roast leg of lamb, $8.95, on Fridays; prime rib, $13, on Saturdays). We skipped Sunday's roast turkey ($8.75) for chicken breast in lobster sauce ($8.50) and broiled swordfish ($9.95), thick and moist. Appetizers included mussels steamed in wine, herring in sour cream and trout pate. The clam chowder ($1.85) was creamy and full of clams. Large, fresh salads came with a fine creamy dill dressing. Other entrees ($6.50 to $12.75) included broiled scallops, a fisherman's platter, shrimp scampi, charbroiled lamb chops and fried chicken. Fresh rolls, baked potatoes or rice, and vegetables — in our case, summer squash — fill out the meal. If you have room left, try a pistachio bombe ($1.75) or cheesecake with strawberries ($2.25). After dinner, it's fun to walk out by the waterfront and Town Pier, to watch the twinkling lights in houses and on boats, and hear the surf as it hits the rocks. This is coastal Maine at its best. Dinner nightly, 5:30 to 9. Breakfast is also served.

Lawnmeer Inn, Route 27, Southport. (207) 633-2544. This big old white inn has developed a reputation for its dining room, and when we arrived at 6:45 on a Friday evening, we still had to wait more than a half hour for a table. Fortunately we could sit on the porch and look out over the picturesque inlet, part of Townsend Gut. Since no reservations are taken, you're advised to arrive early or late on weekend nights. The main dining room has nice water views, and wooden tables with ladderback chairs. The second room, where we ate, is less charming because of its modernization; its blonde pine wainscoting and beige walls seems anemic, although flowered draperies and old photos help. It was fun to sit at a window table and watch a brief thunderstorm, and a dramatic sky in its wake, over the water. We chose deep sea scallops in a wine and almond sauce ($10 a la carte, add $2 for a complete dinner) and creamed cod au gratin ($8.30). Chicken, pork chops and steaks are on the menu as well. A good salad contained cucumbers, red cabbage, tomatoes, fresh garden lettuce and croutons. You can also choose hearts of lettuce or pears and cottage cheese. Soothing desserts are bread pudding, gingerbread with whipped cream, Indian pudding and Jello. The menu appeals to older people as well as families, both for price and straightforward preparation. There's a small cocktail lounge. Dinner nightly.

Lobsterman's Wharf, Route 96, East Boothbay. (207) 633-3443. Located in a commercial fishing area on the small but picturesque harbor at East Boothbay, this spot captures the flavor of boat building and repairing, fishing, and most importantly, good waterfront dining on the Damariscotta River. The umbrellaed deck overlooking the water is the place to be if it's nice; our lunch on a warm, sunny July day was perfect and we enjoyed watching the small boats (even a canoe) in which people arrived for a meal. The restaurant is in a low building with booths and nautical memorabilia inside; out front where the deck is, a tugboat-like facade is painted red. You sit at picnic tables and — if it's as glaringly sunny a day as ours — try to get one with an umbrella (we didn't succeed, but what nice pink cheeks we sported later)! For lunch you can have a lobster roll ($5.95), sandwich ($6.75) or club ($7.95); crabmeat in the same guises, a crabmeat melt ($6.25) or a bowl of lobster stew ($6.50) or clam chowder ($3.95). Steamed clams and boiled lobsters are available all day, at the market price. For dinner, you can also get broiled halibut ($9.25), a broiled fisherman's platter ($13.50) and broiled scallops ($11.75). Steaks, chicken, lamb chops and mixed grill are there for the landlubbers. Big glasses of iced tea or beer wash it all down, and the blueberry pie, carrot cake, strawberry shortcake and cheesecake are homemade. Lunch daily, 11:30 to 4:30; dinner, 5 to 9.

Lobsterman's Co-op, Atlantic Avenue, Boothbay Harbor. (207) 633-4900. This is supposed to have the best values around, and its outdoor deck, with rows of picnic tables (another section is protected by a roof) is always full, it seems. Certainly the view of the harbor can't be improved upon. You're given a number when you order at the counter, and these are blared out via loudspeaker for pickups. The prices seem right: steamed clams for $4.50; a one-and-one-quarter-pound lobster for $7.25; a jumbo lobster for $6.50 per pound; corn at 75 cents an ear; mussels for $3, and fried scallops for $6.75. And the desserts are enticing: chocolate peanut butter pie ($2.50), blueberry cake (75 cents). Service is on paper goods; there are large garbage barrels for disposing of the debris. Beer, wine, coffee, tea and soft drinks are available. Open daily from 11:30 to 8.

The Chowder House, opposite the footbridge, Boothbay Harbor. (207) 633-5761. Robert and Sally Maroon opened this attractive waterfront restaurant cum shopping arcade nearly 10 years ago. It has lots of atmosphere from the weathered look of the building to the white mismatched chairs at bare wooden tables and an open kitchen area with a serving bar in the shape of a dory. A deck overlooking the harbor is enhanced by flower-decorated lampposts and piled lobster pots. The building's origin as a plumbing warehouse remains intact, all of the reconstruction done by Robert, who is a woodworker with small shop on the premises (specialty: carved signs). Other shops that can be visited before or after dining include a yarn shop, with wool from Boothbay area sheep, and an antiques/junk shop with all sorts of amazing stuff. On the chilly night we visited, we were lucky to snag one of the eight rough pine plank tables indoors. Fresh flowers in milk glass vases and flickering candles in red glass containers are just right touches. Sandwiches and salads are always on the menu, but specialties included baked stuffed haddock ($10.95), sauteed scallops ($11.95) and a bowl of clam ($4.50) or fish ($3.75) chowder, creamy and brimming with seafood. A glass of the house wine, Los Hermanos, provided a good accompaniment, and we all saved room for dessert ($1.95). The strawberry rhubarb pie was excellent; we all saved room for dessert; the carrot cake, on the dry side. There's a small, convivial bar. Lunch and dinner daily.

Andrews' Harborside Restaurant, at the footbridge, Boothbay Harbor. (207) 633-4074. Formerly the Blue Ship, this jauntily awninged and decked restaurant with its exceptional location is much in demand for breakfast, lunch and dinner — especially with tourists browsing through the shops. We had breakfast at one of the wood-look formica tables, set with blue chairs. Floors are bare wood, pillars are white, and there's a fresh, nautical feeling. Tables with blue umbrellas on the deck overlook the harbor. The huge cinnamon rolls popular with the former restaurant's clientele are still on the menu; at 95 cents they cover a breakfast plate and are the piece de resistance in a $2.10 continental breakfast. Another favorite choice is blueberry pancakes for $2.75; you can also get yogurt, fruit and eggs in all guises. Curiously, Asti Spumante is on the breakfast menu at $3.25 a glass. For lunch, shrimp, lobster, crabmeat and chicken rolls are available; the lobster costs $7.50. Dinner emphasizes seafood such as lobster pie, ($13.25), scallops sauteed with mushrooms and served in a cream sauce ($11.95), broiled haddock ($9.65) and fried oysters ($8.95). A country-style chicken pie and sirloin strip steak satisfy the non-fish eaters. Breakfast daily, 7:30 to 11; lunch, 11:30 to 4:30; dinner, 5 to 10.

Brown Brothers Wharf, east side of the harbor, (207) 633-5440. In its 43rd year, the Brown Brothers establishment -- restaurant, condominiums, motel rooms, a wharf and marina — is well known locally. Just look for the statue of the big fisherman in his yellow foul-weather gear. On our first visit to Boothbay nearly 20 years ago, we ate a good seafood dinner here, and we returned recently for breakfast. While the wood tables and captain's chairs, carpeted floor, and a few nautical touches can't mask the commerciality of the place (it's hardly intimate), the location on the harbor is excellent and views from the first three rows of tables quite good. Our breakfasts of french toast ($2.45), oatmeal ($1.50) and a huge muffin of the day (blueberry, not surprisingly) were fine. The dinner menu includes baked stuffed lobster or a lobster clambake (both $15.95), sea kabob ($12.95) and a fried shrimp platter ($8.95). Breakfast daily, 8 to 10; dinner, 5:30 to 9. Open June-September.

Ken Gray's Clam and Lobster Bakes, Pier One, Boothbay Harbor. (207) 633-5629 or 633-2248. Traditional lobster clambakes, steamed on seaweed and served on the deck at red tables or indoors in a huge hall with end-to-end picnic tables, are served at noon, 2, 5 and 6 and it's a good idea to reserve ahead. The $20.50 tab pays for two one-pound lobsters, a hard-boiled egg, corn, steamed clams, pickles, chips and watermelon. A free bottle of champagne is included for two people. You also can just order a lobster for $12 or clams, corn, and various specials a la carte. This is very basic, popular and seems quite good. Wear casual clothes; it's messy!

Other Choices

Russell House, Route 27, Boothbay. (207) 633-6656. Jocelyn and Harvey Oakes have opened a restaurant in this New England farmhouse on the main route leading from Route 1 to Boothbay Harbor and turned it into the most elegant in the area. Bluish gray carpeting, blue calico tablecloths atop white cloths with white napkins, fresh flowers, blond wood chairs and tiny white lights on potted plants all blend softly in a sophisticated manner. The menu is no less so. Appetizers in the $3.50 to $4.95 range include baked artichoke hearts, oysters Rockefeller, country pate and smoked haddock, mussels and scallops in puff pastry. The house salad at $4.95 is fresh greens topped with marinated mushrooms and artichoke hearts, smoked turkey breast and mandarin oranges and served with a raspberry vinaigrette. Spinach salad at $6.95 is locally smoked seafood on a bed of fresh spinach. Seafood and veal are featured entrees ($12.50 to $14.95). Besides veal Oscar, veal gorgonzola, veal dijon and veal au citron, you might try loin lamb chops dijonnaise or the pasta dish, Hay and Straw —

fettuccine with locally smoked seafood sauteed in garlic and herbs, snow peas and fresh mushrooms, tossed with parmesan cheese and heavy cream. The Russell House has five attractively refurbished upstairs guest rooms, all with private baths, dark green carpeting, stenciled walls and dark pine beds with quilts ($55 to $60). Dinner nightly, 5:30 to 9:30; winter, 6 to 9.

Country Greens, Wharf Street, Boothbay Harbor. (207) 633-6242. William Walsh, a former private-school headmaster in Connecticut, and his wife Ruth, an artist, opened this different -- and refreshingly so -- restaurant in Boothbay Harbor in 1982 on the second floor of the Custom House. You go up a narrow flight of stairs from the bustling wharf area, into an all-white dining room (white walls and white tablecloths with white placemats over them.) With fresh flowers on the tables and paintings on the walls, you feel as if you're dining in an art gallery. The view from the small window tables is of the busy street below, and the contrast between the tranquility of the dining room and the street from which you've just come is part of the charm. A small but good salad bar has a choice of sweet poppyseed or dijon mustard dressings and the homemade biscuits are splendid. Choices at luncheon include salad plates — the chicken tarragon and walnut ($4.75) was excellent; three-egg omelets (mushroom and onion, ham and cheddar, cheddar and Swiss, Spanish) in the $5 range; sandwiches such as roast beef and horseradish ($5.75), a husband's favorite, or lobster salad ($7.25). The special dessert of fresh blueberries with lime mousse was light and refreshing. For dinner you might have seafood marinara with fettuccine ($10.75), scallops sauteed in a dijon sauce ($11.75), chilled lobster, shrimp and scallop salad ($12.75) or chicken breast stuffed with gruyere, prosciutto and apricots ($9.75). Dinner entrees are served with the salad buffet and a vegetable. The restaurant has a liquor license. Lunch, Monday-Saturday 11:30 to 2; dinner, Tuesday-Saturday, 5:30 to 8:30. Open June-September.

For breakfast with the locals, try **Everybody's** in a small mall off Route 27. Eggs Benedict is $3; pancakes are 50 cents each, and eggs, 45 cents for one, 70 cents for two. Good home fries and bagels are available.

FOR MORE INFORMATION: Boothbay Harbor Chamber of Commerce, Box 356, Boothbay Harbor, Me. 04538. (207) 633-2353. The information booth is on Route 17 just before the harbor area.

Old boats and waterfront structures are typical of Vinalhaven.

Vinalhaven-Islesboro-Camden, Me.

Penobscot Bay is Maine's largest and most interesting. Dotted with islands and busy with lobster boats and windjammers (more sailing trips leave from Camden than from any other port in Maine), it presents an ever-changing picture to visitors.

Lobster is king here. Lobster buoys dot the water and those sturdy lobster boats head out early in the morning, not to return until the end of a hard day. The result is both picturesque and palate-pleasing; lobsters are offered up by area restaurants in guises ranging from roll to Newburg with the standard New England boiled lobster probably first in popularity.

We love lobster but it isn't that alone which draws us to the Penobscot Bay area. The sea is magnificent, tumbling toward a rocky coast edged with the dark and fragrant pines for which Maine is famed. The skies are alternately brooding and bright, clouds scudding across the blue or forming into thunderheads with little warning.

Sailors must know their stuff, and they do. Windjammers ply the waters with graceful sails unfurled, their bows rising and falling with the rhythm of the sea. The tang of salt air fills our nostrils; we breathe deeply and feel energized. There is something about this part of Maine that beckons us back again and again.

Here we sample three places in or on Penobscot Bay: the two markedly different islands of Vinalhaven and Islesboro, and the picturesque seaside village of Camden. All three are do-able in one trip, and each has a special flavor.

Vinalhaven

One of the more populated island communities off the coast of Maine (some 1,200 year-round residents) and larger than most in size (five by eight miles), Vinalhaven is home to an active fishing community. The harbor is very much a working harbor and the island lobstermen, dressed in yellow foul-weather gear and high black rubber boots, are busily setting and hauling traps much of the time.

Fishing wasn't always the main industry. Quarrying was, and Vinalhaven granite can be found in the Museum of Fine Arts in Boston and the Cathedral of St.

310

John the Divine in New York City. In the center of the island's only town, Carver's Harbor, is a large, bright blue "galamander," a wheeled vehicle used to haul huge pieces of granite from quarry to boat. The abandoned quarries have a new life as spring-fed, freshwater swimming areas; you can sunbathe on the rocks surrounding these clear pools. The rocky coast and cold water aren't conducive to ocean swimming, and few attempt it.

Vinalhaven's distance from shore (90 minutes by ferry) and the size of its ferry (maximum of 10 to 12 cars and trucks) have helped to limit commercialization. When we visited, we were enchanted by its simplicity; there were one motel, two B&Bs and a couple of other homes where residents took in roomers. Three restaurants worthy of the name, eight mopeds available for rent and one museum (charming but small) meant that Vinalhaven hadn't become touristy — yet. There was some concern that a larger ferry would be put into service for the summer of 1987, apparently that threat passed, at least for the time. But the island is being discovered and summer residents are increasing in number.

Vinalhaven won't be overrun by tourists soon, however. There's only so much to do here. It's enough for daytrippers — who love to visit — and enough for weekenders. If you want to stay longer, know that this will be a low-key vacation — the kind where you take books to read, and don't expect to be entertained every minute.

Getting There

Vinalhaven is reached by ferry from Rockland, Me. One innkeeper describes it as "the best boat ride, for the money, in the state of Maine." The schedule for the **Governor Curtis** has been Monday-Saturday at 8:40, 1 and 4:45 and Sunday at 8:40 and 5:10 during the summer from Rockland. Return from Vinalhaven weekdays at 7, 11:20 and 3:20, Sundays at 8:15 and 1:30. Adults $3, round trip; children $1.75. Automobiles are $13 round trip; reservations, far in advance, are a must with Maine State Ferry Service, 517 Main St., Rockland, (207) 594-5543. An extra ferry trip was to be instituted in 1987. The ride *is* exceptional, among the Fox Island group (of which Vinalhaven is the largest) with the possibility of spotting seals (we did).

Where to Stay

As the island's only town, Carver's Harbor is where you have to stay, but it's also the most interesting place. Neat Victorian houses are mixed among the simpler fishermen's homes; a short Main Street has a few stores and a couple of restaurants. The ferry comes into Carver's Harbor and you can walk everywhere.

The Fox Island Inn, Carver Street, Vinalhaven 04863. (207) 863-2122. Anita and Peter Kellogg, an attractive and ambitious young couple, bought this house in 1983 and have turned it into a pleasant B&B. The Kelloggs used to run sailing trips out of Boothbay Harbor on a trimaran that Peter built himself; he is a fanatic about sailing, evidenced by the reading material scattered around the living room and game room in the house. Three doubles and one single on the first floor share a newly tiled bathroom (unfortunately located off the kitchen where guests breakfast); two rooms upstairs share another bath with shower stall. The Kelloggs have stripped floors to expose wide pine floorboards and have mixed antique pieces with simple country furniture for a homey decor. Breakfast is buffet style with scrumptious homemade breads and muffins set out on the kitchen counter with coffee, tea and hot chocolate. Juice is in the fridge. The Kelloggs purchased a second building, the Annex, in 1986. Three of its four rooms have distant views of the harbor and ocean; there are a common living room and deck and just coffee in the morning. Doubles, $35 and up. Open mid-May to mid-October.

The Libby House, Water Street, Vinalhaven 04863. (207) 863-4696. Phil and Paula Roberts, who live most of the year on Long Island where he teaches, opened this B&B in 1985 and were still at work on renovations when last we peeked in. The name comes from the family who were the original owners and occupants of the house from 1869 until the Robertses bought it. White with blue shutters, the Libby House is situated on a street not far from the harbor. The fireplaced living room, with built-in day bed and bookcases, is cozy and welcoming; sprightly flowered wallpaper and a rose-colored rug are just right. An efficiency apartment on the main floor rents for the season; upstairs are two doubles and one twin-bed room that share a bath, and a two-room suite with its own bath. A continental breakfast is served in a cheerful dining room. Doubles, $40; suite, $75. Open June-September.

Tidewater Motel, on the harbor, Vinalhaven 04863. (207) 863-4618. The location of this ordinary looking motel cannot be surpassed. It's right on the harbor and most rooms have water views. Some units have kitchens. Doubles, $40 to $45. Open year-round.

Lori Rudolph, (207) 863-4881, who works in the local library, rents two rooms with a shared bath on the second floor of her High Street home (a stone's throw from the island Historical Society Museum) for $40 a night. There's an attractive deck out back for sitting and sipping a drink, and a simple breakfast (coffee, juice, English muffins) is served in the kitchen. Open year-round. .

Rentals are available but there are not many. Renters negotiate with someone they know, consult *The Wind,* the chatty, weekly newssheet, or contact a real-estate agent like Lorraine Walker, (207) 863-4474.

Where to Eat

There are only three restaurants to speak of, several grocery stores, a small gourmet shop with good takeout food for picnics, and a couple of fast-food spots where you stand at the window to get food to go. No liquor is sold or served on the island; you can bring your own wine or beer.

Sands Cove Lobster & Clambake, Sands Road, Vinalhaven. (207) 863-2171 or 863-2559. This is one of our favorite waterfront restaurants anywhere. "Rustic" was the way a friend described it, and she was right. It is also very good. The restaurant, a rough-hewn log cabin with equally rough-hewn picnic tables and benches inside and out, overlooks Sands Cove. We toted a bottle of white wine, which our waitress cheerfully uncorked and served with paper cups. Our first trip, on a windy, rainy evening, was rewarded by the warmth of a wood stove. The menu is short, but locally inspired. Appetizers include native shrimp cocktail; 15 shrimp with cocktail sauce cost about $3. Rock crab claws at $3 and fried crab "biskits" (four fried crab cakes) at $4 are other appetizer choices. We split a hod of steamers for $3.50. Lobsters can be purchased individually ($6 to $7) or as part of a clambake that also includes a whole boiled crab, steamers, cole slaw and assorted breads for $12.75. Corn on the cob is 75 cents; a garden salad with a good herb dressing, served in a paper container, $1. An assorted bread crate ($3.25) including blueberry bread, anadama bread, a dense and wonderful white bread and a lemon bread was memorable. A pottery crock holds butter; service is on heavy plates or in cardboard cartons of the sort that usually hold french fries. With your lobster you get a good-sized stick instead of a nutcracker; use it to crack open the lobster on a large stone that is on the table. It's much more fun. You can also order a sirloin steak ($12.50) or surf and turf. A couple of days later, we sat outside for lunch and watched lobsters being pulled wriggling from a barrel just before they were cooked to order. Close enough to the ferry slip to walk, this is a great place for daytrippers to have lunch. Lunch and dinner, Memorial Day through Labor Day, weekends to Jan. 1. Closed Tuesdays in summer and Wednesdays for lunch.

The Haven, Main Street, Vinalhaven. (207) 864-4969. On the waterfront, the Haven offers dinner in a cute if small dining room with red and white checked tablecloths on small tables. Dinner is at two sittings, 6 and 8, and reservations are advised. The food is the island's most ambitious and some locals call it the best. Menu items can be eclectic, ranging from broiled strip steak at $12 to ragout of lobster with leeks, tomatoes and shallots for $13. Other choices might be wiener schnitzel or ragout of pork with sage and capers. One of the more tempting desserts is Swedish cream with cranberry-grand marnier sauce. Lunches include crab roll and crab melt with cheddar cheese (both around $4). Light breakfasts are available Tuesday-Saturday. Lunch, Tuesday-Friday; dinner, Tuesday-Sunday. Open spring to late fall.

The Mill Race, Main Street, Vinalhaven. (207) 863-9366. Mismatched tables covered in red oilcloth, a melange of chairs, and a small gift shop up front selling handmade mittens and sweaters — this is a local haunt. Open year-round for all three meals, this is the town's basic restaurant. It's not bad, although cooking can be uneven. Our broccoli, cheese and bacon quiche was good except that we couldn't find the bacon. Sandwiches, soups and a couple of hot dishes form the luncheon menu; at dinner there's very good lasagna, spaghetti and meatballs and seafood specials (like twin lobsters), ranging from $6 to $14. There's an upright piano and a wall gallery of granite quarry memorabilia. Although it's on the water (at the point where Carver Pond joins the harbor), the windows are smallish and high and there aren't really views. Minor detail. Breakfast, lunch and dinner daily. Open year-round.

Other options for eating in Vinalhaven include **The Harbor Gawker**, which is open daily from 10 to 9:30 for sandwiches, hamburgers, hot dogs, fried clams and scallops. It's right in the center of the village. The **Pizza Pit** on High Street, below Candage's Grocery, is what it sounds like. The **Burger Ped** sells fast food (hamburgers, hot dogs) close to the ferry slip and rents mopeds.

Seeing and Doing

There is not much to do, unless you're content to watch harbor activity, sunbathe and swim at the quarries (Booth's Quarry, which serves as a town park, is 2.7 miles from town); stroll around a wildlife preserve (Lane's Island), bike (BYO), poke into a few small shops (pottery and clothing) and just wander around.

Vinalhaven Historical Society Museum on High Street, 863-4969, is open daily July through Labor Day from 11 to 3 and is worth a stop. In one large room are gathered memorabilia from island families, ranging from Cantonese china plates to an old foot-pedal-powered dentist's drill. We enjoyed prints of the Lane-Libby fishing factory, a photo of a 155-pound lobster, a codfish skin and samples of granite quarried on the island. Copies of all yearbooks from the island's school give you a taste of the place. Farther up High Street, one of the island cemeteries has interesting carved headstones.

Lane's Island Preserve is an easy walk from town. Forty-five acres of fields, marsh and moorlands are kept as a recreation preserve by the Nature Conservancy. You'll find a couple of picnic tables and a stony beach where we saw children swimming. The Lane family cemetery is above the beach at this scenic spot.

Those with cars have 38 miles of roads to drive, not all in good condition. Many people drive to the island's northern end to look out at North Haven, a neighboring island with a pretty seafront village, where IBM's Thomas Watson has a place. The lighthouse, Brown's Head Light, is not particularly picturesque, but beyond it you can see the bay, usually studded with sailboats. We liked Tip Toe Mountain, off Crockett River Road. It's an easy climb, and you're rewarded with magnificent views of Crockett's Cove and Dogfish Island.

Carver's Harbor is fun to poke around. **Vinalhaven Pottery** offers a variety of craft items and usually has an exhibit on view. **Robert Indiana**, the graphic artist, has restored the Odd Fellows Hall, a massive and wild-looking building in the center of town, as a workshop-study; it's a sight to see. From different vantage points, the harbor activity is interesting. The island newspaper, a one-sheet weekly called *The Wind*, fills you in on necessary details of life and announces public suppers and bake sales.

Islesboro

This 10-mile-long, narrow island just three miles from the coast has been a retreat for wealthy families for generations. Their mansions are set back from the main road that runs through the center of Dark Harbor, the most socially acceptable address.

The anomaly here is that despite its restrictiveness and privacy, Islesboro is incredibly accessible to daytrippers — the **Governor Muskie** ferry makes nine 25-minute trips in each direction, virtually on the hour, from late May through mid-September. Bikers love the island, but it's also easy to bring your car over; just wait in line for the next available spot. Adults $1.50, round trip; children $1; cars $5.50. Be advised that the ferry terminal in Islesboro is not in, or near, civilization; you should have at least a bike to get around and a car is a good idea.

A day trip is an easy way to see the island; there are a few places to stay for those who want to spend a longer time. For us, one day was enough, but we only spent time on the southern — Dark Harbor — part of the island, which is connected at the Narrows to a northern chunk. There are no road signs, but you can't get too lost.

Where to Stay

The **Islesboro Inn**, Dark Harbor, Islesboro 04848. (207) 734-2222. The most elegant place to stay on the island was built in 1916 as one of the large private summer cottages of the well-to-do who vacationed here. A grand piano in the front living room, a lovely terrace dining area with homespun bluish-gray linens on the tables and a gorgeous view of Penobscot Bay, and a tennis court strike an upscale mood. Women dress for dinner and men wear jackets. Seven of the 16 guest rooms have fireplaces and most have dramatic views of the water. Six of the 15 rooms have private baths. Breakfast may be had in bed, if you want to be decadent, and afternoon tea is served in the dining room. There are a dock with a float and small boats, bicycles, shuffleboard and other lawn games. Doubles, $110 to $200, MAP. Open Memorial Day through Columbus Day.

The Dark Harbor House Inn, Box 185, Dark Harbor, Islesboro, 04848. (207) 734-6669. Built as a turn-of-the-century cottage for a Philadelphia banker, this huge yellow house with white trim has nine guest rooms, four with private baths. An airy public room downstairs has rattan furniture, oil paintings and a canary named Lawrence in a cage. The pretty breakfast room has light wood Windsor style chairs and blue tablecloths; continental breakfast comes with the room, although a full breakfast menu is also available. Doubles, $60 to $80. Open Memorial Day through Columbus Day.

Gablewood, Main Road, Islesboro 04848. (207) 734-6969. This white B&B with black shutters is located in the middle of the island, presided over by enthusiastic Cynthia Buswell. Six guest rooms are furnished with great taste; we like the end room on the first floor with a forest green quilt on the bed. Three of the five rooms on the second floor have private baths, two share. A full breakfast is served in a lovely dining room and relaxing. Doubles, $55 to $70.

Where to Eat

Daytrippers should bring their own lunch or get one at the **Dark Harbor Shop**, where quite good sandwiches are concocted. You can sit at the old-fashioned counter inside or on the front deck, which has two picnic tables. Ice cream cones, including ginger flavor, are popular here; you can buy sweaters and gifts inside. The **Blue Heron Restaurant** in Dark Harbor is simple, but is said to have good dinner selections. You can eat formally at the **Islesboro Inn.**

Seeing and Doing

Bike or drive to **Pendleton Point**, a rocky beach with three picnic tables and the best "skipping stones" we've found. You can stand here for quite a while, skimming them across the water's surface. Stop and browse at **Island Books**, a big red barn full of used and rare books, also located on the Main Road.

The **Sailors Museum** at Grindel's Point Light is at the ferry slip; you can walk up the stairs to the light and get a panoramic view of the bay and the Camden Hills in the distance.

Naturally, you'll enjoy biking and riding past all of the elegant summer homes. And that's all, folks.

Camden

Compared with Vinalhaven and Islesboro, Camden is civilized, commercial and touristy. It got that way because it possesses extraordinary natural endowments. The long, narrow harbor is crowded with tall-masted schooners. Behind the town, the Camden Hills form a kind of natural amphitheater. Who wouldn't love it?

Thousands do. They come year-round, but especially in the summer. Consider the opportunities: Shakespeare in the park, rental boats of all sizes and shapes in the harbor, dining on the wharf, shopping in boutiques, staying in one of the many B&Bs and inns, eating lobsters and steamers and blueberry everything.

Camden serves as an embarkation point for windjammer cruises. Most leave town Monday morning and return the following Saturday. Passengers arrive late Sunday afternoon. If you're around, it's fun to walk the docks and watch the action.

Where to Stay

The Whitehall Inn, High Street (Route 1), Camden 04843. (207) 236-3391. This comfortable white inn with green shutters on the edge of town has a distant view of Penobscot Bay. A Camden classic from the 1800s, it is associated with poet Edna St. Vincent Millay, who grew up in the area and gave a poetry reading here in 1912. A Millay memorabilia room, off the main parlor, displays her high school diploma and several photos. Huge old rockers with rush backs and seats are lined up along the front porch and guests sometimes carry breakfast coffee there to sit and stare out to sea. This is an old-fashioned place, upfront about the fact that there are no TVs in the 51 rooms; you're welcome to work on puzzles in the parlor. There are a shuffleboard court, bicycles to rent, and a 22-foot boat that takes guests on excursions around the harbor. Two Victorian houses across the street offer bed and breakfast and have a longer season than the inn. In the main inn, breakfast and dinner in a country elegant dining room are included in the room rates. Doubles, $90 to $130 MAP. Main inn open late May to mid-October.

Camden Harbour Inn, 83 Bay View St., Camden 04843. (207) 236-4200. This large white inn with 22 guest rooms high on a hill has a magnificent vista of the harbor below. A late 19th century establishment, it has been updated and enlarged; there are four new guest rooms and a solarium dining room with great water views. The renovated main parlor has comfortable chairs and couches plus tables for games and puzzles. Two front guest rooms overlook the bay and have their own decks; a fireplaced suite has a lounge area and private porch with a view ($120 during the summer). Breakfast is included in the room rate. Lunch or dinner in the solarium offers a varied menu with emphasis on seafood. You can have a drink at the Thirsty Whale Bar. Doubles, $65 to $120. Open year-round.

Norumbega, High Street, Camden 04843. (207) 236-4646. One of the great late 19th century villas along the Maine coast is this treasure, opened in 1984 by V. Mark Boland as a B&B. The cobblestone-walled mansion looks like a castle. Inside are endlessly fascinating public rooms (the woodwork alone is priceless) and seven large bedrooms, all with private bath. Five of the bedrooms (the ones in back of the house have breathtaking views of the bay) and two are done in a more country look. Flower-laden decks go off all three floors, and expansive lawns slope down to the bay. Mark pours tea or wine for guests in the afternoon, but breakfast is the day's highlight. Served in a long table in the formal dining room, it is a feast of juices and exotic fruits, all kinds of breads and muffins, and, when we stayed, the best french toast ever, topped with a dollop of sherbet and sliced peaches. Doubles, $100 to $130.

Goodspeed's Guest House, 60 Mountain St. (Route 52), Camden 04843. (207) 236-8077. This Federal home with its cheery patio is about five blocks from the harbor, but it has loads of charm. Most rooms have naturally finished wide pine floors and each is individually decorated. A wicker-filled sitting room on the second floor is especially nice in green and white. Accommodations range from a small single to a suite that sleeps four; most share baths. Continental breakfast may be served outdoors on a flower-bedecked deck. Doubles, $60 to $70. Open late spring to late fall.

Blue Harbor House, 67 Elm St. (Route 1), Camden 04843. (207) 236-3196. The house is white, the shutters blue, and the spirit of innkeeper Lorraine Tedeschi is warm and welcoming. She and her husband Thomas have been operating this B&B since 1984 and their enthusiasm for Camden is contagious. The seven guest rooms in the house dating from 1835 are decorated in traditional, cozy comfort (handmade quilts, ruffled curtains). Guests are served a continental breakfast in summer and fall. Out back are luxury housekeeping apartments in a refurbished carriage house and barn. Doubles, $45 to $75. Open year-round.

Windward House, 6 High St., Camden 04843. (207) 236-9656. Len and Betty Lubrano cheerfully describe themselves as corporate dropouts from Paramus, N.J., who turned this large yellow-shuttered, brown house close to the center of town into a B&B in 1984. Seven rooms share three baths on three floors (that on the main floor is awfully near the main entrance to the house). The top floor is not as homey as the others, but two rooms share a bath and it can work nicely for a family. Len describes the breakfast served in the dining room as "an ample continental breakfast; you won't go away hungry." Doubles, $60-70. Open year-round.

Lord Camden Inn, 24 Main St., Camden 04843. (207) 236-4325. You're right in the center of town, above the shops, when you stay at this newly restored brick inn with an elevator. Rooms are on the third and fourth floor (those on the third have cheerful little decks over the Megunticook River; those on the fourth view the harbor). All 27 rooms are furnished in antique and period style and all have private baths, TV sets and in-room phones. A continental breakfast is brought to your room in the morning. Doubles, $55 to $95.

The Owl and the Turtle, 8 Bay View St., Camden 04843. (207) 236-4769 or 236-2302. Book lovers and tea drinkers will like these three guest rooms located over a good bookstore; there's a tea room in season. Each room has a balcony with a panoramic harbor view; the paneled, pleasant rooms have private baths. The location puts you in the center of harborfront activity. And all those books to choose from for bedtime reading! Continental breakfast is served in your room in the morning. Doubles, $65.

The High Tide Inn, Route 1 north, Camden 04843. (207) 236-3724. This manicured waterfront complex north of town has all sorts of accommodations: rooms in the main house, two motel-style buildings, and individual cottages. It is one of the few places with its own, albeit rocky, beach; there are chaise lounges and chairs for sunning on a velvety lawn as well. An optional breakfast is served on the porch. Inn rooms, $40 to $50; cottages, $50 to $60; motels, $50 to $70. Open late May through mid-October.

CAMPING. Camden Hills State Park has 112 sites, none with electrical hookups. Hot showers are available from June 15 to Labor Day. You're advised to arrive early in the day to claim a site.

Seeing and Doing

Windjammer Cruises. Several gorgeous schooners take passengers on six-day sailing trips along the coast of Maine, leaving Camden Monday and returning

Saturday. Activities include swimming, sunning, helping to sail the boat, and eating hearty meals. At night there's often a songfest or time to explore the shore. Among captains running windjammer cruises: Alan Talbot, Box 696, Camden, 236-4449; Ken and Ellen Barnes, 70 Elm St., Camden, 236-3520, and H.S. Hawkins, Box 798, Camden, 236-2750.

Sea Touring Kayak Center of Maine, 123 Elm St., Camden, 236-9569, sponsors day-long paddle trips on Penobscot Bay. Kayaks are also for rent.

Sail aboard the **Milky Way,** a typical 38-foot ketch, which offers three sails daily from 10 to 2; 1 to 4; and 5 to 7. Two-hour sails are $16; three-hour sails, $24. See Heidi Moore at the Town Landing to make arrangements.

Stroll along the docks and check out the boats in the harbor. There are also several cruises of the harbor offered daily.

Touring and Hiking. Some of the East Coast's best hiking is available on 25 miles of trails in **Camden Hills State Park. Mount Megunticook** is the second highest point on the Eastern Seaboard. If you don't feel like hiking, drive the toll road up **Mount Battie,** an easy one-mile drive; the view is worth the $1 toll. Another scenic drive is out Route 52 to **Megunticook Lake.** A walking tour of Camden and a bicycle or car tour of Camden and Rockport are available through the Camden-Rockport Historical Society.

Cultural Attractions. The Camden Shakespeare Company, founded in 1978, gives three plays in repertory from June 21 to Sept. 1 in the natural, stone-tiered Bok Amphitheater near the harbor. The sylvan setting adds a lot to matinee or evening performances. The **Farnsworth Museum** in nearby Rockland ranks among the finer regional art museums in the country. The collection focuses on American art from the 18th century to the present, with many prized works by the Wyeth family. The **Shore Village Museum,** also in Rockland, has an intriguing collection of lighthouse and Coast Guard memorabilia.

SHOPPING. Sophisticated shopping is available in Camden. **The Smiling Cow,** a large and venerable gift shop with a great collection of Maine items, has a view from its rear porch over a river that ripples down rocks toward the harbor. **Unique 1** specializes in natural fiber sweaters, but also has pottery, baskets and gifts. **Heather Harland** offers interesting kitchen items and cards. **The Admiral's Buttons** specializes in preppy clothing and sailing attire. **Once a Tree** has good wooden items. **Haskell & Corthell** and the **House of Logan** are nice women's apparel stores. **The Winemporium** has an excellent selection of wines and food products, many of them, like the local goat cheese, from Maine.

Where to Eat

Aubergine, 6 Belmont Ave., Camden. (207) 236-8053. The first fine French restaurant in the area, Aubergine is known for inspired nouvelle cuisine. David Grant, who trained in France, is the chef; wife Kerlin is a horticulturist who fills the public rooms with lavish bouquets of flowers from her gardens outside. An aubergine carpet, pictures of eggplants, pale yellow walls trimmed in white, frilly white curtains, white wood chairs and tables topped with white linen and flowers make a romantic setting. The menu, which changes monthly, takes advantage of fresh and colorful ingredients. Appetizers range from $5 to $8.95 for wild game pate, smoked salmon and feuillete of lobster with truffles. Entrees are $12.95 for pasta with saffron, red pepper and crab to $18.95 for filet of beef with peppercorns. Salmon with lobster sabayon, ragout of chicken, sweetbreads with wild mushrooms, and lamb with roasted garlic and sage have been on the menu when we dined. Desserts may include chocolate mint charlotte, lemon Bavarian cake and sorbets. Dinner, Tuesday-Sunday 6:30 to 9. Reservations required.

The Waterfront Restaurant, Harborside Square off Bay View Street, Camden. (207) 236-3747. There is no nicer waterside setting in Camden than this establishment with a large outdoor deck shaded by a striking white canvas tarpaulin that resembles a boat's sails. Blue canvas director's chairs at bare wooden tables continue the nautical feeling. Bread sticks with a crock of cheese and grapes and celery appeared on the table as we were seated; next came a basket of good warm bread. Salads in glass bowls are dressed with any of three outstanding dressings: sweet-and-sour bacon, lemon-parmesan and tomato-pesto. Among appetizers are a smoked fish sampler, all sorts of shellfish from a raw bar, and soups. Dinner entrees ($9.95 to $12.95) include seafood florentine (lobster, crab and scallops with spinach), poached salmon and swordfish grilled over applewood with rosemary, which was juicy and succulent. Mint chocolate chip pie with hot fudge sauce and whipped cream proved to be the ultimate dessert. Lunch daily, 11:30 to 2:30; dinner 5 to 10.

The Secret Garden, 31 Elm St., Camden. (207) 236-8911. This small, creative restaurant with a dining garden out back is a colorful spot indeed: green and pink overcloths atop wild floral cloths; cream-colored walls, green chairs and carpeting, and tall napkins of every color. Fresh flowers in clay pots, white china, silver side plates and huge wine glasses spell sophistication. Equally colorful is a small garden courtyard, where casual fare is served. The menu emphasizes American regional cuisine. Appetizers (from $3.50 for vegetable soup to $6.50 for lobster fiesta) include a rustic pate and a spicy crab Avery, laced with a creamy Louisiana Avery Island sauce. Six entrees run from $11.95 for chicken stuffed with cheeses, basil, spinach, nuts and mangos to $18.50 for double stuffed tenderloin (prime beef wrapped in veal and stuffed with foie gras and truffles). Lamb chops are marinated in petite sirah and served with lemony choron sauce. Finish with mango cheesecake, chocolate marquese in strawberry sauce or homemade blueberry ice cream. Dinner nightly, 6 to 11. Open June-September.

Cappy's Chowder House, Main Street, Camden. (207) 236-2254. Right in the center of town, Cappy's is *the* place for breakfast, and is in demand for lunch and dinner, too. Lobster traps hang above the bar, one wall is exposed brick, and green billiard-room lamps hang above bare pine tables. Your placemat is your breakfast menu and offers "pure eggstasy" (country eggs prepared any style, $1.85 for two), the "omelette shoppe" (ham and cheese, seaman's and other omelets, $2.95 to $3.95), and pancakes including Maine blueberry and apple spice ($2.50). The grapefruit is do-it-yourself; a knife comes with it. Soft rock plays in the background and young servers rush around. For lunch or dinner you can have the Penobscot, a grilled crab salad sandwich with Swiss cheese, tomato and dijon mustard ($5.25) or pasta and shrimp salad served on greens ($5.95). The Crow's Nest with a raw bar is a good spot for happy hour; it has a similar menu and a view of the harbor. Dinner includes seafood stir-fry and skewered scallops in the $10 range. Buy goodies at the bakery below. Open daily, 7 to midnight.

FOR MORE INFORMATION: Rockport-Camden-Lincolnville Chamber of Commerce, Public Landing, Box 919, Camden, Me. 04843, (207) 236-4404. For the islands, contact the Maine Publicity Bureau, 97 Winthrop St., Hallowell, Me. 004347. (207) 289-2423.

Historic John Perkins House overlooks the water at Castine.

Castine, Me.

Poised on a peninsula jutting into East Penobscot Bay, Castine is an enclave of peace and quiet.

Therein lies a certain irony, for this sedate little town was forged from a military heritage and a maritime disposition. Founded in 1613 as a French trading colony that became the first permanent settlement in New England, Castine was a major battlefield in the French and Indian wars, the American Revolution and the War of 1812. No fewer than 16 fortifications have been built on the peninsula since 1635, so it's little wonder that the town's only through street is named Battle Avenue.

Its maritime bent is evident in the windjammers in its harbor and by the Maine Maritime Academy, the dominant presence in Castine today. In their rowdier off-duty moments, academy cadets may tie one on in the boisterous waterfront Reef Tavern when their enormous training vessel State of Maine is tied up at the town dock.

Otherwise, all is prim and proper in this quietly prosperous town, which local historian Gardiner E. Gregory says was the second wealthiest per capita in the United States in the 19th century. Long a summer colony, Castine is evolving into a year-round community. Culture thrives in a quaint summer theater and an impressive museum, and visitors are well cared for in three fine inns.

History is more noticeable here than in most such places, if only because there's a large historical marker at almost every turn. You can marvel at them all on a couple of walking tours, climb around the embankments of Revolutionary forts, tour the pre-Revolutionary John Perkins House and watch a blacksmith at work. You can see the inside of the State of Maine ship, look for seals on a harbor cruise, thrill to the windjammers near the yacht club and feast on unusual

320

seafood at one of the most atmospheric waterside restaurants in all of Maine. You can play golf or tennis, swim at the beach or a saltwater pool, or hike around Dyce's Head lighthouse and Witherle Park.

Castine is a haven for rest and relaxation, blessedly off by itself and away from the mainstream.

Getting There

About 40 miles due south of Bangor, Castine is located at the tip of a peninsula, opposite Belfast across East Penobscot Bay. From Route 1 at Orland, take Route 175 and Route 166 to Castine.

Where to Stay

The Manor, Battle Avenue, Box 276, Castine 04421. (207) 326-4861. The sprawling turn-of-the-century summer cottage designed by Mead, McKim and White for Commodore Fuller of the New York Yacht Club in 1895 looks the way an elegant Maine lodge should. You arrive up a long driveway to an edifice of brown wood and stone, a flower-bedecked terrace and an entry archway tunneling between the main house and a wing with the second floor overhead. Young innkeepers Sara and Paul Brouillard are known for their hospitality and fine cuisine. Sara grew up in the house, which they have grandly restored since saving it from demolition in 1980. Paul, a creative dynamo, is the Manor's chef in the off-season and oversees his busy Dennett's Wharf restaurant on the waterfront in summer. Among public rooms are a large sitting room with three velvet sofas to sink into, two small dining rooms (and a table in the library for intimate private parties), and an enclosed cocktail porch with a magnificent green marble and mahogany bar. Throughout are Earle Bakeman's collection of carved birds — one of a bald eagle with a salmon in his beak was coveted by Walter Cronkite, but Paul wouldn't part with it. He also won't part with his new $40,000 billiard table in his "office," the former suite fashioned from the old billiard room in which we once stayed. All 10 guest rooms have private baths, and the Brouillards were readying an 11th room with a water view on the third floor. With five acres of lawns near the end of a dead-end street, the inn is so quiet that the only sound at night is made by the melodic harbor bell. Sara serves a hearty continental-plus buffet breakfast of smoked meats, cheeses, pastries and bran muffins, all decorated with fresh fruits and nasturtiums. Doubles, $55 to $95. Open year-round.

Pentagoet Inn, Main Street, Box 4, Castine 04421. (207) 326-8616. New owners Lindsey and Virginia Miller from Arkansas — he a physician and she a nurse — have upgraded the venerable Pentagoet since acquiring it late in 1985 and have lengthened its season to April through New Year's. Their downstairs parlors (one a well-outfitted library and the other with a nifty windowseat looking toward the harbor) are smashingly refurbished in greenish-gray seafoam shades. The pristine dining room (see Where to Eat) has an addition looking out over terraced gardens, and there's a sparkling new kitchen. Two-night minimum stays, MAP meal requirements and limited dining for the public are intended "to make this a highly desirable experience for our house guests," in Virginia Miller's words. The turreted main inn has twelve guest rooms, six with private baths, and antique furnishings. From a large armchair near the brass bedstead in the third-floor turret you can glimpse the harbor; outside the door, some of Virginia Miller's collection of teddybears are seated on a sofa. The nicest rooms are in the 200-year-old house (called 10 Perkins Street) behind the inn. All six rooms with oriental rugs on wide-planked wood floors have private baths; two have church-pew benches, one has a small sitting room with fireplace and another is a small room rented as a single. Guests who don't want the nightly turn-down service are advised to hang the special "napping" sign on their door while at dinner. The changing breakfast menu might include cantaloupe, homemade granola, sourdough blueberry pancakes and Canadian bacon. And the toast, made from homemade whole wheat bread, is delectable. Doubles, $110 to $140, MAP. Closed January-March.

Castine Inn, Main Street, Box 41, Castine 04421. (207) 326-4365. Perfect for people-watching, a pleasant front porch with polka-dot covered seats and a profusion of flowers welcomes guests to the Castine Inn, built in 1898 and operated continuously since. New owners Mark and Margaret Hodesh have redone the front parlor and are spiffing up the fourteen guest rooms, nine with private baths, opening hotel-style off a long wide corridor. The carpeted rooms are plain but comfortable; two new ones on the third floor have bright wallpapers and colorful accents, and six more were to be opened on the third floor. Complimentary breakfast includes hash every day, pancakes, sausages and fresh muffins. The dark cozy pub tucked away in a corner is inviting indeed in English hunting green. A table in the large entry foyer contains all manner of local brochures, including the inn's own informative guides to diversions and shopping. Doubles, $50 to $60. Closed November to mid-May.

Castine Cottages, Route 166, Box 224, Castine 04421. (207) 326-8809. Believe it or not, these six log-cabin housekeeping cottages lined up on a secluded bluff with 1,500 feet of waterfront north of town are the only other public accommodations we could find in Castine. But they're so prized and so reasonable that they're booked for the summer by March, according to owners Lloyd and Susan Snapp, who live nearby. Each has a fully equipped kitchenette, a paneled living room with Franklin fireplace and a sofabed, two bedrooms, and a screened porch. The Snapps say the clamming is great in Hatch's Cove, which has a good beach below the cottages. Weekly rentals starting Saturday, $260.

RENTALS. House and cottage rentals are hard to come by. Check with Castine's two real-estate agencies, Water Street Realty, Box 139, (207) 326-4477, or Endicott Insurance and Real Estate, Main Street, Box 359, (207) 326-8741.

Seeing and Doing

WALKING TOURS. "The Story of Castine," a brochure you find everywhere, with maps and a history by Gardiner E. Gregory, details two walking tours which take in most of Castine. There's a short tour, which covers Main and Water steets and the quaint, out-of-the-mainstream village common that's as picturesque as any in New England. The longer tour, which can be driven although we prefer to poke along on foot, embraces Perkins Street and Battle Avenue. Included are the major fortifications (Fort Madison consists of a few embankments with two picnic tables beside the water; Fort George is larger with earthen ramparts and ditches), historic sites, a public path to the water from Dyces Head lighthouse and such unexpected pleasures as a tiny circular shorefront house and the enormous stucco summer home, Guerdwood. Interestingly, you encounter more historic markers denoting more sites than the tour map desigrates ("since we want to give visitors a pleasant walk without confusing them, some had to be left out," the historical society brochure acknowledges).

HARBOR TOURS. Castine's colorful harbor always has been dotted with yachts, sailboats, the tall-masted windjammers (usually tied up on Mondays and Tuesdays) and the ultimate incongruity for a small and sedate harbor, the towering and massive State of Maine ship. New in 1986 were historic harbor and seal-watch tours offered by the **Hattie E**, 326-9494, with daily cruises from Dennett's Wharf, starting at 6:45 a.m. for coffee cruises and continuing throughout the day and evening. Special picnic runs go to the fine Holbrook Island Sanctuary across Castine Harbor on Cape Rosier on Saturday and Sunday. Adults $10, children $6.50.

Swimming and Other Sports. Swimming off a long, stony beach is available to the public (no facilities) at **Wadsworth Cove.** The **Castine swimming pool** provides saltwater swimming in a dug pool nearby. A nine-hole golf course is open for a fee at the private **Castine Golf Club,** one of America's earliest (1897); its first five holes were originally on the site of adjacent Fort George. The club also has four tennis courts. The **Maine Maritime Academy** offers its gymnasium, pool, weight room, and squash and racquetball courts for a $3 fee daily.

The State of Maine Ship, MMA Dock, 326-4311, Ext. 254. The 534-foot-long, 10-deck-high Maine Maritime Academy training vessel is open to the public when it is in port. MMA cadets give tours on the half hour or as desired on this combination passenger-freighter built in 1949 and in service during the Korean and Vietnamese wars. It's a hulk of a sight on the Castine waterfront, and a sight inside as well. You'll see the vast engine room, the steering mechanisms, some of the cabin rooms used by 300 cadets, the mess hall and kitchens (complete with gigantic hot food vats used one night as hot tubs by the "foodos" and from which no one would eat afterward on the 1986 cruise, our cadet guide informed.) You might be told more than you want to know and climb more stairs than you want to ascend, but touring a hands-on ship used every spring for ocean training cruises is an unusual experience. Open daily, 8 to 4. Free.

The Wilson Museum, Perkins Street, 326-8753. Built in 1921 to house the extensive collections of anthropologist and geologist J. Howard Wilson, this is a highly personal place reflecting the tastes of Dr. and Mrs. Wilson and their world travels. "There's a bit of the whole world here," said the woman on duty; "the way it's laid out tells you the history of mankind back to Cyprus in 3000 B.C." Included are everything from remarkable beaded Indian moccasins and ceremonial leggins, ship models, an Indian pueblo model, firearms, stone artifacts and pottery to modern paintings by 21 artists spilling onto a rear porch above the harbor. The Wilsons' daughter, Mrs. Norman Doudiet, is the museum director and guiding force. The property also contains a working blacksmith shop, a hearse house with Castine's funeral vehicles from a century ago, and the 1763 **John Perkins House,** the area's oldest house, which was moved to the site and restored in 1970. Museum is open free daily except Monday, 2 to 5, Memorial Day through September. Open Sunday and Wednesday 2 to 5 during July and August are the Blacksmith Shop and Hearse House, free, and the Perkins House, $2.

Cold Comfort Summer Theater, Emerson Hall, Court Street, 326-9041. For a decade or so, a local theater company has been staging delightful summer productions in a low-key style. In 1986, a stray tomcat stole the show during

"Carousel" as he sauntered across the stage in the Maine Maritime Academy dock area. After appearing in Gilbert and Sullivan's "The Mikado," Leland J. Witting, editor and publisher of the weekly Castine Patriot newspaper, explained in a column why he would "put on silly clothes and sing 19th Century patter to a room full of people, when you can make a fool of yourself just as easily in print." Residents and visitors are charmed by the summer's four productions in various places, based out of Emerson Hall. Shows are Tuesday-Saturday at 8. Adults $8, students, $5.

SHOPPING. Downtown Castine consists of few but select stores. **Treworgy's Ship Chandlery** offers nautical equipment as well as gifts from around the world, books, jewelry, Gordon Fraser cards and a Caswell-Massey apothecary. At the **Water Witch**, tall, dark and striking Jean de Raat, the water witch herself, sells a variety of fine clothing made of cotton Dutch wax batiks and Java prints, as well as British Viyellas and Maine woolen fabrics; she also has an interesting mail-order catalog. An historic and handsome yellow brick house is the site of **Yellow Brick Antiques**, with choice antiques and a gallery. Owner Leila Day has branched out into a shop for contemporary crafts, **Oakum Bay, Ltd.** Also new were **Compass Rose**, a shop with books and prints and a special section of Penguin books; the **French Creek Decoy Shop**, where Castine transplant Chris Murray sells his award-winning carved wildfowl. Model ship builder Fred Nichols has a showroom on Main Street as well. The corner **Castine Variety Store**, locally called Sylvia's for its owner, carries everything from sewing machine bobbins to camera batteries; it's the place where the locals congregate starting at 6 a.m. for coffee and gossip — be advised, the counter stools are "reserved" by local custom and a visitor who sits down to order coffee is apt to be politely but firmly admonished, "that's to go."

Where to Eat

Dennett's Wharf, Sea Street, Castine. (207) 326-9045. Paul Brouillard of the Manor oversees this bustling and casual oyster bar and lobster pound right on the water below Sea Street. Colorful sailing flags hang from the vaulted ceiling of the former sail and rigging loft built in the early 1900s. Patrons dine semicommunally at heavy tables for ten, or outside at hexagonal or regular picnic tables spaced well apart on a large deck over the water. The nine-pin bowling lane discovered under the floorboards was turned into the world's longest oyster bar; here customers sip and snack while awaiting a table. There's non-stop activity and incredible atmosphere, and the all-day menu offers everything from sea urchins and razor clams to shore dinners to an excellent seafood pasta salad ($7.95) featuring halibut, cod and smoked mussels. The smoked seafood sampler ($8.95) was not what we expected — no sliced salmon but rather heavily smoked chunks of monkfish, trout, bluefish and mackerel along with shrimps, scallops and mussels, served with a delicious homemade chutney and several pieces of French bread. Those who dislike fish can order chili or teriyaki steak. The house muscadet wine is bone dry, the Coor's beer cooling and the strawberry shortcake made with fresh strawberries and real biscuits. On a sunny day the deck is glorious — alas, it gets too buggy for use at night. Weekend entertainment ranges from a calypso band to classical music by the Kneisel Hall String Quartet from nearby Blue Hill. Stop by in the morning and you might find Castine carver-fisherman Earle Bakeman delivering his catch of crabs, mussels and sea urchins, or local children gathering the periwinkle snails for the steamer. Open daily from May to mid-October.

The Manor, Battle Avenue, Castine. (207) 236-4861. When he's not at Dennett's Wharf, which is to say in the off-season, energetic Paul Brouillard cooks up a storm at the Manor. His range is as wide as his interests: shrimp saute on pasta or carpaccio for appetizers, duck breast armagnac, roast pheasant with champagne and truffles, or Atlantic salmon with a sauce of fume, French sorrel and creme fraiche for entrees ($13.50 to $16.75) Bourbon walnut pie is one of the good desserts. You may want to end your meal with cordials at the elegant bar, surrounded by all kinds of carved birds. The two small dining rooms look most luxurious at night, what with white linens, peach napkins, china in the "bittersweet" pattern, shell-patterned cutlery, pale pink stemware and candles in crystal holders. The cozy library is also available for intimate dinners. Dinner nightly, 5 to 9, mid-October through April.

The Pentagoet Inn, Main Street, Castine. (207) 326-8616. All is serene and sophisticated in Virginia and Lindsey Miller's expanded dining room. Virginia did the decorating; her rose-colored walls are a backdrop for bare wood floors and well-spaced tables draped in white linens, each formal place setting containing two wine glasses and a crystal water glass. To the rear, a new dining area has six tables beside a small deck with gardens beyond. Inn chef Jim Remick has gained a large, all-new kitchen in which to prepare changing dinner fare. Appetizers might be shrimp piccata, mushrooms stuffed with Maine crabmeat or a lobster crepe. Entrees range from $9 for broiled filet of haddock or breast of chicken sauteed with lemon and fresh rosemary to $15 for lobster pie or steamed lobster. Other offerings might be peppered rib eye steak or grilled halibut, both $11. The well-chosen wine list contains some good values. Classical music is played through a compact disc system and occasionally there is live harp and flute background music. Dinner, 5:30 to 8, by reservation only.

Castine Inn, Main Street, Castine. (207) 326-4365. The dinner menu changes daily but the specialties remain the same: crabmeat cake with mustard sauce ($3.50 as an appetizer, $11 as an entree), billi-bi bisque, roast pork loin with fresh peach chutney, chicken and leek pot pie, and baked Indian pudding and fresh fruit cobblers and crisps for dessert. The price of the meal ($10 to $14) includes biscuits, potato, vegetables and salad. Later in the evening, desserts and nightcaps are served in the living room or on the front porch. Dinner nightly except Tuesday, 6 to 8:30.

The Quarterdeck, Water Street, Castine. (207) 326-4001. Fish in three glass aquariums float above diners in booths at this casual establishment. The fish are popular with children, and the aquariums serve as dividers between the dining room and a bar with a piano. The semi-open kitchen serves up seafood and family-type fare, with such daily specials as chicken dijon with rice ($8.95), prime rib ($9.25), a crabmeat roll ($2.95) and spinach quiche ($3.50) A lobster salad plate is $4.95, and a limited breakfast menu is offered in summer from 7 to noon. Otherwise, open daily from 11 to 9, weekends 7 a.m. to 9.

Petty's Pizza, Water Street, Castine. (207) 326-4047. The sign out front states that on May 8, 1768, "this was declared the first condemned building in North America." Today it houses a tiny restaurant with four booths in which good breakfasts and excellent pizzas are served. For breakfast, try the Eggemoggin muffin ($1.50) or an omelet with home fries ($2.95). Muffins, baked each morning, go for 75 cents. Grinders, calzones and pizzas are served the rest of the day. The pizzas ($3 to $10.95) are notable for homemade white or whole wheat dough and varied toppings, including jalapeno peppers, black olives and ricotta cheese. The Hawaiian includes crushed pineapple. Petty's favorite "As We Like It" has a whole wheat crust, spinach and ricotta, is covered with mozzarella and topped with fresh mushrooms. Draft beer, wine and natural fruit juices are available. Open Monday-Saturday 7 a.m. to 10 p.m., Sunday 8 to 10, with brunch from 8 to noon.

The Breeze, Town Dock, Castine. (207) 326-9034. Good for lunch or casual supper is this snack bar in a shack, from which you take your food to picnic tables on the dock (and often share it with hungry seagulls). The fried clam roll is $3.50, a crabmeat roll $2.80, and you can get such things as a fried haddock sandwich, hamburger and a fried chicken plate for a song. Soft ice cream is available, as are shakes ($1.25) and sundaes (75 cents). The owners were planning to add boiled lobsters to the menu. Hours vary.

FOR MORE INFORMATION: Castine has no tourist information center and no Chamber of Commerce to contact. The Town Office is in Emerson Hall, Court Street, Castine, Me. 04421. (207) 326-4502.

Stonington harbor is on view from deck at Captain's Quarters.

Stonington/Deer Isle, Me.

Turn south off busy Route 1, which is apt to be filled with a steady stream of cars between Belfast and Bar Harbor, and prepare yourself for a different pace in a timeless place.

From the scenic lookout atop Caterpillar Hill as you head down Route 176 is one of the best views in all New England. Blue waters, green islands and mountains meld into one astonishing panorama as far as the eye can see.

Cross the high, unexpectedly imposing suspension bridge over the fine sailing waters of Eggemoggin Reach to Deer Isle and enter another world: one of little traffic, no neon, no fast food, few residents and fewer tourists.

Deer Isle, the second largest island off the Maine coast, is a world removed from its busy and larger neighbor, Mount Desert Island. It's more like Isle au Haut, the offshore island that embraces a remote portion of Acadia National Park, whose better known section surrounds Bar Harbor.

Back in the mid-18th century, Deer Isle ranked second only to Gloucester,

327

Mass., as a fishing port. Later, it was the source of granite for New York's bridges, Rockefeller Center and the John F. Kennedy Memorial in Arlington National Cemetery. At its height, Stonington, its biggest village, had 3,500 people, steamer service, a theater-opera house and something of a boomtown atmosphere.

Today, the commercial fishing fleet remains active, and lobster traps are piled all around town. But Stonington's population has dwindled to 1,300 hardy types who, we're told, rise with the sun and go to bed when it gets dark. "We used to have beer joints but they were nothing but trouble," reported the clerk in the state liquor store. "You'd need two trained gorillas for bouncers!" So the town, commercially at least, is dry and ever so quaint and quiet.

A sign outside the island's little information center says it's open from 10 til ? on weekdays and 11 til ? on Sundays. But it was closed every time we passed on three successive July days.

Never mind. The appeal of Deer Isle is not in the tourist attractions (there aren't any, to speak of). It's in the endearing charms of tiny towns like Deer Isle (the name of the island, as well as of the island), Sunshine and Sunset, which remain much as they were 50 or more years ago. It's in the wonderful views that appear at every turn of the island roads that meander hither and yon. It's in the remarkable crafts turned out by artisans attracted by the seaside Haystack Mountain School of Crafts and a simpler lifestyle.

As potter William Mor's wife Carolyn suggested when we visited: "Out here we have a peaceful way of life — a community where you can live and let live."

Getting There

Deer Isle is about 50 miles south of Bangor, at the end of a peninsula crossed at its top by U.S. Route 1 between Bucksport and Ellsworth. From Route 1, take Routes 175, 15 or 172 to Little Deer Isle, and Route 15 out to Stonington.

Where to Stay

A few choice inns and B&Bs are available (including one offshore in a lightkeeper's station), plus a few older motels.

Motels

Beachcomber Motel, Little Deer Isle 04650. (207) 348-6115. This 20-unit motel has a convenient waterfront location right at the foot of the Deer Isle suspension bridge. Our quarters were small but had wall-to-wall carpeting, TV and outside chairs looking onto Eggemoggin Reach. Picnic tables are scattered across the lawn leading down to the shore, where you gather mussels at low tide and swim at high tide, but can't do either in between, so great is the difference in tides here. The adjacent **Beachcomber Restaurant** has a takeout where you can get a lobster roll for $6.80, and a sitdown restaurant where dinners range from $8.50 for baked stuffed haddock to $16.95 for a deluxe shore dinner. When we dined, many customers were ordering the prime rib specials, $6.95 and $10.95. Restaurant open 7:30 a.m. to 9 p.m. Doubles, $36 to $42; open June-September.

Captain's Quarters Inn & Motel, Main Street, Box 83, Stonington 04681. (207) 367-2420. Another fine waterfront location and a magnificent, large deck with a mix of picnic tables, loungers and a little wooden church perched atop a post commend this ramble of rooms, efficiencies and apartments. You enter through a gift shop, office and coffee bar. Seventeen rooms on two floors vary from small doubles with shared baths to two-bedroom apartments with kitchens and living rooms. Best, of course, are the eight facing the water, especially a couple with their own private decks. Here, as opposed to the street side, you're lulled to sleep by the sounds of gulls and foghorns. All rooms have black and white TVs and electric blankets; some have unexpected touches like modern fireplaces and one has a spiral staircase. It takes a diagrammed map to figure out what you want and to find your way there. All the prolific flowers in pots and gardens result from the gardening talents of owner Robert Dodge, who also owns the Bayview Restaurant. Doubles, $26 to $60; apartments, $55 to $90. Open year-round.

Boyce's Motel, Water Street, Box 94, Stonington 04681, (207) 367-2421 or 367-2253. With our children, we once stayed in this small motel, which back then had seen better days. The five original units remain, but Barbara and George Boyce have added six new rooms in outbuildings to the rear, including a two-story structure with three units and decks. The biggest has a living room, kitchen and two bedrooms, while two others have sitting room and bedroom. All rooms have color TV and, while they're not on the water, the Boyces have the next best thing: a small private waterfront deck for guests' use across the street. Doubles, $29 to $50.

Inns and B&Bs

The Pilgrim's Inn, Deer Isle 04267. (207) 348-6615. This striking, dark red 1793 house occupies a grand location on a spit of land between Northwest Harbor in front and the Mill Pond in back. Innkeepers Jean and Dud Hendrick have refurbished the rooms in sprightly Laura Ashley style. Eight of the thirteen guest rooms have private baths; all have wood stoves and are furnished with antiques, oriental rugs and quilts. Parlors are on either side of the front hallway; one was being converted into a reading room with comfortable furniture when we visited. A stairway leads down to a cozy common room, its bay window overlooking the Mill Pond; a tap room where Dud Hendrick mixes a neat raspberry daiquiri upon request, and beyond, an attached barn in which Jean Hendrick serves exceptional dinners (see Where to Eat). The Hendricks' latest attraction is No. 15, a sweet seaside cottage, perfect for honeymooners, a block down Main Street. It has a living room with cathedral ceiling and open beams, fireplace and an intimate window seat, a full kitchen and dining area and an upstairs bedroom. A rear deck overlooks terraced gardens and the water. Meals may be made here or taken in the inn; double, $100 EP, $150 MAP. Homemade granola, scones, fresh melon and omelets are served at breakfast in the inn. Doubles, $120 to $140 MAP; three-night minimum in August. No credit cards; no smoking in bedrooms or dining room. Open mid-May to mid-October.

Goose Cove Lodge, Goose Cove Road, Sunset 04683. (207) 348-2508. A 1.5-mile long dirt road leads to the End of Beyond — the loveliest sight in the world, according to the lodge brochure. This 70-acre preserve marked by trails, wide sandy beaches and tree-lined shores is a paradise for nature lovers; at low tide, you can walk across a sand bar to Barred Island, a nature conservancy filled with birds and wildlife. Innkeepers Eleanor and George Pavloff offer seven secluded cottages and four attached cottages, each with ocean view, sundeck, kitchenette or refrigerator and fireplace, plus ten rooms or suites in two annexes off the main lodge. The hillside lodge is the epitome of a Maine lodge: an enormous stone fireplace and a mishmash of lodge chairs, benches, sofas and

329

bookcases. The shiny pine tables in the paneled, wraparound dining room — with windows onto the water below — are graced by William Mor stoneware and bud vases holding field flowers. Guests gather for hors d'oeuvres and BYOB drinks in the lodge before dinner at 6:30; counselors entertain children, who have their own dinner beforehand. Weekly rates, $375 to $425 per person MAP in annexes, $430 to $460 per person MAP in cottages. Shorter stays possible in June and September. Open June to mid-October.

Ocean View House, Main Street and Sea Breeze Avenue, Box 261, Stonington 04681. (207) 367-5114. Jack Custer took a glass-blowing class at nearby Hays-tack Mountain School of Crafts and liked the area so much that he and his wife Christine, who live in a Detroit suburb where he is a teacher and she a physical therapist, bought this turn-of-the-century inn about ten years ago for a summer home. They have fixed up the house, originally built to board quarry workers employed on Crotch Island, over the past few years and lately have opened it to the public as a B&B. Simple and fresh, the Ocean View has eight bedrooms sharing two baths on the second and third floors. Colorful hooked rugs are on painted floors, curtains are tied with multicolored ribbons, and there are nice touches like shell soaps, Kleenex in little houses with the tissue coming out of the chimney, and Poland Spring mineral water in every room. Colorful thick towels, pretty linen on the beds and lots of fresh flowers are other attractions. A couple of the rooms have fine views of the water; for the best view climb up to the cupola, with its 360-degree panorama. There's a small sitting room where Christine sells jams and syrups; in the sunny breakfast room, she serves muffins and sweet breads, fresh orange juice, strawberry sorbet, and (trust us, we tasted one) the best tart ever, with a seashell of pastry filled with raspberries, cream cheese, whipped cream and a blueberry glaze — the berries are local, of course. Doubles, $35. Open July and August only.

Torrey Farm B&B, King Row, Box 83, Deer Isle 04627. (207) 348-9976. Ray Malone, a most affable former choir director from Greenwich, Conn., fell in love with the island when he first visited a decade ago. In 1983, he bought his handsome farmhouse, dating from the early 19th century. As he tells it, he became an innkeeper when his friends Jean and Dud Hendrick from the Pilgrim's Inn sent up a couple for whom they had no room. "I had to race upstairs and clean the bathroom," he laughs, "and when I asked Jean how much I should charge and she suggested $50, I said, $50, just for sleeping in the bed? Holy mackerel!" Four bedrooms, of varied sizes and all interestingly decorated, share two baths. Guests have use of a front sun parlor with solar heating, cheerful with brick floor, bright yellow corduroy sofa and exotic plants like birds of paradise. A parlor with TV is also available. From his wonderful beamed kitchen, filled with baskets he makes himself, Ray serves up a breakfast of fresh fruit and homemade strawberry sorbet, bagels, coffeecake, bran muffins and maybe a French omelet with mushrooms, or waffles with real maple syrup. Ray also makes a variety of special vinegars with herbs from his large garden in back. An antiques store in an adjacent barn is also in the works. Doubles, $50. Closed in winter.

The Keeper's House, Box 26, Isle au Haut 04645. (207) 677-3678. For a change of pace, how about staying in a restored lightkeeper's station? You take the mailboat from Stonington to this remote six-mile-long island, part of Acadia National Park and eight miles offshore from Deer Isle. Innkeepers Jeffrey and Judi Burke also operate the Little River Inn in Pemaquid. Jeff came upon the

330

1907 Coast Guard lightkeeper's house atop the craggy sea cliff for the first time in 1985 and "immediately saw that it was the most wonderful possibility for an inn anywhere." After pouring $300,000 into acquisition and renovations, the Burkes feel they now offer "a living museum where guests step back in time." No cars, no electricity, no phones nor commercial development mar the simplicity of an island containing a few Acadia Park campsites and 50 residents. The light tower still operates, and beacons from five other lighthouses can be seen at night. The inn offers four large guest rooms, all with water views and furnished with antiques, sea chests, rocking chairs and coastal memorabilia, plus a separate cottage. Modern baths with hot showers (water is heated by a wood stove) are shared. Judi bakes her breads and pastries, and serves a variety of native seafood and complimentary wine at candlelight dinners; afterward, guests chat amid the glow of gas lights. The daily rate includes all expenses from parking on the mainland and round-trip passage on the mailboat to all meals and a tour of the island. Doubles, $165 AP. Two-night minimum in summer; no mailboat on Sundays or postal holidays. Open June-October.

The Inn at Ferry Landing, 108 Old Ferry Road, Deer Isle 04627. (207) 348-7760. A more perfect waterfront location — at a point along Eggemoggin Reach where the ferry from Sargentville once landed — could scarcely be imagined. And the 1850s farmhouse for sale, which we eyed longingly the previous summer, was gloriously renovated in 1987 into a trim B&B by young Bostonians Stephen and Donna Gormley, who now offer five guest rooms, two with private baths. Rooms are handsomely furnished with period pieces and antiques, and patchwork quilts top every bed. The showplace is the large, contemporary-style living room with large windows onto the water on three sides. Donna will hand you a pair of binoculars, the better to view the seals asleep on the rocks by the shore. Guests relax on a side deck facing the water; the intrepid can swim or dig mussels. A hearty breakfast is served in the dining room. Doubles, $50 to $70; open all year.

Maplehurst Inn, Route 175, Sargentville 04673. (207) 359-8806. Just across Eggemoggin Reach from Deer Isle is this 1837 estate surrounded by stately maples. Starting with three guest rooms sharing one bath in 1985, Philadelphians Dennis Mitchell and Harry Harihan have been restoring their B&B to the point where, last we knew, they had five guest rooms and four baths. From the back porch with its comfortable redwood furniture you can see the water. The sitting room has Victorian furnishings and a TV. Two dining rooms, one quite formal, are ready for breakfast or dinner. Dennis and his partner serve full breakfasts of poached eggs with hollandaise sauce or fresh blueberry pancakes. Optional BYOB dinners, by reservation, are priced from $6 to $12, depending on choice of predetermined entrees — perhaps fish chowder, London broil or Harry's spaghetti, and locally made pies. The men plan to restore the original front porch one of these days for dining. Doubles, $55.

RENTALS. Listings may be available from Green's Landing Realty, Box 500, Stonington, (207) 367-5140; Sea Breeze Real Estate, Box 26, Stonington, (207) 367-2305, or Shepard's, Box 115, Stonington, (207) 367-2790.

Seeing and Doing

Boat cruises among the islands off Deer Isle are a must, if only on a mailboat ride to Isle au Haut. Among the choices:
Palmer Day III Excursions, Stonington, 367-2207. The best trip is offered

by Capt. Reginald Greenlaw, who conducts daily cruises on his 45-passenger boat in the waters off Stonington. He is as entertaining as is his excursion, which offers closeup views of untold varieties of birds, deer and even an island full of seals, one of whom leaps beside the boat to get the raw fish the captain brings along. The seal-feeding session is more fun than any aquarium's, and we particularly enjoyed the five-mile ride along the shore of Isle au Haut. It's one of the most interesting nature cruises we've taken, as well as the most informative. Only a meanie would take the captain up on his offer to refund the fare of anyone "who will stand up in front of my guests and say they're not happy with the trip." Daily at 3, July 4 to Sept. 1; adults $7, children under 10, $4.

On Wednesdays, the Palmer Day sails to Vinalhaven and North Haven, with stops on each island, leaving at 8:30 and returning at 1:30; adults $10, children $7. Captain Greenlaw also offers special charters and bird and whale watch excursions, the latter from 6 a.m. or earlier for those who want to see the auks and puffins at Matinicus Rock and whales off outer Isle au Haut. The cost is $500 for up to 20 passengers.

Isle au Haut Co., Isle au Haut, 367-5193 days, 348-6038 evenings. Passengers can ride the **U.S. Mail boat** from Stonington to Isle au Haut and-or Duck Harbor. The trip out takes about 40 minutes, with a 15-minute stop, and Duck Harbor is 20 minutes beyond. Trips run two to five times daily except Sunday and postal holidays. One-way trips in summer are $5 adults, $3 children. The company also runs scenic excursions aboard Miss Lizzie, which departs from the Atlantic Avenue Hardware Dock, Stonington, at 2:30 daily between June 23 and mid-September for cruises among the islands of Penobscot Bay.

The Aladdin, Buck's Harbor Marine, South Brooksville, 326-9051. On their classic 40-foot Owen's cutter, Capt. David Whitney and his wife Lynn offer three sailings of three hours each daily at 10, 2 and 6. The Whitneys also will arrange moonlight cruises and picnic charters to spruce-covered islands. Scheduled sailings are $18 per person and require a minimum of six passengers.

Sailways, Goose Cove Lodge, Deer Isle, 348-2279. Based at a resort with half a mile of ocean frontage, Sailways offers a variety of boats for rent, sailing instruction and weekend lessons in sea kayaking. Owners Frank and Vicki Hull also take people on boats to haul lobster traps set out by Sailways and have expanded their rental fleet with a facility at Burnt Cove.

Other Attractions

The Island Country Club on Sunset Road, Deer Isle, offers "friendly golf and tennis," according to an advertisement. It has a nine-hole golf course and a tennis court, and lunch is available from 11 to 2.

Crockett Cove Woods Preserve, Crockett Cove, Stonington. If Deer Isle has a tourist attraction, this is it, we suppose. It's hard to find, off Whitman Road at Burnt Cove on the Stonington-Sunset Road. The persistent will be rewarded with a pleasant quarter-mile walk through part of a 100-acre coastal rain forest. The self-guided tour is enhanced by a brochure that helps the already knowledgeable identify what they see. Even the uninitiated will be impressed by the beautiful shades of greens, the exotic mosses, a bog, the lush growth and huge rocks. It really is like a rain forest. Free, parking for three or four cars only.

SCENIC DRIVES. You'll need to follow the Chamber of Commerce map, but the rewards are great for those with wanderlust. We particularly enjoy the little

Sand Beach Road along the channel known as the Deer Island Thorofare, with a stop for rock climbing or a hasty swim at Fifield Point or Burnt Cove. To the east of town is Ames Pond with some rare pink water lilies. There is a particularly scenic drive out to Oceanville, where you stumble upon a tiny beach with calm water beside a bridge. Another drive goes out past the hamlet of Sunshine (at the opposite side of the island from Sunset) to Haystack Mountain School of Crafts, where the waterfront vistas from on high are something else, and where the hardy can descend what seem like endless wooden stairs to the rocky shore. Follow almost any side road and you'll come to a dead end at the water.

Crafts and Shopping

Haystack Mountain School of Crafts, Sunshine Road, Deer Isle, 348-6946. A long gravel road finally brings you to this noted crafts school, perched on a hillside with wondrous views through deep green spruce trees of sparkling blue waters below. We found the various artists' studios and the school's layout interesting but were surprised not to see many crafts on display. This is a working school, however, and no items are for sale. Visitors welcome Thursday-Sunday 10 to 4 only.

Almost at the end of the Sunshine Road is **Clutter Inn Crafts**, a crazy-looking house that on first glance you'd probably decide to skip. Don't. Inside, Lois Albro displays wares from her studio in New Ipswich, N.H. She makes everything herself. We especially liked her nice mats adorned with ducks and birds, and bought an apron decorated with racquets for a tennis-loving friend.

Ronald Hayes Pearson, whose jewelry is exhibited across the country, has a shop in his striking home along Reach Road in North Deer Isle. Pearson works in silver and gold; his twist earrings at $65 for silver and $230 for gold are especially in demand. He and his wife Carolyn Hecker, executive director of the growing Maine Crafts Association which started locally, welcome visitors Monday-Saturday from 10 to 5.

Farther along Reach Road, which parallels Eggemoggin Reach, is the home and studio of potter **William Mor**. His functional stoneware is neatly displayed in a sheltered outdoor sales area surrounded by flower gardens and a pond. We were surprised that the pottery is kept outside, but Carolyn Mor assured us that everything is safe; "people leave their houses unlocked and their keys in their cars in Deer Isle," she explained. Nearby is a studio showroom in which you may view work in progress and see Mor's gas-fired kiln. The sales area is open daily from 10 to 5, and we predict you'll come away with a purchase or two.

The **Deer Isle Artists Association** conducts a series of four-person shows all summer in its gallery on the second floor of the old Deer Isle High School, hours from 2 to 4:30 daily. Items are for sale at moderate prices in the Little Gallery, housed in the former library.

Timeless Designs, a gallery and gift shop run by Jane Weiss, has an extraordinary stock of local crafts, from textiles to jewelry, plus gadgets and gifts for the gourmet. Also in Deer Isle, the new **Hoy Gallery**, where two enormous American flags were draped over the entrance, has fine watercolors. The **Turtle Gallery** has changing exhibits of watercolors, oils, drawings, photographs and wood carvings by area artists. The **Periwinkle Shop** stocks books, cards, knit goods, stuffed animals and local crafts.

At **Once Upon an Island**, a country gift shop of note, Cathy D'Errico offers wonderful Maine things, from axes and fireplace tools to jewelry by a neighbor, Ronald Hayes Pearson. She makes her own jams and jellies, and will bake her cheesecakes, blueberry cakes and whipped cream cakes to order.

STONINGTON SHOPS. For a remote and isolated town, Stonington has a disproportionate number of interesting galleries and shops along Main Street.

The Eastern Bay Cooperative Gallery, its rear windows providing a harbor view for an arty backdrop, is operated by local artists. On display is "the best of the island," according to one, from the more than 40 who work in a variety of media. We were struck by the colorful quilts, hooked rugs, one-of-a-kind clothing, the wall hangings, and some remarkable pottery. The **Lower Deck** below has clothes and cute country things.

Island Supply Co. has exotic clothing from the Far East, Greece and Mexico, especially things appropriate for summer by the seashore, of course, and puts out a spiffy four-color catalog. Its new **Summer House** in the rear offers home furnishings, wall hangings, batik placemats, paper lanterns and such. The **Dry Dock** is another fine shop with imported gifts — pottery from Portugal, glassware from Mexico and cooking utensils from across the world — plus colorful clothing from India, handknit sweaters, wool, cards and a children's corner. The **Dockside Bookstore**, right beside the water with chairs for reading on a little deck, specializes in Maine and marine books and nautical gifts.

The jumble of stuff in front of the second-hand shop on Sea Breeze Avenue is such that we passed several times before deciding to stop. A 10-cent box is crammed with gadgets, as are the 50-cent table and the $1 table. Go inside and you'll find everything from clam rollers to whale trivets to furniture. Owner Pete Palmieri said the shop's name, which we otherwise wouldn't have known, is **Chairs, Chairs, Chairs.** We're not sure exactly why.

Where to Eat

Pilgrim's Inn, Deer Isle. (207) 348-6615. Inn guests as well as about 10 lucky outsiders feast on the island's best meals at Pilgrim's Inn. Following cocktails and appetizers at 6 p.m. in the common room, Jean Hendrick serves a single-entree, prix-fixe dinner for $18.50 at 7 in the former goat barn, where you're surrounded by candlelight, fresh flowers, farm utensils and quilts on the walls, mismatched chairs and 10 outside doors that open to let in the breeze. The changing menu might have roast tenderloin with cornichon tarragon sauce, roast lamb with herbs, chicken breast stuffed with pesto, ricotta and pignoli nuts, or stuffed sole mousseline. Jean's salads may contain Japanese greens; her vegetables from the backyard garden might be fresh peas or new potatoes. We had a remarkable Sunday night dinner of a salad with goat cheese, homemade peasant bread, a heavenly paella decorated with nasturtiums, and a raspberry chocolate pie on a shortbread crust. The wines are good and exceedingly reasonable. Dinner nightly at 7, by reservation only.

The Fishermen's Friend, School Street, Stonington. (207) 367-2442. The outside is unprepossessing, to say the least, and the interior is zilch: a front room with booths and tables, a smaller back room with windows onto a field, and tables covered with oilcloth, paper mats and fake flowers. Hanging plants are the only "decor." But this decade-old restaurant run by Henry and Susan Bray doesn't need any. It's got down-to-earth food at the lowest prices around. For lunch, we enjoyed a wonderful clam chowder and a shrimp stew, plus a superior crabmeat roll laden with meat and the best fried clams ever for $14.50. For dinner, start with scallop stew ($2.25) or Port Clyde brand sardines, packed in Stonington and served on lettuce with saltines ($1.85). Entrees, served with a huge house salad at lunch and a salad bar at night, hot rolls and "real mashed potatoes" or french fries, range from $6.50 for haddock to a lobster dinner for

$10.95. A seafood platter is $10.75; broiled Atlantic salmon, $7.25. Friday night's fish fry is $4.99 with "seconds on us," according to the menu. Non-fish eaters like the roast beef dinner ($6.95), ham steak with pineapple or perhaps just a hot dog (85 cents). Open daily 11 to 9. BYOB; no credit cards.

Bayview Restaurant, Sea Breeze Avenue, Stonington. (207) 367-2274. Again there's not much in the way of decor -- pressed-tin ceiling and walls, linoleum floor and mismatched Scandinavian cutlery, blue mats and an arrangement of wildflowers at each table (at night, the mats give way to tablecloths and candlelight). And, despite the name, there's not much of a water view except, perhaps, from the rear kitchen. But the food is fresh and reasonably priced, from $5.95 for baked or boiled scrod and fried shrimp to $11.95 for Nellie's sauteed lobster meat served on toast points ("a la Nova Scotia, from an old family recipe," according to the makeshift menu). You can get almost any of the local fish fried, broiled or baked, and the seafood platter is a hefty serving for $9.25. Breakfast from 6, lunch 11 to 3, dinner 5 to 9 or later. BYOB.

Eaton's Lobster Pool, Blastow's Cove, Little Deer Isle. (207) 348-2383. It was dark by the time we reached this cavern of a room, with bare tables covered with "how to eat your lobster" paper placemats, bare light bulbs hanging from the ceiling beams, a fireplace in the middle and lobster cut-outs in the doors. We got the manager to unscrew the light bulb right over our heads, drank wine from water glasses, poured our own water from a pitcher, helped ourselves to dressings from a couple of bottles brought along with our iceberg-lettuce salads, and settled in for a lobster feast like everyone else. The lobster dinner ($15) was fine, and the steamed clams some of the most succulent we've tasted. We didn't have room for the only dessert, a homemade blueberry pie. Not til the next day when we returned for another look did we realize that tables near the windows had wondrous water views, or that there was a wraparound outdoor deck by the water with, inexplicably, no tables. Dinner, Monday-Saturday 5 to 9; Sunday, noon to 9. Seasonal.

Austin's, Water Street, Stonington. (207) 367-5871. In what was an ice cream shop with seven tables, the owners expanded the menu in 1986, and now one can lunch very pleasantly inside or on an outdoor deck over the water. The Austin family, who also operate Austin Woods in Machias, make their chowder from scratch with butter, cream and salt pork from a family recipe, they poach their own turkey at night, obtain their rye bread and bagels from a deli in Bangor, and import their water from Burnt Cove. They were in their shakedown period when we visited and had just run out of pita bread for the sandwiches. But we were after the ice cream anyway. It's made by a cooperative of Hancock County farmers, has a high butterfat content and is absolutely delectable. Open from 11:30, June-September.

The Penguin Peddler, Water Street, Stonington. Nancy Brooks sets up the grill behind her little street stand from 11 to 3 in the summer and cooks up hot dogs with kraut (85 cents), chili, sandwiches and other lunchy things. A bagel with herbed cream cheese is $1.30; a BLT pocket, $2.10. She also has potato salad and cole slaw, and her fudge is 50 cents a piece.

FOR MORE INFORMATION: Deer Isle-Stonington Chamber of Commerce, Box 268, Stonington, Me. 04681. (207) 348-6124.

Sand Beach offers ocean swimming for the hardy in Acadia National Park.

Bar Harbor/Acadia National Park, Me.

Anyone who has succumbed to the enticements of Acadia National Park can believe full well its claim to having more scenic variety per square mile than any other part of the national park system.

Rugged ocean coastline first comes to mind when one thinks of Acadia, which occupies the better part of Mount Desert Island — the country's third largest (after Long Island and Martha's Vineyard).

There also are towering cliffs and mountain summits (including Cadillac Mountain, the highest along the East Coast), the East's only natural fjord, fresh-water lakes, sandy beaches, and wetlands and forests full of wildlife.

Such scenic diversity produces the widest range of outdoor activity in one place in Maine, if not the East. The visitor can explore the jagged shoreline, climb mountains, swim in the ocean or lakes, go sailing or lobstering, canoe through salt marshes and kayak along the coast, watch for birds and whales, walk along nature trails and through exotic gardens, hike or bicycle or go horseback riding on 50 miles of carriage paths, and camp near the sea, among other pursuits.

They used to call it "rusticating," when thousands of city folk descended in the 19th century on Bar Harbor — the island's largest town — to pursue the active outdoor life, eschewing what they considered the pretentious activities of such summer colonies as Newport, Lenox and Saratoga. In the 1880s, Bar Harbor's 18 hotels could accommodate more than 25,000 guests, and the elite began building fashionable cottages that were the largest in Maine.

Residents like John D. Rockefeller Jr., fearing commercial encroachments, bought up vast tracts of land. In 1919, they donated them to the federal government for the first national park in the East. The advent of the automobile made the island more accessible, the hotels disappeared and the Great Fire of 1947 destroyed many of the large homes remaining from Bar Harbor's heyday.

336

Today's visitors find vestiges of the island's Golden Era in the mansions of West and Eden streets, and the enclaves at Seal Harbor and Northwest Harbor. But they're more likely to find campers and hikers and bicyclists who appreciate the outdoor wonderland that led the residents who settled Bar Harbor in 1796 to name the town Eden.

With four million visitors annually, Acadia is said to rank second only to the Great Smokies as the nation's most visited national park. Most are rusticators — the kind of people whom local innkeeper Frank Matter describes as "more bohemian than sophisticated." After all, he says, the old Bar Harbor was the bohemian resort for the wealthy. Although elements of high-living and luxury creep in this far Down East, Acadia National Park gives the island a sense of rugged individualism in sync with nature.

Getting There

Bar Harbor and Acadia National Park are about 180 roundabout miles northeast of Portland and 45 miles southeast of Bangor. Take coastal U.S. Route 1 to Ellsworth or Interstate 95 to Bangor and Route 1A to Ellsworth. Route 3 from Ellsworth leads to the park entrance and, beyond, to Bar Harbor. An airport just off island in Trenton is served by airlines from New England cities. The Blue-nose ferry connects Bar Harbor with Yarmouth in Nova Scotia.

Where to Stay

About 950 rooms were added in Bar Harbor in 1986 alone, bringing the total to 6,400, according to local innkeepers. The options are so varied and numerous that we can offer only a choice sampling of those near the water.

Cottages and Camping

You'll find more old-fashioned cabins and cottage colonies (and motels) along the approaches to Acadia National Park and Bar Harbor than you thought existed. Even in high season if you arrive without a reservation, with luck you'll be able to find room in one. A few of the better choices:

Emery's Cottages on the Shore, Sand Point Road, Box 172, Bar Harbor 04609. (207) 288-3432. Many cottage colonies aren't near the water, are decrepit and packed close together. This complex is one of the best; it has 14 housekeeping and 8 sleeping cottages, the latter closest to the water. All have electric heat, color TV and private baths, some with new tub-shower combinations. Efficiency cottages vary in size. The sleeping cottages have one double bed, a refrigerator and coffeemaker. A pleasant lawn leads to a gravel beach; lawn chairs, picnic tables and grills are provided. Weekly rates, non-housekeeping $325; efficiencies, $375 to $425; daily rates off-season and when available. Open late April to late October.

Hinckley's Dreamwood Motor Court, Route 3, Box 15, Bar Harbor 04609. (207) 288-3510. It's not on the water, but its location among the pines is the next best thing. Twenty-nine rooms are available in duplex motel units and cottages, 16 with kitchenettes. All are carpeted and have television; several have screened porches and fireplaces, and there's an appealing small pool. A four-bedroom house is available for $125 a night and a four-bedroom cottage for $100. Housekeeping units require a three-day minimum in season; weekly rates are available. Doubles, $38 to $45 in motel units, $48 to $54 in housekeeping ($56 to $74 for up to four persons). Open May to Oct. 15.

Woodland Park, Route 3, Box 1590, Bar Harbor 04609. (207) 288-4016. Three generations of our family stayed here for a couple of summer vacations in the 1960s. The seven housekeeping cottages vary in size and quality (some of us were put up in a trailer), but the location away from the highway beside the water in a secluded cove is good, and the swimming from a raft exhilarating — if you can last in the 50-degree water. Weekly rates, $275 to $500 for up to four people.

Seaside Cottages, Clark's Cove, RD 1, Box 2340, Bar Harbor 04609. (207) 288-3674. Fully equipped cottages of one to three bedrooms are offered by the Leland family beside the waters of Clark's Cove. A wide lawn leads to a private beach for swimming and clam digging, and free rowboats are available for fishing. Weekly rates for two, $400. Open May–October.

CAMPING. Mount Desert Island is a paradise for campers, and five private campgrounds are happy to oblige in Bar Harbor. Closest to town is **Bar Harbor Campground,** whose rates of $10 to $13 a night for a party of four are typical. **Mount Desert Narrows Campground** is on the ocean. Purists prefer the two campgrounds in Acadia National Park — **Blackwoods,** five miles south of Bar Harbor off Route 3, and **Seawall,** near Southeast Harbor. Both are in woods near the ocean, and offer naturalist talks and special activities. Fees are $4 a night, for a maximum of two weeks. Sites can be reserved at Blackwoods; Seawall is first-come, first-served. Contact the National Park Service, Acadia National Park, RD 1, Box 1, Bar Harbor 04609.

RENTALS. Many cottage colonies rent by the week or longer. Realtors such as Island Realty, 110 Main St., 288-9778, and the Bar Harbor Chamber of Commerce can advise on house or cottage rentals.

Inns/Motor Inns

Bar Harbor Inn & Motor Inn, Newport Drive, Bar Harbor 04609. (207) 288-3351. The Bar Harbor Motor Inn's name was changed in 1986 to reflect the extensive restoration of the original inn building, which now looks and feels as its predecessor (the private Oasis Club's Reading Room) must have at the turn of the century. Rebuilt following the 1947 fire as the Bar Harbor Hotel, the inn now has a handsomely appointed lobby. Owner Barry Harris also added an outdoor dining terrace and planned a hotel addition for what has to be the most watery spot in town — on seven landscaped acres with the sea on two sides. The 54 rooms in the main inn have been beautifully refurnished in Colonial elegance, but possessing such modern accoutrements as cable TV, clock radios and pushbutton phones. Some inn rooms have views of the harbor, and some over the lobby are enormous. We've always been partial to the motel section, whose balconies back up to the water with wonderful views and considerable privacy. We didn't know there was such a pleasant walk around the point along Frenchman Bay until we stayed there. There's a large heated pool, as well as a small public beach adjacent. Daily sailing excursions are offered on the schooner Janet May, which is moored at its 164-foot pier. Three meals a day are available at the outdoor **Gatsby's Terrace** or the striking, windowed **Reading Room** (see Where to Eat). Doubles, $86 to $110. Open May–October.

Bayview Hotel & Inn, 111 Eden St, Bar Harbor 04609. (207) 288-3173 or 288-4353. In 1983, Texas businessman John Davis converted his family's 30-room white brick Georgian-style summer home built in the 1930s into a smashing inn (with four spacious and opulent guest rooms) and restaurant overlooking

Frenchman Bay. He then added condominium townhouses, set well back from the water, and a 26-room three-story hotel next to the inn and, some would say, made it into Neiman-Marcus North. We think the hotel a bit glitzy for Bar Harbor, and are partial to the elegance and seclusion of the inn (it's like staying in a private mansion). Unfortunately, the rooms in the hotel have only fake balconies, but everything else is fit for a visiting Texan, from the crystal lamps and TVs hidden in the armoires to the bubblebath presented in a silver swan. The hotel's waterside restaurant and bar, all in tones of pink, peach and rust, with rose wing chairs, look out onto a terrace, above a small swimming pool and large whirlpool. Only breakfast and lunch are served here. For dinner one may go to the inn, where the setting is unforgettable (see Where to Eat). Doubles in hotel, $135 to $155; in inn, $95 to $175. Open year-round.

The Bar Harbor Regency, 123 Eden St., Bar Harbor 04609. (207)288-9723. Most of Bar Harbor's hostelries were Mom-and-Pop operations until this one was erected by a Florida outfit and landscaped almost overnight for a delayed opening in 1986. But this is the newcomer with which oldtimers now compete, and compete they do (see above). It occupies the site of the former home of Dr. William Procter of Procter & Gamble, who'd never recognize the four-story hotel with 179 rooms, all rather sophisticated for Down East Maine (there's even a glass elevator from which riders can view Frenchman Bay). Most rooms have tiny balconies and are tastefully furnished in soft greens with kingsize or two double beds. The grounds include tennis courts, a jogging path, a small pool and jacuzzi. A seafood restaurant was due to open. Doubles, $120 to $150.

Atlantic Oakes By-the-Sea, Route 3, Bar Harbor 04609. (207) 288-5801. Until the newcomers arrived, this 109-room resort motel beside the Bluenose Ferry Terminal on the 10-acre estate once owned by Sir Harry Oakes was one of Bar Harbor's most deluxe and expensive. Each spacious room in this brown-shingled low-rise has large windows onto a balcony or patio with a grand ocean view. The attractive grounds include five tennis courts (two of them lighted and with a tennis pro in residence), a heated pool and a pebble beach with a float and a pier, where boats may be rented and sailing lessons are given. In season, a complimentary breakfast is served in the mansion each morning, and lobster cookouts and clambakes are available. Doubles, $76 to $103. Open year-round.

Atlantic Eyrie Lodge, Highbrook Road, Bar Harbor 04609. (207) 288-9786. The owner of Atlantic Oakes By-the-Sea opened this four-story motor inn high atop a hill above Cleftstone Manor in 1986. Most of the 57 rooms have great ocean views from private balconies (the top two floors carry higher prices). All rooms have cable TV and two double beds except for larger kitchenette rooms that have one king bed and a sofabed. A continental breakfast of donuts, juice and coffee is provided in the lobby. The swimming pool has a slide, which youngsters like. Doubles, $75 to $90. Open May 25 through Oct. 15.

Park Entrance Motel, Route 3, Bar Harbor 04609. (207) 288-3306. Located on a hillside opposite the main park entrance, this established motel is almost always booked and we're disappointed when we call too late, which is usually. It's a low-key kind of place, away from town and caring not a whit about the rat race engendered by newer hoteliers. It advertises "an ocean view from every room," if it advertises at all, and the lawns slope down to a pebble beach graced by a pier and the biggest mussels we ever saw, ready for gathering by the handful at low tide. Rowboats are free, the outdoor pool has a curving slide, picnic tables and grills are available for cookouts, and there's an 18-hole putting green. The 53 rooms on two floors are comfortable and priced right, and five efficiencies are available. Doubles, $70. Open mid-May to mid-October.

Golden Anchor Inn & Pier, 55 West St., Bar Harbor 04609. (207) 288-5033 or (800) 242-1231. Don't be deceived by the name; this is a sprawling 88-room motel of some years, right in the heart of town. It does have a large pier and it's right on the water, all but six rooms having sliding doors onto private balconies with water views — as close as 25 feet to the ocean, our guide pointed out. Best of the two buildings is the one farther from the street and facing directly onto Frenchman Bay. Rooms have two double beds, TV and modern baths, and look like those in any older motel, except for the view. There's a large outdoor pool, and coffee and donuts are served in the morning. Cruises leave from the pier, which is the site of the **Chart Room** restaurant (see Where to Eat). Doubles, $80 to $101. Open year-round.

Inns/Guest Houses

Cleftstone Manor, Eden Street, Bar Harbor 04609. (207) 288-4951. A larger-than-life portrait of Queen Victoria greets you rather unapprovingly at the entrance to this 33-room summer home built atop a cliff in 1884 by the Blair family of Washington (D.C.) Blair House fame. Surely, the queen would approve of what Don and Phyllis Jackson, formerly of Connecticut, have done since 1981 to transform the rambling 19th century mansion into a treasure trove of formal Victoriana, with a heavy dose of Britain to boot. White lace, ribbons and bows, dolls, velvet-covered chairs, priceless antiques and art objects are everywhere. Thirteen of the 18 guest rooms have private baths; one has a private balcony overlooking Frenchman Bay, five have fireplaces, and all have goose-down comforters, handmade quilts and plush carpeting accented with orientals. Rooms vary in size from small to sumptuous. The prized Romeo & Juliet honeymoon suite — one of three fashioned from the original ballroom on the main floor — has a brass bed canopied in lace and a wondrous pillow-laden sofa in front of the fireplace. A hearty breakfast of fruit and yogurt salad, coffee cake, bagels, datenut bread and crumpets is served in the magnificent sunroom, a sight to behold with its white wicker furniture, blue cushions and Dutch blue Delft collection. "The secret is to feed them well," Phyllis says of her guests. At 4 o'clock, she serves high tea, with cucumber and watercress sandwiches plus four or five sweets; in the evenings, she says, world affairs are settled in the parlor over complimentary wine and three kinds of English cheese. In the inn's tiny gift shop, Phyllis sells a small cookbook she compiled.. Outside, the Jacksons lavish attention on their fine English garden, which provides English lavender for their potpourris and yarrow for their dried flower arrangements. Doubles, $70 to $125. Open May-October.

The Inn at Canoe Point, Route 3, Box 216, Hulls Cove 04644. (207) 288-9511. One of Mount Desert Island's few small inns right on the ocean, this is a stunner of a place. After getting his feet wet with a couple of B&Bs in Southwest Harbor, Don Johnson provided the crowning touch by turning this Tudor-style home hidden from the highway in an acre and a half of woods into a stylish B&B. A large, L-shaped deck takes full advantage of the location beside Frenchman Bay. Five guest rooms, all with private baths, have water views and are decorated in exquisite taste. Check out Don's collection of Life and Esquire magazines dating from the 1930s and '40s in the upstairs hall. Guests enjoy a pleasant living room, where an elegant grouping of seats faces the fireplace, and the waterfront Ocean Room with a huge sectional, fireplace and stereo. The latter is the setting for a breakfast of fresh fruit and a main course like blueberry pancakes, cinnamon french toast or spinach and cheddar quiche. Iced tea is served on warm afternoons on the waterfront deck, which is so seductive as to keep guests from touring the rest of the island. Don also can be persuaded to take guests out on his boat. Doubles, $75 to $150; open all year.

The Tides, 119 West St., Bar Harbor 04609, (207) 288-4968. Susan and Barry Fox-Jackson, he the son of the Clefstone owners, opened their inn in an imposing Greek-Revival mansion in 1986. No Victorian clutter here — ''I don't like dusting,'' says Susan. The couple aims for a mood of casual elegance, they say. We'd say it is more elegant than casual. Our room, the master bedroom, was the epitome of class, from the beige or blue velvet wing chairs, the queensize bed with fishnet canopy, eyelet dust ruffle, and lace-trimmed sheets to the large dressing room with makeup table, the arrangement of daisies and mums, and the attention to every detail. There was even a small porch off the bathroom where we could sit and enjoy the salt air. And in the bathroom were Crabtree & Evelyn bath cubes, Yardley skin cream and posh towels of deep burgundy with eyelet edges. Two crystal glasses flanked a bottle of Perrier, and ice came in a crystal ice bucket on a silver tray with silver tongs, set on a linen napkin. The two other bedrooms, the East Room and Amy's Room, are not as large but are equally well-equipped. Guests have use of an upstairs living room with a huge sofa in front of a fireplace; most pieces were picked up at auctions in New Hampshire and finished by the couple. Susan serves an outstanding breakfast, either on the pillared rear porch overlooking Frenchman Bay or in the gorgeous dining room. From orange juice in a cut-glass pitcher to Royal Worcester napkin rings, this is a remarkable repast. We were served cantaloupe, blueberry muffins, coffeecake and two eggs on toast ringed with bacon, but Susan has a big repertoire of breakfast dishes like baked french toast with raisin bread and streusel topping or a sausage, egg and cheese casserole. The one-and-a-half-acre property, landscaped with lovely old lilac trees and Japanese maples, has 156 feet of bay frontage. You couldn't ask for a better place to unwind. Doubles, $125 to $150. Open mid-May to mid-October.

Seeing and Doing

Acadia National Park, the largest national park in the East, is Mount Desert Island's big draw. The 38,000 acres encompass 44 miles of dramatic coastline, all the island's major mountains, part of the Somes Sound fjord, all or part of every major lake shore, 120 miles of trails and bike paths, and a scenic 20-mile Loop Road and Ocean Drive that allow drivers to see the highlights.

The **Visitor Center** on Route 3 south of Hull's Cove is a must for orientation purposes (you can also tune your car radio in to a special frequency detailing park events and highlights). Up a two-minute walk from an expanded parking lot is a rustic contemporary building in which a 15-minute movie is shown on the half hour from 8 a.m. to 8 p.m., park rangers offer advice about trips and naturalist programs, and you can rent a self-guiding cassette-tape tour of the park (rental of player and tape, $8.95; tape only, $5.95). Here also you get your first panoramic view of Frenchman Bay from on high.

PARK LOOP ROAD. Starting from the Visitor Center, this 20-mile loop can take three hours (with stops) or a day. The limited-access two-lane roadway can be entered or left at several points, but the Ocean Drive segment is one-way outbound. The first two overlooks provide good views of Frenchman Bay, Bar Harbor and the area burned in the 1947 fire.

Sieur de Monts Spring, covered by a small octagonal structure but still bubbling water from a fountain in the adjacent nature center, is a favorite stop. The **Robert Abbe Museum of Stone Age Antiquities** tells most of what you could want to know of the area's history, especially of the Indians (admission 50 cents). The wonderful **Wild Gardens of Acadia** has more than 300 plants indigenous to the area's forests, mountains and shores labeled and grouped in 13 sections, from deciduous weeds to dry heath and bog. Well-maintained gravel paths lead past some rare specimens, with benches placed strategically along the way. (If the Wild Gardens whet your appetite, stop later at the showy **Asticou Terrace and Thuya Gardens** in Northeast Harbor.)

The 1.4-mile **Precipice Trail** rises sharply from the Champlain Mountain overlook. The males in our family climbed it and returned with the report that it took 90 minutes to get up, 40 minutes to come down, and that there were two tunnels and countless firemen-type ladders to traverse, with sheer drops to contemplate. Wild blueberries along the way and the view from the barren summit made the hike worthwhile.

Going from the sublime to the ridiculous, cool off after your climb at **Sand Beach,** the only saltwater beach in the park and an arc of sand between two cliffs. You may notice hundreds of people on the beach and only a few brave souls in the ocean. Feel and you'll know why; the water temperature rarely tops 55. If you like to get numb, head for the changing room, don your suit and c'mon in, the surf's fine. Otherwise, soak up some sun — if it's not obliterated by fog — or hike the easy 1.8-mile Ocean Path along the water.

Thunder Hole is where the waves rush into a small cave and roar out with a sound of distant thunder, if tides and surf coincide. At **Otter Cliffs,** look out to sea from the highest headlands on the East Coast. Beyond is **Otter Point,** a rocky place good for sunning and picnicking.

Leaving the ocean, the Park Loop Road turns inland toward Jordan Pond. Stop for lunch or tea at the venerable **Jordan Pond House** (see Where to Eat) and admire the view of the two rounded mountains known as the **Bubbles** (named by a long-ago youth for the bosom of his amour). At the end of Jordan Pond is a huge boulder balancing atop a cliff.

Pass beautiful **Eagle Lake,** which gets smaller and bluer as you drive the 3.2-mile side trip up **Cadillac Mountain.** The road is excellent and gradual (an 8 percent grade, which our son bicycled up) and the view from the top is incredible in all directions. A short summit trail has interesting interpretive signs. The Sunset Parking Area near the top is where everyone gathers to watch the sunset — the mountains and waters to the west a changing rainbow of greens, blues, oranges and reds. It's an enlightening sight to anyone who thinks Key West or Carmel sunsets are the ultimate.

Descend Cadillac Mountain and you've completed the loop. Follow the signs to Bar Harbor or other destinations.

OTHER DRIVES. So far, you've seen only a portion of the park, albeit the most popular part. Head for Northeast Harbor and **Sargent Drive,** which borders the fjord-like **Somes Sound.** There are scenic views all the way around to quaint **Somesville.** Down the west side of Somes Sound is **Echo Lake,** which has a fine beach, changing rooms, and water far warmer than the ocean. It's a short hike or a long drive around Echo Lake to **Beech Cliff,** which has a great view of the lake below and where if you holler, you may hear your echo. Farther down the peninsula past Southwest Harbor is a section of the park containing **Seawall, Wonderland,** and the **Ship Harbor Nature Trail** (which is well worth taking), and the **Bass Harbor Light.** These are the high spots of Acadia National Park on Mount Desert Island; other sections of the park are off-island on Isle au Haut and on the mainland Schoodic Peninsula.

CARRIAGE PATHS. Fifty miles of carriage paths were planned and built by John D. Rockefeller Jr. in the 1920s to provide a refuge for carriages from the intrusions of the auto. The 10-foot-wide paths follow the land's contours, protected by stone culverts and retaining walls and notable for 13 interesting, hand-cut stone bridges. About 18 miles of the paths have been specially surfaced for bicycles; the rest are better for hikers, wide-tire bicyclers and horseback riders.

Active Pursuits

NATURALIST PROGRAMS. The park offers a remarkable range of programs and tours, from boat cruises to mountain hikes to nature walks to evening activities. They follow a set daily schedule (available from the park visitor center), starting with a three-hour birder's walk at 7:30 and ending at 9:30 with Stars over Acadia from the summit of Cadillac Mountain. Among the more appealing titles are Life between the Tides, Shoreline Discovery Walk, Boulders and Beaches, Beaver Watch and Night Prowl. The park naturalists or their assistants are personable and enlightening, and we've enjoyed every tour or program we've tried.

BIKING. Although the terrain is hilly, biking opportunities abound throughout Acadia National Park and Mount Desert Island. The park visitor center offers detailed maps of roads and trails through the park. Cyclists can take the same routes as listed above on the Park Loop and other drives. They can get away from cars and trailers on the park's carriage paths. The Eagle Lake-Witch Hole Loop is a five-hour carriage park ride with spectacular views of lakes, mountains and ocean. For shore-viewing, bike the road to Seawall and Wonderland. A longer excursion is to take the 40-minute ferry ride from Bass Harbor to **Swan's Island,** a world apart. We once picnicked in an eerie fog at deserted Hockamock Head Lighthouse high on a cliff with a bell buoy ringing off shore and an abundance of raspberries, blueberries and gooseberries waiting to be picked. Swan's Island seems not to have a level stretch, however, and pedaling up all the hills isn't easy for aging legs. Bicycles are available for rent in Bar Harbor at **Mopeds of Maine,** 116 Main St.; **Bar Harbor Bicycle Shop,** 114 Cottage St., and **Acadia Bike & Canoe,** 48 Cottage St.

HIKING. Besides 50 miles of carriage paths, 120 miles of hiking trails await the hiker. They vary from mountain climbs (naturalists lead hikes up Acadia, Gorham and Beech mountains) to self-guided walks for casual strollers — the Jordan Pond nature path and the Ships Harbor nature trail. The park visitor center provides trail maps.

HORSEBACK RIDING. Wildwood Stables, Park Loop Road near Seal Harbor, 276-3622, offers one-hour guided horseback rides five times daily from 9:30 for $8 per rider. Hour-long horse-drawn tours over the carriage roads leave four times a day starting at 10 (adults $6, children $4). A 90-minute sunset hayride to the summit of Day Mountain leaves at 6:30 in June and July, at 6 in August and September (adults $6, children $4).

CANOEING AND KAYAKING. The lakes of Mount Desert Island are considered a canoeist's paradise. Locals recommend Long Pond, the island's largest with three access points; secluded Seal Cove Pond, Echo Lake, Eagle Lake and Jordan Pond. Tidal currents in Somes Sound are dangerous for light craft; you also might be surprised by frolicking porpoises. Canoeing the Bass Harbor Marsh at high tide is quite an experience, especially on a moonlit night when you may hear and see herons, owls, beavers and deer. Canoes may be rented from **Acadia Bike & Canoe**, 48 Cottage St., Bar Harbor, or **National Park Canoe Rental** at Pond's End in Somesville (mornings, $12.50; afternoons, $13.50, and full day, $19.50). **Coastal Kayaking Tours,** 48 Cottage St., Bar Harbor, 288-5483, conducts a variety of tours and rents kayaks.

SWIMMING. The only ocean beach is **Sand Beach** (see Acadia National Park). Lifeguards staff it and the park's **Echo Lake.** Explore or ask around and you may come upon a little beach or swimming area on others of the numerous freshwater lakes. If you're adventurous (some would say foolhardy), you can swim off the rocks or in the coves of Frenchman Bay.

Walk the Bar. For two hours on either side of low tide, you can walk across a sand bar from the end of Bar Harbor's High Street (just west of the Bar Harbor Club) to Bar Island. There are trails and shoreline to explore, and the shallow water is considerably warmer than at Sand Beach. Bring a picnic and a bathing suit, but don't tarry or you may have to swim back against the current.

Boat Cruises

NATURALIST SEA CRUISES. Park naturalists conduct cruises aboard privately owned boats, and these are among the more informative of all the island's cruises. Tours as scheduled in 1986: Frenchman Bay, Municipal Pier, Bar Harbor, 288-3322, two-hour cruise in search of eagles, ospreys and porpoises, daily except Thursday at 8:30, adults $6.50, children $4. Bass Harbor, Swan's Island Ferry Terminal, 244-5365, two hours of Down East scenes related to the lobster industry, daily except Sunday at 1, adults $6, children $4. Islesford Historical Cruise, Municipal Pier, Northeast Harbor, 276-5352, three hours through Somes Sound and Cranberry Isles to Little Cranberry Island to visit Islesford Historical Museum, daily except Wednesday at 9, adults $7, children $4. Baker Island, Municipal Pier, Northeast Harbor, 244-3366, four-hour cruise to isolated, storm-sculptured Baker Island, daily except Monday at 1, adults $9, children $4.

Frenchman's Bay Boating Co., 1 West St., Bar Harbor, 288-3322, offers boat rentals, sailing cruises and at least 11 sightseeing cruises of Frenchman Bay daily in summer. Costs range from $5 adult, $3 child for one-hour cruises to $7.75 adult, $4.50 child for a two-and-one-half-hour cruise covering the estates, Seal Harbor, the Rockefeller compound and the Porcupine Islands. Half-day deep-sea fishing tours leave at 8 and 1:30, $15 per person. The Bay Lady II gives windjammer cruises five times daily: adults $13.50, children $9.

The Janet May, Bar Harbor Motor Inn Pier, Bar Harbor, 288-4585. With bright red sails, this 91-foot replica of a 19th century wooden coasting schooner offers three sailing excursions daily of two to three hours. Prices vary from $14 to $17.50; children half price. Also sailing from the Motor Inn Pier is the Marion G, a 1938 wooden sailing yacht, taking up to six passengers on a five-hour island sail at 10 ($35), plus a harbor sail from 3:30 to 5 and an evening sail from 6 to 7:30 (both $15).

Aunt Elsie's Lobster Fishing Trips, 60 West St., Bar Harbor. 288-9505. The Aunt Elsie takes passengers aboard to watch lobster traps being hauled up and to enjoy lobster and crab cooked on board. Ninety-minute trips leave five times daily starting at 8. Tickets $12.

Acadia Whale Watch, Golden Anchor Pier, West Street, Bar Harbor, 288-9794. Billed as the largest and fastest whale-watch boat on the East Coast, this cruises the open Atlantic for four to five hours to look for whales, sharks, seals, porpoises, dolphins and birds. Tickets $20.

The Golden Eagle, Golden Anchor Pier, West Street, Bar Harbor, 288-9505. Bald eagles are the theme of this cruise of two to three hours; they sometimes come within 20 feet of the ship to pick fish out of the ocean. Passengers also may see seals, ospreys, fish hawks and porpoises. Tickets $8.

Harbor Boat Rentals, 1 West St., Bar Harbor, 288-3757. Boston Whalers with outboard motors are priced by size from $25 for two hours to $95 for eight hours.

Sea Fun Day Cruise, Bar Harbor Ferry Terminal, Bar Harbor, 288-3395. The CN Marine-operated **Bluenose** ferry leaves daily at 8 for a six-hour crossing to Yarmouth, N.S. Most of the passengers go one way or for extended trips, but the ferry offers round trips with about a 90-minute layover in Yarmouth, returning about 9:30. The day trip includes a buffet breakfast and dinner, as well as a complete lunch. The highlight for many is gambling at the slot machines; it certainly isn't the view (there isn't any except at either end) or downtown Yarmouth. Be sure to pick a calm day. Our latest crossing to Yarmouth was so rough that almost everyone got seasick; we pitied the poor souls who had to turn around and endure six more hours. Adults $49.50, children $32.50.

Other Attractions

Museums. The Natural History Museum of the College of the Atlantic, Route 3, Bar Harbor, has exhibits relating to the island's marine mammal, seabird and plant life. Visitors are encouraged to disassemble and reassemble the backbone of a 20-foot whale skeleton and to walk nature trails. Open daily 9 to 4, mid-June to Labor Day. Adults $1.50, children 50 cents. The **Bar Harbor Historical Museum** in the basement of the Jesup Memorial Library has a collection of early photographs, hotel registers and a large scrapbook on the 1947 fire. Open weekdays 1 to 4; free.

Music. Band concerts are presented by the Bar Harbor Town Band Monday and Thursday evenings at 8 on the Village Green. The green also is the site of other events, including a mid-July **Dulcimer Festival. The Bar Harbor Festival** presents weekend concerts in the summer, and the **Acadia Repertory Theater** has a full summer season in Somesville. New in 1986 and a big hit was the **Music Theater of Bar Harbor's** dinner-theater cabaret of "Oklahoma" and other movie themes at the Bar Harbor Club. The $18 tab included dinner and entertainment.

SHOPPING. Bar Harbor shops are concentrated along Main, Cottage and Mount Desert streets. **Island Artisans**, a co-op, is owned by the two dozen artists who are represented in the handsome shop by a variety of wares. The Bar Harbor headquarters of the **Acadia Shops**, which also are located in the national park and have an exceptional shop at the Jordan Pond House, features the crafts, gifts and foods of Maine. The **Dancing Deer** has interesting gifts, and **A Potter's Choice** and the **Blue Heron** are good for crafts. **J.H. Butterfield Co.** is a gourmet grocery store of the old school, and **Trehan's Candies** serves up sweets.

Where to Eat

With only 7,000 year-round residents to support them in the off-season, most island restaurants operate seasonally — generally from April or May to October or November.

A Seaside Feeling

George's, 7 Stevens Lane, Bar Harbor. (207) 288-4505. Run by a local high-school history teacher, this summery place in a little Southern-style house off Main Street behind First National Bank doles out our favorite food on the island, imaginatively and with a Greek orientation. White organdy curtains flutter in the breeze, classical guitar music plays in the background and everything is served on clear glass plates atop pink-linened tables. On our latest visit, hot crusty French bread and the best little Greek salads ever preceded our entrees — a distinctive plate of smoked scallops on fettuccine ($8.95) and a special of shrimp on a fresh tomato sauce with feta cheese, rice pilaf and fresh New Zealand spinach with orange juice and orange zest ($12.50). Only a lemon cloud with a slightly soggy crust was not up to snuff. The appetizers are assertive (artichoke hearts baked in phyllo with bechamel and kasseri cheese boiled with garlic), and the entrees inventive (mustard shrimps, lamb seared with pepper and onion, veal sauteed with lime, and mushrooms baked in French bread with cream and tarragon), priced from $7.50 to $15.50. The seafood strudel is a knockout, the house Greek wine tangy, and the desserts usually first-rate. Dinner nightly, 5:30 to 10, lighter dishes until midnight.

The Bayview Inn, 111 Eden St., Bar Harbor. (207) 288-3173. Dine as the elite did in days gone by in the formal dining room or the dark paneled library at this mansion overlooking Frenchman Bay. First, however, have a drink on the flower-bedecked rear terrace, to which you might want to return to watch the Bluenose ferry pass as you sip an after-dinner cordial. The fine complimentary soups and salads that came with dinner when we first dined here now cost extra. Entrees are priced from $12.50 for vermicelli primavera to $19.95 for surf and turf (Maine lobster and filet mignon). Turbans of salmon, lobster Delmonico and beef Wellington are other choices on the continental menu. Among appetizers ($5.50 to $8.50) are gravlax, carpaccio and oysters Romanoff. A grand marnier-soaked orange cake with ice cream and very good brewed decaf followed our dinners. A small but select wine list is on the pricey side for Maine. Dinner nightly from 6; Sunday brunch.

The Reading Room, Newport Drive, Bar Harbor. (207) 288-3351. The re-decorated circular dining room of the Bar Harbor Inn and Motor Inn is prettier than ever, all in deep rose and green colors accented by pots of yellow and white mums and the finest ocean panorama around. You feel as if you're sitting right over the water as you dine on such continental specialties as haddock en papillote, crabmeat au gratin, broiled lamb chops, veal marsala or chateaubriand ($40 for two). Entrees start at $12.95 for chicken Paula; most are in the mid to high teens. Lobster parfait and artichoke hearts stuffed with crabmeat are the most appealing appetizers; chocolate chambord cake and strawberry amaretto torte the best desserts. The new outdoor **Gatsby's Terrace** is lovely for waterside meals. Lunch daily, 11:30 to 2:30; dinner, 5:30 to 8:30.

Jordan Pond House, Park Loop Road, Acadia National Park. (207) 276-3316. A tradition since 1895 (except for a year's absence following a 1979 fire), the rebuilt Jordan Pond House is more popular than ever. The interior is strikingly contemporary, with cathedral ceilings, huge windows and fieldstone fireplace. For lunch, we like to sit outside on the "porch," which is more like a covered terrace, where you can look down the lawns to Jordan Pond and the Bubbles, past the picnic tables where afternoon tea with popovers ($4.75) is a must for residents and visitors alike. The menu is limited but appealing. Our most recent lunch included a fine seafood pasta ($5.50) and a curried chicken salad ($4.75) garnished with red grapes and orange slices; we shared a popover — a bit steep at $2, considering it was hollow! Popovers come with dinners, priced from $8 for blueberry chicken or seafood pasta to $15.75 for lobster pie. Steamed lobster is $13.75. Accompaniments range from fresh lemonade, homemade ice cream and bread pudding to exotic international coffees. Lunch 11:30 to 2:30; tea 2:30 to 5:30; dinner 5:30 to 9. Open summer only.

The Chart Room, Golden Anchor Pier, West Street, Bar Harbor. (207) 288-9740. The former Flying Bridge on a pier jutting into the harbor has been gussied up. Two interior dining rooms with beige tablecloths and colorful director's chairs are flanked by an outdoor wraparound deck, where cocktails are served, and topped by an open-air deck on the roof. What a place for a drink or a casual meal! You'll be lucky to get a seat at peak periods, but if you do you'll enjoy a reasonably priced dinner ($7.95 for chicken parmesan or sirloin tips to $16.95 for surf and turf). A boiled lobster dinner was $11.95 in 1986; at lunch it went for $7.95. Open daily, 11 to 10.

Fisherman's Landing, West Street, Bar Harbor. (207) 288-4632. Even more casual is this long-established place on a working fishing pier, to which we head whenever we're in the mood for Maine lobster. It was the first outdoor restaurant in a town which suddenly has many. You order in a steamy shack, pick up beer or a carafe of wine from the adjacent bar and find a table under a pavilion or, preferably, outside by the water. Soon you'll enjoy the most succulent lobster ever to be boiled ($5.95 for a one-pounder, $6.95 a pound for those over 1 1/2 pounds). The french fries are terrific, and a good lobster roll costs only $4.95. Open daily, 11:30 to 8:30.

The Quarterdeck, 1 Main St., Bar Harbor. (207) 288-5292. Boiled lobster goes for $10.95 in this plain restaurant with a nautical decor and windows onto West Steet toward the water. Entrees range from $8.95 to $12.95 for things like shrimp scampi, lobster fra diavolo, lobster crepes and sole marguery. Dinner nightly, 4:30 to 10.

Other Choices

124 Cottage Street, 124 Cottage St., Bar Harbor. (207) 288-4383. There's a new rear courtyard dining area at this exceptionally popular restaurant with several cozy dining rooms in a converted house. The long waits for a table and the advertised 60-item gourmet salad bar turn us off, but the locals love it; the salad bar even has everything from pea pods to pumpkin seeds to gumdrops! What the owners call artful cuisine runs from $7.95 to $13.95 for such dishes as almond shrimp oriental and a sampling of scallops, shrimp, crab and sole broiled in garlic butter. Szechwan shrimp, seafood stir-fry and the seafood primavera are popular choices. Dinner nightly, 5 to 11.

Central House, 60 Cottage St., Bar Harbor. (207) 288-4242. Striking black, blue and pink floral wallpaper, sheer pink curtains, old framed pictures and votive candles flickering on white linened tables create a romantic setting in this downtown Victorian inn with 12 guest rooms upstairs. The long narrow side porch decked out in fine linen, candles in hurricane lamps and floral china particularly appeals. For starters, try the marinated scallops or smoked trout with curried mayonnaise. Main courses run from $9.50 for halibut Nicoise to $14.95 for filet Oscar. In between are items like crab florentine, smoked haddock fettuccine and smoked Cornish game hen with a spiced apricot glaze. Fresh fruit strudel and lemon mousse are worthy desserts. The cocktail lounge is known for its fresh fruit daiquiris, and there's piano music nightly. Dinner nightly from 5:30; appetizers and desserts to midnight.

Brick Oven Restaurant, 21 Cottage St., Bar Harbor. (207) 288-3708. A 35-seat coffee shop catering to local families just grew and grew into a two-story affair that bills itself as a turn-of-the-century museum. Six small dining rooms are outfitted with items from old mansions, stables, shops and even a drugstore. Up a circular staircase are the antiques shop, the railroad parlor car, the English pub (where you may view an antique puppet theater), the tavern room and the captain's room. We dined downstairs in the English library, filled with drugstore display cases, old signs and a huge toy collection. It was very cluttered and bright, with bare tables, no candles and like no English library we know of. But the fresh haddock heavily flavored with herbs ($8.95) was one of the better fish dishes we've had, the excellent tossed salads contained everything from peas and sprouts to raisins and apples, and the sole St. Albert wrapped around crabmeat in newburg sauce was too rich to finish. Dinner nightly, 4:30 to 9 or 10.

Parkside, 185 Main St, Bar Harbor. (207) 288-3700. A most pleasant sidewalk cafe is the main attraction at this summery house overlooking the village green, with a wraparound veranda and a garden in which colorful flags wave. The home of the late lamented Norumbega Mountain Shop, it was taken over in 1985 by Larry Duffy of the Quarterdeck. Laura Ashley wallwapers, brass wall sconces, bare polished floors and stained-glass windows enhance the interior setting. A lobster salad roll ($4.95) and a seafood fettuccine ($6.95) are popular at lunch. Dinner brings a boiled lobster for $8.95 plus a wide range of seafood and meats from $6.95 for broiled haddock to $10.95 for roast duckling a l'orange. Watermelon and peach daiquiris are bar favorites. Open daily, 11 to 9:30.

Poor Boy's Gourmet, 137 Cottage St., Bar Harbor. (207) 288-4148. Aptly named is this tiny storefront restaurant with wooden booths and knotty pine walls, dispensing interesting fare at bargain prices. The menu lists eight dinner entrees for $6.95, including lemon chicken, veal oregano, beef stroganoff and baked stuffed shrimp en casserole. Crab bisque and curried chicken and grape salad, both $2, are among starters; wines are $1 a glass, and desserts could be an ice cream almond ball with a chocolate-creme de cacao sauce, banana sabayon and grasshopper pie. How they can do it for the prices is amazing, but they've survived two good summers. Dinner nightly, 5:30 to 9:30.

FOR MORE INFORMATION: Bar Harbor Chamber of Commerce, 93 Cottage St., Box 158, Bar Harbor, Me. 04609. (207) 288-5103. Visitor centers are located at the entrance to Mount Desert Island on Route 3, the Bar Harbor Ferry Terminal and the Municipal Pier.

Franklin D. Roosevelt Cottage overlooks the water on Campobello Island.

Campobello, N.B./Lubec-Eastport, Me.

The East Coast's U.S. Route 1 dwindles away. The craggy coastline seems more remote with each mile, until you reach the northeasternmost tip of the United States, where the forested coast, offshore islands and wispy fog envelop the Bay of Fundy shoreline into a sheltered time warp. The birds start twittering with the summer sunrise at 4 in the morning, and the salmon, sardines, puffins and whales add a northern maritime flavor.

This is Maine's distant Washington County and, across the Roosevelt International Bridge over the Lubec Narrows, Franklin Delano Roosevelt's beloved island of Campobello in New Brunswick. It's a wonderland of nature at its most primitive.

Of course, it takes the better part of a day to drive up the Maine coast to this area which marks the beginning of Atlantic Canada and which the Roosevelt family cherished for its very isolation. And once here, you may not be able to get there from here, as the saying goes. Although Lubec is less than three miles from Eastport across Cobscook Bay, it's a circuitous 40 miles by land or a roundabout trip by water via two ferries and Canada's Campobello and Deer islands.

Campobello, the private estate of the Owen family for nearly a century, was acquired in 1881 by a Boston development corporation that erected two large hotels and turned part of the Canadian island into a summer playground for wealthy Americans. Today, one-third of it is the unique Roosevelt Campobello International Park, site of the Roosevelt summer home and 2,600 acres of nature preserves.

Lubec (accent second syllable, as in Quebec), the closest point to Campobello, is the largest town on Cobscook Bay and is the sardine packing capital of the world. A roaring seaport back in the days when there were 15 bars, 13 canneries and 3,000 people, Lubec is now dry, its population has slipped to 2,000 and only two sardine canneries survive.

Lubec is endearingly old-fashioned and quiet compared with Eastport, which seems bigger than its population of 1,982 suggests. At the foot of a long peninsula and maddeningly difficult to reach by car, America's easternmost city is emerging as an important deepwater seaport for ocean-going vessels and is a surprisingly up-and-coming place.

Campobello, too, is about to grow now that a new development company is selling residential lots "like hotcakes," according to Robert Voigt, a Lubec motel owner and one-man chamber of commerce. "The boom is just starting, but it will change the whole community here," he says.

What won't change is the rustic remoteness of this area or stark beauty. As the movie in the Campobello park visitor center suggests, the fog, the cold water and some of the highest tides in North America create a distinctive nature and water life, a world of beauty so quiet that you must listen for it.

Getting There

Interstate 95, U.S. Route 1 and Maine Route 9 lead motorists to the Lubec-Eastport area. Route 190 dead-ends at Eastport. Route 189 goes to Lubec and across the short FDR International Memorial Bridge to Campobello Island. Ferries to and from Letete connect Campobello and Easport with the New Brunswick mainland via Deer Island.

Campobello operates on Atlantic Time, you must pass through Customs (in 1986, there was an overzealous Canadian Customs officer asking, among other things, if we were bringing in weapons), and prices quoted there are in Canadian funds.

Where to Stay

Campobello and Lubec are closely allied in spirit and geography. Eastport is harder to get to (and from). Each has its merits as a base for exploration.

Campobello-Lubec

The Owen House, Welshpool, Campobello, N.B. E0G 3H0. (506) 752-2977. You can see water from every room of the Owen House, an historic Colonial inn on ten acres of grounds, beloved by artists and birders. Innkeeper Joyce Morrell is a painter who exhibits in Blue Hill, Me., and St. Andrews, N.B.; she conducts workshops here from time to time. In August, many Audubon groups visit and are apt to give slide shows at night in the gallery. Other common rooms are a side porch filled with old bottles, ship's mementos and the like, a homey parlor full of wicker furniture and colorful afghans, and a dining room with colorful wallpaper and hooked rugs. Here is where guests are served full breakfasts of bacon and eggs or pancakes and sausage or "sometimes I'll do a quiche type thing," says Joyce. Five bedrooms on the second floor have private baths; four on the third floor share. Hudson's Bay blankets and bright quilts and pillows adorn the beds. Some rooms have fireplaces. The house was built in 1829 by Admiral William Fitzwilliam Owen, son of the British captain who was granted the island in 1769. It seems as solid as it did then, and has been well-preserved. Guests love the peace and quiet, the gatherings around a fireplace in the evenings, the comings and goings of the ferry to Deer Island and the fishing boats at the Welshpool wharf next door, and the path to the beach, if not the 45-degree water. Doubles, $45 to $55. Open May-September.

Campobello Island Club Lodge, Route 774, Box 16, Welshpool, N.B. E0G 3H0. Or Box 20, Lubec, Me. 04652. (506) 752-2487. Owned by the Campobello Island Club, which is selling residential lots, this 10-room lodge is available for transients if it is not booked for prospective purchasers. The lodge consists of a main cottage with restaurant and three log cottages built early in this century as a summer home for a prosperous family. The Bayview cottage has four rooms with private baths; the Woodhaven Cottage contains five smaller rooms (each with washbowl in the room) sharing two baths and the Lobster Trap Suite (with living room, kingsize water bed and three twin water beds). All rooms retain the original Douglas fir walls, but have carpeting, new plumbing, ceiling fans and queensize water beds, and the decor is surprisingly sprightly. The main cottage has a contemporary-style living room full of comfy chairs and sofas and lots of pillows as well as one of the biggest fieldstone fireplaces we ever saw. Dinners are served semi-family style in the dining room or beside the fire; guests have a choice among two or three entrees, perhaps a fried seafood platter or beef, served with gravy, mashed potatoes, vegetables, rolls and salad. If the lodge is not full, the public may have dinner for $15. Otherwise, breakfast and dinner are included in the room price. Doubles, $58.50 to $84, MAP; suite, $110 for two, $20 each additional.

Quoddy View Cabins and Motel, Campobello, N.B. E0G 3L0. (506) 752-2981. Atop a hill in the Wilson's Beach section, this complex of seven basic cabins and two motel units is considered the nicest on the island. Six of the cabins have kitchenettes; one has two bedrooms and the rest have two double beds. There's not much in the way of grounds, but it's only a short trek down to the waterfront. Cabins, $32 to $40; motel, $32.

Home Port Inn, 45 Main St., Lubec, Me. 04652. (207) 733-2077. Six guest rooms, five with private baths, and a distinguished dining room (see Where to Eat) are offered in an appealing 1880 home by new innkeepers Bob and Claire Studley. Guests gather in a large parlor, which has TV, VCR, stereo and piano, and ice for BYO drinks. Rooms are interestingly decorated with antiques. One looks like a library with walls of books and paneling; another has a corner china cabinet and a carved oak bedstead; the rear room with twin beds gets a great view of the sunset over the bay. A complimentary continental breakfast of coffee cake and blueberry muffins is served in the morning. Doubles, $45 to $55. Open May 15-Nov. 15.

Eastland Motel, Route 189, Lubec, Me. 04652. (207) 733-5501. The area's largest place to stay (20 rooms), it was the only one when Robert and Christie Voight bought an eight-unit motel in 1977. They added 12 modern units in a separate wing a year later, and offer spacious rooms with two double beds or a double and single, wall-to-wall carpeting and cable TV. We asked for a water view when we booked, only to be told you couldn't see the ocean, but that that they were by the airport with a view of a pond. We anticipated a lot of noise, but now we doubt that more than a few small planes a week take off or land on the grass airstrip, and those probably not at night. Coffee and donuts are available for purchase in the office, where you also can pick up the Voights' handy guide, "What to Do in Lubec for Four Enjoyable Days." Mrs. Voight says her husband, who has "done more than anyone to promote tourism here," published it because he feels the state travel bureau ignores Lubec-Eastport. His recommendations might not take four days; then again, they could take you a week. Doubles, $40 to $45. Open year-round.

Due East B&B, Route 191, Box 113, Lubec 04652. (207) 733-2413. "Andrew Wyeth's art comes alive in the surrounding fields, pastures, rock-bound coast, sand beach and sheltered harbor," says the brochure of this B&B which opened in 1986. Indeed, it would be hard to imagine a more watery setting, beside an ocean cove near Eastern Head on what owners Carl and Barbara Chamberlain call "a natural environment saltwater farm." The former Connecticut residents bought the 1800 farmhouse in 1978 and spent eight years making it livable. Now they have five guest rooms and a remarkable long dining room/solarium complete with a 10-foot-high rosebush abloom ("Not only do we have the best view, but we have the best room to view it from," Barbara says). Beyond the solarium is a parlor with TV, wood stove and baskets hanging from the beams. All five guest rooms face the water; two on the main floor share a bath. The Chamberlains serve hearty breakfasts of creamed fish with hot biscuits or ham and cheese omelets (with eggs from their own chickens), and Carl pushes his porridge with brown sugar and cream. They also serve dinner by reservation. The main course depends on the catch of the day by "the young man next door." A typical meal ($12) would be clams stuffed with crabmeat, spinach salad, boiled lobster and rhubarb custard pie. Doubles, $42. Open year-round.

Eastport Area

Weston House, 26 Boynton St., Eastport, Me. 04631. (207) 853-2907. Eastport lawyer-politician Jonathan Weston built this majestic yellow Federal-style house in 1810 on a hill overlooking Passamaquoddy Bay. In 1985, it was acquired by Californians Jett and John Peterson, who operate it as a B&B with exceptional flair. The five upstairs rooms share two-and-one-half baths. The bayview Audubon Room, in which John James Audubon once stayed, has a four-poster queensize bed with eyelet-edged sheets and lovely scatter rugs on polished floors. The Weston Room offers a kingsize bed, fireplace, TV and telephone. The public rooms are even more impressive: a library with books and TV, a formal front parlor where afternoon tea and sherry are poured in front of the fireplace beside a century-old melodion, and a more casual kitchen-dining area in which meals are served. Jett Peterson wants guests to "enjoy all of our house." They certainly enjoy her breakfasts of fresh orange juice, melon balls with mint, and silver-dollar pancakes doused with lingonberry or hot apricot syrup one day, muffins and coddled eggs the next. Jett will dish up gourmet dinners by reservation for $6 to $15 — perhaps broccoli soup, Spanish fish salad and rhubarb pie. Doubles, $35 to $45. Open year-round.

Eastport Artists Retreat, 29 Washington St., Eastport, Me. 04631. (207) 853-4239. This really is an artists' retreat, run by painter Joyce Weber, who welcomes guests or artists to her skylit studio at the rear of the third floor and runs three July workshops for artists each summer. It's also a Victorian B&B, an 1846 home with intricately carved, marble-topped furniture and knickknacks. Opened in 1983, it has five guest rooms sharing two baths on the second and third floors, which also have a small library and sitting area. Downstairs is a large, comfortable double parlor with TV and fireplace, and a dining room in which hearty breakfasts of quiche, blueberry pancakes and such are served. Family-style dinners ($8) may be arranged. Doubles, $40. Open year-round.

Todd House, Todd's Head, Eastport, Me. 04631. (207) 853-2328. Here you can stay in a Revolutionary War-era house overlooking the bay. This five-room B&B served as a barracks during the Civil War and exudes history from every side. Listed on the National Register of Historic Places, it has a huge center chimney and an unusual front staircase. A continental breakfast, including what innkeeper Ruth McInnis calls "the best blueberry muffins ever," is served in the original common room in front of an enormous fireplace with bake oven and cooking tools from yesteryear. The large back yard above the bay is available for cookouts. Three of the five guest rooms have working fireplaces, two have water views and two have cable TV. Doubles, $35 to $40.

Lincoln House Country Inn, off Route 1, Dennysville, Me. 04628. (207) 726-3953. Also on the National Register, this expansive yellow Georgian Colonial, built in 1787 by an ancestor of Abraham Lincoln, has been restored by Jerry and Mary Carol Haggerty, who acquired it in 1976. Although not on the ocean, it overlooks the Denny River on substantial property off Route 1, halfway between Lubec and Eastport. The six comfortable upstairs guest rooms share four baths; most have working fireplaces or wood stoves. All four rooms in the main section open onto a back hall, a large area with chairs and the original floors. Two rooms in the oldest ell of the house are particularly well furnished with antiques. Much of the furniture has been refinished by Jerry, who fashioned a bar from a 4,000-pound elm trunk for the pub he created in the old woodshed. Guests gather in the pub, a popular spot with locals, as well as in a large parlor with an open hearth in what was the original kitchen, or in the summer kitchen. This is a choice nature area and from the inn's grounds you can see bald eagles, ospreys and seals; birders spotted more than 100 species on one July day. Mary Carol serves wonderful dinners in the dining room (see Where to Eat) and offers breakfasts for house guests. Doubles, $50 to $55 EP. Open May-November.

CAMPING. Herring Cove Provincial Park, (506) 752-2396, a fine park on Campobello with beach and golf course, has 78 campsites. More than 100 large, well-spaced campsites are available at Maine's **Cobscook Bay State Park**, off Route 1 six miles south of Dennysville. A private full-service campground is the **Seaview**, Route 190, Eastport, (207) 853-4471.

Seeing and Doing

Roosevelt Campobello International Park, Campobello Island. (506) 752-2997. A unique example of international cooperation, this 2,600-acre park established in 1964 is administered by a joint commission of three Canadians and three Americans, including Franklin D. Roosevelt Jr. Known as FDR's "beloved island," it was ranked in his affections second only to Hyde Park. From 1883 when he was a newborn until 1921 when he was stricken by polio here, he spent most of his summers on Campobello. After 1921, he returned only three times for short visits, all while he was President. Here are the cottage and the grounds where the Roosevelts vacationed, the waters where they sailed, and the beaches, bogs and woods where they hiked and relaxed.

The park **reception center** provides an excellent introduction both to the Roosevelts' tenure here and to the island. Movies — "Campobello, the Outer Island" and "Beloved Island" and "FDR, the Man Who Changed America" — are shown on the hour; the former, in particular, helps you understand the unusual nature of this area. "The fog rolls in and provides a distinctive nature and water "life," the narrator relates. The four-part movie ends with a welcome by FDR Jr. The park is open daily 9 to 5, late May to mid-October. Free.

The Roosevelt Cottage, Campobello Island. The homey red 34-room house high above Passamaquoddy Bay is one of the most pleasant we've seen. It's so open and unrestricted that you can walk right into most rooms; unobtrusive hostesses answer questions or leave you on your own. The home still looks lived in; it's filled with fresh field flowers and beautiful views are afforded from all the window seats. Most of the furnishings were used by the Roosevelts; only the curtains and bedspreads are reproductions of the originals, we were told. You'll see the megaphone used for hailing latecomers to meals, a collection of canes, the large chair used to carry the handicapped President, the family telescope, and 18 simple but inviting bedrooms that would make a great summer B&B today! Outside are lovely gardens and paths to the shore.

The Hubbard Cottage. Next door to the Roosevelt property is this cottage, also called the Gables, acquired by the park commission in 1970 when it was the last remaining Victorian summer residence in the park. Under park operation, it serves as a conference center for government and non-commercial groups; participants can stay here or in the nearby Prince and Wells-Shober cottages. The oval window in the dining room, about 10 feet wide, is a sight to behold. The main floor is open for tours Wednesday-Sunday, except when conferences are in session.

THE PARK. Nearly 16 miles of scenic drives and nine miles of walking trails let you see the coves, duck ponds, bogs and fog forests that typify the area. The bays still contain fishing wiers, used for catching herring. The wildflowers — especially the aroma of wild roses and the brilliant splashes of lupin all along the roads in June and July — are out of this world. Among the park's features:

Friar's Head. A short walk leads to an observation deck on the site of the original Friar's Head Pavilion, which provides interesting maps and plaques with descriptions of the panorama all around. Here is the best vantage point to see the entire area; it's a good place to get your bearings. Picnic tables and grills are scattered about.

Herring Cove Provincial Park and Golf Course. A nine-hole golf course and fine campsites are among the attractions here. The mile-long Herring Cove Beach is good for beachcombing, picnicking and an invigorating dip in the Bay of Fundy; a seawall separates it from Lake Glen Severn. FDR and his family used to swim in the lake and gather multi-colored stones on the beach.

Beyond Herring Cove is **Con Robinson Point,** with two picnic tables on a bluff and stairs down to a secluded dark sand beach. **Liberty Point Road** leads on around Raccoon Beach to Liberty Point, near the Sugar Loaves rocks and the Boring Stones, which emerge only at low tide. Trails take hikers to Ragged Point and Owen Head, for some rugged scenery, and to Lower and Upper Duck ponds, saltwater coves and barrier beaches that are repositories for driftwood and migratory waterfowl.

East Quoddy Head Lighthouse. You can walk across at low tide to the craggy headland, but at high tide when we were there the barrier was 10 feet under a fierce current flowing two ways. We had to console ourselves with the sight of whales cavorting a quarter-mile offshore; we wished we'd brought binoculars, as had the party that pointed them out. Here was a most scenic and isolated spot, seemingly at the end of the earth. Back toward the settlement of Wilson's Beach, a road leads east to Head Harbour, the protected harbor where the commercial fishing fleet is berthed.

FERRY RIDES. From Welshpool on Campobello, a summer car ferry to Deer Island runs from the last weekend in June to Labor Day, roughly every hour and a half. The ferry is the most scenic way to get from Lubec to mainland New Brunswick, via Deer Island, a New Brunswick fishing island so unmarked and low-key that we got lost trying to find the free provincial ferry connection to Letete on the mainland. At Deer Island, you also can take a ferry to or from Eastport; it runs hourly mid-June to mid-September. The Deer Island-Campobello ferry costs $10 for car and driver, $2 for passengers; the Eastport ferry costs $7 and $2 (prices are Canadian.) A tugboat hauls the small, six-car ferry. The captain said we'd get to observe some seals (we didn't) and the Old Sow, the largest tidal whirlpool in the world off Deer Island (we didn't).

LUBEC. Back in Maine, the sardine capital of the world is down to two surviving canneries, **Peacock Canning Co.** on Water Street and **Booth Fisheries Co.** on Commercial Street. Visitors may tour these plants on weekdays and watch how the employees cut, clip and pack the herrings in each can. Also still in operation is the only smoked herring plant in the United States, run by the McCurdy family on Water Street and open for tours. The **Sardine Village Museum,** the only one of its kind, is located in an old barn on Route 189 near the turnoff to Quoddy Head. It's open periodically and the owner guides visitors through the process of transforming herring into sardines.

West Quoddy Head Lighthouse. West Quoddy Head is shrouded in fog an average of 59 days a year, a sign near the 1809 lighthouse informs. We happened to visit this easternmost point in the United States on one of the clearer days, the fog that had enveloped Lubec in the morning having vanished by midday. You might spot groups of whales surfacing in the tidal waters between West Quoddy Head and Grand Manan Island, N.B.

West Quoddy State Park. Besides offering picnic facilities, the park has trails to the lighthouse, an island and a bog, and a two-mile trail leads along the shoreline to Carrying Place Cove. A raised boardwalk goes through the bog, which has been declared a National Natural Landmark; its dense moss and heath vegetation are unusual.

The **West Quoddy Head Marine Research Station,** which focuses on whales, has a small visitor center.

BOAT TOURS. In Lubec, Capt. E. Butch Huntley, 733-5584, takes visitors on his **Seafarer** for whale-watching, bird sighting or island-hopping by appointment.

Reversing Falls, Pembroke, Me. Signs off Route 1 lead to Leighton Neck and Young's Cove Road and a 140-acre picnic area beside this unusual attraction. The incoming and outgoing tides hit a series of rocks, creating saltwater falls that are quite a sight. **Cobscook Bay State Park,** south of Dennysville, juts out into the bay and provides an abundance of birds and flowers as well as clams for digging.

EASTPORT. A Norwegian freighter docked in 1985 at the municipal pier, marking the debut of one of Maine's more important deepwater seaports. The town is bustling—comparatively—with activity these days and local promoters see it evolving from an isolated Down East fishing village into a tourist destination in the future. **Overlook Park** on Water Street is a good place to view the bay, Campobello Island and Lubec. The **Cannery Wharf** is fun for snacks or meals, and the ferry leaves from the adjacent pier for Deer Island, N.B.

Where to Eat

Home Port Inn, 45 Main St., Lubec. (207) 733-2077. The rear dining room with captain's chairs is cheery in peach and white and shines like a beacon in rocky culinary shoals. The handwritten menu offers three entrees ($9.95 to $12.50), seafood casserole of crabmeat and-or scallops in a cream sauce, chicken parmesan or rib-eye steak. Start with one of the interesting soups (cheddar cheese, cauliflower with cinnamon or cold tomato, basil and walnut) and finish with chocolate mousse, pecan pie with ice cream or sour cream pound cake with cherries. Entrees come with rice, vegetable, salad with dijon vinaigrette and homemade bread. Claire Studley's spinach and sour cream casserole topped with pecans is a local favorite. Dinner nightly, 6 to 8:30; reservations requested. BYOB.

Herring Cove Lodge, Herring Cove Provincial Park, Campobello. (506) 752-2467. A contemporary shingled building at the entrance to the golf course is considered the best place for value. Three tables in the L-shaped dining room have water views (on clear days you can see Grand Manan); the rest look onto the golf course to the rear. Heavy modern wood and leather chairs are at tables covered with linoleum cloths; fake carnations sit in assorted vases. Full-course dinners served with vegetable, cole slaw and potato go for $5.95 for roast turkey or baked chicken to $9.95 for New York sirloin. A combination plate of steamed clams plus fried haddock and scallops is $13.50 and a steamed lobster, $14.50 — these are Canadian prices, remember. We'd try the sauteed Bay of Fundy scallops or the smoked pollock, done by a unique process known only to Campobello folk, according to the menu, served in a milk and butter broth with optional onion garnish. Lunches are pleasantly priced as well, from $1.35 for a hot dog to $6.25 for sweet and sour fish. You can get a tuna roll with french fries and cole slaw for $2.95, or a lobster roll for $5.65. The house red or white wine, from Moncton, N.B., is $1.95 a glass. Lunch and dinner daily, 11 to 9.

Hillside Restaurant, Route 189, West Lubec. (207) 733-4323. Gary Mc-Connell started in 1979 with a takeout stand and added a dining room with a counter in 1986. "We're not fancy and we don't have a view," he says, "but we serve the kind of food that brings people back." It's so casual that we sat at the counter, along with three local geezers who came in for ice cream sundaes, and had a Saturday night dinner of an excellent seafood chowder, a lobster roll ($4.95) and a plate of fried clams ($7.95) with french fries and cole slaw. It is so Down East and so utterly unpretentious that we didn't even mind the purple bug zapper or the lack of beer or wine (Lubec is a dry town). You can get a hot dog for 85 cents or baked haddock with lobster sauce for $8.75. The fresh fruit pies are said to be great, and we found the strawberry shortcake simply yummy. Open daily except Tuesday, 11 to 9.

Other Lubec Choices. According to Robert Voigt of the Eastland Motel, it used to be that if visitors didn't get to Lubec before Uncle Kippy's Place closed at 6, they had to go to the grocery store to make a sandwich for supper. Now, besides the Home Port and Hillside, locals recommend: **Richard's Seaview Restaurant**, Route 189, offering a menu from $6.50 for haddock to $12.85 for steak and shrimp. **Uncle Kippy's Place**, a waterfront shack, has pizzas, grinders, and lobster or crab rolls, $2.75 to $4.75. **Tip's at the Marina**, open from 5:30 a.m. to 6:30 p.m. (closed Sunday), serves chicken nuggets and fries for $3, a lobster dinner for $6

356

Lincoln House, Dennysville. (207) 726-3953. The pub is where the locals go, but the finest meals between Lubec and Eastport are served in the 30-seat dining room of this out-of-the-way inn. People drive for miles, and no wonder. An aura of history is conveyed by the prim white room with tan trim and wainscoting, narrow-board floors, a few prints and wreaths on the walls, and tables set with green cloths, floral napkins and pewter cutlery. Mary Carol Haggerty's menu is thoroughly up to date; she serves a full-course, prix-fixe meal for $16, the single entree changing nightly. Sunday it's shrimp provencale, Tuesday lobster, Wednesday veal Amelio and "Thursday chicken "every way — piccata, Diana, apricot glaze or the chef's way." Friday is seafood casserole and Saturday brings roast loin of beef with bearnaise sauce. Soup could be brandied pumpkin, crab bisque, celery walnut or New England fish chowder; salad could be artichoke, waldorf, spinach-egg or tossed. Homemade breads like cheese or fennel, or sour cream and chive rolls accompany. A special dessert is fresh strawberry pie. The wine list is excellent for this area, starting at $6 for Mondavi white and going to $19 for chateauneuf du pape. Cocktails from 5:30; dinner nightly at 7 by reservation.

The Cannery, North Water Street, Eastport. (207) 853-4800. Right on the waterfront, this restaurant complex includes the **Pickling Shed** bar and the **Clam Kibben** for light meals. The main dining room in the Cannery is notable for a full-length wall of boulders covered with lobster traps, bare floors and large wood tables. Dinner entrees run from $8.50 for chicken breast with orange mustard sauce to $17.95 for reef and beef (a one-pound lobster and half a pound of beef). In between are baked salmon or swordfish, scallops en casserole, linguini with scallops and clams in mornay or white sauce. Fish chowder for $1.95 and scallop cocktail for $2.95 are bargain appetizers. Tables on the wharf are available for patrons of the Clam Kibben, where you can order steamers, lobster, crab or seafood rolls and salads, fish and chips, sandwiches and such for $2.50 to $6.95. Both establishments are fully licensed. Clam Kibben, open daily 11 to 7; Cannery, nightly 5 to 9:30; June-September.

Rolando's Italian Harborview Restaurant, 118 Water St., Eastport. (207) 853-2334. This 19th century sea captain's home overlooking the harbor was recommended by regular visitors from St. Andrews. We had seen and admired it from the outside, but did not stop. The regulars say there is a wonderful seafood platter and a combination of things Italian and they love it. The entire menu, from seafood to steaks to fresh-dough pizzas, is available to go.

FOR MORE INFORMATION: Roosevelt Campobello International Park, Executive Secretary, Welshpool, Campobello, N.B. or Box 97, Lubec, Me. 04652, (506) 752-2997. Eastport Area Chamber of Commerce, Box 254, Eastport, Me. 04631. (207) 853-4644.

Algonquin Hotel is a landmark for visitors in St. Andrews.

St. Andrews-By-the-Sea, N.B.

For many Canadians, no resort — not Mont Tremblant, not Banff nor even Jasper — has the mystique of St. Andrews-by-the-Sea. Since the late 19th century, it has been a low-key watering hole for old-money Canadians and Americans attracted by pollen-free air and a protected, picturesque setting surrounded by water on three sides at the southwestern tip of New Brunswick.

In the 1940s, the Canadian among us cherished the summers she spent with a friend whose family from Montreal owned a house in St. Andrews. Lazy days and nights, swimming at Katy's Cove, having sundaes at the counter and listening to the jukebox in the local teenage hangout, going to first-run films several times a week at the local movie palace (they reached St. Andrews even before Montreal), dropping into Cockburn's Corner Drug Store to be sprayed with the French perfume of choice by owner Bobby Cockburn on the way to the weekly dance, and a first summer romance are lasting memories.

Though the dance hall, movie theater and hangout are gone, St. Andrews still looks and feels much as it did in our teenage years. That's probably because this historic town, settled by British Loyalists fleeing Castine, Me., in 1783 — a year before the province of New Brunswick was born — has been passed over, in a way, by time and tourism.

The new arterial Route 1 from St. Stephen to St. John skips St. Andrews, 10 miles to the south. The Canadian Pacific Railroad, whose founders built summer estates in the area, no longer stops there, and the Grand Manan ferry has moved its base from St. Andrews to Black's Harbour. Today, the traveler has to be aware of and want to visit St. Andrews to make the detour.

Canada's Old Guard resort peaked in the 1940s, says M. Jean Stinson, descendant of original Loyalist settlers and head of Osprey Travel & Promotions Ltd., which provides a number of visitor guide services in town. "The moneyed people have gone elsewhere," she says. "When the older generation died off, the younger generation didn't have the same ties with the community. St. Andrews was sort of at the end of the line. But now the town is waking up."

The air of optimism and the improvements for visitors in the decade since we last visited are obvious. The Algonquin Hotel has been renovated, newcomers have moved to town to become innkeepers and shopkeepers or to work for the Biological Station, and St. Andrews is "poised on a period of growth," in the words of Robert Estes, the Texan who recently took over the Rossmount Inn.

Sensing its incipient revival, Connecticut resident Kathleen Lazare purchased the delightful Pansy Patch cottage for an antiques and rare books shop and then opened a B&B. "There's a little bit of heaven here," she claims.

You'll find it along the shady streets dotted with historic homes and churches, along the shoreline forged by tides that rise and fall up to 25 feet a day, and on the sparkling waters of Passamaquoddy Bay.

But as ex-Bostonian Bill Dalton, a university professor and innkeeper, advises visitors, St. Andrews is "a place where you have to get yourself going. Touristy things aren't laid on you. It's so quiet and private that you really get in touch with nature here."

Getting There

Facing easternmost Maine just across Passamaquoddy Bay, St. Andrews is at the southwestern tip of New Brunswick off Route 1, about 50 miles west of Saint John. Take Route 127 south to St. Andrews. Calais is the main border entry point from Maine. Two short ferry rides provide a more scenic route from Lubec and Eastport, Me., via Campobello and Deer Island to Letete, N.B. They offer a glimpse of the area's maritime flavor, but run in summer only.

Prices are quoted in Canadian funds, which in 1986 represented a discount of about 36 percent for Americans. New Brunswick is in the Atlantic time zone, one hour ahead of Eastern time.

Where to Stay

Accommodations range from the manorial, veranda-swathed Algonquin Hotel to small B&Bs and a Kiwanis-run campground.

The Old Guard

The Algonquin Hotel, 184 Adolphus St., St. Andrews EOG 2X0. (506) 529-8823. (800) 268-9411 (Canada) or (800) 828-7447 (US). One of the grand old Canadian Pacific hotels that span the country, the 187-room Algonquin preserves a tradition of gracious resort life that has nearly vanished. One look at the turreted, Tudoresque hotel surrounded by lavish flower beds atop a hill overlooking St. Andrews and Passamaquoddy Bay indicates that this is a special place. Add bellhops in kilts of the New Brunswick tartan, the long lobby with comfortable peach chairs on which people actually are sitting, the enormous 375-seat Passamaquoddy Dining Room with windows onto the grounds, the book-lined Library Bar with nightly piano music, a large pool, tennis courts, a championship golf course and good conference facilities, and the result is a resort of world renown. That the historic hotel which had been started by Boston businessmen in 1883 as a private club had fallen on tough times in the post-war era is no longer of import. Rescued by the provincial government in 1974 and managed since by CP Hotels, the Algonquin was immediately upgraded. When we last visited in 1986, it was in the midst of a five-year renovation program in which 40 guest rooms were being redone each year. Those we saw had queensize beds with quilts in gray and peach, two upholstered chairs, cable-TVs hidden in armoires, and modern bathrooms with baskets of toiletries; the melon-colored towels and sheets are a CP trademark. Some of the older rooms off rambling corridors in angled wings are larger with twin beds, and many connect for family suites. Rooms on the third and fourth floors have water views. Because the hotel was rebuilt with concrete walls, ceilings and floors after a 1914 fire, the rooms are solid and unusually quiet. Three meals a day are served in the dining room (see Where to Eat). Doubles, $89 to $95; suites $137 to $242; MAP available. Open late May to early October.

Tara Manor Inn, 559 Mowat Drive (Hwy. 127), Box 30, St. Andrews E0G 2X0. (506) 529-3304. A former private estate, Tara occupies 20 secluded acres crisscrossed by sculptured century-old hedgerows on a hill overlooking Passamaquoddy Bay. Innkeepers Norman and Sharon Ryall started with two rooms in their residence in 1971, opened a dining room in 1980, and were planning what Norman called four ultra rooms to be "the best in the Maritimes." The existing 20 rooms in the old carriage house, boat house and servant's quarters, all with full baths and cable TV, are comfortable indeed. Decor varies from French provincial to early American. All rooms are different but have striking draperies and Tara's signature collections of plates displayed in bays on the walls. Some have adjoining sun rooms or private balconies with views of the sea. The park-like grounds include a pleasant swimming pool. Doubles, $66 to $78; deluxe rooms with balconies, $94. Open May-October.

Rossmount Inn, Hwy 127, R.R. 2, St. Andrews E0G 2X0. (506) 529-3351. This venerable Victorian manor house also overlooks the bay from a hill, this one at the base of Chamcook Mountain, highest in the area. Behind the inn are woods that are part of an 87-acre wildlife preserve; in front is a rather barren lawn leading up to a square building with yellow awnings that is almost comical-looking. You'd never suspect that the interior is the height of opulent Victoriana. Energetic young Texans Robert and Lynda Estes took over in 1986 from longtime innkeepers George and Marion Brewin, devoted Anglophiles who had given the Rossmount a wide reputation for haute cuisine and luxury lodging. A wide reception hall boasts the chair used by the king of Belgium at the coronation of Queen Elizabeth, a crystal chandelier and a floor covered with oriental rugs. A formal staircase leads to the second and third floors, where 16 guest rooms (all with private baths) go off central hallways furnished with Victorian sitting areas (fine for sitting, but we had to go to a vacant west-facing room to be able to read in the late afternoon since our room lacked both comfortable chairs and good lights). Though covered with oriental rugs (which sometimes clash with the flowery bedspreads), the floors are thin and so are the doors, and a grandfather's clock chimes every 15 minutes all night. Best rooms are those in the front corners with water views. All are furnished with fine antiques and Victorian accoutrements. The main floor has a small parlor and an intimate bar in which resides a piano originally intended for Kaiser Wilhelm before World War I. A large raised deck surrounds a swimming pool beside the inn. Doubles, $65 to $70; two-night minimum on weekends. Open April-December.

Other Choices

The Pansy Patch, 59 Carleton St., St. Andrews E0G 2X0. (506) 529-3384. A fairy-tale white stucco cottage, with small-paned windows, towers and turrets and a roof that looks as if it should be thatched, stands across the street from the Algonquin Hotel. Built in 1912 by the superintendent of Canadian Pacific Hotels, it was fashioned after a Cotswold cottage. Kathleen Lazare of Connecticut, an antiques dealer, fell in love with it when vacationing in St. Andrews; she and husband Michael bought it and now have the largest rare book store in Atlantic Canada, plus an antiques business and four bedrooms for a B&B. A fire in the huge fireplace glows in the living room with its beamed ceiling; here guests may sit in the evenings, surrounded by Mrs. Lazare's 6,000 volumes. In the tiny breakfast room or on the back deck overlooking terraced gardens, she serves homemade blueberry waffles, french toast or scrambled eggs for breakfast. Homemade granola, local honey and strawberries are often on the docket. Four bedrooms upstairs share two bathrooms; the bedrooms are nicely decorated with antique furniture and one has a fireplace, a sleigh bed and a wing chair. The Lazares also operate **Canadian Trading Co.** on Main Street, dealing in primitive antiques and crafts. Doubles, $55. Open May 15 to Oct. 1.

Best Western Shiretown Inn, 218 Water St., Box 145, St. Andrews E0G 2X0. (506) 529-8877. Built in 1881, this curbside hostelry in downtown St. Andrews bills itself as Canada's oldest summer hotel, though purists might find the Best Western connection a bit disconcerting. The white clapboard hotel has a pillared veranda that becomes a sidewalk cafe with umbrellaed tables in summer. Waitresses in Colonial garb scurry around two dining rooms with pressed-tin ceilings and lace curtains and tablecloths, and an English-style pub serving "pub grub." The inn's 26 rooms have been modernized to Best Western standards, including color TV, phones and private baths. But the original dressers and tables from the old Kennedy Hotel have been refinished to blend with the atmosphere of the period. Innkeeper Ian MacKay, the town's most active entrepreneur, also owns the **Smuggler's Wharf** and **Lighthouse** restaurants, as well as the **Smuggler's Village** efficiency apartments across Water Street with views of the harbor. The 14 units vary from one to three rooms; all have kitchenettes, TV and patios, and rent for $50 to $65 daily, $275 to $450 weekly. Doubles in inn, $38 to $48. Open year-round.

Seaside Beach Resort, 351 Water St., Box 310, St. Andrews E0G 2X0. (506) 529-3846. This complex of 22 housekeeping cottages with access to the waterfront is good for families, as we found in the mid-1970s on our first family trip to St. Andrews with children. At that time, we found no one restaurant to suit our varied (make that outspoken) tastes, so ended up barbecuing a steak outside our cottage. And our older son was kept amused at night playing Scrabble across the street with an elderly guest at the Sea Side Inn, then under joint ownership. The cottages have been upgraded a bit from the state we remember them; some are quite large, some have two bedrooms, and every unit has black and white cable TV. A spacious lawn leads to the waterfront, where rowboats are available. Doubles, $45. Seasonal.

Snore by the Shore, 153 Water St., St. Andrews E0G 2X0. (506) 529-4255. Another good place for families, or those on limited budgets, is this amusingly named B&B operated since 1984 by ex-Bostonians Bonnie and Bill Dalton, she a goldsmith and he a professor at the University of New Brunswick in Fredericton. Three of the five guest rooms in the bright red structure have private baths. Its rooming house heritage is reflected in small, plain rooms (yours might have a card table placed between two chairs), brightened by colorful afghans made by the Daltons' daughter. An adjacent cottage offers kitchen, living room and beds for five. A full breakfast, including ham and eggs and homemade muffins, is served in a living-dining area or outside on the balcony, both of which look onto the water. Bill Dalton encourages guests to sail, windsurf or go scuba diving from his beach, which he describes as "very friendly at low tide." His wife keeps busy with her crafts and gift shop on the main floor. Doubles, $35; cottage, $60.

Picket Fence Motel, 102 Reed Ave., Box 424, St. Andrews E0G 2X0. (506) 529-8985. Bright yellow doors, lawn chairs and flowers in log pots make this 19-unit motel the most inviting in town. It's across from the Algonquin golf course, and set back a bit from the road beyond a lawn. A housekeeping unit for two is available. Doubles, $38 to $50. Open mid-May to mid-October.

CAMPING. Passamaquoddy Park Campground, Indian Point Road, St. Andrews E0G 2X0. (506) 529-3439. The Kiwanis Club of St. Andrews runs this spacious, well-equipped tent and trailer park at Indian Point, which has a clear view across a little-used road to Passamaquoddy Bay. The beach here is fine, and the campground is off by itself a mile from the center of town. It has 49 full hook-up sites, 40 with water and electricity and 32 unserviced sites. Reservations are not required. Daily rates, $7 to $9.50.

Cozy Cove, a private campground located in Chamcook just beyond the Rossmount Inn, has a pool and miniature golf. It has easy access to swimming at Chamcook Lake.

Island View, another campground on Route 127 West in Bayside, overlooks St. Croix Island, where Samuel de Champlain spent the winter of 1604-05. It has a pool, but campers can also swim in the St. Croix River from Sandy Point.

Seeing and Doing

Surrounded by water on three sides, St. Andrews is naturally geared to water pursuits, which may be affected by the 26-foot rise and fall of the Passamaquoddy Bay tides (influenced by the Bay of Fundy, which has the highest tides in the world). The area's rich marine life has made it an important center for marine biological research.

Water Attractions

SWIMMING. Katy's Cove, operated by the St. Andrews Swimming Club in cooperation with the Algonquin Hotel at the end of Acadia Road, is a favorite spot. Gates at the old railroad bridge at the mouth of the cove prevent the replacement of water at every high tide, so the cove is warmer than beaches on the bay (a sign said the water temperature was a relatively mild 63 when we were there in early July). Lifeguards staff the sandy beach, and there's a clubhouse where the porches are lined with old Adirondack lawn chairs. Admission is $1 daily. The beach at **Indian Point**, opposite the Kiwanis Club campground, is good for those who like ocean-bay swimming. Beyond Katy's Cove and reached by Bar Road, the bar to **Minister's Island**, across which you can drive at low tide, provides more sheltered swimming. **Chamcook Lake** is a favorite with locals who like its crystal-clear waters and a secluded beach. North of town along the St. Croix River is **Sandy Point**, one of the few expanses of truly sandy beach in the St. Andrews area.

SAILING AND BOATING. Passamaquoddy Bay is protected from the open ocean by Deer and Campobello islands, so the sailing is better than off the open coasts of nearby Maine and New Brunswick. For the first time in 1986, Coastal Sailboat Rentals, Town Wharf, rented rowboats, dinghies and sloops starting at $5 an hour. A variety of boat cruises and whale-watching expeditions are offered; they can be arranged through **Osprey Travel**, 222 Water St., 529-8844. A four-hour whale-watch tour goes past Campobello and Quoddy Point. Island-hopping, an eight-hour tour run by Osprey Travel, leaves at 9 a.m. Fridays from St. Andrews for St. George, Deer Island and Campobello; 4 to 14 people are transported via ferries in a mini-van for $35 each.

BEACHCOMBING. Because of the enormous range of the tides, a wide variety of marine life can be found in the area between high and low tides. Walk the beaches or explore the shore near Minister's Island to find shells, mussels, sea urchins, starfish, sand dollars and such.

Minister's Island. The bar to Minister's Island, which we remember nervously driving across a decade ago, is under 17 feet of water at high tide, so you don't want to get stranded out there. The island can be visited under auspices of Osprey Travel. Jean Stinson leads tours of **Covenhoven**, the abandoned 19-bedroom estate of CP railroad magnate Sir William Van Horne. Only the pool room remains fully intact after a developer whose dream died conducted an auction of the island's contents. It's said that when movers were emptying the place, the 5,000-pound billiards table could not be dismantled before the tide came in.

Other Activities

GOLFING. The Algonquin's famed golf course was not patterned nor named after the "Old Course" in St. Andrews, Scotland, contrary to belief. Algonquin officials say that golfers who have played both find that this has more hazards, is more capricious and requires a greater variety of shots than the Scotland course. Thirteen of the holes are played near or within sight of Passamaquoddy Bay, making it a particularly scenic setting. The first nine holes were constructed in 1894 and an additional nine holes were laid out in 1900. Another short nine-hole course with narrow fairways and small greens was added in 1921.

WALKING TOURS. Settled in 1783 by United Empire Loyalists who floated their dismantled homes here from Castine, Me. (they were rebuilt and three are still standing.). St. Andrews is said to have more examples of fine New England Colonial architecture than any other Canadian town. Everything from Cape Cod cottages to saltboxes to large Georgian houses with Federal detailing can be seen scattered across a grid of neatly squared lots laid out by town planners two centuries ago. More than 250 structures, many of them legacies of the prosperous era when St. Andrews was a port of call on the West Indies trade route, are over 100 years old. The 1824 **Greenock Presbyterian Church** looks like any white Colonial New England church, except for the unusual bright green oak tree carved on the exterior beneath its spire; other St. Andrews churches, particularly those along King Street, are architecturally interesting. Two-hour guided walking tours of the town depart daily at 10 from Osprey Travel, $5; two-hour bus tours leave at 2, $9.

Ross Memorial Museum, 188 Montague St., 529-3906. Here is a true house museum, acquired and given to the town by Henry Phipps Ross and his wife Sarah as a means to display their extensive collections acquired from world travels. Mr. Ross, a onetime Episcopal minister, and his wife, the daughter of the Bradstreet of Dun & Bradstreet in New York, were Americans who summered here from 1902 to 1945. The imposing red brick Neo-Classical house was built in 1824 and acquired by the Rosses in 1938 for a museum. Their collection of decorative arts and furniture was accumulated mainly prior to World War I. When we were there, the special exhibit, which changes annually, showed their fascinating photographs and travel mementos from the 1925-26 world cruise of the S.S. Carinthia, the maiden voyage of the Cunard Lines ship. Guided tours, Monday-Saturday 10 to 4:30, mid-May to early October; also Sunday 1:30 to 4:30 from early July. Free.

Huntsman Marine Laboratory Aquarium, Brandy Cove Road, 529-4285. This is a fun spot for youngsters. They'll probably pass quickly through the basic exhibits, a slide show on "Quoddy Seas and Shores" and a movie, "The Sea." Ahead lies a heart-shaped touch pool surrounded by a raised platform where kids can get close to shells, starfish, wolffish and a rare black sea bass. Harbor seals cavort in an open water tank and are fed at 10 and 4 daily. Don't miss Clyde, a stuffed 27-pound lobster, caught in 1962 off Campobello. Open daily, 10 to 8, July to mid-September, 10 to 4:30 in June. Adults $2, students $1.50, family $6.

Sunbury Shores Arts and Nature Center, 139 Water St., 529-3386. Based in Centennial House, an old general store on the waterfront, the center has a year-round gallery presenting about 15 exhibitions annually, two artists' studios, a children's nature room, a pottery studio and an extensive summer instruction program. Special programs range from week-long workshops for adults and children to beach walks, nature hikes, birdwatching, whale-watching and bonfire get-togethers on Friday nights. The center also has a conservation area in which a marked nature trail winds through woods and meadows off Brandy Cove Road near the Huntsman Aquarium. Open daily 9 to 5, May-September. Free.

St. Andrews Blockhouse, adjacent to Centennial Park, off Water Street. This restored, two-story National Historic Site was built of hand-hewn timbers in 1813 to protect St. Andrews from American privateers. Of 12 such blockhouses built in New Brunswick, it is the only survivor. Guides and interpretive displays explain the role of the blockhouse in the War of 1812. Open daily, June to Sept. 15. Free.

Sir James Dunn Arena, 24 Reed Ave. Public ice-skating is available most evenings at the arena, home of one of North America's oldest summer hockey schools. The arena also has bowling lanes and movies are shown in its theater each night.

SHOPPING. The stores of St. Andrews along Water Street range, we think, from the ridiculous to the sublime. Fortunately there are getting to be more of the latter:

Cottage Craft, on the waterfront at Town Square, stocks beautiful knit goods, including a knitted lobster resting on a trap, knitting bags (one shaped like a house in which the door opens), men's tweed jackets, sweaters and the neatest collection of mittens you ever saw. **Sea Captain's Loft** is suavely filled with English china, ladies' wear including Geiger jackets and woolens, children's books and toys, and John Putnam's Heritage House miniatures. The **China Chest** imports English bone china, Welsh and Scottish woolens and Canadian gifts.

Hollyhock & Vine purveys a little bit of everything in exquisite taste, from a shelf of beautiful glass paperweights to baby gifts, glassware, paper goods and silk flowers. **Boutique La Balena** has cute things like stuffed animals, cards, apparel and a large toy section. **Carriage House Studio**, in the same building as the B&B Snore by the Shore, is where Bonnie Dalton sells gold and enamel jewelry, as well as interesting crafts, gifts and wooden things. **Windridge Country Store and Bakery** uses flour ground at its own farm (which it sells to other health-food stores) for its breads and seafood muffins (that's right, a lunchtime treat at $1.35). Apple cider, preserves, butter tarts, Scottish oatcakes and fabulous ice creams are all homemade.

Stickneys Wedgwood Store, founded in 1842, is the oldest Wedgwood store in North America and the oldest store in St. Andrews. Operated by the Stickney family until 1976, it is now expanded with a complete range from Christmas plates to commemorative pieces. It appears extremely cluttered compared to Tom Smith's fine **Bocabec Pottery** next door. Nearby is the **Leather Shop**,

Presents in the Algonquin Hotel, owned by Duncan Hutchinson of the Whale of a Cafe, is one of the better hotel gift shops we've seen. **The Pansy Patch** across the street is crammed with antiques and paintings, and has an extraordinary rare book collection.

Where to Eat

L'Europe, 48 King St., St. Andrews. (506) 529-3818. Just off Water Street in the heart of town is this rustic low brown building which, it turns out, is a remodeling of the aforementioned dance hall. There are Tiffany lamps in one dining room and fabric-covered lamps in the other, over tables outfitted with fine linen and china. Since 1984, it's been serving up what many consider to be the best food in town from an extensive menu. A small dish of pate precedes dinner, but for those who want more substantial appetizers ($4.70 to $34.50), how about mackerel in aspic, smoked eel, lobster crepes or Beluga caviar? Main courses go from $9.50 for perch in a jacket to $27 for filet mignon with morels. Other choices include haddock sauteed with almonds, red snapper, salmon provencale, curried pork, ragout of lobster with morels, Hungarian stew and German rouladen. The haddock is served with vegetables, salad (which often costs extra elsewhere in the Maritimes) and the ubiquitous mashed potatoes. Among desserts are peach cream cheesecake, butter cream mocha cake and Black Forest cake. Dinner nightly except Monday, 6 to 11. Closed in winter except for Christmas week.

Evening Star at Tara Manor Inn, 559 Mowat Drive, St. Andrews. (506) 529-3304. Burgundy draperies and carpeting, pink linens, crystal chandeliers and live piano music create an elegant big-city setting in a country-inn dining room with a fancy name, one that you might not expect to find in little old St. Andrews. Although we had dinner reservations for 8:30, we endured a long wait in an elaborate Victorian parlor and then a long wait at our table before a cheese spread with six symmetrical crackers arrived, followed by an undistinguished salad of iceberg lettuce, a tray of three dressings (the best was the sour cream and chive), and an ordinary little loaf of bread, with a crock of soft butter. Things rapidly got better with braised citrus pork, accompanied by rice, green beans and slivered almonds, and curried lamb and rice (much more rice than lamb), served with a tray of sliced almonds, chutney and bananas in sour cream. A $17 bottle of B&G Cotes du Rhone accompanied, and a light blueberry cheesecake and Spanish coffee were worthy endings for a splurge of a meal.

Other entrees ($14.50 to $18.75) from the large continental menu included seafood linguini, red snapper, sole amandine, poached salmon, roast rack of lamb and delmonico steak. Start with New Brunswick fiddlehead soup or fish terrine, among other interesting soups and appetizers. Dinner nightly, 6 to 9:30.

Passamaquoddy Dining Room, Algonquin Hotel, St. Andrews. (506) 529-8823. The airy, windowed veranda with large tables overlooking the gardens and pool is the most inviting section of the 375-seat dining room, elegantly appointed with damask linens, lace doilies on the china, fresh flowers and a particularly striking display of breads — one shaped like an alligator — near the entrance. Upwards of 500 people turn out for the Sunday brunch, a bargain at $10.95 for all you can eat; the daily lunch buffet for $9 also is well-received. The dinner menu is innovative for the area and pleasantly priced. You might start with shrimp caprice, smoked Atlantic salmon or a hefty seafood chowder before sampling roast loin of pork, grilled New Zealand lamb steaks, baked sole with tarragon sauce or seafood casserole (all under $12), among a dozen choices priced from $9.75 to $19.50. Prime rib with Yorkshire pudding and boiled lobster are popular, of course. Desserts range from ice creams to fancy pastries. The wine list — sorely limited, as is the norm in New Brunswick — has 10 dinner wines, rated as to sweetness and priced from $12.50 to $37. Lunch and dinner daily.

Whale of a Cafe, 173 Water St., St. Andrews. New in 1986 and an instant hit with local food mavens was this small place by the water behind Boutique la Balaena. Concerned about a lack of interesting dining, boutique owner Sheila Simpson converted a rear storage room into a cafe and turned it over to Duncan Hutchinson, a caterer and teacher at the Community College of New Brunswick. The result: SRO for lunch and light supper. It's self-service; you place your order with a counter girl or the chef himself, then take your food to one of a handful of tables inside, outside on an outdoor deck, or to colorful picnic tables by the shore. The food is fresh as can be. There's a choice of two soups (cream of fiddlehead or fish chowder when we visited), four salads (an innovation for St. Andrews), half a dozen sandwiches on croissant rolls, and nice desserts. We found the whale of a salad (greens, ham, mushrooms, shrimp, nuts, mandarin oranges and strawberries with Caesar, curry or sour cream dressings) to be the ultimate in chef's salads for $3.75. The shrimp salad was a bargain at $3.95, and the ham, turkey and roast beef sandwiches were generous, to say the least. Tarts are 55 cents, tortes $2.95 and the ubiquitous Black Forest cake ($3.25) is considered the best in town. Open daily in summer, 10 to 9, continental breakfast from 8:30.

Rossmount Inn, Hwy. 127, St. Andrews. (506) 529-3351. Three stained-glass windows from an 18th century chapel in Great Britain make up the bay window in the elegant, formal Victorian dining room at the Rossmount. Flickering candles in heavy red glass are overpowered by the light from overhead chandeliers, making the room rather too bright for our taste, and we felt almost as if we were eating in a museum. The style set by longtime innkeepers George and Marion Brewin was being maintained by new owners Robert and Lynda Estes. Lynda, trained in French cooking, is chef and changes her menu nightly, her prix-fixe meals ranging from $16 to $23. We started with French onion soup and a green salad with a radish-cream dressing. Main courses of very lemony but good scallops and poached halibut were served with crisp zucchini

366

slices, plus a baked potato that didn't do anything for the seafood. A fruit trifle and a Black Forest cake surrounded by strawberries were delicious desserts. Lynda's menu ranges from Atlantic salmon, swordfish, pollock and lobster to filet mignon. Dinner nightly, 6 to 8:30. No smoking.

The Gables, 143 Water St., St. Andrews. (506) 529-3440. A nice, three-level deck beside the water appeals for breakfast, lunch or supper. The spare dining room has bare wood tables and a dance floor (with dancing nightly) and the adjacent Brass Bull Pub is a lively spot. A lobster roll is $6.50 and a hamburger, $1.45, but the locals suggest springing for the Bull Burger, thick and terrific, or the chicken and almond sandwich, $2.95 and $2.75 respectively. The dinner menu offers two boiled lobsters for $11.95, baked or curried scallops, grilled haddock and beef tenderloin, served, as the menu says, with salad, "real mashed potato" and fresh vegetable; prices are $6.95 to $11.95. The super champagne breakfast — three eggs, three strips of bacon, three pancakes and three glasses of champagne, $9.99 — sounds as if it would finish you off before the day starts. Breakfast, 7:30 to 11; lunch, 11 to 10; dinner, 5 to 10.

Lighthouse Restaurant, Lower Patrick Street, St. Andrews. (506) 529-3082. A nautical dining rom dressed in brown and white has windows overlooking Passamaquoddy Bay at a point beside the lighthouse. It's the choicest waterfront spot in town, and tourists like it for its lobsters (a seafood feast of steamed clams, fish chowder, deep-fried seafood sampler, lobster, dessert and beverage is $19.95). The fisherman's choice offers lobster stew, lobster roll or steak sandwich, salad bar and beverage for $9.95. Other possibilities are seafood casserole, coulibiac of salmon, haddock amandine, coquilles St. Jacques and rainbow trout stuffed with crabmeat, $11.95 to $13.95. The wine list is not one of the area's better, but the view certainly is. Open nightly 5 to 10, May-October.

FOR MORE INFORMATION: St. Andrews Chamber of Commerce, Box 89, St. Andrews, N.B. E0G 2X0, (506) 529-3000. Tourist Bureau is at Market Wharf, foot of King Street. Local guide and excursion services are offered by Osprey Travel, 222 Water St., Box 583, St. Andrews, (506) 529-8844.

Mahone Bay is on view from terrace at the Galley at South Shore Marine.

Chester-Lunenburg, N.S.

For those who have searched for a perfect seaside shangri-la along the Northeast Coast — search no longer. We've found it, in a place that until recently we never realized was there.

It's the Chester-Mahone Bay-Lunenburg area along Nova Scotia's South Shore, about 50 miles southwest of Halifax. People call it variously Lunenburg County, the South Shore, Bluenose Country, the Lighthouse Trail. We call it wonderful.

Centered around Mahone Bay and its 365 islands, this low-key stretch of rather sophisticated villages civilizes an otherwise provincial, seafaring area. Its undulating inlets are tranquil refuges from the generally rugged Nova Scotia coastline.

The area brings to mind the Maine coast as it used to be -- secluded, unspoiled, yet with a welcome air of civility. It's not so isolated that you have to forego the amenities of good restaurants, inns, galleries and shops. But it's unfrequented enough that you have no sense of the crowds that jam similar areas in New England.

Chester, a village of 1,100 settled in 1759 by New Englanders, is on a peninsula at the head of Mahone Bay. Today it is a resting place for wealthy Canadians and Americans and, perhaps, Captain Kidd's buried bounty.

368

Lunenburg, called the Gloucester of Canada, was founded in 1753 by German Protestants and is Canada's oldest fishing port. With a population of 3,000, it's the colorful home of working fishermen and Bluenose schooners, and is reputed to be the most architecturally interesting town in Canada.

The village of Mahone Bay (population 1,200) is poised at the head of an inlet from the bay, whose sailing waters are considered among the best in the world. "We love the beauty around us and welcome you to share it," proclaim the endearing signs at the village limits.

Here is the one rural area in the Maritimes that matched our expectations for a balance of quaint charm and urbane shops, good dining on outdoor decks, picturesque harbors and peaceful beaches.

Perhaps you'll feel like Lunenburg painter-shopkeeper Gail Patriarche, who fell in love with the area and moved from Ontario in 1981. Said she: "I'm an artist, and I felt I'd been cheated all my life until I got here."

Getting There

This area is easily reached in less than an hour via Route 103 from Halifax, Atlantic Canada's largest city and a major air and rail destination. It's about a three-hour drive via Route 103 from Yarmouth, where the ferries land from Bar Harbor and Portland, Me. Prices are quoted in Canadian funds. The province is on Atlantic Time, one hour ahead of Eastern.

Where to Stay

Lunenburg and Mahone Bay are about 10 miles apart from each other, while Chester is about 20 miles northeast of Mahone Bay. The accommodations are grouped here by location.

Lunenburg and Mahone Bay

Boscawen Inn, 150 Cumberland St., Box 1343, Lunenburg B0J 2C0.(902) 634-3325. Perched astride a steep hill, this restored 1888 Victorian mansion has 18 guest rooms (11 with private bath), a couple of formal parlors, an acclaimed dining room and an outdoor deck with a view over treetops and houses of Lunenburg Harbor. Although it is considered to be the best inn in the area, we think it could be more welcoming. The Victorian parlors, furnished in museum-quality pieces by innkeeper Leslie Langille, a local antiques dealer, did not afford comfortable seats or good lamps for reading, and the smaller and more cozy den was always occupied. Since our small room had space only for twin beds, one chair and a bureau, we put on sweaters and went out to read on the deck. The much larger upstairs rooms are elegant indeed with canopy or four-poster beds, fancy curtains and upholstered chairs. The top-of-the-line room, with a view of the harbor, has oriental rugs and a working fireplace. Although we did chat after dinner with a few other guests in the parlor, this is not a jolly kind of inn, and it is not a B&B. Three meals daily are served in the downstairs dining room (see Where to Eat.) Doubles, $30 to $65. Open May-October.

Chillingsworth Guest House, 52 MacDonald St., Box 1391, Lunenburg B0J 2C0. (902) 634-3701. The man who once owned Boscawen built this 1928 New England Colonial Georgian house with a Grecian portico entrance, but there the connection ends. This four-bedroom B&B sharing two large bathrooms, located on half a block of treed and manicured lawns in an out-of-the-way residential neighborhood, is a decorator's dream made very livable by personable host Peter Greve. A Dane who emigrated to Canada in 1958, he was an interior decorator in Toronto before opening Chillingsworth — named after the famed Cape Cod restaurant — in 1985. Guests have the run of the house and grounds. The large and comfortable drawing room is notable for two European crystal chandeliers, cream-colored draperies purchased from the estate of the late Emperor Haile Selassie of Ethiopia, Chinese accessories and large mural wallpaper depicting the fictional Tara plantation. An inviting den has fireplace, television and library for guests' use. Peter serves a continental breakfast of fresh orange juice, his own muffins and jams, and Danish cheese in the oak-paneled dining room, its bay window looking onto the gardens. The guest rooms are decorated with antiques and traditional art. The fireplaced Senator's Suite has a queensize brass bed, two apricot chairs and a blue loveseat; the Tara Suite in dusty rose has lace curtains and Chippendale furniture. The green Garden Suite in Florida style has wicker bedsteads and a dear little balcony surrounded by Norwegian spruce trees overlooking the garden. Bowls of fresh fruit are placed in the halls, as are vases of flowers from the gardens. Outside are open and covered patios. Doubles, $45 to $55. Open year-round.

Atlantic View Motel and Cottages, Mason's Beach, R.R. 2, Lunenburg B0J 2C0. (902) 634-4545. Nine motel units (five with kitchens) and five housekeeping cottages date back 40 years, but they're thoroughly up to date in terms of furnishings. And, my, what a view! Across the narrow, untrafficked road is the open Atlantic, and this is one of the few places in the area where you get to see it. From the motel efficiency units (kitchenette and living room in front, bedroom with two double beds in the rear), each back door leads to a picnic table; Adirondack chairs are out front for gazing at Battery Point Light. Longtime owners David and Betty Steele, who greet most of their guests by name, offer a heated swimming pool and a couple of rowboats for exploring the tidal pond in the rear; a hike along the path through the woods may reveal turtles and muskrats. Obviously, this is a good place for families. Doubles, $35 to $45, each additional $3. Open May-October.

Belroy Motel, 39 Knickle Road, Lunenburg B0J 2C0. (902) 634-8867. It's not near the water, but this is Lunenburg's newest motel and it's adjacent to the community swimming pool. The 18 contemporary rooms on two floors have wood-paneled ceilings and brick walls, TV and radio. A dining room is open daily from 7 a.m. to 10 p.m. In 1986, owners Gene and Yvonne Tanner acquired the **Topmast Motel** on Mason's Beach Road, (902) 834-4661; they planned to refurbish its 12 rooms and add balconies to take advantage of the great view of Lunenburg Harbor across the greens of the Bluenose Golf Club (doubles $38). When we visited, Gene Tanner also had acquired a downtown site overlooking the Fisheries Museum of the Atlantic and planned to open the **Rum Runner's Inn**. Doubles at Belroy, $34 to $38. Open year-round.

The Compass Rose, 15 King St., Box 1267, Lunenburg B0J 2C0. (902) 634-8509. The striking house painted maroon with cream trim, built for a sea captain in 1825 in the center of Lunenburg, offers five guest rooms for B&B and an excellent restaurant (see Where to Eat). Suzanne and Rodger Pike moved here in 1984 from Vancouver and have turned this into a going concern. Interestingly, the original Georgian facade was later Victorianized, its exterior dressed up in gingerbread style. The five guest rooms share one full bathroom and two washrooms. Each is charmingly furnished with puffy quilts and nice pillows on the beds, scatter rugs on painted floors, hanging Tiffany lamps and all kinds of colorful accents. One has a loveseat and two white-iron double beds; another with 1920s art deco furniture has a queensize waterbed. A full breakfast is served. Doubles, $35 to $45. Open March-November.

Harbour Watch, 85 Pelham St., Box 1348, Lunenburg B0J 2C0. (902) 634-8818. A Victorian home built in 1882 was converted into a small but appealing B&B in 1986 by Ron and Doreen Cook, who also own and operate **Victoria's Historic Inn** with a Cajun restaurant in Wolfville in Nova Scotia's Annapolis Valley. Their manager here, Margaret Reid, showed us four pleasant guest rooms, one with queen bed in Victorian style and another with two beds done up in lavender. The second-floor shared bath in front has the best view of the harbor; a clown is perched on the windowsill here, and another one is on a shelf in the front corner bedroom. A second full bath is available in the basement. There's an inviting parlor with TV and a player piano. Guests are served a full breakfast at a long table in the formal dining room. Doubles, $39. Open year-round.

Mahone Bay Inn, 680 Main St., Mahone Bay B0J 2E0. (902) 624-8078. Across from Government Wharf and facing the bay, this yellow Victorian B&B with white gingerbread trim was opened in 1983 by Gordon and Esther Bryant, who moved here from California after deciding this was "a good place to raise our family and ourselves." Guests have use of a living room with fireplace and stereo, a den with TV, games and piano, and a basement sauna and exercise room. One ground-floor bedroom has a crazy bathroom angled under a stairwell. Four upstairs rooms with original floors showing are plainly but nicely furnished; two have water views, and all share one large bathroom. Full breakfasts, including homemade muffins and jams, are served in the dining room, where there's a large aquarium beside the table. The Bryants have bicycles and ping-pong and pool tables for their guests. Doubles, $40. Open year-round.

Chester Area

Best Western Oak Island Inn & Marina, Route 3A, Western Shore B0J 3M0. (902) 627-2600. This motel with 69 units and four suites has everything, including the area's largest conference center, banquet hall, game room, indoor pool and sauna, room service, and dancing in the Anchorage Lounge. The best of the large rooms with two double beds and a pink and green decor are the half which face the water; otherwise you could be in any decent motel. From your room you can look across to Oak Island and dream of buried treasure. There's a private beach beside the bay, and the marina offers boat rentals, fishing charters and scenic cruises of Mahone Bay. Dinner in the **Atlantic Room**, with water views on three sides, is standard motel fare, priced from $7.95 for fried trout to $16.95 for a Nova Scotia seafood platter. The dining room is open for three meals a day; dinner from 5 to 10. Doubles, $49 to $67. Open year-round.

The Tall Ships Inn, King Street, Box 837, Chester B0J 1J0. (902) 275-5559. A resident Austrian couple runs this fine B&B for Halifax owners who have outfitted it handsomely indeed. The front parlor has a spinning wheel and velvet sofas; ship's instruments are displayed on a table in a rear parlor, and there's a small TV room with a spring water dispenser. Upstairs are five guest rooms, three with private bath and two sharing. One has a canopied bed covered by an antique quilt, a loveseat and scatter rugs. A continental breakfast of croissants and muffins is served in a pleasant dining room, set with speckled blue plates on colorful quilted placemats, and filled with antiques. Doubles, $65 to $68; one single, $45. Open May 1-Oct. 15.

Windjammer Motel, Route 3, Chester B0J 1J0. (902) 275-3567. Built in the late 1950s, this is still the only motel in Chester. Its season is short and "we could rent 100 rooms for 50 days," new owners Richard and Kim Johnson said of their 15-room establishment. Each room has two double beds, full bath and color cable TV. Although the motel faces the road, its rear lawn slopes down to tiny Stanford Lake, and there are lawn chairs and picnic tables. The Windjammer Restaurant, under separate management, is next door, serving lunch and dinner ($5 to $13). Doubles, $42.

The Cove B&B, Big Tancook Island, Lunenburg County B0J 3G0. (902) 228-2054. A 45-minute ferry ride from Chester takes people seven miles out in Mahone Bay to Big Tancook Island, three miles long and one mile wide. The island has a general store, gift shop, canteen, church and — hard to believe — a tourist bureau, plus the Cove B&B, just over a mile from the ferry landing (transportation arranged by phone). David and Martha Farrar offer two double rooms, two singles, two baths and bunkhouse facilities, plus ample lawn space for tenters. A hearty breakfast is included in the room price, and other meals from picnics to high tea may be arranged. The beach and nature trails are nearby. There are special rates for families and extended stays (once you get out here you may not want to leave). Doubles, $35; children $5 each. Open June 15-Oct. 15.

CAMPING AND CABINS. Risser's Beach Provincial Park, Route 331 south of Bridgewater, 688-2034, is a beautiful park with an ocean beach and 90 unserviced campsites, both open and wooded; $6 nightly. The **Lunenburg Board of Trade**, Box 1300, Lunenburg, 634-8100, offers twenty serviced and eight unserviced sites in an open area beside the Tourist Bureau on Blockhouse Hill Road; nightly, $8 to $10. **Ovens Natural Park**, Box 41, Riverport, 766-4621, has 85 serviced and 85 unserviced sites near the ocean and scenic caves; nightly, $9 up. Two miles east of Chester, **Graves Island Provincial Park**, Route 3, 275-9917, has 64 unserviced sites in an open and wooded campground beside the ocean; nightly, $6.

RENTALS. Several cottage colonies offer cabins by the week or longer. **Lily Point Motel & Cottages**, RR2, Lunenburg, 634-8085, has four efficiency motel units and two housekeeping cottages on a point in the bay five minutes from Lunenburg; doubles, $32 to $40. The Lunenburg Board of Trade, Box 1300, 634-8100, may have suggestions.

Seeing and Doing

Lunenburg

Situated on a peninsula between "front" and "back" harbors, this historic fishing and boat-building village is the county's principal business center. It is also becoming an arts center of note.

The **Lunenburg Craft Festival**, the largest in Nova Scotia with more than 100 participating craftsmen, is held annually in mid-July. The annual Nova Scotia Fisheries Exhibition and Fishermen's Reunion is an attraction in September.

The visitor's first stop should be at the tourist bureau, located in a lighthouse atop Blockhouse Hill. Climb to the top for a panoramic view of the village and its front and back harbors.

"Experience Lunenburg: Talk to a Pilot," say notices posted on stores around town. They advise that "these special people will be happy to act as your pilots and navigate you around our intriguing port." You're supposed to look for townsfolk wearing flag pins. Although we never found any, it's a great idea.

The schooner Bluenose, depicted on the back of the Canadian dime, was built here in 1921 and was the racing champion of the North Atlantic fishing fleet. The Bluenose II, a replica of the original, was built here in 1960 was the HMS Bounty, used in the filming of "Mutiny on the Bounty." It caused quite a stir when it returned in the summer of 1986 for only its second visit in 26 years to its birthplace. Moored along the wharf, it lived up to its billing as "the last of the full-riggers — the near ultimate in man's creation of beautiful ships." Along the front harbor are the shipbuilding yards and commercial fisheries that give Lunenburg its title, the Gloucester of Canada. Today, the fishing fleet of modern trawlers and scallop draggers makes Lunenburg a major fish landing port on the North Atlantic seaboard.

The Fisheries Museum of the Atlantic, Foot of Duke Street, Lunenburg, (902) 634-4794. The bright red buildings of a former fish processing plant — typical of Atlantic Canada. Inside are an aquarium with 25 tanks and three floors of exhibits. You may see a fish being filleted in a demonstration room. Boats are on display in the Hall of Inshore Fisheries. In the Dory Shop, you can watch a dory being built. The Bank Fishery/Age of Sail, a Parks Canada exhibit, traces the 400-year history of fishing along the banks of the continental shelf off Canada's East Coast. Another exhibit portrays the triumphs of the Bluenose. On the third floor are the Rum Runners exhibit, reflecting the Prohibition era when fishermen trafficked illicit liquor to the U.S.A, a sailmaker's exhibit, a typical fish company office from the 1920s, ice harvesting equipment, photographs of old Lunenburg and the Ice House Theater, which shows half-hour films on fishing. Outside the museum you can board the Theresa E. Connor, built here in 1938 and the last Lunenburg schooner to fish the Grand Banks with dories, and the steel-hulled side trawler Cape North, first of the fresh fish draggers to sail out of Lunenburg. The museum has a restaurant and gift shop. Open May 15-Oct. 15, daily 9:30 to 5:30. Adults $2, children 50 cents, family $5.

Schooner tours of Lunenburg harbor and deep-sea fishing expeditions leave from the Fisheries Museum Dock. The S.S. Timberwind, 634-8966, a traditional Lunenburg schooner, sails daily at 10:30, 12:30, 2:30 and 4:30. Adults $10, children $7.

WALKING TOUR. The bright colors of the buildings will impress you as much as the architecture along the historic streets on the hillside above the harbor. They're particularly striking against the background of blue harbor and the lush greens of the Bluenose Golf Club on the hillside beyond. St. Andrew's Presbyterian and Zion's Lutheran churches are the oldest of their denominations in Canada. St. John's Anglican (1754) is the second oldest Protestant church in Canada; guided tours are given daily in summer. The hilltop Lunenburg Academy built in 1894, visible for miles around, is a Provincial Heritage Property still used as an elementary school.

ARTS AND CRAFTS. Lunenburg's galleries and shops are relatively few but exceptional. **Montague Woollens,** at Montague and King streets, is a choice shop purveying 100 percent Icelandic wool sweaters and lovely angora sweaters among a wide selection of handwoven and handknit wearing apparel for men and women. Upstairs is **Teddy Bear Knits,** which has knitted outfits for children and a selection of children's gifts. Framed on a wall up the stairway was a

373

wonderful two-tone down vest with sweater and turtleneck, size 6, for $31.95. Owners Gail and John Patriarche also had the **Morash Gallery, 55 Montague St.**, with paintings and gifts in a restored 1876 house that is among the most photographed in Lunenburg.

Houston North Gallery, 110 Montague St., specializes in folk art and Inuit (Eskimo) art on three fascinating floors with views of the harbor. Owner Alma Houston and son John both spent many years in the Arctic, an experience reflected in their selection of works and exhibits. We were intrigued by hand-painted chairs portraying local scenes, larger-than-life sea birds carved of wood, a porch on which dwelt a gigantic moose, and an enormous musk ox rug complete with head, horns and hooves.

The **Black Duck Handcrafts Cooperative,** 8 Pelham St., is Nova Scotia's first craft cooperative. Now more than a decade old, it's a showplace for members to display their wares, including clothing, eye-catching kites, pottery, baskets and local books; all the herbal items smelled great. **Olson's Blue Rocks Studio II,** 178 Pelham St., was relocated in 1982 from the nearby Blue Rocks arts colony. **The Shop at 54 Pelham St.** displays local crafts, gifts, weavings, toys, books and kitchen gear. The **Lunenburg Art Gallery** at 19 Pelham St., sponsored by the town's active Heritage Society, shows works of local artists.

Mahone Bay

Mahone Bay is the dominant bay of the area and ringing the head of a harbor is the small town of the same name. It's known for three landmark churches facing the waterfront side by side and, lately, for some fine crafts shops and boutiques along Main Street, the shore Route 3.

Amos Pewterers has been operating from an old boat building shop beside the bay since 1974. You may see Greg and Suzanne Amos at work; you'll certainly see some amazing pewter pieces — many of them surprisingly sleek and contemporary — from bowls to picture holders to jewelry. Across the street at the **Birdsall-Worthington Pottery Ltd.**, Tim Birdsall and Pam Worthington make Nova Scotian earthenware pottery with a decorating technique known as slip trailing. Their delicate floral painting over clay vases and dishes is exquisite. **The Teazer,** named for the legendary ghost ship said to still haunt Mahone Bay, has five rooms of crafts, sweaters, kitchenware, children's items and fine clothing and accessories from the British Isles.

At the eastern edge of town is **Kedy's Landing,** a complex of a dozen distinctive shops fashioned in 1985 from a couple of restored historic buildings facing the bay. Our favorite store here is **Admiral Benbow,** where everything is from the British Isles — all the clothing and gifts "and even us," volunteered the owners from Cornwall. Fishermen's smocks from Wales or Cornwall are particularly attractive. **Candleriggs** offers Maritime handcrafts and designer sweaters. **Bali Sekali** has contemporary clothing in natural materials, the **P.G. Joost Co.** specializes in maritime and local books, and the **Kettle Creek Canvas Co.** shows cotton clothing, bags and accessories.

Chester

Called "possibly the prettiest village in Nova Scotia" by the Windjammer Motel brochure, this looks like a typical New England coastal town, thanks to its rolling green topography and its early New England settlers. Located on a hilly peninsula, it has a front harbor, a back harbor and various inlets, all emanating from Mahone Bay for a pervasive water presence. It's a summer refuge for the affluent, including, we're told, Phyllis Diller and Pierre Elliott Trudeau. The summer population doubles, most of them regular visitors and many of their cars bearing American license plates.

Sailing is the village's principal preoccupation. Mahone Bay is a rainbow of colorful sails during **Chester Race Week**, an annual event in August (as is **Old Home Week.**) Just west of Chester is South Shore Marine, billed as Atlantic Canada's largest marina complex. All the coves and inlets with which the Chester area abounds are mooring places for fine powerboats and sailboats, quite in contrast to the old fishing boats in most Maritimes harbors. "There aren't many such places where you can sail and not hit open ocean," said Chris Morin, co-proprietor with her sister of the Chester Basin Coffee House, from whose deck one gets a good view of the boating activity. An even better place to view the yacht races is from what villagers call the Parade Grounds, a green hillside with lawns and flowers. Here on a spit of land separating the front and back harbors (connected by a canal) is the Chester Yacht Club founded in 1901, the War Memorial Monument, the Victorian gazebo bandstand still used for concerts by the Chester Brass Band and a bridge across the canal to Peninsula Road.

An **Historic Walking Tour** brochure guides visitors past landmarks you might not otherwise recognize or find, including several examples of what it calls "Picturesque architecture, an interpretation of Gothic Revival," using decorative trim, steeply pitched gables and lapped siding. Water Street along the front harbor leads to Government Wharf, where ferry service is provided several times daily to Big and Little Tancook Islands. Chester has a golf club, tennis courts and a saltwater pool near the Canal Bridge on the back harbor.

Come-a-Long II, a 40-foot cape boat owned by South Shore Marine, 275-4700, operates harbor and bay tours out of Chester, evening cruises and charters. Scheduled Mahone Bay cruises take 25 people at 10 and 1 daily except Tuesday and Thursday in summer from the Parade Grounds in Chester. Evening cruises depart from South Shore Marine at 7 nightly except Tuesday and Thursday. Adults $10, children $6.

Oak Island. Out in Mahone Bay just off the community of Western Shore is an eerie island of buried treasure. Long a haven for smugglers and privateers, it has a money pit discovered in 1795 by three Chester youths on a camping expedition; they started digging, and treasure hunters have been digging in vain since for what is believed to be Captain Kidd's bounty. Six lives and more than $2 million have been spent on the most expensive treasure hunt in the world. All agree that the designer of the pit was a genius, for the treasure has defied discovery. Since 1969, Triton Alliance Ltd. — a syndicate of Canadian and American businessmen — has been conducting a highly technical hunt on the island. You can tour the island under auspices of Triton Alliance, which has a small museum and gift shop at the entrance, where you listen to a 10-minute tape before getting in a guide's car or a bus for a 25-minute tour. A number of digging sites, shafts, a bore hole, the 100-foot-deep cave-in pit and the money pit heighten one's interest in the Oak Island tale, subject of three books. By the time you finish you may share the guide's optimism that the treasure will be uncovered within the year. It's hokey, but fascinating. Tours daily, June 1-Sept. 15. Adults $3, children $1.50.

The M.V. Tageshelle, 627-2600, gives boat tours and fishing charters past the Oak Island money pit and through the Chester islands from the Best Western

Oak Island Inn & Marina, Western Shore. Cruises are scheduled daily at 5:30, 6:30 and 7:30.

SHOPPING. Probably because Chester is less tourist-oriented and its residents are busy sailing, the village lacks the number of choice shops found in Lunenburg and Mahone Bay. Queen Street, the main street, has the **Needle's Eye,** featuring machine-embroideredNova Scotia scenes, quilted tea cosies, pillows and appliqued children's hangings. **The Owl and the Pussy Cat** offers books, toys, handcrafts and imported gifts. Two good shops are beside the harbor on Water Street. **The Warp and Woof,** at the venerable age of 60, is one of Nova Scotia's oldest gift shops, featuring handcrafts, wood carvings, apple dolls, an art gallery and gift items from around the world; its **Sweater Annex** has imported woolens and accessories. Jim Smith's **Nova Scotia Folk Pottery,** charmingly housed in the old Corner Store, features especially colorful plates and pitchers in striking purples and greens.

Other Attractions

BEACHES. You have to go off the main roads to find them, but if you do you'll luxuriate in their tranquility and relative privacy. Some of the best are to the southwest of Lunenburg along the scenic shore Route 331 from East Medway. **Beach Meadows,** almost a horseshoe of white sand and clear water, is a beach lover's dream. A long dirt road leads to **Cherry Hill Beach,** where you're rewarded by beaches facing both west and south, and may find shells and driftwood. **Risser's Beach** is a superb provincial park with a wonderful beach where the breakers roll in neatly in single lines, a 1.5-mile boardwalk traverses a salt marsh, a canteen dispenses food, and there are picnic areas. East of Lunenburg, there's a lovely little unnamed beach on a bay four miles down Second Peninsula. East of Chester is **Graves Island Provincial Park,** which has a small stony beach and picnic tables. Out the next peninsula is **Bayswater Beach,** with a view of the open ocean near Blandford. Queensland, on St. Margaret's Bay, is the home of three beaches, **Cleveland, Queensland** and **Black Point.**

Poking and Browsing. A particularly scenic route leads from East Medway along Route 331 to LaHave and Lunenburg. Besides visiting beaches (above), you'll want to make side trips. A road from Petite Riviere leads to the charming summer colony of **Green Bay.** Turn right at Crescent Beach for the quaint **LaHave Islands;** stop at the free Marine Museum housed in a tiny church after crossing a strange one-lane, wood-floor bridge. **LaHave** is an appealing town, where a ferry crosses the LaHave River — known as the Rhine of Canada — on the hour to Lower LaHave. The unusual ferry is drawn by cable; the ride takes five minutes and costs 50 cents.

The **Ovens Natural Park,** near Riverport, has 200 acres of caves and rock formations that are scenic, we're told, but a bit over-commercialized for our taste. Gold was found here in 1861, and a miniature Klondike started when gold miners arrived in hopes of striking pay dirt; their town was soon abandoned, but tunnels and pits remain. Cunard's Cove, named for the founder of the Cunard Lines, is where his son conducted a successful venture gathering gold from the beach. This is essentially a private campground with a swimming pool, and there's a day-use charge which discourages a quick look at the caves. Open daily, May 20-Sept. 10.

Several scenic roads lead from Route 3 toward the ocean between Lunenburg and Chester. Everyone heads out to **Blue Rocks,** a tiny weatherbeaten fishing village somewhat like famed Peggy's Cove before it was overrun; it's a favorite with artists and photographers. The road down **Second Peninsula** hugs the shoreline and we saw a cormorant spreading its wings and a big blue heron feeding in shallow water at low tide. **Second Peninsula Provincial Park** has picnic tables beneath a stand of tall fir and spruce trees beside a rocky shore. You can take a circle tour around **Indian Point**, where Micmac Indians once lived, and out to **Martins Point**. Beyond Chester on the other side of St. Margaret's Bay is storied **Peggy's Cove**, which we enjoyed on a May weekday almost 20 years ago — the latest time at noon on a September Sunday we felt almost claustrophobic with the many bus loads of tourists. But the awesome rocks, the lighthouse and the crashing surf are must sights to see, if you can avoid the hordes.

Where to Eat

This is one of the few areas in the Maritimes which we have found to have appealing restaurants, both in terms of cuisine and settings — a result, no doubt, of the sophisticated tastes of residents and summer visitors.

Near the Water

The Captain's House, 129 Central St., Chester. (902) 275-3501. Folks from Halifax and even farther away flock to this imposing Georgian house, built in 1822 on a lot owned by one of Chester's first settlers. The draw is the famed Sunday brunch, with seatings at 11 and 1:30 — price $19.95. On several long tables are displayed smoked and fresh fish, oysters, pates, seafood crepes, roast beef, apple and rum crepes and just about anything else good to eat you could think of. The three classic dining rooms downstairs are done up in white linens, heavy draperies and lots of fresh flowers. Waitresses glide by in long skirts, and Scottish music plays in the background. The dining rooms in back have a grand view of the front harbor. Owner Ron Philips, who also owns the acclaimed **Blomidon Inn** in Wolfville and **Bread and Roses** in Annapolis Royal, has plans to turn the upstairs rooms into bedrooms, and then the Captain's House will be a B&B. The dinner menu, with its lovely watercolor drawing of the building by famed Canadian artist Dorothy Clark McClure, lists entrees from $12.25 for supreme of chicken to $19.95 for tournedos Bras D'Or, stuffed with oysters. Quebec duckling, rack of lamb, Digby scallops and haddock poached in chablis and garnished with lobster and prawns are some choices. At lunch, try the south shore casserole, with lobster, scallops and shrimp for $8.95, or oyster stew, $4.95. Grand Pre wines are $2.95 a glass; the wine list is better than most around here. Lunch daily, noon to 3; dinner from 5; Sunday brunch. Open April-October.

The Rope Loft, Water Street, Chester. (902) 275-3430. Would that every restaurant could have such a felicitous setting. This popular place at water's edge has a second-story deck with rustic wood furniture, a new lower deck with spiffy white tables and chairs, a soaring upstairs Rope Loft dining room and a timeworn, timbered 1815 sea shanty downstairs. Obviously it can handle scores of people, so we were surprised to be the only diners when we arrived about 9:30 on a July weeknight. We wished we'd been earlier to have enjoyed a drink on the upper-level deck right beside the front harbor, with boats moored all around. The candlelit dining room was casual and the service solicitous (after all, we were the only ones there, but the help probably wanted to go home). We shared an appetizer of solomon gundy (Nova Scotia pickled herring) before digging into our entrees of grilled halibut ($11.25) and Digby scallops marinated in vermouth ($13.25), generously served on huge plates filled with carrots and either rice or new potatoes. The limited menu is priced from $10.75 for poached haddock or Lake Bras d'Or rainbow trout stuffed with prawns and mushrooms to $15 for sirloin steak. A Maritime parfait with dark rum and maple syrup is the most interesting of the desserts, unless you feel like splurging for chocolate fondue for two ($14.50). Lunch in the **Old Wharf** downstairs or outside on the decks would be worthwhile as well. Open daily, noon to 10, May to mid-October.

The Galley at South Shore Marine, off Route 3, Chester. (902) 275-4700. New in 1984 and part of a marina, this contemporary restaurant with an outdoor deck and picnic tables overlooks Mahone Bay. The view from the two-level dining room is pretty as a picture, as is the entire restaurant in its nautical setting. The eight-page menu is a bit cutesy, but the prices are right for mussel chowder, lobster stew or seafood sampler for appetizers ($3 to $6.50), and stuffed sole, clams over pasta, fishermen's casserole, stir-fried vegetables and mussels over rice, or, if you must, chicken or pepper steak for entrees ($7.95 to $16.50). The desserts and wines are limited; the fancy "fog-cutter" cocktails and "hot grog" liqueured coffees are not. In front is the Loft, a marine store stocking nautical clothing, equipment and gifts, and outside are tables and chairs under clumps of birch trees. Open daily, noon to 9.

Cape House Inn, Route 3, East Mahone Bay. (902) 624-8211. A long driveway up a hill leads to a red house with a statue of a baker at the entrance. Built in 1765, the house has a great view of Mahone Bay, the harbor and the village. Ann Cavezan and her late physician husband Raymond started out in 1978 serving English tea in the afternoon, adding chowder lunches and finally dinners of renown. The huge fireplace with bake oven dominates the country-pretty dining room filled with local antiques and art work. Aperitifs may be served in the lounge or on the front canopied deck looking down on the bay. The handwritten menu starts with such appetizers as house pate, poached scallops, spicy Acadian peppered shrimp or brie and smoked salmon in puff pastry with onion chutney. Entrees ($11.50 to $17.95) include sauteed scallops, lobster cardinal, filet of beef bearnaise, chicken in puff pastry with a champagne-mustard sauce, and roast duckling. Finish with grand marnier cream puffs, raisin custard bread pudding with hot rum sauce, bittersweet chocolate mousse or Peninsula Farm homemade ice cream. Mrs. Cavezan has a sure, deft touch in the kitchen, so we were sorry to learn she was planning to sell in 1987, but were assured that any purchaser would run it in the Cavezan tradition. They'd be foolish not to. Dinner Tuesday-Sunday, seatings at 6 and 8:15. Open June-October.

Zwicker's Inn, 662 Main St., Mahone Bay. (902) 624-8045. Here's another special place, run with panache by Jack and Katharine Sorenson, who in 1980 restored to its original use the first posthouse between Chester and Lunenburg, circa 1800. The inviting interior has several small dining rooms with soft yellow walls hung with local art works, red cloths over white linen, lace curtains and begonias in the windows. British music plays in the background. It's a homey setting for some imaginative food, like an outstanding mussel soup from a Maxim's of Paris recipe, piping hot and served with wonderful thick herb bread: a tasty mushroom-almond pate served with a small crock of potato salad, raw veggies and crisp rye toast; a seafood chowder and a Danish-style open-face roast beef sandwich with horseradish sauce. Accompanied by the local Keith beer, this was a memorable lunch. For dinner, we'd start with the mussel soup again and perhaps soused shrimps or smoked salmon (both $4.25) and then try the seafood Skibbereen, poached halibut or maybe barbecue-braised lamb shank or broiled pork tenderloin with thyme glaze ($9.50 to $12.95). We might try Zwicker's own noodles with chicken or shrimps, or shrimp Louis. Desserts run the gamut from lemon-honey cheesecake monogrammed "Z" for Zwicker's to homemade ice creams to potted cheese, whipped with butter and sherry and accompanied by a few grapes. These people do have fun and serve interesting food at wallet-pleasing prices. The wine list is one of Nova Scotia's most extensive. Open daily, summer 11:30 to 9:30, rest of year noon to 5 and 5 to 10.

Silver Spoon Terrace Restaurant, Kedy's Landing, Mahone Bay, (902) 524-8371. If the dessert case at the front entrance doesn't entice you, surely the front terrace or the spiffy licensed cafe will. This is an offshoot of Silver Spoon Desserts in Halifax, and offers the same kind of appealing menu and culinary flair. For lunch, you might try a spinach salad nouvelle, chicken pasta or Atlantic scallops in pesto sauce, $3.95 to $7.50. The limited dinner fare might include curried chicken and shrimp, a casserole of Nova Scotia seafood in bechamel sauce or seafood in pastry shell, $8.95 to $9.95. A three-course dinner, which changes weekly, is served weekends only for $12.95. Desserts are to die for: an almond cognac torte, raspberry hazelnut swirl, Swiss mocha orange log, creme de menthe truffle and all the other delectables that have Halifax on a perpetual sweets kick. Open Tuesday-Sunday, 11:30 to 8:30, mid-April to Dec. 24.

Away from the Water

Compass Rose, 15 King St., Lunenburg, (902) 634-8509. Music, candlelight and all kinds of art and little mementoes on walls and shelves transform three small dining rooms into romantic, intimate settings for fine fare. Delicious rolls, both white and herbed, preceded a good appetizer ($4.50) of pickled mussels and marinated herring with sour cream and a summer salad ($3.95 — a bit steep, we think, for a simple tossed salad like we make at home). Among entrees from $7.95 for mussels mariniere to $15.95 for steak au poivre, we were happy with the fettuccine with scallops and the spicy Lunenburg sausage, a local dish served with diced potatoes, tangy sauerkraut and hot dijon mustard, a good and hearty dish that would be a real winner in winter. Other choices included baked halibut, chicken Veronique and teriyaki steak. The dessert recitation intrigued enough that we shared a yummy creme de menthe ice cream pie with chocolate wafer crust, topped with whipped cream and chocolate sauce; the recipe for the Bavarian torte was requested by Gourmet magazine. A bottle of the house Compass Rose white wine was great, tasting like a fume blanc. While husband Rodger handles kitchen duties, Suzanne Pike oversees the dining room and makes sure her guests feel welcome. At lunch, try the lobster quiche with salad (a steal at $5.95), or some of the other items we sampled at dinner. Lunch daily, 11:30 to 2; dinner from 5. Open March-November.

Boscawen Inn, 150 Cumberland St., Lunenburg, (902) 634-3325. The downstairs dining room is simple and pretty with linens, candles, fresh flowers and sheer curtains on the windows, but could use more music to make things convivial. The menu appeals, although we regretted that the night's special of lamb was unavailable and the prime rib with Yorkshire pudding and rich gravy was overdone for our taste. The apricot chicken had a lovely sauce, but was a bit overcooked; the accompanying broccoli and carrots were undercooked. Solomon gundy, grilled scallops and bacon, and Lunenburg pudding (a pate made with ground pork and spices) are among appetizers, $2.50 to $3.95; the seafood chowder is rich and creamy, and a lobster salad ($3.50) is a bargain. The menu's seven entrees range from $9.95 for poached haddock or apricot chicken to $12.95 for coquilles St. Jacques or sauteed scallops. Among desserts are gingerbread with whipped cream, blueberry shortcake and amaretto cheesecake. Lunch, noon to 2; dinner, 5:30 to 9. Open May-October.

Casual Choices

Mug Up Chowder House, 128 Montague St., Lunenburg. (902) 634-3118. The menu explains that the term "mug up" denotes a snack or bite to eat aboard fishing vessels — to tide you over until the cook prepares the main meal. So here two women serve up eight kinds of chowder (from mussel to scallop to haddock to corn, $2.50 to $3, except $5.50 for seafood chowder of lobster and shrimp), a lobster sandwich for $5 and a concoction of scallops or lobster with cheese sauce on an English muffin, $5.25. At breakfast, all eggs are poached (two eggs on white or whole wheat go for $3). The place has no atmosphere other than what its owners say is the essence of Maritime cookery — fresh food in simple surroundings. We only wished the dining room shared the view of the harbor afforded by the rear kitchen. Open daily, 8 to 7, May 15-October, 8 to 3 rest of year.

Tingle Bridge Tea House, Mader's Cove, Mahone Bay. (902) 624-9770. The outdoor deck under the green and white awning is the place to stop for chowders, tea and homemade scones, and desserts with a grand view of the bay below. Inside are a handful of tables for cool days. Bill and Betty Amos, with son David, handle the cooking chores and keep lunch simple: chicken and biscuits, $4.95; fish chowder and bread, $3.95. Regulars come for the variety of teas and scones ($3.50) as well as shortcake, seasonal fruit pies, cheesecake and southern pecan pie. Open Wednesday-Sunday, 11 to 5:30, June-September; weekends only in spring and fall.

Thirsty Thinkers Tea Room, 297 Queen St., Chester. (902) 275-4747. A white house with blue window boxes on Chester's main street is a tea room-plus, serving seafood chowder, sandwiches, and steamed clams or mussels. Under a community outreach training program for Bonny Lea Farm participants, handicapped people serve a limited but good menu for $2.50 to $4.25. We liked the sound of a pizza for one topped with homegrown herbs. Open daily 9 to 5 and Sunday noon to 5, May to October.

Dolphin Beverage Room, 90 Pelham St., Lunenburg. (902) 634-4242. Genteel visitors might not want to set foot in the bar, but the original Lunenburg lobster supper served downstairs every Friday night is said to have good food in a casual atmosphere. The price is in the $14 range, a full menu is available, and the owner was thinking of adding a terrace dining area for 1987.

Chester Basin Coffee House, Route 3, Chester Basin. You can get a full breakfast of eggs, bacon, toast and coffee for $3, cooked and served to you with local color by friendly proprietor Chris Morin and her sister. The open rear deck looks right over the water, and we lingered to watch a loon — "one of two who live with us," said Chris, who also reported that minks live under the rocks and seals visit two or three times a year. Open daily in summer.

FOR MORE INFORMATION: South Shore Tourism Association, Box 82, Bridgewater, N.S. B4V 2W6, (902) 543-5391. Lunenburg Board of Trade, Box 1300, Lunenburg B0J 2C0, (902) 634-8100.

View of downtown Halifax is afforded from harbor excursion boat.

Halifax, N.S.

Imagine a waterfront city served by two competing bus-tour lines, two excursion boat tours, commuter ferries, half a dozen sailing cruises, Rolls-Royce and rickshaw tours, and even a sightseeing helicopter. A city with eight downtown hotels and a World Trade and Convention Center. A city with half a dozen downtown shopping complexes, five colleges and universities, and countless pubs, nightclubs and restaurants.

Such a city has to be a major commercial and destination center like Boston or New Orleans or San Francisco. This particular city, however, is Halifax. With barely 100,000 inhabitants, it is indeed a commercial and destination center far out of proportion to its size.

It happens also to be the largest city on Canada's East Coast and "the city" revered and visited by more than one million outlanders from throughout the Maritime Provinces. The world's second largest natural harbor and a heritage as the first English settlement in Canada have granted Halifax an importance beyond its size.

Situated on a hilly peninsula, Halifax is very much geared to the water. Its historic dominance as a seaport has brought it military vessels, freighters and ocean liners; these share the waters today with an inordinate number of private sailboats and yachts.

The once-decrepit waterfront has been rejuvenated into a model unmatched along the Atlantic coast. Considered the leading North American city in historic building renovations, Halifax has restored its waterfront to maximum advantage and nothing gets in the way of access to the water.

"We've strived for a balance between commercial and people-oriented activities," says Gerald G. Etienne, president and chief executive officer of Waterfront Development Corp. Ltd., the 10-year-old provincial crown corporation which oversees restoration efforts.

All Halifax, indeed, is a people-oriented city. Downtown office workers jog or take their lunch breaks beside the harbor, in the heart of the restored area called Historic Properties, or on the slopes leading to the hilltop fortress, the Citadel. Downtown sidewalks and connecting skywalks are crowded by day, in the evening and on weekends. Eight major parks in this "City of Trees" are fully used and off-limits to cars. Cars also stop for pedestrians at crosswalks, which may prove unnerving for Americans who pause at curbside to get their bearings, unintentionally stopping all traffic in the process.

Halifax also is a city of plaques, befitting its history and proud tradition. You can seldom go far on any of the city's walking tours — or anywhere else, for that matter — without pausing to read a commemoration.

The daily blast of the Citadel cannon at noon accentuates the city's military past, inviting the visitor to explore a fascinating, lively area replete with history and water activities.

Getting There

Halifax is a main entry point to the Maritimes by rail and air. Nova Scotia's major highways — Routes 101, 102 and 103 converge on Halifax from all directions. You can sail from Maine to Yarmouth via a twelve-hour ferry trip from Portland or a six-hour ferry trip from Bar Harbor, and from New Brunswick via a two-and-one-half-hour ferry trip from Saint John to Digby. Or you can drive all the way around on express (though not necessarily four-lane) highways through New Brunswick and Truro to Halifax. Each way has reasons to commend it, and we lean to driving around one way, taking the Bar Harbor ferry shortcut the other.

Prices are quoted in Canadian funds. Halifax is on Atlantic Time, one hour ahead of Eastern.

Where to Stay

Since this is a city-oriented area, you'll probably want to stay at a downtown hotel. Be advised there are outlying motels and several small bed-and-breakfast houses as well.

Halifax Sheraton Hotel, 1919 Upper Water St., Halifax B3J 3J5. (902) 421-1700. Superbly located beside the harbor, this new-in-1985 hotel is the most convenient to all the waterfront goings-on. About half the 350 guest rooms on six floors have partial harbor views; ours was literally perched over the water and fortunately had a small window which could be opened to let in all the water sounds. Others which face the city or an indoor pool-courtyard are not so inviting. The hotel's award-winning design is based on the military ordinance building which formerly occupied the property. It includes an historic clock tower and is so low-rise and in harmony with its surroundings that you would not suspect it to be a modern hotel. The **Cafe Maritime,** crowned by a skylight, is the open-to-the-lobby restaurant serving three meals a day; it's known especially for a lavish Sunday brunch, and has the most interesting dinner menu of any Halifax hotel. A harborside outdoor cafe for $5.50 in the **Harbourfront Bar.** Doubles, $110 to $130.

Delta Barrington, 1875 Barrington St., Halifax B3J 3L6. (902) 429-7410. Just a couple of blocks above the harbor and blending in with the Historic Properties renovation (its east side looks onto the Granville Pedestrian Mall), this hotel sometimes calls itself the Barrington Inn and rightly so. The most requested of the 202 rooms on three floors face onto two inner courtyards; they're quieter and away from the street. Rooms have mini-bars and large baths;

the 35 Signature Service rooms have Gucci accessories and complimentary Perrier as well as continental breakfast. A new Nautilus fitness center and a children's playground plus a supervised weekend children's center are attractions. Doubles, $97 to $122.

Chateau Halifax, 1900 Barrington St., Halifax B3J 1P2. (902) 425-6700. Across the street and uphill from the Delta Barrington, the 305-room Canadian Pacific hotel built in 1974 is part of the Scotia Square retail complex and rests atop a five-level parking garage, with a lobby beneath. One-third of the rooms have views up the harbor to the north. All were being renovated in 1987 to produce long credenzas with built-in TVs and mini-bars, marble bathrooms and dressing areas with vanities. The indoor-outdoor pool area is Halifax's nicest; an enclosed dome with a jacuzzi is part of Halifax's renovation project. The **Crown Cafe** is considered one of the best hotel dining rooms, and Sunday brunch in the rooftop Bluenose Room offers a fantastic view of the harbor and city (our suggestion that they open it for dinner was not the first). Doubles, $90 to $100.

Prince George Hotel, 1725 Market St., Halifax B3J 2N9. (902) 425-1986. This spiffy 217-room hotel opened in 1986 across the street from Halifax's World Trade and Convention Center to cater to the business trade — it's even linked to the center by underground tunnel. There aren't many water views, our guide conceded, but the sixth-floor rooms have a perfect view instead of the historic town clock on Citadel Hill. All is luxurious, from the art deco lobby with neon lights and gray and plum decor to the spacious guest quarters, all with two phones in the room, remote-control TV, large work tables and dressing areas with hair driers. The Prince George boasts Halifax's only deep-end hotel pool, plus a landscaped garage roof for walking and relaxation. The hotel is part of a small local chain embracing the Citadel Inn and the new **Cambridge House**, opening in 1987 with 200 "travel suites" at Brunswick and Sackville streets. Doubles, $90 to $100.

Citadel Inn, 1960 Brunswick St., Halifax B3J 2G7. (902) 422-1391. The closest hostelry to the Citadel, this two-tower complex has 280 rooms, half facing up the harbor. Strangely, only the lower floors have balconies, which look onto highrise apartments across the street. Rooms have refrigerators and mini-bars, and a solarium contains a swimming pool and jacuzzi. The windowed restaurant, **Arthur's**, features a prime rib dinner buffet with Yorkshire pudding, seafood newburg and salad bar for $14.50. Doubles, $85 to $115.

Lord Nelson Hotel, 1515 South Park St., Halifax B3J 2T3. (902) 423-6331. A classic older hotel with ornate lobby and a front porch sporting a lineup of chairs facing the Public Gardens, the Lord Nelson is favored by bargain-seekers and people who like the fashionable uptown Spring Garden location. The early section was built in 1928 and the North Towers were added in 1967. "A good majority of our guests prefer the older rooms of some distinction," said the desk clerk. A free swimming pool and health spa is adjacent to the hotel. The lower-priced among the 312 rooms lack air-conditioning and cable TV. Doubles, $60 to $84.

The Haliburton House Inn, 5184 Morris St., Halifax B3J 1B3. (902) 420-0658. Taken by the lifestyle of Nova Scotia, Yale University graduate William McKeever moved his family from Colorado to Halifax in 1987 to open the Haliburton House Inn, Atlantic Canada's first European-style urban inn. Its 40 rooms and suites have been grandly refashioned from three downtown townhouses. Rooms are spacious, have comfortable chairs and TV, and those in the rear have balconies onto a courtyard. Continental breakfast is served in a main-floor dining room. Doubles, $65 to $95.

BED AND BREAKFAST. **Halifax Metro Bed & Breakfast,** Box 1613, Station M, Halifax B3J 2Y6, (902) 434-7283, is a listing service for B&Bs. Diana Mills, co-author of *A Guide to Nova Scotian Bed and Breakfast*, has three rooms with shared bath at **Birdland B&B** at 14 Bluejay St., Halifax B3M 1V1, (902) 443-1055; doubles, $35. Carolyn Lock advertises friendly comfort and good food at her **Old 362 B&B,** 1830 Robie St., Halifax B3H 3G3, (902) 422-4309, three rooms with shared bath; doubles, $35. The **Queen Street Inn,** 1268 Queen St., Halifax B3J 2H4, (902) 422-9828, has six double rooms with Nova Scotia antiques; doubles, $40. **Hilton Hall,** 1263 South Park St., Halifax B3J 2K8, (902) 423-1961, offers nine Victorian rooms with private and shared baths, period antiques and a continental breakfast in a small tea room; doubles, $45 to $55. Full breakfast and afternoon tea are served at Halifax's first downtown B&B, **Heritage House Inn,** 1253 Barrington St., Halifax B3J 1Y2, (902) 423-4435.

Seeing and Doing

There's much to do in and around Halifax, and a variety of tours and excursions are designed to acquaint you with the city, its history and harbor. For quick and easy orientation purposes, start with an auto drive around the Citadel, a walk through the Historic Properties and a passenger-ferry ride across the harbor to Dartmouth and back.

On the Water

THE HARBOR. The world's second largest natural harbor extends inland from the open Atlantic past downtown and through the Narrows into Bedford Basin; a fjord appropriately called the Northwest Arm juts into the northwest residential areas, creating a peninsula for Halifax and a sheltered waterfront haven for the fortunate. The harbor is exceedingly busy, what with traffic on two soaring suspension bridges connecting Halifax and Dartmouth, commuter ferries, ocean-going ships, numerous sailboats and yachts, and often military planes buzzing overhead. We even saw several parachutists trailing red smoke in a military operation, You can get a feel for it all by boarding the **Dartmouth Ferry,** North America's oldest saltwater ferry service in continuous operation, which takes passengers back and forth between downtown Halifax and Dartmouth on eight-minute trips for 35 cents; this is a commuter ferry and they really know how to move people, with red lights blocking entrances, green lights allowing you to board and a series of escalators, walkways and parks at the Dartmouth end.

WATER EXCURSIONS. The **Haligonian II,** Privateer's Wharf, Historic Properties, 423-1271. The beginning and the end of its two-hour narrated cruise are inexplicably silent, but there's a running commentary in the middle. The cruise goes up-harbor to the McKay Bridge, with a view of the Bedford Institute of Oceanography, the world's second largest. It proceeds back past the 1917 Halifax Explosion site (the world's worst manmade explosion before the atom bomb — caused by the collision of a ship and a munitions ship), the oldest naval dockyard in North America, ocean-going piers and the continent's second-largest container loading freighter piers (we saw both a Soviet freighter taking on grain and a passenger liner about to leave), two deep-sea oil-drilling rigs, and McNab's and George's Islands. As the boat turns into the Northwest Arm, you may see a mounted policeman among the joggers in Point Pleasant Park. You'll certainly see plenty of pleasure craft at the Royal Nova Scotia Yacht Squadron, North America's first yacht club and the terminus for the noted Marblehead to Halifax Yacht Race, several other private clubs and an interesting array of waterfront homes.Tours daily May 31-Oct. 12, 10 and 1:30 (also 4 and 7 in season). Adults $9.50, children $4.50.

When in port, the **Bluenose II**, 422-2678, Canada's most famous racing schooner, takes passengers on three two-hour sailing cruises daily except Monday from its berth beside the Halifax Sheraton.

Captain Murphy's Boat Tours, 423-8471, include the Harbour Queen, a 250-passenger paddlewheeler with morning, afternoon, dinner and dancing cruises. Gerard Murphy's 75-foot Danish sailboat, the **Mar II**, offers daily one or two-hour cruises as well as lunch cruises and moonlight excursions. **Polaris**, 422-3888, a 75-foot ketch, gives 90-minute sailing cruises from Cable Wharf four times daily for $12. **Halifax Harbour Tours and Charters**, 455-4751, offers sailing cruises of the harbor and the South Shore aboard the 45-foot ketch Rorqual.

Particularly popular with Haligonians is the **McNab's Island Ferry**, 422-9523. The Vera III transports passengers to McNab's Island at the entrance of the harbor for hiking, swimming or a visit to the Island Tea Room, where lobster, seafood, sandwiches and afternoon tea and corn boils are served in a stone cottage set in a century-old garden overlooking the ocean. Round trips are $6.75 for adults, $3.50 for children; ferry departs hourly daily in summer, weekends in spring and fall.

On the Shore

LAND TOURS. A different Halifax is seen on any number of city tours. **Gray Line**, 454-9321, offers three narrated, two-and-one-half-hour city-wide tours daily with stops at the Citadel and the Maritime Museum of the Atlantic; adults $9, children $4.50. Similar prices are charged by **Halifax Double Decker Tours Limited**, 455-0676, which gives two-hour tours on red British buses daily from Historic Properties. Private tour guides offer such options as Rolls-Royce tours and rickshaw tours and taxis.

If these don't suffice, you can get a bird's-eye view of the city via **Cougar Helicopters**, from the Waterfront Heliport on Lower Water Street opposite the Brewery Market.

WALKING TOURS. A good walking tour map guides you in some detail through historic Halifax. Other walking tours are outlined in the Halifax Visitors' Guide and Metro Guide. Obviously you'll want to explore the waterfront, the central **Grand Parade** (former militia drilling ground) between the Old City Hall and **St. Paul's Anglican Church** (1750), oldest Protestant church in Canada, and the **Spring Garden** area.

The Halifax Citadel, 426-5080, Canada's most visited National Historic Park commands a steep hill overlooking downtown and the harbor. Considered one of the finest remaining examples of a bastioned fortification of the 19th century, it is a maze of period barracks, garrison cells and museum rooms, including the independent **Army Museum of Canadian and British Militaria**. To get the most out of it, take a free 45-minute guided tour; otherwise you're on your own and signs and information are notably lacking. A 50-minute audio-visual presentation, the "Tides of History," begins every 15 minutes and tells the history of Halifax and its military defenses. In summer, the fortress is garrisoned by university students who portray British military personnel of the 19th century Royal Artillery and 78th Highlanders. You'll hear the crack of rifle fire and the skirl of bagpipers as they drill in the parade, patrol the beats and hoist signals on the masts. The Friends of the Citadel Society also sponsor occasional candlelight tours and **Her Majesty's Cavalier Dinner,** a candlelight feast and show. "Victoria and Albert," a love story with music. Presented during the four-course chicken marengo dinner, the show proved so popular in 1986 that its six-week nightly summer run was extended to include weekends through October (tickets, $25; reservations, 425-3923). If you can't have dinner, get a feel for the old military days with a basic lunch in the restaurant. The slopes and greens called Halifax Commons around the Citadel are great for lounging. At the foot of Citadel Hill is the Town Clock, Halifax's best-loved landmark. It was given to the town in 1803 by Prince Edward, son of King George III — he had been head of the garrison in Halifax from 1794 to 1800. Citadel open daily 9 to 8 in summer (nominal admission), 9 to 5 and free rest of year.

RESTORATIONS. Much of Halifax's rejuvenation has been guided by Waterfront Development Corp. Ltd., a government-backed corporation providing land and planning services for private development. "The whole waterfront area was a disaster not long ago," recalled Gerald G. Etienne, its president and CEO. "Nobody would come down here." Ten years later, this public-private partnership is credited with making Halifax the North American leader in historic restorations — from the rebirth of the oldest waterfront wharf complex to St. Paul's Church, Canada's first Parliament Building, Government House, the Brewery Market, Granville Pedestrian Mall and lately the historic City Hall. Next, Waterfront Development planned to complete a walkway along the waterfront from the Sheraton to the Brewery, add a waterfront park next to the Maritime Museum and seek an aquarium. Halifax's downtown, which has shifted north from the Spring Garden focal point of two decades ago to Historic Properties, is edging back along the waterfront to Spring Garden once again.

Historic Properties, a once-abandoned four-acre waterfront site, is the keystone of Halifax's restoration efforts. Recipient of a Heritage Canada Award for historic preservation, it is a mix of boutiques, restaurants, lounges and the facilities of the Nova Scotia College of Art and Design, as well as a good visitor information center and launching point for tours. The **Brewery Market,** a newer anchor to the south end of the waterfront, was fashioned from the old Keith's Brewery. Somewhat dwarfed by the towering Maritime Center overhead, it's primarily a food and drink emporium with a few stores and offices.

PARKS. This city of parks offers some special places: the **Grand Parade,** a pleasant place to relax in the historic heart of the city, is the scene of many a noontime entertainment extravaganza and perhaps the best people-watching point in Halifax. **Point Pleasant Park,** 186 acres of forest surrounded by water at the southern tip of the city, is great for boat-watching, hiking, picnicking, horseback riding, exploring nature trails and the seawall, as well as swimming (the sandy Black Rock Beach is sheltered by a rocky point at Harbour Lookoff). This is a pedestrian's park; no cars are allowed and even bicycling is banned on weekends and holidays. **Fleming Park** along the North West Arm offers swimming at another sheltered beach and views of the city from the top of the imposing stone Dingle Tower. The **Halifax Public Gardens** is a shady, 16-acre oasis at downtown's edge. The oldest Victorian formal gardens in North America, it has lovely walks, bridges, a gazebo for Sunday band concerts, a free-form pond with an island and, of course, ample flower beds, few of them identified. We were struck by the gardens' southern air, enhanced by gnarled old trees and an exotic cactus garden, and the friendly ducks and geese seeking handouts from one and all. **Seaview Park**, a rather barren new 12-acre waterfront park under the Murray MacKay Bridge, affords a good view of all the shipping and boating operations in Bedford Basin.

Maritime Museum of the Atlantic, 1675 Lower Water St., 429-8210. This is the marine history branch of the decentralized Nova Scotia Museum. Housed in an old ship chandlery and warehouse with modern addition, it has plenty of room for well-displayed exhibits, among them a collection of boats including Queen Victoria's Royal Barge under a three-story vaulted ceiling. We were especially taken by the inside of a vessel cabin in which the cabinet door was swinging and the horizon tilting through the window, giving one a dizzying if momentary sense of sea motion. The Canadian scientific ship Acadia is docked outside for exploration. Open daily most of the year; free.

SHOPPING. As in other cities, the large chain and department stores are in the suburban malls. Halifax is blessed, however, with a number of new and restored downtown shopping complexes, some of them connected by pedestrian skywalks. **Scotia Square** is the largest; **Barrington Place** and **Maritime Center Mall** are close contenders. An uptown section around Spring Garden Street is funky and upscale, filled with university students, yuppies and the Old Guard. **Spring Garden Place** has the most chic shops, a Texas-style galleria with hanging white lights, and a good new basement market which contains Prime Cuts of Meat Ltd., Veggies Produce, Spring Garden Bakery and a branch of Desserts Plus. Outside, **Jennifers** is a large gift and craft shop which carries almost everything you see that's good all over Nova Scotia. We like the wide variety of shops in **Historic Properties**, especially **A Pair of Trindles Bookshop**, which carries every book ever written by a Canadian author. We picked up a couple of the Anne of Green Gables paperbacks, as well as Hugh MacLennan's classic novel about the Halifax explosion, *Barometer Rising*.

Where to Eat

Although Halifax has traditionally been considered a meat and potatoes or fried seafood town, many of its restaurants are changing their menu horizons with the times. Today, its dining establishments offer some of the best, most interesting food to be found in Eastern Canada.

Gourmet Favorites

Upper Deck, Historic Properties, Halifax. (902) 422-1289. The Privateer's Warehouse and Wharf was one of the first buildings to be restored in Historic Properties, and the three-decker sandwich of restaurants owned by Michael Lindthaler has been going strong since 1975. The Upper Deck is the culinary gem of the operation. Although it lacks a water view, "we make up for it with our food and service," manager Bradley Mast told two tourists who were ready to eat at 6 o'clock but wanted to be beside the water. After dark, of course, it doesn't matter all that much, and the Upper Deck is stunning indeed with its original stone walls and timbered ceiling, heavy wood tables topped with dark leather mats, brocade runners and candles in etched glass hurricane lamps on the main level, tiny table lamps on the loft level. Mussels bourguignon and mussel soup flavored with rosemary and gin are good starters. Among entrees ($13.50 for filet of sole meuniere or amandine to $22.95 for Privateers' brochettes — shrimp, scallops and beef), we savored the rack of lamb persille and the filet mignon. The accompanying vegetables (roesti potatoes, tiny brussels sprouts, cauliflower and tomatoes) were exceptional. Our only regret was that the special venison with bourbon sauce (around which we'd planned our choice of the sommelier's special Wynns Oven Australian cabernet for $17), turned out to be unavailable. Like the food, the wine list is fairly extensive and on the pricey side for Halifax, but the dining experience is generally considered to be consistently the best in the city. The **Middle Deck Lounge** serves up nightly entertainment as well as lunch, while the lively **Lower Deck Pub**, packed at night with young Haligonians enjoying singalong entertainment, offers pub snacks. Dinner, Monday-Saturday from 5:30.

La Perla, 71 Alderney Drive, Dartmouth. (902) 469-3241. When we visited this expanding two-year-old northern Italian restaurant across the street from the Dartmouth Ferry Terminal, there was not even a sign to identify it. But word of its excellence preceded it everywhere we went, and the quick ferry trip across the harbor to Dartmouth for lunch rewarded us with our finest meal in Nova Scotia. Maurizio Bertossi and his Dartmouth-born wife Stephanie started with an upstairs cafe, expanded downstairs to the main floor, and were adding a larger seafood restaurant, to be called **San Remo**, next door. La Perla's decor was designed around the distinctive tall red upholstered seats acquired from a railroad car; they form four booths along one wall on the first and second floors, and the rest of the seating is at four tables for two on each floor. Since the restaurant started upstairs, the kitchen is there, and the staff maneuver back and forth to the main floor along a narrow stairway they share with customers. But what food the kitchen produces! There are intriguing salads like one with thinly sliced marinated veal, heavenly pastas and exceptional entrees ($8.50 to $12.95) such as veal scaloppine with a walnut, mustard, brandy and cream sauce, quail with buttered polenta and rabbit stewed in herbs, tomato and wine. Delicious hot rolls served with butter squeezed through a pastry tube, a fettuccine in basil cream sauce and a penne with peas and salami made a memorable lunch, accompanied by a carafe of the house white Colli Albani and topped off with cappuccino and a smooth ice cream crepe smothered in hot orange sauce. And, crowning glory, our crisply linened table happened to be the only one with a water view. Reservations are advised, far in advance for weekends. Lunch, 11:30 to 2; dinner, 5:30 to 9:45; closed Sunday.

Rosco's Mediterranean Restaurant, 1489 Hollis St., Halifax. (902) 423-4560. This comfortable, clubby English Tudor-style restaurant with airy greenhouse is beside an open courtyard in the restored Brewery complex. It emerged in 1986 from the former Sanford's with Mediterranean fare and a new concept in eating that young but well-traveled owner Ross (Rosco) MacLean calls modular cuisine. Classic dishes from France to Spain to Greece to North Africa are prepared in full and half portions to encourage sampling. The menu recommends that you order by round or course, share and when finished, select the next round. Now that's the ultimate in grazing! Halifax trendies were catching on when we visited and the Spanish and Moroccan items were proving most popular. We made a dinner by sharing a Mediterranean fish soup that had more bite than fish, a Spanish red onion and orange salad, excellent warm sourdough bread with swirled butter, a Moroccan lamb tagine, and a Spanish pork tenderloin with pickled raw onions, carrots and zucchini. Lamb couscous, veal kidneys, blackened fish and shrimp with feta also appealed ($4 to $7 for half portions; $7 to $12 for full). A trio of lemon, orange and cranberry sherbets made a refreshing ending. Rosco's inherited an extensive wine cellar, but also offers house wines by the glass or half carafe for sampling. Open Monday-Friday from 11:30, Saturday from 5:30.

The Silver Spoon Restaurant, 1865 Hollis St., Halifax. (902) 422-1519. Although this establishment is noted for desserts, we recommend it for lunch and dinner as well. Deanna Silver's main-floor cafe has a mere 13 glass-topped tables with pink cloths, small lamps and candles. A table d'hote menu that changes every two weeks is only $16.95 and could include a first course of waterfront salad (with smoked salmon, mango and orange slices), a seafood antipasto and poached halibut with French tarragon butter. On the regular menu, entrees run from $7.95 for cassoulet of chicken to $16.95 for seafood Silver Spoon on a bed of homemade pasta. Stuffed pork tenderloin, sweetbreads dijonnaise and navarin of lamb are some of the intriguing possibilities. Even more intriguing are the desserts served here and down below at Silver Spoon Desserts, 1866 Water St., where it seems that half of Halifax comes in at night to indulge a sweet tooth. Many customers have had dinner at another spot but stop here for dessert. Listening to classical music, perched at little glass-covered tables, you can hardly choose between several fabulous truffles, cakes like Queen of Sheba gateau or, our downfall, a raspberry hazelnut cheesecake. Of course there are all kinds of coffees and teas, and the glass of water comes with a slice of lemon. Cafe, Monday-Saturday 11:30 to 11; Desserts, Monday-Saturday from 9:30 a.m., Sunday 11:30 to 7; take-out service available.

Scanway, The Courtyard, 1569 Dresden Row, Halifax. (902) 422-3733. If you like Scandinavian food as much as we do, you'll head for this nifty place off Spring Garden Road. Unni Simensen from just outside Oslo owns it, and when you dine here you almost feel you are in Norway. The old (150 years) house has been done over with pine walls and track lighting but the six original fireplaces remain, and the two second-floor dining rooms and adjacent outdoor decks ringed with purple petunias contain lots of nooks and crannies. The comfortable chairs are made of local pine, and red candles are at every table. Everyone flocks to Scanway at lunchtime for the wide selection of open-faced sandwiches, 22 in all, from $4.25 for egg and tomatoes to $7.25 for "tartarbiff." Smoked salmon with egg custard is one of the most requested. Among salads is an excellent plate of smoked salmon, shrimp on egg and marinated herring. At night entrees ($5.95 to $12.95) include lobster and shrimp in a white wine sauce and sole stuffed with crab. You could start with smoked eel and end with one of Scanway's fabulous desserts like marsipankake, a delightful creation of light cake layered with fruit and whipped cream and covered with a layer of marzipan. Aquavit comes right from the freezer, as it should; there's Tuborg beer and a quite decent wine list. Downstairs is **Scanway Gourmet** for snacks, desserts and takeout. Lunch 11:30 to 3; dinner 5 to 10 or 11; closed Sunday.

Fat Frank's, 5411 Spring Garden Road, Halifax. (902) 432-6618. "Purveyors of fine foods to the nobility and gentry since 1974," says the plaque in front of the brick townhouse, and that about sums it up. So do all the clippings and photos discretely lining the staircase of this local institution run by Frank Metzger who, we understand, is tall and heavyset but not really fat. Your wallet may have to be to get through a full dinner, however. The smoked salmon appetizer is $8.75, a tossed salad $4 (salad almost always costs extra in Halifax), entrees start at $17.95 and desserts include a fresh vanilla-poached fruit with cinnamon for $5.50. Among the interesting entree offerings: sweetbread fritters, curried shrimps with assorted fruits, halibut with capers and cream in a mille-feuille pastry, a trio of chicken breasts with cranberries and peppercorns, and poached scallops and pears with pernod and melon pearls. There's tableside flambeeing, formal service and furnishings and crisp white linen, brocade banquettes and walls hung with portraits in three dining rooms. A five-course menu degustation for $37.50 lets you sample several specialties. Downstairs is the new **Bentley's Bistro**, a particularly pleasant spot with tile floors, stone walls and three enormous potted palms that frequently must be replaced because they don't fare well in a Halifax basement. An appealing and reasonable menu is served all day from 11:30 to 10 or 11, closed Sunday. Lunch, Monday-Friday 11:30 to 2; dinner nightly, 6 to 10:30.

Other Choices

Clipper Cay, Historic Properties, Halifax. (902) 423-6818. Local detractors contend that this lives up to the first part of its name and sells windows rather than food, and we admit we were so put off by a haughty maitre-d' who failed to produce a window table as requested that we gave up our coveted dinner reservation. There's no denying that Clipper Cay has the best water view in Halifax, its expansive windows taking full advantage. The main second-floor dining room is supremely elegant, pink and pricey. Dinner entrees run from $12.95 for filet of sole or grilled sirloin steak to $19.95 for filet of beef with bearnaise sauce. The Cajun platter of seafood prepared from an Acadian recipe sounds interesting, as does the Arctic char topped with seafood and served Harlequin style. Lunches are simpler and cheaper, and the popular downstairs **Cayside Lounge** offers snacks, sandwiches and pasta, as well as light entrees. Lunch, Monday-Friday from 11:30; dinner nightly, 5 to 11.

Five Fishermen, 1740 Argyle St., Halifax. (902) 422-4421. The tourists also pack this place, and when we stopped by one weeknight we overhead a party of two being told they would have a two-hour wait until 9 for dinner as eight conventioneers were ushered upstairs. Although Haligonians think it has slipped under its recent ownership, out-of-towners like the nautical decor with a statue at a ship's wheel atop the stairs, high-back chairs, bare wood floors and window seats beside the Grand Parade. They also like the complimentary salad bar and seafood bar with steamed mussels and clams. Fish from the restaurant's own boat appears in many forms, from Arctic char and mako shark ($13.95) to house specialties like prawns with cheese, lobster thermidor and Digby scallops with rice ($17.95). Lunch is offered in the **My Apartment Lounge** next door, one of nine beverage rooms launched by new owner Gary Hurst. Dinner nightly.

Ryan Duffy's, Spring Garden Place, Halifax. (902) 421-1116. This is the latest incarnation of Le Grand, Duffy's Bar and the Rainbow Grill. Newly expanded, formal yet casual and attractive with well-spaced tables flanked by brocade upholstered arm chairs, soaring windows onto the street and, surprisingly, candles dripping in old wine bottles, it specializes in corn-fed beef and steak carved to size at your table. The raw meat literally is brought to the table, you choose your portion, it's carved and weighed, and you pay by the pound — "the record so far is 25.7 ounces," the maitre-d' informed us. A few seafood dishes complement the beef, which run from $9.50 for catch of the day to $18.50 for lobster. We would have chosen almost anything from the changing "outdoors" menu —roast medallions of wild Russian boar with hot cumberland sauce, two boned quails with perigourdine sauce, fresh salmon baked on a cedar plank or grilled Bras d'Or lake trout stuffed with baby shrimp and wild rice, all preceded by

390

pate in puff pastry or soup and Duffy's special Icelandic baby shrimp salad with mandarins and tossed with toasted coconut and papaya dressing. Quite a bargain for $15.95 complete. Lunch, 11:30 to 3; dinner 5 to 11, Sunday to 9.

Le Bistro, 1333 South Park St., Halifax. (902) 423-8428. Don't let its location in the main-floor corner of a high-rise apartment deceive you. This is as French a bistro as you'll find this side of the Left Bank. An enclosed atrium has umbrella-covered tables looking onto the street; the interior is dimly lit, candles drip over Perrier bottles and the hanging lamps are covered in red and white to match the tablecloths. And the inexpensive food appeals to the nearby Dalhousie University crowd. We were stunned to find a Sunday brunch with eggs Benedict or crepes florentine for $5.25, including champagne or bloody mary (the latter, as we brunched on shrimp Creole and chicken livers with poached eggs. A classical guitarist played regular menu appeals as well, and people rave about the "Ancient Mariner" Caesar salad garnished with grilled scallops, Icelandic shrimp, crab and mussels ($8.75). Open daily from 11:30 to 1 a.m., Sunday from 11 to midnight.

MacAskill's Dining Room & Lounge, Dartmouth Ferry Terminal, Dartmouth. (902) 466-3100. New in 1986 was this large establishment seating 285 atop the Dartmouth Ferry Terminal, with a glorious view of the Halifax skyline and water on three sides. A statue of the Cape Breton giant for which the restaurant is named stands beside the oven, called Angus' Mill and Bakery, where four kinds of bread are baked. The rather standard meat and seafood menu seems expensive ($12.95 for pan-fried haddock or lasagna to $19.95 for salmon in phyllo or top strip loin), but the price includes a choice of any two "great beginnings," from seafood chowder and newburg or curried chicken with pasta to salads of spinach or seafood pasta. The oversize menu, encased in glass, is brought to your table with a flashlight. The airy dining room is cheery and contemporary in beige and cranberry; nicely angled tables have large spindle arm chairs. Lunch and dinner daily.

McKelvie's, 1680 Lower Water St., Halifax. (902) 421-6161. "Delishes Fishes Dishes," proclaims the menu of this casual place with the intriguing interior in a restored firehouse across from the Maritime Museum. It's a hodgepodge of lattice work with rope dividers, arches, hanging lamps and centered by a long boat, which is flanked by seats for large parties or drinks while awaiting dinner. The mussels are extra-good here, the halibut and swordfish are blackened with Cajun spices, and there's a strip steak for those who don't want seafood. Dinner entrees run from $8.50 for haddock and chips to $14.95 for shrimp in pernod, honey and garlic. Open daily from 11:30.

The Sandwich Tree, Xerox Building, Purdy's Wharf, Halifax. This is where office workers go for a healthy breakfast or lunch at a bargain, inside in a sleek gray, cane and chrome setting or outside on a vast upper deck with harbor view beyond. We marveled at the breakfast specials, eggs Benedict and eggs florentine, both $1.99, ordered cafeteria style but brought to the table with coffee refills. There are six kinds of muffins, several other egg dishes, and many sandwiches, soups and salads for lunch. The 1 + 1 + 1 for $3.99 brings you soup or salad plus a shrimp quiche or shepherd's pie or any sandwich plus beverage. Open weekdays, 8 to 4.

FOR MORE INFORMATION: Tourism Halifax, P.O. Box 1749, Halifax, N.S. B3J 3A5. (902) 421-8736. It operates a Visitor's Information Center in Old City Hall, Duke and Barrington streets, as well as a handy waterfront visitor center in Historic Properties.

Marker details points of interest along Cabot Trail.

Cabot Trail/Cape Breton Island, N.S.

Cape Breton Island — and particularly its Cabot Trail — has long been a destination for knowing travelers who like breathtaking oceanfront and mountain scenery, interesting history and customs, and a distinct change of pace.

Although internationally known, its location out of the mainstream and its distance from the rest of civilization leave Cape Breton a delightful world unto itself. Yes, Americans and off-island Canadians can get there and do, but it's no quick trip.

The 184-mile-long Cabot Trail, its best-known claim to fame, is a sharply rising and falling highway that hugs the most scenic oceanside cliffs this side of California's Big Sur. It alone is worth the five-hour drive from Halifax, the one-day drive from eastern Maine.

But there's much more. For scenery and sailing, the shimmering Bras d'Or Lakes make up an inland sea which so captivated Alexander Graham Bell that he made the lakeside resort village of Baddeck his summer home for 35 years. Today, visitors find Baddeck a good base for exploring the island.

The partly restored Fortress of Louisbourg, the largest national historic park in Canada, is an absorbing recreation of the 18th century village known as the Gibraltar of Canada. Here you relive the history of the costly site that helped France to lose its empire and Britain her American colonies, changing the destiny of North America.

To the French legacy at Louisbourg and the French-Acadian still dominant at Cheticamp, add the Micmac Indians at four reservations along the Bras d'Or Lakes and the prevailing Scottish presence for a unique mix of cultures.

Nowhere in Nova Scotia (which means New Scotland in Latin) is the Scottish influence more pronounced than in the Cape Breton Highlands. They so resemble the Scottish Highlands that a New York Times article on Cape Breton was headlined "Scotland on a Nearer Shore." You quickly recognize the Scottish dialect and place names, the preponderance of last names beginning with "mac," and the fondness for the foods and traditions of Scotland.

So isolated are parts of Cape Breton that they remain much as John Cabot found them when he landed, it's believed, in 1497 at Aspy Bay on the northernmost tip of Nova Scotia. Except for the mining interests in the populated area called Industrial Cape Breton centered around Sydney, fishing and tourism are the main occupations.

Both are quite different from what you might expect, however. The fishing is done as of old from weatherbeaten boats of many hues; they are moored in picturesque harbors or can be seen at work off the soaring coastline. The tourism scene is straight out of the past as well — no chain motels or fast-food eateries here. Instead you find Mom & Pop motels and a few traditional lodges, fried-seafood restaurants, Scottish or Acadian souvenir stands and shops, and offbeat surprises everywhere.

Cape Breton is a world apart — a place of history, tradition and scenery so powerful that you can't help but yield to its allure.

Getting There

Although there is air service from major cities to Halifax and Sydney, most travelers drive (or rent a car) to see Cape Breton Island. This is a large island, and unless you go by tour bus, it's difficult to get around without wheels. Although great for hiking, we saw few cyclists, probably because of the mountains and distances involved.

The island is easily reached via the Trans-Canada Highway (Routes 104 and 105), which meets the Cabot Trail in the vicinity of Baddeck.

Prices are quoted in Canadian funds. Cape Breton is in the Atlantic time zone, one hour ahead of Eastern time.

Where to Stay

Your choice of accommodations depends on time, budget and personal preferences. Those in the Cape Breton Highlands run the gamut, with the exception of chain motels. Several fine resort lodges are located in or near Cape Breton Highlands National Park. Baddeck, beside Lake Bras d'Or at the beginning and end of the circular Cabot Trail, is the best interior location for exploring all of Cape Breton. The Margarees, Cheticamp and Ingonish are close to the park on the south side; Pleasant Bay is beyond. Toll-free reservations can be made at many places by the provincial reservations service, Check Inns, from the U.S. (800) 341-6096, from Maine (800) 492-6043, the Maritimes (800) 565-7105, Quebec (800) 565-7180, and most of Ontario (800) 565-7140.

Resort Retreats

Keltic Lodge, Box 70, Ingonish Beach B0C 1L0 (902) 285-2880. World-famous as a full-service resort operated by the provincial government, Keltic Lodge couldn't be more superbly situated. It's off by itself in an idyllic setting, commanding a smashing view of the ocean on two sides from its perch astride a long high promontory called Middle Head. You'll likely see it from the road, long before you pass the renowned Highlands golf course and enter the grounds through graceful birches arched over profuse flower borders. On your right is the resort's newer and more motel-like **White Birch Inn**; on the left is the **Atlantic Coffee Shop** and gift shop, and beyond is the striking white, red-roofed **Main Lodge**. We booked one of the 40 rooms in the White Birch Inn, which had two picture windows overlooking a narrow lawn beside the cliff and nothing but ocean and the craggy shoreline opposite. At least that's what was in view when we arrived; shortly after, it began raining and the next morning we and everything else north of Baddeck were enveloped in fog and a howling gale. Under those conditions, one night was enough; had the weather cooperated, even the most driven traveler might have lingered to laze beside the heated saltwater pool, hike around Middle Head, play golf or tennis and enjoy the usual resort amenities. Before the deluge, we did manage a 90-minute hike out to Tern Point, spotting cormorants, viewing the pounding surf below and picking wild raspberries for sustenance. Our spacious room had a double and a twin bed, pale blue walls and carpeting, two yellow rocking chairs beside a red table, a telephone and a small AM-FM radio for company on a rainy evening under circumstances that best could be described as lonely. Downstairs were two large lounges, one with a TV set, where movies are shown at night. Why the White Birch Inn is air-conditioned we'll never know (the temperature never neared 70 the entire eight days we were in Nova Scotia either in July or early September). It's also heated and remains open in winter for skiers at the Cape Smokey ski area (a site for Canada's 1987 Winter Games hosted by Cape Breton). Thirty-two more rooms with private bath are located in the Main Lodge. Twenty-six rooms with private bath are available in cottages, some with fireplaces and sitting rooms. The lodge has large, comfortable sitting rooms, a downstairs bar and a long main dining room with windows onto the ocean on both sides. Three meals a day are served (see Where to Eat). The lodge is booked long in advance. Doubles, MAP only, $147 in Main Lodge, $152 in White Birch Inn, $167 in cottages. Main Lodge open June to Oct. 20.

Inverary Inn Resort, Shore Road, Box 190, Baddeck B0E 1B0. (902) 295-2674. An expanding resort with a Scottish theme beside Lake Bras d'Or, this has 90 guest rooms, two restaurants (see Where to Eat), a new indoor pool and an appealing gift shop. The MacAuley family have operated it since 1971, and their Scottish heritage is evident from the names of the diverse buildings to the salty kippered herring and untoasted bannoch served at breakfast. The eight original rooms in the inn are appointed with antique furnishings; four on the second floor have private baths, four on the third floor share. Guests can relax in an old-fashioned, book-filled parlor with TV, or outside on the many chairs scattered around the lawns. Our lakefront room in the two-story **Argyle Lodge**, the main motel unit, was comfortable with pine paneling and furniture (the pine chairs, made near Halifax, are especially handsome), autumn-patterned draperies and bedspreads, flowered sheets and cable TV. Other rooms are in **Culloden House** and eight cottages. The 24 newest rooms, in the **Glasgow House** with an indoor pool and jacuzzi, are open all year. They're thoroughly up to date in pink and blue with comforters on the beds, thick carpeting and bar-refrigerators. Three fine tennis courts are beside the lake, as is **Scottie's Fish House** and a blue-canopied pontoon boat which takes guests on lake cruises. Don't miss the **gift shop**, chock full of handknitted sweaters, toys, china, and tapes and records of Cape Breton music; if you're a grandparent, this is a great place to shop for the kiddies. Between the bustling restaurant and the

Many bus tours, Inverary is apt to convey a busy feeling; at least we found it so, our car and only two others being sandwiched between four tour buses. Doubles, $50 to $85. Glasgow House open year-round.

The Normaway Inn, Egypt Road, Margaree Valley B0E 2C0. (902) 248-2987. Although not on the water, this out-of-the-way 1920s resort with 31 rooms is perfect for those who seek tranquility and a welcoming atmosphere. "We get people who want to get away and have peace and quiet," says innkeeper David MacDonald. The 250-acre property is in a wooded valley two miles off the Cabot Trail, and we saw a deer as we approached via the long driveway lined with pines. Breakfast and lunch are served in the dining room, considered one of the island's best (see Where to Eat). A folksinger entertains at night in the huge living room, equipped with a fieldstone fireplace, old stuffed sofas and lots of books; a connecting sunroom is cheery by day. Downstairs is a TV room, where red chairs are lined up for local-interest films at night. The inn's nine rooms, each with private bath and located so no two are adjacent, are comfy with one or two double beds and decorated in lodge style. Extra privacy is afforded in six cabins, plus eleven new one-bedroom pine chalets clustered near the tennis court. For breakfast, try the Eggs Hughie D ($5.50), a local creation of two poached eggs on Margaree muffins, with Canadian back bacon, topped with a light tomato sauce and cheddar cheese. Doubles, $60 or $70 in inn, $55 to $65 in cabins. Open June to Oct. 15.

Glenghorm Resort, Cabot Trail, Box 39, Ingonish B0C 1K0. (902) 285-2888 or 285-2049. Chris and Clarence Meisner claim to be the deans of seasonal resort operators in the province, having started Glenghorm in 1952. Since then it just grew and grew. They now have 950 feet of beach frontage, a restaurant, gift shop, and 90 motel units, efficiencies and housekeeping cottages in two separate complexes. The first and original is close to the shore and dining room; the newer complex is a bit more distant but near the pool. Picnic tables and some cottages face the water, as do a couple of the six motel buildings with private balconies; we liked them better than the newer motels away from the water. The 130-seat dining room has a view of the ocean at the foot of the 22-acre property. The dinner menu runs from $7.50 for meat loaf to $12 for deep-fried scallops. Says Chris Meisner: "These local ladies know how to cook fish, and people tell us ours are the best meals they've had since leaving home." She has printed her recipe for oatcakes to share with inquiring guests. Doubles, $50 to $60; cottages, $50 to $75, usually booked weekly. Open May 20-Oct. 15.

Baddeck Bases

Silver Dart Lodge, Shore Road, Baddeck B0E 1B0. (902) 295-2340. Despite its name, this is a modern motor inn with 82 units (12 of them chalets and 24 with kitchen facilities) and a bar and dining room. Although we had expected it to be on the water, it is across Shore Road and up a hill. Our room with two double beds and TV was fine and the view of Lake Bras d'Or from the balcony was inspiring, even though we had to ask for chairs and then had to dodge a thunderstorm; the ensuing rainbow was a colorful substitute for the missing sunset. The bright red lighting in the chalet-style dining room would compete with the sunset anyway. What we thought was a rather strange dinner — our first in Nova Scotia — turned out to be not so strange for Cape Breton. Our entrees of lake trout ($9.95) and salmon with egg sauce ($12.95) came with cubed turnips, carrots, two scoops of lumpy mashed potatoes, one piece of iceberg lettuce and a tomato slice, plus a $16 bottle of pinot blanc. An accordion-playing Scotsman in a kilt entertained. Dinner, 5:30 to 9. Doubles, $50 to $67. Open May 15-October.

Telegraph House, Chebucto Street, Box 8, Baddeck B0E 1B0. (902) 295-9988. Built in 1861 in the midst of tiny downtown Baddeck, the main building contained the office of the first Trans Oceanic Cable Co. Some of the first telegraph messages in North America were sent from here, and part of the original cable can be seen. Alexander Graham Bell's Room No. 1 is preserved in much the same style as when he stayed here in the 1880s. Other rooms in the three-story inn are furnished in Victoriana and a number share baths. Out back is an L-shaped motel. All told there are 47 guest rooms, 37 with private bath, a pleasant common room in which a fire is lit on cool mornings, and a beamed and paneled dining room serving three meals a day. Owners Buddy and Mary Dunlop are the fourth generation of the founding innkeepers. Doubles, $56 to $65. Open year-round.

Gisele's of Baddeck, Shore Road, Baddeck B0E 1B0. (902) 295-2849. Many think the area's most interesting food is served in Gisele's fancy dining room (see Where to Eat). Helen and Hans Sievers took over the complex from his mother (Gisele, who retired to Florida) in 1975 and have added on. One two-room suite and three efficiency cottages are located near the restaurant; up a hill out back is a new two-story motel with 26 units, each with two beds, color TV and unusual bow windows that let you see more of the distant lake and provide some solar heat on cool days. Rooms are nicely outfitted with local pine furniture designed by Hans and made by an Indian cooperative. Gisele handpainted the plates hanging on the walls and the tiles on walls and tables, and she still sends pieces of her craft up from Florida, decorated with shells and such. Doubles, $50 to $70. Open May 15-October.

Motels along the Cabot Trail

Since the preferred direction around the Cabot Trail is clockwise from Baddeck, lodging is listed in that order.

Duck Cove Inn, Margaree Harbour B0E 2B0. (902) 235-2658. This is not an inn, but a motel, although one with a restaurant and smashing vistas of the harbor. Amusing tables with checkers games built in are just outside the main entrance. The dining room is comfortable and homey with paper mats on pine tables, captain's chairs and nothing too striking to detract from the view. Dinners (from $7.75 for grilled cod fillets to $11.95 for grilled or poached salmon) include fish chowder or soup and beverage. The 24 motel units are standard with two double beds and TV. The 12 newer units in the two-story motel closest to the water have balconies or sliding doors onto a terrace. Canoes are available for rent in a little park beside the river. Doubles, $44 to $48. Open June-Oct. 20.

Laurie's Motel, Main Street, Box 1, Cheticamp B0E 1H0. (902) 224-2400. Laurie McKeown's father started this growing lodging and dining complex in 1938 with five cabins in the heart of French-Acadian Cheticamp. The cabins are long gone, replaced by an 11-unit motel behind the restaurant. A later 10-room section was double-decked in 1985 to provide 31 units. Laurie refurbished the older units in 1985, and acquired a liquor license (permitting a suave upstairs cocktail lounge) for the restaurant (see Where to Eat). He's proud of the six family suites with sitting areas in the new motel section, especially the large second-story end suite with a view of the Gulf of St. Lawrence from the chesterfield and chair grouping by the window — "you'll have a hard time finding a better room in all of Nova Scotia," he claims. Doubles, $45 to $53; suites, $52 to $65. Open year-round.

Park View Motel, Box 117, Cheticamp B0E 1H0. (902) 224-3232. Located five miles north of Cheticamp at the West Gate of Cape Breton Highlands National Park, this is exactly what its name says. The low one-story red building has 17 units with wall-to-wall carpeting and color TV. There's an oval outdoor pool with a diving board. A licensed dining room serves three meals a day. Doubles, $43 to $45. Open May 24-Oct. 15.

Beachside Motels and Restaurant, Pleasant Bay B0E 2P0. (902) 224-2467. This motel comes in two sections, one with twelve units (four of them billed as deluxe and two with private decks) and another with eight efficiency units. The location atop a hill overlooking the quaint fishing harbor, Pleasant Bay and headlands is better than the facilities. The licensed restaurant is open for three meals; you can get burgers and sandwiches for lunch, or a complete dinner of roast turkey, pork chops, Atlantic salmon or lobster ($7.99 to $15.99). Doubles, $40 to $45. Open June 10-Oct. 15.

Mountain View Motel, Pleasant Bay B0E 2P0. (902) 224-3100. Better looking than its neighboring Beachside but away from the water is the Mountain View. Formerly the Bonnie Doon, it has 18 motel units with TV and radio, four efficiency cottages and three cabins. A swimming pool, tennis courts, shuffleboard and volleyball are attractions, and the licensed dining room serves three meals daily. Doubles, $40 to $45. Open May 15-Oct. 20.

Amber Gate, Box 177, Ingonish Beach B0C 1L0. (902) 285-2525. A large TV satellite is the first thing you notice at this small place in the trees near the beach. "We're the only ones with satellite TV," the office staffer explained. The rooms in the six-unit motel up close to the road have one or two double beds and TV. Near the sand beach are four efficiency cottages and two beachfront houses, the latter with fireplaces and accommodating six or seven people. Doubles, $50 to $75 in motel, $65 to $150 in cottages. Open May-December.

Other Options

Cape Breton Bed & Breakfast. About 60 homes that take in travelers are marked by distinctive small signs across the island and listed in a brochure prepared by the Cape Breton Development Corp., Box 1750, Sydney B1P 6T7. Most have one or two rooms and charge $20 single, $24 double, for bed and breakfast. The island tourist association information bureaus assist in making reservations.

CAMPING. Numerous campgrounds are detailed in the Nova Scotia Tourism Department's travel guide. Two private ones that appeared are the **Baddeck Cabot Trail KOA,** Box 417, Baddeck, 295-2288, with 115 serviced and 36 unserviced sites, and **Bras d'Or Lakes Campground,** Box 392, Baddeck, 295-2329, with 56 serviced and 33 unserviced sites and 500 feet of shoreline on the lake. The **National Park** has eight campgrounds, which have varied facilities and rates (most $7.50 daily), some on the ocean.

COTTAGES. Among the choices are **Cape Breton Highlands Bungalows,**

Box 151, Ingonish Beach, 285-2000, with 25 cottages built by the National Parks Service on a lake overlooking Ingonish Beach, doubles $45, and **Whale Cove Summer Village**, RR 1, Margaree Harbour, 235-2202, 30 housekeeping cottages with porches on a bluff beside the ocean, $40 to $65 daily.

Seeing and Doing

Because Cape Breton's weather is fickle and you can get socked in by fog, it's best to allow two or three days there in order to pick the clearest day to drive the Cabot Trail. Plenty of diversions are available for marginal weather.

THE CABOT TRAIL. The 184-mile-long trail around the outermost tip of Cape Breton embraces some of North America's most spectacular scenery. The road is good and the complete trip can be done in a day, or you can linger and retrace your steps.

Pick a clear day — preferably sunny, although we've never seen it that way (both times we had clouds but good visibility). The most breathtaking scenery (and slowest driving) is along relatively short stretches in Cape Breton Highlands National Park, up and down cliffs on the eastern and western shores and in the mountainous northern interior near Big Intervale. Although you might choose as we did to go counterclockwise against the prevailing traffic and for right-hand access to scenic pull-offs, don't. The second time we went the other way and concluded that the clockwise direction offers better vistas.

Cape Breton Highlands National Park, Ingonish Beach. Established in 1936, this is Eastern Canada's largest national park and the heart of the Cabot Trail. The park's main feature is an extensive plateau, criss-crossed by rivers and valleys between mountains and a rugged coastline of bold headlands, steep cliffs, hidden coves and sandy beaches. To us, it's a cross between Scotland's Highlands, Portugal's Algarve and California's Big Sur, and the wilderness is so vast and the signs of civilization so different that you could imagine yourself in a foreign land.

Naturalists appreciate the many varieties of wildlife and vegetation. Hikers like the 140 miles of trails leading to the interior plateau, the rugged coast or to 1,000-foot viewpoints overlooking it all; the 28 trails are detailed in a special brochure. Swimmers will find two supervised beaches and any number of salt and freshwater beaches. Picnicking is offered at numerous "picnic parks." The 18-hole Highlands Links is one of the world's more challenging golf courses. Three tennis courts are available at the Ingonish Beach Day Use Area. In winter there's skiing on Cape Smokey, site of the ski competition in Canada's 1987 Winter Games hosted by Cape Breton Island. The park's interpretive program includes a variety of roadside markers and exhibits, self-guided trails and, in summer, guided walks and evening talks by park rangers.

Information centers are open from mid-May to mid-October at the Cheticamp and Ingonish entrances to the park. Park admission is $3 per car daily or $10 annually.

Trail and Park Highlights

The Cabot Trail and the park have as many interesting (if not quite as diverse) attractions as Yellowstone or Yosemite. Going clockwise, we were particularly struck by the colorful old boats and the loons in the harbor at **Grand Etang** and the austere, barren French Acadian fishing village of **Cheticamp** (pause to view the ornate interior of **St. Peter's Roman Catholic Church**), the ride up

French Mountain (with views behind) and then down the switchbacks to **Pleasant Bay**. Atop French Mountain are the **Skyline Trail**, from which you peer down on the Cabot Trail and see fishing boats and maybe a whale, and the **Bog Trail** where signs along a boardwalk attempt to make the bog interesting.

As you head into the interior, stop at the **Lone Shieling**, a replica of an open Scottish sheep crofter's hut dwarfed by 300-year-old sugar maples. The descent down North Mountain provides awesome views toward Aspy Bay. Take the one-mile side trip on a dirt road to **Beaulach Ban Falls**, a 50-foot-high waterfall and picnic area that's worth the detour.

At **Cape North**, leave the trail to head out to the northernmost tip of Cape Breton. Stop at **Cabot Landing**, where English explorer John Cabot and his son Sebastian are thought to have set foot on the sandy beach in 1497. The view across the church spire and colorful houses as you descend the hill into the harbor at Bay St. Lawrence is unforgettable.

Back in Cape North, leave the Cabot Trail to take the coastal route off to **White Point** and **Neil's Harbor**. It provided even more spectacular views than much of the Cabot Trail, and so unexpectedly. We liked the multi-colored bluff near Smelt Brook, which ends with a formation that looks like the profile of Richard Nixon. Drive down to White Point, a working dock reeking of fish, with colorful boats and lobster traps all around. Neil's Harbor is as picturesque a fishing village as you'll find.

Rejoin the Cabot Trail and stop at **Black Brook Cove**, one of the many picnic parks in the area and this one with grass, a sandy beach and a bluff on one side. Go into the Keltic Lodge grounds and hike, if you have time, out to the end of **Middle Head. Ingonish Beach** is long, sandy and reminiscent of Ogunquit's the first time we saw it; the surf was crashing in a storm the second time. The beach is actually a spit of land with the ocean on one side and a freshwater lake on the other. The Cabot Trail climbs **Cape Smokey**, which may be clouded in mist, for its last steep descent toward the open Atlantic. At **North Shore**, you may be able to see in the distance the famous **Bird Islands**, home of the Atlantic puffin and a favorite with bird-watchers (who can visit by tour boat from Big Bras d'Or). At the **Gaelic College** in St. Ann's, the only one of its kind in North America, is the **Great Hall of the Clans**, which depicts the history and culture of the Scots and was described by one irreverent visitor we know as much ado about nothing. It's open daily, June-September 9 to 5, July-August 8 to 8, adults $1.

Stops and Shops along the Trail

Starting clockwise, note the Margaree River, one of North America's most beautiful (and prolific) salmon rivers. It offers 20 fishable miles of crystal-clear water and an abundance of salmon pools. Visitors are welcome to view salmon and trout at the **Margaree Fish Hatchery** in Northeast Margaree. Also at Northeast Margaree is the **Margaree Salmon Museum**, operated by the Margaree Anglers Association, a diverting experience for anyone interested in salmon and fishing; open June 15-Oct. 15, daily 9 to 5, adults 50 cents.

The sandy ocean beach at Margaree Harbour, as well as others along the west shore, are said to have the warmest waters north of the Carolinas. **Schooner Village** is a must stop for anyone with an ounce of Scottish blood and a taste for the offbeat. It's a funky, crowded indoor complex of five gift shops with British facades, where you can find anything from kilted tartan skirts and Hudson's Bay coats to Quebec wood carvings, Beatrix Potter figures, T-shirts and souvenir spoons. (You can also get a snack at the coffee shop, eat on the Schooner restaurant and go below decks to the Schooner Museum.) As you head north toward Cheticamp, you'll spot **Joe's Drive-in Theater of Scarecrows,** a bizarre outdoor stage near Cap LeMoine where about 50 scarecrows, all dressed differently, flap in the breeze. The butterflies you see decorating many houses are for sale in the shops.

Around Cheticamp you'll come to **Flora's,** a vast emporium of souvenirs and Cheticamp hooked rugs and smaller pieces made by more than 100 local women; you may get to see Flora at work. **Les Trois Pignons** (The Three Gables) is a highly touted center of Acadian history with a rather overpriced museum and gallery of hooked rugs and tapestries by Elizabeth LeFort, the Cheticamp native whose works are in the Vatican, Buckingham Palace and the White House (open May-October, daily 9 to 5, summer 9 to 9). Beyond, the world's largest lobster trap catches your eye as it envelops **Le Gabion,** a gift shop with more hooked rugs, souvenirs and local crafts.

Whale cruises leave the Government Wharf at Cheticamp on the 40-foot Bonnie Maureen daily at 9, 1 and 6 in July and August. The three-hour cruise shows sea caves, unusual rock formations, cormorants, perhaps a bald eagle and an average of 20 Atlantic pilot whales ($15 per person).

Near Cape North you'll find **Arts North,** a small two-story contemporary building selling local pottery, fibers and especially nice jewelry (daily 9 to 6, mid-June to mid-October). In the last hamlet of **Meat Cove** at the end of the road at the end of the northernmost Cape Breton coast, you can visit the **Meat Cove Pottery** workshop, where artisans are at work year-round. At South Harbor, the **Teapot Pottery Shop** is the retail outlet for the craftsmen of Meat Cove, with a full line of their stoneware, painting and sculpture plus other crafts; meals also are available.

Ingonish is one of the oldest settlements on the Atlantic coast. Today it's a golfing, beach and ski resort. Works of painter Christopher Gorey are shown by his wife at **Lynn's Craft Shop and Gallery** in Ingonish.

Baddeck and Bras d'Or Lakes

Baddeck is on a hillside beside Lake Bras d'Or, and world-class sailboats dock in its harbor before cruising the inland saltwater lakes. From a park near the Bras d'Or Yacht Club you can see where Alexander Graham Bell's Silver Dart flew off the ice in 1909 to become the first manned flight in the British Commonwealth and where his hydrofoil set a world speed boating record in 1919. You also can see **Beinn Breagh,** the mountain he owned and the 1892 summer estate he built there.

At the government wharf is **Seawinds Chandlery,** a smart shop with heavy Prince Edward Island sweaters, local handcrafts and nautical gifts. From here, a free boat run by the Baddeck Lions Club takes swimmers back and forth in summer to a beach on **Kidston Island.** Just east of town is **Bute Arran Gift Shop,** which has fine British woolens, Nova Scotia tartans, blankets, china, local crafts and books. Owners Don and Margot MacAuley also offer four rooms for bed and breakfast, 295-2786, from $27 to $32. Incidentally, Centre Bras d'Or at Baddeck presents a lively **Festival of the Arts,** starting in mid-July with three weeks of nightly performances by name entertainers and a special theater series at Baddeck Rural High School.

Alexander Graham Bell National Historic Park, Route 205, Baddeck.

(902) 295-2069. If when you think of Mr. Bell all you think of is the telephone, think again. This fascinating place shows the remarkable range of his inventive genius, from genetics and medical science to the Silver Dart airplane and the hydrofoil. By films, audio displays and such you'll learn of his romance with his deaf pupil Mabel, whom he later married, hear his famous "Dr. Watson, Dr. Watson" phone message, enjoy his early telephones and airplane models, view hundreds of historic photographs and see the remains of the hydrofoil. The priceless collection that makes up the museum was donated by his family, some of whom still live at Beinn Breagh, which you can see from the gardens on the roof of the striking tetrahedon-shaped museum. Open July-September, daily 9 to 9; rest of year 9 to 5. Free.

Bras d'Or Lakes. Anyone coming this far to Cape Breton ought not to miss the majestic, mountain-ringed sprawl of inland lakes. Their reach is 50 miles long and 20 miles wide, creating 600 miles of shoreline. The tides flow in from the Atlantic through two narrow passages at the north, Great Bras d'Or and Little Bras d'Or. Boats can get to the Atlantic from the southern end via St. Peters Canal. The drive up the lake's east side along Route 4 affords spectacular hilltop views. Returning south toward Baddeck from Sydney around Great Bras d'Or at sunset was unforgettable, matching in its own way the grandeur of the Cabot Trail. You may cross through the middle of the lakes via a five-minute ferry ride (50 cents a carload) at **Grand Narrows.** Stop at **Iona** to see the **Nova Scotia Highland Village Museum,** a recreated Scottish village overlooking the Barra Strait (June 15-Sept. 15, Monday-Saturday 10 to 6, Sunday 11 to 5, adults $2.50). A good place to eat or stay here is the **Highland Heights Inn,** Route 223, Iona, 622-2360, an attractive hilltop building with 26 units with private bath and color TV, doubles $51; serving three meals daily.

A Side Trip to Louisbourg

Fortress of Louisbourg National Historic Park, Louisbourg, (902) 733-2280. We don't know when we last were so surprised and impressed by a restored village as here. We expected to spend a couple of hours and ended up having to drag ourselves away after six.

Louisbourg, for the uninitiated (which included us), is the Canadian government's $26 million recreation of the abandoned 18th century walled city established by the French between 1713 and 1745 to defend their possessions in the New World. Until it was ambushed by Americans in 1745 and destroyed by the British in 1760, it was the mightiest fortress on this continent, the third busiest seaport (after Boston and Philadelphia) and the center of French civilization in North America. It is the only Colonial town of import without a modern city superimposed on top, so one-fourth of it has been authentically restored as it was in 1744.

After orienting yourself in the visitor center via a five-minute slide show as you proceed through four small theaters to a bus loading area, you are transported two miles out to the fortress, poised on a point beside the ocean. Outside is a scene of melancholy desolation; inside, the physically austere fortress masks a lively working village of soldiers and seafaring families. Here, 175 costumed guides, most of them in their 20s and unusually articulate, interpret the town as it was in 1744, and the intriguing story of the rise and fall of Louisbourg gradually unfolds.

Although guided tours are offered periodically, you're on your own as you go through guardhouses, barracks, vegetable gardens, warehouses, homes, taverns, the military bakery, government buildings and the elegant Governor's Quarters. Guides will volunteer information if spoken to (they and their stories are fascinating). Take the time to chat and also to listen (by telephone) to exceptionally interesting recordings detailing facets of Louisbourg life pertaining to the building you're in.

Stop for a meal or snack at the **Hotel de la Marine** or **L'Epee Royale**. At the former, you'll be seated communally and served by waitresses in 18th century garb. For $7 each (about $4.50 American) we had a lunch of pea soup, chicken fricassee and bread pudding, plus a pewter container of red wine. You sit on low chairs at a table covered with a sheet and huge serviettes, using a single pewter spoon for the entire meal. Quite an experience, we thought, as did our tablemates from Arizona and a California man whose wife was lunching in L'Epee Royale because she liked the sound of the stew there better!

There's so much to see and absorb that you could easily spend an entire day. Don't miss the building detailing the restoration of Louisbourg; that story is almost as interesting as the story of Louisbourg. Usually between 600 and 1,800 people a day visit for a yearly total of about 125,000, which isn't many considering the significance of the site. It's apt to be windy, lonely and cold out there (wear something warm and windproof), and you'll understand why Louisbourg — planned as the New World's capital — didn't make it. Open daily, July and August 9 to 7, June and September 10 to 6. Adults $4, children $1, family $8.

The village of Louisbourg, as opposed to the fortress, has a handful of restaurants, shops and motels, but most visitors prefer to stay in Sydney or commute from Baddeck. One shop not to be missed is the **Louisbourg Craft Workshops**, an airy building on four levels showing exceptional crafts, many made next door. Here also you can get tea, coffee and local oatmeal and molasses cookies and relax in a glass enclosure or outside at tables by the water.

Where to Eat

The food of Cape Breton was not what we had hoped for: interesting seafood, simply yet imaginitively prepared, served with fresh vegetables and produce at small restaurants beside the ocean. Instead, the fish is generally deep-fried, the vegetables heavy-handed, the salads extra and everything geared to tour buses. We found only one oceanside seafood shanty and two outdoor decks in all our travels. Some of the Scottish specialties were fun, however.

Baddeck Area

Gisele's of Baddeck, Shore Road, Baddeck. (902) 295-2849. One guest wrote that its food is "an oasis in a gourmet desert," and friends reported they had a fine dinner here. The curved dining room has windows onto Lake Bras d'Or across the road. The striking blue tile tables were designed by Hans Sievers; more tiles and local art are on the walls. With her mother-in-law Gisele retired in Florida, Helen Sievers does the cooking; the cuisine is seafood with a touch of French. Among appetizers ($2.95 to $5.95) are marinated herring, Atlantic mackerel smoked on the site, a house pate glazed in cognac, or escargots bourgignon flambeed in brandy; for main courses ($12.95 to $15.95), sole meuniere, poached salmon, seafood coquille, wiener schnitzel or filet mignon bearnaise. Desserts, baked on the premises, include pies, tortes, cakes and cheesecakes, and you might finish with Gisele's special flambeed coffee with crème de cacao, whipped cream and grand marnier. The wine list features good French, German, Spanish and Nova Scotia wines. Dinner, 5:30 to 10.

Inverary Inn, Shore Road, Baddeck. (902) 295-2674. Old bottles of all colors are lined up on the windowsills in the airy outer dining room looking across the lawns to Lake Bras d'Or. The Royal Stuart tartan on the overcloths is repeated in the waitresses' skirts. The limited dinner menu (entrees $10 to $15) contains few surprises, except perhaps for stupad, a Scottish dish combining sweet cream, oatmeal, scotch whiskey and sugar, served with crackers — and that for an appetizer! We passed, thank you, and settled for a prime rib that tasted better than it looked and a New York strip steak that was too thin and rather fatty and tough. The steak came with mashed potatoes and frozen peas, the prime rib with cole slaw and horseradish. A basket of oatcakes and buns was served first, and a side Caesar salad ($3.25) was very good. A tangy lemon snow made a nice, light ending. Dinner nightly, 5:30 to 8:30.

Scottie's Fish House, Shore Road, Baddeck. (902) 295-3155. This is the new casual, waterside restaurant at the side of the Inverary Inn property, opened by Scottie MacAuley, son of the innkeepers. And while we wished we had eaten here rather than in the main dining room, friends who preceded us had dinner at Scottie's and thought the inn would have been a better choice. Such are the vagaries of eating on Cape Breton. The red-linened interior has generous windows overlooking the water, but we'd choose the outside porch beside the cove, where luxury sailboats and yachts are moored. This is the kind of outdoor place we'd been looking for, where you can watch the waterfront goings-on as you savor a lobster roll for $6.95. You can get a lobster dinner for $14.95 (about $9.95 in American funds), a seafood platter for $11.25 and a scallop kabob for $12.25. Open daily 11:30 to 9, June 15 to Oct. 15.

Taj Restaurant, MacLeod Street, Baddeck. (902) 295-2915. Who'd ever expect to find an Indian restaurant on Cape Breton, much less one in an ordinary brick house fronted by an ornate wooden temple facade facing the parking lot behind the Alexander Graham Bell Museum? Otherwise you might never know it was there, and even so it's hard to get to, but for those of us who crave Indian food, it's a treat. The Madhur family from New Delhi (he's a teacher at Baddeck Rural High School) serve sandwiches, seafood and standard dinners as well as East Indian specialties at prices not to be believed. How about chicken curry for $5.95 or tandoori murgha for $7.95? That's the same price as for T-bone steak or poached salmon, and nothing's higher except lobster ($10.95). Pakoras and samosas are $2.50; those irresistible Indian breads like poori and paratha are 50 cents or $1.25. End with mango pulp and ice cream, $1.40. The Madhurs started with a gift shop and expanded with their licensed restaurant a decade ago. Lunch and dinner daily, June-October.

Around the Cabot Trail

Normaway Inn, Egypt Road, Margaree Valley. (902) 248-2987. Big windows on both sides of the dining room look onto a tranquil rural landscape. With tables covered with dark green linen, Wedgwood china and fresh flowers, it's a simple but pleasant setting and the food is considered some of the best around. Complete dinners are priced according to the choice of entree ($10.50 to $19.50) on the blackboard menu, which changes nightly. Main courses might be coquilles St. Jacques, pork tenderloin oriental, stuffed Cornish hen with orange sauce or mint barbecued lamb chops. Start with raspberry soup, gazpacho, clam chowder or smoked salmon; succumb finally to a cheesecake with raspberry puree, raspberry lemon cake with ice cream and rum sauce, or honeydew melon and sherbet. Vegetables and salads come from the inn's gardens. The wine list is better than the norm in Nova Scotia, most bottles in the $14.50 range. Dinner nightly, 5:30 to 8:30.

Schooner Restaurant, Cabot Trail, Margaree Harbour. (902) 235-2317. You can dine aboard the schooner Marian Elizabeth, built in 1918 and one of only two remaining Lunenburg fishing schooners, listen to cocktail music played on the piano by Stephanie May and perhaps chat with John May, who's unmistakable in long gray beard and MacDonald tartan kilt. The May family moved here in 1974 from Hartford, Conn., where she was a widely known political activist and he a comptroller for Aetna Life & Casualty. They reopened the Schooner restaurant and have vastly expanded the rambling Schooner Village Gift Shop complex of five boutiques with half-timbered facades under one roof, a coffee shop and the Schooner Museum. Dinners run from $4.75 for two chicken dishes (creamed or Southern fried) to $15 for lobster. Other reasonably priced choices include grilled halibut, poached salmon, cod Portuguese and Margaree River trout. Chowders, sandwiches and salads are the fare at lunch, and among desserts are strawberry shortcake and hot gingerbread with applesauce and whipped cream. Lunch daily, 11:30 to 2:30; dinner, 5:30 to 8 or 9, June 15-Oct. 15.

Harbour Restaurant, Main Street, Cheticamp. (902) 224-2042. The pleasant, rustic dining room in orange and brown tones looks onto the water beside a lighthouse. We could see cows grazing along the shore across the cove, near a spit of sand covered with birds, as we lunched on a spicy noodle soup (which contained everything but the kitchen sink), a lobster roll and a plate of fried clams with cole slaw, both $6.95, washed down with the local Oland beer. The menu offered a variety from egg rolls to salads to butterscotch meringue pie. Open 7 a.m. to midnight, 11 to 8:30 in winter.

Laurie's Dining Room, Main Street, Cheticamp. (902) 224-2400. Energetic Laurie McKeown has been upgrading his family's motel and restaurant operation, obtaining a liquor license in 1986, adding an upstairs cocktail lounge, and planning to add a second-story deck for waterview dining in 1987. The mainfloor dining room seats 60 at white-linened tables covered with Cape Breton paper maps. The upstairs lounge is unexpectedly chic with plush rust velvet chairs at good-looking ash tables; you'd almost think you were in a city hotel. For 40 years, Laurie's father John has reigned in the kitchen, where his homemade soups and chowders, breads and pastries, and seafood obtained from the wharf across the street have won acclaim. The halibut, haddock and grey sole fillets are broiled in foil and served with tartar sauce ($8.95 to $10.95) — not exactly the way we like them, but better than the deep-fried and heavily breaded treatment indigenous to the area. The salmon is steamed Acadian style (again served with tartar sauce); other choices might be baked ham with scalloped potatoes or pork chops with apple jelly. Some say the special mince pie is the best they've tasted. Lunch, 11:30 to 2; dinner, 5 or 5:30 to 8 or 8:30; winter, Saturday-Sunday 5:30 to 8.

The Black Whale, Cabot Trail, Pleasant Bay. (902) 224-2185. We'd seen the publicity and drove quite a distance -- which you often have to do on the Cabot Trail — to have lunch at this "internationally famous" seafood restaurant. The only problem was that it had no lunch items, just a few seafood dinners chalked on the blackboard ($6 to $9) and served in the local (heavy dinner) manner. We longed for a lobster roll or chowder and salad, so moved on after glancing at the homey interior of the unusual pine and log building seating 150 in several sections. Owners Bill and Jean Atwell say theirs is not a gourmet restaurant; instead they aim to provide good, fresh seafood to thousands of travelers at a fair price. The tourists respond in droves, and are especially fond of the fish. Open 11 to 9, June 15-Sept. 30.

Keltic Lodge, Ingonish Beach. (902) 285-2880. The food in the famed lodge's 200-seat dining room is good if unremarkable, and non-guests are welcome by reservation. In resort style, the menu changes daily and meals are prix-fixe. Our dinner for two started with solomon gundy (four pickled herring, a local specialty) and a ham and asparagus feuillette, followed by Ingonish clam chowder and creamed vegetable soup, and good salads. For main courses we chose Cornish game hen, which came with a large baked potato and red braised cabbage, and a rather dry poached salmon doused with hollandaise. Desserts of assorted sherbets and a fresh plum tart were the best part of the meal; we also appreciated the good rolls and oatcakes which arrived, mercifully, with butter which you didn't have to unwrap as you must elsewhere in the province. Although we skipped the porridge and kippered herring, the next day's breakfast was filling as well: a fresh fruit cup (more canned than fresh, we're afraid), cream of wheat, a poached egg on English muffin with good Canadian sausage, and scrambled eggs with ham. Prix-fixe, $27 for dinner, $10.50 for lunch and $8 for breakfast. Jackets required for dinner. Breakfast 7 to 9:30, lunch noon to 2, dinner 6 to 9.

The Lobster Galley, Cabot Trail, St. Ann's Harbor. (902) 295-3100. The Lobster Galley wasn't open either time we went by, but we did get a breakfast one foggy July morning at **Marie's Takeout** stand next door. At least it was a breakfast of sorts. The closest thing was a grilled cheese sandwich and instant coffee; when we ordered, the owner phoned his wife to come over to help him grill the sandwich. At any rate, the Lobster Galley advertises a sunny deck overlooking the harbor (we never saw any sun), a lobster pound and "a full exciting menu from breakfast to lunch and dinner." Tell us about it! Open May-October.

Special Treats

The Gingerbread Man, Cabot Trail, Cape North. (902) 383-2942. A mile west of tiny Cape North in the 1876 Middle Ridge Schoolhouse is a quaint Scottish bakery, gift shop and restaurant run by Roseanne and Don MacInnis. The restaurant, like none we ever saw before, resembles a camp building with screened windows which can be covered from the outside on cool days; a portable heater was going the September afternoon we dined alone, sitting on black stools at round pink tables. Three complete dinners are served for $6.95: a Scottish baked fish roll, Forfar Bridie or seafood chowder. All include carrots and three-bean salad, bannoch, white and brown bread, oatcakes, Scottish jam, beverage and dessert, perhaps a gingerbread man or woman. Breakfasts are $3.95 for egg and Canadian bacon pie or oatmeal raisin cinnamon porridge, accompanied by juice, coffee and all those marvelous breads and oatcakes. If you can't be there at mealtime, stop in for a chocolate chip cookie (35 cents) or an apple turnover ($1.50); maybe you'll be lucky enough to hit a day when they have one of our favorite Canadian treats, butter tarts -- they didn't, nor did nearby **Angel's Bakery**, to which we drove off for another try. Open 8 a.m. to 7 p.m., June to mid-October.

Chowder House, Lighthouse Road, Neil's Harbor. Just past the lighthouse on the point at Neil's Head, this is the kind of eatery we'd expected to find all over the island. You place your order and pick it up at the counter, then sit down at red picnic tables inside or out on a deck beside the ocean. Even though we'd had a light lunch at the Gingerbread Man less than two hours before, we had to split a bowl of seafood chowder ($3.65), which was the essence of fishiness, chock full of lobster, haddock and clams, and served with a biscuit. Other choices ranged from clams and chips ($5) to scallops and chips ($7.50); they had a good-looking lobster burger for $6, and for dessert, oatcakes or pie. The owner told us there once were four such places across Cape Breton, but they and a place near Margaree were the only survivors. Open summer, 11 to 8; fall, 11 to 4.

Herring Choker Deli, Route 105, Nyanza. (902) 295-2275. A mile from where the Cabot Trail heads toward Margaree west of Baddeck is this super deli and health food store with four tables. Regulars were enjoying Greek salads or soup and a sandwich for $4.95. The Indian Bay Bakery on premises makes granola, bagels and breads. Someone advised that "this is the most with-it place on Cape Breton" as we picked up a few slices of smoked salmon ($17.95 a pound) and French bread for a picnic beside the water.

Manigo-Island View, Route 105, Micmac Indian Refuge, Whycocomagh. This place wasn't open when we stopped, but we heard that chef Dixon Cole of Montreal was building its reputation as one of the finer dining spots on Cape Breton. Digby scallops, halibut steak, seafood casserole with shellfish, salmon and halibut in pastry, eel parmesan and lamb chops were among the offerings on the sample menu, $7.95 to $12.95. We peered in the window to find pictures of Indians, baskets and wall hangings decorating two small dining rooms and a small bar in the middle. Supposedly open 9 to 9.

FOR MORE INFORMATION: Superintendent, Cape Breton Highlands National Park, Ingonish Beach, N.S. BOC 1L0. (902) 285-2270. Or write Tourism Nova Scotia, Box 456, Halifax B3J 2R5.

Also by Wood Pond Press

Getaways for Gourmets in the Northeast. This book by Nancy Webster and Richard Woodworth is for anyone who likes good food and wine. It guides you to the best dining, lodging, specialty food shops and culinary attractions in 22 areas from the Brandywine Valley to Montreal, the Finger Lakes to Cape Cod. Published in 1984; fully revised and expanded in 1988. 474 pages to read and savor. $12.95.

Inn Spots & Special Places in New England. Much more than an inn guide, the second book by Nancy Webster and Richard Woodworth tells you where to go, stay, eat and enjoy in 30 of the region's choicest areas. It details 200 of the best inns, 300 restaurants, and 400 sights to see and things to do. Published in 1986. 334 pages of timely tips. $11.95.

Weekending in New England. The best-selling travel guide by Betsy Wittemann and Nancy Webster details everything you need to know about 18 of New England's most interesting vacation spots: nearly 1,000 things to do, sights to see and places to stay, eat and shop year-round. Published in 1980; fully updated and revised in 1984 and 1988. Full of facts and fun. $10.95.

The Best of Daytripping & Dining. The new book by Betsy Wittemann and Nancy Webster, this is a companion to their original Southern New England and all-New England editions. It pairs 25 featured daytrips with 25 choice restaurants, among 200 other suggestions of sites to visit and places to eat, in Southern New England and nearby New York. Published in 1985. 186 pages of fresh ideas. $7.95.

The Originals in Their Fields

These books may be ordered from your local bookstore or direct from the publisher, pre-paid, plus $1.50 handling for each book. Connecticut residents add sales tax.

Wood Pond Press
365 Ridgewood Road
West Hartford, Conn. 06107
(203) 521-0389

Index to Major Accommodations, Attractions and Restaurants

The Black Pearl, Newport, R.I. 172
Black Swan Tavern, Ogunquit, Me. 285
The Black Whale, Pleasant Bay, N.S. 404
The Blue Anchor Motel, Plymouth, Ma. 220
Blue Harbor House, Camden, Me. 317
Blue Heron Restaurant, Isleboro, Me. 315

The Blue Ribbon, Stockton, N.J. 36
Blue Shutters Inn, Gloucester, Ma. 229
Blue Water Inn, Ogunquit, Me. 286
The Boarding House, Nantucket, Ma. 205

The Boardwalk, Lake George, N.Y. 95
The Boat House, Montauk, N.Y. 69
Boathouse Restaurant, Rockport, Ont.
Boldt Castle, Alexandria Bay, N.Y. 102
Bonnie Castle Resort, Alexandria Bay, N.Y. 98

Boothbay Region Art Gallery, Boothbay Harbor, Me. 305
Boothbay Region Historical Society, Boothbay Harbor, Me. 305
Boscawen Inn, Lunenburg, N.S. 369 and 379
Boscobel, Garrison, N.Y. 80
Boulders Inn, New Preston, Ct. 119 and 124

Boyce's Motel, Stonington, Me. 329
The Brass Bed, Cape May, N.J. 43
The Brass Bed, Oak Bluffs, Ma. 191
Brass Lantern Inn, Nantucket, Ma. 196
The Breakers Ristorante, Spring Lake, N.J. 62

The Breeze, Castine, Me. 326
Brick Oven Restaurant, Bar Harbor, Me. 348
The Bridge, Tilghman Island, Md. 11
Bridgeton House, Upper Black Eddy, Pa. 30

Brown Brothers Wharf, Boothbay Harbor, Me. 308
Brownie's Cabins, South Wellfleet, Ma. 210

Bucks County Playhouse, New Hope, Pa. 34
Bull's Bridge Inn, Kent, Ct. 126
The Cabot Trail, Cape Breton Island, N.S. 398
Cafe Etcetera, Alburg, Vt. 242
Cafe la Fraise, Hanover, N.H. 254
Cafe on the Green, Newport, R.I. 175
Camden Harbour Inn, Camden, Me. 316

Camden Shakespeare Company, Camden, Me. 318
Campobello Island Club Lodge, Welshpool, N.B. 351
The Cannery, Eastport, Me. 357
Canoe Island Lodge, Diamond Point, N.Y. 87

Cape Breton Highlands National Park, Nova Scotia 398
Cape Cod National Seashore, Ma. 211
Cape House Inn, East Mahone Bay, N.S. 378
Cape Motor Inn, Cape May, N.J. 44
Cape Neddick Inn, Cape Neddick, Me. 283
Cappuccino's, Newport, R.I. 176
Cappy's Chowder House, Camden, Me. 319
Capt. Thomson's Motor Lodge, Alexandria Bay, N.Y. 100
Captain Daniel Packer Inne, Mystic, Ct. 150
Captain Dexter House, Vineyard Haven, Ma. 179
Captain Elias Davis House, Gloucester, Ma. 235
Captain Higgins Seafood Restaurant, Wellfleet, Ma. 215
Captain Mey's Inn, Cape May, N.J. 43
Captain Sawyer's Place, Boothbay Harbor, Me. 302
The Captain's House, Chester, N.S. 377
Captain's Quarters Inn & Motel, Stonington, Me. 328
The Captain's Table, Nantucket, Ma. 206
Carriage House, Rye, N.H. 274
The Carriage House, Spring Lake, N.J. 57

Casa Rossi, Narragansett, R.I. 159
Casey Farm, Saunderstown, R.I. 158
Castine Cottages, Castine, Me. 322
Castine Inn, Castine, Me. 322 and 325
Cavallario's Steak and Seafood House, Alexandria Bay, N.Y. 105
Center Cafe, Wakefield, R.I. 159
Central House, Bar Harbor, Me. 347
Centre Bridge Inn, New Hope, Pa. 29 and 35

Chalet Leon Motel-Resort, Watkins Glen, N.Y. 109
The Chalfonte, Cape May, N.J. 44
Chantecleer Inn, Siasconset, Ma. 203
The Charlotte Inn, Edgartown, Ma. 181
The Chart Room, Chester, Vt. 138
Chateau Halifax, Halifax, N.S. 383
The Chateau Motel, Spring Lake, N.J. 57
Chesapeake Bay Maritime Museum, St. Michaels, Md. 6
Chester Basin Coffee House, Chester Basin, N.S. 380
Chestnut Hill on the Delaware, Milford, N.J. 31
Chicatabut Inn, Rockport, Ma. 231
The Chieftain Motel, Hanover, N.H. 249
Chillingsworth Guest House, Lunenburg, N.S. 369
The Chowder House, Boothbay Harbor, Me. 307